BARRON'S
GED

HIGH SCHOOL EQUIVALENCY EXAM

15TH EDITION

Murray Rockowitz, Ph.D.
Former Chairman, Board of Examiners,
New York City Board of Education
Former Principal,
John Philip Sousa Junior High School,
New York City
Former Chairman, English Department,
Charles Evans Hughes High School,
New York City

Samuel C. Brownstein
Former Chairman, Biology Department,
Wingate High School, Brooklyn, New York

Max Peters
Former Chairman, Mathematics Department,
Wingate High School, Brooklyn, New York

Ira K. Wolf, Ph.D.
Former Teacher of Mathematics,
Benjamin N. Cardozo High School,
Bayside, New York

Johanna M. Bolton
Instructor, Adult High School Program,
Daytona Beach Community College,
Daytona Beach, Florida

Robert Feinstein
GED Instructor for Adult Educational Services,
Northport-East Northport School District,
Northport, New York

Sally Ramsey
Former GED Instructor,
Southeastern Illinois College,
Harrisburg, Illinois

Louis Gotlib
Science Teacher,
Wissahickon Senior High School,
Ambler, Pennsylvania

Kelly A. Battles
Language Arts Teacher,
Fredericksburg, Virginia

BARRON'S

All inquiries should be addressed to:
Barron's Educational Series, Inc.
250 Wireless Boulevard
Hauppauge, New York 11788
www.barronseduc.com

Library of Congress Control Number: 2009032067

ISBN-13: (book only) 978-0-7641-4463-9
ISBN-10: (book only) 0-7641-4463-4

ISBN-13: (book with CD-ROM) 978-0-7641-9742-0
ISBN-10: (book with CD-ROM) 0-7641-9742-8

Library of Congress Cataloging-in-Publication Data

GED, high school equivalency exam / Murray Rockowitz ... [et al.].— 15th ed.
    p.   cm.
  Includes index.
  ISBN-13: 978-0-7641-4463-9 (book)
  ISBN-10: 0-7641-4463-4 (book)
  ISBN-13: 978-0-7641-9742-0 (package)
  ISBN-10: 0-7641-9742-8 (package)
    1. General educational development tests—Study guides.   2. High school
equivalency examinations—Study guides. I. Rockowitz, Murray. II. Barron's
Educational Series, Inc.   III. Title: General educational development test, high
school equivalency exam.   IV. Title: High school equivalency exam.

LB3060.33.G45R63   2010
373.126'2—dc22   2009032067

PRINTED IN THE UNITED STATES OF AMERICA
9 8 7 6

Contents

SOCIAL STUDIES

SCIENCE

LANGUAGE ARTS, READING

MATHEMATICS

TWO PRACTICE EXAMS

Preface

This edition includes what you need to know to pass the tests of General Educational Development (GED) in order to qualify for a High School Equivalency Diploma. The authors, all specialists in various areas of the high school curriculum, have developed practice exercises and tests that will help prepare you for the GED Examination.

TO THE READER

"Until recently, all we asked of job applicants was that they be able to sign their names and find their way to the time clock. Now they've got to have a high school diploma." These words of an electronics manufacturer are a warning to the student and jobseeker alike. In today's world you must have a high school diploma

- if you want to advance your education by enrolling in college;

- if you want to say to your family and friends, "Yes, I have a high school diploma.";

- if you want an interesting job—one that does not lead to a dead end;

- if you want to continue your studies at a technical school;

- if you want to get a technical or junior professional Civil Service position;

- if you want to be accepted in a specialized assignment in the Armed Forces.

If you have not yet completed high school, this book will help you earn that precious diploma by passing a High School Equivalency Examination. All fifty states, the District of Columbia, many U.S. territories, and most Canadian provinces have programs that enable you to do this.

To help you, we have carefully analyzed the latest GED tests, and, on the basis of that analysis, have prepared materials that provide:

- explanations of key ideas,

- concise summaries of each topic,

- thorough drill exercises,

- realistic practice tests.

All you need to add is the determination to use these materials according to the schedule we have suggested. If you do, you will gain the confidence and knowledge you need to pass the High School Equivalency Examination and earn your high school diploma.

TO THE INSTRUCTOR

If you are using this book in a class preparing for the High School Equivalency Examination, please note that:

- all necessary background materials have been included;

- after every principle, appropriate illustrations may be found;

- after each topic and subtopic, there are ample drill exercises;

- sample reading selections have been thoroughly analyzed;

- answers for all exercises have been included and, in most cases, explanations for the correct answer are given.

You will **not** have to go to any other sources for additional materials. We have included more than enough practice and drill for any student in your class who seeks the High School Equivalency Diploma.

INTRODUCTION TO
THE GED EXAM

Preparing for the GED Exam

CHAPTER 1

THE IMPORTANCE OF THE GED EXAM

The General Educational Development (or GED) Examination offers anyone who has not completed his or her high school diploma a way to earn a High School Equivalency Certificate. This is the equivalent of a high school diploma, and it is necessary for those who want to continue their education in college or another career-oriented program. Having a high school diploma today is also very important if you want a good job.

High school graduates typically earn much more than high school dropouts. *It pays to have a high school diploma.*

This book has been written to help you prepare to take the GED Examination. It contains reviews of the subject material, practice exercises, and even practice tests, all of which will familiarize you with the content and format of the actual examination. Over two million people have already used this book to help them pass the GED Examination. You can, too!

THE FIVE GED TEST AREAS

The GED Examination is divided into five tests:

1. Language Arts, Writing

2. Social Studies

3. Science

4. Language Arts, Reading

5. Mathematics

The five tests are designed to measure the knowledge and skills that a student should have acquired after four years in high school. One important thing about the tests is that, even though the questions may involve a specific area of study such as science, you don't have to memorize specific facts, details, dates, or even exact definitions. Much of this information is given to you in the test itself. You have to be able to read and understand the material that is presented and then to answer questions about it.

With the exception of the essay part of the Writing Skills test, and ten alternate format questions in the Math test, all of the questions in the GED Examination are multiple-choice. You will be given a brief statement, short passage, map, table, or diagram, and then you will have to answer one or more multiple-choice questions about this material. This book will help you learn how to analyze and use information presented in these various ways.

TIMETABLE OF A
HIGH SCHOOL EQUIVALENCY EXAMINATION
TOTAL: 7 HOURS, 5 MINUTES

	Section	Time Allowed	Number of Test Items	Description
Test 1	The Language Arts, Writing Test Part I	75 minutes	50	Sentence Structure (30%) Usage (30%) Mechanics (25%) Organization (15%)
	Part II	45 minutes		Essay on a given topic
Test 2	The Social Studies Test	70 minutes	50	History (40%) Geography (15%) Civics and Government (25%) Economics (20%)
Test 3	The Science Test	80 minutes	50	Biology (50%) Earth Science Chemistry } 50% Physics
Test 4	The Language Arts, Reading Test	65 minutes	40	Literary Text (poetry, drama, prose before 1920, prose 1920–1960, prose after 1960) (75%) Nonfiction Text (nonfiction prose, critical reviews, business documents) (25%)
Test 5	The Mathematics Test Part I (with a calculator)	45 minutes	25	Numbers and Operations (25%) Geometry (25%) Measurement and Data Analysis (25%) Algebra (25%)
	Part II (without a calculator)	45 minutes	25	(same as above)

COMMONLY ASKED QUESTIONS
ABOUT THE GED TESTS

1. ***Who can take the GED tests?*** Adults who meet the eligibility requirements established by their state, territorial, or provincial departments of education can take the GED tests.

2. ***Where are the GED tests given?*** The American Council on Education (ACE) maintains an informative Web site (*http://www.acenet.edu/clll/ged*) that lists testing centers in all 50 states and several territories outside the United States, along with other valuable GED-related material. For testing centers and administrative contacts nearest your home, you can also try calling or visiting your local high school.

3. ***What score is required to earn a High School Equivalency Diploma?*** The standard score requirements vary for each state, territory, or province. You will find that in some states a candidate must earn a minimum score of 410 on each of the five test areas or a minimum average score of 450 for the five tests. (200 is the lowest score; 800, the highest.) The majority of states require a minimum average score of 450 and no individual test score below 350 or 410.

4. ***What types of questions are on the GED tests?*** Part II of the Writing Skills test requires a written essay. For most of the other test questions, you will be given information in the form of a written passage, graph, diagram, map, or table, and asked to answer one or more multiple-choice questions based on the information presented. Five answer choices are given for each question, except for the alternate format math questions.

5. ***How can experience outside the classroom help me pass the GED tests?*** Many people worry about the difficulty of taking the GED Examination, especially if they've been out of school for a long time. What you should realize is that learning continues after you leave school. You read newspapers and follow political events; you travel and talk to many different people; you listen to the radio, watch television, and go to the movies. All of these experiences are forms of learning and add to your educational background.

6. ***Why are maturity and motivation strong assets?*** More mature students have experiences that will help them visualize or understand situations that may be involved in a problem on the GED Examination. Also, older students understand the need for good study habits and have the self-discipline to work regularly in this book. With the mature decision to study for the GED tests, half the battle is over. Many educators know that motivation, the desire to learn, is the first step toward success.

7. ***When are you ready to take the GED Examination?*** After reviewing and doing the practice exercises, take the practice tests in the back of the book, and score your results. If your scores are in the category Good or Excellent, you are probably ready to walk into the examination room with confidence. If, however, you did not attain such scores, do not apply for the GED Examination until you have studied further. Concentrate on the areas in which you are weak.

ORGANIZING YOUR PLAN OF STUDY

SOME STUDY HINTS

Educators agree that, for learning to be efficient, certain steps must be followed. As a mature person, you will probably appreciate the value of carefully following these ten tips for successful study.

1. **Physical conditions.** Find a quiet place. Tolerate no distraction—noise or music. Do not work in an overheated room.

2. **Timing.** You will learn faster and remember longer if you study in several short sessions rather than in one long session. Do not attempt to study for an entire weekend. Fatigue will set in after a few hours. It is wiser to spend some time each day rather than to "cram" your work into one or two days.

3. **Schedule for study.** A study schedule must be workable, realistic, practical, and, above all, suited to you and your other obligations. Decide which days and hours you can spare for study. Make a schedule, and stick to it.

4. **Using odd moments.** Put spare time and wasted moments to work. Riding on the bus or train may be a good time to memorize troublesome spelling words and to study rules of grammar or definitions of unfamiliar terms.

5. **Efficiency.** Most people find that learning occurs faster in the early part of the day. Perhaps you can work into your schedule some time for study before your day's work begins or on weekend mornings. Certainly you should not schedule study in the later hours of the evening.

6. **Review periods.** On certain days, plan to review. Take stock of yourself in these study periods. This review will serve at least two purposes. It will definitely reinforce the learning, and the gratification of knowing that you have acquired new material will stimulate you to learn more.

7. **Writing while you learn.** Wherever possible, write what you are studying. Spelling can best be learned by writing. Get into the habit of writing down key ideas of the passages you read. This writing will focus attention on your learning, will help you avoid distractions that may cause your mind to wander, and will provide an opportunity to check up on yourself. Also, educators believe that the more senses employed while studying, the more effective the learning will be.

8. **Reading.** The best way to improve reading comprehension is by practicing reading. You will find that a great part of the test involves the interpretation of reading material. Read your newspaper very carefully. Make it a habit to read the editorials. If possible, engage a member of your family or a friend in frequent discussions of the ideas presented in your newspaper. Of course, this book has specific reading exercises on the various phases of the test. But remember: there is no substitute for general reading.

9. **The dictionary.** The most important single book, in addition to this one, that can help you prepare for the High School Equivalency Examination is a dictionary which you can find online or in any book store. It is important to have one nearby as you study. A suggested inexpensive dictionary is the pocket-size paperback edition of *Webster's New World Dictionary of the American Language.*

10. **S Q 3R.** A popular way to remember the five important steps needed to study effectively is the S Q 3R method.

- S stands for *survey.* You examine the material to be learned to get a general idea of the content.

- Q stands for *question.* You turn the topic, the title of the section you are studying, into a question or questions. For example, if the title of the section is "Drawing Conclusions," you turn it into a challenging question: "How do I draw conclusions from what I read?"

- The first of the three R's stands for *read.* You use the reading skills that are taught in this book, such as locating the main idea, finding details, reading critically, detecting propaganda, determining cause and effect, and comparing and contrasting ideas.

- The second R stands for *recite.* You close the book and speak aloud from memory. Include especially the main ideas you have located and any name, word, or fact you find difficult to remember.

- The third R stands for *review*, which literally means to "view" or see again. You look over your notes, the lines you have highlighted, or the outline you have made. Do this again until you are sure you have mastered the material, for example, spelling words that trouble you or a rule of punctuation you find hard to remember.

This is a summary of the S Q 3R method of study:

S urvey
Q uestion
R ead
R ecite
R eview

BEFORE THE TEST DATE

1. **Use this book wisely.** It can help you achieve your goal—the High School Equivalency Diploma. After you take the Diagnostic Test, you will discover your specific weaknesses and can concentrate your review on these areas. Study the examination strategies, and apply them when you do the exercises and take the practice tests.

2. **Practice reading and writing.** Besides using the material in this book, spend more time reading. Read the local newspaper and some magazines. Also practice writing. Write letters to friends and relatives. Instead of using the telephone, use your pen.

3. **Don't rush to take the tests.** Don't be in too big a hurry to apply for the GED Examination. First be sure that you are prepared by taking the exercises and tests in this book. Even though most states will let you retake the tests after a waiting period, a notice that you failed the first time is unpleasant and may even discourage you from trying again. Instead of rushing into the examination and trusting to good fortune for a passing grade, it's better to wait until you know that you're ready. Also, don't procrastinate and cram all your study into the last few days. This rarely works. It's much better to set a realistic study schedule that gives you enough time to prepare.

4. **Know what to expect.** By the time you finish the preparation material in this book, you will be familiar with all the kinds of questions you will encounter on the GED tests. The exercises and practice test questions in this book are very similar to the actual test questions. Knowing what to expect will relieve some of your anxiety about taking the exam.

5. **Relax.** It's a good idea to relax the evening before you take the GED Examination. A good night's sleep will help you to think logically; you'll be well rested and alert. Also, do not eat a heavy meal, which will make you feel dull and sleepy, before you take the test.

TACTICS AND STRATEGIES IN THE EXAM ROOM

1. **Allow plenty of time to get to the test site.** Taking a test is pressure enough. You don't need the extra tension that comes from worrying about whether you will get there on time.

2. **Read all directions and questions carefully.** Answer the question given, not one you expected. Look for key words, such as *except*, *exactly*, and *not*. Carefully examine tables, graphs, and diagrams so you don't miss important information.

3. **Don't expect trick questions.** A straightforward presentation is used in all test sections.

4. **When you have difficulty finding an answer, eliminate choices that are definitely wrong.** Then consider the remaining choices.

5. **Don't let one or two challenging questions upset you.** Some questions are definitely harder than others. Remember you do not have to get 100 percent on this examination. No one does.

6. **Don't get bogged down on any one question.** If a question is taking too much time, circle it and make a guess. Then, if you have time at the end of the examination, go back and review the circled questions.

7. **Change answers only if you have a good reason for doing so.** Don't change your answer on a hunch or a whim. Most often the first judgment that you make is correct.

8. **Check answer order frequently.** Make sure you are putting your answers in the right spaces.

9. **Use your time wisely.** After taking the practice tests in this book, you will be familiar with the proper pace needed to complete each test.

10. **Do not make stray pencil marks on the answer sheet.** These may interfere with the rating of your performance. If you wish to change an answer, be sure to erase your first mark completely. Also, do not fold or crease the answer sheet.

11. **Answer all questions, even if you have to guess.** Your score will be determined by the number of correct answers; no points are deducted for wrong answers. For this reason it is better to guess at an answer than to not respond at all. Of course, wherever possible, eliminate as many wrong answers as you can before guessing.

12. **Remain as calm as possible.** Psychologists claim that more than 90 percent of us think we don't perform well on tests *of any kind*. But more than 80 percent of the people who have taken the High School Equivalency tests in the New York area, for example, have passed them. They must be doing something right. And so can you—with the right attitude and careful preparation.

A SUGGESTED STUDY PLAN

The task of reading this book and learning the material may seem impossible—after all, it's a big book! If, however, you divide everything up into small lessons, the job suddenly becomes much easier. The teachers who prepared this material for you have done just that—they have arranged everything into relatively small chapters, which you can review and master before moving on to the next one.

A Word About Time

Don't try to learn everything or take every practice test in one session. Work at your own speed and in your own way. A book can't be completely flexible—but we urge you to be flexible. Use this book to suit your individual needs. If you need review in math but feel pretty confident about English, concentrate on math. If you want to try the exams first and skip a study section, do so. Remember that High School Equivalency Examinations are given frequently. Remember also that in most states you can take one test at a time—or two, or three, or all five. Remember especially that, if you fail one test, you can take another...and another. However, you will probably take all five tests and pass them all the first time you try. That is what this book aims to help you do.

GED WEB SITES

GENERAL WEB SITES

For further information regarding the GED exam, visit the following web sites.

www.ged-online.com/index-google.html

www.literacydirectory.org/

www.acenet.edu/AM/Template.cfm?Section=GEDTS

www.floridatechnet.org/GED/LessonPlans/Lessons.htm

en.wikipedia.org/wiki/GED

www.gedonline.org/facts/facts.html

education-portal.com/articles/All_About_the_GED

www.oltraining.com/catalog/be_ged/loc.html (listing of all states' GED web sites)

www.studyguidezone.com/ged.htm

www.4tests.com/training/

www.testprepreview.com/modules/socialstudies.htm

STATE WEB SITES

Be sure to check out your state's web site for specific information about testing times, places, and requirements.

Alabama: www.acs.cc.al.us/ged/ged.aspx

Alaska: www.ajcn.state.ak.us/abe/ged.htm

Arkansas: dwe.arkansas.gov/ged.htm

Arizona: www.ade.state.az.us/adult-ed/

California: www.cde.ca.gov/ta/tg/gd/

Colorado: www.cde.state.co.us/cdeadult/GEDindex.htm

Connecticut: www.state.ct.us/sde/deps/Adult/ged/index.html

Delaware: www.k12.de.us/adulted/ged.html

Florida: www.aceofflorida.org/ged/

Georgia: www.dtae.tec.ga.us/adultlit/ged.html

Hawaii: doe.k12.hi.us/communityschools/diplomaged.htm

Idaho: www.idahoptv.org/learn/careers.cfm

Illinois: www.gedillinois.org/

Indiana: www.doe.state.in.us/adulted/

Iowa: www.readiowa.org/GED/gedfacts.html

Kansas: www.kansasregents.org/adult_ed/ged.html

Kentucky: kyae.ky.gov/students/ged.htm

Louisiana: www.doe.state.la.us/lde/family/525.html

Maine: www.maine.gov/education/aded/dev/index.htm

Maryland: www.marylandpublicschools.org/MSDE/programs/GED/

Massachusetts: www.doe.mass.edu/ged/

Michigan: www.michigan.gov/mdcd/0,1607,7-122-1680_2798_2801---,00.html

Minnesota: mnabe.themlc.org/GED.html

Mississippi: sbcjcweb.sbcjc.cc.ms.us/adulted/ged/default.asp

Missouri: www.gedonlineclass.com/

Montana: www.opi.state.mt.us/GED/Index.html

Nebraska: www.nde.state.ne.us/ADED/home.htm

Nevada: www.literacynet.org/nvadulted/programs-ged.html

New Hampshire: www.ed.state.nh.us/education/doe/organization/
adultlearning/Adulted/new_hampshire_ged_testing_program.htm

New Jersey: www.state.nj.us/njded/students/ged/

New Mexico: www.ped.state.nm.us/div/ais/assess/ged/gedfaq.html

New York: www.emsc.nysed.gov/ged/

North Carolina: www.ncccs.cc.nc.us/Basic_Skills/ged.htm

North Dakota: www.dpi.state.nd.us/adulted/index.shtm

Ohio: www.ohioliteracynetwork.org/ged.html

Oklahoma: ok.cls.utk.edu/ged_tests.html

Oregon: www.oregon.gov/CCWD/GED/index.shtml

Pennsylvania: www.able.state.pa.us/able/cwp/view.asp?a=5&Q=39791&g=
176&ableNav=|2620|2786|&ableNav=|2766|&ableNav=|2759|2766|

Rhode Island: www.ridoe.net/adulted_ged/Default.htm

South Carolina: www.sclrc.org/ged.htm

South Dakota: www.state.sd.us/dol/abe/ged_testing_home.htm

Tennessee: www.state.tn.us/labor-wfd/AE/aeged.htm

Texas: www.tea.state.tx.us/ged/

Utah: www.usoe.k12.ut.us/adulted/GED/tv/tips.htm

Vermont: www.state.vt.us/educ/new/html/pgm_adulted/ged/info.html

Virginia: www.pen.k12.va.us/VDOE/Instruction/Adult/ged.html; www.vaged.vcu.edu/index.shtml

Washington: www.sbctc.ctc.edu/ged/default.asp

Washington, DC: www.dcadultliteracy.org/services/ged.html

West Virginia: www.wvabe.org/ged_centers.htm

Wisconsin: dpi.wi.gov/ged_hsed/gedhsed.html

Wyoming: www.wyomingworkforce.org

A Diagnostic Exam

The direction sheets, mathematics formulas,* and question formats of this exam are constructed like the actual test you will take. The exam consists of five parts.

Tests		Questions	Time Allowance	
Test 1:	The Language Arts, Writing Test, Part I	50	1 hour,	15 minutes
	The Language Arts, Writing Test, Part II	Essay		45 minutes
Test 2:	The Social Studies Test	50	1 hour,	10 minutes
Test 3:	The Science Test	66	1 hour,	35 minutes
Test 4:	The Language Arts, Reading Test	40	1 hour,	5 minutes
Test 5:	The Mathematics Test, Part I	25		45 minutes
	The Mathematics Test, Part II	25		45 minutes
*More science questions are on the diagnostic test than are on the actual GED exam		**Total:**	7 hours, 20 minutes	

For this exam, we have included an answer sheet and a self-appraisal chart. Mark yourself on each test, checking your answers against the answer key. Read the answer explanations to be sure you understand the correct answer choices. After you have calculated the scores for all five tests, refer to the self-appraisal materials to determine your subject area strengths and weaknesses as well as your total GED score.

The main purpose of the test is to help you discover your strengths and your weaknesses. IMPORTANT: You should spend more time studying those chapters that deal with the tests in which you are weakest. In that way, you will improve your score when you take the two practice exams at the end of this book.

SIMULATE TEST CONDITIONS

To make conditions similar to those on the actual exam, do not take more time than that allowed for each test.

*Directions and mathematics formulas are reprinted by permission of the GED Testing Service of the American Council on Education.

ANSWER SHEET FOR
THE DIAGNOSTIC EXAMINATION

TEST 1: LANGUAGE ARTS, WRITING

1. ① ② ③ ④ ⑤
2. ① ② ③ ④ ⑤
3. ① ② ③ ④ ⑤
4. ① ② ③ ④ ⑤
5. ① ② ③ ④ ⑤
6. ① ② ③ ④ ⑤
7. ① ② ③ ④ ⑤
8. ① ② ③ ④ ⑤
9. ① ② ③ ④ ⑤
10. ① ② ③ ④ ⑤
11. ① ② ③ ④ ⑤
12. ① ② ③ ④ ⑤
13. ① ② ③ ④ ⑤
14. ① ② ③ ④ ⑤
15. ① ② ③ ④ ⑤
16. ① ② ③ ④ ⑤
17. ① ② ③ ④ ⑤
18. ① ② ③ ④ ⑤
19. ① ② ③ ④ ⑤
20. ① ② ③ ④ ⑤

21. ① ② ③ ④ ⑤
22. ① ② ③ ④ ⑤
23. ① ② ③ ④ ⑤
24. ① ② ③ ④ ⑤
25. ① ② ③ ④ ⑤
26. ① ② ③ ④ ⑤
27. ① ② ③ ④ ⑤
28. ① ② ③ ④ ⑤
29. ① ② ③ ④ ⑤
30. ① ② ③ ④ ⑤
31. ① ② ③ ④ ⑤
32. ① ② ③ ④ ⑤
33. ① ② ③ ④ ⑤
34. ① ② ③ ④ ⑤
35. ① ② ③ ④ ⑤
36. ① ② ③ ④ ⑤
37. ① ② ③ ④ ⑤
38. ① ② ③ ④ ⑤
39. ① ② ③ ④ ⑤
40. ① ② ③ ④ ⑤

41. ① ② ③ ④ ⑤
42. ① ② ③ ④ ⑤
43. ① ② ③ ④ ⑤
44. ① ② ③ ④ ⑤
45. ① ② ③ ④ ⑤
46. ① ② ③ ④ ⑤
47. ① ② ③ ④ ⑤
48. ① ② ③ ④ ⑤
49. ① ② ③ ④ ⑤
50. ① ② ③ ④ ⑤

TEST 2: SOCIAL STUDIES

1. ① ② ③ ④ ⑤
2. ① ② ③ ④ ⑤
3. ① ② ③ ④ ⑤
4. ① ② ③ ④ ⑤
5. ① ② ③ ④ ⑤
6. ① ② ③ ④ ⑤
7. ① ② ③ ④ ⑤
8. ① ② ③ ④ ⑤
9. ① ② ③ ④ ⑤
10. ① ② ③ ④ ⑤
11. ① ② ③ ④ ⑤
12. ① ② ③ ④ ⑤
13. ① ② ③ ④ ⑤
14. ① ② ③ ④ ⑤
15. ① ② ③ ④ ⑤
16. ① ② ③ ④ ⑤
17. ① ② ③ ④ ⑤
18. ① ② ③ ④ ⑤
19. ① ② ③ ④ ⑤
20. ① ② ③ ④ ⑤

21. ① ② ③ ④ ⑤
22. ① ② ③ ④ ⑤
23. ① ② ③ ④ ⑤
24. ① ② ③ ④ ⑤
25. ① ② ③ ④ ⑤
26. ① ② ③ ④ ⑤
27. ① ② ③ ④ ⑤
28. ① ② ③ ④ ⑤
29. ① ② ③ ④ ⑤
30. ① ② ③ ④ ⑤
31. ① ② ③ ④ ⑤
32. ① ② ③ ④ ⑤
33. ① ② ③ ④ ⑤
34. ① ② ③ ④ ⑤
35. ① ② ③ ④ ⑤
36. ① ② ③ ④ ⑤
37. ① ② ③ ④ ⑤
38. ① ② ③ ④ ⑤
39. ① ② ③ ④ ⑤
40. ① ② ③ ④ ⑤

41. ① ② ③ ④ ⑤
42. ① ② ③ ④ ⑤
43. ① ② ③ ④ ⑤
44. ① ② ③ ④ ⑤
45. ① ② ③ ④ ⑤
46. ① ② ③ ④ ⑤
47. ① ② ③ ④ ⑤
48. ① ② ③ ④ ⑤
49. ① ② ③ ④ ⑤
50. ① ② ③ ④ ⑤

TEST 3: SCIENCE

1. ① ② ③ ④ ⑤
2. ① ② ③ ④ ⑤
3. ① ② ③ ④ ⑤
4. ① ② ③ ④ ⑤
5. ① ② ③ ④ ⑤
6. ① ② ③ ④ ⑤
7. ① ② ③ ④ ⑤
8. ① ② ③ ④ ⑤
9. ① ② ③ ④ ⑤
10. ① ② ③ ④ ⑤
11. ① ② ③ ④ ⑤
12. ① ② ③ ④ ⑤
13. ① ② ③ ④ ⑤
14. ① ② ③ ④ ⑤
15. ① ② ③ ④ ⑤
16. ① ② ③ ④ ⑤
17. ① ② ③ ④ ⑤
18. ① ② ③ ④ ⑤
19. ① ② ③ ④ ⑤
20. ① ② ③ ④ ⑤
21. ① ② ③ ④ ⑤
22. ① ② ③ ④ ⑤

23. ① ② ③ ④ ⑤
24. ① ② ③ ④ ⑤
25. ① ② ③ ④ ⑤
26. ① ② ③ ④ ⑤
27. ① ② ③ ④ ⑤
28. ① ② ③ ④ ⑤
29. ① ② ③ ④ ⑤
30. ① ② ③ ④ ⑤
31. ① ② ③ ④ ⑤
32. ① ② ③ ④ ⑤
33. ① ② ③ ④ ⑤
34. ① ② ③ ④ ⑤
35. ① ② ③ ④ ⑤
36. ① ② ③ ④ ⑤
37. ① ② ③ ④ ⑤
38. ① ② ③ ④ ⑤
39. ① ② ③ ④ ⑤
40. ① ② ③ ④ ⑤
41. ① ② ③ ④ ⑤
42. ① ② ③ ④ ⑤
43. ① ② ③ ④ ⑤
44. ① ② ③ ④ ⑤

45. ① ② ③ ④ ⑤
46. ① ② ③ ④ ⑤
47. ① ② ③ ④ ⑤
48. ① ② ③ ④ ⑤
49. ① ② ③ ④ ⑤
50. ① ② ③ ④ ⑤
51. ① ② ③ ④ ⑤
52. ① ② ③ ④ ⑤
53. ① ② ③ ④ ⑤
54. ① ② ③ ④ ⑤
55. ① ② ③ ④ ⑤
56. ① ② ③ ④ ⑤
57. ① ② ③ ④ ⑤
58. ① ② ③ ④ ⑤
59. ① ② ③ ④ ⑤
60. ① ② ③ ④ ⑤
61. ① ② ③ ④ ⑤
62. ① ② ③ ④ ⑤
63. ① ② ③ ④ ⑤
64. ① ② ③ ④ ⑤
65. ① ② ③ ④ ⑤
66. ① ② ③ ④ ⑤

TEST 4: LANGUAGE ARTS, READING

1. ① ② ③ ④ ⑤
2. ① ② ③ ④ ⑤
3. ① ② ③ ④ ⑤
4. ① ② ③ ④ ⑤
5. ① ② ③ ④ ⑤
6. ① ② ③ ④ ⑤
7. ① ② ③ ④ ⑤
8. ① ② ③ ④ ⑤
9. ① ② ③ ④ ⑤
10. ① ② ③ ④ ⑤
11. ① ② ③ ④ ⑤
12. ① ② ③ ④ ⑤
13. ① ② ③ ④ ⑤
14. ① ② ③ ④ ⑤
15. ① ② ③ ④ ⑤

16. ① ② ③ ④ ⑤
17. ① ② ③ ④ ⑤
18. ① ② ③ ④ ⑤
19. ① ② ③ ④ ⑤
20. ① ② ③ ④ ⑤
21. ① ② ③ ④ ⑤
22. ① ② ③ ④ ⑤
23. ① ② ③ ④ ⑤
24. ① ② ③ ④ ⑤
25. ① ② ③ ④ ⑤
26. ① ② ③ ④ ⑤
27. ① ② ③ ④ ⑤
28. ① ② ③ ④ ⑤
29. ① ② ③ ④ ⑤
30. ① ② ③ ④ ⑤

31. ① ② ③ ④ ⑤
32. ① ② ③ ④ ⑤
33. ① ② ③ ④ ⑤
34. ① ② ③ ④ ⑤
35. ① ② ③ ④ ⑤
36. ① ② ③ ④ ⑤
37. ① ② ③ ④ ⑤
38. ① ② ③ ④ ⑤
39. ① ② ③ ④ ⑤
40. ① ② ③ ④ ⑤

TEST 5: MATHEMATICS, PART I

1. ① ② ③ ④ ⑤
2. ① ② ③ ④ ⑤
3.

4. ① ② ③ ④ ⑤
5. ① ② ③ ④ ⑤
6.

7. ① ② ③ ④ ⑤
8. ① ② ③ ④ ⑤
9. ① ② ③ ④ ⑤
10. ① ② ③ ④ ⑤

11. ① ② ③ ④ ⑤
12. ① ② ③ ④ ⑤
13. ① ② ③ ④ ⑤
14.

15. ① ② ③ ④ ⑤
16. ① ② ③ ④ ⑤
17. ① ② ③ ④ ⑤
18. ① ② ③ ④ ⑤
19.

20. ① ② ③ ④ ⑤

21. ① ② ③ ④ ⑤
22.

23. ① ② ③ ④ ⑤
24. ① ② ③ ④ ⑤
25.

TEST 5: MATHEMATICS, PART II

26. ① ② ③ ④ ⑤

27.

28. ① ② ③ ④ ⑤

29. ① ② ③ ④ ⑤

30. ① ② ③ ④ ⑤

31. ① ② ③ ④ ⑤

32. ① ② ③ ④ ⑤

33. ① ② ③ ④ ⑤

34. ① ② ③ ④ ⑤

35. ① ② ③ ④ ⑤

36. ① ② ③ ④ ⑤

37. ① ② ③ ④ ⑤

38. ① ② ③ ④ ⑤

39. ① ② ③ ④ ⑤

40. ① ② ③ ④ ⑤

41. ① ② ③ ④ ⑤

42. ① ② ③ ④ ⑤

43. ① ② ③ ④ ⑤

44. ① ② ③ ④ ⑤

45. ① ② ③ ④ ⑤

46. ① ② ③ ④ ⑤

47.

48. ① ② ③ ④ ⑤

49. ① ② ③ ④ ⑤

50.

DIAGNOSTIC EXAM

TEST 1: LANGUAGE ARTS, WRITING, PART I

DIRECTIONS

The first part of the GED exam measures the test taker's ability to correctly and sufficiently analyze the English language. This section focuses on the written, not spoken, word and consists of both multiple-choice questions and an essay.

The first half of this section consists of multiple-choice questions with paragraphs that have numbered sentences. Some of these sentences contain errors such as usage, sentence structure, and mechanics. Multiple-choice questions follow each of these passages. For questions that refer to sentences that are already correctly written, choose the answer that doesn't change the sentence. Sometimes the best answer is the one that makes a sentence's point of view or verb tense consistent with the rest of the paragraph.

You are given 120 minutes (two hours) for this section of the exam. We recommend that you spend 75 minutes working on the multiple-choice questions, and 45 minutes on the essay. A separate set of directions is given for the essay after the multiple-choice questions.

To mark your answer, darken the corresponding circle on the answer sheet.

FOR EXAMPLE:

Sentence 1: **We were all honored to meet governor Phillips.**

What correction should be made to this sentence?

(1) insert a comma after <u>honored</u>   ① ② ● ④ ⑤
(2) change the spelling of <u>honored</u> to <u>honered</u>
(3) change <u>governor</u> to <u>Governor</u>
(4) replace <u>were</u> with <u>was</u>
(5) no correction is necessary

In this example, the word "governor" should be capitalized; therefore, answer space 3 would be marked on the answer sheet.

GO ON TO THE NEXT PAGE

TEST 1: LANGUAGE ARTS, WRITING, PART I

<u>Questions 1–9</u> refer to the following paragraph.

(1) A combination of attributes make vegetable gardening a national hobby with both young and old. (2) For an ever-increasing number of individuals seed catalogs and the thoughts of spring gardening provide a happy escape from the winter doldrums. (3) Vegetable gardeners unanimously agree that many home-grown vegetables picked at their peak of maturity have quality. seldom found in vegetables purchased from commercial markets. (4) From Spring to late Fall, a well-planned and maintained garden can provide a supply of fresh vegetables, thus increasing the nutritional value of the family diet. (5) Freezers make it possible to preserve some of the surplus vegetables to be enjoyed at a later date other vegetables can be stored for a few months in a cool area. (6) Not to be overlooked is the finger-tip convenience of having vegetables in the backyard; this in itself justifies home gardening for many individuals. (7) In addition, vegetable gardening provides excercise and recreation for both urban and suburban families. (8) Although your initial dollar investment for gardening may be nominal, one cannot escape the fact that gardening requires manual labor and time. (9) Neglecting jobs that should be performed on a regular basis may result in failure and a negative feeling toward gardening.

1. Sentence 1: **A combination of attributes make vegetable gardening a national hobby with both young and old.**

   What correction should be made to this sentence?

   (1) insert a comma after <u>attributes</u>
   (2) change <u>make</u> to <u>makes</u>
   (3) capitalize vegetable gardening
   (4) reverse <u>with</u> and <u>both</u>
   (5) no correction is necessary

2. Sentence 2: **For an ever-increasing number of individuals seed catalogs and the thoughts of spring gardening provide a happy escape from the winter doldrums.**

   What correction should be made to this sentence?

   (1) remove the hyphen from <u>ever-increasing</u>
   (2) change <u>number</u> to <u>amount</u>
   (3) insert a comma after <u>individuals</u>
   (4) insert a comma after <u>catalogs</u>
   (5) no correction is necessary

3. Sentence 3: **Vegetable gardeners unanimously agree that many home-grown vegetables picked at their peak of maturity have <u>quality. seldom</u> found in vegetables purchased from commercial markets.**

   Which of the following is the best way to write the underlined portion of this sentence? If you think the original is the best way, choose option (1).

   (1) quality. seldom
   (2) quality. Seldom
   (3) quality seldom
   (4) quality; seldom
   (5) quality, seldom

4. Sentence 4: **From Spring to late Fall, a well-planned and maintained garden can provide a supply of fresh vegetables, thus increasing the nutritional value of the family diet.**

   What correction should be made to this sentence?

   (1) remove capitals from <u>Spring</u> and <u>Fall</u>
   (2) remove the hyphen from <u>well-planned</u>
   (3) remove the comma after <u>vegetables</u>
   (4) change <u>thus</u> to <u>however</u>
   (5) no correction is necessary

GO ON TO THE NEXT PAGE

TEST 1: LANGUAGE ARTS, WRITING, PA

5. A new paragraph can

   (1) be started after sentence 3
   (2) be started after sentence 4
   (3) be started after sentence 6
   (4) be started after sentence 7
   (5) not be started

6. Sentence 6: **Not to be overlooked is the finger-tip convenience of having vegetables in the backyard; this in itself justifies home gardening for many individuals.**

   What correction should be made to this sentence?

   (1) insert a comma after <u>overlooked</u>
   (2) change the spelling of <u>vegetables</u> to <u>vegtables</u>
   (3) replace the semicolon after <u>backyard</u> with a comma
   (4) change the spelling of <u>gardening</u> to <u>gardning</u>
   (5) no correction is necessary

7. The topic sentence of this paragraph is

   (1) sentence 1
   (2) sentence 2
   (3) sentence 3
   (4) sentence 8
   (5) sentence 9

8. Sentence 8: **Although your initial dollar investment for gardening may be nominal, one cannot escape the fact that gardening requires manual labor and time.**

   What correction should be made to this sentence?

   (1) change <u>Although</u> to <u>Because</u>
   (2) remove the comma after <u>nominal</u>
   (3) change <u>one</u> to <u>you</u>
   (4) change <u>requires</u> to <u>require</u>
   (5) no correction is necessary

9. Sentence 9: **Neglecting jo... be performed on a regular ... result in failure and a negativ... toward gardening.**

   What correction should be made to thi... sentence?

   (1) insert a comma after <u>jobs</u>
   (2) insert a comma after <u>basis</u>
   (3) change <u>may result</u> to <u>results</u>
   (4) change <u>and</u> to <u>despite</u>
   (5) no correction is necessary

<u>Questions 10–19</u> refer to the following paragraph.

(1) In coming years, families will need to learn to turn to there computers for assistance. (2) With the increasing amounts of information a family is required to process, the home computer will become a necessity for both decision making and family record storage and retrieval. (3) A home communications revolution is predicted with the arrival of the home computer. It will serve as a source and processor of information. (4) A virtually infinite amount of information from many sources will be at the instantaneous disposal of the family for more efficient decision making. (5) The computer will plan meals, turn lights on at appropriate times keep track of family members' schedules, calculate budget information, and oversee credit, spending, and bank accounts. (6) Just as home equipment frees the homemaker from the labor of housekeeping, the computer release's family members from some repetitious managerial duties. (7) The home terminal may serve as a home education center for children's homework and part of the lifelong learning program of parents and elderly family members. (8) The change that will have the most immediate effect on family decision making will be increased discretionary time. (9) For economic reasons, many families will decide to use their "free" time to hold a second job. (10) With the increasing interest in personal development, a segment of the time might be allotted by some to develop alternative interests through lifelong educational programs that will

GO ON TO THE NEXT PAGE

TEST 1: LANGUAGE ARTS, WRITING, PART I

facilitate career changes, to increase skills for effective citizenship, and learning new skills to enhance their family living.

10. Sentence 1: **In coming years, families will need to learn to turn to there computers for assistance.**

    What correction should be made to this sentence?

    (1) remove the comma after <u>years</u>
    (2) change <u>will need</u> to <u>need</u>
    (3) change the spelling of <u>assistance</u> to <u>assistence</u>
    (4) change the spelling of <u>there</u> to <u>their</u>
    (5) no correction is necessary

11. Sentence 2: **With the increasing amounts of information a family is required to process, the home computer will become a necessity for both decision making and family record storage and retrieval.**

    What correction should be made to this sentence?

    (1) change <u>With the</u> to <u>Despite</u>
    (2) change <u>is</u> to <u>are</u>
    (3) remove the comma after <u>process</u>
    (4) change the spelling of <u>necessity</u> to <u>neccesity</u>
    (5) no correction is necessary

12. Sentence 3: **A home communications revolution is predicted with the arrival of the home <u>computer. It</u> will serve as a source and processor of information.**

    Which of the following is the best way to write the underlined portion of the sentence? If you think the original is the best way, choose option (1).

    (1) computer. It
    (2) computer, It
    (3) computer, it
    (4) computer it
    (5) computer; It

13. Sentence 4: **A virtually infinite amount of information from many sources will be at the instantaneous disposal of the family for more efficient decision making.**

    What correction should be made to this sentence?

    (1) insert a comma after <u>information</u>
    (2) insert a comma after <u>sources</u>
    (3) insert a comma after <u>family</u>
    (4) change the spelling of <u>efficient</u> to <u>eficient</u>
    (5) no correction is necessary

14. Sentence 5: **The computer will plan meals, turn lights on at appropriate times keep track of family members' schedules, calculate budget information, and oversee credit, spending, and bank accounts.**

    What correction should be made to this sentence?

    (1) remove comma after <u>meals</u>
    (2) insert comma after <u>times</u>
    (3) change <u>members'</u> to <u>member's</u>
    (4) change the spelling of <u>schedules</u> to <u>skedules</u>
    (5) no correction is necessary

15. Sentence 6: **Just as home equipment frees the homemaker from the labor of housekeeping, the computer release's family members from some repetitious managerial duties.**

    What correction should be made to this sentence?

    (1) change <u>Just as</u> to <u>Although</u>
    (2) change <u>release's</u> to <u>releases</u>
    (3) remove the comma after <u>housekeeping</u>
    (4) change the spelling of <u>equipment</u> to <u>equiptment</u>
    (5) no correction is necessary

GO ON TO THE NEXT PAGE

TEST 1: LANGUAGE ARTS, WRITING, PART I

16. Sentence 7: **The home terminal may serve as a home education center for children's homework and part of the lifelong learning program of parents and elderly family members.**

    If you rewrote sentence 7 beginning with

    <u>Children's homework and part of the lifelong learning program of parents and elderly family members</u>

    the next words should be

    (1) are served
    (2) may serve
    (3) may be served
    (4) serve
    (5) will serve

17. Sentence 8: **The change that will have the most immediate effect on family decision making will be increased discretionary time.**

    What correction should be made to this sentence?

    (1) change <u>will have</u> to <u>having</u>
    (2) change the spelling of <u>effect</u> to <u>affect</u>
    (3) change <u>family</u> to <u>family's</u>
    (4) change <u>will be</u> to <u>is</u>
    (5) no correction is necessary

18. Sentence 9 should be

    (1) left as it is
    (2) placed last
    (3) placed after sentence 2
    (4) placed after sentence 6
    (5) omitted

19. Sentence 10: **With the increasing interest in personal development, a segment of the time might be allotted by some to develop alternative interests through lifelong educational programs that will facilitate career changes, to increase skills for effective citizenship, and learning new skills to enhance their family living.**

    What correction should be made to this sentence?

    (1) change the spelling of <u>development</u> to <u>developement</u>
    (2) change the spelling of <u>through</u> to <u>thorough</u>
    (3) remove the comma after <u>changes</u>
    (4) change <u>learning</u> to <u>to learn</u>
    (5) no correction is necessary

<u>Questions 20–28</u> refer to the following paragraphs.

(1) To lessen the threat of faulty car repair work or repair frauds, they're a number of constructive steps you can take. (2) While these measures can't offer full protection, it is wise insurance against dented pocketbooks and expanded time schedules.
(3) First, never wait until a small problem becomes a big and costly one. (4) Always takes your car in for a check at the first sign of trouble.
(5) But before you take the car in, make a list of all problems and "symptoms" so you are prepared to describe the trouble as accurately and specifically as possible.
(6) Don't just ask to have the car put in "working order," (7) that kind of general statement can lead directly to unnecessary work.
(8) On your initial visit, make certain you get a copy of the work authorization that you sign or a general estimate of the total cost of the repairs. (9) Don't leave until you do.
(10) Ask the repair garage to telephone you when the exact work to be done has been determinned. (11) When you receive the call, say you now want to return to the station to obtain another work order itemizing the cost of each repair to be made.

GO ON TO THE NEXT PAGE

TEST 1: LANGUAGE ARTS, WRITING, PART I

20. Sentence 1: **To lessen the threat of faulty car repair work or repair frauds, they're a number of constructive steps you can take.**

    What correction should be made to this sentence?

    (1) change <u>lessen</u> to <u>lesson</u>
    (2) remove the comma after <u>frauds</u>
    (3) change the spelling of <u>they're</u> to <u>there are</u>
    (4) change <u>can</u> to <u>might</u>
    (5) no correction is necessary

21. Sentence 2: **While these measures can't offer full protection, it is wise insurance against dented pocketbooks and expanded time schedules.**

    What correction should be made to this sentence?

    (1) change <u>While</u> to <u>Nevertheless</u>
    (2) change <u>it is</u> to <u>they are</u>
    (3) change <u>insurance</u> to <u>insurence</u>
    (4) insert a hyphen in <u>pocketbooks</u>
    (5) no correction is necessary

22. Sentence 3: **First, never wait until a small problem becomes a big and costly one.**

    What correction should be made to this sentence?

    (1) change <u>first</u> to <u>firstly</u>
    (2) remove the comma after <u>first</u>
    (3) change the spelling of <u>until</u> to <u>untill</u>
    (4) change <u>becomes</u> to <u>will become</u>
    (5) no correction is necessary

23. Sentence 4: **Always takes your car in for a check at the first sign of trouble.**

    What correction should be made to this sentence?

    (1) change <u>takes</u> to <u>take</u>
    (2) change <u>always</u> to <u>allways</u>
    (3) change <u>your</u> to <u>your'e</u>
    (4) insert a comma after <u>check</u>
    (5) no correction is necessary

24. Sentence 5: **But before you take the car in, make a list of all problems and "symptoms" so you are prepared to describe the trouble as accurately and specifically as possible.**

    What correction should be made to this sentence?

    (1) change <u>take</u> to <u>will take</u>
    (2) remove the comma after <u>in</u>
    (3) change <u>are</u> to <u>will be</u>
    (4) change the spelling of <u>specifically</u> to <u>specificaly</u>
    (5) no correction is necessary

25. Sentences 6 and 7: **Don't just ask to have the car put in "working <u>order," that</u> kind of general statement can lead directly to unnecessary work.**

    Which of the following is the best way to write the underlined portion of this sentence? If you think the original is the best way, choose option (1).

    (1) order," that
    (2) order" that
    (3) order": that
    (4) order". that
    (5) order." That

GO ON TO THE NEXT PAGE

TEST 1: LANGUAGE ARTS, WRITING, PART I

26. Sentence 8: **On your initial visit, make certain you get a copy of the work authorization that you sign or a general estimate of the total cost of the repairs.**

    What correction should be made to this sentence?

    (1) change the spelling of <u>initial</u> to <u>initail</u>
    (2) remove the comma after <u>visit</u>
    (3) insert a comma after <u>sign</u>
    (4) change the spelling of <u>estimate</u> to <u>estemate</u>
    (5) no correction is necessary

27. Sentence 10: **Ask the repair garage to telephone you when the exact work to be done has been determinned.**

    What correction should be made to this sentence?

    (1) insert a comma after <u>you</u>
    (2) insert a comma after <u>work</u>
    (3) insert a comma after <u>garage</u>
    (4) change the spelling of <u>determinned</u> to <u>determined</u>
    (5) no correction is necessary

28. Sentence 11 should be

    (1) left as it is
    (2) placed first
    (3) placed after sentence 5
    (4) placed before sentence 9
    (5) omitted

<u>Questions 29–37</u> refer to the following paragraphs.

(1) Total dollars available, family tastes storage and preparation facilities, end use, and item cost all affect a buying decision. (2) Unit pricing can help by taking the guesswork out of the price factor and simplifying cost comparisons.

(3) Unit price is just what its name implies—the price per unit. (4) To be more specific, unit pricing gives you the cost per ounce or per pound or per 100 or per square foot. (5) This price per unit enables you to ready find the best buy, dollarwise, among several items in different-size packages with different total prices.

(6) Thousands of retail food chain stores now have unit pricing programs. (7) Such programs are required by local laws in several areas, but generally the programs are voluntary.

(8) Stores that offer unit pricing generally use a shelf tag system—a label on the shelf edge below the item gives the name of the item, the size, the total price, and the unit price.

(9) When unit pricing was first introduced the shelf tag system posed some problems because keeping the tags on the shelves in the right location can be difficult. (10) But as unit pricing has gained acceptance, some of these mechanical problems has been overcome, and the label information has become more usable from the shoppers' standpoint.

29. Sentence 1: **Total dollars available, family tastes storage and preparation facilities, end use, and item cost all affect a buying decision.**

    What correction should be made to this sentence?

    (1) insert a comma after <u>tastes</u>
    (2) change <u>all</u> to <u>each</u>
    (3) change <u>affect</u> to <u>effect</u>
    (4) change the spelling of <u>buying</u> to <u>bying</u>
    (5) no correction is necessary

GO ON TO THE NEXT PAGE

TEST 1: LANGUAGE ARTS, WRITING, PART I

30. Sentence 1: **Total dollars available, family tastes storage and preparation facilities, end use, and item cost all affect a buying decision.**

    Sentence 1 should be

    (1) left as is
    (2) placed last
    (3) placed after sentence 2
    (4) placed before sentence 10
    (5) omitted

31. Sentence 2: **Unit pricing can help by taking the guesswork out of the price factor and simplifying cost comparisons.**

    What correction should be made to this sentence?

    (1) change <u>can</u> to <u>could</u>
    (2) change <u>by taking</u> to <u>to take</u>
    (3) insert a hyphen in <u>guesswork</u>
    (4) insert a comma after <u>factor</u>
    (5) no correction is necessary

32. Sentences 3 and 4: **Unit price is just what its name implies—the price per unit. <u>To be more specific,</u> unit pricing gives you the cost per ounce or per pound or per 100 or per square foot.**

    Which of the following is the best way to write the underlined portion of these sentences? If you think the original is the best way, choose option (1).

    (1) . To be more specific
    (2) , To be more specific
    (3) ; To be more specific
    (4) : To be more specific
    (5) —To be more specific

33. Sentence 5: **This price per unit enables you to ready find the best buy, dollarwise, among several items in different-size packages with different total prices.**

    What correction should be made to this sentence?

    (1) remove the commas before and after <u>dollarwise</u>
    (2) change <u>ready</u> to <u>readily</u>
    (3) change <u>among</u> to <u>between</u>
    (4) change <u>size</u> to <u>sized</u>
    (5) no correction is necessary

34. Sentences 6 and 7: **Thousands of retail food chain stores now have unit pricing <u>programs. Such programs are</u> required by local laws in several areas, but generally the programs are voluntary.**

    The most effective combination of sentences 6 and 7 would include replacing the underlined words with which of the following groups of words?

    (1) programs and such programs
    (2) programs; although such programs
    (3) programs, whereas such programs
    (4) programs that are
    (5) programs, some being

35. Sentence 8: **Stores that offer unit pricing generally use a shelf tag <u>system—a label</u> on the shelf edge below the item gives the name of the item, the size, the total price, and the unit price.**

    Which of the following is the best way to write the underlined portion of this sentence? If you think the original is the best way, choose option (1).

    (1) system—a label
    (2) system. a label
    (3) system; a label
    (4) system: a label
    (5) system, a label

GO ON TO THE NEXT PAGE

TEST 1: LANGUAGE ARTS, WRITING, PART I

36. Sentence 9: **When unit pricing was first introduced the shelf tag system posed some problems because keeping the tags on the shelves in the right location can be difficult.**

    What correction should be made to this sentence?

    (1) change <u>was</u> to <u>had been</u>
    (2) insert a comma after <u>introduced</u>
    (3) change <u>the right</u> to <u>their right</u>
    (4) insert commas before and after <u>in the right location</u>
    (5) no correction is necessary

37. Sentence 10: **But as unit pricing has gained acceptance, some of these mechanical problems has been overcome, and the label information has become more usable from the shoppers' standpoint.**

    What correction should be made to this sentence?

    (1) change the spelling of <u>acceptance</u> to <u>acceptence</u>
    (2) remove the comma after <u>acceptance</u>
    (3) change the spelling of <u>usable</u> to <u>useable</u>
    (4) change <u>has been overcome</u> to <u>have been overcome</u>
    (5) no correction is necessary

Questions 38–47 refer to the following paragraphs.

(1) You are going to move. (2) That statement will ring true for most Americans. (3) You will be the exception if you maintain your present residence for the rest of your life. (4) About one in five persons moves each year, put another way, the average person moves once every 5 years. (5) Again dealing in averages most moves of household goods are completed without difficulty, although some are not. (6) The moving experience can be uneventful, but it should be recognized that many of the factors involved can lead to frustrations, uncertainties, and expected course of action that suddenly must be changed. (7) Most moves envolve fulfillment of a positive development. (8) A promotion has come through,

(9) or perhaps an opportunity to move to a better climate. (10) Maybe there's a long-sought chance to be closer to the home folks or the grandchildren.

(11) On the other side of the coin, a familiar neighborhood is being left behind. (12) The personal effort that must be put into a move can leave family members exhausted just at the time when they need to be at their sharpest.

38. Sentences 1 and 2: **You are going to move. That statement will ring true for most Americans.**

    The most effective combination of sentences 1 and 2 would include which of the following groups of words.

    (1) would be a statement that will ring
    (2) is a statement that will ring
    (3) might be a statement that will ring
    (4) being a statement that will ring
    (5) will be a statement that will ring

39. Sentence 3: **You will be the exception if you maintain your present residence for the rest of your life.**

    What correction should be made to this sentence?

    (1) change <u>will be</u> to <u>are</u>
    (2) change the spelling of <u>exception</u> to <u>exeption</u>
    (3) insert a comma after <u>exception</u>
    (4) change <u>your</u> to <u>you're</u>
    (5) no correction is necessary

40. Sentence 4: **About one in five persons moves each <u>year, put</u> another way, the average person moves once every 5 years.**

    Which of the following is the best way to write the underlined portion of this sentence? If you think the original is the best way, choose option (1).

    (1) year, put
    (2) year, although put
    (3) year, and put
    (4) year, because put
    (5) year, or put

GO ON TO THE NEXT PAGE

TEST 1: LANGUAGE ARTS, WRITING, PART I

41. Sentence 5: **Again dealing in averages most moves of household goods are completed without difficulty, although some are not.**

    What correction should be made to this sentence?

    (1) insert a comma after <u>averages</u>
    (2) insert a hyphen in <u>household</u>
    (3) change the spelling of <u>difficulty</u> to <u>dificulty</u>
    (4) remove the comma after <u>difficulty</u>
    (5) no correction is necessary

42. Sentence 6: **The moving experience can be uneventful, but it should be recognized that many of the factors involved can lead to frustrations, uncertainties, and expected course of action that suddenly must be changed.**

    What correction should be made to this sentence?

    (1) change the spelling of <u>experience</u> to <u>experiance</u>
    (2) remove the comma after <u>uneventful</u>
    (3) change <u>but</u> to <u>and</u>
    (4) change <u>course</u> to <u>courses</u>
    (5) no correction is necessary

43. Sentence 7: **Most moves envolve fulfillment of a positive development.**

    What correction should be made to this sentence?

    (1) change <u>most moves</u> to <u>most every move</u>
    (2) change <u>envolve</u> to <u>could envolve</u>
    (3) change <u>envolve</u> to <u>involve</u>
    (4) change the spelling of <u>development</u> to <u>developement</u>
    (5) no correction is necessary

44. Sentences 8 and 9: **A promotion has come <u>through, or</u> perhaps an opportunity to move to a better climate.**

    Which of the following is the best way to write the underlined portion of these sentences? If you think the original is the best way, choose option (1).

    (1) through, or
    (2) through. or
    (3) through: or
    (4) through; or
    (5) through—or

45. Sentence 10: **Maybe there's a long-sought chance to be closer to the home folks or the grandchildren.**

    What correction should be made to this sentence?

    (1) change <u>there's</u> to <u>they're is</u>
    (2) remove the hyphen from <u>long-sought</u>
    (3) add an apostrophe to <u>folks</u>
    (4) change the spelling of <u>grandchildren</u> to <u>grandchildern</u>
    (5) no correction is necessary

46. The topic sentence of this paragraph is

    (1) sentence 1
    (2) sentence 4
    (3) sentence 6
    (4) sentence 9
    (5) sentence 11

GO ON TO THE NEXT PAGE

TEST 1: LANGUAGE ARTS, WRITING, PART I

47. Sentence 12: **The personal effort that must be put into a move can leave family members exhausted just at the time when they need to be at their sharpest.**

    What correction should be made to this sentence?

    (1) insert commas around that <u>must be put into a move</u>
    (2) change <u>can</u> to <u>could</u>
    (3) change the spelling of <u>exhausted</u> to <u>exausted</u>
    (4) insert a comma after <u>time</u>
    (5) no correction is necessary

<u>Questions 48–50</u> refer to the following paragraphs.

(1) In fishing, the first step for the angler is to upgrade his equipment so that the availible range of lures, line weights, distances, etc., is substantially increased. (2) Usually a spinning reel and rod are selected as the next phase in advancement.

(3) The spinning reel consist's of a stationary spool carrying a length of monofilament line, a bail, or pickup device to direct the line onto the reel; and a crank that rotates the pickup device, restoring the line to the spool.

(4) In operation, the lure, attached to the monofilament line and dangling several inches beyond the rod tip, is cast by swinging the rod from a position slightly behind the shoulder through a forward arc to a position in front at approximately eye level.

(5) Proper timing of the finger pressure on the line as it leaves the reel, combined with the rod acceleration, control the distance the lure will travel.

(6) Lures as light as a sixteenth of an ounce with two-pound test monofilament line will provide enjoyable sport with any of the panfish; heavier lures and lines will more than adequately subdue far larger fish.

(7) Lures are available in a near infinite range of weights, sizes, shapes, and colors and include such items as spoons, spinners, jogs, plugs, and bugs as well as natural baits.

(8) With adequate spinning gear, anyone is prepared to pursue the fascinating and challenging game fish. (9) This category includes the world-famous and aristocratic salmon, the trout, the chars, the grayling, the basses, and the pike family.

48. Sentence 2 should be

    (1) left as it is
    (2) placed last
    (3) placed after sentence 5
    (4) placed before sentence 8
    (5) omitted

49. Sentence 2: **Usually a spinning reel and rod are selected as the next phase in advancement.**

    If you rewrote sentence 2 beginning with

    <u>The next phase in advancement</u>

    the next words would be

    (1) are selected a spinning
    (2) are selecting a spinning
    (3) selects a spinning
    (4) is the selection of a spinning
    (5) will be selecting a

50. Sentence 3: **The spinning reel consist's of a stationary spool carrying a length of monofilament line, a bail, or pickup device to direct the line onto the reel; and a crank that rotates the pickup device, restoring the line to the spool.**

    What correction should be made to this sentence?

    (1) change <u>consist's</u> to <u>consists</u>
    (2) change the spelling of <u>length</u> to <u>lenth</u>
    (3) remove the comma after <u>line</u>
    (4) insert a comma after <u>device</u>
    (5) no correction is necessary

GO ON TO THE NEXT PAGE

TEST 1: LANGUAGE ARTS, WRITING, PART II

This part of the Writing Skills test is intended to determine how well you write. You are asked to write an essay that explains something, presents an opinion on an issue, or concentrates on retelling a personal experience.

Prompt

As a child we have many experiences ranging from funny to unfortunate. In the Mark Twain story, *Tom Sawyer*, we find young Tom in many unforgettable situations from being lost in a cave to returning in time for his own funeral. Each of us has a personal story from childhood that seems to be told over and over at family reunions, birthdays, or around friends. Perhaps your personal experience happened on a fishing trip, at school, or on a campout.

Discussion Question

Think of a personal childhood experience that seems to be told over and over again. It may be funny, sad, exciting, or just something out of the ordinary. What personal experience comes to mind?

DIRECTIONS

Write an essay of about 250 words in which you recount this personal event. Give supporting details in your essay. You have 45 minutes to write on this topic.

Check Yourself

- Read carefully the prompt, discussion question, and directions.
- Decide if the prompt is expository, persuasive, or narrative.
- Plan your essay before you begin.
- Use scratch paper to prepare a simple outline.
- Write your essay on the lined pages of a separate answer sheet.
- Read carefully what you have written and make needed changes.
- Check for focus, elaboration, organization, conventions, and integration.

END OF EXAM

TEST 2: SOCIAL STUDIES

DIRECTIONS

This section is made up of multiple-choice questions, most of which are based on readings that will often include a figure, graph, or chart. Study the information given to answer each question correctly.

Answering the multiple-choice questions should take you no longer than 70 minutes. It's best not to spend too much time on one question. There is no penalty for incorrect answers so be sure to answer every question.

To mark your answer, darken the corresponding circle on the answer sheet.

FOR EXAMPLE:

Early colonists of North America looked for settlement sites that had adequate water supplies and were accessible by ship. For this reason, many early towns were built near

(1) mountains
(2) prairies
(3) rivers   ① ② ● ④ ⑤
(4) glaciers
(5) plateaus

The correct answer is "rivers"; therefore, answer space 3 would be marked on the answer sheet.

GO ON TO THE NEXT PAGE

TEST 2: SOCIAL STUDIES

Questions 1–3 are based on the following passage.

The governor is empowered to veto single items of the budget bill, appending to each a message, and to return the same to the legislature if it is still in session. Such items can be enacted over his veto. This authority, not possessed by the president of the United States, lays a heavy responsibility on the governor for the integrity of the budget in all its parts.

All bills passed within the last ten days of a legislative session fall under what is called the "30-day" rule. None can become a law unless within 30 days (Sundays included) it has been signed by the governor.

The veto power is not used sparingly. More than one out of four bills falls to the deadly stroke of the executive pen.

1. The passage indicates that the governor

    (1) vetoes about one fourth of the bills
    (2) vetoes about three fourths of the bills
    (3) vetoes all bills during the legislative session
    (4) vetoes no bills during the legislative session
    (5) uses the veto power very sparingly

2. The "30-day" rule applies to

    (1) the time limit for exercising the veto
    (2) the pocket veto
    (3) the amount of time in which to appeal the governor's action
    (4) bills passed within the last ten days of a legislative session
    (5) the limitation on passing a law over the governor's veto

3. The governor's veto power is greater than that of the president in that the governor has the ability to

    (1) take as much time as he wishes before signing a bill
    (2) veto a bill in less than 10 days
    (3) ignore all bills during the last month of the legislature
    (4) veto single items of the budget bill
    (5) override the two-thirds vote of the legislature

Questions 4–6 are based on the following passage.

The consumer's first line of defense is information. Before you buy any product— especially before you make a major purchase of any kind—get all the information you can about the manufacturer's guarantee or warranty provisions.

Remember, a guarantee is a statement by the manufacturer or vendor that he stands behind his product or service. Guarantees and warranties usually have limitations or conditions, so get all promises in writing.

Before you buy any product or service covered by a guarantee or warranty, make sure you resolve these questions:
    —What, exactly, is covered?
    —Whom should you call when you need repairs under the warranty?
    —Must repairs be made at the factory or by an "authorized service representative" to keep the warranty in effect?
    —Who pays for parts, for labor, for shipping charges?
    —How long does the warranty last?
    —If pro rata reimbursement is provided, what is the basis for it?
    —If the warranty provides for reimbursement, is it in cash or credit toward a replacement?
Keep the warranty and sales receipt for future reference.

4. The advice given to the consumer in this passage deals chiefly with

    (1) business ethics
    (2) unconditional guarantees
    (3) product safety
    (4) unwarranted promises
    (5) pre-purchase information

5. Guarantees and warranties, the passage implies, should be

    (1) conditional
    (2) in writing
    (3) made by the salesman
    (4) cancelable
    (5) dependent on the use of the product

GO ON TO THE NEXT PAGE

TEST 2: SOCIAL STUDIES

6. Warranties usually include all of the following EXCEPT

    (1) what is covered
    (2) who does the repairs
    (3) where the repairs are made
    (4) who pays for expenses incurred in doing the repairs
    (5) return of monies paid

<u>Questions 7 and 8</u> are based on the following chart.

MEDIAN AGE IN THE UNITED STATES

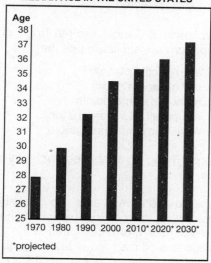

*projected

7. Which situation will be most likely to occur after the period shown in the graph?

    (1) Advertisers will increase their emphasis on youth.
    (2) The size of the average family will increase.
    (3) School districts will build more elementary schools.
    (4) The cost of the Social Security program will rise.
    (5) Population will begin to decline.

8. Which factor would most likely reverse the direction of the trend indicated by the graph?

    (1) development of a cure for cancer
    (2) a large increase in the birth rate
    (3) a prolonged period of economic depression
    (4) an increase in infant mortality
    (5) pollution control

9. Government policies designed to foster economic growth by encouraging greater consumption would probably meet with the greatest opposition from which group?

    (1) labor leaders
    (2) business executives
    (3) military leaders
    (4) environmentalists
    (5) individual entrepreneurs

<u>Questions 10 and 11</u> are based on the following cartoon.

10. What is the main idea of the cartoon?

    (1) The world lacks sufficient energy resources to survive much longer.
    (2) Concerns of environmentalists have had little impact on the actions of industrialists.
    (3) The struggle between energy and the environment cannot be resolved.
    (4) The need to produce energy comes into conflict with the need to preserve the environment.
    (5) A stalemate has been arrived at between industrialists and environmentalists.

GO ON TO THE NEXT PAGE

TEST 2: SOCIAL STUDIES

11. In dealing with the situation referred to in the cartoon during the late 1970s, the United States federal government generally followed a policy that

    (1) gave priority to energy demands over environmental concerns
    (2) sided with environmentalists against corporations
    (3) sought new energy sources outside the United States
    (4) attempted to divert national attention to other issues
    (5) dealt evenhandedly with industrialists and environmentalists

12. The presidents of the United States from the time of World War II to the present have been most influential in the area of

    (1) civil rights
    (2) urban affairs
    (3) foreign affairs
    (4) states rights
    (5) human rights

Questions 13 and 14 are based on the following passage.

Not all place names on maps refer to visible locations. When a name refers to a specific place, it can be easy to get a mental picture of it. When you see a name such as Arctic Circle, Antarctic Circle, Tropic of Cancer, or Tropic of Capricorn, you do not get a mental picture in the same way. These imaginary markers on the Earth's surface usually appear on maps as dotted blue lines. When you travel across one of them, you cannot detect it with the human eye or feel it against your skin.

The Tropics of Cancer and Capricorn are named after constellations of stars. Historians believe that ancient Roman geographers were the first to refer to these two imaginary lines as Cancer and Capricorn.

The Tropic of Cancer runs parallel to the equator at latitude 23°27'N. It marks the northernmost point at which the sun appears directly overhead at noon. The name refers to the constellation Cancer (the Crab), which first becomes visible in the Northern Hemisphere on June 20, 21, or 22, near the summer solstice.

The Tropic of Capricorn runs parallel to the equator at about latitude 23°27'S. It designates the southernmost point at which the sun appears directly overhead at noon. The name refers to the constellation Capricorn (the Goat), which first becomes visible in the Southern Hemisphere on December 21 or 22, near the winter solstice.

13. The Arctic and Antarctic Circles are

    (1) mental pictures
    (2) imaginary markers
    (3) dotted blue lines
    (4) visible locations
    (5) easily detected

14. The Tropic of Cancer and the Tropic of Capricorn are similar in that they

    (1) are specific places
    (2) are of recent origin
    (3) mark the same points
    (4) run parallel to the equator
    (5) were named by navigators

Questions 15 and 16 are based on the following passage.

Fourscore and seven years ago our fathers brought forth on this continent a new nation, conceived in liberty, and dedicated to the proposition that all men are created equal.

Now we are engaged in a great civil war, testing whether that nation, or any nation so conceived and so dedicated, can long endure. We are met on a great battlefield of that war. We have come to dedicate a portion of that field as a final resting-place for those who here gave their lives that that nation might live. It is altogether fitting and proper that we should do this.

But, in a larger sense, we cannot dedicate—we cannot consecrate—we cannot hallow—this ground. The brave men, living and dead, who struggled here, have consecrated it far above our poor power to add or detract.

—Abraham Lincoln

15. In the first paragraph, the speaker refers to

    (1) the Declaration of Independence
    (2) the Articles of Confederation
    (3) the United States Constitution
    (4) the Northwest Ordinance
    (5) the Monroe Doctrine

GO ON TO THE NEXT PAGE

TEST 2: SOCIAL STUDIES

16. The purpose of the speech was to

    (1) commemorate a battle
    (2) remember the founding of our nation
    (3) dedicate a cemetery
    (4) deplore civil war
    (5) seek political support in an election

Questions 17–19 are based on the following chart, which lists some characteristics of Nations *A* and *B*.

Factors of Production	Nation A
Land (natural resources)	Relative scarcity
Labor	Relative abundance
Capital	Relative abundance
Business management	Relative abundance

Factors of Production	Nation B
Land (natural resources)	Relative abundance
Labor	Relative abundance
Capital	Relative scarcity
Business management	Relative scarcity

17. Which economic decision would most probably be in the best interests of Nation *A*?

    (1) permitting an unfavorable balance of payments
    (2) seeking foreign markets
    (3) attracting investments from foreign nations
    (4) encouraging immigration
    (5) increasing imports

18. During the early 19th century, which nation most nearly resembled Nation *A*?

    (1) the United States
    (2) Great Britain
    (3) Russia
    (4) Turkey
    (5) China

19. If Nation *B* wishes to industrialize, how can it best encourage its own citizens to invest their capital in domestic industries?

    (1) by permitting an unfavorable balance of payments and seeking colonies
    (2) by permitting an unfavorable balance of payments and encouraging immigration
    (3) by attracting investments from foreign nations and encouraging immigration
    (4) by instituting high protective tariffs and giving tax concessions to business
    (5) by lowering taxes on imports

20. "Our policy in regard to Europe . . . is not to interfere in the internal concerns of any of its powers"—President Monroe, 1823

    "It must be the policy of the United States to support free peoples who are resisting attempted subjugation by armed minorities or by outside pressures."—President Truman, 1947

    The most valid conclusion to be drawn from these statements is that

    (1) President Truman followed President Monroe's theory of foreign relations
    (2) during the 19th and 20th centuries, the United States was not interested in international affairs
    (3) during the 19th century, events in Europe did not affect the United States
    (4) President Truman changed the policy of President Monroe
    (5) armed minorities threatened the United States

Questions 21 and 22 are based on the following graphs.

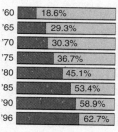

Of all women with children under 6 and living with their husbands, how many work?

'60	18.6%
'65	29.3%
'70	30.3%
'75	36.7%
'80	45.1%
'85	53.4%
'90	58.9%
'96	62.7%

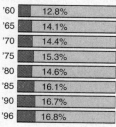

Of all women who work, how many have children under 6 years old?

'60	12.8%
'65	14.1%
'70	14.4%
'75	15.3%
'80	14.6%
'85	16.1%
'90	16.7%
'96	16.8%

Of all working women with children under 6 and living with their husbands, how many work...

	FULL TIME	PART TIME
'60	69.6%	30.4%
'65	68.8%	31.2%
'70	64.9%	35.1%
'75	64.9%	35.1%
'80	64.9%	35.1%
'85	65.7%	34.3%
'90	64.2%	35.8%
'96	62.8%	37.2%

Source: Bureau of Labor Statistics

GO ON TO THE NEXT PAGE

TEST 2: SOCIAL STUDIES

21. The period with the greatest increase in the percentage of working women having children under 6 and living with their husbands was

    (1) '60–'65
    (2) '70–'75
    (3) '80–'85
    (4) '85–'90
    (5) '90–'96

22. The percentage of women working part time remained steadiest between

    (1) '60 and '70
    (2) '70 and '80
    (3) '75 and '85
    (4) '80 and '90
    (5) '90 and '96

Question 23 is based on the following graph.

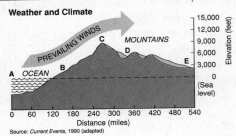

Weather and Climate

Source: *Current Events*, 1990 (adapted)

23. Which area, as illustrated in the graph, would be warmest and driest?

    (1) A
    (2) B
    (3) C
    (4) D
    (5) E

Question 24 is based on the following diagram.

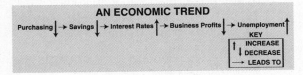

24. Which is occurring in the economy illustrated above?

    (1) increase in real income
    (2) devaluation of currency
    (3) growth
    (4) recession
    (5) recovery

25. "All forms of life developed from earlier forms. In every case the fittest survived and the weak died out. It is the same for people and nations."

    This passage expresses a view most often found in

    (1) fundamentalism
    (2) social Darwinism
    (3) liberalism
    (4) utopian socialism
    (5) egalitarianism

Questions 26–28 are based on the following table.

A Snapshot of Family Finances

	1992	1995	1998	2001
Family income *median, before-tax*	$30,400	$32,700	$33,400	**$39,900**
Family net worth *median*	56,800	60,900	71,600	**86,100**
Percentage of all families with stock holdings *direct or indirect*	36.7%	40.4%	48.8%	**51.9%**
Median value of holdings *for families with holdings*	$12,000	$15,400	$25,000	**$28,000**
Debt as a percentage of total family assets	14.6%	14.7%	14.4%	**12.5%**
Families with debt payments that are 40 percent or more of income	10.9%	10.5%	12.7%	**11.0%**

Source: *Federal Reserve*

26. From 1992 to 2001, the median family income (before taxes) has

    (1) rapidly increased
    (2) rapidly declined
    (3) steadily increased
    (4) steadily declined
    (5) stayed the same

27. The debt as a percentage of total family assets probably declined between 1998 and 2001 because

    (1) their debt payments went down
    (2) their holdings were worth more
    (3) their net worth jumped more than in previous years
    (4) their income had increased
    (5) their stock holdings had increased significantly.

GO ON TO THE NEXT PAGE

TEST 2: SOCIAL STUDIES

28. According to the table, the following declined every year except one:

    (1) family income
    (2) family net worth
    (3) debt as a percentage of total family assets
    (4) median value of holdings
    (5) percentage of all families with stock holdings

Questions 29–31 are based on the following passage.

   We must pursue a course designed not merely to reduce the number of delinquents. We must increase the chances for young people to lead productive lives.
   For these delinquent and potentially delinquent youth, we must offer a New Start. We must insure that the special resources and skills essential for their treatment and rehabilitation are available. Because many of these young men and women live in broken families, burdened with financial and psychological problems, a successful rehabilitation program must include family counseling, vocational guidance, education and health services. It must strengthen the family and the schools. It must offer courts an alternative to placing young delinquents in penal institutions.

   —Lyndon B. Johnson

29. The emphasis in this speech is on

    (1) diagnosis and research
    (2) prevention and rehabilitation
    (3) rehabilitation and research
    (4) treatment and diagnosis
    (5) research and diagnosis

30. The main purpose of this speech is to

    (1) provide federal financial aid
    (2) give advice to broken families
    (3) support research and experimentation
    (4) praise "halfway houses"
    (5) advocate legislation to combat juvenile delinquency

31. The passage implies that

    (1) delinquents cannot lead productive lives
    (2) detention of delinquents is unnecessary
    (3) delinquency is caused by family problems
    (4) the federal government must assume responsibility for preventing juvenile delinquency
    (5) courts must place young delinquents in the proper penal institutions

Questions 32 and 33 are based on the following photograph.

32. The purpose of this photograph is to show

    (1) how dangerous it is to transport merchandise without a cover
    (2) how vulnerable merchandise is when in the open
    (3) how milk was gathered and stored
    (4) how milk jugs once were transported
    (5) the first covered wagon to transport milk

33. The photograph was probably taken

    (1) during the 1940s
    (2) during the 1950s
    (3) during the 1960s
    (4) during the 1970s
    (5) during the 1980s

GO ON TO THE NEXT PAGE

TEST 2: SOCIAL STUDIES

Question 34 is based on the following graph.

2004 Presidential Election Results

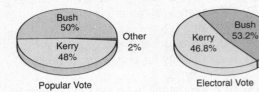

Popular Vote   Electoral Vote

34. Which generalization is supported by the information provided by the graph?

   (1) The electoral vote often fails to reflect the popular vote.
   (2) The House of Representatives settles presidential elections in which third-party candidates participate.
   (3) The electoral college system weakens the two-party system.
   (4) Electoral college members usually vote for their party's candidates.
   (5) Electoral votes result in closer elections.

Questions 35–37 are based on the following graph.

Average Amount of Time Each Day Spent Doing Each Activity
(*hours:minutes*)

	Children 2 to 7	Children 8 to 18
Watching TV	1:59	3:16
Listening to CDs or tapes	0:21	1:05
Reading	0:45	0:44
Listening to the radio	0:24	0:48
Using the computer	0:07	0:31
Playing video games	0:08	0:27
Using the Internet	0:01	0:13

Percentage of Children Who Use a Computer Each Day

All children	42%
2–7 years old	26
8–18 years old	51
White	45
Black	39
Hispanic origin	28
Low income	29
Middle Income	40
High income	50

35. The survey mentions all of the following media EXCEPT

   (1) TV
   (2) reading
   (3) radio
   (4) Internet
   (5) movies

36. The most likely computer user according to the graph would be

   (1) an 8- to 18-year-old white
   (2) a low-income 2- to 7-year-old
   (3) a middle-income Hispanic
   (4) a high-income 2- to 7-year-old
   (5) a 2- to 7-year-old black

37. The dominant medium for children from 2 to 18 is

   (1) TV
   (2) reading
   (3) radio
   (4) computer
   (5) Internet

38. A primary source is an eyewitness account of an event or events in a specific time period. Which would be an example of a primary source of information about life in the 18th-century American colonies?

   (1) a diary of a colonial shopkeeper
   (2) a painting of the colonial period by a 20th-century artist
   (3) a novel about the American Revolutionary War
   (4) a reproduction of furniture used during the colonial period
   (5) a social history of the period

GO ON TO THE NEXT PAGE

TEST 2: SOCIAL STUDIES

Questions 39 and 40 are based on the following graph.

Median Weekly Earnings of Full-Time Female Workers, 25 and Over, by Educational Attainment (In 1998 dollars)

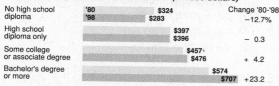

		Change '80–'98
No high school diploma	'80 $324 / '98 $283	−12.7%
High school diploma only	$397 / $396	− 0.3
Some college or associate degree	$457 / $476	+ 4.2
Bachelor's degree or more	$574 / $707	+23.2

Women's Median Earnings by Race and Educational Attainment, 1998

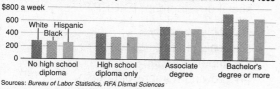

Sources: *Bureau of Labor Statistics, RFA Dismal Sciences*

39. Between 1980 and 1998, weekly earnings fell the most for women with

    (1) no high school diploma
    (2) a high school diploma
    (3) some college study
    (4) an associate degree
    (5) a bachelor's degree

40. By background, women's earnings for whites and Hispanics exceeded that of blacks who had

    (1) no high school diploma
    (2) a high school diploma
    (3) an associate degree
    (4) a bachelor's degree
    (5) more than a bachelor's degree

Questions 41–43 are based on the statements made by Speakers A, B, C, D, and E.

Speaker A: Government could not function very well without them. The flow of information they provide to Congress and the federal agencies is vital to the functioning of our democratic system.

Speaker B: Yes, but the secrecy under which they generally operate makes me suspicious that they are influencing lawmakers in improper ways.

Speaker C: Don't forget that they not only try to influence Washington opinion but also attempt to shape public opinion across the nation in order to create a favorable climate for their views.

Speaker D: That's true. Any politician who ignores 40,000 letters does so at great risk. We have to pay attention to them whether we accept their views or not.

Speaker E: I agree with Speaker C. Public opinion is essential to the functioning of our American way of life.

41. Which group are the speakers most likely discussing?

    (1) lawyers
    (2) reporters
    (3) government workers
    (4) media analysts
    (5) lobbyists

42. Which speaker is most concerned about the impact of the methods used by this group upon democratic government?

    (1) A
    (2) B
    (3) C
    (4) D
    (5) E

43. Which speaker implies that lawmakers frequently must deal with a great many issues about which they know very little?

    (1) A
    (2) B
    (3) C
    (4) D
    (5) E

GO ON TO THE NEXT PAGE

TEST 2: SOCIAL STUDIES

Question 44 is based on the following cartoon.

"AND A HAPPY ELECTION YEAR TO YOU, TOO"

44. Which statement best summarizes the main point of the above cartoon?

   (1) The citizen's vote is a powerful means of influencing legislators seeking reelection.
   (2) Citizens are dependent upon the legislative branch of government for protection.
   (3) Federal and state legislators usually agree on major campaign issues.
   (4) The public generally does not favor consumer protection legislation.
   (5) Voters are easily fooled by politicians seeking votes.

Questions 45–47 are based on the following passage.

   The people and groups that provide the stimulation and contact necessary for social development—the socializing agents—usually fall into two classes: (1) those people with authority over the individual, such as parents and teachers, and (2) those in positions of equality with him or her—age peers, such as playmates or a circle of friends. Since the family is the socializing agent during the critical first years of life, it naturally has had great influence. But because of the increased specialization of the functions of the family, the rapidity of social change that tends to divide the generations, and the high degree of mobility and social fluidity, the peer group is of growing importance in modern urban life.

45. Parents, teachers, and age peers share the role of

   (1) people with authority over the individual
   (2) peer group members
   (3) the friendly circle
   (4) the family circle
   (5) socializing agents

46. All of these reasons are given for the increased role of peers in an individual's social development EXCEPT

   (1) social mobility
   (2) social fluidity
   (3) generation gap
   (4) growing number of peers
   (5) specialization of family functions

47. The family, in modern urban life, is

   (1) exerting influence
   (2) growing in importance
   (3) being replaced by the peer group
   (4) filling a broadening role
   (5) influential only in the early years of life

Questions 48 and 49 refer to the following statements made by Speakers A, B, and C.

Speaker A: Increased contact among nations and peoples is characteristic of our times. A single decision by OPEC or a multinational corporation can send ripples of change throughout our global society.

Speaker B: If we are to survive, all passengers on our Spaceship Earth must participate in efforts to solve the issues that threaten humankind—poverty, resource depletion, pollution, violence, and war.

GO ON TO THE NEXT PAGE

TEST 2: SOCIAL STUDIES

Speaker *C:*   We must understand that no single culture's view of the world is universally shared. Other people have different value systems and ways of thinking and acting. They will not see the world as we do.

48. Which concept is discussed by both Speakers *A* and *B*?

   (1) self-determination
   (2) nationalism
   (3) conservation
   (4) interdependence
   (5) protectionism

49. Speaker *C* indicates a desire to reduce

   (1) ethnocentrism
   (2) globalism
   (3) social mobility
   (4) religious tolerance
   (5) interdependence

Question 50 is based on the following cartoon.

"Witnesses for the Prosecution"

50. The cartoon is concerned primarily with determining responsibility for which situation?

   (1) use of poison gas during World War I
   (2) slave labor camps in the Soviet Union during the Stalin era
   (3) the Holocaust in Europe during the 1930s and 1940s
   (4) apartheid practices in South Africa
   (5) the blitzkrieg of World War II

END OF EXAM

TEST 3: SCIENCE

DIRECTIONS

You are given 95 minutes to complete the Science section of the GED. This section is focused on your knowledge of general scientific concepts. All questions are in multiple-choice format and require the test taker to study the given information (graph, figure, charts, etc.) to reach a correct answer.

You will not be penalized for incorrect answers, so remember to answer every question.

To mark your answer, darken the corresponding circle on the answer sheet.

FOR EXAMPLE:

Which of the following is the smallest unit?

(1) solution
(2) molecule
(3) atom
(4) compound
(5) mixture

① ② ● ④ ⑤

The correct answer is "atom"; therefore, space 3 would be marked on the answer sheet.

Note: *The science sections of the two practice tests at the end of this book, like the science section on the actual GED exam, consist of 50 questions. This section has 66 questions in order to diagnose better your strengths and weaknesses in science.*

GO ON TO THE NEXT PAGE

TEST 3: SCIENCE

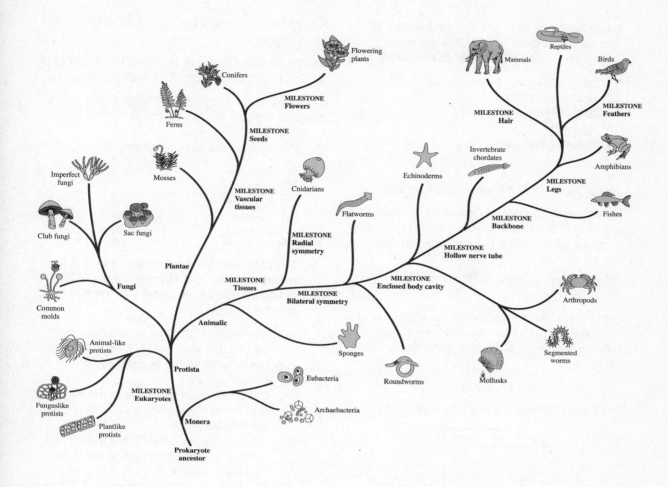

Questions 1–4 refer to the figure above.

The figure above shows the evolutionary relationships between the major classes of organisms. Branch points show common ancestors, and each branch represents a new class of organisms.

1. Which milestone came latest in evolution?

    (1) tissues
    (2) bilateral symmetry
    (3) feathers
    (4) flowers
    (5) backbone

2. Which of the following shows the correct order of emergence, from earliest to latest?

    (1) mosses, ferns, conifers
    (2) conifers, mosses, ferns
    (3) ferns, mosses, conifers
    (4) ferns, conifers, mosses
    (5) conifers, ferns, mosses

3. If groups that shared common ancestors are more likely to be closely related, which groups are most closely related evolutionarily?

    (1) echinoderms and mollusks
    (2) birds and reptiles
    (3) round worms and segmented worms
    (4) protists and molds
    (5) echinoderms and fishes

GO ON TO THE NEXT PAGE

TEST 3: SCIENCE

4. Later developments are more advanced and specialized. Which of the following is the most specialized evolutionary development?

    (1) hair
    (2) radial symmetry
    (3) backbone
    (4) feathers
    (5) bilateral symmetry

Questions 5–8 refer to the following information.

The density of an object can often be used to help identify it. Density is defined as the ratio of the mass of a substance to its volume, or as an equation:

$$\text{Density} = \frac{\text{mass}}{\text{volume}}$$

If the object has a shape such as a block or a cube, then the volume can be determined by multiplying the length times the width times the height or

$$V = l \times w \times h$$

Three samples are provided to a student:

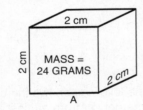

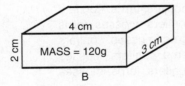

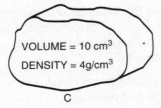

Sample A is a cube 2 cm on a side, with a mass of 24 grams.

Sample B is a 120 gram block with a height of 3 cm, and a width of 2 cm, and a length of 4 cm.

Sample C is an irregularly shaped object with a mass of 4 g/cm^3 and a volume of 10 cm.

5. What is the density of sample B?

    (1) 2 g/cm^3
    (2) 3 g/cm^3
    (3) 4 g/cm^3
    (4) 5 g/cm^3
    (5) 6 g/cm^3

6. Suppose sample A were to be cut into two unevenly sized and shaped pieces. What would be true of the density of the two new, smaller pieces?

    (1) The larger of the two would have a greater density.
    (2) The smaller of the two would have a greater density.
    (3) The two pieces would have the same density, which would be different from the original piece.
    (4) The two pieces would have the same density, which would be the same as the original piece.
    (5) There is not enough information to tell.

7. When a balloon is heated its volume doubles. What happens to its density?

    (1) The density doubles.
    (2) The density quadruples.
    (3) The density stays the same.
    (4) The density is cut in half.
    (5) There is not enough information to tell.

8. What is the mass of sample C?

    (1) 20 g
    (2) 30 g
    (3) 40 g
    (4) 60 g
    (5) 80 g

GO ON TO THE NEXT PAGE

TEST 3: SCIENCE

9. An island may form when material expelled by an undersea volcano gradually builds up and rises above the surface of the water. This has happened in numerous places in the Pacific Ocean. Over time, however, another island may begin to form some distance from the first. It is possible that chains of islands, such as the Hawaiian Islands, were formed in this way. One reason for this may be that

   (1) the volcano moves along the bottom of the ocean
   (2) the plates of earth and rock that cover the interior of planet Earth are slowly moving, taking the islands with them
   (3) when the first island was finished, some leftover lava started another island
   (4) volcanoes erupted in places where islands were going to be formed
   (5) volcanic eruptions have had nothing to do with the formation of islands

10. The figure above shows a sonar wave being sent out from a ship, hitting the bottom of the ocean and bouncing back to the ship. By knowing the speed of the sound wave and the time the wave travels, the depth to the bottom of the ocean can be determined. The sonar wave travels at 1,000 meters per second. If it takes 4 seconds for the wave to travel to the bottom of the ocean and return, how deep is the ocean at that location?

   (1) 500 meters
   (2) 1,000 meters
   (3) 2,000 meters
   (4) 4,000 meters
   (5) 8,000 meters

Questions 11–13 refer to the following passage.

Most of us have played with magnets from the time we were very young. Magnets may be man-made or occur naturally. The earliest of magnets came from the ancient Greeks, who used a mineral known as magnetite, which they noticed could repel or attract certain metals. Interestingly, if a magnet is broken in half, each piece will then have its own north and south poles.

In general, all magnets, no matter what their shape, have both a north and south pole. Like poles repel each other; unlike poles attract each other. A compass works because it uses a freely rotating magnet that be attracted or repelled by the naturally magnetic poles of the Earth.

One of the most common applications of magnets is in creating an electromagnet, which is caused when an electric current moves through a magnetic material, such as an iron nail.

11. What type of magnet can be controlled by adjusting the flow of electric current, such as might be used in a scrap yard to pick up, and then drop large pieces of metal?

   (1) magnetite
   (2) an electromagnet
   (3) a naturally occurring magnet
   (4) a bar magnet
   (5) a magnet with two north poles

12. Which end of a compass will face north?

   (1) the north pole
   (2) the south pole
   (3) either end, depending on whether it is above or below the equator
   (4) it depends what the magnet is made of
   (5) it depends what metals are around the compass

13. Alnico magnets are used in industry because they have a great deal of strength for their size. What must be true of an alnico magnet?

   (1) It must have an electric current going through it.
   (2) It must be attracted to all metals.
   (3) It must be a naturally occurring magnet.
   (4) It must have both a north and a south pole.
   (5) None of the above must be true.

GO ON TO THE NEXT PAGE

TEST 3: SCIENCE

Questions 14–16 refer to the following article.

The two most common types of engines are the gasoline internal combustion engine and the diesel engine. Each has its own advantages and disadvantages in specific situations. In the gasoline internal combustion engine used in most automobiles and lawn mowers, a mixture of gasoline and air is mixed together and ignited by a spark from a spark plug. The air provides the necessary oxygen that allows combustion to take place.

The diesel engine works by mixing the fuel and air under very high pressures, which heats the mixture to a very high temperature, causing it to ignite. The high pressures used require a very strong construction for the walls of the cylinders and engine. Diesel engines can be more difficult to get started, but once going, they are inexpensive to run, as the fuel they require costs less than gasoline.

14. Which of the following is true of the internal combustion engine but not the diesel engine?

   (1) It requires both fuel and air.
   (2) It is less expensive to operate.
   (3) It requires a spark plug.
   (4) It operates by compressing the air and fuel mixture to ignite it.
   (5) It needs less air.

15. Why are diesel engines used for trucks that travel long distances?

   (1) Gasoline is not available everywhere.
   (2) Diesel engines get better mileage than gas fuel engines.
   (3) Internal combustion engines pollute.
   (4) Spark plugs are unreliable.
   (5) The engines have stronger walls.

16. Which type of engine would a race car use and why?

   (1) internal combustion because it is cheaper to operate
   (2) internal combustion because it weighs less
   (3) internal combustion because it uses less fuel
   (4) diesel because it does not require a spark plug
   (5) diesel because the engine is stronger

Questions 17–19 refer to the following article.

All nations agree that cooperative efforts are needed in research to study and predict earthquakes. In July 1956 the first World Conference on Earthquake Engineering was held in Tokyo. Its purpose was to share information about the prediction of earthquakes and methods of constructing buildings and bridges that can withstand the shocks.

What causes earthquakes? The crust of the Earth is a broken mosaic of pieces, bounded by deep cracks called faults. When forces deep inside the Earth move these pieces, tremendous shock waves start from the faults. Shock waves in the crust, from whatever source, can be detected by seismographs all over the world. If the earthquake occurs beneath the ocean, it produces an enormous wave, called a tsunami, that can do much damage when it arrives at a shore.

17. What is the most frequent cause of major earthquakes?

   (1) movements within the Earth
   (2) folding
   (3) landslides
   (4) submarine currents
   (5) tsunamis

18. How can earthquake destruction be minimized?

   (1) more frequent use of seismographs
   (2) better construction of buildings
   (3) quicker methods of evacuation
   (4) early detection and warning
   (5) better control of tsunamis

19. Nuclear explosions can be detected by seismographs because they

   (1) cause tsunamis
   (2) occur on geologic faults
   (3) cause earthquakes
   (4) produce shock waves in the crust
   (5) compress the rock

GO ON TO THE NEXT PAGE

TEST 4: LANGUAGE ARTS, READING

DIRECTIONS

This section of the exam consists of questions based on articles about literature, excerpts from different literary periods (pre-1920, 1920–1960 and post-1960 literature), and business documents. Each of these excerpts will be followed by multiple-choice questions you must answer.

You should read each excerpt carefully before answering the accompanying questions and refer to the passages as often as necessary to help you answer the questions.

Before each excerpt is a "purpose question" designed to show you why you're reading the passage, and what to focus on. These purpose questions do not need to be answered as they are only there to help you in your reading.

You will not be penalized for incorrect answers so be sure to answer every question. This section's questions should take you no more than 65 minutes.

To mark your answer, darken the corresponding circle on the answer sheet.

FOR EXAMPLE:

It was Susan's dream machine. The metallic blue paint gleamed, and the sporty wheels were highly polished. Under the hood, the engine was no less carefully cleaned. Inside, flashy lights illuminated the instruments on the dashboard, and the seats were covered in rich leather upholstery.

The subject ("It") of this excerpt is most likely

(1) an airplane
(2) a stereo system   ① ② ● ④ ⑤
(3) an automobile
(4) a boat
(5) a motorcycle

The correct answer is "an automobile"; therefore, answer space 3 would be marked on the answer sheet.

GO ON TO THE NEXT PAGE

TEST 4: LANGUAGE ARTS, READING

Questions 1–5 refer to the following business document.

HOW MUST EMPLOYEES' WORK ENVIRONMENT BE FLEXIBLE?

Window Solutions for Networks Employee Handbook

Telecommuting

(1) The Company is committed to creating a flexible work environment that balances the needs of our customers, employees, and the Company. (2) Therefore, the Company tries
(5) to be creative in its approach to work styles and location. (3) Telecommuting arrangements may be made on an "as needed basis" or set up on a regular schedule. (4) In either case, it is preferred that
(10) employees spend time working in the office whenever possible. (5) This allows employees to be accessible to customers and creates a sense of consistency and cooperation among work groups. (6) When
(15) employees desire to work at home, the Company asks that they do so in a manner that is in keeping with a workstyle of accessibility, communication, and productivity. (7) All telecommuting arrangements are subject to
(20) approval by the employee's manager. (8) In general, the following principles should be used in telecommuting.
 • (9) Employees should make arrangements with their manager at least 1 week before
(25) telecommuting.
 • (10) Employees should check in with the office on a regular basis.
 • (11) Employees should inform their manager of their whereabouts so they may
(30) be reached easily.
 • (12) Working at home means working for the Company, not taking time off to do projects not related to the Company.
 • (13) Employees should not routinely work
(35) at home on days before or following vacations or holidays.
 • (14) Under regular circumstances, telecommuting should not be used more than 1 day a week or more than 3 days a
(40) month.

1. What is the meaning of "telecommuting"?

 (1) working primarily on the phone
 (2) working from home
 (3) working at the office
 (4) working on a computer
 (5) answering phones for the Company

2. According to the document, which one of the following is a principle used in telecommuting (lines 19–40)?

 (1) telecommuting should be done at least 4 days a month
 (2) working from home on days before or following vacations or holidays is acceptable
 (3) check in with the office at least once every hour
 (4) employees should give their manager information of their whereabouts
 (5) taking a vacation is the same as working at home

3. Which of the following would be an example of "a manner that is in keeping with a workstyle of accessiblity, communication, and productivity" (lines 16–18)?

 (1) employee routinely checks in with his manager
 (2) employee communicates via cell phone
 (3) employee calls customers from the office
 (4) employee informs manager of his whereabouts only once
 (5) employee produces less work while telecommuting

4. If the Company wanted to dismiss an employee for improper telecommuting, which of the following would be a valid reason?

 (1) employee regularly used telecommuting more than 3 days each month
 (2) employee checked in with the office
 (3) employer didn't give time off to the employee
 (4) employer failed to inform employee of telecommuting policy
 (5) Company has a no-fault policy

GO ON TO THE NEXT PAGE

TEST 4: LANGUAGE ARTS, READING

5. What is the main purpose of the Company's telecommuting policy?

   (1) to reduce the employees' workload
   (2) to create a more flexible and balanced work environment for today's employees
   (3) to give more vacation time
   (4) to allow for direct communication between customer and employee
   (5) to save the Company money

<u>Questions 6–10</u> refer to the following excerpt from a work of prose fiction.

WHAT CAN A BEREAVED FATHER DO?

Iona sees a hall porter with some sacking, and decides to talk to him.

"Friend, what sort of time is it?" he asks.

"Past nine. What are you standing here for? Move on."

Iona moves on a few steps, doubles up, and abandons himself to his grief. He gives a tug at the reins; he can bear it no longer. "The stables," he thinks, and the little horse, as if it understood, starts off at a trot.

One of the cabdrivers around the stove half gets up, grunts sleepily, and stretches toward a bucket of water.

"Do you want a drink?" Iona asks him.

"Don't I want a drink!"

"That's so? Your good health! But listen, mate—you know, my son is dead...Did you hear? This week, in the hospital...It's a long story."

Iona looks to see what effect his words have, but sees none—the young man is fast asleep again. Just as much as the young one wants to drink, the old man wants to talk. Is it nothing to tell?

"I'll go and look after my horse," thinks Iona; "there's always time to sleep. No fear of that!"

When he is alone, he dares not think of his son; he can speak about him to anyone, but to think of him, and picture him to himself, is unbearably painful.

"That's how it is, my old horse. There's no more Kuzma Ionitch. Now let's say, you had a foal, you were this foal's mother, and suddenly, let's say, that foal went out and left you to live after him. It would be sad, wouldn't it?"

The little horse munches, listens, and breathes over its master's hand...

Iona's feelings are too much for him, and he tells the little horse the whole story.

6. In this story it is ironic that

   (1) the cabdriver wants a drink
   (2) the hall porter tells Iona to move on
   (3) Iona tells his story to his horse
   (4) Iona has run out of food for his horse
   (5) the horse had a foal

7. Iona goes to take care of his horse. He does so most probably to

   (1) have something to do
   (2) protest the high cost of feed
   (3) show his great love for his horse
   (4) prove that he does not resent the cabdriver's action
   (5) remove his feelings of guilt

8. The setting for this story is probably a 19th-century

   (1) American city
   (2) eastern European city
   (3) northern European farm
   (4) American small town
   (5) English city

9. The author's purpose in using the present tense is most probably to

   (1) make the story seem modern
   (2) increase the length of the story
   (3) heighten the reader's sense of immediacy
   (4) write the story as consciously as possible
   (5) reinforce the first-person point of view

10. Iona's situation is brought home to the reader when he

    (1) asks the hall porter for the time
    (2) asks the cabdriver for a drink
    (3) talks to himself
    (4) fights off sleep
    (5) compares himself to a foal's mother

GO ON TO THE NEXT PAGE

TEST 4: LANGUAGE ARTS, READING

Questions 11–15 refer to the following excerpt from a work of prose nonfiction.

HOW DID A FRONTIER WOMAN LIVE?

She was always there, just outside the front door, to welcome their visitors, having been warned of their approach by the sound of hoofs and the rumble of wheels on the

(5) wooden bridge. If she happened to be in the kitchen, helping her Bohemian cook, she came out in her apron, waving a buttery iron spoon, or shook cherry-stained fingers at the new arrival. She never stopped to pin up a

(10) lock; she was attractive in dishabille, and she knew it. She had been known to rush to the door in her dressing-gown, brush in hand and her long black hair rippling over her shoulders, to welcome Cyrus Dalzell,

(15) president of the Colorado & Utah; and the great man had never felt more flattered. In his eyes, and in the eyes of the admiring middle-aged men who visited there, whatever Mrs. Forrester chose to do was

(20) "lady-like" because she did it. They could not imagine her in any dress or situation in which she would not be charming. Captain Forrester himself, a man of few words, told Judge Pommeroy that he had never seen

(25) her look more captivating than on the day when she was chased by the new bull in the pasture. She had forgotten about the bull and gone into the meadow to gather wild flowers. He heard her scream, and as he ran

(30) puffing down the hill, she was scudding along the edge of the marshes like a hare, beside herself with laughter, and stubbornly clinging to the crimson parasol that had made all the trouble.

(35) Mrs. Forrester was twenty-five years younger than her husband, and she was his second wife. He married her in California and brought her to Sweet Water a bride. They called the place home even then, when they

(40) lived there but a few months out of each year.

—Willa Cather

11. The narrator describes Mrs. Forrester as a young woman who was not only hospitable, but also charming in her

   (1) education
   (2) appearance
   (3) intelligence
   (4) agility
   (5) devotion

12. Which literary device is used in line 31?

   (1) understatement
   (2) hyperbole
   (3) simile
   (4) onomatopoeia
   (5) metaphor

13. The word *they*, as used in line 20, is intended to mean the

   (1) neighbors of Mrs. Forrester
   (2) middle-aged men
   (3) summer days
   (4) narrator's thoughts
   (5) passers-by

14. The narrator portrays the natural elegance of Mrs. Forrester with which of the following words?

   (1) "charming"
   (2) "attractive in dishabille"
   (3) "captivating"
   (4) all of the above
   (5) none of the above

15. What does the imagery in lines 22–34 convey about Captain Forrester's opinion of his wife?

   (1) Her attitude made her attractive.
   (2) She often neglected her duties as a housewife.
   (3) She was a frail woman, prone to injury.
   (4) She was defeated by the adversity of life.
   (5) She was stubborn when dealing with her husband.

GO ON TO THE NEXT PAGE

TEST 4: LANGUAGE ARTS, READING

Questions 16–20 are based on the following poem.

WHAT IS IT LIKE WHEN ELECTRIC POLES REPLACE TREES?

On their sides, resembling fallen timbers
without rough
Barks—a hundred feet apart—lie power
poles.
Just yesterday, this road was edged
With eucalyptus; in aisles
Between rows of trees, seats for the aged.
Now tree odors hover in the air, residues of
life.
The poles are erected. The frigid,
Passionless verticals
Strive
To fill the socket-shaped holes
Left by trees. Identical, cement-wedged
Below, parasitically fastened to live wires
above,
Tree imposters, never to be budged
From a telegraphic owl's
Knowitallness, they stand—rigid!
Sad children, wishing to climb, scan the
miles
And miles of uninterrupted electric forests for
leaves.

16. Which phrase best expresses the ideas of this poem?

    (1) the new trees
    (2) the promising verticals
    (3) improving the landscape
    (4) on climbing trees
    (5) tree odors

17. The poet seems to resent the power poles'

    (1) rough barks
    (2) new odors
    (3) lifelessness
    (4) expensiveness
    (5) electric charge

18. In this poem, the children are sad because

    (1) the poles are too slippery to climb
    (2) the poles are too rigid to climb
    (3) they have been forbidden to climb the poles
    (4) the poles have replaced the trees
    (5) they have grown to love the owls

19. The poet's point of view is expressed by the use of such phrases as

    (1) fallen timbers
    (2) power poles
    (3) passionless verticals
    (4) socket-shaped holes
    (5) live wires

20. An example of a poetic figure of speech is found in the words

    (1) tree odors
    (2) cement-wedged
    (3) tree imposters
    (4) sad children
    (5) scan the miles

GO ON TO THE NEXT PAGE

TEST 4: LANGUAGE ARTS, READING

Questions 21 to 25 refer to the following poem.

WHAT IS THE REACTION OF A TEACHER TO HIS STUDENT'S DEATH?

I remember the neckcurls, limp and damp
    as tendrils;
And her quick look, a sidelong pickerel
    smile;
(5) And how, once startled into talk, the light
    syllables leaped for her,
And she balanced in the delight of her
    thought,
A wren, happy, tail into the wind,
(10) Her song trembling the twigs and small
    branches.
The shade sang with her;
The leaves, their whispers turned to kissing;
And the mold sang in the bleached valleys
(15)   under the rose.

Oh, when she was sad, she cast herself
    down into such a pure depth,
Even a father could not find her:
Scraping her cheek against straw;
(20) Stirring the clearest water.

My sparrow, you are not here,
Waiting like a fern, making a spiny shadow.
The sides of wet stones cannot console me,
Nor the moss, wound with the last light.

(25) If only I could nudge you from this sleep,
My maimed darling, my skittery pigeon.
Over this damp grave I speak the words of
    my love:
I, with no rights in this matter,
(30) Neither father nor lover.
        —Theodore Roethke, "Elegy for Jane"

21. The poet wrote this poem mainly to
    (1) describe Jane
    (2) criticize Jane
    (3) mourn Jane
    (4) remember Jane
    (5) forget Jane

22. The poet's feeling for Jane, as indicated in the poem, is one of
    (1) awe
    (2) reverence
    (3) regret
    (4) nostalgia
    (5) love

23. To what does the poet repeatedly compare Jane?
    (1) a flower
    (2) a shooting star
    (3) a bird
    (4) a small pet
    (5) a lovely song

24. The change that takes place in the poem starting on line 21 is that the poet
    (1) becomes resigned
    (2) recollects further details
    (3) compares himself to a father
    (4) talks directly to the dead student
    (5) becomes more angry at his loss

25. The poem is powerful in its impact on the reader because the poet feels he
    (1) is like a father to Jane
    (2) is like a lover to Jane
    (3) is like a teacher to Jane
    (4) has no right to write the poem
    (5) is responsible for her tragedy

GO ON TO THE NEXT PAGE

TEST 4: LANGUAGE ARTS, READING

Questions 26–30 refer to the following excerpt from a play.

HOW DOES THE FAMILY RESPOND TO LINDNER'S OFFER?

WALTER: I mean—I have worked as a chauffeur most of my life—and my wife here, she does domestic work in people's kitchens. So does my mother, I
(5) mean—we are plain people . . .

LINDNER: Yes, Mr. Younger—

WALTER: [*Really like a small boy, looking down at his shoes and then up at the man*] And—uh—well, my
(10) father, well, he was a laborer most of his life.

LINDNER: [*Absolutely confused*] Uh, yes—

WALTER: [*Looking down at his toes once again*] My father almost beat a
(15) man to death once because this man called him a bad name or something, you know what I mean?

(20) LINDNER: No, I'm afraid I don't.

WALTER: [*Finally straightening up*] Well, what I means is that we come from people who had a lot of pride. I mean—we are very
(25) proud people. And that's my sister over there and she's going to be a doctor—and we are very proud—

LINDNER: Well—I am sure that is very
(30) nice, but—

WALTER: [*Starting to cry and facing the man eye to eye*] What I am telling you is that we called you over here to tell you that we
(35) are very proud and that this is—this is my son, who makes the sixth generation of our family in this country, and that we have all thought about your
(40) offer and we have decided to move into our house because my father—my father—he earned it. [MAMA *has her eyes closed and is rocking back and*
(45) *forth as though she were in*

church, *with her head nodding the amen yes*] We don't want to make no trouble for nobody or fight no causes—but we will
(50) try to be good neighbors. That's all we got to say. [*He looks the man absolutely in the eyes*] We don't want your money. [*He turns and walks*
(55) *away from the man*]

LINDNER: [*Looking around at all of them*] I take it then that you have decided to occupy.

BENEATHA: That's what the man said.

(60) LINDNER: [*To* MAMA *in her reverie*] Then I would like to appeal to you, Mrs. Younger. You are older and wiser and understand things better I am sure...

(65) MAMA: [*Rising*] I am afraid you don't understand. My son said we was going to move and there ain't nothing left for me to say. [*Shaking her head with double*
(70) *meaning*] You know how these young folks is nowadays, mister. Can't do a thing with 'em. Good-bye.

LINDNER: [*Folding up his materials*]
(75) Well—if you are that final about it... There is nothing left for me to say. [*He finishes. He is almost ignored by the family who are concentrating on*
(80) WALTER LEE. *At the door* LINDNER *halts and looks around*] I sure hope you people know what you're doing. [*He shakes his head and exits*]

—Lorraine Hansberry, *A Raisin in the Sun*

26. The story Walter tells about his father almost beating a man to death for calling him a name is

(1) an anecdote
(2) a lie
(3) a warning
(4) a dream
(5) an allusion

GO ON TO THE NEXT PAGE

TEST 4: LANGUAGE ARTS, READING

27. From this point on, the family will

    (1) stay in the ghetto
    (2) try for a new life
    (3) sell their house
    (4) retreat to the South
    (5) fight for causes

28. After this incident, the head of the house will be

    (1) Travis
    (2) Mama
    (3) Walter
    (4) Ruth
    (5) Beneatha

29. Mr. Lindner

    (1) understands the Youngers
    (2) despises the Youngers
    (3) is sympathetic to the Youngers
    (4) is tolerant of the Youngers
    (5) disagrees with the Youngers

30. The word that best describes Walter's family is

    (1) plain
    (2) vicious
    (3) proud
    (4) trouble-making
    (5) uncooperative

Questions 31–35 refer to the following passage.

HOW DOES AN INDIAN CHIEF REMEMBER HIS CHILDHOOD?

I have acted in the movies and in Wild West shows, and served as an interpreter between the Indian and the White man. I have met presidents and kings, writers, scientists, and artists. I have had much joy and received many honors, but I have never forgotten my wild, free childhood when I lived in a tepee and heard the calling of the coyotes under the stars . . . when the night winds, the sun, and everything else in our primitive world reflected the wisdom and benevolence of the Great Spirit. I remember seeing my mother bending over an open fire toasting buffalo meat, and my father returning at night with an antelope on his shoulder. I remember playing with the other children on the banks of a clean river, and I shall never forget when my grandfather taught me how to make a bow and arrow from hard wood and flint, and a fishhook from the rib of a field mouse. I am not sentimental but memories haunt me as I review scenes from those days before I was old enough to understand that all Indian things would pass away.

The average American child of today would enjoy the privileges I had out there on the unspoiled prairie one hundred years ago. I was usually awake in time to see the sun rise. If the weather was warm, I went down to the river that flowed near our village and dipped water out of it with my hands for a drink, then plunged into it. The river came down out of the hills, ferrying leaves, blossoms, and driftwood. Fish could be seen in the pools formed near the rapids over which it rippled. Birds nested and flew among the banks, and occasionally I would see a coon or a fox in the brush. Hawks circled overhead, searching the ground for mice or other small animals for their breakfast, or to feed the young in their nests. There were never enough hours in a day to exhaust the pleasure of observing every living creature—from the orb spider spinning his magic and all but invisible web to the bald eagles on their bulky nests atop the tallest trees, teaching fledglings how to eject safely.

—Memoirs of Chief Red Fox

31. The mood of the selection is one of

    (1) nostalgia
    (2) bitterness
    (3) resignation
    (4) envy
    (5) anticipation

GO ON TO THE NEXT PAGE

TEST 4: LANGUAGE ARTS, READING

32. One of the most important of the chief's memories is that of

    (1) Wild West shows
    (2) many honors
    (3) meeting presidents and kings
    (4) family members
    (5) coyotes

33. The writer's primitive world was characterized by

    (1) evidence of the Great Spirit
    (2) fishhooks
    (3) bow and arrow
    (4) the call of the coyotes
    (5) night winds

34. The writer's love of nature led him to

    (1) observe it closely
    (2) benefit from its warmth
    (3) collect specimens
    (4) search for small animals
    (5) sleep late

35. Nature a hundred years ago was preferable to nature today because it was more

    (1) varied
    (2) wild
    (3) magical
    (4) friendly
    (5) unspoiled

Questions 36–40 refer to the following commentary on the plays *Romeo and Juliet* and *West Side Story*.

HOW DO *ROMEO AND JULIET* AND *WEST SIDE STORY* COMPARE?

What glorious verse falls from the lips of Shakespeare's boys and girls! True, there is a rollicking jazzy vigor in such songs of *West Side Story* as the one of Officer Krupke, but it
(5) pales alongside the pyrotechnical display of Mercurio's Queen Mab speech. There is tenderness in "Maria," but how relatively tongue-tied is the twentieth-century hero alongside the boy who cried, "He jests at scars
(10) that never felt a wound." "Hold my hand and we're halfway there," say Maria and Tony to each other, and the understatement touches us. But "Gallop apace, you fiery-footed steeds" and the lines that follow glow with a glory that
(15) never diminishes. The comparisons of language could be multiplied, and always, of course, Shakespeare is bound to win.

Without its great poetry *Romeo and Juliet* would not be a major tragedy. Possibly it is
(20) not, in any case; for as has frequently been remarked, Shakespeare's hero and heroine are a little too slender to carry the full weight of tragic grandeur. Their plight is more pathetic than tragic. If this is true of them, it
(25) is equally true of Tony and Maria: for them, too, pathos rather than tragedy. But there is tragedy implicit in the environmental situation of the contemporary couple, and this must not be overlooked or underestimated.
(30) Essentially, however, what we see is that all four young people strive to consummate the happiness at the threshold on which they stand and which they have tasted so briefly. All four are deprived of the opportunity to do
(35) so, the Renaissance couple by the caprice of fate, today's youngsters by the prejudice and hatred engendered around them. All four are courageous and lovable. All four arouse our compassion, even though they may not
(40) shake us with Aristotelian fear.

Poets and playwrights will continue to write of youthful lovers whom fate drives into and out of each other's lives. The spectacle will always trouble and move us.

GO ON TO THE NEXT PAGE

TEST 4: LANGUAGE ARTS, READING

36. The author of the selection implies that

    (1) the songs of *West Side Story* lack strength
    (2) the language of *West Side Story* leaves us cold
    (3) the language of *Romeo and Juliet* lacks the vigor of that of *West Side Story*
    (4) the poetry of *Romeo and Juliet* will prevail
    (5) the speech of *West Side Story* can compete with the verse of *Romeo and Juliet*

37. In comparing the language of *Romeo and Juliet* with that of *West Side Story* the author

    (1) takes no position
    (2) likes each equally
    (3) favors that of *Romeo and Juliet*
    (4) favors that of *West Side Story*
    (5) downplays the differences

38. Both plays share a common weakness. That weakness is

    (1) the stature of their heroes and heroines
    (2) the absence of deep emotion
    (3) their dramatic construction
    (4) the lack of substance of their themes
    (5) the lack of linguistic power

39. The couples in the two plays share all of the following EXCEPT

    (1) a pathetic situation
    (2) lack of opportunity to achieve happiness
    (3) courage
    (4) inability to instill fear in the reader
    (5) inability to arouse pity in the reader

40. The couples in the two plays differ in the nature of

    (1) their plight
    (2) their ultimate fate
    (3) the cause of their tragic situation
    (4) their attractiveness
    (5) their love for one another

END OF EXAM

TEST 5: MATHEMATICS

DIRECTIONS

The Mathematics portion of the GED exam consists of both multiple-choice and alternate format questions. The goal of this section is to measure your general math skills and problem-solving abilities. Each question is based on a short reading that could include a diagram, graph, or chart.

The questions in this section should take you no longer than 45 minutes. There's no penalty for incorrect answers so be sure to answer every question. Also, be careful not to spend too much time on each question.

Formulas you need are given on page 68. Only some of the questions will require you to use a formula. Not all the formulas given will be needed.

The questions will give you varying amounts of information—some will provide more information than you need to solve the problem, while other questions will not provide enough to solve the problem. When a question does not provide enough information to solve the problem, then the correct answer will be "Not enough information is given."

You may use a calculator on Part 1.

To mark your answer, darken the corresponding circle on the answer sheet.

FOR EXAMPLE:

If a grocery bill totaling $15.75 is paid with a $20.00 bill, how much change should be returned?

(1) $5.26
(2) $4.75
(3) $4.25
(4) $3.75
(5) $3.25

① ② ● ④ ⑤

The correct answer is "$4.25"; therefore, answer space 3 would be marked on the answer sheet.

GO ON TO THE NEXT PAGE

TEST 5: MATHEMATICS

FORMULAS

Description	Formula
AREA (A) of a:	
square	$A = s^2$; where s = side
rectangle	$A = lw$; where l = length, w = width
parallelogram	$A = bh$; where b = base, h = height
triangle	$A = \frac{1}{2} bh$; where b = base, h = height
trapezoid	$A = \frac{1}{2}(b_1 + b_2)\, h$; where b = base, h = height
circle	$A = \pi r^2$; where π = 3.14, r = radius
PERIMETER (P) of a:	
square	$P = 4s$; where s = side
rectangle	$P = 2l + 2w$; where l = length, w = width
triangle	$P = a + b + c$; where a, b, and c are the sides
circumference (C) of a circle	$C = \pi d$; where π = 3.14, d = diameter
VOLUME (V) of a:	
cube	$V = s^3$; where s = side
rectangular container	$V = lwh$; where l = length, w = width, h = height
cylinder	$V = \pi r^2 h$; where π = 3.14, r = radius, h = height
square pyramid	$V = \frac{1}{3}(\text{base edge})^2 h$
cone	$V = \frac{1}{3}\pi r^2 h$
Pythagorean theorem	$c^2 = a^2 + b^2$; where c = hypotenuse, a and b are legs, of a right triangle
distance (d) between two points in a plane	$d = \sqrt{(x_2 - x_1)^2 + (y_2 - y_1)^2}$; where (x_1, y_1) and (x_2, y_2) are two points in a plane
slope of a line (m)	$m = \dfrac{y_2 - y_1}{x_2 - x_1}$; where (x_1, y_1) and (x_2, y_2) are two points in a plane
MEASURES OF CENTRAL TENDENCY	mean = $\dfrac{x_1 + x_2 + \ldots + x_n}{n}$; where the x's are the values for which a mean is desired, and n = number of values in the series
	median = the point in an ordered set of numbers at which half of the numbers are above and half of the numbers are below this value
simple interest (i)	$i = prt$; where p = principal, r = rate, t = time
distance (d) as function of rate and time	$d = rt$; where r = rate, t = time
total cost (c)	$c = nr$; where n = number of units, r = cost per unit

GO ON TO THE NEXT PAGE

TEST 5: MATHEMATICS, PART I

Directions: You will have 45 minutes to complete this section. You may use a calculator.

1. On 5 successive days a deliveryman listed his mileage as follows: 135, 162, 98, 117, 216. If his truck averages 14 miles for each gallon of gas used, how many gallons of gas did he use during these 5 days?

   (1) 42
   (2) 52
   (3) 115
   (4) 147
   (5) 153

2. Parking meters in Springfield read: "12 minutes for 5¢. Maximum deposit 50¢." What is the maximum time, in hours, that a driver may be legally parked at one of these meters?

   (1) 1
   (2) 1.2
   (3) 12
   (4) 2
   (5) Not enough information is given.

Question 3 is based on the following figure.

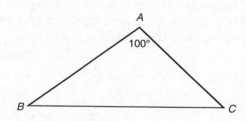

3. If $AB = AC$ and m $\angle A = 100°$, what is the measure of $\angle B$ in degrees?
   Mark your answer in the circles on the grid on the answer sheet.

4. The Clothing Zone had a special sale on shirts. One style sold at $20 per shirt, and another group sold at $25 per shirt. If 432 shirts were sold at $20 and 368 shirts were sold at $25 each, the number of dollars taken in at the shirt sale may be represented as

   (1) 800(20 + 25)
   (2) (20)(368) + (25)(432)
   (3) (20)(800) + (25)(800)
   (4) 45(432 + 68)
   (5) (20)(432) + (25)(368)

5. A hockey team won X games, lost Y games, and tied Z games. What fractional part of the games played were won?

   (1) $\dfrac{X}{X + Y + Z}$

   (2) $\dfrac{X}{XYZ}$

   (3) $\dfrac{X}{XY}$

   (4) $\dfrac{X}{X + Y}$

   (5) $\dfrac{X}{X - Y - Z}$

6. One-half the students at Madison High School walk to school. One-fourth of the rest go to school by bicycle. What part of the school population travels by some other means?
   Mark your answer in the circles on the grid on the answer sheet.

GO ON TO THE NEXT PAGE

TEST 5: MATHEMATICS, PART I

7. Which of the following graphs shows the solution set for the inequality $2x > 4$?

   (1) ←——————————————————→
       -3 -2 -1   0   1   2   3

   (2) ←——————————————————→
       -3 -2 -1   0   1   2   3

   (3) ←——————————————————→
       -3 -2 -1   0   1   2   3

   (4) ←——————————————————→
       -3 -2 -1   0   1   2   3

   (5) ←——————————————————→
       -3 -2 -1   0   1   2   3

8. An aquarium is in the form of a rectangular solid. The aquarium is 3 feet long, 1 foot 8 inches wide, and 1 foot 6 inches high. What is the volume, in cubic feet, of the aquarium?

   (1) 6.16
   (2) 6.4
   (3) 7.5
   (4) 7.875
   (5) 8.64

9. A flagpole casts a shadow 16 feet long. At the same time, a pole 9 feet high casts a shadow 6 feet long. What is the height, in feet, of the flagpole?

   (1) 18
   (2) 19
   (3) 20
   (4) 24
   (5) Not enough information is given.

10. The enrollment of a college is distributed as follows:

    360 freshmen
    300 sophomores
    280 juniors
    260 seniors

    The freshman class makes up what percent of the total enrollment?

    (1) 18%
    (2) 20%
    (3) 25%
    (4) 30%
    (5) Not enough information is given.

11. A purse contains 6 nickels, 5 dimes, and 8 quarters. If one coin is drawn at random from the purse, what is the probability that the coin drawn is a dime?

    (1) $\frac{5}{19}$

    (2) $\frac{5}{14}$

    (3) $\frac{5}{8}$

    (4) $\frac{5}{6}$

    (5) $\frac{19}{5}$

12. The leaders in the Peninsula Golf Tournament finished with scores of 272, 284, 287, 274, 275, 283, 278, 276, and 281. What is the median of these scores?

    (1) 273
    (2) 274
    (3) 276
    (4) 278
    (5) 280

13. Lee brings a bucket to soccer practice and fills it halfway with water. Approximately how many gallons does it hold?

    1 cu. in. = .0043 gallon

    (1) 10
    (2) 15
    (3) 18
    (4) 20
    (5) 28

    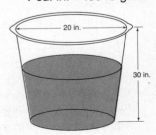

GO ON TO THE NEXT PAGE

TEST 5: MATHEMATICS, PART I

14. The scale on a map is 1 inch = 150 miles. The cities of Benton and Dover are $3\frac{1}{2}$ inches apart on this map. What is the actual distance, in miles, between Benton and Dover?

    Mark your answer in the circles on the grid on the answer sheet.

Question 15 is based on the following figure.

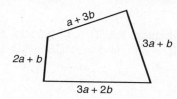

15. What is the perimeter of the figure?

    (1) $8a + 5b$

    (2) $9a + 7b$

    (3) $7a + 5b$

    (4) $6a + 6b$

    (5) $8a + 6b$

Question 16 is based on the following chart.

SPEAKER SALE	
1/3 off listed prices	
40 Watts	$159.99
60 Watts	$183.99
80 Watts	$219.99
All Installations	$150

16. Kirsten wants to purchase a pair of car speakers. The list above indicates prices for each pair, not including the 1/3 discount. If she buys the 40-watt speakers at the discounted price and has them installed, what will her total bill be, including 8% sales tax?

    (1) over $400

    (2) between $225 and $250

    (3) between $250 and $260

    (4) between $260 and $270

    (5) between $270 and $280

17. The Men's Shop advertised a spring sale, including the following sale items.

    ties: 3 for $42
    shirts: 3 for $60
    slacks: $32.75 per pair
    jackets: $158.45 each

    What is the price of 6 ties, 3 shirts, 2 pairs of slacks, and 1 jacket?

    (1) $350.45

    (2) $180.20

    (3) $242.15

    (4) $212.95

    (5) $367.95

18. In which of the following lists are the numbers written in order from greatest to smallest?

    (1) 0.80, 19%, 0.080, $\frac{1}{2}$, $\frac{3}{5}$

    (2) 0.80, $\frac{1}{2}$, 0.080, $\frac{3}{5}$, 19%

    (3) 0.80, $\frac{3}{5}$, $\frac{1}{2}$, 19%, 0.080

    (4) $\frac{1}{2}$, 0.80, $\frac{3}{5}$, 19%, 0.080

    (5) $\frac{3}{5}$, $\frac{1}{2}$, 19%, 0.080, 0.80

19. If an airplane completes its flight of 1,364 miles in 5 hours and 30 minutes, what is its average speed, in miles per hour? Mark your answer in the circles on the grid on the answer sheet.

20. The distance between two heavenly bodies is 85,000,000,000 miles. This number, written in scientific notation, is

    (1) 8.5×10^{-10}

    (2) 8.5×10^{10}

    (3) 85×10^{9}

    (4) 0.85×10^{-9}

    (5) 850×10^{7}

GO ON TO THE NEXT PAGE

TEST 5: MATHEMATICS, PART I

21. What is the value of $3ab - x^2y$ if $a = 4$, $b = 5$, $y = 3$, and $x = 2$?

    (1) 18

    (2) 24

    (3) 48

    (4) 54

    (5) 72

Question 22 is based on the following graph.

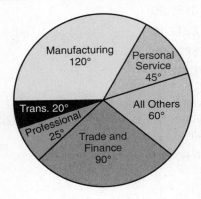

This circle graph shows how 180,000 wage earners in a certain city earned their livings during a given period.

22. The number of persons engaged in transportation in the city during this period was?

    Mark your answer in the circles on the grid on the answer sheet.

23. A hiker walks 12 miles due north. Then he turns and walks 16 miles due east. At this point, how many miles is the hiker from his starting point?

    (1) 12

    (2) 16

    (3) 18

    (4) 20

    (5) Not enough information is given.

Question 24 is based on the following figure.

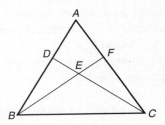

24. If $\overline{BF}$ bisects $\angle ABC$, $\overline{CD}$ bisects $\angle ACB$, m$\angle ABC = 68°$, and m$\angle ACB = 72°$, then m$\angle BEC =$

    (1) 90°

    (2) 98°

    (3) 100°

    (4) 110°

    (5) 120°

25. The dimensions of the hallway below are 6.5 ft. and 7.2 ft. If the area is to be covered with carpet at $2.10 per square foot, how much would carpeting for the hallway cost?

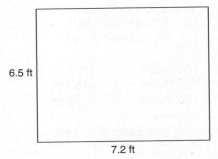

Mark your answer in the circles on the grid on the answer sheet.

GO ON TO THE NEXT PAGE

TEST 5: MATHEMATICS, PART II

Directions: You will have 45 minutes to complete questions 26–50. You may NOT use a calculator; otherwise, directions are the same as in Part I. You MAY refer to the *Formulas* sheet.*

26. John weighed 192 pounds. His doctor put him on a diet, which enabled him to lose at least 4 pounds per month. What was John's exact weight after 6 months on the diet?

    (1) 160 lb.
    (2) 165 lb.
    (3) 167 lb.
    (4) 168 lb.
    (5) Not enough information is given.

27. Mr. Ames bought a bond for $10,000. The bond yields interest at $8\frac{1}{2}$% annually. If the interest is paid every 6 months, how much is each interest payment in dollars?
    Mark your answer in the circles on the grid on the answer sheet.

28. Given the equation $x^2 - x - 12 = 0$, which of the following give(s) a complete solution of the equation?

    (1) 4 only
    (2) −4 only
    (3) 3 and 4
    (4) −3 and 4
    (5) −4 and 3

29. The ratio of men to women at a professional meeting was 9:2. If there were 12 women at the meeting. Which equation could be used to find the number of men at the meeting?

    (1) $\frac{12}{x} = \frac{9}{2}$
    (2) $24x = 180$
    (3) $\frac{9}{2} = \frac{x}{12}$
    (4) $7x = 24 + 9$
    (5) Not enough information is given.

30. What is the slope of the line that passes through point A (2,1) and point B (4,7)?

    (1) $\frac{1}{3}$
    (2) $\frac{2}{3}$
    (3) $\frac{3}{2}$
    (4) 2
    (5) 3

31. In a basketball game Bill scored three times as many points as Jim. Together they scored 56 points. How many points did Bill score?

    (1) 14
    (2) 28
    (3) 42
    (4) 48
    (5) Not enough information is given.

Question 32 is based on the following graph.

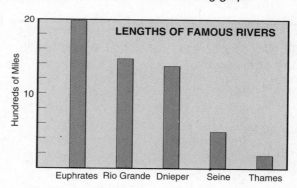

32. The graph shows the lengths of some famous rivers correct to the nearest hundred miles.

    Which one of the following statements is correct?

    (1) The Thames is more than one-half as long as the Seine.
    (2) The Dnieper is 1,200 miles long.
    (3) The Euphrates is about 250 miles longer than the Rio Grande.
    (4) The Rio Grande is about 1,000 miles longer than the Seine.
    (5) The Thames is about 100 miles long.

GO ON TO THE NEXT PAGE

TEST 5: MATHEMATICS, PART II

Question 33 is based on the following graph.

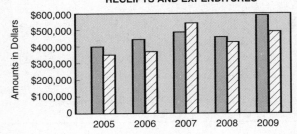

RECEIPTS AND EXPENDITURES

33. The graph shows receipts and expenses for the years indicated. The receipts are designated by shaded bars and the expenses by striped bars. The year in which receipts exceeded expenses by $100,000 was

   (1) 2005
   (2) 2006
   (3) 2007
   (4) 2008
   (5) 2009

34. If 1 pencil costs y cents, then 6 pencils will cost, in cents,

   (1) $6y$

   (2) $\dfrac{y}{6}$

   (3) $\dfrac{6}{y}$

   (4) $y + 6$

   (5) $\dfrac{y}{2}$

35. Mr. Martin earns $12 per hour. One week Mr. Martin worked 42 hours; the following week he worked 37 hours. Which of the following indicates the number of dollars Mr. Martin earned for the 2 weeks?

   (1) $12 \times 2 + 37$
   (2) $12 \times 42 + 42 \times 37$
   (3) $12 \times 37 + 42$
   (4) $12 + 42 \times 37$
   (5) $12(42 + 37)$

36. Kwan's recipe for lemonade requires 8 ounces of lemon juice for every quart of water used. To prepare for a large party, he uses 4 gallons of water. How much lemon juice is needed?

   (1) 108 ounces
   (2) 5 quarts
   (3) 96 ounces
   (4) 1 gallon
   (5) $2\frac{1}{2}$ quarts

Question 37 is based on the following figure.

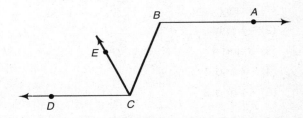

37. In the figure $\overleftrightarrow{AB} \parallel \overleftrightarrow{CD}$, $\overrightarrow{CE}$ bisects $\angle BCD$, and m$\angle ABC = 112°$. Find m$\angle ECD$.

   (1) 45°
   (2) 50°
   (3) 56°
   (4) 60°
   (5) Not enough information is given.

GO ON TO THE NEXT PAGE

TEST 5: MATHEMATICS, PART II

38. Mrs. Garvin buys a bolt of cloth 22 feet 4 inches in length. She cuts the bolt into four equal pieces to make drapes. What is the length of each piece?

    (1) 5 ft.
    (2) 5 ft. 7 in.
    (3) 5 ft. 9 in.
    (4) 6 ft. 7 in.
    (5) Not enough information is given.

<u>Questions 39 and 40</u> are based on the following graph.

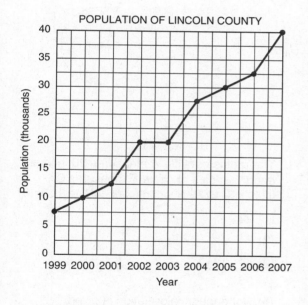

POPULATION OF LINCOLN COUNTY

The graph shows the growth in population in Lincoln County between the years 1999 and 2007.

39. What was the population of Lincoln County in the year 2004?

    (1) 20,000
    (2) 25,000
    (3) 26,000
    (4) 27,500
    (5) 30,000

40. The amount of population growth in Lincoln County between 1999 and 2000 was the same as which of the following?

    (1) 2000–2001 as well as 2001–2002
    (2) 2000–2001 as well as 2004–2005
    (3) 2004–2005 as well as 2006–2007
    (4) 2001–2002 as well as 2002–2003
    (5) 2002–2003 as well as 2004–2006

41. A box is in the form of a rectangular solid with a square base of side x units in length and a height of 8 units. The volume of the box is 392 cubic units. Which of the following equations may be used to find the value of x?

    (1) $x^2 = 392$
    (2) $8x = 392$
    (3) $8x^3 = 392$
    (4) $8x^2 = 392$
    (5) $8 + x^2 = 392$

42. There were three candidates at a school board election. Mrs. Clay received twice as many votes as Mr. Dunn, and Mr. Arnold received 66 votes more than Mr. Dunn. How many votes did Mrs. Clay receive?

    (1) 209
    (2) 275
    (3) 320
    (4) 402
    (5) Not enough information is given.

GO ON TO THE NEXT PAGE

TEST 5: MATHEMATICS, PART II

Question 43 is based on the following figure.

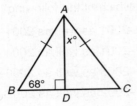

43. If $AB = AC$, $\overline{AD} \perp \overline{BC}$, and m$\angle B = 68°$, what is the value of x?

    (1) 12°
    (2) 22°
    (3) 32°
    (4) 44°
    (5) 68°

Question 44 is based on the following information.

In the figure below line $\overleftrightarrow{PQ}$ is parallel to line $\overleftrightarrow{RS}$.

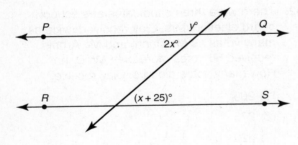

44. What is the value of x?

    (1) 15
    (2) 20
    (3) 25
    (4) 30
    (5) 35

45. The square root of 30 is between which of the following pairs of numbers?

    (1) 3 and 4
    (2) 4 and 5
    (3) 5 and 6
    (4) 6 and 7
    (5) 15 and 16

Question 46 is based on the following figure.

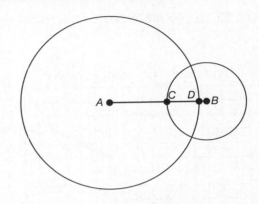

46. The radius of circle A measures 20 inches, and the radius of circle B measures 8 inches. If $CD = 6$ inches, find AB, in inches.

    (1) 22
    (2) 24
    (3) 25
    (4) 28
    (5) Not enough information is given.

GO ON TO THE NEXT PAGE

TEST 5: MATHEMATICS, PART II

47. The graph of a square is shown on the grid below.

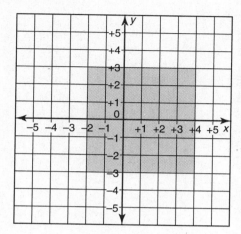

What point is the location of the center of the square?

Mark your answer on the coordinate plane grid on your answer sheet.

---

48. A woman buys n pounds of sugar at c cents a pound. She gives the clerk a $10 bill. The change she receives, in cents, is

(1) $nc - 1000$

(2) $n + c - 1000$

(3) $1000 - (n + c)$

(4) $1000 - nc$

(5) Not enough information is given.

49. If $x = 10$, each of the following is true **EXCEPT**

(1) $3x + 1 > 12$

(2) $2x - 3 < 25$

(3) $x^2 + 1 > x^2 - 1$

(4) $4x - 1 = 39$

(5) $2x - 7 < 7 - 2x$

Question 50 is based on the following figure.

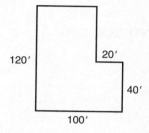

50. Mr. Denby planned to build a house on the plot of ground shown. What is the area, in square feet, of this plot of ground?

Mark your answer in the circles on the grid on the answer sheet.

END OF EXAM

ANSWER KEYS, SUMMARIES OF RESULTS, AND SELF-APPRAISAL CHARTS

TEST 1: LANGUAGE ARTS, WRITING, PART I/PAGE 19

I. CHECK YOUR ANSWERS, using the following answer key:

1. **2**	10. **4**	19. **4**	28. **1**	37. **4**	46. **2**
2. **3**	11. **5**	20. **3**	29. **1**	38. **2**	47. **5**
3. **3**	12. **1**	21. **2**	30. **1**	39. **5**	48. **1**
4. **1**	13. **5**	22. **5**	31. **5**	40. **5**	49. **4**
5. **5**	14. **2**	23. **1**	32. **1**	41. **1**	50. **1**
6. **5**	15. **2**	24. **3**	33. **2**	42. **4**	
7. **1**	16. **3**	25. **5**	34. **4**	43. **3**	
8. **3**	17. **5**	26. **5**	35. **3**	44. **1**	
9. **5**	18. **1**	27. **4**	36. **2**	45. **5**	

II. SCORE YOURSELF:

Number correct:

Excellent _____
45–50

Good _____
39–44

Fair _____
33–38

III. EVALUATE YOUR SCORE: Did you get at least 35 correct answers? If not, you need more practice for the Language Arts, Writing, Part I test. In any event, you can improve your performance to Excellent or Good by analyzing your errors.

IV. ANALYZE YOUR ERRORS: To determine your areas of weakness, list the number of correct answers you had under each of the following categories (which correspond to the content areas of the Language Arts, Writing, Part I test), and compare your score with the average scores specified in the right-hand column. Review the answer analysis section beginning on page 84 for each of the questions you got wrong, and give yourself more practice in your weak areas with the appropriate material in Chapters 3–7 before attempting Practice Exam One.

Content Areas	Items	Your Score	Average Score
Sentence Structure	3, 12, 16, 25, 29, 32, 34, 38, 40, 44, 49		7
Usage	1, 8, 19, 20–21, 23–24, 33, 37, 42		7
Mechanics			
Possessives/contractions/ homonyms	10, 15, 43, 50		3
Punctuation	2, 14, 26, 35, 36, 41		3
Capitalization	4		1
Organization	5, 7, 18, 28, 30, 46, 48		4
No correction	6, 9, 11, 13, 17, 22, 27, 31, 39, 45, 47		7

Total _____

TEST 2: SOCIAL STUDIES/PAGE 31

I. CHECK YOUR ANSWERS, using the following answer key:

1. **1**	11. **1**	21. **1**	31. **3**	41. **5**
2. **4**	12. **3**	22. **2**	32. **4**	42. **2**
3. **4**	13. **2**	23. **5**	33. **1**	43. **1**
4. **5**	14. **4**	24. **4**	34. **4**	44. **1**
5. **2**	15. **1**	25. **2**	35. **5**	45. **5**
6. **5**	16. **3**	26. **3**	36. **1**	46. **4**
7. **4**	17. **2**	27. **4**	37. **1**	47. **1**
8. **2**	18. **2**	28. **3**	38. **1**	48. **4**
9. **4**	19. **4**	29. **2**	39. **1**	49. **1**
10. **4**	20. **4**	30. **5**	40. **3**	50. **3**

II. SCORE YOURSELF:

Number correct:

Excellent _____
                              45–50

Good _____
                              40–44

Fair _____
                              35–39

III. EVALUATE YOUR SCORE: Did you get at least 35 correct answers? If not, you need more practice for the Social Studies test. In any event, you can improve your performance to Excellent or Good by analyzing your errors.

II. ANALYZE YOUR ERRORS: To determine your specific weaknesses, list the number of correct answers you had under each of the following categories (which correspond to the content areas of the Social Studies test), and compare your score with the average scores specified in the right-hand column. Review the answer analysis section beginning on page 87 for each of the questions you got wrong, and give yourself more practice in your weak areas with the appropriate material in Chapters 10–12 (including the "Glossary of Social Studies Terms") before attempting Practice Exam One.

Content Areas	Items	Your Score	Average Score
Political Science	1–3, 12, 29–31, 34, 41–43, 44, 48–49		8
Economics	4–6, 9, 17–19, 21–22, 24 26–28, 35–37, 39–40		10
History	15–16, 20, 25, 32–33, 38, 50		5
Geography	7–8, 10–11, 13–14, 23, 45–47		7

Total _____

TEST 3: SCIENCE/PAGE 42

I. CHECK YOUR ANSWERS, using the following answer key:

1. **3**	12. **2**	23. **3**	34. **3**	45. **4**	56. **2**
2. **1**	13. **4**	24. **5**	35. **5**	46. **3**	57. **4**
3. **2**	14. **2**	25. **3**	36. **5**	47. **3**	58. **1**
4. **4**	15. **2**	26. **5**	37. **3**	48. **2**	59. **2**
5. **4**	16. **2**	27. **4**	38. **4**	49. **2**	60. **2**
6. **4**	17. **1**	28. **3**	39. **3**	50. **2**	61. **2**
7. **4**	18. **2**	29. **4**	40. **3**	51. **1**	62. **3**
8. **3**	19. **4**	30. **5**	41. **1**	52. **4**	63. **1**
9. **2**	20. **2**	31. **5**	42. **3**	53. **4**	64. **2**
10. **3**	21. **2**	32. **4**	43. **3**	54. **5**	65. **2**
11. **2**	22. **4**	33. **1**	44. **3**	55. **5**	66. **4**

II. SCORE YOURSELF:

Number correct:

Excellent _____
60–66

Good _____
49–59

Fair _____
40–48

III. EVALUATE YOUR SCORE: Did you get at least 40 correct answers? If not, you need more practice for the Science test. In any event, you can improve your performance to Excellent or Good by analyzing your errors.

IV. ANALYZE YOUR ERRORS: To determine your specific weaknesses, encircle the number of each question that you got wrong. This will reveal the specific science area that needs emphasis in planning your study program. After studying the answer analysis section beginning on page 90 for each of the questions you got wrong, list the terms that you feel need further explanation and study them in the "Glossary of Scientific Terms." Then give yourself more practice in your weak areas with the appropriate material in Chapters 13–15 before attempting Practice Exam One.

Content Areas	Items	Your Score	Average Score
Biology	1–4, 24–39, 41–43, 45–49, 59, 61–66		24
Earth Science	9–13, 17–19, 40, 44, 55–58		7
Chemistry	20–23, 44, 50–53		6
Physics	5–8, 14–16, 54, 60		7

Total _____

TEST 4: LANGUAGE ARTS, READING/PAGE 57

I. CHECK YOUR ANSWERS, using the following answer key:

1. **2**	9. **3**	17. **3**	25. **4**	33. **1**
2. **4**	10. **5**	18. **4**	26. **3**	34. **1**
3. **1**	11. **2**	19. **3**	27. **2**	35. **5**
4. **1**	12. **3**	20. **3**	28. **3**	36. **4**
5. **2**	13. **2**	21. **3**	29. **5**	37. **3**
6. **3**	14. **4**	22. **5**	30. **3**	38. **1**
7. **1**	15. **1**	23. **3**	31. **1**	39. **4**
8. **2**	16. **1**	24. **4**	32. **4**	40. **3**

II. SCORE YOURSELF:

Number correct:

Excellent _____
36–40

Good _____
32–35

Fair _____
28–31

III. EVALUATE YOUR SCORE: Did you get at least 28 correct answers? If not, you need more practice for the test on Language Arts, Reading. In any event, you can improve your performance to Excellent or Good by analyzing your errors.

IV. ANALYZE YOUR ERRORS: To determine your specific weaknesses, first list the number of correct answers you had under each of the following categories and compare your score with the average scores specified in the right-hand column. After studying the answer analysis section beginning on page 95 for each of the questions you got wrong, study the material in the section *Basic Reading Skills* and the section *Reading Prose, Poetry, and Drama,* as well as the "Glossary of Literary Terms," all in Chapter 16, to strengthen your weak areas before attempting Practice Exam One.

Reading Skills	Items	Your Score	Average Score
Locating the Main Idea	5, 16, 21		3
Finding Details	2, 12, 17–18, 23–24, 32–33, 38–40		11
Inferring Meaning	1, 13–15, 19–20, 22, 34–35		6
Making Inferences	3, 4, 7, 10, 25, 36–37		5
Determining Tone and Mood	6, 9, 26–27, 31		4
Inferring Character	11, 28–30		3
Inferring Setting	8		1

Total _____

Now, to see how your scores in the content area of Language Arts, Reading test compare with the average scores in the right-hand column, list your score for each of the following:

Literary Forms	Items	Your Score	Average Score
Prose Fiction	6–15		7
Prose Nonfiction	1–5, 31–40		17
Poetry	16–25		7
Drama	26–30		3

Total _____

TEST 5: MATHEMATICS/PAGE 67

I. CHECK YOUR ANSWERS, using the following answer key:

1. **2**	11. **1**	21. **3**	31. **3**	41. **4**
2. **4**	12. **4**	22. **10,000**	32. **4**	42. **5**
3. **40**	13. **4**	23. **4**	33. **5**	43. **2**
4. **5**	14. **525**	24. **4**	34. **1**	44. **3**
5. **1**	15. **2**	25. **98.28**	35. **5**	45. **3**
6. **3/8, or .375**	16. **5**	26. **5**	36. **4**	46. **1**
7. **5**	17. **5**	27. **425**	37. **3**	47. **(1,0)**
8. **3**	18. **3**	28. **4**	38. **2**	48. **4**
9. **4**	19. **248**	29. **3**	39. **4**	49. **5**
10. **4**	20. **2**	30. **5**	40. **2**	50. **10,400**

II. SCORE YOURSELF:

Number correct:

Excellent _____
40–50

Good _____
32–49

Fair _____
28–31

III. EVALUATE YOUR SCORE: Did you get at least 28 correct answers? If not, you need more practice for the Mathematics test. In any event, you can improve your performance to Excellent or Good by analyzing your errors.

IV. ANALYZE YOUR ERRORS: To determine your specific weakness, list the number of correct answers you had under each of the following skill areas, and compare your score with the average scores specified in the right-hand column. After studying the answer analysis section beginning on page 97 for each of the questions you got wrong, give yourself more practice in your weak areas with the appropriate material in Chapters 18–25 before attempting Practice Exam One.

Content Areas	Items	Your Score	Average Score
Numbers and Basic Operations	1, 2, 4, 12, 19, 26, 35, 45		5
Fractions and Measurements	6, 11, 36, 38		2
Decimals and Percents	10, 18, 20, 27, 29		3
Data Analysis	14, 16, 17, 22, 32, 33, 39, 40		4
Algebra	5, 7, 8, 15, 21, 28, 31, 34, 41, 42, 48, 49		7
Geometry	3, 9, 13, 23, 24, 25, 30, 37, 43, 44, 46, 47, 50		7

Total _____

Your Total GED Score

The Language Arts, Writing Test _____

The Social Studies Test _____

The Science Test _____

The Language Arts, Reading Test _____

The Mathematics Test _____

Total _____

ANSWER ANALYSIS

TEST 1: LANGUAGE ARTS, WRITING, PART I/PAGE 19

1. **2** There is an error in usage. The subject of the sentence is *combination*, which is singular. A singular verb, *makes*, is required for agreement.

2. **3** The error is in punctuation. A comma is needed to set off an introductory phrase.

3. **3** There is a sentence fragment beginning with *seldom*. This is corrected by removing the period and joining the fragment to the rest of the sentence.

4. **1** There is an error in capitalization. Seasons are *not* capitalized.

5. **5** This paragraph has one main idea and cannot be divided in two.

6. **5** No correction is necessary.

7. **1** The first sentence makes a general statement about the attributes of vegetable gardening. The other sentences in the paragraph support this main idea.

8. **3** The usage error is in the shift in person in two pronouns that refer to the same person. The second-person pronoun *your* in the introductory clause requires a continuation of the second person, *you*, in the main clause.

9. **5** No correction is necessary.

10. **4** The correct homonym is *their*, meaning belonging to them. The computers belong to them (families).

11. **5** No correction is necessary.

12. **1** The original is correct. Two sentences are needed.

13. **5** No correction is necessary.

14. **2** A comma is required to set off items in a series.

15. **2** There is no need for an apostrophe in *releases*. The verb must agree with its subject, and in this sentence, both should be singular.

16. **3** The meaning of the sentence requires *may be served*.

17. **5** No correction is necessary.

18. **1** Sentence 9 should be left as it is because it elaborates on *discretionary time* in the previous sentence.

19. **4** There is an error in usage. Parallel structure requires the use of infinitives: *to develop, to increase, to learn* (rather than *learning*).

20. **3** The sentence requires the use of *there are* rather than *they are (they're)*. *They are a number of...steps* doesn't make sense.

21. **2** The pronoun *they* agrees with plural noun *measures*.

22. **5** No correction is necessary.

23. **1** The subject of the sentence is you (understood). Therefore, the verb to agree with a singular subject is *take*.

24. **3** The future tense should be used for an action taking place in the future, that is, when you take the car in.

25. **5** Two sentences are necessary to correct the run-on sentence. To accomplish this, a period after *order* and a capitalized *That* are needed.

26. **5** No correction is necessary.

27. **4** The correct spelling is *determined*.

28. **1** Sentence 11 should be left as it is because it is the logical last course of action for the passage.

29. **1** A comma is needed to set off items in a series.

30. **1** Sentence 1 should be *left as is* because it is the best introductory sentence. It doesn't make sense in any other part of the literature.

31. **5** No correction is necessary.

32. **1** The original way is the best among the choices offered.

33. **2** *Readily* is an adverb that modifies the verb *to find*.

34. **4** The relative pronoun *that* avoids the unnecessary use of the words *such programs*.

35. **3** A semicolon is used to separate independent clauses in a sentence.

36. **2** A comma is used after an introductory clause.

37. **4** The plural subject, *some*, requires the verb *have been overcome*.

38. **2** Making "You are going to move" the subject of the verb *is* eliminates the need for "That statement" and effectively combines the two sentences.

39. **5** No correction is necessary

40. **5** *Or* is correct because another way to state the fact is given.

41. **1** A comma is used after an introductory phrase.

42. **4** There is more than one course of action; therefore, *courses* is the correct choice.

43. **3** The proper word for this sentence is *involve*.

44. **1** The original is correct because *or* connects two independent clauses (*has come through* is understood after *an opportunity to move to a better climate*).

45. **5** No correction is necessary.

46. **2** The main idea of this passage is that *the average person moves once every 5 years*.

47. **5** No correction is necessary.

48. **1** The first sentence tells the first step of fishing; therefore, it must be left as the first sentence of the first paragraph in order to keep the chronologic order of steps.

49. **4** Rewriting the sentence with *The next phase* as the subject requires a singular verb, *is*, in the present tense.

50. **1** A verb that agrees with a singular subject does not require an apostrophe.

TEST 1: LANGUAGE ARTS, WRITING, PART II/PAGE 30

SAMPLE ESSAY

I remember the day that I fell off the back of my brother's bicycle. The memory is still so vivid in my mind. I will always remember it.

It was a beautiful spring day when my older brother and I decided to go bike riding on the same bike. My brother's bicycle was an old Easy Rider with a saddle seat and a fender that went over the back tire. The fender was my "seat." As I straddled the back tire on the fender and we began our journey up a large hill I remember telling him, "I'm slipping off the fender!" "Just hold on," was his reply. I tried but my little seven-year old hands just couldn't do the trick. I slid right onto the asphalt roadway. My hands and knees took the brunt of the force and as I got up I looked down to see two very badly skinned knees. Crying, my brother helped me hobble back to the house where my mother was none too sympathetic with the sight of my terribly skinned knees. In fact, she was upset with me too because I was to wear a short dress the next night for my Bible School Program. She had warned me not to ride on the back of the bike. I suppose I should have listened.

What a day that was. It still seems like yesterday when I sat straddled on that old bicycle just before slipping off. I'll never forget it.

TEST 2: SOCIAL STUDIES/PAGE 31

1. **1** The last paragraph of the passage states clearly that the governor's veto power is not used sparingly, and that more than one out of four bills fails to receive approval.

2. **4** The second paragraph of the selection deals with the "30-day" rule. The first sentence of this paragraph states that all bills passed within the last ten days of the legislative session are covered by this rule.

3. **4** The first sentence of the first paragraph states that the governor has the power to veto single items of the budget bill. This is an authority not possessed by the president of the United States.

4. **5** Nearly all of the selection deals with a plan of action for use before the consumer buys. See the second sentence and also the first words of the third paragraph.

5. **2** The consumer is advised to get all promises in writing.

6. **5** It is specifically mentioned that pro rata (or partial) return of moneys and credit toward a replacement may be part of a warranty.

7. **4** By 2030, increasing numbers of Americans will reach the age that makes them eligible for Social Security benefits.

8. **2** A large increase in the birth rate would cause the average age to become lower since the many babies added to the population would counteract the older Americans.

9. **4** Persons concerned with the natural environment fear that an emphasis on greater production and consumption will mean further pollution of the air (by factory smokestacks and apartment house incinerators) and of rivers, lakes, and streams (by industrial wastes and sewage disposal); and increased problems of solid waste disposal and rising noise levels.

10. **4** There is no movement toward a solution to the energy problem as long as the two cyclists representing energy and environment keep pedaling in different directions.

11. **1** A fivefold increase in the price of imported crude oil from 1973 to 1980 severely affected the U.S. economy and forced a search for alternative domestic sources of energy, despite possible immediate negative effects on the environment.

12. **3** This is directly related to the big change from isolationism to internationalism in U.S. foreign policy. From 1920 to 1940 we had no political or military ties to non-American countries, and we never joined the League of Nations. Since World War II, which ended in 1945, the United States has pursued policies of collective security. President F. D. Roosevelt called for the United Nations, of which we are a charter member. President Truman committed U.S. aid to Europe through the Marshall Plan, the Truman Doctrine, and NATO. Subsequent presidents have continued economic aid to Asia and Africa, military assistance to Middle East and Asian nations, and commitments to Korea and Vietnam. President Kennedy started the Peace Corps, and President Nixon tried to negotiate peace in Vietnam and in Israel. Each of the other choices involves areas in which the Congress, the Supreme Court, and the states have been more influential than the president.

13. **2** The passage states that the Arctic and the Antarctic are "imaginary markers on the Earth's surface."

14. **4** It is stated that both the Tropic of Cancer and the Tropic of Capricorn run parallel to the equator.

15. **1** The Gettysburg Address was delivered in 1863. Fourscore and seven years earlier—that is, 87 years earlier—the Declaration of Independence had been signed. It declared the liberty of the thirteen colonies and stated that all men are created equal.

16. **3** The speech was delivered at the Gettysburg cemetery. In the second paragraph, Lincoln states that this is the purpose of the occasion.

17. **2** Lacking land for agriculture, Nation *A* will use its abundant labor, capital, and management skills to develop industry. The resulting products can be sold to domestic and foreign markets.

18. **2** In the 1800s, Great Britain led the world in manufacturing and resembled Nation *A* in factors of production.

19. **4** Nation *B*, with its natural resources and labor, must encourage new industries by protectionist tariffs and by tax concessions to attract capital investment.

20. **4** The purpose of the Truman Doctrine, as opposed to President Monroe's policy of noninterference, was to support the governments of Greece and Turkey against direct and indirect Communist aggression. In 1947 Greece was in especially weakened condition following Nazi occupation during World War II, and was under attack by Communist guerrilla bands.

21. **1** From '60 to '65, the increase was 29.3% minus 18.6%, or 10.7%, greater than for any other interval.

22. **2** Between '70 and '80, the percentage of women working part time remained unchanged at 35.1%.

23. **5** Area E is farthest from a large body of water and moisture from the ocean by the prevailing winds would fall as rain before reaching Area E.

24. **4** A recession takes place in the economy when purchasing, saving, and business profits go down. The result is an increase in unemployment and a period of reduced economic activity—a recession.

25. **2** Social Darwinism became popular in the second half of the 19th century. It applied Darwin's theory of natural selection to people and nations, attempting thereby to justify the widening gap between the rich and the poor in the United States.

26. **3** From 1992 to 2001, the median family income (before taxes) steadily increased a couple thousand dollars each year.

27. **4** The debt as a percentage of total family assets probably declined between 1998 and 2001 because income had increased by more than $6,000.

28. **3** According to the table, debt as a percentage of total family assets declined every year except 1995.

29. **2** The purpose of this speech by President Lyndon Johnson was to help troubled young people lead productive lives. In dealing with delinquent and potentially delinquent youth, he was concerned first about preventing them from getting into trouble; then, if they did, in helping them to become useful citizens. These ideas are stated in the first two paragraphs.

30. **5** President Johnson states that he recommends the Juvenile Delinquency Prevention Act of 1967.

31. **3** Family counseling is recommended because so many delinquents "live in broken families, burdened with . . . problems."

32. **4** The photograph depicts an early transportation method of milk.

33. **1** The photograph was taken when trains were still the most common form of transportation of goods, which was during the 1940s.

34. **4** Comparing the two graphs reveals that the electoral vote reflected the popular vote in 2004.

35. **5** The movies are not mentioned as a media type.

36. **1** The 8- to 18-year-olds have the highest percentage, 51%, and whites at 45% have a higher computer use than Blacks and Hispanics.

37. **1** As an activity, watching TV is well ahead of the other six mentioned.

38. **1** A primary source is an eyewitness account of an event, such as a description in a diary, or an artifact constructed in a specific time period.

39. **1** With a drop of 12.7%, the weekly earnings fell the most for women with no high school diploma.

40. **3** The graph indicates that median earnings for whites and Hispanics exceeded those for blacks with an associate degree.

41. **5** Lobbyists are representatives of special-interest groups who attempt to influence congressmen by providing information, preparing bills, and testifying at hearings.

42. **2** (B) Lobbyists sometimes use undesirable ways of influencing legislation by giving gifts and campaign contributions. The laws they sponsor may not benefit the general public.

43. **1** (A) Thousands of bills in many areas are introduced during each session of Congress. These must be handled by standing committees who try to bring expertise to each subject.

44. **1** Out of concern for their own reelection, legislators (the Boy Scouts in the cartoon) introduce consumer protection bills during an election year.

45. **5** Parents, teachers, and age peers are mentioned in the two classes of socializing agents.

46. **4** In the last sentence, all of the reasons are mentioned except the *number* of peers. The group is mentioned as being of increasing importance.

47. **1** The passage, in the second sentence, refers to the great influence of the family.

48. **4** Speaker A is talking about a world made smaller by modern technology. Speaker B agrees and adds that the problems of any area now become the problems of all humankind. Both feel that, as the world becomes one community, interdependence is a factor in world survival.

49. **1** Ethnocentrism is the view that one's own culture is superior to all others. Speaker C is calling for the appreciation of other people's value systems and ways of life.

50. **3** The extermination of over six million people, nearly all Jews, by the Nazi regime in Germany is called the Holocaust.

TEST 3: SCIENCE/PAGE 42

1. **3** Feathers are a late branch on this tree and thus came later in evolution. Notice that tissues came much earlier in the branching process.

2. **1** The branch coming straight up from plantae shows that mosses came before ferns, which came before conifers.

3. **2** Birds and reptiles are late branches on the animal branch of the phylogenetic tree. Notice that they are also right next to each other.

4. **4** The latest of these evolutionary developments is feathers, which appear at the end of the animal branch of the tree.

5. **4** The volume of the block is 3 cm × 2 cm × 4 cm or 24 cm³. The mass is given as 120 grams. Using the density formula provided, $120g/24cm^3 = 5$ g/cm³, Choice 4.

6. **4** Cutting an object into smaller pieces does not change its identity, and does not change its density. It is true that the volume of the new piece would be smaller, but the mass would be smaller as well. Notice that Choice 3 looks similar to Choice 4, but that the second part of the response is different. Make sure you read all of the choices completely before you select your answer.

7. **4** A balloon that is heated does not undergo any change in mass. You are told that the volume doubles. Thus, when doing a density calculation, you would be dividing the same mass by twice the volume. Dividing by twice as big a number gives half the answer. For example, a 100 gram balloon with a volume of 50 cm³ would have a density of 2 g/cm³. If the volume doubles to 100 cm³, the new density would be 1 g/cm³ (half of the original).

8. **3** If density is mass divided by volume, then mass is density times volume, so 4g/cm³ times 10 cm³ = 40g.

9. **2** According to the theory of continental drift and plate tectonics, the surface of the Earth is moving. The undersea volcanic vent, however, opens deep into the center of the Earth and is stable. One theory about the formation of the Hawaiian Islands suggests that a section of the Earth moves over the volcanic vent, which spews forth enough material to form an island; then, as a new section of Earth moves over the vent, another island is formed.

10. **3** The total time for the sound wave to go from the boat to the bottom and back is 4 seconds. It took 2 seconds to go down and 2 seconds to return. Therefore, 2 seconds × 1,000 meters/second = 2,000 meters.

11. **2** Only an electromagnet has the ability to be turned on or off. Notice that Choice 5 is an impossibility, so that you could disregard this answer at once.

12. **2** Since opposite poles of a magnet attract, the north pole of the Earth should attract the south pole of a compass needle. It does not matter where on Earth you are, this is always true.

13. **4** The passage clearly states that all magnets have a north and a south pole, so that must be true of the magnet referred to in the question, regardless of the type of magnet it is.

14. **2** The passage states that the diesel engine is less expensive to operate. Choice 1 is true of both engines. The amount of air used is not mentioned at all in the passage (Choice 5).

15. **2** On long trips, diesel engines get better mileage on the same amount of fuel as gasoline engines.

16. **2** Internal combustion engines weigh less and a race car is concerned with speed and little else. Cost is not a factor, nor is availability of spark plugs.

17. **1** Earthquakes are the result of the movement of rock masses below the Earth's surface, resulting in breaking rock layers and displacement (fault) of segments of the layer at the breaking point. The folding of rock layers results from the action of lesser forces acting over a longer period of time. The forces produced by landslides are too small to create an earthquake.

18. **2** The 1989 earthquake in San Francisco killed many people because older buildings and roadways were not built to withstand such a severe shock. The more modern buildings survived.

19. **4** It is shock waves in the crust that a seismograph detects, whether they are produced by earthquakes or by nuclear explosions.

20. **2** The mass of an atom comes from its protons and neutrons, each of which weighs 1 amu. If an atom has a mass of 7 amu, then the number of protons and neutrons must total 7. 7 total − 3 protons = 4 neutrons.

21. **2** A neutral atom has an equal number of protons and electrons. A positive ion has extra protons (or a shortage of electrons). An atom with 12 protons and 10 electrons would have a +2 charge.

22. **4** An Al ion has a charge of +3 and a Cl ion a charge of −1. It takes 3 −1 charges to cancel (or balance out) a +3 ion charge. Thus, there are three Cl ions for each Al ion.

23. **3** An atom that loses an electron will have an "extra" proton and a +1 charge. The passage states that the mass of the electron is so small that it can be ignored for most calculations. Only Choice 3 meets both of these conditions.

24. **5** Many parts of the plant are involved, but it is in the chloroplasts that the actual chemical process takes place.

25. **3** Water from the soil is conducted through the xylem.

26. **5** Chemical energy is needed to split water into H^+ (combined in the glucose) and O_2.

27. **4** Hydrogen and carbon dioxide are successively built up into sugars.

28. **3** Chlorophyll in the chloroplasts of the cells transforms the energy of light into chemical energy.

29. **4** The stomata are openings through which carbon dioxide enters the leaf.

30. **5** Note that the figure shows you that light, water, and carbon dioxide all go into the plant system to produce sugars. Thus all three are required, and Choice 5 is the correct answer.

31. **5** Since carbon dioxide is used in photosynthesis, increasing the supply would speed up the process.

32. **4** The birds have come to resemble each other because they have evolved to adapt to the same lifestyle. Choices 2, 3, and 5 contradict the statement that the birds are unrelated.

33. **1** According to the information, the white moths were invisible to predators against the light-colored bark. When the trees were darkened by soot, however, the moths were very easy to see.

34. **3** The only life process that a snake cannot perform alone is reproduction.

35. **5** Since the heart is a muscle with nerves that conduct impulses, potassium is an important nutrient. Many prescription drugs that heart patients take have a tendency to remove excess water. Dissolved potassium is thus lost.

36. **5** Stack gases combine with atmospheric water to produce acid rain, which can damage embryos, buildings, trees, and lungs.

37. **3** Mice have many offspring, with a short time between generations. Choice 1 is wrong because bacteria do not reproduce sexually. Choices 2 and 4 are wrong because dogs and humans, while of great practical interest, are not as prolific as mice. Oak trees are extremely prolific, but they have to grow for many years before they produce acorns.

38. **4** The passage implies that green bacteria evolved from nongreen forms, which must have been on Earth first. Animal life requires oxygen, so it must have come after the green bacteria changed the atmosphere.

39. **3** The wolf population peaked a year after the peak of the moose population, so many wolves must have been born when the moose population was at its highest.

40. **3** The fossils in rock layer *D* are older than those in layer *A*. Fossils are found in sedimentary rocks. Sedimentary rocks are formed as layer upon layer of material is deposited. The oldest sediment layer *D* was laid down first and appears at the bottom. The youngest layer is at the top.

41. **1** Breathing air is not a form of direct transmission of body fluids. In sexual intercourse, each person has intimate contact with the body fluids of the other, so Choice 2 is wrong. Choices 3, 4 and 5 all involve transmission of blood from person to person.

42. **3** The breeder's problem is to locate the immune plants, which will be those that survive when herbicides are applied.

43. **3** Reasons to use new strains of plants are those that provide benefits to both farmers and consumers. Both options I and II would be beneficial, but using more water and fertilizer would cost more and would not be beneficial to either the grower or the consumer.

44. **3** For a substance to melt it must take in energy. The opposite of melting is freezing, which involves the release (or loss) of energy. When a substance evaporates, it gains energy and when it condenses (the opposite process), it releases energy. Thus, options I and III, but not II, are correct.

45. **4** Cloning is used to produce a large number of plants in a short period of time. According to the passage, one million plants can be cloned in about six months.

46. **3** According to the passage, each cell contains chromosomes, a complete blueprint for reproducing itself.

47. **3** The hormones auxin and cytokinin stimulate the production of new plants. Hormones are substances that regulate the growth and reproduction of organisms.

48. **2** Cloning is defined as a form of vegetative propagation. Vegetative propagation is a form of asexual reproduction; that is, only one parent is required.

49. **2** Sexual reproduction processes mix the heredities of the two parents, and produce offspring different from both. In cloning and other vegetative methods, there is no change in the genotype.

50. **2** The medicine is a suspension, not a solution. All incorrect choices are characteristic of solutions.

51. **1** Sour substances such as juice and vinegar have low (acidic) pH values. Only Choice 1 has a pH value for an acid. The others are either neutral (Choice 2) or basic (Choices 3, 4, and 5).

52. **4** A pH of 10.5 is quite basic and would be expected to have properties similar to soapy water and ammonia. Both of these taste bitter and turn litmus blue, which is a match with Choice 4.

53. **4** A bitter substance suggests a base. Bases turn litmus blue and methyl red yellow, so the correct answer is Choice 4. Notice that the information needed is provided within the table and that you do not need to know the details of acids, bases, or indicators to solve the problem.

54. **5** Heat is a form of energy that moves spontaneously from regions of higher temperatures to lower. Cold is not a thing; the word here is used as an adjective.

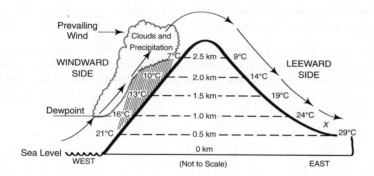

55. **5** On the west side of the mountain, the temperature is dropping 3°C for each 0.5 km. At 2.5 km the temperature is 7°C. At the top it is 3° less, or 4°C. The same results would be obtained by using data from the east side of the mountain, where the temperature is dropping 5°C for each 0.5 km.

56. **2** When precipitation occurs, the relative humidity is 100%. In the diagram, precipitation is occurring on the windward side of the mountain at an elevation of 2.5 km.

57. **4** As the air rises, it expands. When it expands, it cools. You may have noticed that the air rushing out of a tire feels cool. This is because the air is expanding.

58. **1** As the air descends on the leeward side of the mountain, it becomes warmer. As a result, there will rarely be precipitation there. The lack of precipitation will produce an arid region. The deserts in the southwestern part of the United States are located on the leeward sides of mountain ranges.

59. **2** Some plants release pollen to the atmosphere. Human activity does not greatly affect the amount of pollen in the atmosphere. Substances are usually considered pollutants when they are added to the environment by human activity. Any portion of the environment can become polluted,

including the atmosphere, the hydrosphere, or the lithosphere. The environment is said to be polluted when more of some substance is added than would normally be present. If, for example, large amounts of waste are dumped into a river, the water becomes polluted. Fish and other living organisms in the river may die if the pollution level becomes too great.

60. **2** The block and the weight are tied together, so they must always have the same speed. If the force moving the block becomes larger than the friction, the block must accelerate.

61. **2** Although a turtle has a hard outer shell similar to an exoskeleton, it also has an internal skeleton and is classified as a vertebrate.

62. **3** The independent variable in an experiment is the factor or variable directly manipulated by the experimenter, in this case the presence of the flypaper.

63. **1** Bottle 1 has flypaper in it, which although not a "natural" thing, in this case could create a situation where not flying was an advantage.

64. **2** The most obvious variable to be measured to see if there was a genuine advantage to wingless or winged flies is the number of flies that have survived. Choice 2 is the best answer.

65. **2** Mutations are changes in the genes in an organism. Although they are the result of gene changes (or different alleles appearing), the actual change is known as a mutation.

66. **4** In most circumstances in nature, it must be expected that wings are useful. This experiment sets up an artificial environment in which the survival values are reversed. Some such environment might well exist in nature.

TEST 4: LANGUAGE ARTS, READING/PAGE 57

1. **2** The document describes a flexible form of working from home, telecommuting.

2. **4** The third principle listed says that "employees should inform their manager of their whereabouts so they may be reached easily."

3. **1** An employee who "routinely checks in with his manager" shows that he is communicating well.

4. **1** The last principle states that telecommuting should not be used more than 3 days in a month.

5. **2** The policy's first statement says, "The Company is committed to creating a flexible work environment. . . ."

6. **3** Only an animal is awake to listen to Iona.

7. **1** Iona feels he must do something since he can always sleep later.

8. **2** The name of Iona's son, Kuzma Ionitch, is a clue to an eastern European setting.

9. **3** The present tense gives a feeling that the events described are happening now.

10. **5** Iona asks the horse to put herself in the position of a foal's mother who loses her foal.

11. **2** Mrs. Forrester's appearance is described as "attractive" and "lady-like" among other things.

12. **3** Mrs. Forrester "was scudding . . . like a hare." This is a simile, because it is a direct comparison that uses the word *like* or *as*.

13. **2** The pronoun *they* refers to the middle-aged men who came to admire Mrs. Forrester.

14. **4** Mrs. Forrester's natural elegance is described in all of the words listed: "charming," "attractive in dishabille," and "captivating."

15. **1** Captain Forrester described his wife as "captivating" in the incident with the bull, implying that he believed her attitude in such a precarious situation made her attractive to him.

16. **1** The power poles are replacing the eucalyptus and thus are, in a sense, new trees.

17. **3** The poet calls the power poles "frigid" and "passionless."

18. **4** The children realize they cannot climb the "new trees" and miss the old ones.

19. **3** The poet considers the electric poles incapable of feeling ("passionless verticals") since they are not like trees, which are members of the Plant Kingdom and draw life from the Earth.

20. **3** "Tree imposters" is a metaphor in which the poles are compared to false-pretending people.

21. **3** Line 25 states that the poet cannot be consoled. He wishes he could wake Jane from "this sleep"—death.

22. **5** In line 28, he speaks of "my love."

23. **3** Jane is referred to as "a wren," "my sparrow," and "my skittery pigeon."

24. **4** The poet goes from "she" to "her" to "you."

25. **4** In line 29, he indicates he has "no rights in this matter."

26. **3** Walter indirectly indicates that Lindner can expect the same treatment if Lindner insults him.

27. **2** It can be inferred that a better home will be part of a new life.

28. **3** Mama says, "My son said we was going to move," so Walter will be the head of the house.

29. **5** As he leaves, Lindner shakes his head in disagreement.

30. **3** Walter says, "We are very proud people."

31. **1** The author repeats "I remember" and says he has "never forgotten" and "shall never forget."

32. **4** The chief remembers his mother cooking, his father returning from hunting, his grandfather teaching him.

33. **1** The writer says his world reflected the wisdom and benevolence of the Great Spirit.

34. **1** The author writes, "There were never enough hours in a day to exhaust the pleasure of observing every living creature."

35. **5** The author describes the privileges he had on the "unspoiled prairie one hundred years ago."

36. **4** The author says that, in comparisons of language, Shakespeare is bound to win.

37. **3** The author says, among other unfavorable comparisons, that the songs of *West Side Story* pale next to the speech of Mercurio.

38. **1** The passage states that Romeo and Juliet "are a little too slender" to carry the play and this is "equally true of Tony and Maria."

39. **4** The passage observes that the heroes and heroines do "not shake us with...fear."

40. **3** Romeo and Juliet suffer from "the caprice of fate," while Tony and Maria suffer from prejudice and hatred.

TEST 5: MATHEMATICS/PAGE 67

1. **2** First find the total mileage.

$$135 + 162 + 98 + 117 + 216 = 728 \text{ mi.}$$

Divide the total mileage (728) by the number of miles covered for each gallon of gas used (14) to find the number of gallons of gas needed.

$$728 \div 14 = 52 \text{ gal.}$$

2. **4** Since 5¢ will pay for 12 min. $0.50 will pay for $10 \times 12 = 120$ min. 120 min. = 2 hr.

3. **40** If $AB = AC$, then $\angle ABC$ is an isosceles triangle and base angles B and C have equal measures: $\text{m}\angle B = \text{m}\angle C$.
Let $x = \text{m}\angle B = \text{m}\angle C$.

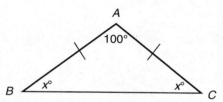

The sum of the measures of the angles of a triangle is 180°, so

$$
\begin{aligned}
x + x + 100 &= 180 \\
2x + 100 &= 180 \\
2x &= 180 - 100 = 80 \\
x &= 40
\end{aligned}
$$

4. **5** Since 432 shirts were sold at $20 each, the number of dollars taken in was 20×432.
Since 368 shirts were sold at $25 each, the number of dollars taken in was 25×368.
The total amount taken in was $20 \times 432 + 25 \times 368$, which may be written as

$$(20)(432) + (25)(368).$$

5. **1** The total number of games played was $X + Y + Z$.
The number of games won was X.

The fractional part of the games won was $\dfrac{X}{X + Y + Z}$

6. **3/8 or .375**

$\dfrac{1}{2}$ of the pupils walk to school.

$\dfrac{1}{4}$ of the other $\dfrac{1}{2} = \dfrac{1}{4} \times \dfrac{1}{2} = \dfrac{1}{8}$ use bicycles.

$\dfrac{1}{2} + \dfrac{1}{8} = \dfrac{4}{8} + \dfrac{1}{8} = \dfrac{5}{8}$ of the pupils either walk or use bicycles.

Therefore, $1 - \dfrac{5}{8} = \dfrac{3}{8}$ use other means.

7. **5** Since $2x > 4$, then

$$x > \frac{4}{2} = 2.$$

The only choice that is greater than 2 is 3.

8. **3** Since the aquarium is in the shape of a rectangular solid, its volume is given by the formula $V = lwh$. To find the volume in cubic feet, express each of l, w, and h in feet.

Length, l, is 3 ft.

Width, $w = 1$ ft. 8 in. $= 1\frac{2}{3}$ ft. $= \frac{5}{3}$ ft.

Height, h, is 1 ft. 6 in. $= 1\frac{1}{2}$ ft. $= \frac{3}{2}$ ft.

$$V = 3 \times \frac{5}{3} \times \frac{3}{2} = \frac{15}{2} = 7.5 \text{ cu. ft.}$$

9. **4** Let $x =$ height of flagpole. The two poles and their shadows can be represented by two triangles.

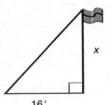

Since the triangles are similar, the lengths of corresponding sides are in proportion.
Set up the proportion:

$$\frac{h \text{ (flagpole)}}{h \text{ (pole)}} = \frac{l \text{ (flagpole shadow)}}{l \text{ (pole shadow)}}$$

$$\frac{x}{9} = \frac{16}{6}$$

$$6x = 9 \times 16 = 144$$

$$x = \frac{144}{6} = 24$$

10. **4** The total enrollment is $360 + 300 + 280 + 260 = 1{,}200$

The part of the total enrollment that represents the freshmen is

$$\frac{360}{1{,}200} = \frac{36}{120} = \frac{3}{10} = 30\%.$$

11. **1** The purse contains $6 + 5 + 8 = 19$ coins, 5 of which are dimes.

Therefore, the probability of drawing a dime is $\frac{5}{19}$.

12. **4** When an odd number of scores are arranged in increasing order, the median is the middle number. In this case, there are 9 numbers, so the median is the fifth number.

272, 274, 275, 276, 278, 281, 283, 284, 287
↓
median

13. **4** Volume of a cylinder: $\pi r^2 \times h$

$$3.14 \times 10^2 \times 30 = 9{,}420 \text{ cu. in.}$$

$$9{,}420 \times .0043 = 40.5 \text{ gallons}$$

If the bucket is filled halfway, then it holds approximately 20 gallons.

14. **525** Since 1 in. on the map represents 150 mi., 3 in. represents $3(150) = 450$ mi., and $\frac{1}{2}$ in. represents $\frac{1}{2}(150) = 75$ mi.

Then $3\frac{1}{2}$ in. represents $450 + 75 = 525$ mi.

15. **2** To find the perimeter of the figure, find the sum of the lengths of the four sides:

$$2a + b + a + 3b + 3a + b + 3a + 2b = 9a + 7b.$$

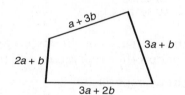

16. **5** $\$159.99 \times \frac{2}{3} = \$106.66$ (40-watt speakers after discount)

$\$106.66$
$+ \$150$ (installation)
$\$256.66$
$\times \quad 1.08$ (sales tax)

$\$277.19$, which falls between $270 and $280

17. **5** Since 3 ties sold for $42,
6 ties cost 2($42) = $84.
3 shirts cost $60.
Since slacks sold for $32.75 per pair,
2 pairs of slacks cost 2($32.75) = $65.50.
1 jacket cost $158.45.
$84 + $60 + $65.50 + $158.45 = $367.95

18. **3** Write all the numbers as decimals, so that it is easier to arrange the numbers in order of size.

$$19\% = 0.19,$$

$$\frac{1}{2} = 0.50, \text{ and } \frac{3}{5} = 60.$$

The correct order from greatest to smallest is

$$0.80, \ 0.60, \ 0.50, \ 0.19, \ 0.080$$

or $0.80, \ \dfrac{3}{5}, \ \dfrac{1}{2}, \ 19\%, \ 0.080$

The correct choice is (3).

19. **248** To find the average speed, in miles per hour, divide the distance, in miles, by the time, in hours. Since 5 hr. and 30 min. is $5\dfrac{1}{2}$, or 5.5 hr., divide 1,364 by 5.5: $1364 \div 5.5 = 248$.

20. **2** To write a number in scientific notation, write it as the product of a number between 1 and 10 and a power of 10. In this case, the number between 1 and 10 is 8.5. In going from 8.5 to 85,000,000,000, you move the decimal point 10 places to the right. Therefore $85,000,000,000 = 8.5 \times 10^{10}$.

21. **3** $\quad 3ab - x^2y = 3(4)(5) - (2)(2)(3)$
$$= 60 \quad\quad - 12 = 48$$

22. **10,000** The sum of the measures of the angles around the center of the circle is 360°. The fraction that represents the part of the total number of workers engaged in transportation is $\dfrac{20}{360} = \dfrac{1}{18}$.

$$\frac{1}{18} \text{ of } 180,000 = \frac{180,000}{18} = 10,000$$

23. **4** In the right triangle use the Pythagorean theorem.

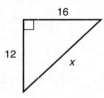

$$x^2 = (12)^2 + (16)^2$$
$$x^2 = \ 144 + 256 = 400$$
$$x = \sqrt{400} = 20$$

24. **4** Since m∠ABC = 68° and $\overline{BF}$ bisects ∠ABC, then m∠EBC = $\dfrac{1}{2}$ (68) = 34°.

Since m∠ACB = 72° and $\overline{CD}$ bisects ∠ACB, then m∠ECB = $\dfrac{1}{2}$ (72) = 36°.

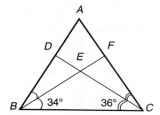

Since the sum of the measure of the angles of a triangle is 180°,

$$m\angle EBC + m\angle ECB + m\angle BEC = 180°$$
$$34 + 36 + m\angle BEC = 180°$$
$$70 + m\angle BEC = 180°$$
$$m\angle BEC = 180 - 70 = 110°$$

25. **98.28**

$$\begin{array}{r} 6.5 \\ \times\ 7.2 \\ \hline 46.8 \end{array}$$ sq. ft. (area of hallway)

$$\begin{array}{r} \times\ 2.10 \end{array}$$ (price of carpet/sq. ft.)

$98.28 (total price of the carpet)

26. **5** You know that John Davis lost *at least* 4 lb. each month. But he may have lost much more. Not enough information is given to determine his *exact* weight after the 6-month period.

27. **425** The annual interest on $10,000 at $8\dfrac{1}{2}$% is $10,000 × 0.085 = $850.

Thus, every 6 months Mr. Ames receives $\dfrac{1}{2}$ of $850 = $425.

28. **4** Factor the left-hand side of $x^2 - x - 12 = 0$:

$(x - 4)(x + 3) = 0,$
$x - 4 = 0$ **or** $x + 3 = 0$
$x = 4$ **or** $x = -3$

29. **3** Using the first ratio of 9:2, set up a second with the information given, then convert to an equation using fractions.

$$\dfrac{9\ \text{(men)}}{2\ \text{(women)}} = \dfrac{x\ \text{(unknown \# of men)}}{12\ \text{(known \# of women)}}$$

30. **5** Slope of $\overleftrightarrow{AB}$ = $\dfrac{\text{change in } y\text{-coordinates}}{\text{change in } x\text{-coordinates}}$

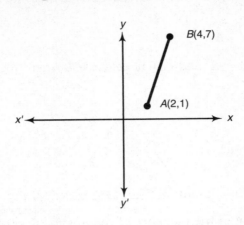

$$\text{Slope of } \overleftrightarrow{AB} = \frac{7-1}{4-2} = \frac{6}{2} = 3$$

31. **3** Let x = number of points scored by Jim, and $3x$ = number of points scored by Bill.

$$\begin{aligned} x + 3x &= 56 \\ 4x &= 56 \\ x &= 56 \div 4 = 14 \\ 3x &= 3(14) = 42 \end{aligned}$$

32. **4** Note that each subdivision line on the vertical axis represents 200 mi. The Rio Grande is about 1,500 mi. long, and the Seine is about 500 mi. long. Therefore, the Rio Grande is about 1,000 mi. longer than the Seine.

33. **5** In 2009, the receipts were $600,000 and the expenses were $500,000.

$$\$600,000 - \$500,000 = \$100,000$$

34. **1** Six pencils will cost 6 times as much as 1 pencil. Since y is the cost of 1 pencil, the cost of 6 pencils is 6 times $y = 6y$.

35. **5** In 2 weeks Mr. Martin worked a total of (42 + 37) hr. and earned $12 for each hour. Therefore, the total number of dollars he earned was 12(42 + 37).

36. **4** There are four quarts in a gallon. Kwan has multiplied the usual recipe by 16 (1 qt. × 16 = 4 gal.) for the party.
    Thus, multiply the lemon concentrate by 16.
    16 × 8 = 128 oz. then divide by 32 (oz./qt.)
    4 qt. = 1 gal.

37. **3** Since pairs of alternate interior angles of parallel lines have equal measures, m∠BCD = m∠ABC. Thus m∠BCD = 112°.

$$\text{m}\angle ECD = \frac{1}{2} \, \text{m}\angle BCD$$

$$= \frac{1}{2}(112°) = 56°$$

38. **2** 22 ft. 4 in. = 22(12) + 4 = 268 in.

268 ÷ 4 = 67 in. per piece

$$\frac{67}{12} = 5\frac{7}{12}$$

Each piece is 5 ft. 7 in. in length.

39. **4** According to the graph, the population in 2004 was midway between 25,000 and 30,000.

$$25,000 + 30,000 = 55,000$$
$$55,000 \div 2 = 27,500$$

40. **2** Lincoln County's population increased by 2,500 (or one vertical line up on the graph) between 1999 and 2000. This is true of both 2000–2001 and 2004–2005. The other choices can be eliminated because either one or both years did not show the 2,500-person increase.

41. **4** Use the formula $V = lwh$ to represent the volume of the rectangular solid.

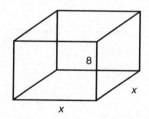

$$V = x \cdot x \cdot 8 = 8x^2$$
$$8x^2 = 392$$

42. **5** Since the total number of votes cast is not given, an equation to solve the problem cannot be set up.

43. **2** If $AB = AC$, $m\angle C = m\angle B = 68°$. Since $\overline{AD} \perp \overline{BC}$, $m\angle ADC = 90°$.

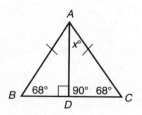

Since the sum of the measures of the angles of a triangle is 180°:

$$68 + 90 + m\angle x = 180$$
$$158 + m\angle x = 180$$
$$m\angle x = 180 - 158 = 22°$$

44. **3** Since *PQ* is parallel to *RS*, alternate interior angles are equal:
$2x = x + 25$. Subtracting x from each side yields $x = 25$.

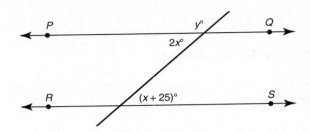

45. **3** Since $5^2 = 25$ and $6^2 = 36$, $\sqrt{30}$ is between 5 and 6.

46. **1** *AD* = radius of large circle = 20 in. *BC* = radius of small circle = 8 in.

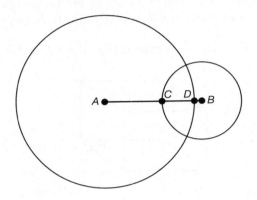

$CD = 6$
$DB = BC - CD = 8 - 6 = 2$
$AB = AD + DB = 20 + 2 = 22$ in.

47. **(1,0)** The square measures 6 units × 6 units. Its center coordinates are (1,0). Your grid should be marked accordingly.

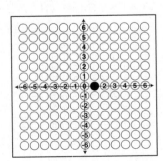

48. **4** To find the cost of *n* lb. of sugar at *c* cents per pound, multiply *n* by *c* to obtain *nc*.
To find the change received subtract *nc* cents from 1000 cents.
The result is $1000 - nc$.

49. **5** Check each inequality or equation in turn.

  (1) $3(10) + 1 > 12$, $30 + 1 > 12$. True

  (2) $2(10) - 3 < 25$, $20 - 3 < 25$. True

  (3) $10^2 + 1 > 10^2 - 1$. $100 + 1 > 100 - 1$. True

  (4) $4(10) - 1 = 39$, $40 - 1 = 39$. True

  (5) $2(10) - 7 < 7 - 2(10)$, $20 - 7 < 7 - 20$. Not true

  The correct choice is (5).

50. **10,400**   Divide the given figure into two rectangles by drawing a dotted line.

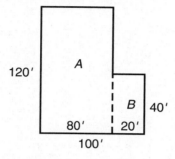

  Width of rectangle $A = 100 - 20 = 80$

  Length of rectangle $A = 120$

  Area of rectangle $A = (80)(120) = 9,600$ sq. ft.

  Area of rectangle $B = 40 \times 20 = 800$ sq. ft.

  Area of figure $= 9,600 + 800 = 10,400$ sq. ft.

LANGUAGE ARTS, WRITING, PART I

Sentence Structure

A sentence is the basic means of communicating an idea.

A sentence may be defined as a group of words having a subject and a predicate (see Glossary of Usage, pages 148–151) and expressing a complete thought. Each sentence should be separated from the one that follows it by some form of end punctuation such as a period, a question mark, or an exclamation point.

RUN-ON SENTENCES

One of the most common writing mistakes is the failure to separate two or more sentences using the proper punctuation. Instead, there's either no punctuation at all or an incorrect use a comma. The general term for this group of errors is the *run-on sentence* or, if a comma is incorrectly used, the *comma splice*.

Here are frequently made errors and the ways in which they may be corrected.

The first type of run-on sentence results from an incorrectly used or omitted conjunction (connecting word) or adverb.

> **TIP**
>
> Run-ons are two complete thoughts improperly joined.

WRONG:
Joe was elected class president he is very popular.

CORRECT:
Joe was elected class president *because* he is very popular.

"Joe was elected class president" and "he is very popular" are both independent sentences. The two sentences have been run together because there is no end punctuation between them. This error can be corrected by simply placing a period between the two sentences. A better way to correct this error, however, is to look for a relationship between the two sentences. The first sentence, "Joe was elected class president," is a result of the second, "he is very popular." Therefore, it is possible to join the two sentences using the conjunction *because*. Joe was elected president *because* he is very popular. Here are a few more examples.

WRONG:

Joe is very popular therefore he was elected class president.

Joe is very popular thus he was elected class president.

CORRECT:

Joe is very popular and, as a result, he was elected class president.

Joe is very popular. Therefore, he was elected class president.

WRONG:

Joe worked hard he was bound to succeed.

CORRECT:

Joe worked *so* hard *that* he was bound to succeed.

WRONG:

Joe disliked English he got a good mark anyhow.

CORRECT:

Joe disliked English, *but* he got a good mark anyhow.

CORRECT:

Although Joe disliked English, he got a good mark.

WRONG:

Joe disliked English however he got a good mark.

CORRECT:

Joe disliked English. *However*, he got a good mark.

WRONG:

Joe is excellent in mathematics he is also good in English.

CORRECT:

Joe is excellent in mathematics, *and* he is also good in English.

WRONG:

Joe is always imitating the coach, he respects him greatly.

CORRECT:

Joe is always imitating the coach *whom* he respects greatly.

In the above example, *coach* is the word (noun) described and *whom he respects greatly* is the descriptive clause.

WRONG:

Did Joe win he was the best candidate.

CORRECT:

Did Joe win? He was the best candidate.

"Did Joe win?" is an interrogative sentence that asks a question. "He was the best candidate" is a declarative sentence that makes a statement. Often students combine, in error, the question and the answer given to it.

PRACTICE

Some of the following sentences have errors; others are correct. Write "correct" for those that have no errors. Rewrite the sentences that contain errors. (Answers can vary.)

1. Hector studied very hard, so he passed the test.

2. Maria was very beautiful therefore she was chosen queen of the prom.

3. Avital has lots of friends she is very good-natured.

4. Since the employer required a high school diploma, I had to pass the GED test.

5. Helena was a good shopper she saved lots of money.

6. The politician did not do much campaigning nevertheless he was elected.

7. Although the team rallied, it lost the game.

8. Fernando is an excellent violinist he is a fine violist as well.

9. The telecast raised much money for muscular dystrophy research, furthermore it was very entertaining.

10. The class elected Juan president of the class they liked him best of all the candidates.

11. Anna was the best student the class admired her.

12. Is Conchita home? I have to speak to her.

13. Did you go to see the play it was very entertaining.

14. "Come in," said the hostess, "I'm happy to see you."

15. "Study hard," advised the teacher. "You'll pass the test."

ANSWERS

1. Correct.

2. Maria was very beautiful. Therefore, she was chosen queen of the prom.

3. Avital is very good-natured and, as a result, she has lots of friends.

4. Correct.

5. Helena was a good shopper. She saved lots of money.

6. The politician did not do much campaigning. Nevertheless, he was elected.

7. Correct

8. Fernando is an excellent violinist; he is a fine violist as well.

9. The telecast raised much money for muscular dystrophy research. Furthermore, it was very entertaining.

10. The class elected Juan president of the class because they liked him best of all the candidates.

11. Anna, whom the class admired, was the best student.

12. Correct.

13. Did you go to see the play? It was very entertaining.

14. "Come in," said the hostess. "I'm happy to see you."

15. Correct.

SENTENCE FRAGMENTS

Another common mistake is the failure to complete a sentence. (You will remember that a sentence is defined as a group of words having a subject and a predicate and expressing a complete thought.) In the kind of error called a *sentence fragment*, either the subject is left out, so that a predicate is left standing by itself (e.g., "Wish you were here.") or a part of the predicate is broken off from the sentence and made to stand by itself (e.g., "Walking down the street.").

WRONG:
Am having a wonderful time. Wish you were here.

CORRECT:
I am having a wonderful time. *I* wish you were here.

WRONG:
Joe studied hard. Passed all his tests and graduated.

CORRECT:
Joe studied hard, passed all his tests, and graduated.

WRONG:
Joe got a good mark in English. Although he doesn't like the subject.

CORRECT:
Joe got a good mark in English, although he doesn't like the subject.

WRONG:
Joe has an English teacher. Whom he likes very much.

CORRECT:
Joe has an English teacher whom he likes very much.

WRONG:
Joe got up early. To go to school.

CORRECT:
Joe got up early to go to school.

WRONG:
Joe went to the movies. With his friend.

CORRECT:
Joe went to the movies with his friend.

WRONG:
Joe enjoyed himself. At the movies.

CORRECT:
Joe enjoyed himself at the movies.

WRONG:
Joe admires the captain of the team. Ron Jones.

CORRECT:
Joe admires the captain of the team, Ron Jones.

IMPORTANT NOTE

A clause and a phrase can be detached in error either at the *beginning* or at the *end* of the sentence.

WRONG:

Joe has excelled in his studies. Also in sports and extracurricular activities.

CORRECT:

Joe has excelled in his studies, in sports, and in extracurricular activities.

WRONG:

Joe enjoys all sports. Baseball, football and swimming.

CORRECT:

Joe enjoys all sports: baseball, football, and swimming.

Sports is the object; baseball, football, and swimming are nouns in apposition equivalent in meaning. Note that the colon is used to introduce listings. See the section "Basic Rules of Punctuation" beginning on page 157.

PRACTICE

1. Miss you. Will be home tomorrow.
2. Great idea. Wish you luck.
3. Don collected baseball cards. Played the piano and excelled in sports.
4. Donna went to school. Worked as a baby-sitter.
5. Fern is popular. Because she is considerate.
6. I enjoy being with Jill. Who is very amusing.
7. Looking around the room. Cynthia saw her friend.
8. Frances practiced daily, doing her exercises on the piano.
9. I was too tired. To go to the supermarket.
10. Miguel collects antiques. Stamps and coins.
11. Dick met his fiancee's mother, Mrs. Ellis.
12. Noel spent his spare time at the movies. Also at the pool and at the gym.
13. Sheila helped at home, in school, and at church.

ANSWERS

1. I miss you. I'll be home tomorrow.
2. That's a great idea. I (We) wish you luck.
3. Don collected baseball cards, played the piano, and excelled in sports.
4. While Donna went to school, she worked as a baby-sitter.
5. Fern is popular because she is considerate.
6. I enjoy being with Jill, who is very amusing.
7. Looking around the room, Cynthia saw her friend.
8. Correct.
9. I was too tired to go to the supermarket.
10. Miguel collects antiques, stamps, and coins.
11. Correct.
12. Noel spent his spare time at the movies, the pool, and the gym.
13. Correct.

PRACTICE WITH RUN-ON SENTENCES AND SENTENCE FRAGMENTS

Beneath each sentence you will find five ways of writing the underlined part. Choose the answer that makes the best sentence. Answer 1 is always the same as the underlined part and is sometimes the right answer. This is the sentence revision type of multiple-choice item.

1. Yolanda had a passion for <u>fruits; melons,</u> pineapples, grapefruits, and pears.

   (1) fruits; melons,
   (2) fruits. melons,
   (3) fruits, melons,
   (4) fruits: melons,
   (5) fruits. Melons,

2. "Take your umbrella," suggested the boy's <u>mother. "It</u> might rain."

   (1) mother. "It
   (2) mother," it
   (3) mother,". It
   (4) mother: "It
   (5) mother:" it

3. "Why he didn't come home on <u>time." stated</u> the parent, "is beyond me."

   (1) time." stated
   (2) time? "stated
   (3) time"? stated
   (4) time, "Stated
   (5) time," stated

4. The teacher told her <u>student to bring his</u> books to class every day.

   (1) student to bring his
   (2) student that he should bring his
   (3) student he should bring his
   (4) student: bring your
   (5) student—bring your

5. Arnold studied <u>a lot he</u> wanted to make the honor roll.

   (1) a lot he
   (2) a lot because he
   (3) a lot: He
   (4) a lot, he
   (5) a lot. since he

6. Have you been to the <u>museum it</u> has an excellent exhibition.

   (1) museum it
   (2) museum, it
   (3) museum? it
   (4) museum? It
   (5) museum which

7. "The Red Sox won the <u>pennant," said the sportscaster, "I</u> thought they were the best team."

   (1) pennant," said the sportscaster, "I
   (2) pennant." said the sportscaster, "I
   (3) pennant", said the sportscaster, "I
   (4) pennant," said the sportscaster. "I
   (5) pennant." said the sportscaster. "I

8. The student replied <u>that he is</u> living here for the last three years.

   (1) that he is
   (2) that "He is
   (3) that, "He is
   (4) that he was
   (5) that he has been

9. <u>I should agree to the proposal if I were</u> in your situation.

   (1) I should agree to the proposal if I were
   (2) I would agree to the proposal if I would be
   (3) I would agree to the proposal if I was
   (4) I would agree to the proposal, if I was
   (5) I would agree to the proposal; if I were

10. The employer refused the worker the <u>raise besides,</u> he threatened to fire him.

    (1) raise besides,
    (2) raise, besides,
    (3) raise: besides.
    (4) raise. besides
    (5) raise. Besides,

11. <u>Studying hard. Miss you. Write.</u>

    (1) Studying hard. Miss you. Write.
    (2) I am studying hard. Miss you. Write.
    (3) I am studying hard. I miss you. Write.
    (4) Studying hard; miss you; write.
    (5) Studying hard: miss you. Write.

12. To succeed in <u>school: Juan</u> attended regularly, did his homework, and studied hard.

    (1) school: Juan
    (2) school. Juan
    (3) school, Juan
    (4) school—Juan
    (5) school Juan

13. Why didn't you <u>come I</u> waited for hours for your arrival.

    (1) come I
    (2) come, I
    (3) come; I
    (4) come: I
    (5) come? I

14. Joanne didn't like to <u>study she</u> passed the examination anyhow.

    (1) study she
    (2) study and she
    (3) study, and she
    (4) study: but she
    (5) study, but she

15. They objected to <u>me staying. Nevertheless, I</u> remained at the gathering.

    (1) me staying. Nevertheless, I
    (2) me staying, nevertheless I
    (3) my staying, nevertheless, I
    (4) my staying. Nevertheless I
    (5) my staying. Nevertheless, I

16. <u>Can't be at your wedding send</u> all our love.

    (1) Can't be at your wedding send
    (2) Can't be at your wedding; send
    (3) Can't be at your wedding; we send
    (4) Can't be at your wedding, we send
    (5) We can't be at your wedding, but we send

17. Although Vincent and <u>Giuseppe, buddies during the Vietnam War, hadn't met</u> for over five years.

    (1) Giuseppe, buddies during the Vietnam War, hadn't met
    (2) Giuseppe buddies during the Vietnam War hadn't met
    (3) Giuseppe, buddies during the Vietnam War, didn't meet
    (4) Giuseppe were buddies during the Vietnam War yet hadn't met
    (5) Giuseppe were buddies during the Vietnam War, they hadn't met

18. Will you come to my <u>party I'd</u> be happy to have you there.

    (1) party I'd
    (2) party. I'd
    (3) party; I'd
    (4) party: I'd
    (5) party? I'd

19. "This is most unusual," said <u>Jorge, "the</u> mail has never come late before."

    (1) Jorge, "the
    (2) Jorge, "The
    (3) Jorge. "The
    (4) Jorge; "The
    (5) Jorge: "The

Answer Key

1. **4**	5. **2**	9. **1**	13. **5**	17. **5**
2. **1**	6. **4**	10. **5**	14. **5**	18. **5**
3. **5**	7. **4**	11. **3**	15. **5**	19. **3**
4. **1**	8. **5**	12. **3**	16. **5**	

WHAT'S YOUR SCORE?

_____ right,	_____ wrong
Excellent	18–19
Good	15–17
Fair	12–14

If you scored lower, study the kinds of run-on sentences and sentence fragments illustrated in this section.

Answer Analysis

1. **4** See Type 5 under "Sentence Fragments." The nouns in apposition with *fruits* should be preceded by a colon. See Rule 1 under "The Colon."

2. **1** No error.

3. **5** See "The Comma," as it refers to the divided quotation where commas are used to set off the speaker.

4. **1** No error.

5. **2** See Type 1 under "Run-on Sentences." A cause for Arnold's studying hard is needed to bring the two sentences together.

6. **4** See Type 6 under "Run-on Sentences." Two sentences of different kinds are improperly run together.

7. **4** See Type 7 under "Run-on Sentences." The two sentences are improperly run together because there is a divided quotation.

8. **5** The present perfect tense is required since the student has been living here up to the present time.

9. **1** Correct as is.

10. **5** See Type 4 under "Run-on Sentences." In this run-on sentence, an additional idea is incorrectly connected to the first idea.

11. **3** See Type 1 under "Sentence Fragments." The subjects of the first two sentences are improperly left out. In *Write*, the subject *you* is understood.

12. **3** See Type 4 under "Sentence Fragments." The Important Note mentions that a phrase may, in error, be detached at the beginning of the sentence. Here, it is "To succeed in school." The colon detaches the phrase; the comma connects it to the sentence.

13. **5** Two sentences of different kinds are incorrectly run together.

14. **5** See Type 3 under "Run-on Sentences." A conflicting idea is incorrectly connected to the idea it apparently contradicts.

15. **5** See Problem 3 under "Some Special Problems" of "Case of Nouns and Pronouns."

16. **5** See Type 1 under "Sentence Fragments." The subject of the sentence is improperly left out. In addition, see Type 3 under "Run-on Sentences." A conflicting idea is incorrectly connected to the idea it apparently contradicts.

17. **5** See Type 4 under "Sentence Fragments" (particularly **Important Note**). This is an example of a detached clause at the beginning of the sentence.

18. **5** See Type 6 under "Run-on Sentences." Two sentences of different kinds are incorrectly run together. "Will you come to my party?" is an interrogative sentence; "I'd be happy to have you there" is a declarative sentence.

19. **3** See Type 7 under "Run-on Sentences." Two different sentences are run together improperly because there is a divided quotation.

PARALLEL STRUCTURE

A major error in structure is failure to keep parts of the sentence that perform the *same purpose* in the *same form*. This is called an error in parallel structure.

WRONG:

Joe likes *swimming, fishing,* and, if he has the time, *to take* a long walk.

The sentence tells us three things Joe likes. They are related to us by words that are the objects of the verb *likes,* and they serve the same purpose. But are their forms alike? Let us line them up vertically.

> Joe likes swimming
> fishing
> to take a long walk

No, they are not. *Swimming* and *fishing* are verbs used, in the *-ing* form, as nouns. *To take,* however, is an infinitive. Words having the same function should have the same form. Then, the sentence has parallel structure. The sentence should read:

> Joe likes swimming
> fishing
> taking a long walk

CORRECT:

Joe likes *swimming, fishing,* and, if he has the time, *taking a long walk.*

WRONG:

Jane and Jim took part *in* baseball games, *in* swimming *contests,* and *in learning* about golf.

The sentence tells us three things in which Jane and Jim took part. All three are objects of the preposition *in.* They serve the same purpose, yet the form of one of them is different.

> Jane and Jim took part
> in baseball *games*
> in swimming *contests*
> in *learning* about golf

Two are nouns; the third is a verb used, in the *-ing* form, as a noun. To maintain parallel structure, the third must also be a noun.

> Jane and Jim took part
> in baseball *games*
> in swimming *contests*
> in *golf lessons*

Lessons is a noun. The structure of the items in the sentence is now parallel.

CORRECT:

Jane and Jim took part *in* baseball *games, in* swimming *contests,* and *in* golf *lessons.*

WRONG:
The backers failed to realize *the success of the show* or *how long it would run.*

Two things were realized: both are objects of the infinitive *to realize.* Yet one is a noun, *success;* the other a noun clause, *how long it would run.* Since both fill the same purpose in the sentence, they should have the same form. Either both should be nouns or both should be noun clauses. You may correct this sentence in either of two ways to achieve parallel structure.

CORRECT:
The backers failed to realize the *success* of the show or the *length* of its run. [Two nouns]

The backers failed to realize *how successful the show would be* or *how long it would run.* [Two noun clauses]

WRONG:
Chiquita was *both* asked to work the switchboard *and* to address envelopes.

Note that only one of the words, *and,* precedes an infinitive, *to address.* Both should precede the infinitives, *to work* and *to address.*

Chiquita was asked   *both* to work
                  and to address

CORRECT:
Chiquita was asked *both* to work the switchboard *and* to address envelopes.

WRONG:
The basketball star *not only* was popular *but also* modest.

The basketball star was   *not only* popular
                       but also modest

CORRECT:
The basketball star was *not only* popular *but also* modest.

TIP

If you want to remember the idea behind parallel structure, here is a simple example.

Something *old*
Something *new*
Something *borrowed*
Something *blue*

Note that *Something* is followed by four different adjectives.

Here is another great example from Abraham Lincoln's Second Inaugural Address. (The parallel elements are underlined.) "With malice toward none, with charity for all, with firmness in the right as God gives us to see the right, let us finish the work we are in, to bind up the nation's wounds, to care for him who shall have borne the battle and for his widow and his orphan, to do all which may achieve and cherish a just and a lasting peace among ourselves and with all nations."

PRACTICE

1. Irene enjoys baking, cooking, and to prepare meals.
2. Julie excels at embroidering, crocheting, and hooking rugs.
3. Ben took courses in computers, in mathematics, and in learning about fine arts.
4. Jesse couldn't decide on a career in education, in business, or becoming a doctor.
5. Jane needed financial support and being encouraged.
6. Arnold was not aware of his strength or how good-looking he was.
7. The movie was entertaining and it instructed us as well.
8. Carmen was interested neither in sports nor in books.
9. He was not only smart but also handsome.

ANSWERS

1. Irene enjoys baking, cooking, and preparing meals.
2. Correct.
3. Ben took courses in computers, in mathematics, and in fine arts.
4. Jesse couldn't decide on a career in education, in business, or in medicine.
5. Jane needed financial support and encouragement.
6. Arnold was not aware of how strong or how good-looking he was.
7. The movie was entertaining and instructive.
8. Correct.
9. Correct.

PRACTICE WITH PARALLEL STRUCTURE

Beneath each sentence you will find five ways of writing the underlined part. Choose the answer that makes the best sentence. Answer 1 is always the same as the underlined part and is sometimes the right answer. These are included in the sentence correction type of multiple-choice item.

1. <u>To strive for perfection, to serve one's fellow man, to help</u> the needy are ideals all should try to follow.

   (1) To strive for perfection, to serve one's fellow man, to help
   (2) To strive for perfection, serving one's fellow man, helping
   (3) Striving for perfection, serving one's fellow man, and to help
   (4) Striving for perfection, to serve one's fellow man, helping
   (5) To strive for perfection. To serve one's fellow man. To help

2. Jones, the president of the union and <u>who is also a member of the community group,</u> will be in charge of the negotiations.

   (1) who is also a member of the community group,
   (2) since he is a member of the community group
   (3) a member of the community group
   (4) also being a member of the community group
   (5) , in addition, who is a member of the community group

3. Marie is good-looking, <u>with intelligence, and has youth.</u>

   (1) with intelligence, and has youth
   (2) intelligent, and has youth
   (3) intelligent, and is youthful
   (4) , with intelligence, and youthful
   (5) intelligent, and youthful

4. The instructor told the student <u>to hold the club lightly, keeping his eye on the ball and drawing the club back quickly, but too much force should not be used</u> on the downward stroke.

   (1) to hold the club lightly, keeping his eye on the ball and drawing the club back quickly, but too much force should not be used
   (2) to hold the club lightly, keep his eye on the ball, and drawing the club back quickly, and too much force should not be used
   (3) to hold the club lightly, keep his eye on the ball, draw the club back quickly and not use too much force
   (4) to hold the club lightly, keep his eye on the ball, draw the club back quickly and too much force should not be used
   (5) he should hold the club lightly, keeping his eye on the ball, drawing the club back quickly, and not using too much force

5. He is rude, gruff, <u>and doesn't think of the feelings of others or of showing consideration to</u> others.

   (1) and doesn't think of the feelings of others or of showing consideration to
   (2) and doesn't think of or show consideration to
   (3) thoughtless, and inconsiderate of
   (4) thoughtless of others and of showing consideration to
   (5) thoughtless of others' feelings, and lacking in consideration to

Answer Key

1. **1**   2. **3**   3. **5**   4. **3**   5. **3**

Answer Analysis

1. **1** No error.

2. **3** The nouns in apposition must be parallel to one another. "Jones, the *president*...and a *member*...."

3. **5** This is a case of parallel structure involving three adjectives.

4. **3** Four infinitives in parallel form are much clearer than the mixture of an infinitive (*to*

hold), two participles (*keeping* and *drawing*), and a clause (*too much force should not be used*).

5. **3** Parallel structure requires the use of four adjectives (*rude, gruff, thoughtless,* and *inconsiderate*) instead of two adjectives (*rude, gruff*) and two phrases (*of the feelings..., of showing...*) following the unnecessary verb *doesn't think.*

MISPLACED MODIFIERS

A modifier is a word or a group of words that help describe another word or group of words by giving a more exact meaning. The modifier may be an adjective (a *big* house) or an adverb (walk *slowly*), an adjective clause (the man *who came to dinner*) or an adjective phrase (Jeanie *with the light brown hair*), an adverbial clause (he arrived *when the clock struck twelve*) or an adverbial phrase (he arrived *on time*). Very often, confusion in meaning takes place when a modifier is used incorrectly.

A modifier that is misplaced in a sentence may cause confusion in meaning.

WRONG:
Fred cut himself while shaving *badly.*

The word *badly* is a misplaced modifier. It is an adverb that modifies the meaning of the verb *cut* and, therefore, should be placed where there is no doubt about what it modifies. (It certainly isn't intended to modify *shaving.*)

CORRECT:
Fred cut himself *badly* while shaving.

The meaning is completely changed by the placement of the modifier. Now the sentence means what the writer intended to say.

WRONG:
The fire was put out before any damage was done *by the firefighters.*

The phrase *by the firefighters* is a misplaced modifier. It modifies the verb *put out* and, therefore, should be placed near the verb it modifies. The writer certainly did not mean to say that the firefighters did any damage, yet this is the message conveyed. Once again, the misplaced modifier completely confuses the meaning.

CORRECT:
The fire was put out *by the firefighters* before any damage was done.

WRONG:
What do you think of Bill Clinton *as a foreign diplomat?*

The adjective phrase *as a foreign diplomat* is obviously not intended to modify Bill Clinton, who cannot possibly be one. It should be placed near the word it modifies, *you.*

CORRECT:
As a foreign diplomat, what do you think of Bill Clinton?

What do you, *as a foreign diplomat,* think of Bill Clinton?

> **TIP**
>
> *Always place the modifier, be it a word or a group of words, as near as possible to the word it modifies* so that the reader will not be in any doubt about the meaning of the sentence.

Here's a humorous example of a misplaced modifier to help you remember the rule.

WRONG:
They were *almost* married for five years.

To save the couple from gossip, you must place the modifier, *almost*, near the word it modifies, *five*.

CORRECT:
They were married for *almost* five years.

PRACTICE

1. Julia almost won all the prizes that were awarded.

2. The girl was dancing with her boyfriend in the red dress.

3. What do you think of Shakespeare as an English teacher?

ANSWERS

1. Julia won almost all the prizes that were awarded.

2. The girl in the red dress was dancing with her boyfriend.

3. As an English teacher, what do you think of Shakespeare?

DANGLING MODIFIERS

In the preceding examples, the modifier was misplaced. It should have been placed clearly and unmistakably near the word or words it modified. At least, though, there was a word in the sentence with which the modifier belonged. In the case of the *dangling modifier*, the problem is that there is no word or words to which the modifier clearly refers.

WRONG:
Speeding down the track at ninety miles an hour, *the stalled car* was demolished by the train.

The stalled car obviously can't be speeding. The dangling modifier, *speeding*, can refer only to the train. This is an easy one to correct.

CORRECT:
Speeding down the track at ninety miles an hour, *the train* demolished the stalled car.

WRONG:
At ten, my parents took me on a trip to California.

The phrase *at ten* is dangling since it does not have a noun it clearly modifies. Who was ten? Surely not the parents. The phrase has to be converted into a clause to correct the error.

CORRECT:
When I was ten, my parents took me on a trip to California.

TIP

Dangling modifiers can be avoided by following an introductory phrase immediately with the word it modifies.

WRONG:

To get good grades, *lessons* must be prepared carefully.

CORRECT:

To get good grades, *you* must prepare your lessons carefully.

WRONG:

After graduating from school, my father got me a good job.

CORRECT:

After I was graduated from school, my father got me a good job.

WRONG:

Watching the baseball game, the hot dogs tasted delicious.

CORRECT:

Watching the baseball game, I ate delicious hot dogs.

WRONG:

His leg was injured *while playing* tennis.

CORRECT:

He injured his leg *while playing* tennis.

WRONG:

Walking through the zoo, my eye was caught by the gorilla.

Did you ever see an eye walking?

CORRECT:

As *I* was *walking through the zoo*, the gorilla caught my eye.

Now we come to the case of the modifier that can modify, not one, but two words or phrases.
Here's an example.

WRONG:

Does a man live here with a wife and a child *named Johnny?*

Who is named Johnny, the man or the child? The sentence is unclear as it stands. If the man is named Johnny, then this is how the question should have been written.

CORRECT:

Does a man *named Johnny* live here with a wife and a child?

If, however the child is named Johnny, the sentence has to be changed to put *Johnny* near the word *child*, thus making them equivalent.

CORRECT:

Does a man live here with a wife and a child, *Johnny?*

Here are some other two-way modifiers.

WRONG:
Plans for withdrawing troops *gradually* were drawn up by the government.

There are two possible meanings here: that the troops will be withdrawn gradually *or* that the plans were drawn up gradually. The writer probably meant:

CORRECT:
Plans for the gradual withdrawal of troops were drawn up by the government.

WRONG:
Because we studied *for a week* we were ready for the examination.

Did we study for a week, or were we ready for the examination for a week? It is not clear from the sentence what the writer intended. A comma, put in the right place, will help get rid of the two-way modifier.

CORRECT:
Because we studied for a week, we were ready for the examination.

PRACTICE

1. Sightseeing in Washington, D.C., the White House was my first stop.

2. Struggling in the water, the lifeguard saw me.

3. To earn an equivalency diploma, the GED test must be passed.

4. Because we had no classes for a week we were on vacation.

5. After I passed the GED test with the help of the teacher I got a job.

6. Hopes for recovering from the operation quickly were dashed by the doctor.

ANSWERS

1. When I was sightseeing in Washington, D.C., the White House was my first stop.

2. The lifeguard saw me while I was struggling in the water.

3. To earn an equivalency diploma, you must pass the GED test.

4. Because we had no classes, for a week we were on vacation.

   or

   Because we had no classes for a week, we were on vacation.

5. After I passed the GED test, with the help of the teacher I got a job.

   or

   After I passed the GED test with the help of the teacher, I got a job.

6. Hopes for recovering quickly from the operation were dashed by the doctor.

   or

   Hopes for recovering from the operation were quickly dashed by the doctor.

PRACTICE WITH MODIFIERS

Beneath each sentence you will find five ways of writing the underlined part. Choose the answer that makes the best sentence. Answer 1 is always the same as the underlined part and is sometimes the right answer.

1. <u>Turning</u> the corner, my eye caught sight of the house where I used to live.

   (1) Turning
   (2) After turning
   (3) Having turned
   (4) When turning
   (5) When I turned

2. The <u>horse, ridden by the experienced jockey with the broken leg, had</u> to be destroyed.

   (1) horse, ridden by the experienced jockey with the broken leg, had
   (2) horse ridden by the experienced jockey with the broken leg had
   (3) horse with the broken leg ridden by the experienced jockey had
   (4) horse with the broken leg ridden by the experienced jockey, had
   (5) horse with the broken leg, ridden by the experienced jockey, had

3. The interviewee was <u>asked, "What is your opinion of Elizabeth Taylor as a movie critic?"</u>

   (1) asked, "What is your opinion of Elizabeth Taylor as a movie critic?"
   (2) asked his opinion of Elizabeth Taylor as a movie critic.
   (3) asked "What his opinion was of Elizabeth Taylor as a movie critic?"
   (4) asked, "As a movie critic, what is your opinion of Elizabeth Taylor?"
   (5) asked as a movie critic "What is your opinion of Elizabeth Taylor?"

4. <u>Wagging its tail, the dog food was quickly consumed by the happy puppy.</u>

   (1) Wagging its tail, the dog food was quickly consumed by the happy puppy.
   (2) Wagging it's tail, the dog food was quickly consumed by the happy puppy.
   (3) The happy puppy quickly consumed the dog food wagging its tail.
   (4) Wagging its tail, the happy puppy quickly consumed the dog food.
   (5) The dog food was quickly consumed by the happy puppy wagging it's tail.

5. <u>At the age of ten, my parents took me</u> to Disneyland.

   (1) At the age of ten, my parents took me
   (2) At the age of ten my parents took me
   (3) My parents took me at the age of ten
   (4) My parents took me aged ten
   (5) At the age of ten, I was taken by my parents

6. <u>The secretary located the picture of the senator looking through the files.</u>

   (1) The secretary located the picture of the senator looking through the files.
   (2) The secretary located the senator's picture looking through the files.
   (3) Looking through the files, the senator's picture was located by the secretary.
   (4) Looking through the files, the secretary located the picture of the senator.
   (5) Looking through the files the picture of the senator was located by the secretary.

7. The Smiths <u>were almost married</u> ten years before they had their first child.

   (1) were almost married
   (2) were married almost
   (3) almost were married
   (4) had been almost married
   (5) had been married almost

8. We finally agreed on a price for the <u>picture of the ship that hung</u> in the balcony.

    (1) picture of the ship that hung
    (2) picture of the ship that was hung
    (3) picture of the ship that hanged
    (4) ship's picture that hung
    (5) ship's picture that hanged

9. Our guest let us know <u>that he would be arriving next week in his last letter</u>.

    (1) that he would be arriving next week in his last letter
    (2) that he was arriving next week in his last letter
    (3) that he will arrive next week in his last letter
    (4) in his last letter that he would be arriving next week
    (5) in his last letter that he was arriving next week

10. My mother lives in the <u>house on the hill that she just bought</u>.

    (1) house on the hill that she just bought
    (2) house on the hill she just bought
    (3) house she just bought on the hill
    (4) house on the hill which she just bought
    (5) house, she just bought, on the hill

Answer Key

| 1. **5** | 3. **4** | 5. **5** | 7. **5** | 9. **4** |
| 2. **5** | 4. **4** | 6. **4** | 8. **4** | 10. **3** |

WHAT'S YOUR SCORE?

_____ right,	_____ wrong
Excellent	9–10
Good	8
Fair	7

If you scored lower, review the corrected examples in this section

Answer Analysis

1. **5** The way the sentence reads with the dangling modifier, the *eye* is *turning the corner.*

2. **5** *With the broken leg* is a misplaced modifier. Also see Rule 8 under "The Comma." In this sentence, commas are required to set off *ridden...jockey.*

3. **4** Again there is a misplaced modifier. *Movie critic* should be placed near the word it modifies—*interviewee.*

4. **4** The dangling modifier gives the impression that the *dog food was wagging its tail.* The possessive pronoun *its* does not have an apostrophe.

5. **5** The dangling modifier, *At the age of ten,* erroneously modifies *parents.*

6. **4** The dangling modifier *looking through the files* gives the mistaken impression that *the picture* was doing the looking.

7. **5** The modifier, *almost,* is misplaced. It should be near *ten years,* which it modifies. Also see "Misplaced Modifiers." The past perfect tense, *had been married,* is needed because the years of marriage in the past *preceded* the birth of the child, also in the past.

8. **4** The modifier, *that hung in the balcony,* should be near the noun, *picture,* which it modifies. See "Misplaced Modifiers." The past tense of *hang* (an object) is *hung.*

9. **4** The misplaced modifier, *in his last letter,* gives the mistaken impression that the guest would be arriving *in* the letter. The phrase should be near *know,* which it modifies.

10. **3** *She just bought* modifies *house* and should be placed next to it.

Usage

CHAPTER 4

AGREEMENT

SUBJECT AND VERB

The most common error in writing is the lack of agreement between subject and verb. The basic rule is:

> **THE VERB MUST AGREE WITH ITS SUBJECT IN *NUMBER* AND IN *PERSON*.**
>
> ***Number***
>
> 1. If the subject is *singular* (there is only one person or thing spoken about), the verb must be *singular*.
> 2. If the subject is *plural* (there is more than one person or thing spoken about), the verb must be *plural*.
>
> ***Person***
>
> The verb must agree with the subject in *person*.
>
> **Singular**
> I study   –First Person
> You study   –Second Person
> He ⎫
> She ⎬ studies   –Third Person
> It ⎭
> **Plural**
> We study   –First Person
> You study   –Second Person
> They study   –Third Person

What is the subject?

Ordinarily, determining the subject is easy. But when the *subject and the verb are separated* by a number of intervening words it can be a bit tricky to figure out the subject.

Joe, despite the fact that he was a newcomer, *was* elected president.
[*Joe* is still the subject—singular.]

It's even more confusing when intervening phrases contain a plural.

Joe, together with all his friends, *was* welcomed warmly.
[*Joe* is still the subject—singular.]

Is the subject singular or plural?

A *box* of chocolates *is* on the table.
[*Box*, the subject, is singular.]

Most of the time, *pronouns* are the cause of this type of error.

Singular Pronouns		Singular or Plural Pronouns
anybody	neither	any
anyone	nobody	all
each	no one	more
either	one	most
everybody	somebody	none
everyone	someone	some

However, *compound subjects* also cause confusion. When a subject has more than one part and the parts are connected by *and* or by a word or groups of words similar in meaning to *and*, the *compound subject* takes a plural verb.

Joe *and* his friend *are* here.

To study hard, to play hard, to enjoy life *are* desirable aims.

Her outstanding contribution to school athletics, her service as class officer, and her excellent scholastic record *qualify* her for the position of president.

EXCEPTION: A compound subject that consists of two singular subjects connected by *either...or*, or *neither...nor*, is considered a singular subject.

Neither Joe nor his friend *is* here.

Sometimes the subject comes after the verb. It is still the subject and may be singular or plural.

Pasted in the upper right-hand corner of the envelope were two ten-cent stamps.
[*Stamps* is the subject, even though it is the last word in the sentence. The verb is plural because the subject, *stamps*, is plural.]

REMEMBER

The subject nearest the verb determines whether that verb should be singular or plural.

Some Special Problems

1. AGREEMENT OF SUBJECT AND CERTAIN IRREGULAR VERBS

The addition of the negative contraction *n't*, should not result in an error you would not make if the *n't* were omitted.

> WRONG:
> It don't matter.

> CORRECT:
> It doesn't matter.

You would never say, "It do matter." You would say, "It does matter."

2. USE OF SINGULAR OR PLURAL AFTER *THERE* AT THE OPENING OF A SENTENCE

The use of *is* or *are* depends on the *noun or pronoun that follows* the verb.

> WRONG:
> There's many ways to show you care.

> CORRECT:
> There are many ways to show you care.

3. SUBJECTS THAT ARE PLURAL IN FORM BUT SINGULAR IN MEANING

The mere fact that a noun ends in *s* doesn't automatically make it plural.

NOUNS WITH SINGULAR MEANINGS	
economics	mumps
mathematics	news
measles	physics

4. SUBJECTS THAT ARE SINGULAR IN FORM BUT PLURAL IN MEANING

Despite what you might think, these subjects take a *singular* verb when the group involved is thought of as a single unit.

The crowd *was* dispersed by the police.

NOUNS WITH PLURAL MEANINGS	
army	group
class	orchestra
club	team
crowd	

PRACTICE

1. Economics is my most difficult subject.

2. The group of students are gathering at the office.

3. Neither Jules nor I are coming to the meeting.

4. There's a great many problems to be solved.

5. The teacher, together with her students, are going to the theater.

ANSWERS

1. Correct.

2. The group of students is gathering at the office.

3. Neither Jules nor I am coming to the meeting.

4. There are a great many problems to be solved.

5. The teacher, together with her students, is going to the theater.

PRONOUN AND ANTECEDENT

Another common error is failure to provide agreement between a pronoun and the noun it is replacing, its *antecedent*.

**A PRONOUN MUST AGREE WITH ITS ANTECEDENT
IN *NUMBER, GENDER,* AND *PERSON.***

Number

If the antecedent is singular, the pronoun replacing it is singular.

Joe does *his* homework.
[The pronoun *his* takes the place of Joe. *Joe* is singular (one person); therefore, the pronoun is singular.]

Gender

If the antecedent is masculine, the pronoun replacing it is masculine. If the antecedent is feminine, the pronoun replacing it is feminine.

Susan does *her* homework.

Person

Both *Joe* and *Susan* are in the third person. Therefore, the pronouns replacing each must be in the third person—*his, her.*

How do you find the antecedent? Sometimes it is not easy to determine what noun the pronoun is replacing. The *antecedent may be separated from the pronoun* that takes its place by a number of words or by a phrase.

Joe is a *boy* who does *his* work.
[*boy*—antecedent; *his*—pronoun]

One of the boys who walked to school was late to *his* class.
[*one*—antecedent; *his*—pronoun]

The same procedure should be used to *determine the number of the pronoun when it replaces a compound subject.*

Joe and his *friend* brought *their* books.

When *either...or* or *neither...nor* connects singular subjects, the pronoun is singular.

Neither Joe *nor* his friend brought *his* book.

However, a pronoun that refers to a singular and a plural antecedent connected by *or* or *nor* agrees in number with the closer antecedent.

Either Kathy *or* the boys should explain *their* reasons.

Some Special Problems

1. PRONOUNS THAT APPEAR TO BE PLURAL BUT ARE, IN FACT, SINGULAR

Some pronouns appear to refer to more than one person, but they never refer to more than one person *at a time*. Others may be either singular or plural.

Singular Pronouns		**Singular or Plural Pronouns**
anybody	neither	any
anyone	nobody	all
each	no one	more
either	one	most
everybody	somebody	none
everyone	someone	some

The following sentence may sound a little strange to you, but it is correct.

Every student must do *his* homework every day.

2. PRONOUNS THAT REFER TO NOUNS THAT APPEAR TO BE PLURAL BUT ARE SINGULAR IN FORM

These pronouns require a verb in the singular.

The team continued *its* winning streak.

3. PRONOUNS WITH INDEFINITE ANTECEDENTS

The antecedent must be clear or the sentence rephrased.

> WRONG:
> Frank told Joe to take *his* books to school.
> [To whom does *his* refer—to Frank or to Joe? The sentence must be rewritten to clear up this confusion.]
>
> CORRECT:
> Frank told Joe to take Frank's books to school for him.
>
> OR
>
> Frank said to Joe: "Take my books to school for me."

PRACTICE

1. Will everyone who has the right answer raise their hands?

2. Every participant must do his best.

3. The mother told her daughter to take her laundry to the laundromat.

4. One of my friends who went to school with me lost his mother.

5. Either the workers or the foreman are expected to attend.

ANSWERS

1. Will everyone who has the right answer raise his hand?

2. Correct.

3. The mother told her daughter, "Take my laundry to the laundromat."

4. Correct.

5. Either the workers or the foreman is expected to attend.

PRACTICE IN AGREEMENT

In each sentence, five parts are underlined and numbered. Where there is an error in agreement, choose the number of the under-lined part that contains the error. If there is no error, choose answer 5. No sentence contains more than one error. These are included in the sentence correction type of multiple-choice item.

1. Luis, accompanied by his friend are
   (1)   (2)
   waiting to see whether you and I are
                            (3)(4)
   joining them. No error
                   (5)

2. There, Mr. Chairman, is all the
   (1)   (2)
   reports that the committee prepared
   in its work as well as the notes that
      (3)   (4)
   were taken. No error
                (5)

3. There's several ways for the city to
   (1)
   solve its fiscal problems, but one of
       (2)   (3)
   them is not to lose its integrity.
                       (4)

   No error
   (5)

4. News from abroad <u>is</u> that each country
                    (1)

   is supporting <u>its</u> own policies despite
                 (2)

   the fact that <u>ours</u> <u>are</u> superior to
                 (3)   (4)

   theirs. <u>No error</u>
           (5)

5. Let everyone who <u>agrees</u> raise <u>his</u>
                    (1)   (2)

   hand so that neither George nor I <u>am</u>
                                     (3)

   in doubt about what the majority opinion
   <u>is.</u> <u>No error</u>
   (4)   (5)

6. Margaret asked Rosa to take <u>her</u>
                              (1)

   clothes to the cleaners and to make
   certain that <u>none</u> of <u>them</u> <u>were</u> in need
               (2)   (3)   (4)

   of repair. <u>No error</u>
              (5)

7. Watching <u>our</u> game <u>were</u> Fred and his
            (1)   (2)

   father and his mother, together with
   <u>their</u> other children and <u>their</u> neighbors.
   (3)   (4)

   <u>No error</u>
      (5)

8. <u>Each</u> American must ask <u>himself</u>:
   (1)   (2)

   "<u>Don't</u> it matter if we pollute <u>our</u>
    (3)   (4)

   environment?" <u>No error</u>
                 (5)

9. "Neither <u>I</u> nor <u>they</u> <u>are</u> attending
           (1)   (2) (3)

   the game," we said to <u>its</u> promoter.
                         (4)

   <u>No error</u>
      (5)

10. <u>Everyone</u> gave <u>her</u> opinion that a blue
    (1)   (2)

    and white suit <u>was</u> the best choice for
                   (3)

    Liz to wear although there <u>were</u>
                               (4)

    exceptions. <u>No error</u>
                (5)

Answer Key

1. **2**	3. **1**	5. **5**	7. **5**	9. **5**
2. **2**	4. **5**	6. **1**	8. **3**	10. **5**

WHAT'S YOUR SCORE?

_____right,   _____wrong

Excellent   9–10
Good   8
Fair   7

If you scored lower, restudy this section, concentrating on the rules and examples.

Answer Analysis

1. **2** Luis, the subject of the sentence, is singular, so the verb should be singular: *is* instead of *are*.

2. **2** The subject of the sentence, *reports*, follows the verb. Since the subject is plural, the verb should be plural: *are*, not *is*.

3. **1** The subject is *ways*, which follows the verb. The verb must be plural to agree with the plural subject. *There's* should be *There are*.

4. **5** No error.

5. **5** No error.

6. **1** The antecedent of *her* is not clear. Is it Margaret or Rosa? Depending on the answer, *her* should be changed to *Margaret's* or *Rosa's*.

7. **5** No error.

8. **3** The correct form of the third person singular of the verb *do* is *does*. *Doesn't it...is* correct.

9. **5** No error.

10. **5** No error.

CASE OF NOUNS AND PRONOUNS

NOUNS

In English, the form of a noun rarely changes because of its case (its relation to other words in the sentence). Only in the *possessive case* do the forms of most nouns change.

Nominative Case

> *Frank* hit Joe.
> [*Frank* is the subject.]

Objective Case

> Joe hit *Frank*.
> [*Frank* is the object.]

> Ellen ate the *salad*.
> [*Salad* is the object.]

Possessive Case

> *Cesar's* friend went away.
> [A noun requires an apostrophe to indicate possession.]

PRONOUNS

Nearly all pronouns have different forms in the nominative, objective, and possessive cases. Only the pronoun forms *you* and *it* do NOT change when the case changes from *nominative* to *objective* or vice versa.

Nominative Case (for subjects)	Possessive Case	Objective Case (for objects)
I	my, mine	me
you	your, yours	you
he	his	him
she	her, hers	her
it	its	it
we	our, ours	us
they	their, theirs	them
who	whose	whom
whoever	–	whomever

Basic Rules for the Case of Pronouns

NOMINATIVE

1. The subject of a verb (a noun or a pronoun) is in the nominative case. This is true whether the subject is singular or compound.

   WRONG: Me and Frank are good friends.
   CORRECT: Frank and *I* are good friends.

2. A predicate pronoun, whether singular or plural, is in the nominative case.

   They thought that the visitor was *he*.

   Frank and Joe knocked on the door. "It is *they*," Sue said.

3. Pronouns in apposition with nouns in the nominative case are also in the nominative case.

   The two *contestants, she* and *I*, were tied for first place.

OBJECTIVE

4. The object of a verb (a noun or pronoun) is in the objective case. This is true whether the object is singular or compound.

   They applauded *him* and *her*.

   Did they face Frank and *us* in the contest?

5. The object of a proposition is in the objective case. This is true whether the object is singular or compound.

   Everyone but *her* did the homework.

   Between *you* and *me*, Sue is my best friend.

6. Pronouns in apposition with nouns in the objective case are also in the objective case.

   They gave the prizes to the *winners, her and me*.

   For *us amateurs*, it is fun to watch professionals perform.

7. The subject of an infinitive is in the objective case; the same is true for the object of an infinitive.

   We asked *him* to go.

   We wanted him to ask *them* to come along.

POSSESSIVE

8. Pronouns in the possessive case, unlike nouns in the possessive case, *never* have an apostrophe.

   The dog wagged *its* tail.

   We have met the enemy and they are *ours*.

   She has *hers;* they have *theirs*.

Some Special Problems

1. THE CASE OF PRONOUNS COMING AFTER A COMPARISON INVOLVING *THAN* OR *AS*

CORRECT: Joe received more votes than *I*.

The problem of deciding the case, and therefore the form, of the pronoun is complicated by the fact that the verb following *I* is understood.

CORRECT: Joe received more votes than I (did).

This is, therefore, a special instance of Rule 1: The subject of a verb is in the nominative case. This rule is true even if the verb is understood.

2. THE CASE OF THE RELATIVE PRONOUN *WHO* OR *WHOM*

Determine whether the relative pronoun is the subject or the object in its clause, and don't be fooled by words that come between the subject and the verb.

CORRECT: *Who* do you think *was elected* president?
[*Who* is the subject of *was elected* and is therefore in the nominative case.]

CORRECT: *Whom did you invite* to the party?
[*Whom* is the object of *did invite* and is therefore in the objective case.]

The same rule applies to *whoever* and *whomever*.

CORRECT: Give the book to *whoever asks* for it.
[*Whoever* is the subject of *asks* and is in the nominative case.]

CORRECT: He impressed *whomever he approached*.
[*Whomever* is the object of *approached* and is in the objective case.]

3. THE CASE OF PRONOUNS (OR NOUNS) COMING BEFORE VERBS ENDING IN *-ING* AND USED AS NOUNS

CORRECT: I do not object to *his* going with me.

Going is a verb form ending in *-ing* and used as a noun—object of the preposition *to*. The possessive case, *his*, must be used. This is a fine point, but it often appears on tests.

Here are several more examples:

CORRECT: Fatigue was the cause of *Frank's* falling asleep at the wheel.

CORRECT: *My* going to school daily helped my work.

CORRECT: The television program interfered with *Sue's* and *Joe's* doing their homework.

4. THE CASE OF SHIFT IN PRONOUN REFERENCE

Unnecessary shift in pronoun reference is another common error. This involves pronouns that refer to the same person in the same sentence.

WRONG:
If *one* has a good sense of humor, *you* will probably be popular.

CORRECT:
If *one* has a good sense of humor, *one* will probably be popular.

If *you* have a good sense of humor, *you* will probably be popular.

PRONOUN REMINDER

Remember to be consistent in your use of pronouns. Do not shift from a pronoun in one person (*one* is in the third person) to another pronoun in another person (*you* is in the second person) unless the two pronouns refer to different people.

PRACTICE

1. Dolores was prettier than her.

2. Juana didn't like us asking her all those questions.

3. Who can you trust with your money these days?

4. Whoever thought of this idea is a genius.

5. Who do you feel deserves the prize?

6. When one works hard, he feels he deserves a raise.

ANSWERS

1. Dolores was prettier than she.

2. Juana didn't like our asking her all those questions.

3. Whom can you trust with your money these days?

4. Correct.

5. Correct.

6. When one works hard, one feels one deserves a raise.

PRACTICE WITH NOUNS AND PRONOUNS

In each sentence, five parts are underlined and numbered. Where there is an error in case, choose the number of the underlined part that contains the error. If there is no error, choose answer 5. No sentence contains more than one error.

1. If <u>I</u> were <u>she</u>, I would not
   (1)   (2)
   exchange <u>hers</u> for <u>mine</u>. <u>No error</u>
            (3)   (4)   (5)

2. <u>Whom</u>, do you think, should be asked
   (1)
   to send <u>his</u> regrets to <u>them</u> and <u>me</u>?
           (2)   (3)   (4)
   <u>No error</u>
   (5)

3. It is <u>they</u> <u>whom</u> we invited, not <u>him</u>
        (1)   (2)   (3)
   and <u>her</u>. <u>No error</u>
       (4)   (5)

4. <u>She</u> and <u>I</u> decided to give <u>ours</u> to
   (1)   (2)   (3)
   <u>whoever</u> we pleased. <u>No error</u>
   (4)   (5)

5. <u>They</u> and <u>I</u> gave the prize to the
   (1)   (2)
   winners, <u>him</u> and <u>her</u>. <u>No error</u>
            (3)   (4)   (5)

6. The winners, <u>he</u> and <u>she</u>, were
               (1)   (2)
   welcomed to the society by <u>us</u> and
                              (3)
   <u>them</u>. <u>No error</u>
   (4)   (5)

7. Did Joe and <u>him</u> meet John and <u>her</u>
              (1)   (2)
   in the finals when they eliminated
   <u>their</u> opponents and <u>ours</u>? <u>No error</u>
   (3)   (4)   (5)

8. Between <u>you</u> and <u>I</u>, <u>it's</u> their problem,
          (1)   (2) (3)
   not <u>ours</u>. <u>No error</u>
       (4)   (5)

9. <u>Whose</u> going to get more votes than <u>I</u>,
   (1)   (2)
   <u>he</u> or <u>she</u>? <u>No error</u>
   (3)   (4)   (5)

10. For <u>us</u> newcomers, <u>his</u> going upset
       (1)   (2)
    <u>us</u>, <u>me</u> particularly. <u>No error</u>
    (3)   (4)   (5)

Answer Key

1. **5**   3. **5**   5. **5**   7. **1**   9. **1**
2. **1**   4. **4**   6. **5**   8. **2**   10. **5**

WHAT'S YOUR SCORE?

_____right,   _____wrong
Excellent   9–10
Good   8
Fair   7

If you scored lower, restudy this section, concentrating on the rules and examples.

Answer Analysis

1. **5** No error.
2. **1** The relative pronoun that begins the sentence is the subject of *should be asked* and should therefore be in the nominative case, *who*.
3. **5** No error.
4. **4** This word is the object of the preposition *to*, so it should be in the objective case. *Whomever* is correct.
5. **5** No error.
6. **5** No error.
7. **1** This word is part of the subject and should be in the nominative case. *He* is correct.
8. **2** *Me* is correct since the objective case is required for the object of the preposition *between*.
9. **1** A subject and verb are required, not a possessive pronoun. *Who's* (or *who is*) is correct.
10. **5** No error.

VERBS

The *verb*, the part of the sentence that indicates the action carried out by the subject, *also indicates* when the action was carried out. It does so by its tense.

TENSE

The most widely used tenses are the

present,

past, and

future.

An additional tense is the present perfect, which is less frequently used, and sometimes causes difficulty.

This tense requires the use of a helping verb (*have*) and the past participle of the verb.

Verb: *to live*	
Present tense:	live
Past tense:	lived
Future tense:	shall live
Present perfect tense:	has, have lived

Examples of the use of tense:
Note the way in which the rest of each sentence is affected.

Present tense:	I *live* in New York *now.*
Past tense:	I *lived* in New York *last year.*
Future tense:	I *shall live* in New York *next year.*
Present perfect tense:	I *have lived* in New York for *five years.*

VERB FORMS

The principal parts of *to live, to see, to do,* and *to lie* are:

Verb	Past	Past Participle
live	lived	lived
see	saw	seen
do	did	done
lie	lay	lain

Many of the difficulties you have with verbs involve the *irregular verbs*. These change form in either the past or the past participle or in both. The most frequent error is the use of the wrong part of the verb, most often the past participle for the simple past.

WRONG:
I seen him do it.

CORRECT:
I *saw* him do it.

WRONG:
I done it.

CORRECT:
I *did* it.

Note: The present perfect tense is formed with *has* or *have* plus the past participle.

I *have seen* enough; I am glad to leave.

Study the lists of most frequently confused verbs found on pages 141 and 142.

PRACTICE

1. They begun to improve after much practice.

2. Aaron brung the book I needed to school.

3. My friends had drunk all the lemonade at the party.

4. The valise that had lain out in the rain was soaked.

5. The batter swang the bat at the wild pitch.

6. The hostess had laid out the cookies beautifully on the table.

7. The oarsman almost drownded when the winds blew up.

8. The choir sung all the songs on the program.

9. The sun shined all day.

10. The guest awoked before I did.

ANSWERS

1. They began to improve after much practice.

2. Aaron brought the book I needed to school.

3. Correct.

4. Correct.

5. The batter swung the bat at the wild pitch.

6. Correct.

7. The oarsman almost drowned when the winds blew up.

8. The choir sang all the songs on the program.

9. The sun shone all day.

10. The guest awoke before I did.

FREQUENTLY USED IRREGULAR VERBS

Verb	Past Tense	Present Perfect Tense
be	I was	I have been
beat	I beat	I have beaten
become	I became	I have become
begin	I began	I have begun
bite	I bit	I have bitten
blow	I blew	I have blown
break	I broke	I have broken
bring	I brought	I have brought
buy	I bought	I have bought
catch	I caught	I have caught
choose	I chose	I have chosen
come	I came	I have come
dig	I dug	I have dug
do	I did	I have done
draw	I drew	I have drawn
drink	I drank	I have drunk
eat	I ate	I have eaten
fall	I fell	I have fallen
fly	I flew	I have flown
freeze	I froze	I have frozen
get	I got	I have got *or* gotten
give	I gave	I have given
go	I went	I have gone
grow	I grew	I have grown
have	I had	I have had
know	I knew	I have known
lay	I laid (place)	I have laid
lead	I led	I have led
lie	I lay (recline)	I have lain
lose	I lost	I have lost
make	I made	I have made
ride	I rode	I have ridden
ring	I rang	I have rung
rise	I rose	I have risen
run	I ran	I have run
say	I said	I have said
see	I saw	I have seen
shake	I shook	I have shaken
sink	I sank	I have sunk
speak	I spoke	I have spoken
swim	I swam	I have swum
swing	I swung	I have swung
take	I took	I have taken
teach	I taught	I have taught
tear	I tore	I have torn
think	I thought	I have thought
throw	I threw	I have thrown
win	I won	I have won
write	I wrote	I have written

50 OTHER IRREGULAR VERBS

Verb	Past Tense	Present Perfect Tense
arise	I arose	I have arisen
awake	I awaked *or* awoke	I have awaked *or* awoke
bear	I bore	I have borne *or* born
bend	I bent	I have bent
bind	I bound	I have bound
build	I built	I have built
creep	I crept	I have crept
deal	I dealt	I have dealt
dive	I dived, dove	I have dived
drive	I drove	I have driven
drown	I drowned	I have drowned
feed	I fed	I have fed
feel	I felt	I have felt
fight	I fought	I have fought
find	I found	I have found
flee	I fled	I have fled
forget	I forgot	I have forgotten
forgive	I forgave	I have forgiven
hang (an object)	I hung	I have hung
hang (a person)	I hanged	I have hanged
hide	I hid	I have hidden
hold	I held	I have held
kneel	I knelt	I have knelt
leave	I left	I have left
lend	I lent	I have lent
meet	I met	I have met
mistake	I mistook	I have mistaken
pay	I paid	I have paid
prove	I proved	I have proved *or* proven
seek	I sought	I have sought
sell	I sold	I have sold
send	I sent	I have sent
sew	I sewed	I have sewed *or* sewn
shine	I shone	I have shone
shrink	I shrank	I have shrunk
sing	I sang	I have sung
slay	I slew	I have slain
slide	I slid	I have slid
sleep	I slept	I have slept
spend	I spent	I have spent
spring	I sprang	I have sprung
steal	I stole	I have stolen
strike	I struck	I have struck
swear	I swore	I have sworn
sweep	I swept	I have swept
swing	I swung	I have swung
wake	I waked *or* awoke	I have waked *or* woken
wear	I wore	I have worn
weep	I wept	I have wept
wind	I wound	I have wound

A Special Problem

The irregular verbs you have just studied present difficulties when used in simple sentences. Even more difficult are complex sentences (see the "Glossary of Usage" on page 148). In these sentences, you must determine the time (or tense) relationship between the verbs in the two clauses.

What is the proper sequence of tenses for verbs in the main and dependent clauses of a complex sentence?

This can vary, but some common sequences follow.

VERB SEQUENCES	
Main Clause	**Dependent Clause**
Present tense: I *gain* weight	**Present tense:** when I *eat* too much.
Present tense: I *believe*	**Past tense:** that he *studied* for the examination.
Past tense: The audience *applauded*	**Past tense:** when the soloist *finished*.
Future tense: I *shall leave*	**Present tense:** when he *comes*.

PRACTICE WITH VERBS

In each sentence, five parts are underlined and numbered. Choose the number of the underlined part that contains the error. If there is no error, choose answer 5. No sentence contains more than one error.

1. He was <u>suppose</u> to <u>lay</u> the book on
         (1)   (2)
   the table after he <u>brought</u> it home
              (3)
   from the man from whom he had
   <u>taken</u> it. <u>No error</u>
    (4)   (5)

2. After the pitcher <u>threw</u> a fast ball,
              (1)
   the batter <u>swung</u> the bat and
          (2)
   <u>hit</u> the ball to left field, where it was
   (3)
   <u>caught</u>. <u>No error</u>
    (4)   (5)

3. The child <u>awoke</u> when the parent
          (1)
   <u>brung</u> the gift he had <u>chosen</u> and
    (2)   (3)
   <u>gotten</u> into the bedroom. <u>No error</u>
    (4)   (5)

4. After he <u>drunk</u> his milk, the athlete
        (1)
   <u>dived</u> into the pool and <u>swam</u> ten
    (2)   (3)
   laps more than he <u>said</u> he would.
             (4)
   <u>No error</u>
    (5)

5. I <u>lay</u> in bed dreaming of the places I
    (1)
   had <u>seen,</u> the friends I had not
      (2)
   <u>forgotten</u>, and the new friends I had
     (3)
   <u>met</u>. <u>No error</u>
    (4)   (5)

6. When I <u>wrote</u> her that I wanted it
        (1)
   <u>done,</u> Rita <u>hung</u> the picture that had
    (2)   (3)
   <u>lain</u> on the floor. <u>No error</u>
    (4)   (5)

7. The entertainer <u>sung</u> the song I had
                    (1)
   <u>sung</u> when you <u>saw</u> me, and I was
    (2)   (3)
   <u>shaken</u> by the coincidence. <u>No error</u>
    (4)   (5)

8. He would have <u>drownded,</u> had I not
                    (1)
   <u>bent</u> the board which pinned him
    (2)
   down and then <u>broken</u> it with the
                    (3)
   tool I had <u>found.</u> <u>No error</u>
               (4)   (5)

9. I <u>arose</u>; I <u>sprang</u> after the mugger; I
     (1)   (2)
   <u>struck</u> him; I <u>threw</u> him to the ground.
    (3)   (4)
   <u>No error</u>
    (5)

10. The suspect admitted: "I <u>done</u> it. I
                                 (1)
    <u>crept</u> into the apartment. I <u>fought</u>
     (2)   (3)
    with the man. I <u>tore</u> his clothes."
                     (4)
    <u>No error</u>
     (5)

Answer Key

| 1. **1** | 3. **2** | 5. **5** | 7. **1** | 9. **5** |
| 2. **5** | 4. **1** | 6. **5** | 8. **1** | 10. **1** |

WHAT'S YOUR SCORE?

_____right,	_____wrong
Excellent	9–10
Good	8
Fair	7

If you scored lower, restudy this section, concentrating on the rules and examples.

Answer Analysis

1. **1** The past participle of *suppose* is *supposed.*

2. **5** No error.

3. **2** The past tense of *bring* is *brought.*

4. **1** The past tense of *drink* is *drank.*

5. **5** No error.

6. **5** No error.

7. **1** The past tense of *sing* is *sang.*

8. **1** The past participle of *drown* is *drowned.*

9. **5** No error.

10. **1** The past tense of *do* is *did.*

ADJECTIVES AND ADVERBS

An **adjective** is used to describe a noun or pronoun.

He wore a *dark* hat.

An **adverb** is used to modify a verb, an adjective, or another adverb.

He played *very poorly.*
[*Poorly* modifies *played; very* modifies *poorly.*]

There are times, however, when adjectives and adverbs may be confused. This confusion can be caused by

Use of a verb that describes a condition, not an action

If the verb is not used as an action verb, or if the verb describes a condition, then an *adjective rather than an adverb* must follow it. Why? The adjective really modifies the subject and not the verb.

VERBS THAT DESCRIBE A CONDITION	
look	be
feel	am
taste	is
seem	are
become	was
smell	were
grow	has been
sound	had been

He looks *sick.*
[*Sick* describes *he.*]

I feel *good.*
[*Good* describes *I.*]

The fruit tastes *sweet.*
[*Sweet* describes *fruit.*]

Adjectives or adverbs that have the same form

ADJECTIVES AND ADVERBS WITH THE SAME FORM	
fast	long
slow	ill
deep	sharp

He worked very *fast.*

He cut *deep* into the skin.

Some Special Problems

1. ADJECTIVES THAT INDICATE THE DEGREE TO WHICH THEY DESCRIBE NOUNS

Degree is indicated in one of two ways:

- the adverb *more* or *most* is placed before the adjective;
- The suffix *-er* or *-est* is added to the adjective.

He was *more quiet* than she.

He was *quieter* than she.

He was the *most friendly* person there.

He was the *friendliest* person there.

What is the problem? It is that you must use the *more* or *-er* form when two and only two persons or things are involved. Similarly, you must use the *most* or *-est* form when three or more persons or things are involved. Never use *both* in the same sentence.

He was the *shyer* of the two.

He was the *most shy* among the three of them.

NOTE		
Some irregular adjectives do not follow these rules. The most frequently used are:		
	Comparative (Comparison between two people or things)	**Superlative (Comparison among more than two people or things)**
bad	worse	worst
far	farther	farthest
good	better	best
many, much	more	most

2. INCORRECT USE OF A NEGATIVE ADVERB AND A NEGATIVE ADJECTIVE IN THE SAME SENTENCE

WRONG:
He doesn't do *no* work.
[A negative adverb—*n't [not]* and a negative adjective—*no*]

CORRECT:
He doesn't do *any* work.

PRACTICE

1. The orchestra sounded superb.

2. Alfredo waited long for his reward.

3. Enrique was the noisier student in the class.

4. Of the three children, the youngest was the baddest.

ANSWERS

1. Correct.

2. Correct.

3. Enrique was the noisiest student in the class.

4. Of the three children, the youngest was the worst.

PRACTICE WITH ADJECTIVES AND ADVERBS

In each sentence, five parts are underlined and numbered. Choose the number of the underlined part that contains the error. If there is no error, choose answer space 5. No sentence contains more than one error.

1. Hardly <u>hadn't</u> he <u>quietly</u> and <u>painfully</u>
         (1)   (2)   (3)
   built the sand castle than it was
   <u>swiftly</u> torn down. <u>No error</u>
   (4)   (5)

2. Although I feel <u>good</u>, I look <u>sick</u>
              (1)   (2)
   because I ate <u>sparingly</u> and
              (3)
   <u>improperly</u>. <u>No error</u>
   (4)   (5)

3. <u>Gladly</u> I'll say that he <u>surely</u> hit the
    (1)   (2)
   ball <u>real</u> <u>well</u>. <u>No error</u>
      (3) (4)   (5)

4. Anita was the <u>most</u> <u>intelligent</u> girl
              (1)   (2)
   although she didn't dress <u>well</u> or act
                     (3)
   <u>properly</u>. <u>No error</u>
   (4)   (5)

5. The lunch, which was <u>lovingly</u> and
                 (1)
   <u>carefully</u> prepared, tastes <u>deliciously</u>
    (2)   (3)
   and is <u>healthful</u>. <u>No error</u>
        (4)   (5)

6. He worked <u>fast</u>; I worked <u>slow</u>. He
         (1)   (2)
   rested <u>frequently</u>; I worked <u>continuously</u>.
       (3)   (4)
   <u>No error</u>
   (5)

7. It doesn't seem <u>right</u> that some
              (1)
   flowers that look <u>ugly</u> smell <u>sweet</u>
             (2)   (3)
   while others that look pretty smell
   <u>bad</u>. <u>No error</u>
   (4) (5)

8. Doesn't Chico succeed just as <u>good</u>
                         (1)
   as Carlos though he isn't as
   <u>hard-working</u>, <u>serious</u>, and
    (2)   (3)
   <u>conscientious</u>? <u>No error</u>
   (4)   (5)

9. The <u>worse</u> of the two storms ended
       (1)
   as <u>quickly</u> and <u>suddenly</u> as it had
      (2)   (3)
   begun, leaving us <u>ill</u> with fear.
               (4)
   <u>No error</u>
   (5)

10. He spoke <u>deliberately</u> and chose
           (1)
    his words <u>carefully</u>, with the result
          (2)
    that his speech cut <u>deep</u> and he was
              (3)
    the <u>more</u> effective of the two speakers.
       (4)
    <u>No error</u>
    (5)

Answer Key

1. **1**	3. **3**	5. **3**	7. **5**	9. **5**
2. **5**	4. **5**	6. **5**	8. **1**	10. **5**

WHAT'S YOUR SCORE?

_____right,	_____wrong
Excellent	9–10
Good	8
Fair	7

If you scored lower, restudy this section, concentrating on the rules and examples.

Answer Analysis

1. **1** To avoid a double negative, the correct word is *had*.

2. **5** No error.

3. **3** The word modifies the adverb *well*, so it should be an adverb—*really*.

4. **5** No error.

5. **3** The verb *tastes* requires a predicate adjective. *Delicious* is correct.

6. **5** No error.

7. **5** No error.

8. **1** This word modifies the verb *Does(n't) succeed*, so an adverb, *well*, is required.

9. **5** No error.

10. **5** No error.

GLOSSARY OF USAGE

ACTIVE VERB   Verb whose subject is the doer of the action that the verb is indicating. (The batter *hit* the ball.)

ADJECTIVE   Part of speech that helps describe a noun or pronoun by giving it a more exact meaning. (*big* house; *many* friends; *this* pencil)

ADVERB   Part of speech that helps describe a verb, an adjective, or another adverb by giving it a more exact meaning. (walks *slowly*; *very* pretty)

AGREEMENT   This refers to parts of a sentence that are alike in gender, number, and person such as a subject and its verb and a pronoun and its antecedent. (*I study. He studies.* The *dog* wagged *its* tail.)

ANTECEDENT   Noun that is replaced with a pronoun. (*EVERYONE* will please remove *his* hat. *WALKING* is *what* I like to do most.)

ANTONYM   Word that is opposite in meaning to another word. (happy, sad)

APPOSITION   Condition describing two nouns, next to each other in a sentence, that are equivalent in meaning. (my brother, Joe; Mrs. Brown, the secretary)

AUXILIARY VERB   Verb that helps another word show voice or tense. (I *would have* forgotten. She *had* left.)

CASE   Form of a noun or pronoun that shows its relation to the other words in a sentence.

Nominative case of pronouns has the forms *I, you, he, she, we, they, who*, and is used as the subject of a verb or as a predicate noun. (*They* go. It is *we.*)

Possessive case shows possession. In nouns, it is formed with the apostrophe: (Frank's). Possessive pronouns include *mine, yours, his, hers, its, ours, theirs, whose.* (Note: There is no apostrophe in any possessive pronoun.)

Objective case of pronouns has the forms *me, you, him, her, us, them, whom*, and is used as the object of a verb, object of a preposition, subject or object of an infinitive. (They hit *him.* They gave it to *him.* I want *him* to go. I want to hit *him.*)

CLAUSE Group of words in a sentence that contains a subject and a predicate.

Independent clauses can stand alone. (He played well.)

Dependent clauses (adverb, adjective, or noun clauses) cannot stand alone. (He played well *although he was hurt.* The book *that I read* was very interesting. *That he recovered* was a miracle.)

COMPARISON Change of form in adjectives and adverbs to show increase in amount or quality. (strong, strong*er*, strong*est*; good, bet*ter*, be*st*)

Comparative refers to a greater degree in quality or quantity of one item or person with respect to another. (smart*er* of the two)

Superlative refers to a greater degree in the quality or quantity of one item or person with respect to two or more others. (larg*est* of the three)

COMPLEX SENTENCE Sentence that has one independent clause and at least one dependent clause. (We are happy *that you came.*)

COMPOUND-COMPLEX SENTENCE Sentence that has two independent clauses and at least one dependent clause. (*Joe sang* and *Joan played the song that she had been studying.*)

COMPOUND PREDICATE Two or more predicates usually joined by *and* or *or.* (He *goes to school by day* and *works at night.*)

COMPOUND SENTENCE Sentence that has two independent clauses. (*Joe sang* and *Joan played the piano.*)

COMPOUND SUBJECT Two or more subjects that take the same verb. (*Frank* and *I* will come.)

CONJUNCTION Part of speech that connects words, phrases, or clauses. (bread *and* butter; "to be *or* not to be"; She came *when* I left.)

CONSONANT Letter other than *a, e, i, o, u* (which are considered vowels) or *y* (which is considered a semivowel).

DASH Punctuation mark that shows a pause or break in a sentence. (He may not come—but why should I worry?)

DIRECT OBJECT Noun or pronoun that receives the action of the verb. (Jon struck *him.* Give *it* to Gerry.)

DIRECT QUOTATION Use of the exact words of the speaker. (The teacher said, "Do your homework.")

FIRST PERSON Pronoun and verb forms that refer to the person or persons speaking. (*I, we; my, our; me, us; am, are*)

FUTURE TENSE Time of verb that shows a happening yet to take place. (He *will retire* next year.)

GENDER Classification of nouns and pronouns into three groups: masculine, feminine, and neuter. A *masculine* pronoun is *he;* a *feminine* pronoun is *she;* a pronoun in the *neuter* gender is *it.*

GLOSSARY Listing of difficult or unusual words occurring in a book with their definitions. It is usually found in the back of the book. This glossary is at the end of the chapter to which it relates.

HOMONYM Word with the same sound as another word or words but with a different spelling and meaning. (to, too, two; pear, pair)

HYPHEN Mark (-) used to form a compound adjective (two-faced), to join certain prefixes to words (ex-president) or to separate words into syllables (En-glish).

IDIOM Group of words that, taken together, differs in meaning from the individual words used separately. (once upon a time)

INDIRECT OBJECT Word that shows, without any preposition, to whom or for whom the action in the sentence is taking place. (He gave *me* a pen.)

INDIRECT QUOTATION Quotation that does not use the exact words of the speaker. (The candidate said [that] he would accept the nomination.)

INFINITIVE Verb form that is usually indicated by *to* before the verb. Sometimes *to* is understood. (I want *to go.* He made me *laugh.*)

INTERJECTION Independent word that expresses strong feeling. (ah! oh! alas!)

INTERROGATIVE SENTENCE Sentence that asks a question. (Did he leave?)

INTRANSITIVE VERB Verb that has no object. (He *stands.* I *sit.)*

MODIFIER Word or group of words that help describe another word or group of words by giving a more exact meaning. See ADJECTIVE, ADVERB.

NOMINATIVE CASE Form of the noun or pronound that is the subject or predicate noun in a sentence. *(She* is *president.)*

NOUN Part of speech that is the name of a person, place, or thing. (George Washington; New York; toy)

NUMBER Change in the form of a noun, pronoun, adjective, or verb to show whether there is one *(singular)* or more than one *(plural)* (man, men; he, they; this, these; is, are)

OBJECT Noun or pronoun that names the person or thing acted upon by the verb. (She brought the *book.* I admire *her.)*

OBJECTIVE CASE Form of the noun or pronoun that shows it is the person or thing that receives the action. (I hit *him.)*

OBJECT OF A PREPOSITION Noun or pronoun that follows a preposition that controls it. (with *me*; between *you* and *me*; among *him* and *them)*

PARALLELISM (PARALLEL STRUCTURE) Two parts of a sentence that are given the same form, and therefore have the same importance, in the sentence. (He eats *both* meat *and* vegetables. *Not only* the relatives were invited *but also* the friends. Beth enjoys *jogging, skating,* and *skiing.)*

PARTICIPLE Form of a verb that is used both as an adjective and as part of a verb. (the *sleeping* child; am *going*; have *gone)*

present participle (going)

past participle (gone)

PART OF SPEECH One of eight categories into which words in a sentence are assigned: *noun, pronoun, verb, adjective, adverb, preposition, conjunction, interjection.*

PASSIVE Form of verb that is used when the subject of the sentence receives the action. (The watch *was given* to Joe. The man *was laid* to rest.)

PAST TENSE Time of verb that shows that an action has been completed. (He *went.* We *did go.)*

PERSON Form of pronoun or verb that tells whether the person (or persons) speaking is doing the action (*first person*); a person being spoken to is doing the action *(second person);* or the person spoken about is doing the action *(third person).* (*We* left for home. *You* stayed here. *They* arrived late.)

PHRASE Group of words without a subject and predicate, usually introduced by a preposition, that has a use in a sentence like that of a noun, adjective, or adverb. (*In the park* is where I like to sit. Jeannie *with the light brown hair.* He ran *to first base.)*

PLURAL Form of noun, pronoun, adjective, or verb that indicates that more than one person, place, or thing is being spoken about in the sentence. (boys; they; these; are)

POSSESSIVE Form of noun or pronoun that shows ownership. (*girl's* pencil; *ladies'* hats; *its* paw)

PREDICATE Part of the sentence that tells something about the subject (what the subject does, what is done to the subject, or what is true about the subject). (The boy *went home quickly.* This milk *tastes sour.)*

PREFIX Addition (usually a single syllable) to the beginning of a word that adds to or changes the meaning of the word. (*im*possible; *ex*-president; *re*view; *pre*fix)

PREPOSITION Part of speech that shows the relationship between a noun or pronoun that is its object, and some other word in the sentence. (Mary went *to* the library.)

PRESENT PERFECT TENSE Time of verb that shows an action that started in the past and is continuing or has just been completed in the present. It requires the use of an auxiliary verb in the present tense and the past participle. (He *has been* our friend for years.)

PRESENT TENSE Time of verb that shows an action that is going on now. There are three forms of this tense—he *says,* he *is saying,* he *does say.*

PRONOUN Part of speech that is used in place of a noun. (John came. *He* was welcome.) The four main kinds of pronouns are:

demonstrative (this, that, these, those);

personal (I, you, he, she, it, we, they);

possessive (mine, yours, his, hers, ours, theirs);

relative (that, what, who, which).

PROPER NOUN Noun that refers to an individual person, place, or thing. (George Washington; New York City; City Hall)

ROOT Basic part of a word, without prefixes or suffixes, that gives the main meaning of the word. (*cred*—believe; with prefix *in* and suffix *ible*—in *cred* ible—unbelievable)

RUN-ON (or COMMA SPLICE) SENTENCE Two sentences that are made into one by mistake. They are separated either by a comma or by no punctuation at all. (Wrong: Kay is class president, she is my friend. Correct: Kay is class president. She is my friend.)

SENTENCE Group of words containing a subject and a predicate and expressing an independently complete thought. (*He came early.*) Three chief kinds of sentences are:

declarative (makes a statement);

interrogative (asks a question);

imperative (gives a command).

SENTENCE FRAGMENT Group of words that may contain a subject and a predicate but that fails to express a complete thought and is, by error, punctuated as if it did. (Wrong: Hoping to hear from you. Correct: I am hoping to hear from you.)

SINGULAR Form of noun, pronoun, adjective, or verb that refers to one person, place, or thing in a sentence. (boy; he; this; is)

SUBJECT Part of the sentence that does the action or is spoken about. (*He* hit the ball. *The watch* was given to the man.)

SUFFIX Addition to the ending of a word that adds to or changes its meaning. (hand*ful*; quick*ly*; act*or*)

SYLLABLE Smallest group of sounds, consisting of a vowel sound, and one or more consonant sounds that are pronounced as a unit. (con-so-nant)

SYNONYM Word that is very similar in meaning to another word. (happy—glad)

TENSE Time of an action, indicated by the verb as *present, past, future, present perfect.* These are the most widely used tenses in English.

USAGE Actual use of language by the people at large. *Good usage* is the actual use of language by educated persons and other persons in positions of importance.

VERB Part of speech that indicates the action carried out by the subject or that tells something about the subject. (He *hit* the ball. She *was* in the garden.)

VOWELS Letters representing the sounds *a, e, i, o, u.* The letter *y* is considered a semivowel, as in *slowly.*

Mechanics

Mechanics deals with capitalization, punctuation, and spelling (especially homonyms, possessives, and contractions).

Capitalization. Fifteen basic rules are provided with applications for each.

Punctuation. Basic rules and examples are given for each of the major punctuation marks: period, question mark, exclamation point, comma, semicolon, colon, apostrophe, parentheses, and quotation marks.

Spelling. A total of 650 words has been included in three lists for you to study. Study the basic rules for homonyms, possessives, and contractions.

CAPITALIZATION

ALWAYS CAPITALIZE

1. The first word of a sentence.

   We went to the theater.

2. The first word of a direct quotation.

   He said, "Don't give up."

3. The first word of a line of poetry.

   "Poems are made by fools like me..."

4. Proper nouns (names of specific persons, places, or things).

   Winston Churchill; Mr. James Jones; New York City; Main Street; City Hall

   Note: Capitalize names of family members when used in place of their actual name.

   CORRECT: I need you, Mom.
   Grandma went to the store today.

5. Proper adjectives (adjectives formed from proper nouns).

   American; Shakespearean

6. Names of specific organizations or institutions.

   Sousa Junior High School; Columbia University; American Red Cross; Federal Bureau of Investigation

7. Days of the week, months of the year, and holidays. (*Note:* Do *not* capitalize seasons, e.g., winter.)

   Sunday; June; Thanksgiving

8. Languages. (*Note:* These are the *only* school subjects that are capitalized.)

   French; Hebrew
   I study English, Spanish, biology, mathematics, and social studies.

9. Races and religions.

   Hindu; Christian

10. References to the Deity and to the titles of holy books.

    the Almighty; the Old Testament; the Koran

11. Titles of people when they are followed by a name; capitalize both the title and the name. (*Note:* If a specific person is meant, the name may, at times, be omitted.)

    President Lincoln; Dr. Schweitzer; Her Majesty the Queen

12. Titles of works of literature, art, and music.

    War and Peace (note that articles, short prepositions, and conjunctions such as *and* are not capitalized in titles); *American Gothic;* Beethoven's Fifth Symphony

13. The pronoun *I* at all times.

    How do I get there?

14. Sections of the country, but not directions.

    I lived in the South for five years.
    We traveled south.

15. Specific places and addresses, but do not capitalize the second half of a hyphenated number.

    Times Square; 25 Main Street; 65 West Thirty-third Street.

PRACTICE

1. Junior belongs to the Boy scouts.
2. My favorite subject in school is English.
3. New York City is about 250 miles south of Boston.
4. The bible is a holy book to millions.
5. Salt Lake city is in Utah.
6. My cousin shouted, "be careful!"
7. Maria's cat was named sandy.
8. My home is located near broadway.
9. Most inhabitants of Israel are jewish.
10. Labor day occurs in September.

> **TIP**
>
> Remember the rules of capitalization. They're important! Without proper capitalization, your writing can be confusing.

ANSWERS

1. Junior belongs to the Boy Scouts.
2. Correct.
3. Correct.
4. The Bible is a holy book to millions.
5. Salt Lake City is in Utah.
6. My cousin shouted, "Be careful!"
7. Maria's cat was named Sandy.
8. My home is located near Broadway.
9. Most inhabitants of Israel are Jewish.
10. Labor Day occurs in September.

PRACTICE WITH CAPITALIZATION

The following sentences contain problems in capitalization. If there is an error, select the one underlined part that must be changed to make the sentence correct. If there is no error, choose answer 5. No sentence contains more than one error. These are included in the sentence correction type of multiple-choice item.

1. Peter Winkle of West Virginia, the last
     (1)
   doubtful republican name to be called
                (2)
   on May 16, was, like Ross, a "nobody."
       (3)   (4)
   No error
     (5)

2. Most of our compound words
   beginning with Indian can be traced
                    (1)
   to the white man's contact with these
   original Americans; thus we have
              (2)
   Indian summer, Indian file and Indian
   (3)   (4)
   giver. No error
          (5)

3. Her sons have used books in the way
   her father, the Hon. John F.
                    (1)   (2)
   Fitzgerald, mayor of Boston, used
              (3)
   Thanksgiving turkeys as elaborate
   (4)
   calling cards. No error
                    (5)

4. As the 800-foot-long tanker *Houston*
          (1)
   passed beneath the Verrazano Bridge,
              (2)   (3)
   the captain ordered its speed
       (4)
   reduced. No error
             (5)

5. The English teacher assigned the
          (1)
   Poe story "Murders in The Rue
   (2)   (3)   (4)
   Morgue." No error
             (5)

6. He lived on Twenty-First Street, at
              (1)   (2)   (3)
   the corner of Broadway. No error
                   (4)   (5)

7. The Frick Museum is located East of
       (1)   (2)   (3)
   Central Park. No error
             (4)   (5)

8. He failed Chemistry and French but
              (1)   (2)
   passed English and Spanish. No error
           (3)   (4)   (5)

9. I attended Dawson School and
              (1)   (2)
   Southern University. No error
   (3)   (4)   (5)

10. Mr. and Mrs. Jones and Family invite
    (1)   (2)   (3)   (4)
    you to a party at their home.
    No error
        (5)

Answer Analysis

1. **2** See Rule 6. Capitalize names of specific organizations.

2. **5** No error.

3. **5** No error.

4. **5** No error.

5. **4** Unimportant words in the title of a literary work are not capitalized.

6. **2** In an address, the second part of a hyphenated number is not capitalized.

7. **3** Directions are not capitalized.

8. **1** Only languages, among school subjects, are capitalized.

9. **5** No error.

10. **4** This word refers to a general group and, therefore, is not capitalized.

Answer Key

1. **2**	3. **5**	5. **4**	7. **3**	9. **5**
2. **5**	4. **5**	6. **2**	8. **1**	10. **4**

PUNCTUATION

BASIC RULES OF PUNCTUATION

The Period

The period is used after

- a sentence that makes a statement

    He arrived on time.

- a sentence that gives a command

    Sit up straight.

- some abbreviations and contractions

    Mr., A.M., etc.

The Question Mark

The question mark is used after a sentence that asks a question.

    Did you like the game?

The Exclamation Point

The exclamation point is used after a sentence that emphasizes a command or that conveys strong feeling.

    Stop writing immediately!

    What a pleasant surprise!

The Comma

The comma is used

- to separate a word or words that indicate the person to whom a remark is addressed, known as direct address

    John, please come here.

- to separate a word or words that add information about the noun, known as appositives;

    Pat, my secretary and receptionist, is very efficient.

- to set off expressions or phrases that are inserted in the sentence and that interrupt the normal word order

    Notre Dame, in my opinion, will win the championship.

- after introductory phrases and clauses, particularly when they are long (more than three words) or when the meaning may be temporarily confused if the comma is omitted

  When the dog jumped up, Darryl's parents became frightened.

- to separate independent clauses of a compound sentence joined by a conjunction such as *and, but, for, nor, or, so,* or *yet,* unless the sentences are short

  Joe decided to attend the game, but I remained at home.

  but (if the sentences are short)

  Joe returned but I remained.

- to separate items in a series

  The box contained books, toys, games, and tools.

- before the text of a quotation; in a divided quotation, commas are used to set off the speaker

  The teacher said, "Return to your seats."

  "Return to your seats," said the teacher, "so we may continue the lesson."

- to set off clauses and phrases that are not essential to the meaning of the sentence

  Jan, who was seated beside me, left early.

  [Note that the clause "who was seated beside me" is not essential to the sentence, which, without it, would read, "Jan left early."]

  but

  The students who studied hard passed the test.
  [The clause "who studied hard" is essential since only the students who studied hard passed. Without this clause the meaning intended by the writer—that students who did not study hard failed—would not be clear to the reader.]

- after the salutation in a friendly letter

  Dear Dad,

- after the complimentary close in all letters

  Sincerely,

- between the day of the month and the year when writing a date

  May 23, 2009

- between the city and the state when writing an address.

  St. Augustine, FL 32086

Note: **Do NOT use commas . . .**

- between a subject and its verb when the verb immediately follows the subject

    The boys on the team celebrated their victory.

- to separate parts of a compound predicate or a compound subject.

    They enjoyed a good dinner and saw a play.

    Sally and Jose make great teammates.

The Apostrophe

The apostrophe is used

- in a contraction to show that letters have been omitted

    Don't stop pretending to have a good time.

- to show possession

    My brother's dog has been through obedience training.

- to show plural of single letters

    Susan made straight A's in geography class.

> **IMPORTANT NOTE**
>
> With very few exceptions, the quote's punctuation will go inside the quotation marks.

Quotation Marks

Quotation marks are used

- around titles of songs or poems

    My favorite song is "Imagine" by John Lennon.

- around titles of chapters

    I particularly enjoyed Chapter 3, "Your Pet as a Companion."

- around titles of articles

    In today's paper, there was an article entitled "Hurricane looms in Florida keys."

Parentheses

Parentheses are used to enclose any words that explain or add to a thought contained in a sentence. Parentheses are always used in pairs (that is, one opens and the other closes the included word or words).

    Frank Jones (author of *Ideas That Work*) has written many best sellers.

The Semicolon

The semicolon is used . . .

- to separate independent clauses in a sentence; either a semicolon or a comma may be used when the clauses are short

    I came; I saw; I conquered. (or I came, I saw, I conquered.)

- to separate items in a series when these items contain commas

    The guests included George W. Bush, President of the United States; Colin Powell, former Secretary of State; and Edward Kennedy, Senator.

The Colon

The colon is used . . .

- to introduce a series or a list of items

    These items were included on the shopping list: fruit, vegetables, meat, fish, and ice cream.

- before a restatement, an illustration, or an explanation of the main idea of the sentence

    I have but one rule of conduct: Always arrive on time to appointments.

- after the salutation of a business letter

    Dear Sir:

PRACTICE

1. Invite Constance my sister to the dance.
2. What nonsense!
3. Eli, if you ask me, is the smartest of them all.
4. After Ruth rested at home she felt better.
5. The childrens' clothing department was well stocked.
6. Your country expects only one thing from you citizens; do your duty.
7. Present at the meeting were General Smith, Army Chief of Staff: Admiral Jones, Chief of Naval Operations: and General Gray, Commanding General of the Marine Corps.
8. Maria indicated that she wouldnt come.
9. My parents warned me, "Dont be late."

ANSWERS

1. Invite Constance, my sister, to the dance.

2. Correct.

3. Correct.

4. After Ruth rested at home, she felt better.

5. The children's clothing department was well stocked.

6. Your country expects only one thing from you citizens: Do your duty.

7. Present at the meeting were General Smith, Army Chief of Staff; Admiral Jones, Chief of Naval Operations; and General Gray, Commanding General of the Marine Corps.

8. Maria indicated that she wouldn't come.

9. My parents warned me, "Don't be late."

PRACTICE WITH PUNCTUATION

The following sentences contain problems in punctuation. Choose the number of the under-lined part that must be changed to make the sentence correct. <u>No sentence contains more than one error.</u> If there is no error, choose answer 5. These are included in the sentence correction type of multiple-choice item.

1. Consider, for example, the widespread
        (1)   (2)
   notion that a clean environment can
   be obtained by reducing our
   dependence on "technology". <u>No error</u>
           (3)   (4)   (5)

2. However, we often get careless; we
        (1)   (2)
   say, "It's close enough," or "Who cares
                (3)
   anyway." <u>No error</u>
     (4)   (5)

3. Gasoline and whisky have much in
   common: <u>they're</u> both blended, both
       (1) (2)   (3)
   distilled—and both have something of
        (4)
   a kick. <u>No error</u>
         (5)

4. The object therefore, is to clean up
        (1)   (2)
   the air: the higher the vapor
       (3)
   pressure, the more likely it is that
        (4)
   gasoline will evaporate. <u>No error</u>
                   (5)

5. At 6 <u>PM</u> tomorrow, however, they will
       (1)   (2)   (3)
   be fed into a 12-inch diameter
   pipeline, each entering at a different
           (4)
   point. <u>No error</u>
        (5)

6. Mr. James Smith, President
             (1)
   The Line Company
          (2)
   16 Fifth Street
        (3)
   Lansing, Arizona 47962
   Dear Mr. Smith,
          (4)
   <u>No error</u>
    (5)

7. 1413 Sixth Street_
                     (1)
   Columbus_Florida_
          (2)   (3)
   March 5, 1984
          (4)
   <u>No error</u>
   (5)

8. "Are you coming?" he asked.
                      (1)
   "Yes."
    (2)
   "When?"
     (3)
   "Now."
    (4)
   <u>No error</u>
   (5)

9. "You take care of your problems."
                                    (1)
   said those to whom we addressed our
   questions, "and we'll take care of
         (2)(3)
   ours". <u>No error</u>
     (4)   (5)

Answer Key

1. **4**	3. **5**	5. **1**	7. **2**	9. **4**
2. **4**	4. **1**	6. **4**	8. **5**	

Answer Analysis

1. **4** At the end of a sentence, the period should be placed between the word and the quotation marks (*technology*.").

2. **4** The question mark is used after a sentence that asks a question.

3. **5** No error.

4. **1** See rule 3 under "The Comma." The comma is used to set off expressions or phrases that are inserted in the sentence and that interrupt the normal word order.

5. **1** See rule 3 under "The Period." The period is used after most abbreviations.

6. **4** A colon is required after the salutation of a business letter.

7. **2** In an address, a comma is used between the city and the state.

8. **5** No error.

9. **4** The period should be enclosed within the quotation marks.

SPELLING

Spelling mistakes on the GED test consist of improper homonyms, contractions, and possessives. First, review the basic rules of spelling. Then, move on to the list of homonyms and the practice exercises. Finally, study the rules for contractions and the rules for forming possessives. Complete all practice exercises, and you will be well prepared for this section of the test.

BASIC RULES OF SPELLING

1. Plurals of most nouns are formed by adding *s* to the singular.

   house, house*s*

2. When the noun ends in *s*, *x*, *ch*, or *sh*, the plural generally is formed by adding *es*.

   gas, gas*es*

   box, box*es*

   witch, witch*es*

   dish, dish*es*

3. The plural of a noun ending in *y* preceded by a consonant is formed by changing *y* to *i* and adding *es*.

   lady, lad*ies*

   The plural of a noun ending in *y* preceded by a vowel does not change *y* to *i* EXCEPT for words ending in *quy*.

   toy, toy*s*

   but

   soliloquy, soliloqu*ies*

4. A word that ends in *y* preceded by a consonant usually changes *y* to *i* before a suffix unless the suffix begins with *i*.

   beauty, beaut*iful*

   A word that ends in *y* preceded by a vowel usually keeps the *y* when a suffix is added.

   boy, boy*ish*

5. A word that ends in silent *e* generally keeps the *e* when a suffix beginning with a consonant is added.

   care, care*ful*

   A word that ends in silent *e* generally drops the *e* when a suffix beginning with a vowel is added.

   believe, believ*able*

   move, mov*ing*

6. Words ending in *ce* and *ge* keep the letter *e* before *able* and *ous*, an exception to Rule 5.

   notice, notic*eable*

   change, chang*eable*

   courage, courag*eous*

7. A one-syllable word that ends in one consonant following a short vowel generally doubles the consonant before a suffix that begins with a vowel.

   big, big*gest*

   thin, thin*ner*

8. A word of more than one syllable that ends in one consonant following one short vowel generally doubles the final consonant before a suffix beginning with a vowel *if* the accent is on the last syllable.

   omít, omit t ed

   regrét, regret t ing

   allót, allot t ed

9. The letter "i" is generally used before "e" except after "c."

   bel*ie*ve, rec*ei*ve

   There are many exceptions, as:

   > either
   >
   > neither
   >
   > neighborhood
   >
   > weigh
   >
   > leisure

10. An apostrophe is used to show that a letter has been omitted in a contraction.

    it's for it is

    they're for they are

11. An abbreviation is always followed by a period.

    etc.

    Mr.

    yr.

12. Nouns of Latin origin that end in

   us—become *i* in the plural,

   rad*ius*, rad*ii*

   a—become *ae* in the plural,

   formul*a*, formul*ae*

   um—become *a* in the plural,

   medi*um*, medi*a*

   is—become *es* in the plural.

   ax*is*, ax*es*

13. The suffix *ful* is spelled with a single *l.*

   help*ful*

   tablespoon*ful*

   (*Note:* The word *full* itself is the only exception.)

MOST FREQUENTLY CONFUSED HOMONYMS

A common error is the confusion of two words having the <u>same pronunciation</u> but <u>different spellings and meanings</u>. These are called *homonyms.* In this humorous sentence—"A doctor must have lots of patients (patience)"—there is no way of our knowing which word the speaker means if the sentence is spoken. Therefore, we don't know how to spell the word. The words *patients* and *patience* are homonyms.

Forty-four groups of homonyms follow. Be certain to check the meaning of each word in each group in order to determine the spelling from the meaning of the word as it is used in a sentence.

air; heir	him; hymn	road; rode
all together; altogether	hole; whole	sew; so; sow
ate; eight	hour; our	stationary; stationery
aunt; ant	knew; new	steal; steel
blew; blue	know; no	straight; strait
bough; bow	lead; led	some; sum
brake; break	mail; male	son; sun
buy; by	meat; meet	their; there; they're
cent; scent; sent	pail; pale	threw; through
coarse; course	pair; pear	to; too; two
for; four	patience; patients	way; weigh
forth; fourth	peace; piece	witch; which
grate; great	principal; principle	wood; would
groan; grown	read; red	your; you're
hear; here	right; write	

CONTRACTIONS AND POSSESSIVES

Knowing where and when to use the apostrophe is an important skill. Use the following guidelines to help you.

RULES FOR CONTRACTIONS

1. When forming a contraction, always place the apostrophe in the spot of the missing letter(s).

   cannot = can't

   is not = isn't

   they are = they're

   should not = shouldn't

   you are = you're

2. There are some irregularly formed contractions.

   will not = won't

RULES FOR POSSESSIVES

1. When forming possessives, write " 's" after the word that is possessing.

   Sally's book (the book belongs to Sally)

   children's books (the books belong to the children)

   author's viewpoint (the viewpoint belongs to the author)

2. When forming possessive plural nouns, just place an apostrophe after the "s."

   authors' viewpoints (the viewpoints belong to more than one author)

   books' pages (the pages belong to more than one book)

PRACTICE WITH SPELLING

For each sentence, choose the correct homonym, contraction, or possessive noun/pronoun to fill in the blank.

1. Prince William is the _____ to the English throne.

   (1) air
   (2) heir

2. Our school's _____ communicates well with his students.

   (1) principal
   (2) principle

3. If there is one thing I _____, it's that many countries fear the United States military.

   (1) know
   (2) no

4. Of _____ I want to take a vacation!

   (1) course
   (2) coarse

5. We set _____ on our great adventure to the Florida Keys.

   (1) fourth
   (2) forth

6. My cousin has _____ many pets.

   (1) to
   (2) too
   (3) two

7. In church, the choir sang a beautiful _____.

   (1) him
   (2) hymn

8. The shortstop _____ the ball just in time to make the third out.

   (1) through
   (2) threw

9. When my family members are finally _____, we have a great time.

   (1) all together
   (2) altogether

10. I _____ wait to tell my best friend that I got a job!

    (1) ca'nt
    (2) can't

11. The economy _____ improve when people are afraid to buy stocks.

    (1) wo'nt
    (2) won't

12. My dog likes the smell of _____.

    (1) daisies'
    (2) daisies

13. Susan wants to be an illustrator for _____ books.

    (1) children's
    (2) childrens'

14. _____ cousin works for the CIA.

    (1) Sallys'
    (2) Sally's

15. My _____ Judy is a stay-at-home mom.

    (1) aunt
    (2) ant

16. A letter carrier delivers _____.

    (1) mail
    (2) male

17. Pencil _____ can be poisonous if swallowed by young children.

    (1) led
    (2) lead

18. I learned to _____ clothes from my mother.

    (1) sew
    (2) so
    (3) sow

19. The gym has a set of _____ bikes that I like to ride.

    (1) stationary
    (2) stationery

20. The _____ group decided to do volunteer work together as a service project.

    (1) hole
    (2) whole

21. It _____ my fault that the vase was broken by the puppy; I told you to place it on a higher shelf.

    (1) wasn't
    (2) was'nt

22. The doctor sees about one hundred _____ a day.

    (1) patients
    (2) patience

23. If you are over _____, you should try diet and exercise.

    (1) wait
    (2) weight

24. When _____ homework becomes too much to complete, it is time to start budgeting your time.

    (1) your
    (2) you're

25. _____ are many types of American Indian tribes that still live in the United States.

    (1) There
    (2) Their
    (3) They're

26. The soccer team _____ three tournaments in a row!

    (1) one
    (2) won

27. A spider actually eats _____ own web when he's finished with it.

    (1) his
    (2) it's

28. When _____ work to be done, I'd rather take a nap!

    (1) theirs
    (2) there's

29. The boys thought the bowling alley was all _____ for the evening.

    (1) theirs
    (2) there's

30. When _____ finished debating an issue, the senators return to their offices in the capitol building.

    (1) there
    (2) their
    (3) they're

Answer Key

1. **2**	7. **2**	13. **1**	19. **1**	25. **1**
2. **1**	8. **2**	14. **2**	20. **2**	26. **2**
3. **1**	9. **1**	15. **1**	21. **1**	27. **1**
4. **1**	10. **2**	16. **1**	22. **1**	28. **2**
5. **2**	11. **2**	17. **2**	23. **2**	29. **1**
6. **2**	12. **2**	18. **1**	24. **1**	30. **3**

Organization

CHAPTER 6

BASIC RULES OF ORGANIZATION: UNITY AND COHERENCE

On the GED exam, questions referring to organization in writing make up 15% of the exam. Organization means that the writing has both unity and coherence. Unity and coherence make written works clear and easy to comprehend.

UNITY

Unity: To bring individual thoughts and ideas together in an organized manner.

• In a sentence, it is important to write only *one thought* at a time.

• In a paragraph, it is important to organize several supporting sentences that relate to only *one idea.*

• In an essay, it is important to organize several paragraphs of ideas that support only *one thesis.*

> **TIP**
>
> The key to writing with unity is proper organization of ideas.

Topic Sentences

The unifying idea in a paragraph is demonstrated through the use of a topic sentence. A topic sentence may occur in one of four places in a paragraph:

1. at the beginning, stating the unifying idea of the paragraph

2. at the middle, building up to a point, then expanding on an idea

3. at the end, presenting a well-developed argument followed by a convincing conclusion

4. nowhere; sometimes the topic sentence may not be stated, but implied

Find the topic sentence in the following paragraph.

> She has shown me the awesome tranquility of nature. She gives me the bigger half of the cookie when there's only one left. She doesn't buy me fancy clothes, or take me to expensive restaurants. Instead, she tells me about the rose garden she planted a few years back and the quilt she just started. She always seems to know the answer to my "Why?" questions. She is my mother, my best friend and confidant.

The topic sentence was the last sentence: "She is my mother, my best friend and confidant."

COHERENCE

Coherence: To bring several related ideas together around a central theme and in an organized manner.

- Use transitions in paragraphs from sentence to sentence and in essays from paragraph to paragraph.

> Pasta is easy to make. To make enough pasta for four people, **first** put two cups of water and a teaspoon of salt in a large pot. Bring the salted water to a boil over high heat. **Then** add 16 ounces of pasta. **When** the water returns to a boil, lower the heat to medium high and slightly stir the pasta to keep pieces from sticking together. Let the pasta cook for 8 to 10 minutes, and **then** remove the pot from the heat. **Immediately** pour the pasta into a colander to remove the water. **Finally**, run cool water over the pasta to keep it from becoming sticky. **Now** you may serve it with your favorite sauce.

- Use parallelism (phrases and clauses that have the same grammatical structure).

> Rabbits can become as tame and domesticated as cats **if they are** handled gently on a daily basis and **if they are** taught to use a litter box.

- Use an organizational pattern: chronological order, spatial order, order of importance, specific to general or general to specific, and problem/solution.

> Travelers must be aware of the restrictions for carry-on items today. When **first** arriving at the airport, travelers must check any luggage that will not fit in the overhead bins. Any ordinary objects with a sharp point that could be used as a weapon, such as nail files, needles, and knives, must be checked at this stage in the traveling. **Secondly**, travelers must be prepared to be searched at the passenger screening station. Here, federal security officers direct travelers through metal detectors and assist them in placing all carry-on items through the x-ray machines. At this point, if any contraband items are spotted, they are confiscated. **Finally**, the traveler may be randomly searched again just before boarding the plane.

TIP

Use transitions, parallelism, and organizational patterns to create coherence in your writing.

Common Transitions

Without transitions, your writing will not flow smoothly. Transitions are words and phrases that connect one idea to the next, one sentence to the next, or one paragraph to the next.

Transitions are important because they are the "glue" that holds your ideas together. But be careful not to overuse transitions in your writing; too many transitions can cause as much confusion as too few.

Therefore, you don't necessarily need a transition between every idea or every sentence, but it is a good idea to use a transition between each paragraph. Transitions usually come near the beginning of a paragraph. However, you should use a transition wherever it works best.

Nine Types of Transitions

1. *Transitions that* **add**: additionally, again, along with, also, and, another, as well, besides, equally important, finally, for example, for instance, further, furthermore, in addition, likewise, moreover, next, together with, too.

2. *Transitions that* **signal time**: about, after, afterward, as soon as, at, at the same time, before, during, earlier, finally, first, immediately, in the meantime, later, last, meanwhile, next, next week, next time, next year, now, prior to, second next, soon, then, third, till, today, tomorrow, until, when, yesterday.

3. *Transitions that* **indicate place**: above, across, against, along, alongside, amid, among, around, away from, back of, behind, below, beneath, beside, between, beyond, by, down, here, in front of, in the center of, in the middle of, inside, into, near, off, on top of, outside, over, there, throughout, to the left, to the right, under, up.

4. *Transitions that* **emphasize**: again, another key point, first thing to remember, for this reason, frequently, important to realize, indeed, in fact, in short, in summary, key point, most important information, on the negative side, on the positive side, surprisingly, to emphasize, to point out, to repeat, with this in mind.

5. *Transitions that* **illustrate**: for example, for instance, in other words, put another way, seems clear from this, simply stated, stated differently, that is, to clarify, to illustrate the point.

6. *Transitions that* **show cause and effect**: as a result, for this reason, then, therefore.

7. *Transitions that* **compare**: accordingly, also, as, by comparison, comparable to, in conjunction with this, in the same manner, in the same way, just as, like, likewise, similarly, sometimes.

8. *Transitions that* **contrast**: although, as opposed to, but, conversely, counter to, even so, even though, however, in spite of this, in the meantime, nevertheless, on the contrary, on the other hand, otherwise, sometimes, still, yet.

9. *Transitions that* **summarize**: accordingly, all in all, as a result, consequently, due to, in closing, in conclusion, in short, in summary, in the last analysis, finally, lastly, logical conclusion is, therefore, thus, to conclude.

PRACTICE

Circle the best transition to complete the sentence.

1. I looked across/behind the basketball court to find my opponent about to shoot a three-pointer.

2. When/Before I woke up from my nap, I found the dog had eaten my cake!

3. I learned how to read quicker; as a result/for example I have been making better grades.

4. The store owner locked up each night; however/accordingly, the thief was still able to break in and steal more than a thousand dollars worth of merchandise.

5. My sister has yet/therefore to discover what she wants to do with her life.

ANSWERS

1. across

2. When

3. as a result

4. however

5. yet

Parallel Structure

Parallelism in a coherent paragraph occurs when phrases and clauses have the same grammatical structure. This provides clarity in the writing. On the other hand, faulty parallelism disrupts the balance of grammatical structure. Parallelism appears in the following: outlines, lists, compound structures, comparisons, and contrasted elements. Study the two basic guidelines for parallel structure:

1. It is important to balance

   • nouns with nouns; adjectives with adjectives, etc.

   The History of Sports

   I. Famous **Players**

   A. Deceased

   B. Living

   II. Great **Coaches**

   III. Championship **Teams**

- phrases with phrases

  To wonder about the planet is **to question** the entire universe.

- clauses with clauses

  I wanted to know **that I was safe** and **that everyone else was safe**, too.

2. To make your writing parallel, repeat

   - a preposition
   - an article
   - the "to" of the infinitive
   - the introductory word of a phrase or clause

PRACTICE

Rewrite each sentence, correcting the faulty parallelism.

1. She learned to pay attention and take notes.
2. My brother and sister love to play volleyball.
3. The dog chased the cat behind the table and a wall!

ANSWERS

1. She learned to pay attention and to take notes.
2. My brother and my sister love to play volleyball.
3. The dog chased the cat behind the table and up a wall!

Paragraph Organization

There are four main ways to organize a paragraph:

1. Start with a topic sentence, then add supporting sentences.
2. Start with detailed sentences that support one idea and end with a topic sentence.
3. Start with a statement of the topic, then restrict the idea and illustrate it.
4. Start with a question or statement of problem, then answer and explain a solution.

1. **What type of organization does this paragraph illustrate?**

What I have most wanted to do throughout the past ten years is to make political writing into an art. My starting point is always a feeling of partisanship, a sense of injustice. When I sit down to write a book, I do not say to myself, "I am going to produce a work of art." I write it because there is some lie that I want to expose, some fact to which I want to draw attention, and my initial concern is to get a hearing. But I could not do the work of writing a book, or even a long magazine article, if it were not also an aesthetic experience. Anyone who cares to examine my work will see that even when it is downright propaganda it contains much that a full-time politician would consider irrelevant. I am not able, and I do not want, completely to abandon the world view that I acquired in childhood. So long as I remain alive and well I shall continue to feel strongly about prose style, to love the surface of the earth, and to take a pleasure in solid objects and scraps of useless information. It is no use trying to suppress that side of myself. The job is to reconcile my ingrained likes and dislikes with the essentially public, non-individual activities that this age forces on all of us.

—George Orwell, "Why I Write"

2. **What type of organization does this paragraph illustrate?**

Dealing with the [lime]stone itself involves a whole new set of machines. Great mobile engines called channelers, powered by electricity, chug on rails from one side of the bed to the other, chiseling ten-foot-deep slots. Hammering and puffing along, they look and sound and smell like small locomotives. By shifting rails, the quarries eventually slice the bed into a grid of blocks. The first of these to be removed is called the keyblock, and it always provokes a higher than usual proportion of curses. There is no way to get to the base of this first block to cut it loose, so it must be wedged, hacked, splintered and worried at, until something like a clean hole has been excavated. Men can then climb down and, by drilling holes and driving wedges, split the neighboring block free at its base, undoing in an hour a three-hundred-million-year-old cement job.

—Scott Russell Sanders
from "Digging Limestone"

3. **What type of organization does this paragraph illustrate?**

In October 1347 a Genoese fleet made its way into the Messina harbor in northeast Sicily. Its crew had "sickness clinging to their very bones." All were dead or dying, afflicted with a disease from the Orient. The Messinese harbor masters tried to quarantine the fleet, but it was too late. It was not men but rats and fleas that brought the sickness, and they scurried ashore as the first ropes were tied to the docks. Within days, the pestilence spread throughout Messina and its rural environs and, within six months, half the region's population died or fled. This scene, repeated thousands of times in ports and fishing villages across Eurasia and North Africa, heralded the coming of the great natural disaster in European history—the Black Death.

—Robert S. Gottfried, *The Black Death*

4. **What type of organization does this paragraph illustrate?**

American humor rested less on inherent wit or sharp observation of human filings than on rough drolleries full of exaggeration and strange usage for its own sake. The speech became noisy and profuse. It imitated sounds of sucking and smacking and cracking and slicing and chipping and sawing and thumping and poking and digging and clapping and exclaiming and hushing. It stuck in extra syllables for elegance and comic surprise. It liked to repeat in the same word the sound of dental consonants that gave a jerky, droll effect. It made comedy out of mouth-widening vowel sounds and speech-yodels whose effect depended upon a swallowed 1—the gobble of the North American turkey. It was at times almost an abstract sound. Its character stripped of known words and their meaning, and left only with sound, might still suggest the meaning intended, along with the hard, simple, and at times lyrically beautiful life from which it came.

—*Sons of Democracy*

ANSWERS

1. Starts with topic sentence, then adds supporting sentences.
2. Starts with statement of problem, then explains a solution.
3. Starts with detailed sentences and ends with topic sentence.
4. Starts with a statement of the topic, then restricts and illustrates it.

Text Division

In a piece of writing, it is important to organize all of the paragraphs around a central theme and to separate the paragraphs appropriately from each other.

The most logical time to make a paragraph break (or beginning of a new paragraph) is when there is a shift in

• time or place

• a sequence from one point to the next

• emphasis for the sake of clarity

• dialogue from one speaker to another

• focus from one idea to the next

BASIC GUIDELINES FOR UNITY AND COHERENCE

To achieve and identify unity and coherence in writing, there are a few basic guidelines to follow. Ask yourself the following questions to identify whether or not the piece of writing has unity and coherence:

1. Is there a topic sentence that states only one main idea?

2. Are enough details (elaboration) given to clearly explain the main idea?

3. Is there unity? (Does every sentence refer to the main idea?)

4. Are the ideas arranged in a logical order?

5. Are the ideas connected with transitions?

PRACTICE

Practice Paragraphs and Questions on Organization

Questions 1–3 refer to the following passage.

What is the purpose of chess?

(1) People know little about this fascinating game. (2) A common saying among those who know this game best is that the winner of the game is the one who makes the next-to-the-last mistake. (3) Even among grandmasters, the secret of success is not superior strategy but the failure to make tactical errors. (4) The purpose of the game is the opponent's skillful exploitation of a mistake made at any point in the game. (5) It is rare, nonetheless, that a game lasts for 100 moves. (6) The average number of moves is usually somewhere around 45, and the shortest game can consist of only 2 moves.

1. The topic sentence of this paragraph is

   (1) sentence 1
   (2) sentence 2
   (3) sentence 3
   (4) sentence 4
   (5) sentence 5

2. Sentence 1 should be

   (1) left as it is
   (2) placed last
   (3) placed after sentence 3
   (4) placed after sentence 6
   (5) omitted

3. A new paragraph can

   (1) be started after sentence 2
   (2) be started after sentence 3
   (3) be started after sentence 4
   (4) be started after sentence 5
   (5) not be started

Questions 4–6 refer to the following passage.

Who caused the Soviet Union's revolution?

(A)

(1) Although the peasants occasionally rioted and rebelled, they continued to believe the old myths about how much their tsar loved them. (2) So their uprisings were usually directed against the nobility and local government officials, and were poorly organized and easy to suppress. (3) Russia's factory workers prior to the twentieth century were too few and unorganized to sustain a coherent movement. (4) Russia's revolutionary movement did not emerge from the peasants or workers, the two most oppressed groups in Russia. (5) Instead, it was Russia's small, educated classes, those exposed to foreign ideas, that beginning in the 1820s produced its revolutionaries. (6) At first they were nobles—the only people in Russia at the time with a Western-type education. (7) In 1825 a group of noble army officers tried to overthrow the tsar. Their effort failed, and harsh punishment followed.

(B)

(8) Beginning in the 1840s and especially after 1860, as education spread, most revolutionaries came from the middle and lower classes. (9) The crucial point about these people is what they wanted for Russia. (10) Most of them did not want a society with a constitutional, democratic government and a free-enterprise economic system similar to what they saw in Western Europe or the United States. (11) Instead, Russian revolutionaries were socialists who believed a country's economy should be in the hands of the people as a whole and that every person should receive an equal share of that economy's wealth. (12) Some Russian socialists hoped the economy would be controlled at the local level, while others believed it should be run by a powerful, centralized state. (13) All of them, however, opposed the free-enterprise, capitalist system because they felt it caused inequality and forced most people to live in poverty. (14) They also distrusted constitutional democracy as it existed in the West, mainly because they felt that political institutions in capitalist societies were manipulated and controlled by the rich at the expense of the poor.

—"The Rise and Fall of the
Soviet Union" by Michael Kort

4. The topic sentence of paragraph (A) is

   (1) sentence 1
   (2) sentence 2
   (3) sentence 3
   (4) sentence 4
   (5) sentence 5

5. Sentence 4 should be

   (1) left as it is
   (2) placed first
   (3) placed after sentence 1
   (4) placed after sentence 8
   (5) omitted

6. A new paragraph can

   (1) be started after sentence 2
   (2) be started after sentence 3
   (3) be started after sentence 4
   (4) be started after sentence 5
   (5) not be started

Questions 7–9 refer to the following passage.

What would happen if animals were allowed their freedom?

(1) Among watchdogs in Seattle, Berkeley was known generally as one of the best. (2) Not the smartest, but steady. (3) A pious German shepherd (Black Forest origins, probably), with big shoulders, black gums, and weighing more than some men, he sat guard inside the glass door of Tilford's Pet Shoppe, watching the pedestrians scurry along First Avenue, wondering at the derelicts who slept ever so often inside the foyer at night, and sometimes he nodded when things were quiet in the cages behind him, lulled by the bubbling of the fishtanks, dreaming of an especially fine meal he'd once had, or the little female poodle, a real flirt, owned by the aerobic dance teacher (who was no saint herself) a few doors down the street; but Berkeley was, for all his woolgathering, never asleep at the switch. (4) He took his work seriously. (5) Moreover, he knew exactly where he was at every moment, what he was doing, and why he was doing it, which was more than can be said for most people, like Mr. Tiflord, a real gumboil, whose ways were mysterious to Berkeley. (6) Sometimes he treated the animals cruelly, or taunted them; he saw them not as pets but profit. (7) Nevertheless, no vandals, or thieves had ever brought trouble through the doors or windows of Tilford's Pet Shoppe, and Berkeley, confident of his power but never flaunting it, faithful to his master though he didn't deserve it, was certain that none ever would.

—"Menagerie, A Child's Fable"
by Charles Johnson

7. The topic sentence of this paragraph is

   (1) sentence 1
   (2) sentence 2
   (3) sentence 3
   (4) sentence 4
   (5) sentence 5

8. Sentence 1 should be

   (1) left as it is
   (2) placed first
   (3) placed after sentence 4
   (4) placed after sentence 8
   (5) omitted

9. A new paragraph can

   (1) be started after sentence 2
   (2) be started after sentence 3
   (3) be started after sentence 4
   (4) be started after sentence 5
   (5) not be started

Answer Key

1. **2**	3. **3**	5. **2**	7. **1**	9. **5**
2. **5**	4. **4**	6. **3**	8. **1**	

Answer Analyses

1. **2** The main idea of the paragraph is the role of errors in the playing of chess.

2. **5** The sentence is irrelevant to the topic.

3. **3** The paragraph shifts from its main idea to a subordinate one after sentence 4—the length of games.

4. **4** The main idea of paragraph (A) is to make the point that Russia's revolution did not come from the peasants or workers; the rest of the paragraph proves that statement.

5. **2** Because sentence 4 is the main idea, it would read clearly if it were placed first.

6. **3** A new topic, the educated Russians who tried to overthrow the tsar, is mentioned in sentence 5 and the following sentences support it; therefore, it should be the beginning of a new paragraph.

7. **1** The entire passage describes who Berkeley is, and sentence 1 introduces the reader to Berkeley.

8. **1** Because it is important to know who Berkeley is, sentence 1 must remain the first sentence, for coherence.

9. **5** A new paragraph cannot be started because the entire passage is just introducing the reader to Berkeley.

WHAT'S YOUR SCORE?

_____right,   _____wrong

Excellent	9
Good	8
Fair	7

If you scored lower, review the examples in this section.

Additional Writing Skills

CHAPTER 7

CORRECT USE OF WORDS

Here are thirty pairs of words that are frequently confused and misused. Study the distinctions between the words in each pair. An example of the correct use of each member of the pair is given.

Accept, Except

The verb **accept** means "to receive something" or "to agree to something." **Except** is most frequently used as a preposition meaning "leaving out." The use of *except* as a verb meaning "to leave out" is rare.

> He was chosen to *accept* the gift.

> Everyone came *except* him.

Aggravate, Irritate

The verb **aggravate** means "to make worse." The verb **irritate** means "to annoy." In general, a person is *irritated*; a situation or a condition is *aggravated*.

> Constant rubbing tended to *aggravate* the already painful wound.

> The behavior of the child *irritated* all the guests.

Already, All Ready

Already is an adverb of time meaning "previously." **All ready** means exactly what the two words indicate—all prepared.

> When I arrived, he had *already* left.

> When I arrived, I found them *all ready* for the meeting.

Altogether, All Together

Altogether is an adverb of degree meaning "completely." **All together** means exactly what the two words indicate—all the persons in a group.

He was *altogether* unprepared for the assignment.

We found the team *all together* in the locker room.

Among, Between

Among is used when more than two persons or things are involved. **Between** is used when only two persons or things are involved. (You needn't be concerned with the rare exceptions to these rules.)

Frank, Joe, and Ed shared the expenses *among* themselves.

Jane and Joan shared the expenses *between* themselves.

Amount, Number

Amount is used for things or ideas that cannot be counted, and is usually followed by a singular noun—*money, talent, courage.* **Number** is used for persons or things that can be counted.

Sue carried a large *amount* of cash.

The *number* of accidents this year is greater than we thought.

I needed a large *amount* of money.

I needed a large *number* of dollars to pay my bills.

In the third example, the word *money* is thought of as a single unit. In the fourth, the word *dollars* is thought of as individual items that can be counted.

Around, About

Around is correctly used to indicate direction in a circle around an object. **About** should be used when number or size is indicated.

They walked *around* the house.

There were *about* 50,000 fans in the stadium.

The rug was *about* nine feet wide.

As, Like

Only **as** can introduce a clause. **Like** cannot serve as a conjunction to introduce a clause; it is most frequently used as a preposition meaning "similar to."

WRONG:
This cereal tastes good *like* a cereal should.

CORRECT:
This cereal tastes good *as* a cereal should.

CORRECT:
He wanted everyone to be *like* him.

Beat, Bet

Beat means "to defeat." **Bet** means "to wager," or "to gamble something of value," on the result of a game.

Frank *beat* Jack in straight sets in their tennis match.

I *bet* five dollars that Joan would outrun Jane.

Beside, Besides

Beside means "at the side of." **Besides** means "in addition."

He came over to sit *beside* me.

There were nine others present *besides* Joe.

Borrow, Lend

Borrow means that the borrower is on the taking end of the transaction. **Lend** means that the lender is on the giving end of the transaction.

Please let me *borrow* ten dollars from you.

I'll be glad to *lend* the ten dollars to you.

Both, Each

Both refers to two objects or persons taken together. **Each** refers to one or more objects or persons taken individually.

Both my pens cost ten dollars.

(**Note: Don't** use *both* in the above example if you mean that the cost of the two pens was twenty dollars. *Both* means the pair of pens.)

Each of my pens costs five dollars.

Bring, Take

Bring is used when the movement in the sentence is toward the speaker or the writer. **Take** is used when the movement in the sentence is away from the speaker or the writer.

Bring the pencils to me, please.

Take these books to the principal's office.

Can, May

Can is used to indicate the ability to do something. **May** is used when permission is sought to do something, most frequently in the form of a question.

I *can* tie a slip knot.

May I have the car tonight?

Fewer, Less

The correct use of these words follows the same rules as those indicated for **amount** and **number**. **Fewer** is used for persons or things that can be counted. **Less** is used for things or ideas that cannot be counted. (Note that *less* is usually followed by a singular noun, *fewer* by a plural noun.)

> The number of accidents this year is *fewer* than we thought.
>
> We enjoyed *less* freedom this year than last.

Hanged, Hung

Hanged refers to a specific kind of execution that has taken place. **Hung** refers to something that has been suspended from an object.

> The murderer was *hanged*.
>
> The picture was *hung* on the hook attached to the wall.

Imply, Infer

Imply is used to indicate that the speaker or the writer is making a hint or suggestion. **Infer** is used to indicate that the hint or suggestion made by the speaker was taken by the audience, which drew a conclusion from it.

> I mean to *imply* that he didn't get the job done.
>
> I *infer* from your remarks that he was lazy.

In, Into

In is used to indicate that something is already in a place. **Into** is used to indicate that someone or something is moving from the outside to the inside of a place.

> The dog is *in* the living room.
>
> The dog dashed *into* the living room from the kitchen.

Latest, Last

Latest means "the most recent in a series." **Last** means "final."

> The popular candidate was seen talking with his *latest* rival.
>
> He appeared on television for the *last* time before his retirement.

Learn, Teach

Learn is used to indicate that knowledge or behavior is being acquired. **Teach** is used to indicate that knowledge or behavior is being provided.

> He tried to *learn* how to hang-glide.
>
> I tried to *teach* him how to hang-glide.

Myself, Me

Myself may be used properly in one of two ways. It can be used for emphasis, or it can be used as the object of an action verb with *I* as the subject. (*Never* use *myself* when *I* or *me* is correct.)

Me may be used only as a direct object, never as a subject of a sentence. In order to determine if *me* is appropriate, eliminate any other nouns or pronouns near it and see how it sounds.

I *myself* will attend to this matter.

When the director cast parts, he chose *me* to play the lead.

WRONG:
He gave the awards to Frank and myself.

CORRECT:
He gave the awards to Frank and me.

WRONG:
Frank and myself will get the awards.

CORRECT:
Frank and I will get the awards.

Pour, Spill

Pour means "to cause a liquid to flow deliberately." **Spill** means "to cause a liquid to flow accidentally or unintentionally."

The hostess *poured* coffee for her guests.

The hostess was embarrassed when she *spilled* the coffee on her guest's dress.

Precede, Proceed

Precede means "to come or go before" something or someone. **Proceed** means "to go on," particularly after an interruption.

Jimmy Carter *preceded* Ronald Reagan as president of the United States.

The speaker *proceeded*, after he was interrupted by a heckler.

Principal, Principle

Principal may be used in two ways. It can denote the head of a school, or it can be used as an adjective meaning "the main" or "the most important." **Principle** is used to indicate a law or a rule of conduct.

The *principal* addressed the teachers and the parents.

He was the *principal* speaker at the graduation exercises.

We are dedicated to the *principle* that all men are created equal.

Quite, Quiet

The adverb **quite** means "completely" or "very." The adjective **quiet** means "still" or "calm."

He was *quite* angry when he lost the game.

After his fit of temper, he became *quiet.*

Raise, Rise

Raise means "to lift" or "to bring up" something or someone. **Rise** means "to get up" or "to go up"; it does *not* take an object.

The guard *raised* his rifle when he heard a sound.

He *rises* in the morning when the sun rises.

Rob, Steal

One is said to **rob** a *person* or an *institution* such as a bank by taking property or valuables from it. One is said to **steal** an *object* such as personal property or valuables from someone or some institution.

The criminal was caught in the act of trying to *rob* the bank.

The criminal tried to *steal* the man's wallet.

Set, Sit

Set means "to put something in a certain place." **Sit** means "to be seated."

The delivery boy *set* the packages on the kitchen floor.

Please *sit* in this chair.

Stand, Stay

You **stand** when you are on your feet. (The past tense is *stood.*) You **stay** when you remain in a given place. (The past tense is *stayed.*)

He *stood* all the way home in the bus.

He *stayed* at the stadium until the game was over.

Stationary, Stationery

Stationary means "not moving" or "still." **Stationery** refers to writing paper, envelopes, and other office supplies.

The *stationary* animal provided an excellent target for the hunter.

The student bought his notebooks at the *stationery* store.

FREQUENT ERRORS IN WORD USE

1. **DON'T USE** the expression *could of, should of,* or *would of.* Instead, use the correct expression (with *have*) for which any of these spoken distortions is an incorrect substitute.

   WRONG:

   He could of been the winner if he had tried.

   CORRECT:

   He *could have* been the winner if he had tried.

2. **DON'T USE** the expression *different than.* Instead, use *different from.*

   WRONG:

   Playing baseball is different than playing softball.

   CORRECT:

   Playing baseball is *different from* playing softball.

3. **DON'T USE** incorrect prepositions.

   WRONG:

   May I borrow a dollar off you?

   CORRECT:

   May I borrow a dollar *from* you?

   WRONG:

   Come over our house for a party.

   CORRECT:

   Come *to* our house for a party.

4. **DON'T USE** *don't* in the third person singular. Use *doesn't,* which is the contraction of *does not.*

   WRONG:

   He don't belong here.

   CORRECT:

   He *doesn't* belong here.

5. **DON'T USE** *who's* when you mean *whose. Whose* should be used to show possession. *Who's* is a contraction of *who is.*

   WRONG:

   I know who's book this is.

   CORRECT:

   I know *whose* book this is.

PRACTICE WITH CONFUSED AND MISUSED WORDS

In each sentence, five parts are underlined and numbered. Choose the number of the underlined part that contains the error. If there are no errors, choose number 5. This kind of error is included in the sentence correction type of multiple-choice item.

1. The <u>number</u> of persons present this
        (1)
   time <u>was</u> much different <u>than</u> the
        (2)   (3)
   number <u>that</u> came last time.
          (4)
   <u>No error</u>
     (5)

2. <u>Fewer</u> visitors were allowed <u>in</u> our
      (1)   (2)
   hospital <u>than</u> <u>yours</u>.   <u>No error</u>
            (3)   (4)   (5)

3. We were <u>already</u> to leave <u>as</u> we had
             (1)   (2)
   been instructed had it not been for
   <u>him</u> and <u>her</u>. <u>No error</u>
   (3)   (4)   (5)

4. <u>Bring</u> this book to <u>whoever</u> you
   (1)   (2)
   think is most deserving <u>besides</u> <u>me</u>.
                           (3)   (4)
   <u>No error</u>
     (5)

5. Geraldo and <u>I</u> asked Conchita and
              (1)
   <u>him</u> whether <u>they'd</u> <u>except</u> the gift.
   (2)   (3)   (4)
   <u>No error</u>
     (5)

6. Anyone <u>may</u> ask a question about
           (1)
   any problem bothering <u>him</u> because
                         (2)
   it's the <u>kind of</u> situation which is
            (3)
   most <u>aggravating</u>. <u>No error</u>
        (4)   (5)

7. <u>Enclosed</u> <u>are</u> checks that
   (1)   (2)
   cover all the expenses <u>except</u> <u>hers</u>.
                         (3)   (4)
   <u>No error</u>
     (5)

8. Give the book to <u>whoever</u> asks for
                    (1)
   it despite the large <u>number</u> of
                        (2)
   requests and say it is a gift from
   <u>him</u> and <u>myself</u>. <u>No error</u>
   (3)   (4)   (5)

9. He considered it <u>altogether</u> <u>likely</u>
                    (1)   (2)
   that <u>less</u> accidents would occur
        (3)
   this year than last <u>since</u> the speed
                        (4)
   limit was changed. <u>No error</u>
                        (5)

10. Hector felt that, <u>among</u> the three of
                      (1)
    us who ran for office, the <u>number</u>
                               (2)
    of votes <u>should have proven</u> that
             (3)
    the winners were Enrique and
    <u>myself</u>. <u>No error</u>
    (4)   (5)

Answer Key

1. **3**	3. **1**	5. **4**	7. **5**	9 **3**
2. **2**	4. **1**	6. **4**	8. **4**	10. **4**

WHAT'S YOUR SCORE?

_____ right, _____ wrong

Excellent	9–10
Good	7–8
Fair	6

If you scored lower, restudy this section, concentrating on the differences between the pairs of words and the ten errors in word use to avoid.

Answer Analysis

1. **3** Use *different from* rather than *different than*.

2. **2** *Into* must be used to indicate that the visitors are moving from the outside to the inside of the hospital.

3. **1** *All ready* must be used in the meaning of *all* prepared.

4. **1** *Take* should be used when the movement in the sentence is away from the speaker or writer.

5. **4** *Accept* is used to mean "to receive something."

6. **4** The verb *irritate* should be used since the required meaning is "annoying."

7. **5** No error.

8. **4** Since neither emphasis nor an object of an action verb is required, *me* should be used.

9. **3** *Fewer* should be used since the accidents can be counted.

10. **4** Since neither emphasis nor an object of an action verb is needed in this sentence, *I* should be used.

WORDINESS: THE PROBLEM OF TOO MANY WORDS

Wordiness, the use of more words than is necessary, is a frequent weakness of many speakers and writers. It is particularly undesirable when it confuses the reader.

Some sentences contain words or phrases that are unnecessary.

My friend *he* is a baseball fan.

In this sentence, both the noun *friend* and the pronoun *he* are unnecessary when referring to the same person. Either *friend* or *he* may be used, but not both words.

This *here* pen writes better than that *there* one.

Both *here* and *there* are not needed. *This* means nearer than another person or thing referred to as *that.*

Take your feet off *of* the table.

Off means "so as to be no longer on." The word *of* in the sentence is superfluous.

Whatever he does, he does *it* well.

The pronoun *it* isn't needed. In fact, the pronoun replaces nothing in the sentence and what *it* refers to isn't clear.

Some sentences contain words that are repetitive since they restate parts of the meaning of other words in the sentence.

I have a friend *of mine* who helps me with my housework.

In this sentence, *mine* means "belonging to me," and the idea is already contained in the words *I have.* Therefore, *of mine* should be eliminated from the sentence.

I have to be at work at 9 A.M. *in the morning.*

In this sentence, A.M. means "ante meridiem" or "before noon." It conveys the idea of *morning.* Therefore, the phrase *in the morning* isn't needed.

Congress has decided to refer the matter *back* to committee.

The word *refer,* contains a prefix (*re-*) which means "back." Therefore, the word *back* is unnecessary. A similar incorrect expression is "return back."

Some sentences contain words that unnecessarily repeat other words in the sentence.

We left after *the conclusion of* the concert.

After means "later than," so the words *the conclusion of* are unnecessary.

Helen Keller wrote an autobiography *of her life.*

An *autobiography* is the story of one's life; *of her life* should be omitted.

In my opinion, *I think* the criminal should be pardoned.

In this sentence, *think* means to "hold an opinion," so either *in my opinion* or *I think* can safely be dispensed with.

PRACTICE

1. That there book belongs to me.
2. Despite the rain, the umpires decided to continue on with the game.
3. Please refer back to page 12 in the book.
4. My parents they are completely devoted to me.
5. I usually go to bed at 11:00 P.M. at night.
6. When I was eighteen years old, I graduated from high school.

ANSWERS

1. That book belongs to me.
2. Despite the rain, the umpires decided to continue the game.
3. Please refer to page 12 in the book.
4. My parents are completely devoted to me.
5. I usually go to bed at 11:00 P.M.
6. When I was eighteen, I graduated from high school.

PRACTICE WITH WORDINESS

Beneath each sentence you will find five ways of writing the underlined part. Choose the answer that makes the best sentence. Answer 1 is always the same as the underlined part and is sometimes the right answer.

1. <u>After the conclusion of the game, my friend, he decided to return back</u> home.

   (1) After the conclusion of the game, my friend, he decided to return back
   (2) After the conclusion of the game, my friend decided to return back
   (3) After the conclusion of the game, my friend decided to return
   (4) After the game, my friend decided to return back
   (5) After the game, my friend decided to return

2. At this <u>point in time, type up five copies of this here</u> contract.

   (1) point in time, type up five copies of this here
   (2) point in time, type five copies of this here
   (3) time, type five copies of this
   (4) time, type five copies of this here
   (5) time, type up five copies of this

3. Because we cooperated <u>together, we divided up the work on the report that was assigned.</u>

   (1) together, we divided up the work on the report that was assigned
   (2) together, we divided the work on the report that was assigned
   (3) , we divided up the work on the report that was assigned
   (4) , we divided the work on the assigned report
   (5) , we divided up the work on the assigned report

4. Mr. Steele, <u>who was president of the company, repeated again what he had said while we were having</u> dinner.

   (1) who was president of the company, repeated again what he had said while we were having
   (2) who was president of the company, repeated what he had said while we were having
   (3) president of the company, repeated what he had said while we were having
   (4) president of the company, repeated again what he had said during
   (5) president of the company, repeated what he had said during

5. At 8:00 P.M. <u>in the evening, he continued on his walk, which was enjoyable.</u>

   (1) in the evening, he continued on his walk, which was enjoyable
   (2) he continued on his walk, which was enjoyable
   (3) he continued on his enjoyable walk
   (4) in the evening, he continued his enjoyable walk
   (5) he continued his enjoyable walk

6. <u>A large crowd of people waited outside of</u> the building.

   (1) A large crowd of people waited outside of
   (2) A crowd waited outside
   (3) A crowd waited outside of
   (4) There was a large crowd of people who waited outside of
   (5) There was a large crowd who waited outside of

7. The senator <u>rose up to say that, in his opinion, he thought the bill should be referred back to</u> committee.

(1) rose up to say that, in his opinion, he thought the bill should be referred back to
(2) rose up to say that he thought the bill should be referred back
(3) rose up to say that he thought the bill should be back
(4) rose up to say that, in his opinion, the bill should be referred
(5) rose to say that he thought the bill should be referred

8. My wife wanted <u>that I should return to school when I was thirty years of age</u>.

(1) that I should return to school when I was thirty years of age
(2) that I should return back to school when I was thirty years of age
(3) me to return back to school when I was thirty years of age
(4) me to return to school when I was thirty years of age
(5) me to return to school when I was thirty

Answer Key

| 1. **5** | 3. **4** | 5. **5** | 7. **5** |
| 2. **3** | 4. **5** | 6. **2** | 8. **5** |

WHAT'S YOUR SCORE?

_____ right,   _____ wrong

Excellent	7–8
Good	6
Fair	5

If you scored lower, review the four kinds of wordiness illustrated in this section.

Answer Analysis

1. **5** *The conclusion of, he,* and *back* are all included in the meanings of other words in the sentence.

2. **3** *Point in, up,* and *here* are all included in the meanings of other words in the sentence.

3. **4** *Together* and *up* are included in the meanings of other words in the sentence. The adjective *assigned* is preferable stylistically to the adjective clause *that was assigned.*

4. **5** *Again* is unnecessary. The appositive, *president,* is preferable to the adjective clause *who was president.* The preposition *during* is preferable to the adverb clause *while we were having.*

5. **5** *In the evening* and *on* are included in the meanings of other words in the sentence. The adjective *enjoyable* is preferable to the adjective clause *which was enjoyable.*

6. **2** The words *large* and *of* are unnecessary. *That* is preferable to *who* when it refers to a neuter noun such as *crowd.*

7. **5** The words *up, in his opinion,* and *back* are unnecessary.

8. **5** The words *years of age* are unnecessary. The expression *that I should* is clumsy and can easily be replaced by the words *me to.*

A BASIC 650-WORD VOCABULARY

Here is a list of 650 basic words to help you build your vocabulary. For each word, a definition is provided. You should use these lists together with a good dictionary such as *Webster's New World Dictionary of the American Language.*

200 USEFUL NOUNS

ACCESS (means of) approach or admittance (to records)

ACCORD agreement

AFFLUENCE abundance; wealth (age of _____)

AGENDA list of things to be done or discussed (at a meeting)

ALIAS assumed name (Fred Henry, _____ John Doe)

ANIMOSITY great hatred (toward strangers)

ANTHOLOGY collection of writings or other creative work such as songs

ATLAS book of maps

AUDACITY boldness

AVARICE greed for wealth

AWE feeling of respect and wonder (in _____ of someone's power)

BIGOTRY unwillingness to allow others to have different opinions and beliefs from one's own

BLEMISH defect (on one's record)

BONDAGE slavery

BOON benefit (a _____ to business)

BRAWL noisy fight

BREVITY shortness

BULWARK strong protection (a _____ against corruption)

CALIBER quality (a person of high _____)

CAMOUFLAGE disguise, usually in war, by changing the appearance of persons or material

CASTE social class or distinction

CATASTROPHE sudden disaster (an earthquake)

CHRONICLE historical record

CLAMOR uproar

CONDOLENCE expression of sympathy (extended _____ to a bereaved)

CONNOISSEUR expert judge (of paintings, food)

CONSENSUS general agreement

CONTEXT words or ideas just before or after a given word or idea (meaning of a word in a given _____)

CRITERION standard of judgment (good or poor by this _____)

CRUX the essential point (the _____ of the matter)

DATA known facts (_____ were found through research)

DEBUT first appearance before an audience (actor, pianist)

DELUGE great flood (rain or, in a special sense, mail)

DEPOT warehouse

DESTINY predetermined fate (it was his _____ to)

DIAGNOSIS determination of the nature of a disease or a situation

DILEMMA situation requiring a choice between two unpleasant courses of action (he was in a _____)

DIN loud, continuing noise

DISCORD disagreement

DISCREPANCY inconsistency (in accounts, in testimony)

DISSENT difference of opinion (from a decision)

DROUGHT long spell of dry weather

ELITE choice part or element (of society)

ENVIRONMENT surrounding influences or conditions

EPOCH period of time associated with an important person or event (the _____ of spaceflight)

ERA period of time marked by an important person or event (the Napoleonic _____)

ESSENCE basic nature (of the matter)

ETIQUETTE rules of social behavior that are generally accepted

EXCERPT passage from a book or a document

EXODUS departure, usually of large numbers

FALLACY mistaken idea; reasoning that contains an error

FANTASY imagination (he indulged in _____)

FEUD continued deadly hatred (between two families)

FIASCO complete, humiliating failure

FIEND inhumanly cruel person

FINALE last part or performance

FLAIR natural talent (for sports)

FLAW defect

FOCUS central point (of attention)

FOE enemy

FORMAT physical appearance or arrangement (of a book)

FORTITUDE steady courage (when in trouble)

FORUM a gathering for the discussion of public issues

FOYER entrance hall (to a building or dwelling)

FRAUD deliberate deception

FRICTION rubbing of the surface of one thing against the surface of another

FUNCTION purpose served by a person, object, or organization

GHETTO section of a city where members of a particular group (formerly religious, now usually racial) live

GIST essential content (of a speech or an article)

GLUTTON one who overeats or indulges in anything else to excess

GRIEVANCE complaint made against someone responsible for a situation believed to be unjust

HAVOC great damage and destruction (wreak _____ on)

HAZARD danger

HERITAGE inheritance either of real wealth or of a tradition

HOAX deliberate attempt to trick someone, done either with serious intent or as a joke

HORDE crowd

HORIZON limit (of knowledge, experience, or ambition)

HUE shade of color

HYSTERIA wild emotional outburst

IDIOM expression peculiar to a language that, as a whole, has a different meaning from the words that comprise it (hit the road)

ILLUSION idea or impression different from reality

IMAGE likeness or reflected impression of a person or object

INCENTIVE spur or motive to do something (profit _____)

INCUMBENT present holder of an office

INFLUX flowing in (of money into banks, tourists into a country)

INFRACTION violation of a rule or a law

INITIATIVE desire or ability to take the first step in carrying out some action (often a new plan or idea)

INNOVATION introduction of a new idea or method

INTEGRITY moral and intellectual honesty and uprightness

INTERIM meantime (in the _____)

INTERLUDE period of time between two events (_____ between the acts of a play)

INTRIGUE secret plot

INTUITION knowledge derived through instinct rather than thought

ITINERARY route followed on a trip, actual or planned

JEOPARDY risk of harm (put into _____)

KEYNOTE main theme (He sounded the _____ of the convention)

LARCENY theft (The jury couldn't decide whether the crime was grand or petty _____)

LAYPERSON one who is not a member of a particular profession (from the point of view of a _____)

LEGACY material or spiritual inheritance (from a parent)

LEGEND story passed on from generation to generation and often considered to be true

LORE body of traditional knowledge (nature _____)

MALADY disease (incurable _____)

MANEUVER skillful move (a clever _____)

MARATHON contest requiring endurance

MEDIA means of communication (_____ of radio and television)

MEMENTO object that serves as a reminder (a _____ of the war)

METROPOLIS main city of a state or region (or any large city)

MORALE state of mind as it affects possible future action (The troops had good _____)

MULTITUDE a large number

MYTH a story that is a traditional explanation of some occurrence, usually in nature (the _____ of Atlas holding up the heavens)

NICHE suitable and desirable place (He found his _____ in the business organization)

NOMAD wanderer

NOSTALGIA desire to return to past experiences or associations

ODYSSEY long journey

OMEN something that is believed to predict a future event (an evil _____)

OPTIMUM best possible quantity or quality (He participated to the _____)

OVATION enthusiastic reception usually accompanied by generous applause (He received a tumultuous _____)

OVERSIGHT failure to include something through carelessness (His name was omitted because of an _____)

PAGEANT public spectacle in the form of a stage performance or a parade (a historical _____)

PANORAMA clear view of a very broad area

PARADOX statement of a truth that appears to contradict itself (a 20-year-old who had only five birthdays because he was born on February 29)

PASTIME way of spending leisure time (He took up golf as a _____)

PAUPER very poor person

PEER an equal in age, social standing, ability, or other feature

PHENOMENON event that can be scientifically explained, such as the tides

PITFALL trap

PITTANCE very small sum of money (He survived on a _____)

PLATEAU area of level land located at a height

PLIGHT condition, usually unfavorable (the sorry _____ of the refugees)

POISE calm and controlled manner of behavior (He showed _____ in difficult situations)

PREDICAMENT unpleasant situation from which it is difficult to free oneself (He found himself in a _____)

PREFACE introductory statement to a book or speech

PRELUDE something that is preliminary to a more important act or work

PREMISE statement from which a conclusion is logically drawn (Granted the _____ that..., we may conclude...)

PREMIUM amount added to the usual payment or charge (He paid a _____ for the seats)

PRESTIGE respect achieved through rank, achievement, or reputation

PRETEXT reason given as a cover-up for the true purpose of an action (He gave as a _____ for stealing the ring, his sentimental attachment to it)

PRIORITY something that ranks before others in importance (He gave _____ to his studies)

PROCESS step-by-step system for accomplishing some purpose (the _____ of legislation)

PROSPECT outlook for the future (the _____ of peace)

PROXIMITY nearness

PSEUDONYM assumed name, usually by an author (Mark Twain, _____ of Samuel Clemens)

PUN play on words depending on two different meanings or sounds of the same word (Whether life is worth living depends on the *liver*)

QUANDARY uncertainty over a choice between two courses of action (He was in a _____ between the careers of law or medicine)

QUERY question

QUEST search (_____ for knowledge)

RARITY something not commonly found (A talent like his is a _____)

REFUGE place to which one can go for protection (He found _____ in the church)

REMNANT remaining part (_____ of the troops)

REMORSE deep feeling of guilt for some bad act (He felt _____ at having insulted his friend)

RENDEZVOUS a meeting or a place for meeting

REPLICA an exact copy (_____ of a painting)

REPRIMAND severe criticism in the form of a scolding (He received a _____ from his superior)

RESIDUE remainder

RESOURCES assets, either material or spiritual, that are available for use

RESPITE temporary break that brings relief (_____ from work)

RÉSUMÉ summary

REVERENCE feeling of great respect (_____ for life)

ROBOT one who acts mechanically or like a mechanical man

ROSTER list of names (_____ of guests)

SABOTAGE deliberate damage to vital services of production and supply, usually to those of an enemy in wartime

SAGA long tale, usually of heroic deeds

SALUTATION greeting, written or spoken (The _____ of a letter may be "Dear Sir")

SARCASM use of cutting remarks

SATIRE attack upon evil or foolish behavior by showing it to be ridiculous

SCAPEGOAT person who is blamed for the bad deeds of others

SCENT distinctive smell

SCOPE entire area of action or thought (the _____ of the plan)

SEGMENT part or section of a whole (_____ of a population)

SEQUEL something that follows from what happened or was written before (_____ to a novel)

SILHOUETTE outline drawing in black

SITE location of an object or an action (original _____ of a building)

SLANDER untruth spoken or spread about a person that damages his or her reputation

SLOGAN motto that is associated with an action or a cause (Pike's Peak or bust!)

SLOPE slant (_____ of a line)

SNARE trap

SOLACE comfort (She found _____ in work)

SPONSOR person or organization that endorses and supports an individual, an activity, or a cause

SPUR something that moves one to act (a _____ to sacrifice)

STAMINA ability to fight off physical difficulties such as fatigue and cold

STATURE height reached physically or morally (a man of great _____)

STATUS standing, social or professional

STIMULUS any encouragement to act

STRATEGY skillful planning and execution (the _____ in a battle)

STRIFE conflict (_____ between labor and management)

SUMMIT the highest point (the _____ of his career)

SUPPLEMENT amount added to complete something (_____ to a budget)

SURVEY broad study of a topic (a _____ of employment)

SUSPENSE tenseness brought about by uncertainty as to what will happen

SYMBOL something that is used to represent something else (Uncle Sam is a _____ of the United States)

SYMPTOM indication of something (_____ of disease)

SYNOPSIS brief summary

TACT ability to say and do the appropriate thing

TALLY record of a score or an account (the _____ of the receipts)

TECHNIQUE method or skill in doing work (the _____ of an artist)

TEMPERAMENT natural disposition, often to act in a contrary manner (He displayed a changeable _____)

TEMPO pace of activity (The _____ of life is increasing)

TENSION mental or emotional strain (She was under great _____)

THEME topic of a written work or a talk

THRESHOLD starting point (the _____ of a career)

TINT shade of color

TOKEN sign that stands for some object or feeling (a _____ of esteem)

TONIC something that is a source of energy or vigor

TRADITION body of customs and beliefs received by one generation from another

TRAIT distinguishing feature (_____ of character)

TRANSITION movement from one situation to another (_____ from dictatorship to democracy)

TRIBUTE display of respect or gratitude (He paid a _____ to his parents)

TURMOIL disturbance (great _____ at the meeting)

TUTOR private teacher

ULTIMATUM final ("Take it or leave it") offer

UNREST restless dissatisfaction

UPHEAVAL sudden overthrow, often violent

UTENSIL useful implement (a kitchen _____)

UTOPIA ideal place or society

VALOR courage

VENTURE undertaking that involves risk

VICINITY neighborhood

VICTOR winner

VIGOR vitality

VIM energy

VOW solemn pledge

WAGER bet

WHIM sudden notion or desire

WOE great sorrow (He brought _____ to his friends)

WRATH intense anger (He poured his _____ on his enemies)

ZEAL eager desire

ZEST keen enthusiasm (_____ for competition)

200 USEFUL VERBS

ABSOLVE free from guilt (for a crime)

ACCEDE agree to (a request)

ACCELERATE speed up

ADJOURN put off to a later time (a meeting)

ADVOCATE act in support of (revolution)

ALLEGE claim

ALLOT assign (a share)

ALLUDE refer to (a book)

ALTER change

ASSENT agree

ATONE make up for (a sin)

AUGMENT add to

AVERT prevent

BAN forbid

BAR exclude

CEDE give up (territory)

CHASTISE punish

CITE mention in order to prove something

COERCE force

COLLABORATE work with someone

COMMEND praise

CONCUR agree

CURTAIL cut short or reduce

DEDUCE draw a conclusion from given facts

DEEM consider

DEFER postpone

DELETE remove or erase (a word)

DEPLORE regret

DEPRIVE keep someone from having or getting something

DESPISE scorn

DETAIN delay temporarily

DETECT uncover something that is not obvious

DETEST hate

DETRACT take away from

DEVOUR eat greedily

DIGRESS depart from the subject under consideration

DILUTE weaken by adding something less strong (a mixture)

DISINTEGRATE fall apart

DISPEL drive away

DISPERSE scatter

DISRUPT break up

DISTORT present incorrectly (facts)

DIVERGE go in different directions

DIVULGE reveal

EJECT throw out

ENCOUNTER meet

ENDEAVOR try

ENHANCE increase the quality or value of

ENSUE follow as a result

ERR make a mistake

ERUPT break out

EVADE avoid or escape from someone or something

EXCEED surpass

EXTOL praise highly

FALTER stumble

FAMISH starve

FEIGN pretend

FLOURISH thrive

FOIL prevent

FORSAKE abandon

FRUSTRATE prevent someone from achieving a goal

GAUGE estimate

HARASS disturb constantly

HEAVE lift and throw

HEED pay attention to (advice)

HINDER keep back

HURL throw with force

IGNITE set fire to

IMMERSE plunge into a liquid

IMPAIR damage

IMPLY suggest

INCITE arouse

INFER come to a conclusion based on something known

INSTIGATE spur to action

INTERROGATE question

INTIMIDATE frighten by making threats

IRK annoy

JEER poke fun at (by sarcastic remarks)

LAMENT feel sorrow for

LAUNCH set in motion

LOP cut off

LURE tempt

LURK remain hidden, usually for an evil purpose

MAGNIFY enlarge

MAIM cripple

MIMIC imitate

MOCK ridicule

MOLEST annoy

NARRATE tell (a story)

NAVIGATE steer (a ship)

NEGATE deny

ORIENT adjust oneself or someone else to a situation or place

OUST expel

PEND remain undecided

PERFECT complete

PERPLEX puzzle

PERTAIN have reference to

PERTURB upset greatly

PERUSE read carefully

PRECLUDE prevent something from happening

PRESCRIBE order (for use or as a course of action)

PRESUME take for granted

PREVAIL win out over

PROBE investigate thoroughly

PROCURE obtain

PROSPER be successful

PROTRUDE project

PROVOKE arouse to action out of irritation

PRY look closely into

QUELL subdue

REBATE give back, usually part of an amount paid

REBUKE reprimand

RECEDE move backward

RECONCILE bring together by settling differences

RECTIFY correct

RECUR happen again

REFRAIN keep from

REIMBURSE pay back

REITERATE repeat

REJECT refuse to take

RELINQUISH give up

REMINISCE recall past happenings

REMUNERATE pay for work or other service done

RENOUNCE give up (a claim)

RENOVATE restore (a house)

REPENT regret (a sin)

REPOSE rest

REPROACH blame

REPULSE drive back (an attack)

RESTRAIN hold back

RETAIN keep

RETALIATE return in kind (a blow for a blow)

RETARD delay

RETRIEVE get back

REVERE have deep respect for

SCAN look at closely; look over quickly

SCOFF mock

SCORN treat with contempt

SCOUR clean thoroughly; move about widely in a search

SCOWL look angry

SEEP ooze

SEETHE boil

SEVER divide

SHED throw off (clothing)

SHIRK seek to avoid (duty or work)

SHUN avoid

SHUNT turn aside

SIFT sort out through careful examination (evidence)

SIGNIFY mean

SINGE burn slightly

SKIM read over quickly

SMITE hit hard

SNARL tangle

SOAR fly high in the air

SPURN reject scornfully

STARTLE surprise

STIFLE suppress (feelings)

STREW scatter

STRIVE try hard

STUN daze

SUBSIDE lessen in activity

SUCCUMB yield to

SUFFICE be enough

SURGE increase suddenly

SURMOUNT overcome (an obstacle)

SUSTAIN support

SWAY move back and forth

TAMPER meddle with

TARNISH discolor

TAUNT reproach mockingly

THAW melt

THRASH defeat thoroughly

THRIVE prosper

THROB beat insistently

THRUST push forcefully and suddenly

THWART prevent someone from achieving a goal

TINGE color slightly

TORMENT afflict with pain

TRANSFORM change the appearance of

TRANSMIT send along

TRUDGE walk slowly and wearily

UNDERGO experience

UNDO return to condition that existed before something was done

USURP seize power illegally

UTILIZE make use of

UTTER speak

VACATE make empty

VANQUISH conquer

VARY change

VEND sell

VERIFY prove the truth of

VEX annoy

VIBRATE move back and forth

VIOLATE break (a law)

VOUCH guarantee

WAIVE give up (a right or privilege)

WANE decrease in strength

WAVER sway back and forth

WHET sharpen

WIELD put to use (power or a tool such as a club)

WITHSTAND hold out against (pressure)

WREST pull violently

YEARN long for

YIELD give up

250 USEFUL ADJECTIVES

ADAMANT unyielding

ADEPT skilled

ADROIT skillful

AESTHETIC having to do with beauty

AGILE nimble

AMBIDEXTROUS equally skilled with both hands

AMENABLE disposed to follow (advice)

AMIABLE friendly

APT suitable

ARDENT passionate

ARROGANT over proud

ARTICULATE able to express oneself cleary (an _____ person)

ASTUTE shrewd

AUTHENTIC genuine

BARREN unfruitful

BIZARRE strange

BLAND gentle; soothing

BLATANT overloud

BOISTEROUS rambunctious

BRUSQUE rudely brief

CALLOUS unfeeling

CANDID honest

CASUAL offhand

CHIC stylish

CHRONIC continuing over a long period of time

CIVIC municipal

CIVIL courteous

COLOSSAL huge

COMPATIBLE capable of getting along together

CONCISE brief but complete

CRAFTY sly

CREDIBLE believable

CUMBERSOME bulky

CURT rudely brief

DEMURE modest; reserved

DEROGATORY belittling

DESOLATE lonely

DESTITUTE poverty-stricken

DETERGENT cleansing

DEVIOUS indirect

DEVOID completely free of (feeling)

DEVOUT very religious

DIMINUTIVE tiny

DIRE dreadful

DISCREET careful

DISINTERESTED impartial

DISMAL gloomy

DISTRAUGHT driven to distraction

DIVERSE varied

DOMESTIC having to do with the home

DOMINANT ruling

DORMANT sleeping

DRASTIC extreme (changes)

DREARY gloomy

DUBIOUS doubtful

DURABLE lasting

DYNAMIC energetic

EARNEST intensely serious

EBONY black

ECCENTRIC peculiar (behavior)

EDIBLE fit to be eaten

EERIE weird

ELEGANT tastefully fine

ELOQUENT powerfully fluent in writing or speech

ELUSIVE hard to get hold of

EMINENT distinguished (author)

EPIC heroic in size

ERRATIC not regular

ETERNAL everlasting

ETHNIC having to do with race

EXORBITANT unreasonable (price)

EXOTIC foreign

EXPLICIT clearly indicated

EXTEMPORANEOUS spoken or accomplished with little preparation

EXTENSIVE broad

FANATIC extremely enthusiastic

FEASIBLE possible to carry out (a _____ plan)

FEEBLE weak

FERTILE productive

FERVENT warmly felt

FESTIVE in the spirit of a holiday (celebration)

FICKLE changeable

FLAGRANT noticeably bad (violation)

FLEET swift

FLIMSY not strong (platform)

FLUENT smooth (speech)

FORMIDABLE fear-inspiring because of size or strength (enemy)

FRAGILE easily broken

FRAIL delicate

FRANK outspoken

FRATERNAL brotherly

FRIGID extremely cold

FRUGAL thrifty

FUTILE useless

GALA festive

GALLANT courteously brave (conduct)

GENIAL kindly

GIGANTIC huge

GLUM gloomy

GORY bloody

GRAPHIC vividly realistic

GRATIS free

GRIM sternly forbidding (future)

GROSS glaringly bad (injustice)

GRUESOME horrifying

HAPHAZARD chance

HARSH disagreeably rough

HEARTY friendly (welcome)

HECTIC feverish

HEINOUS outrageous (crime)

HIDEOUS extremely ugly

HILARIOUS very merry, mirthful

HOMOGENEOUS of like kind (group)

HORRENDOUS horrible

HOSTILE unfriendly (unwelcome)

HUMANE merciful

HUMBLE modest

HUMID damp

IMMACULATE spotlessly clean

IMMENSE very large

IMMINENT about to happen (storm)

IMPARTIAL unbiased

IMPERATIVE necessary

IMPERTINENT rude

IMPROMPTU without any preparation (remarks)

IMPUDENT rudely bold

INCESSANT uninterrupted

INCLEMENT rough (weather)

INCOHERENT not clearly connected

INDELIBLE unable to be erased

INDIFFERENT showing no interest

INDIGENT poor

INDIGNANT very angry

INDISPENSABLE absolutely necessary

INDUSTRIOUS hard-working

INEPT ineffective

INFAMOUS having a bad reputation

INFINITE endless

INFLEXIBLE unbending

INGENIOUS clever

INNATE inborn

INNOCUOUS harmless

INSOLENT boldly rude

INTENSIVE thorough (study)

INTERMITTENT starting and stopping (rain)

INTOLERANT unwilling or unable to respect others or their beliefs

INTRICATE complicated

INVINCIBLE unable to be conquered

IRATE angry

IRRATIONAL unreasonable

JOVIAL good-humored

JUBILANT joyous

LABORIOUS demanding a lot of work

LATENT hidden (talent)

LAVISH extremely generous (praise)

LAX loose (discipline)

LEGIBLE easily read (print)

LEGITIMATE lawful (claim)

LETHAL fatal

LOATH reluctant

LOFTY very high

LUCID clear

LUCRATIVE profitable (business)

MAJESTIC grand (building)

MALICIOUS spiteful

MALIGNANT harmful

MAMMOTH gigantic

MANUAL done by the hands (labor)

MARINE of the sea (life)

MARTIAL warlike

MASSIVE bulky and heavy

MEAGER scanty

MENIAL lowly (task)

METICULOUS extremely careful

MILITANT aggressive

MOBILE movable (home)

MUTUAL reciprocal (admiration)

NAIVE innocently simple

NAUSEOUS disgusting

NEGLIGENT neglectful

NEUROTIC describing the behavior of a person suffering from an emotional disorder

NIMBLE moving quickly and easily

NONCHALANT casual and unexcited

NOTABLE important (person)

NOTORIOUS well-known in an unfavorable way (criminal)

NULL having no effect

OBESE very fat

OBJECTIVE free from prejudice (analysis)

OBNOXIOUS extremely unpleasant (behavior)

OBSOLETE out-of-date (machine)

OBSTINATE stubborn

OMINOUS threatening (clouds)

OPPORTUNE timely

ORTHODOX usually approved (religious beliefs)

OUTRIGHT complete

PARAMOUNT chief (importance)

PASSIVE not active (participation)

PATHETIC pitiful

PERILOUS dangerous

PERTINENT relevant

PETTY relatively unimportant

PIOUS devoutly religious

PLACID calm (waters)

PLAUSIBLE apparently true (argument)

POIGNANT keenly painful to the emotions

POMPOUS self-important (person)

PORTABLE capable of being carried (radio)

POSTHUMOUS taking place after a person's death (award)

POTENT powerful (drug)

POTENTIAL possible (greatness)

PRECARIOUS risky

PRECISE exact

PREDOMINANT prevailing

PREPOSTEROUS ridiculous

PREVALENT widespread

PRIMARY fundamental (reason)

PRIME first in importance or quality

PRIMITIVE crude (tools)

PRIOR previous (appointment)

PRODIGIOUS extraordinary in size or amount (effort)

PROFICIENT skilled

PROSAIC ordinary

PRUDENT discreet (advice)

PUNY small in size or slight in strength (effort)

PUTRID rotten

QUAINT pleasantly odd (custom)

RAMPANT spreading unchecked (violence)

RANCID having the bad taste or smell of stale food (butter)

RANDOM decided by chance (choice)

RASH reckless

RAUCOUS harsh (sound)

REFLEX referring to an involuntary response (action)

REGAL royal

RELENTLESS persistent (chase)

RELEVANT pertinent

REMOTE far distant (time or place)

REPULSIVE disgusting

REPUTABLE respectable (doctor)

RESIGNED submitting passively to (one's fate)

RESOLUTE firmly determined

RETICENT speaking little (child)

RIGID stiff

ROBUST strong and healthy

ROWDY rough and disorderly (mob)

RUGGED rough

RUTHLESS pitiless (dictator)

SAGE wise (advice)

SALUTARY healthful (climate)

SANE mentally sound

SCANTY meager

SCHOLASTIC having to do with school and education (record)

SCRUPULOUS careful and honest (accounting)

SEDATE dignified

SERENE calm

SHEER very thin (stockings); utter (nonsense)

SHREWD clever in one's dealings (businessperson)

SIMULTANEOUS happening at the same time (events)

SINGULAR remarkable; strange (behavior)

SINISTER threatening evil

SKEPTICAL showing doubt (attitude)

SLENDER small in size or amount (contribution)

SLUGGISH slow-moving

SNUG comfortable

SOBER serious

SOLEMN grave (occasion)

SOLITARY lone

SOMBER dark and gloomy (outlook)

SOPHISTICATED wise in the ways of the world

SPARSE thinly scattered

SPIRITUAL referring to the spirit or soul

SPONTANEOUS happening as a result of natural impulse (reaction)

SPORADIC happening at irregular times (shooting)

SPRY nimble

STALWART robust

STARK bleak (outlook)

STATELY dignified

STATIC stationary

STATIONARY not moving

STEADFAST firm

STERN severe (look)

STOUT fat; firm (resistance)

STRAIGHTFORWARD honest (answer)

STRENUOUS demanding great energy (exercise)

STURDY strongly built

SUAVE smoothly polite (manner)

SUBLIME inspiring admiration because of noble quality (music)

SUBSIDIARY less important (rank)

SUBSTANTIAL having considerable numbers or size

SUBTLE suggested delicately (hint)

SULLEN resentful

SUMPTUOUS costly (meal)

SUNDRY various

SUPERB of a high degree of excellence

SUPERFICIAL not going beyond the obvious (examination)

SUPERFLUOUS beyond what is needed

SUPERLATIVE superior to all others (performance)

SUSCEPTIBLE easily affected by

TANGIBLE capable of being touched; actual (results)

TARDY late (student)

TART having a sharp taste (food)

TAUT tightly stretched (rope)

TEDIOUS long and tiresome (study)

TENACIOUS holding fast (grip)

TENTATIVE temporary for a period of trial (agreement)

TEPID lukewarm (water)

TERMINAL concluding

TERSE brief but expressive (comment)

TIDY neat (appearance)

TIMELY happening at a desirable time (arrival)

TIMID shy

TIRESOME tiring

TITANIC having enormous size or strength

TORRID intensely hot

TRANQUIL calm (waters)

TRANSIENT passing away after a brief time

TRIFLING having little importance

TRITE ordinary (remark)

TRIVIAL insignificant

TURBULENT agitated

ULTIMATE final (conclusion)

UNANIMOUS in complete agreement (decision)

UNASSUMING modest

UNCANNY unnatural (accuracy)

UNDAUNTED not discouraged

UNDERHAND sly

UNIQUE being the only one of its kind (specimen)

UNRULY disorderly (crowd)

UNWIELDY clumsy to use, usually because of size (implement)

UPRIGHT honest (citizen)

UTMOST most extreme (in distance, height or size)

VAIN futile (attempt); conceited (person)

VALIANT brave

VALID (legally) sound (argument)

VAST very large in extent or size (distances)

VEHEMENT violent in feeling (protest)

VERBATIM word for word (report)

VERSATILE able to perform many tasks well (athlete)

VIGILANT watchful (sentry)

VILE highly disgusting (conduct)

VISIBLE able to be seen (object)

VITAL essential (contribution)

VIVACIOUS lively

VIVID bright (color)

VULNERABLE open to attack (position)

WARY cautious

WEARY tired

WEE very small

WEIGHTY important (decision)

WHOLESOME causing a feeling of well-being (entertainment)

WILY cunning (magician)

WITTY amusingly clever (remark)

WORDY using too many words (reply)

WORTHY deserving (choice)

WRETCHED miserable

Practice with Sample Test Paragraphs

This chapter presents a fully analyzed sample GED test paragraph and three additional paragraphs, with answers, for practice.

PRACTICE TEST PARAGRAPH 1

The following items are based on a paragraph that contains numbered sentences. Some of the sentences may contain errors in sentence structure, usage, or mechanics. <u>A few sentences, however, may be correct as written.</u> Read the paragraph and then answer the items based on it. For each item, choose the answer that would result in the most effective writing of the sentence or sentences. The best answer must be consistent with the meaning and tone of the rest of the paragraph.

(1) Savings has been referred to as the tool for accomplishing future goals. (2) After a family has decided on a savings plan the decision on how to invest wisely must be made. (3) Life insurance is a way to provide immediate financial protection for the loss of income through the death of the breadwinner. (4) Once children are expected, the need arises for life insurance. (5) Life insurance is purchased to cover the cost of the funeral, to pay the expenses of the last illness, and to provide income for the survivors. (6) When planning for this type of financial protection, be sure to consider all resources the survivors will have to use (earning ability as well as financial) the amount of income that will meet necessities, and finally the cost of such a program. (7)

Concentrate insurance dollars on the breadwinner, and buy the type of insurance that will give the most protection for the cost. (8) A savings account is the second leg of the stool for a savings program. (9) It is here where a family keeps the money that it may need immediately or plans to use within the near future. (10) After the family will protect itself with insurance for the survivors and with a savings account, it is then ready to invest in other possible channels. (11) At this point a family needs to consider these channels in line with its distant goals and with the economy.

1. Sentence 1. **Savings has been referred to as the tool for accomplishing future goals.**

   What correction should be made to this sentence?

   (1) change <u>has</u> to <u>have</u>
   (2) change the spelling of <u>referred</u> to <u>refered</u>
   (3) insert a comma after <u>to</u>
   (4) change the spelling of <u>accomplishing</u> to <u>acomplishing</u>
   (5) no correction is necessary

2. Sentence 2. **After a family has decided on a savings plan the decision on how to invest wisely must be made.**

What correction should be made to this sentence?

(1) change has to have
(2) insert an apostrophe after savings
(3) insert a comma after plan
(4) change the spelling of decision to descision
(5) change how to invest to how to have invested

3. Sentence 3. **Life insurance is a way to provide immediate financial protection for the loss of income through the death of the breadwinner.**

Which of the following is the best way to write the underlined portion of this sentence? If you think the original is the best way, choose option (1).

(1) protection for the
(2) protection. For
(3) protection, for
(4) protection; for
(5) protection—for

4. Sentences 4 and 5. **Once children are expected, the need arises for life insurance. Life insurance is purchased to cover the cost of the funeral, to pay the expenses of the last illness, and to provide income for the survivors.**

The most effective combination of these sentences would include which of the following groups of words?

(1) insurance, life insurance is
(2) insurance that is purchased
(3) insurance, in fact life insurance
(4) insurance, that is to say life insurance
(5) insurance life insurance is then purchased

5. Sentence 6. **When planning for this type of financial protection, be sure to consider all resources the survivors will have to use (earning ability as well as financial) the amount of income that will meet necessities, and finally the cost of such a program.**

What correction should be made to this sentence?

(1) change when planning to having planned
(2) insert a comma after the second parenthesis
(3) substitute quotation marks for the parentheses
(4) change the spelling of necessities to neccessities
(5) remove the comma after necessities

6. Sentence 7. **Concentrate insurance dollars on the breadwinner, and buy the type of insurance that will give the most protection for the cost.**

What correction should be made to this sentence?

(1) capitalize breadwinner
(2) insert a hyphen between bread and winner
(3) change will give to gives
(4) remove the before most protection
(5) no correction is necessary

7. Sentences 8 and 9. **A savings account is the second leg of the stool for a savings program. It is here where a family keeps the money that it may need immediately or plans to use within the near future.**

The most effective combination of these sentences would include which of the following groups of words?

(1) program where a family
(2) program for which a family
(3) program here where a family
(4) program in which a family
(5) program to which a family

8. Sentence 10. **After the family will protect itself with insurance for the survivors and with a savings account, it is then ready to invest in other possible channels.**

What correction should be made to this sentence?

(1) change <u>will protect</u> to <u>protects</u>
(2) insert a comma before <u>and</u>
(3) remove the comma after <u>account</u>
(4) change <u>then</u> to <u>therefore</u>
(5) no correction is necessary

9. The topic sentence of this paragraph is

(1) sentence 1
(2) sentence 2
(3) sentence 5
(4) sentence 8
(5) sentence 11

Answer Key

1. **1**	3. **1**	5. **2**	7. **1**	9. **2**
2. **3**	4. **2**	6. **5**	8. **1**	

Answer Analysis

1. **1** (1) is correct because savings is considered a plural noun; therefore, it requires a verb that agrees. (2) is not correct because *referred* is correctly spelled. (3) is wrong because no comma is needed here. (4) is wrong because *accomplishing* is correctly spelled. (5) is wrong because a correction is necessary.

2. **3** (1) is not correct because *family* may be considered a collective noun in the singular. (2) is wrong because no apostrophe is necessary since the idea of possession is not involved. (3) is correct because a comma *is* necessary after an introductory clause. See rule 4. (4) is incorrect because *decision* is spelled correctly. (5) is wrong because *to invest* is the correct tense since the investment has not yet taken place.

3. **1** This is so because the original is the best way. In (2), a period would result in a sentence fragment. In (3), (4), and (5), no punctuation is necessary after *protection*.

4. **2** In (1) the change would result in a run-on sentence. (2) is correct because *that is purchased* is an adjective clause describing *insurance*. In (3), (4), and (5), all the corrections would result in run-on sentences.

5. **2** In (1), the present tense is correct and should not be changed. In (2), a comma should be inserted in a series according to rule 6, so this is correct. (3) is wrong because no one is being quoted. (4) is incorrect because *necessities* is the correct spelling. In (5), the comma is needed to punctuate a series.

6. **5** This is so because no correction is necessary. (1) is incorrect because breadwinner is not a proper noun (see rule 4) and should not be capitalized. (2) is wrong because breadwinner is a single word that does not need a hyphen. In (3), *will give* is the correct tense because the future tense is required and, therefore, there should be no change. In (4), *the* is necessary because a definite article is needed. Therefore (5) is the correct answer.

7. **1** This is a tricky question because it calls for the *most effective combination*. (1) is the most effective combination because the adjective clause immediately follows the noun, *program*, that it describes. (2), (4), (5) are awkward and not as effective. (3) is incorrect because an adjective clause is required.

8. **1** The family protects itself in the *present* so the present tense, not the future tense, is needed. In (2), no comma is needed where only two items are involved: insurance and savings. In (3), the comma after *account* is necessary after an introductory clause. (4) is wrong because *then* is correct since it means "at that time." (5) is incorrect because there is an error in the sentence.

9. **2** (1) is wrong because it mentions only the relationship between savings and future goals. (2) is correct because the entire paragraph describes how to wisely invest in a savings plan. (3) is wrong because it mentions one way to invest in a savings plan. (4) is wrong because it mentions only a savings account. (5) is wrong because it tells what a family needs to consider before deciding on a savings plan.

THREE ADDITIONAL SAMPLE TEST PARAGRAPHS WITH ANSWER ANALYSES

Refer to page 213 for directions in answering the questions based on these paragraphs.

Important: Do not answer any question until you have read and analyzed all the possible choices. You will have to draw on your knowledge of sentence structure, usage, and mechanics, all of which may be involved in a single question.

PRACTICE TEST PARAGRAPH 2

(1) To improve consumer choice use good buying strategies and tactics to carry out the basic plan. (2) Price's and quality can vary greatly in buying food, auto insurance, or dandruff treatments. (3) A watermelon is a better buy at certain times of the year because of transportation costs. (4) Air conditioning may be a good buy at other times. (5) A used car may be adequate for many purposes. (6) A turnip is nutritious. (7) The choice available makes your personal consumer decision process complex, but the potential savings and improvements is huge compared to poor results from not shopping harder. (8) A great deal of regret can be avoided by obtaining reliable information in consumer education courses consumer magazines, and numerous books and pamphlets. (9) Unfair and deceptive practices of a few businesses would largely disappear, if consumers practiced self-defense. (10) Such defense means being well informed. (11) Consumers can assist in improving product safety, help to maintain reasonable prices, and raising the quality of goods not only by buying wisely, but by addressing themselves to economic and consumer problems. (12) Theres a mutual responsibility among consumers to seek and to improve the ways in which producers make and sell their products and services.

1. Sentence 1. **To improve consumer choice use good buying strategies and tactics to carry out the basic plan.**

   What correction should be made to this sentence?

   (1) insert a comma after <u>choice</u>
   (2) change <u>strategies</u> to <u>stratagies</u>
   (3) insert a comma after <u>strategies</u>
   (4) change <u>to</u> to <u>and</u>
   (5) no correction is necessary

2. Sentence 2. **Price's and quality can vary greatly in buying food, auto insurance, or dandruff treatments.**

   What correction should be made to this sentence?

   (1) remove the comma after <u>insurance</u>
   (2) remove the apostrophe from <u>Price's</u>
   (3) change <u>can</u> to <u>could</u>
   (4) remove the comma after <u>food</u>
   (5) no correction is necessary

3. Sentences 3 and 4. **A watermelon is a better buy at certain times of the year because of transportation costs. Air conditioning may be a good buy at other times.**

   The most effective combination of sentences 3 and 4 would include which of the following words?

   (1) costs, although air
   (2) costs, and air
   (3) costs, but air
   (4) costs, however air
   (5) costs, whereas air

4. Sentence 7. **The choice available makes your personal consumer decision process complex, but the potential savings and improvements is huge compared to poor results from not shopping harder.**

   What correction should be made to this sentence?

   (1) change the spelling of <u>available</u> to <u>availible</u>
   (2) remove the comma after <u>complex</u>
   (3) change <u>but</u> to <u>and</u>
   (4) change <u>is</u> to <u>are</u>
   (5) no correction is necessary

5. Sentence 8. **A great deal of regret can be avoided by obtaining reliable information in consumer education courses consumer magazines, and numerous books and pamphlets.**

What correction should be made to this sentence?

(1) change <u>can</u> to <u>could</u>
(2) change <u>by obtaining</u> to <u>if you obtained</u>
(3) insert a comma after <u>courses</u>
(4) remove the comma after <u>magazines</u>
(5) no correction is necessary

6. Sentence 9. **Unfair and deceptive practices of a few businesses would largely disappear, if consumers practiced self-defense.**

What correction should be made to this sentence?

(1) change the spelling of <u>businesses</u> to <u>busineses</u>
(2) change <u>would</u> to <u>should</u>
(3) remove the comma after <u>disappear</u>
(4) change the spelling of <u>disappear</u> to <u>disapear</u>
(5) no correction is necessary

7. Sentences 9 and 10. **Unfair and deceptive practices of a few businesses would largely disappear, if consumers practiced <u>self-defense. Such</u> defense means being well-informed.**

Which of the following is the best way to write the underlined portion of this sentence? If you think the original is the best way, choose option (1).

(1) self-defense. Such
(2) self-defense such
(3) self-defense, such
(4) self-defense; such
(5) self-defense, nevertheless such

8. Sentence 11. **Consumers can assist in improving product safety, help to maintain reasonable prices, and raising the quality of goods not only by buying wisely, but by addressing themselves to economic and consumer problems.**

What correction should be made to this sentence?

(1) remove the comma after <u>safety</u>
(2) change <u>help</u> to <u>helping</u>
(3) change <u>but</u> to <u>and</u>
(4) change the spelling of <u>addressing</u> to <u>adressing</u>
(5) no correction is necessary

9. Sentence 12. **Theres a mutual responsibility among consumers to seek and to improve the ways in which producers make and sell their products and services.**

What correction should be made to this sentence?

(1) change the spelling of <u>Theres</u> to <u>There's</u>
(2) change <u>among</u> to <u>between</u>
(3) change <u>to seek</u> to <u>and seek</u>
(4) change <u>and</u> to <u>or</u>
(5) no correction is necessary

Answer Key

1. **1**	3. **2**	5. **3**	7. **1**	9. **1**
2. **2**	4. **4**	6. **5**	8. **2**	

Answer Analysis

1. **1** There is an error in punctuation. A comma is used after an introductory phrase.

2. **2** There is an error in spelling. *Prices* does not possess anything; therefore, it does not require an apostrophe.

3. **2** A conjunction is required because the two independent clauses are equally important.

4. **4** There is an error in usage. A plural subject, *savings and improvement*, requires a plural verb, *are*.

5. **3** There is an error in punctuation. A comma is required to separate items in a series.

6. **5** No correction is necessary.

7. **1** The original is correct. All other choices result in run-on sentences.

8. **2** There is an error in usage. The use of the participle *helping* is required to parallel the participles *improving* and *raising*.

9. **1** There is an error in spelling. *There's* is a contraction of *there is*, the subject and verb needed to make this sentence.

PRACTICE TEST PARAGRAPH 3

(1) Household insects seem to have an incredible ability to escape extinction. (2) Cockroaches for example which have been on earth millions of years longer than human beings, can subsist on any kind of food. (3) They thrive in all parts of the world, some species prefer a human home to other habitats. (4) Once they enter it they use countless instinctive tricks to keep from being killed or evicted. (5) You can control household pests. (6) Do systematic house cleaning. (7) The best way to rid your home of practically all insect pests is by a combination of good housekeeping practices and proper use of the right insecticide. (8) It is easier to prevent pests from infesting your home than it is to get rid of them after they are established. (9) Household insects seek available food in places where they can hide and breathe. (10) If one eliminates these attractions from your home, the insects will look elsewhere for them. (11) Keep storage cabinets, kitchen drawers, and washtubs clean. (12) Frequent scrubbings with hot water and soap will do the job.

1. Sentence 2. **Cockroaches for example which have been on earth millions of years longer than human beings, can subsist on any kind of food.**

   What correction should be made to this sentence?

   (1) insert commas before and after <u>for example</u>
   (2) change <u>which</u> to <u>who</u>
   (3) remove the comma after <u>human beings</u>
   (4) change <u>can subsist</u> to <u>have subsisted</u>
   (5) no correction is necessary

2. Sentence 3. **They thrive in all parts of the <u>world, some species</u> prefer a human home to other habitats.**

   Which of the following is the best way to write the underlined portion of this sentence? If you think the original is the best way, choose option (1).

   (1) world, some species
   (2) world. Some species
   (3) world some species
   (4) world but some species
   (5) world because some species

3. Sentence 4. **Once they enter it they use countless instinctive tricks to keep from being killed or evicted.**

   What correction should be made to this sentence?

   (1) change <u>it</u> to <u>man's home</u>
   (2) insert a comma after <u>it</u>
   (3) change <u>being killed</u> to <u>having been killed</u>
   (4) change <u>or</u> to <u>and</u>
   (5) no correction is necessary

4. Sentences 5 and 6. **You can control household pests. Do systematic house cleaning.**

   The most effective combination of sentences 5 and 6 would include which of the following groups of words?

   (1) pests and do
   (2) pests if they try to do
   (3) pests while doing
   (4) pests by doing
   (5) pests having done

5. Sentence 7. **The best way to rid your home of practically all insect pests is by a combination of good housekeeping practices and proper use of the right insecticide.**

   If you rewrote sentence 7 beginning with

   <u>A combination of good housekeeping practices and proper use of the right insecticide is</u>

   the next word(s) would be

   (1) indeed
   (2) therefore
   (3) furthermore
   (4) for example
   (5) however

6. Sentence 8. **It is easier to prevent pests from infesting your home than it is to get rid of <u>them after</u> they are established.**

Which of the following is the best way to write the underlined portion of this sentence? If you think the original is the best way, choose option (1).

(1) them after
(2) them. After
(3) them, after
(4) them; after
(5) them, and after

7. A new paragraph should be started after

(1) sentence 2
(2) sentence 4
(3) sentence 8
(4) sentence 10
(5) sentence 11

8. Sentence 10. **If one eliminates these attractions from your home, the insects will look elsewhere for them.**

What correction should be made to this sentence?

(1) change <u>your</u> to <u>one's</u>
(2) remove the comma after <u>home</u>
(3) change <u>will</u> to <u>would</u>
(4) change <u>elsewhere</u> to <u>somewhere else</u>
(5) no correction is necessary

9. Sentences 11 and 12. **Keep storage cabinets, kitchen drawers, and washtubs clean. Frequent scrubbings with hot water and soap will do the job.**

The most effective combination of sentences 11 and 12 would include which of the following groups of words?

(1) and frequent scrubbings
(2) by frequent scrubbings
(3) because frequent scrubbings
(4) since frequent scrubbings
(5) as a matter of fact frequent scrubbings

Answer Analysis

1. **1** There is an error in punctuation. Commas are used to set off clauses that are inserted into a sentence.

2. **2** There is an error in sentence structure. As written, this is a run-on sentence. A period is needed to divide the two sentences, and the second sentence must start with a capital letter.

3. **2** There is an error in punctuation. A comma is needed to set off the introductory clause.

4. **4** The sentences are best combined by changing the second sentence into an adverbial phrase modifying the verb *control.*

5. **5** *However* is used when the idea in a sentence differs from the idea in the preceding sentence. In this case, the preceding sentence mentioned one method of control. This sentence refers to a combination of methods.

6. **1** The original is correct, since *after they are established* is an adverbial clause modifying *get rid of.*

7. **2** The first four sentences describe how insects seem to thrive. The last eight sentences all elaborate on how you can control household insects.

8. **1** There is an error in the use of the pronouns—a needless shift from the third person *one* to the second person *your.* If you use more than one pronoun to refer to the same person, you must be consistent. The words *If one eliminates* must be followed by *from one's home.*

9. **2** The best combination is *by frequent scrubbings*, which modifies the verb *keep* and makes the words *will do the job* unnecessary.

Answer Key

1. **1**	3. **2**	5. **5**	7. **2**	9. **2**
2. **2**	4. **4**	6. **1**	8. **1**	

PRACTICE TEST PARAGRAPH 4

(1) Among your important records are a thorough household inventory. (2) Before this can be of much value, in case of fire or burglary, youll need to supply some details. (3) Be sure to list the item date bought, purchase price, model number if it applies, brand name, dealer's name. (4) And general description (color, size, style, electric or gas, etc.) (5) Don't forget to include a realistic lump sum in your list for clothes and jewelry if you don't itemize these. (6) This information serves a triple purpose. (7) It helps you to determine the value of your possessions so you can have adequate insurance protection. (8) It helps you if it becomes necessary for you to make an insurance claim. (9) Some families take pictures of they're rooms to help identify possessions. (10) One copy of the household inventory should be put in your safe deposit box; you may wish to give a copy to your insurance company.

1. Sentence 1. **Among your important records are a thorough household inventory.**

   What correction should be made to this sentence?

   (1) change <u>your</u> to <u>you're</u>
   (2) change <u>are</u> to <u>is</u>
   (3) change <u>thorough</u> to <u>through</u>
   (4) change the spelling of <u>inventory</u> to <u>inventary</u>
   (5) no change is necessary

2. Sentence 2. **Before this can be of much value, in case of fire or burglary, youll need to supply some details.**

   What correction should be made to this sentence?

   (1) remove the comma after <u>value</u>
   (2) remove the comma after <u>burglary</u>
   (3) change <u>youll</u> to <u>you'll</u>
   (4) change <u>to supply</u> to <u>to have supplied</u>
   (5) no correction is necessary

3. Sentence 3. **Be sure to list the item date bought, purchase price, model number if it applies, brand name, dealer's name.**

   What correction should be made to this sentence?

   (1) insert a comma after <u>item</u>
   (2) capitalize <u>date bought</u>
   (3) remove the comma after <u>applies</u>
   (4) change <u>dealer's</u> to <u>dealers</u>
   (5) no correction is necessary

4. Sentences 3 and 4. **Be sure to list the item date bought, purchase price, model number if it applies, brand name, dealer's name. And general description (color, size, style, electric or gas, etc.)**

   Which is the best way to write the underlined portion of this sentence? If you think the original is the best way, choose option (1).

   (1) name. And
   (2) name. and
   (3) name and
   (4) name, and
   (5) name, And

5. Sentence 5. **Don't forget to include a realistic lump sum in your list for clothes and jewelry if you don't itemize these.**

   What correction should be made to this sentence?

   (1) change <u>Don't</u> to <u>Dont</u>
   (2) change the spelling of <u>realistic</u> to <u>reelistic</u>
   (3) insert a comma after <u>sum</u>
   (4) change the spelling of <u>clothes</u> to <u>cloths</u>
   (5) no correction is necessary

6. Sentences 6 and 7. **This information serves a triple <u>purpose. It</u> helps you to determine the value of your possessions so you can have adequate insurance protection.**

   Which of the following is the best way to write the underlined portion of this sentence? If you think the original is the best way, choose option (1).

   (1) purpose. It
   (2) purpose it
   (3) purpose It
   (4) purpose, so it
   (5) purpose although it

7. Sentence 8. **It helps you if it becomes necessary for you to make an insurance claim.**

   What correction should be made to this sentence?

   (1) insert a comma after <u>you</u>
   (2) change <u>you</u> to <u>one</u>
   (3) change <u>becomes</u> to <u>will become</u>
   (4) change the spelling of <u>necessary</u> to <u>neccessary</u>
   (5) no correction is necessary

8. Sentence 9. **Some families take pictures of they're rooms to help identify possessions.**

   What correction should be made to this sentence?

   (1) change the spelling of <u>they're</u> to <u>their</u>
   (2) insert a comma after <u>rooms</u>
   (3) change to <u>help</u> to <u>which helps</u>
   (4) change the spelling of <u>possessions</u> to <u>posessions</u>
   (5) no correction is necessary

9. Sentence 10. **One copy of the household inventory should be put in your safe deposit box; you may wish to give a copy to your insurance company.**

   What correction should be made to this sentence?

   (1) change <u>should be</u> to <u>is to be</u>
   (2) change the semicolon after <u>box</u> to a colon
   (3) change <u>may</u> to <u>might</u>
   (4) capitalize <u>insurance company</u>
   (5) no correction is necessary

Answer Key

1. **2**	3. **1**	5. **5**	7. **5**	9. **5**
2. **3**	4. **4**	6. **1**	8. **1**	

Answer Analysis

1. **2** There is an error in usage. The subject of the sentence is *inventory*, which is singular. The verb, therefore, must also be singular, *is*, since subject and verb must agree in number.

2. **3** The error is in spelling. The proper contraction of *you will* is *you'll* with the apostrophe indicating that letters are omitted.

3. **1** There is a punctuation error. Commas are needed to set off items in a series.

4. **4** Inclusion of the phrase *and general description* in the previous sentence removes the sentence fragment. A comma is necessary because the phrase is one of a series of phrases.

5. **5** No correction is necessary.

6. **1** The original is correct. Two separate sentences are required.

7. **5** No correction is necessary

8. **1** The error is in spelling. *Their* is a possessive pronoun meaning "belonging to them."

9. **5** No correction is necessary.

WHAT'S YOUR SCORE?

Total your score on the four practice test paragraphs (the analyzed paragraph and the three additional sample test paragraphs).

____ right,	____ wrong
Excellent	32–36
Good	27–31
Fair	22–26

LANGUAGE ARTS, WRITING, PART II

The Essay

The purpose of the GED Essay test is to test your ability to write. It does this by requiring you to write an essay of about 250 words in which you explain something, present an opinion on an issue, or retell a personal experience. The purpose of the test is not to show how much you know about a particular subject, but how well you can relate your ideas. In this chapter, through examples and practice, you will learn essential skills from sentence structure to completed essays that will help improve your ability to create structured and focused essays.

WHAT IS AN ESSAY?

Before you can begin your essay it is necessary that you understand what it is you are writing. An essay is a short theme based on a main idea and details. On the GED test you will be given a *prompt* to write about. You will write sentences that are complete, varied, and correct. You will build them into focused paragraphs that are combined into your final essay.

The *Language Arts, Writing* section will show you how to write an essay by going through ten segments beginning with the sentence and moving to paragraphs and then the essay.

THE SENTENCE

WHAT IS A SENTENCE?

A sentence is a group of words that make a complete thought. In this complete thought there is a subject that tells what the sentence is about and a predicate that tells what the subject does. Sentences express the thoughts and ideas of people through speaking or writing. To make sure that a thought or idea is completely understood, the sentence must be spoken or written clearly and correctly.

EXAMPLES

CORRECT SENTENCES:

Judy will take the five o'clock train home from work.

Please call for a reservation.

Wow, that was a great baseball game!

What's for supper?

These sentences are all grammatically correct. They are complete, begin with capital letters, and end with correct punctuation marks.

INCORRECT SENTENCES:

Gets up early in the morning.

The long black train.

Jan and Mark and Terry and Lee.

The busy intersection is a dangerous place for children they may get hurt.

The first three sentences in the incorrect examples above are sentence fragments. This means they are lacking a subject or a predicate. The last sentence is a run-on sentence.

Gets up early in the morning is lacking a subject. Who or what gets up early in the morning? We can correct this sentence by adding the subject "cat" to the sentence. *The cat gets up early in the morning.*

The long black train is lacking a predicate. What does it do? This sentence can be corrected by adding the predicate "is loaded with freight." *The long black train is loaded with freight.*

Jan and Mark and Terry and Lee is a sentence fragment; it is written poorly and does not contain a predicate. When there is a multiple subject or series of words, they should be connected with commas such as *Jan, Mark, Terry, and Lee will ride the bus to town.*

The busy intersection is a dangerous place for children they may get hurt may sound like a correct sentence, but actually it is two sentences together. This is called a run-on sentence. It should be made into two complete sentences. *The busy intersection is a dangerous place for children. They may get hurt.* Notice that each new sentence has a subject and a predicate.

TYPES OF SENTENCES

There are four basic types of sentences. They are declarative, interrogative, exclamatory, and imperative.

Declarative sentences make a statement. They are a "telling" sentence. This type of sentence states an idea and ends with a period.

EXAMPLES

The sky is blue.

The roses have thorns.

Sandie and Larry are going shopping in the mall.

Flowers need plenty of water to survive the heat of summer.

Interrogative sentences ask a question. An interrogative sentence ends with a question mark.

EXAMPLES

What are you wearing to the dance?

Does the baby need changing?

Did you forget to buy the milk?

Did Christy pick up the mail?

Exclamatory sentences state strong emotion. An exclamatory sentence ends with an exclamation point.

EXAMPLES

Watch out for that car!

The weather report is saying there is a tornado warning!

That bee is after me!

The damage to the park is unbelievable!

Imperative sentences make a request or command. They are sometimes confused with the interrogative sentences, but imperative sentences do not ask a question. With a request or command, the person to whom the statement is directed does not need to give an answer. These sentences end with a period.

EXAMPLES

Please pick up Jordan from football practice.

Don't smoke around the baby.

Wash the dishes when you are finished with the meal.

Please return the movie to the video store.

PRACTICE—TYPES OF SENTENCES

Decide what each type of sentence is and write the correct letter beside the statement.

A. declarative   B. interrogative
C. exclamatory   D. imperative

1. _____The young boy sat by the lake watching his reflection.

2. _____Where are you going on Saturday?

3. _____Charlie was admiring his new car.

4. _____Please turn the stereo down.

5. _____I just won a stuffed gorilla at the fair!

6. _____There are days when I think time passes very slowly.

7. _____The parade is starting!

8. _____Meet me at the pizza parlor.

9. _____When are you driving Diego to the game?

10. _____There is a wonderful new program on television tonight.

ANSWER KEY

1. **A**	3. **A**	5. **C**	7. **C**	9. **B**
2. **B**	4. **D**	6. **A**	8. **D**	10. **A**

Practice—Sentence Components

In order for a sentence to be written correctly it must have several components such as correct capitalization, punctuation, subjects, and predicates. These components help the reader to correctly determine the intended meaning of the statement.

THE BASIC RULES FOR CAPITALIZATION ARE AS FOLLOWS:

- Always capitalize the first word in a sentence.
- Always capitalize important words in a title.
- Always capitalize proper nouns (specific names of people, places, or things).
- Always capitalize the word *I*.

EXAMPLES

This glass jar would make a lovely vase.

Have you ever seen *The Wizard of Oz*?

The Statue of Liberty is located in New York Harbor.

Marci and I are attending the University of Kentucky in the fall.

USE OF PUNCTUATION

Punctuation is important in a sentence to allow the reader to fully understand the meaning of a sentence. A sentence followed by a question mark clearly shows that a question was being asked. An exclamation point at the end of a sentence shows that a sentence is being said with strong emotion, and a period at the end of a sentence tells the reader that a statement is being said. That statement may be telling a fact, opinion, or making a request or command. There are other punctuation marks that may be included in a sentence such as commas, quotation marks, colons, apostrophes, parentheses, and semicolons. These different types of punctuation may be reviewed in *Language Arts, Writing Fundamentals*.

PRACTICE—ENDING PUNCTUATION

Place the correct punctuation mark at the end of each sentence.

1. I wonder what the weather will be like today

2. Tell me about when you were a child

3. What is the best way to get to New York from Denver

4. Help me wrap this package

5. That is really amazing

6. The museum had over ten thousand visitors in the last month

7. What a wonderful time we had

8. Where is my new watch

9. The keys to the car are on the kitchen table

10. This book is one of the best I have ever read

ANSWERS

1. period

2. period

3. question mark

4. period

5. exclamation mark

6. period

7. exclamation mark

8. question mark

9. period

10. exclamation mark

SUBJECT AND PREDICATES

Every sentence must have a *subject* and a *predicate*. A subject tells who or what the sentence is about. The subject in a sentence can be a noun or pronoun, or it could be simply an understood subject. A noun is a person, place, or thing. A pronoun is a word that takes the place of a noun. An understood subject would be one that is not stated, but understood by the reader such as in an imperative sentence.

EXAMPLES

Grandmother's blue dish/fell to the floor with a crash.

The old quilt/was tattered.

I/gathered the walnuts from the ground

Turn the radio down.

The above subjects and predicates are separated by a slash mark. In the first example *Grandmother's blue dish* is the subject and *fell to the floor with a crash* is the predicate. In the second example, *The old quilt* is the subject and *was tattered* is the predicate. In the third example, *I* is the subject and *gathered the walnuts from the ground* is the predicate. The last example has an understood subject. This is an imperative sentence that makes a command. The understood subject would be the person to whom the sentence is referred.

Subjects

A subject may be simple or complete. A simple subject means the key word that the sentence is about. A complete subject includes the simple subject and all the words that go with it.

EXAMPLES

The limb of the tree scratched the clear window.

The small black fox caught a mouse from the field.

The limb of the tree would be the complete subject, while *limb* would be the simple subject. In the second example, *The small black fox* would be the complete subject and *fox* would be the simple subject.

Subjects in a sentence may also be compound. This means there are two or more subjects that share the same verb.

EXAMPLES

Rodney and Carolee are planning a picnic lunch at the park.

Chicago and St. Louis have similar weather.

Amanda, Paul, and Tom worked overtime at the factory.

The compound subject in the first sentence would be *Rodney* and *Carolee*; the second sentence would be *Chicago* and *St. Louis*. The compound subjects in the third sentence would be *Amanda, Paul,* and *Tom.*

PRACTICE—SUBJECTS

Circle the complete subjects in the following sentences. Underline the simple subjects. If the subject is understood, write *understood* at the end of the sentence.

1. The picture frame sits neatly on the office desk.
2. Follow the light with your eyes.
3. The small yellow car made an illegal turn.
4. He watches scary movies in the dark.
5. Brenda's new jeans have a slight tear in the knee.
6. The green light has turned red.
7. The mall is very crowded with shoppers.
8. Watch the weather report tonight.
9. I heard a bird chirping from a distant tree.
10. Art is a fun hobby.

ANSWERS

1. (The picture <u>frame</u>) sits neatly on the office desk.
2. Follow the light with your eyes. (Understood)
3. (The small yellow <u>car</u>) made an illegal turn.
4. (<u>He</u>) watches scary movies in the dark.
5. (<u>Brenda's new jeans</u>) have a slight tear in the knee.
6. (The green <u>light</u>) has turned red.
7. (The <u>mall</u>) is very crowded with shoppers.
8. Watch the weather report tonight. (Understood)
9. (<u>I</u>) heard a bird chirping from a distant tree.
10. (<u>Art</u>) is a fun hobby.

Predicates

The predicate in a sentence tells what the subject *does*. It has a verb form. The verb form may be an action verb or linking verb. Just like the subject, there may be a simple predicate and a complete predicate. A simple predicate would be the one word that tells what the subject does, while a complete predicate would be all the words that go with the verb.

EXAMPLES

The busy school bus picked up the children for school.

Our main course for dinner is beef stew.

In the first sentence the simple predicate would be *picked* and the complete predicate would be *picked up the children for school*. In the second sentence the simple predicate would be *is* and the complete predicate would be *is beef stew*. The first sentence shows an action verb as the predicate while the second sentence shows a linking verb as the predicate. You may review the difference between these two types of verbs in *Language Arts, Writing Fundamentals*.

Sentences may also contain *compound predicates*. This means there are two or more verbs in the predicate that share the same subject.

EXAMPLES

The bird chirped and fluttered around the cage.

Stadium fans clapped, yelled, and stomped as the team entered.

The compound predicate in the first example would be *chirped* and *fluttered*, and in the second example *clapped*, *yelled*, and *stomped*.

Sentences may also have a *compound subject* and a *compound predicate*.

EXAMPLES

The carpenter and plumber looked over the plans and wrote a report.

The teacher, principal, and students played games and rode rides at the school carnival.

Carpenter and *plumber* are the subjects in the first sentence. *Looked* and *wrote* make up the compound predicate. In the second example, *teacher*, *principal*, and *students* are the subjects and *played* and *rode* are the predicates.

PRACTICE—SUBJECT AND PREDICATE

Part A
Put a check mark next to sentences that contain both the subject and the predicate.

1. _____ There is a large black snake crawling across the road.

2. _____ Where are you going for lunch?

3. _____ June stapled her project papers together.

4. _____ Leaves in the afternoon.

5. _____ Watch out for the car!

6. _____ The local radio station plays country music.

7. _____ The tiny brown mouse.

8. _____ Sandwiches for the party.

9. _____ The twins were wearing identical outfits.

10. _____ The car was making.

Part B
Write the letter that corresponds with the underlined part of the sentence.

A. simple subject   D. complete predicate
B. simple predicate   E. compound subject
C. complete subject   F. compound predicate

1. _____ The <u>motor</u> on the car was running hot.

2. _____ A replacement window <u>was ordered for the house</u>.

3. _____ <u>Dogs and horses</u> are useful animals on a ranch.

4. _____ I <u>attended</u> the Thanksgiving Day Parade.

5. _____ The motorcycles <u>skidded and raced</u> past the crowd.

6. _____ <u>A blaring fire alarm</u> was alarming patients in the hospital.

7. _____ December <u>is</u> a very cold month in the northern states.

8. _____ Several <u>thorns</u> are protruding from the base of the rosebush.

9. _____ The small child <u>picked up the blue crayon from the floor</u>.

10. _____ <u>All available volunteers</u> are helping with the disaster.

ANSWERS

Part A
Sentences 1, 2, 3, 5, 6, and 9 should be checked.

Part B

| 1. **A** | 3. **E** | 5. **F** | 7. **B** | 9. **D** |
| 2. **D** | 4. **B** | 6. **C** | 8. **A** | 10. **C** |

EFFECTIVE SENTENCE STRUCTURE

Types of Sentence Structures

It is important when writing an essay that each sentence written is clear and has correct structure. There are different types of sentences that can be part of an essay. These different types of sentences give the essay variety, depth, and a greater sense of interest for the reader. Try some of these types of sentences when you begin your essay.

A *simple sentence* is usually made of an independent clause. An independent clause simply means the sentence contains a subject and a predicate. An independent clause can stand alone.

EXAMPLE

The fisherman caught a ten-pound catfish.

The fisherman would be the subject; *caught a ten-pound catfish* would be the predicate.

A *compound sentence* contains two independent clauses and they are usually combined with a conjunction such as *and*, *or*, *but*, or *so*.

EXAMPLE

The fisherman caught a ten-pound catfish, but it managed to get away.

This sentence has two complete sentences combined with the word *but*. The first independent clause is *The fisherman caught a ten-pound catfish*, and the second is *it managed to get away*. In the first independent clause *The fisherman* is the subject, and *caught a ten-pound catfish* is the predicate. In the second independent clause *it* is the subject and *managed to get away* is the predicate.

A *complex sentence* is made up of one independent clause and one or more dependent clauses (also called a *subordinating clause*). There are several types of subordinating clauses such as appositives, adjectives, adverbs, nouns, and prepositionals. A dependent clause cannot stand alone as a sentence.

EXAMPLE

Aunt Fay, *my mother's sister*, is a very creative artist.

The italicized part of the sentence is a subordinating phrase called an *appositive*, which tells more about the subject *Aunt Fay*. Make sure that you separate the appositive by commas.

SUBJECT/VERB AGREEMENT

When you write a sentence, make sure that the subject and the verb agree. In other words, make sure to use the correct verb form with the subject. (Review *Language Arts, Writing Fundamentals* for complete listing.)

Incorrect Usage of Subject/Verb Agreement

The mums, in the garden, is beautiful in the fall.
I is going to the festival at the park.
Sue and Jackie brung fresh baked pie for the bake sale.
They gives each year to their favorite charity.

Correct Usage of Subject/Verb Agreement

The mums, in the garden, are beautiful in the fall.
I am going to the festival at the park.
Sue and Jackie brought fresh baked pie for the bake sale.
They give each year to their favorite charity.

Different styles of sentences and ideas develop the essay into a more enjoyable reading experience. Try using some of these ideas in your writing.

COMPARING AND CONTRASTING IDEAS

Comparing and *contrasting* means the way ideas are alike and different. If you are writing a narrative essay about the time you rode a mule into the Grand Canyon, you may want to include some comparing and contrasting.

EXAMPLE

I began the long journey down into the canyon on the back of a mule. The mule was a more sure-footed animal than the horse. I was glad to know that since the path was so narrow.

In this passage there is a contrasting idea of how the mule is unlike the horse. The mule is sure-footed and the horse is not.

You may also want to include some sentences that compare. Suppose you were writing a persuasive essay about why farmers should or should not add growth hormones to cattle feed.

EXAMPLE

The hamburger used in many fast-food restaurants is from cattle that have been fed growth hormones. The hamburger that I use at home is from a cow we raised and later butchered. It was not given any type of growth hormone. It seems to me that the hamburger meat from both types of cattle has the same flavor.

This paragraph compares the taste of hamburger from the two types of cattle.

A Venn Diagram

To make it easier to develop comparing and contrasting ideas you may want to draw a Venn diagram. This will help you outline your ideas. A Venn diagram is a simple diagram made up of two intertwining circles. Each outer loop represents how the two ideas are different. The center loop represents how the ideas are alike.

EXAMPLE

If you wanted to compare and contrast the mule and the horse, this is how the Venn diagram would look.

Mule	**Similar**	**Horse**
sure-footed	looks similar	may slip on rock
very strong	can be ridden	used for pleasure
used for working	used on farms	shorter ears
long-eared		is able to reproduce
braying voice		longer tails
offspring of		fast moving
horse and donkey		

PRACTICE—VENN DIAGRAM

Make a Venn diagram on a separate piece of paper. Choose from the following ideas.

computers and typewriters

daycare and stay-at-home moms

college degree and high school degree

video rental and movie theaters

e-mail and postal letters

ANSWERS

(Answers will vary.)

Computer	**Similar**	**Typewriter**
many programs	use electricity	only a word processor
more equipment	have a keyboard	uses ribbon
more capabilities	word processors	
monitor		

CAUSE AND EFFECT

Another way to make your essay more interesting is by including a cause-and-effect relationship of ideas. A cause is what happens first in the relationship of ideas; the effect is secondary.

EXAMPLES

The fierce storm blew the large straw hat from my head. It promptly landed in a large mud puddle.

A careless match was thrown from the window of a passing car. It landed in a stack of dry leaves, which quickly began to burn.

Over Thanksgiving I ate more than my usual amount. At Christmas the dress I wanted to wear was too small.

In the first example the cause would be the *fierce storm* and the effect would be *the hat landed in a large mud puddle*. Keep in mind that the fierce storm would have to happen before the hat could land in a large mud puddle. This makes the fierce storm the cause. The second example shows *the match* as the cause and *the leaves burning* as the effect. The cause in the last example is *I ate too much at Thanksgiving* and the effect would be *the dress was too small*.

PRACTICE—CAUSE AND EFFECT

Put a check mark next to the sentences that have a cause-and-effect relationship.

1. _____ Greg played his guitar and Jane sang.

2. _____ Monica's hair began to get wet as she walked in the rain.

3. _____ The police officer gave Mike a ticket when he discovered his license had expired.

4. _____ The cereal became soggy soon after it was poured into the milk.

5. _____ Someone had torn a page from the magazine.

6. _____ The milk began to soak into the carpet soon after the baby dropped the bottle from her crib.

7. _____ The paper shredded when the printer jammed.

8. _____ The full moon rose over the lake.

9. _____ Keisha switched on the light just as the bulb blew out.

10. _____ The snow was covering most of the mid-western states.

ANSWERS

Sentences 1, 2, 3, 4, 6, 7, and 9 all contain cause-and-effect relationships.

TIME ORDER

Time order words give the reader a sense of *when* things happen and the *correct order*. These types of words may include, first, second, third, next, later, afterwards, soon, and finally. If you were writing a personal narrative about how to make your favorite cake, you would need to add time order words to help with the correct order. This makes the sequence of events more clearly understood.

EXAMPLE

Before I start baking I always check to make sure I have the proper ingredients. First, I read through the recipe carefully. Then I gather together all the ingredients that I will need. I place them on the counter within easy reach. After I have the ingredients, I begin mixing them in the proper order.

This paragraph shows the use of time order words. It makes the sentences of the paragraph relate to one another by moving from one step to the next in the correct order.

On a separate sheet of paper practice using time order words in paragraphs. Below are some ideas for paragraphs.

My morning routine

How to play tennis

Buying a new car

Learning a new dance

Making a scrapbook

Planting a garden

Baking bread

Preparing for an interview

Assembling a product

Home fire drill

ANSWERS

(Answers will vary.)

EXAMPLE

Planting a garden takes a lot of planning. First, there is finding a perfect place in your yard to place it. Second, you need to buy all the supplies to use such as shovels and seeds. Next, you will have to plant the garden according to the planting instructions. Finally, if you maintain it well, you will have a beautiful garden full of fresh vegetables or flowers.

WORDS IN CONVERSATION

Another way to vary sentences used in an essay is to include conversation. Written conversation is called *dialogue*. The correct way to write dialogue is to put it within quotation marks. However, remember that only the spoken part of the dialogue is put into quotation marks and not who said it. Also remember that the first word in a quotation is capitalized unless it is a continuation.

EXAMPLES

"Where did you go on vacation?" asked Emma.

"We went to the Smokey Mountains in Tennessee," replied Bill.

Emma asked, "Have you ever been there before?"

"No," replied Bill, "last year we went to the Everglades."

You can vary your sentence structure by putting the names of the person speaking at the beginning, middle, or end of your sentences. Notice that if you place the person who is speaking in the middle of the sentence, you will have two sets of quotation marks. You would not capitalize the first word in the continuation of that quotation. If a question is asked in dialogue, make sure you put the question mark at the end of the question being asked and not at the end of the sentence unless the quotation ends there. For example, look at the first and third examples.

A statement such as *Juan said he missed his train* is not dialogue. This is a statement written in the third person and does not contain the person's exact words. This is called an *indirect quotation*. It does not have quotation marks around it.

EXAMPLES

Wendy said that she would leave next Monday.

John said that Minnie is feeling much better today.

The barking dog told its owner that someone was nearby.

Jeremy nodded in reply.

Periods, question marks, and exclamation points must be inside the quotation marks. Names of people that are speaking should not be inside the quotation marks.

PRACTICE—QUOTATIONS

Put a check mark next to the correctly written dialogue.

1. _____ "Jimmy said that his new job started on Monday."

2. _____ "Mommy, can I have another cookie?" asked Jenny.

3. _____ "Wow," said Margaret, "you did a great job!"

4. _____ "Did you know, asked Sammy, That I collect stamps?"

5. _____ "Yes," said Francine, "I knew that!"

6. _____ "While you were gone I cleaned the house," she said.

7. _____ He hurriedly answered, "I'll be right there!"

8. _____ Jack said he would like to go to the movies with us.

9. _____ "When did Jonathan call," asked Danielle?

10. _____ "This morning," mother answered with a smile.

ANSWERS

Sentences 2, 3, 5, 6, 7, 8, and 10 are all correct sentences.

RUN-ON SENTENCES

What makes writing sentences hard is the way we speak. We don't always speak in correct sentences and many times we run our sentences together. Therefore, when we write sentences, we often want to write the way we speak.

Run-on sentences occur when you have more than one sentence combined with only one punctuation mark at the end. This makes for an unusually long, incorrect sentence that will take away from your essay.

When you write your essay, avoid this mistake by checking each sentence for a subject and predicate. If you have more than one subject or predicate in a sentence you may have a run-on sentence. You should always proofread your work.

EXAMPLES

INCORRECT:

William and Beverly walked from the grocery store to the park they watched the children play on the swings.

It was beginning to get cold outside the furnace in the house seemed to keep running on and on.

The traffic accident on Ninth Street was the result of someone falling asleep at the wheel he should have been more careful.

CORRECT:

William and Beverly walked from the grocery store to the park. They watched the children play on the swings.

It was beginning to get cold outside. The furnace in the house seemed to keep running on and on.

The traffic accident on Ninth Street was the result of someone falling asleep at the wheel. He should have been more careful.

PRACTICE—SENTENCE WRITING

Practice writing some sentences of your own and give them to someone to read over. The more you write, the better your writing style will develop.

WHAT IS A PARAGRAPH?

A paragraph is a group of related sentences. It is made up of a main idea (topic sentence) and detail sentences. The main idea focuses on what the paragraph will be about while the detail sentences add support to the topic. The first line in a paragraph must be indented (moved over). Watch the margins on both sides of the paper and do not write more than a few letters over the right margin. In a paragraph remember not to move to the left-hand margin every time you begin a new sentence, but begin the next sentence promptly after the last.

EXAMPLES

INCORRECT PARAGRAPH SETUP:

Computers have greatly affected our lives.
Students use the computer to research classroom projects.
Some people use computers to shop for clothes or even food.
Still others use the computer to keep in touch with family and friends.

CORRECT PARAGRAPH SETUP:

Computers have greatly affected our lives. Students use the computer to research classroom projects. Some people use computers to shop for clothes or even food. Still others use the computer to keep in touch with family and friends.

MAIN IDEAS AND DETAILS

A paragraph needs a main idea. The main idea is usually the first sentence in a paragraph, but it doesn't necessarily have to be. When you write your main idea, make sure that the sentence is a broad statement. This will make it easier for you to write detail sentences.

EXAMPLES

There are several differences between satellite television and cable.

Eating from the four basic food groups will help you stay healthy.

My family is very special to me.

Having a fire safety plan is important.

All of the above examples are broad enough to allow the writer to create numerous detail sentences. Let's use the first example and write some details for it.

There are several differences between satellite television and cable. First, cable usually has fewer channels to choose from while satellite television gives you a greater variety. Second, with satellite television you may be able to rent the equipment or you may purchase it. With cable there is no equipment to purchase. Finally, the price is a factor. Depending on the programs you desire, the satellite system may end up costing you more money.

Notice in the above example that the main idea is the first sentence. All of the sentences in the paragraph relate to it. Each detail sentence has something to do with the differences between satellite television and cable. Notice the use also of time order words and the correct setup of the paragraph. Time order words are not necessary in every paragraph, but can be helpful in setting it up.
Let's use the second main idea example and write a paragraph for it.

Eating from the different food groups will help you stay healthy. Your body needs nutrients supplied by each of the four basic food groups. The meat group supplies the needed proteins to keep your energy level high. The dairy group gives you calcium for strong teeth and bones. The vegetable and fruit group provides many vitamins such as A and C. The bread group gives you carbohydrates, which provide you with energy. Missing out on any one of these groups may cause you to become sick.

Try writing detail sentences for the other two examples. Remember to write details that follow the main idea.

PRACTICE—EDITING DETAIL SENTENCES

Read the following two paragraphs and delete the detail sentences that do not follow the main idea.

My family and I went to the apple orchard last fall. The trees seemed to be loaded down with the sweet juicy fruit. There were many apples that had fallen to the ground. These apples were bruised. There was a large owl sitting in the top of a tree. We picked three bushels of apples before it was time to leave. What a great day at the orchard!

My last camping trip was an experience I would rather forget. It seemed we had been walking for hours before the group leader decided she had found the perfect spot for the night. We had just begun to unpack our gear when I looked down to find a large black snake making its way toward me. I tried to move out of its path but it seemed to follow me. The snake was from a nonpoisonous species. I tripped over a stone and fell back just as the group leader scooted the snake in a different direction with a large stick. I don't think I slept at all that night thinking about that snake.

ANSWERS

Paragraph 1: Remove sentence, "There was a large owl sitting in the top of a tree."

Paragraph 2: Remove sentence, "The snake was from a nonpoisonous species."

COMBINING PARAGRAPHS

Once you understand the basics of writing a paragraph you are ready to combine several paragraphs together. When we combine paragraphs together in a theme or essay, we still have to keep the paragraphs focused on the topic. Each paragraph does not have to follow the same topic sentence, but each must be related to the overall main idea of the essay.

PRACTICE—MAIN IDEA IN PARAGRAPHS

Read through the following example of an essay. Underline the main idea in each paragraph as you read. Notice that each main idea relates to the main topic of recycling. Each paragraph in the essay discusses different aspects of why recycling is important.

EXAMPLE

Topic for essay: Recycling Is Important to the Future of America.

Recycling is an important factor for the future of America. It helps to keep pollution down, keeps our landfills from filling up, and helps save some natural resources.

Recycling helps keep the pollution levels down in our society. Newspapers that were once burned can now be returned for recycling. Aluminum cans are less likely to be thrown on the sides of the road because they can be turned in for money. Old tires that were once discarded have been recycled by being chopped up and made into playground coverings. It seems that there are many innovative ways to convert old trash into useful materials.

By recycling materials we can prevent many tons of garbage from being emptied into public landfills. It takes years for many of the items dumped into landfills to decay. Some items take hundreds of years to decay. This slow decay prevents the reuse of landfills, which in turn causes more land to be used.

The earth has only a limited supply of natural resources, and when they are gone there will be no more. By recycling materials made from natural resources we can prevent or slow down the use of these important natural resources.

In summary, recycling is an important factor for the future of America. It helps to keep pollution down, keeps our landfills from filling up, and helps save some natural resources. It would be nice if everyone in America would participate in this practice.

PRACTICE—PARAGRAPHS WITH MAIN IDEAS AND DETAILS

Choose from the following topics and write a paragraph with a main idea and three to five detail sentences.

My favorite pet

Learning to drive

A rewarding experience

A special person

A nerve-racking experience

Violence on television

My favorite job

A scary encounter

ANSWERS

EXAMPLE

My favorite pet is my dog, Charlie. She is a cute Cocker Spaniel puppy. I have taught her many tricks during the few weeks since she came to live with me. She is very lovable. Each day when I come home from work she greets me at the door. I just love her!

(Other answers will vary.)

PRACTICE

What would be the main idea for each group of sentences below? Write a main idea for each group of sentences and then rewrite each group in paragraph form. Add or delete words as necessary.

Group A
Family and friends are gathered together.

The turkey is roasting in the oven.

The children are watching the parade on television.

Main idea _____

Group B

Jayna walks through the rows of books.

She fills out the card in her book.

It is very quiet inside the room.

Main idea _____

Group C

Joel's knee looks badly injured.

The doctor examines the wound.

Stitches are required for the cut.

Main idea _____

Group D

The copy machine was making a funny noise.

The secretaries tried to correct the problem.

A red light was blinking on the control panel.

Main idea _____

ANSWERS

(Sentences will vary.)

EXAMPLE

Group A—It is Thanksgiving Day at the Harris home.

Group B—Jayna visits the local library.

Group C—Joel gets hurt at the football game.

Group D—The office copy machine is broken again!

TYPES OF ESSAYS

WHAT ARE THE DIFFERENT TYPES OF ESSAYS?

Basically there are three different types of essays. They are persuasive, expository, and narrative. Depending on the topic that will be given to you on your GED test, you will be able to pick out what type of essay you need to write and set it up with ease. Expository and persuasive essays are set up in five paragraphs while narratives can be set up in three or four. In this section we will go through the three different types of essays and what makes each unique. In the next few segments we will go through setting up the essays and actually begin writing.

Remember, you are not graded on how much you know about the subject but how well you can relay your ideas on paper.

THE PERSUASIVE ESSAY

This type of essay requires you to take a stand on an issue and develop an argument explaining why you have made this particular choice. You will need to use personal experiences in your explanations or information that you know. This essay is set up in five paragraphs.

Prompt

Many states have enacted laws throughout the years to help people stay safe. One such law that has been passed in many states is the seat belt law.

Discussion Question

Do you believe that states have the right to tell people they must wear a seat belt in an automobile?

Sample Persuasive Essay

Seat belt laws have been enacted in many states. I feel that they are very important for the safety of all Americans. This law saves countless lives each year, makes sure our children are safe, and gives me a sense of security when I get behind the wheel of a car. I believe that seat belt laws are very important and should be enforced in every state.

There are many people alive today because of the enforced seat belt laws. This law makes sure that people who ordinarily don't wear seat belts in automobiles are restrained in case of an accident. I know personally that the seat belt laws work because I, who was once a non-seat belt wearer, was in an accident. I only wore the seat belt because of this law. I was lucky. It saved my life when my car rolled over one night on a rain-slick road. Instead of being thrown out of the car and possibly killed or injured, I was safe.

Children are also safer because of this law. It is required by law that all children be restrained in a car safety seat or seat belt. This keeps the child safe in case of an accident. It also gives the adult driving the comfort of knowing the child is not moving around the automobile where he or she could be injured by opening a door and falling out.

When I get behind the wheel of a car and snap on my seat belt, I feel comfortable knowing that I have a better survival rate should I be in an accident. I want to make sure that I am here to enjoy life for a long time, and by wearing a seat belt in the car I know that I am increasing my odds of surviving an accident.

Seat belt laws are important to me and should be to everyone! They help save lives, keep our children safe, and give me security in the automobile. I would recommend that every state have seat belt laws.

THE EXPOSITORY ESSAY

This essay requires you to explain, describe, or interpret a particular situation, experience, or idea by again using personal experiences or information. This essay is set up in five paragraphs.

Prompt

There have been many great books written through the years. Think of three books that you have read that have affected your life in some way. It may have affected you in a small way or in a profound way.

Discussion Question

What are three books you have read that have affected you in some way?

Sample Expository Essay

Books have always been a big part of my life. I have read many books through the years but three of my favorite books are, *The King, the Mouse, and the Cheese, Little Women*, and *Silas Marner*. I have read these many times and each time I do, they add joy to my life.

The King, the Mouse, and the Cheese was the first book I remember reading. When I was in second grade we were required to do a book report. This book was my choice. I remember my mother reading the book with me and helping me decide what I would say about the book. On the day of the report I stood at the front of the room and quickly reported on the story. The class loved it and everyone wanted to check the book out of the library. This book gave me the joy of reading and made me want to continue.

When I was a teenager, *Little Women* quickly became a favorite of mine. It was a story of four sisters and how they grew from girls into young women. This story discussed friendship, love, and war. It gave me a sense of family and an appreciation for my own.

The last book on my favorite list is, *Silas Marner*. This is a story written by George Eliot. It is about a man who loved gold and came to realize that a little girl was more important than all the gold in the world. It gave me a wonderful message that there are more important things than material possessions.

Books can be a wonderful asset to anyone's life. These marvelous stories can bring fulfillment, appreciation, and values.

THE NARRATIVE ESSAY

This type of essay requires you to recount a personal experience by using sequencing skills, details, or descriptions. It is basically recounting a "story" of what has happened to you. This essay is set up in three or four paragraphs.

Prompt

Everyone seems to have a memorable event that took place in his or her life. Think of an event that seems to stand out in your memory.

Discussion Question

What made this event different from all of the others? Was it a time of great happiness or sadness? Was it funny?

Sample Narrative Essay

The event that is most memorable to me was a Mother's Day in 2005. This was the day that my brother and I decided to take our mom out for a wonderful day at the museum and dinner. What started out as good intentions ended up costing us more than we anticipated.

The day started out fine as we left our home in my brother's big old clunker car and traveled two hours into the city to the museum. As soon as we arrived at the museum we noticed that the day was already getting warm. We went quickly inside the air-conditioned museum and spent several hours wandering around looking at the entire collection of paintings, statues, and even automobiles. After we looked at everything in the museum, we decided we were getting hungry and were eager to go to eat dinner. We left the building and found the car. As my brother turned the key all we heard was a terrible grinding noise that told us we weren't going anywhere. Stuck! My brother called a tow truck to take the car in for repairs. My mother gave my brother money to fix the car and then she and I waited at the museum for his return. In the meantime, it was getting hotter and we were getting hungrier. We went back into the museum and looked around for several more hours until closing time. We then had no choice but to go outside and sit in the stifling heat. We were miserable! Finally, the familiar big old clunker car came into view and we gladly jumped in. The first place we went was to eat.

What started out as a nice trip ended up being a day of misery. Mother's Day, 2008, will be one I will never forget. I'm sure my mother and brother feel the same way.

SETTING UP AN ESSAY

When you take your GED Language Arts, Writing, Part II test, you will be given a prompt and/or a discussion question. You will write your essay on this question.

The prompt on the Language Arts, Writing, Part II test will be a subject that will be familiar to you. You will not be graded on how much you know about the material but how well you can relate your ideas.

In this segment we will go through the three types of essays (expository, persuasive, and narrative) from beginning to end. There will be explanations for each paragraph included in the essay along with the essay in its entirety. You will be able to see and understand the process of a three-, four-, or five-paragraph essay.

WHAT MUST BE INCLUDED IN AN ESSAY?

An essay must have a clear *focus* that states the *main idea. Details* are needed to support that focus. The essay must be set up in a format that makes sense and allows the essay to be read easily and understood by the reader.

Essays have three main parts:

1. The first is an *introduction.* This is the main idea of the essay. The introduction is the first paragraph of the essay. Without an introduction the essay would have no focus and would be hard to understand.

2. The second part of the essay is the *body.* The body is the "meat" of the essay. This is where the supporting details are added. The body of the essays we will write will have one, two, or three paragraphs.

3. The last part of an essay is the *conclusion.* This is the final paragraph of the essay. Not only is it important to have a focus and supporting details but it is equally important to make sure you summarize your essay by tying all the ideas together at the end.

SETTING UP AN EXPOSITORY ESSAY

Expository Prompt

Throughout the year there are many holidays that people in the United States celebrate. Some are religious holidays such as Christmas and Passover, while other holidays celebrate the lives of famous Americans such as George Washington and Abraham Lincoln.

Discussion Question

Think of some holidays that are important to you. Why are these holidays important to you?

How to Set Up an Expository Essay

Focus: What is the main idea that the essay will be about?

Think: Is it about Christmas, Easter, George Washington, and Abraham Lincoln or is it about you? This essay is about you and particular holidays that you relate to your personal life.

First Step: Decide on *three* specific ideas to explain, describe, or interpret in your essay.

Think: What are three holidays that you enjoy? Let's say that you enjoy Veteran's Day, Independence Day, and Christmas. These three holidays will become your second, third, and fourth paragraphs in your five-paragraph essay once a main idea and details are established. The first paragraph in your essay will be an introduction and the last a summarization.

Main Idea: What is the main idea of the essay going to be? Look again at the prompt and see what the discussion question is asking: "Why are these holidays important to you?" You cannot use this statement as your main idea for the essay, but you can reword it to make it into a main idea: "Holidays are important to me." Now you have your main idea.

First Paragraph: The first paragraph begins with the main idea of the essay and includes the three ideas you want to discuss.

Think: What was the main idea of the essay? What were the three ideas you wanted to explain?

EXAMPLE

Holidays are important to me. There are many holidays I enjoy, but the three I enjoy most are Veteran's Day, Independence Day, and Christmas.

This paragraph now includes your main idea of the essay and the three ideas (holidays, in this case) that will be discussed. You may note that this paragraph is made up of only two sentences, yet it relays perfectly the main idea of the essay and the three ideas you are going to discuss. You may however add an extra sentence to help express the main idea.

EXAMPLE

Holidays are important to me. There are many holidays I enjoy, but the three I enjoy most are Veteran's Day, Independence Day, and Christmas. These holidays all have a special meaning to my family and me.

Second Paragraph: You are now ready to set up your second paragraph. In this paragraph you will take your first idea (Veteran's Day) and create a topic sentence (main idea) for the paragraph and then create detail sentences that support the idea.

Think: What would be a good main idea for your second paragraph if the idea you are writing about is Veteran's Day? Mentally take notes of details about why Veteran's Day is important to you. Is it because you have veterans in your family? Is it because you have lost loved ones in a war? Is it because you get a day off from work to be with your family? Whatever the reason, think of a main idea for this paragraph. When you write your main idea for the paragraph make sure it is broad enough to cover several sentences of discussion; for example, "Veteran's Day is an honorable holiday." This is a broad statement that allows you to add on sentences that *explain* why it is important to you. If your main idea was "Veteran's Day is important to me because my father was in the Vietnam War," your detail sentences would be limited to a discussion of your father in the Vietnam War.

EXAMPLE

> Veteran's Day is an honorable holiday. It is a day when I think about the men and women serving our country in the military. Veteran's Day is a day on which I think about the men and women who gave their life for me so that I may have freedom. On this day I take my children to the Veteran's Day services so that they will learn to appreciate and respect the veterans of the past as well as present in our country.

Third Paragraph: The third paragraph relates to the second idea (holiday) from your introductory paragraph. In this case it is Independence Day. The third paragraph is set up in the same way as the second.

Think: Create a main idea or topic sentence. Mentally think of detail sentences that you want to include. Again, try to think of a broad main idea. It will be easier to think of details to go along with it.

EXAMPLE

> Independence Day is a great summer holiday. On Independence Day my family gathers together for our annual family reunion. The kids have a great time lighting sparklers and playing traditional games outdoors. We top off the end of the day by watching the great display of fireworks.

This paragraph has a broad main idea and all details are focused on it. It also includes personal supporting details.

Fourth Paragraph: The fourth paragraph uses your final or third idea (holiday) from your introductory paragraph. This idea is Christmas. Again, this paragraph is set up just as paragraphs two and three.

Think: Create a main idea for your third idea (holiday). This would be about Christmas. What could you write that would be broad enough to include supporting details? If you wrote, "I receive many gifts for Christmas," your detail sentences would be limited to only those gifts you received. If you wrote, "Of all the holidays, Christmas is my favorite," you would have a much broader approach to adding on details.

EXAMPLE

> Of all the holidays, Christmas is my favorite. Christmas is a time of joy and generosity in my family. It is a time when all of my family gathers together in front of the fireplace to sing Christmas carols. I love to watch the little children in my family open their gifts on Christmas morning. It seems to be almost magical.

Fifth Paragraph: This is the last paragraph and its purpose is to summarize the entire essay. As with the other four paragraphs, this paragraph also needs a main idea. This paragraph may also need special phrases to show closure such as: "In summary," "In conclusion," "In short," etc.

Think: Create a main idea that would summarize the entire essay. This paragraph does not need as many detail sentences as the other paragraphs but one or two would help support the summarization. What was the entire essay about? What do you need to include in your summarization of the entire essay? Make sure to put in the three ideas you have been explaining.

EXAMPLE

> In summary, spending holidays with family is important to me. What makes a holiday special is that it truly brings us together. Each year we create memories to last us a lifetime.

The word count for the entire essay is 256 words. You can clearly see that each paragraph is focused, contains main ideas and details, has structure, and yet is simple. Take a look at what the entire essay would look like written together. Notice how it flows easily from one paragraph to the next.

> Holidays are important to me. There are many holidays I enjoy, but the three I enjoy most are Veteran's Day, Independence Day, and Christmas. These holidays all have a special meaning to my family and me.
>
> Veteran's Day is an honorable holiday. It is a day when I think about the men and women serving our country in the military. Veteran's Day is a day on which I think about the men and women who gave their life for me so that I may have freedom. On this day I take my children to the Veteran's Day services so that they will learn to appreciate and respect the veterans of the past and present in our country.
>
> Independence Day is a great summer holiday. On Independence Day my family gathers together for our annual family reunion. The kids have a great time lighting sparklers and playing traditional games outdoors. We top off the end of the day by watching the great display of fireworks.
>
> Of all the holidays, Christmas is my favorite. Christmas is a time of joy and generosity in my family. It is a time when all of my family gathers together in front of the fireplace to sing Christmas carols. I love to watch the little children in my family open their gifts on Christmas morning. It seems to be almost magical.
>
> In summary, spending holidays with family is important to me. What makes a holiday special is that it truly brings us together. Each year we create memories to last us a lifetime.

SETTING UP A PERSUASIVE ESSAY

Persuasive Prompt

At any given evening, with most any family relaxing at home, there will be the familiar ringing of the telephone. Usually it's neighbors, friends, or family, but every so often it is a telemarketer trying to get us to purchase numerous items ranging from new tires, credit cards, or siding, to insurance. Sometimes we decide to purchase these items, and sometimes we become annoyed at their constant calling.

Discussion Question

How do you feel about telemarketers calling your home? Do you feel they are a vital part of our economy by providing a service to people or do you feel they are interrupting your personal time with your family?

How to Set Up a Persuasive Essay

Focus: What is the main idea of the essay going to be about? It is about telemarketers calling your home. The main question is, how do you feel about this? You are required to take a stand on this issue. Do you feel that these calls are important or are they an invasion of your privacy?

First Step: Decide what your stand is on the issue. Next, think of *three* specific reasons why you feel the way you do.

Think: What are the three reasons that you do or do not like telemarketers calling your home. Let's say your stand is that you do not like them calling your home. Here are your three possible reasons:

1. The first reason you do not like them calling is because you do not want to spend your time at home being pressured by salespeople.

2. Your second reason may be that you do not trust people selling items over the phone.

3. Your third reason may be that you don't need or want the product that is being offered.

Main Idea: Take a look at the essay prompt and question. What is the main idea of the essay going to be? Remember to make your first statement or main idea broad enough that you will be able to write a lot about it. You will begin your first paragraph with the main idea of the essay and include your three reasons. Remember, in a persuasive essay you are required to take a stand so this essay is written in the first person, "I." Your main idea may be stated something like this: "There are many reasons why I don't like telemarketers calling my home."

First Paragraph: The first paragraph is the introduction. It will begin with your main idea and have one or two more sentences that support the main idea. Remember to include in your introduction your three reasons why you feel the way you do. This will be the focus of the body of the essay.

Think: What was your main idea? What were your three reasons?

EXAMPLE

> There are many reasons why I don't like telemarketers calling my home. Three of these reasons are that they interrupt my family time, I don't trust giving out financial information to them over the phone, and I don't always need or want the products they offer.

This paragraph now includes your main idea of the essay and three reasons why you don't like telemarketers calling your home. Notice that the paragraph is made up of only two sentences. You may want to add a third sentence to help support the main idea.

EXAMPLE

There are many reasons why I don't like telemarketers calling my home. Three of these reasons are that they interrupt my family time, I don't trust giving out financial information over the phone, and I don't always need or want the products they offer. I know telemarketers have a job to do, but I just don't like the interruptions they cause.

Second Paragraph: You are now ready for your second paragraph. This begins the body of the essay. In this paragraph you will take the first reason from your introduction and create a main idea. Then you will create supporting details for the main idea.

Think: What would be the main idea for your second paragraph? Your first reason in your introduction states: "They interrupt my family time." You will need to use these words to create your main idea. You may write, "When telemarketers call my home I feel that they interrupt my family time." Now you need to think of at least three more sentences that would support how you feel about this particular reason.

EXAMPLE

When telemarketers call my home I feel that they interrupt my family time. It seems that every time my family and I sit down to dinner, the phone rings. Instead of spending time with my children I end up listening to several minutes of chatter. I hate to be rude and hang up the phone, but I admit that is what I sometimes have to do to get back to my family.

Third Paragraph: The third paragraph relates to your second reason in your introduction. The second reason you don't like telemarketers calling is, "I don't feel comfortable giving out financial information over the phone." The third paragraph is still the body of the essay and it is set up just as the second paragraph with a main idea and details.

Think: Create a main idea using your second reason. It may be, "I don't feel comfortable giving out financial information over the phone to a telemarketer." After you have your main idea, you would need to think of about three sentences that support the main idea of your third paragraph.

EXAMPLE

I don't feel comfortable giving out financial information over the phone. I don't know the person on the other end and it could be someone dishonest. I realize that not all telemarketers are dishonest. It's just that it makes me nervous to give out credit card information when anyone could be listening.

Fourth Paragraph: This paragraph is set up like the second and third paragraphs and is also part of the body of the essay. The main idea of the fourth paragraph relates to your third reason in your introduction. Your third reason was, "I don't always need or want the products they are selling."

Think: What would be a good main idea using your last reason? Think of about three sentences that will support your main idea for the fourth paragraph. Your last main idea may be, "Telemarketers don't usually offer any products that I would be interested in purchasing."

EXAMPLE

Telemarketers don't usually offer any products that I would be interested in purchasing. It seems that most telemarketers who call my home try to send me information on acquiring credit cards. Some try to sell expensive encyclopedias or even light bulbs. One telemarketer even offered to sell me siding for my brick home!

Fifth Paragraph: This the last paragraph in your five-paragraph persuasive essay. It is also called the conclusion. It is important that you summarize your entire essay and draw a conclusion in this paragraph.

Think: Create a main idea that would summarize the entire essay. What was the essay about? What was your stand on the issue? Make sure that you put in the three reasons you explained in your conclusion.

EXAMPLE

In conclusion, I simply don't like telemarketers. Interrupting my family time is an annoyance to me. Plus, I don't like to purchase products over the phone, nor do I like to give out my personal information to someone I can't see. I would rather avoid telemarketers altogether.

You have now completed your persuasive essay. Let's take a look at how the entire essay would look when it is put together. The word count for this essay is 280 words. It doesn't take very many sentences to make up the 250 words you need to write in your essay. The persuasive essay we just wrote has only three or four sentences in each paragraph.

There are many reasons why I don't like telemarketers calling my home. Three of these reasons are that they interrupt my family time, I don't trust giving out financial information over the phone, and I don't always need or want the products they offer. I know telemarketers have a job to do, but I just don't like the interruptions they cause.

When telemarketers call my home I feel that they interrupt my family time. It seems that every time my family and I sit down to dinner, the phone rings. Instead of spending time with my children I end up listening to several minutes of chatter. I hate to be rude and hang up the phone, but I admit that is what I sometimes have to do to get back to my family.

I don't feel comfortable giving out financial information over the phone. I don't know the person on the other end and it could be someone dishonest. I realize that not all telemarketers are dishonest. It's just that it makes me nervous to give out credit card information when anyone could be listening.

Telemarketers don't usually offer any products that I would be interested in purchasing. It seems that most telemarketers who call my home try to send me information on acquiring credit cards. Some try to sell expensive encyclopedias or even light bulbs. One telemarketer even offered to sell me siding for my brick home!

In conclusion, I simply don't like telemarketers. Interrupting my family time is an annoyance to me. Plus, I don't like to purchase products over the phone, nor do I like to give out my personal information to someone I can't see. I would rather avoid telemarketers altogether.

SETTING UP A NARRATIVE ESSAY

The narrative essay is set up differently than the expository or persuasive essays. It can have three, four, or even five paragraphs. It is usually easier to set it up in three or four. In the following example we will set it up into three paragraphs. It still has the same three basic parts: the introduction, body, and conclusion. In the narrative essay each paragraph will represent one of the basic parts. Remember that the narrative essay is written in the first person and discusses a personal issue.

Narrative Prompt

Do you remember when you got your first real job? It may have been one when you were still in high school. Maybe it was at the service station across town or being a waiter or waitress. How did you feel about this job? Try to recall how you felt about your first job.

Discussion Questions

Think about your first job. How did you feel about it? How did you get this job? What made it so special?

How to Set Up a Narrative Essay

Focus: What is the main idea of your essay going to be about? It is about your first job and why it was important to you.

First Step: Decide what you want your main idea sentence to say.

Think: Your first sentence or main idea needs to state what type of job you are going to discuss in your essay.

Main Idea: Suppose that your first job was as a waitress or waiter in a restaurant. Your first sentence may be, "I will never forget my first job as a waitress in a small-town café."

First Paragraph: In your first paragraph you will need to include your main idea sentence and at least one or two other sentences to help support the main idea. Remember that the first paragraph is the focus for the entire essay.

EXAMPLE

I will never forget my first job as a waitress in a small-town café.
I was only sixteen years old and felt so excited. This was the
beginning of my independence.

This simple paragraph focuses on the first job and its importance to the writer.

Second Paragraph: The second paragraph in the narrative essay is the body of the essay. Since the essay is written in the first person and tells about an experience of the writer, it is important to put in time order the words that show sequencing of details. Begin the body of the essay with the first event you want to share. Then continue in order. Put in thoughts and feelings as you write your sentences.

EXAMPLE

> The summer after I turned sixteen my mother thought it was time for me to find a summer job. She had heard that there was an opening for a waitress in a small local café. I wasn't too happy about giving up my life of leisure for the summer, but I decided to give it a try. The pay for the job was a dollar an hour, which I thought was a lot of money. I started my job on the first day washing dishes. I washed and washed. After a few days, I was promoted to pouring coffee at the snack bar. I thought this was great compared to the dishwashing and even managed to make a tip now and then. Later on, I was given the job of waiting on the customers. It wasn't as easy as it looked and I made my share of mistakes. Finally, by the end of the summer I had made a little money, but what was most important was the experience I gained.

Make sure that your detail sentences refer to the main idea of the essay. Keep your sentences in sequence. Notice that the writer above uses time order words such as *after a few days, later on,* and *finally*. This allows the reader to understand in exactly what order the actions in the paragraph are taking place.

Third Paragraph: The final paragraph in the narrative essay is the conclusion. This paragraph sums up the entire essay.

EXAMPLE

> My first job was a great experience for me. It helped me to gain my first taste of independence while also gaining some great experience.

The word count for the entire narrative essay is 227 words. Let's take a look at how it would read when put together.

> I will never forget my first job as a waitress in a small-town café. I was only sixteen years old and felt so excited. This was the beginning of my independence.
>
> The summer after I turned sixteen my mother thought it was time for me to find a summer job. She had heard that there was an opening for a waitress in a small local café. I wasn't too happy about giving up my life of leisure for the summer, but I decided to give it a try. The pay for the job was a dollar an hour, which I thought was a lot of money. I started my job on the first day washing dishes. I washed and washed. After a few days, I was promoted to pouring coffee at the snack bar. I thought this was great compared to the dishwashing and even managed to make a tip now and then. Later on, I was given the job of waiting on the customers. It wasn't as easy as it looked and I made my share of mistakes. Finally, by the end of the summer I had made a little money, but what was most important was the experience I gained.
>
> My first job was a great experience for me. It helped me to gain my first taste of independence while also gaining some great experience.

CREATING QUICK OUTLINES FOR ESSAYS

Creating a quick outline before you write your essay will save you some time in writing. Below we will go through three outlines for the previous essays. When you create an outline, you will need to jot down your ideas on scrap paper and not include this in your actual essay, but only use it as a reference.

THE EXPOSITORY OUTLINE

The expository essay was written in a five-paragraph form. Therefore, you will need to number your outline into five sections and write your main idea for each paragraph beside each number. Remember when writing your outline that your first paragraph is the introduction and contains your three main points. Paragraphs two, three, and four will be about the three main points. Typically, outlines are written in Roman numerals.

EXAMPLE

    I. Holidays are important to me.

    II. Veteran's Day is an honorable holiday.

    III. Independence Day is a great summer holiday.

    IV. Of all the holidays, Christmas is my favorite.

    V. In summary, there are many holidays that are important to my family and me.

Once you have your five main paragraph outlines, you can insert your detail sentence ideas under each main idea.

IMPORTANT HOLIDAYS TO ME

  I. Holidays are important to me.
    A. Holidays I enjoy are Veteran's Day, Independence Day, and Christmas
    B. Holidays have special meaning

 II. Veteran's Day is an honorable holiday.
    A. Men and women in the service
    B. Take children to services

 III. Independence Day is a great summer holiday.
    A. Family reunion
    B. Kids play games
    C. Watch fireworks

 IV. Of all the holidays, Christmas is my favorite.
    A. Generosity
    B. Family gathers together
    C. Opening gifts

 V. In summary, there are many holidays that are important to my family and me.
    A. Veteran's Day
    B. Independence Day
    C. Christmas

TIP

An outline will keep your essay focused and organized.

Do not spend a great deal of time jotting down your outline. The outline is meant to save you time. Your detail sentences do not necessarily have to be written out completely in your outline. They can be fragments that you can add on to when you write your complete essay. From the outline you can use the ideas to create your sentences for your five-paragraph essay. Compare the previous outline of "Important Holidays to Me" to the complete essay.

THE PERSUASIVE OUTLINE

The persuasive essay was also written in five-paragraph form. To begin the persuasive outline number your five paragraphs with Roman numerals and write a main idea for each paragraph. The first sentence in your outline is going to state your stand on the issue you will be writing about. This is the focus of the essay. The next three sentences in your outline will be about your three points explaining why you made this stand. Your final sentence is the main idea for your conclusion.

EXAMPLE

    I. I don't like telemarketers calling my home.

    II. Telemarketers interrupt my family time.

    III. I don't like giving out financial information.

    IV. I don't like the products from telemarketers.

    V. There are many reasons I don't like telemarketers calling.

After writing your main ideas for each paragraph, add details to each paragraph. For each detail sentence assign a letter of A, B, C, etc.

WHY I DON'T LIKE TELEMARKETERS
CALLING MY HOME

I. I don't like telemarketers calling my home.
   A. Interrupt family time
   B. Financial information
   C. Don't need or want products

II. Telemarketers interrupt family time.
   A. Phone rings during family time
   B. Hanging up on callers

III. I don't feel comfortable giving out financial information.
   A. I don't know person calling
   B. Credit card information

IV. Telemarketers don't offer products I need or want.
   A. Offer products such as credit cards
   B. Offer products such as encyclopedias or light bulbs

V. I don't like telemarketers calling my home.
   A. Interrupt family time
   B. Financial information
   C. Products

Compare the previous outline with the persuasive essay on telemarketers. Notice again that some sentences are written as fragments. This is for the purpose of jotting the outline ideas down quickly. You can add more words when you write the actual essay.

THE NARRATIVE OUTLINE

The narrative outline is written in a three-paragraph form. Number your three main idea sentences with Roman numerals and then write the main idea for each paragraph. Remember, in a narrative essay the first paragraph is the introduction, the second is the body, and the third is the conclusion.

EXAMPLE

   I. I will never forget my first job as a waitress.

  II. My mother thought it was time for me to get a job.

 III. My first job was a great experience.

After you have decided what you want your main ideas to be in your narrative essay, continue with detail sentences for each paragraph.

MY FIRST JOB

I. I will never forget my first job as a waitress.
   A. Felt excited
   B. New experience

II. My mother thought it was time for me to get a job.
   A. Heard about an opening
   B. Gave up summer vacation
   C. Was paid a dollar an hour
   D. Washed dishes
   E. Promoted to pouring coffee
   F. Waited on customers
   G. Made some mistakes
   H. Made money and gained experience

III. My first job was a great experience.
   A. Gained independence
   B. Gained experience

Notice in the narrative essay outline that most details are added to the second section, which is the body of the essay. When you add your details, keep them in order of occurrence. Compare the outline to the actual narrative essay.

WRITING THE ESSAY

Before you begin to write your own essay let's take a look at some words and phrases that you may include in your essay to make it more complete and also words that you may want to limit.

VERBS

Use the correct verb tense in your sentence.

create	appreciate	achieve	focus
influence	require	retain	increase
experience	dashed	restrict	inform
commit	develop	support	question
decide	compare	supply	apply
provide	manage	convey	convince
consider	educate	introduce	
recommend	expand		

ADJECTIVES

Use these words before a noun to create a more interesting sentence.

useful	young	simple	careful
tactful	uncertain	beneficial	outspoken
lovely	safe	informative	cautious
elaborate	common	generous	persistent
elegant	modern	weary	powerful
merry	marvelous	historical	vital
keen	knowledgeable	fresh	steady

ADVERBS

Use these words to modify a verb, adjective, or another adverb.

slowly	somewhat	more	suddenly
reassuringly	apparently	sometimes	strangely
perfectly	never	forever	awfully
carefully	really	quietly	near
yesterday	surely	twice	fast
very	easily		

TIME AND SPACE ORDER WORDS AND PHRASES

Use these words in your narrative essay to show sequence or in your expository or persuasive essay to help explain ideas.

first	subsequently	then	to the left
second	then again	last	to the right
third	further	previously	in front
next	after	afterwards	far off
later	above	soon after	nearby
after that	beyond		

WORDS AND PHRASES THAT SHOW CONTRASTING THOUGHTS

although	yet	on the other hand
but	however	on the contrary
nevertheless	rather	still

WORDS AND PHRASES THAT HELP ILLUSTRATE AND EXPLAIN AN IDEA

for example	for this reason	as has been said
for instance	truly	that is to say
to illustrate	to emphasize	in fact
thus	again	
in other words	to repeat	

CONNECTING WORDS

Be careful that you do not overuse these words and create run-on sentences.

and	or	but	nor	for

WORDS THAT SUMMARIZE

These words may be used at the conclusion of your essay.

in conclusion	in brief	in sum	in short
in summary	all in all	finally	therefore
to sum up	as a result		

WORDS THAT ADD INFORMATION			
again	in addition to	finally	for instance
in addition	another	as well as	in other words
for instance	also	also	that is
next	for example		

WORDS TO LIMIT IN YOUR ESSAY			
because	but	then	stuff
and	maybe	so	things (Be specific!)

ESSAY PRACTICE

Below is a prompt for a practice essay. On a separate sheet of paper write a quick outline and then begin your essay. Remember that the outline is for your own benefit and is not to be turned in with the essay. Time yourself as you write.

Prompt

American people have become more health conscious in the past few years. More people seem to be exercising regularly and watching what they eat.

Discussion Question

What are some ways that you can help yourself to become healthier or maintain your own good health?

Write an essay of about 250 words in which you explain or present your reasons for this topic. You have 45 minutes to write on this topic.

Sample Answer

After you finish writing your essay compare it to the sample essay below. You may have come up with similar ideas. Everyone will not choose the same three points to write about in their essay. As long as you can provide clear, focused main ideas and details to back them up, you should be on the road to success!

Since the above prompt was an expository theme, you should have written five paragraphs. Look now at the sample outline.

Sample Outline

I. There are many ways in which I stay healthy.
   A. eat right
   B. exercise daily
   C. try not to worry

II. I always try to eat the right types of food each day.
   A. eat from the four main food groups
   B. drink plenty of water

III. Before I begin each day I make sure I exercise at least ten minutes.
   A. start out with stretching exercises
   B. work up to more strenuous exercise

IV. Worry has a big effect on my health.
   A. simple things don't bother me
   B. relaxing

V. There are many ways to stay healthy but I choose to eat right, exercise, and not worry.

Sample Essay from Outline

MAINTAINING GOOD HEALTH

There are many ways in which I can stay healthy. I try to eat right, exercise daily, and try not to worry. If I do all of these things I feel better emotionally and physically.

I always try to eat the right types of food every day. Eating from the four basic food groups always helps. By doing this I make sure I get all the vitamins and minerals that I need each day. I also drink plenty of water instead of soft drinks with added sweeteners. I feel that this is better for me.

Before I begin each day I make sure I exercise at least ten minutes. I begin with stretching exercises. Later, I work up to more strenuous exercises that really get my heart rate up.

Worry has a big effect on my health. I try not to let things worry me as before. I don't let simple things bother me. I usually take a few minutes each day to relax.

There are many ways to stay healthy, but I choose to eat right, exercise, and not worry. With the combination of these three things, how can I go wrong?

In the above sample the word count is 195 words. Once you have your outline written, the paragraph doesn't take that long to write. Just remember to jot down phrases in your outline and don't worry about trying to come up with the "perfect" outline. No one will see it but you!

Allot Your Time

Remember that you have a maximum time of 45 minutes. Use the following guidelines.

1. Read the instructions completely and decide on a topic—three to five minutes.

2. Make your outline—five to ten minutes.

3. Write the 250-word essay—twenty to twenty-five minutes.

4. Revise and edit your essay—five minutes.

Keep these times in mind as you go in to write your essay.

REVISING THE ESSAY

This segment will give you some ideas on how to revise your essay once you have it written. Remember to always reread your essay once you have completed it. If you have allotted your time appropriately, you should have five to ten minutes to complete this very important part of essay writing.

Below is a set of guidelines to follow when revising your essay.

Check Yourself

1. Check for the main idea.

2. Check for *three* points in first paragraph of a persuasive or expository essay.

3. In the persuasive and expository essays, check the second, third, and fourth paragraphs for topic sentences related to the introduction.

4. Check narrative essay for sequencing and time order words.

5. Do your detail sentences in each paragraph stick to the topic?

6. Eliminate run-on sentences; check for correct punctuation, capitalization, subject/verb agreement, and spelling.

7. Check for a clear ending for your essay.

8. Check for clarity and focus.

9. Approximate whether or not the essay is 250 words.

Editing Exercises

Below is an essay with major mistakes. Jot down in the margins the problems that you see with the essay, then check any that you found with the rewritten essay.

BEING A GOOD CITIZEN

Everyone has ideas on how to be a good citizen. I believe that people need to be aware of current events and help other people.

In order to be a good citizen a person should be aware of the current events. If a person is informed good about what is taking place in the world then that person can in turn act on that information. Such as voting. Voting is something every person should do some people don't like to vote. It is a person's right and responsibility to vote in an election and make sure that we have responsible people running our government. Our government today is in need of strong leaders.

I believe everyone should help other people. I have a friend that volunteers their services at the nursing home. There are several nursing homes near here. Volunteering at your child's school is also a wonderful way to help other people this helps the child with class work or even homework.

I think being a good citizen is a great idea!

In the revision of "Being a Good Citizen," you can see that major reconstruction of the format was needed. In the first paragraph of the original essay there were only two points expressed when there should have been three. There were several run-on sentences and details that didn't pertain to the topic. The paragraphs began to ramble without a focus. The last paragraph was made up of only one sentence. You should never have a one-sentence paragraph in your essay. Introductory words in a sentence should be separated with a comma such as, "In order to be a good citizen, a person should....". Changing the word "good" to "well" and placing it before the verb in the sentence "If a person is informed good about what is taking place in the world...." makes better sense. "Good" is an adjective and is used to describe a noun; "well" is an adverb that tells more about the verb.

REVISION OF "BEING A GOOD CITIZEN"

Everyone has ideas on how to be a good citizen. I believe that people need to be aware of current events, help other people, and keep in touch with public officials.

In order to be a good citizen, I feel that a person should be aware of the current events. If a person is well informed about what is taking place in the world, that person in turn can act on that information.

A good citizen should help other people. There are many ways to help others. A few of these ways would be to volunteer in nursing homes or school.

Citizens should keep in touch with public officials. Everyone should know their local, state, and federal elected public officials that represent them. These people provide valuable input to governmental issues.

Being a good citizen is important. I believe that to be a good citizen a person should be aware of current events, help other people, and keep in touch with public officials.

Here is an essay with a few mistakes. See if you can find them in about five to ten minutes.

THE NEGATIVE IMPACT OF TELEVISION ON CHILDREN

Today it seems that children spend entirely too much time in front of the television. I feel that television has a negative effect on children because it takes up much of their free time it provides a child with much publicized violence and a child doesn't get much exercise while sitting in front of a television for hours on end.

When a child has free time I believe that child should be using it for more constructive things like studying or socializing with friends instead of sitting in front of a television watching it hour after hour and not really learning anything it seems they are just being intertained.

There is entirely too much violence on television. If a child watches television unsupervised they may be watching violent programs that the parents aren't aware of. These types of actions that they see on television may seem acceptable to the child and later the child may become involved in unacceptable behavior and the parents wouldn't want that to happen.

Sitting in front of the television daily also keeps the child from doing any physical activities. A child needs to be actively involved in types of physical stimulation that will burn off calories and keep a child's muscles strong.

I believe that television provides a negative impact on children. When children watch too much television it takes up a lot of their free time, it provides a child with visions of violence, and takes away time that a child could be exercising or playing.

In the revision of "The Negative Impact of Television on Children," there were only a few mistakes that you should have found in your ten-minute revision. First, there are some punctuation errors. There should be two commas in the second sentence of the first paragraph ("time," and "violence,"). There should also be a comma after the introductory words, "When a child has free time, I believe...." The second paragraph is made up of one very long incorrect sentence. It should be broken down into smaller sentences. Some words may be omitted because they are unnecessary and take away from the essay. There is also a spelling mistake in the second paragraph—*intertained* should be spelled *entertained*. The third paragraph has problems with an extremely long sentence. The word "and" should not be used in it. The sentence should be broken down into smaller sentences.

REVISION OF "THE NEGATIVE IMPACT OF TELEVISION ON CHILDREN"

Today it seems that children spend entirely too much time in front of the television. I feel that television has a negative effect on children because it takes up much of their free time, it provides a child with much publicized violence, and a child doesn't get much exercise while sitting in front of a television for hours on end.

When children have free time, I believe they should be using it for more constructive things like studying or socializing with friends. I believe they would learn more by doing this than watching television hour after hour. It seems they are just being entertained.

There is entirely too much violence on television. If children watch television unsupervised, they could be watching violent programs that the parents are not aware of. The type of violent actions children see may become acceptable to them. They may later try some of these violent actions.

Sitting in front of the television daily also keeps children from doing any physical activities. Children need to be actively involved in types of physical stimulation that will burn off calories and keep their muscles strong.

I believe that television provides a negative impact on children. When children watch too much television it takes up a lot of their free time, it provides them with visions of violence, and takes away time that they could be exercising or playing.

ESSAY PRACTICE

It is now time to put everything together that you have read and create your own essay.

Prompt

Most people go though life one day at a time accomplishing things along the way. Some people accomplish great education or wealth; others accomplish skills at writing, music, or nurturing. Sometimes, simple accomplishments mean more than great ones. Try to think of what your greatest accomplishments are in life.

Discussion Question

What are your greatest accomplishments?

Write an essay of about 250 words in which you discuss this topic. Give supporting details and examples for every point you make. You have 45 minutes to write on this topic.

Check Yourself

1. Read carefully the prompt, discussion question, and directions.

2. Decide if the prompt is expository, persuasive, or narrative.

3. Plan your essay before you begin.

4. Use scrap paper to prepare a simple outline.

5. Write your essay on the lined pages of a separate sheet of paper.

6. Read carefully what you have written and make needed changes.

7. Check for focus, elaboration, organization, conventions, and integration.

PRACTICE PROMPTS FOR ESSAYS

This segment will provide you with practice prompts for essays. Remember, the more you practice, the better you will become at writing essays.

EXPOSITORY PROMPTS

Collections	Sticking to a Budget
In the News	Automobile Safety
Fun Games to Play	Weather Hazards
Favorite Television Programs	Celebrations
My Friends	Auction Purchases
My Spare Time	Favorite Animals
Funny Sights	Amusement Parks
Dangerous Experiences	World Problems
Favorite Songs	Women in Politics
Running a Household	What I Hope to Gain by Getting My GED

NARRATIVE PROMPTS

My Greatest Adventure	Moving Day
Relatives Visit	My First Home
The Family Vacation	My Experience with Technology
My Greatest Lesson	Something I Haven't Told
Never Again!	My Last Day of Work
My Favorite Hobby	The Greatest Game I've Ever Seen!
A Joyful Experience	My Most Challenging Day
My Experience in the Army	My Most Nervous Day
My Greatest Luck	A Childhood Experience
A Sad Day	A Proud Day in My Life

PERSUASIVE

Is the death sentence constitutional?

Do talk shows go too far?

Should the Ten Commandments be posted in schools?

Should the number of immigrants be restricted in the United States?

Should all work places have mandatory drug testing?

Should high school students be required to pass a test to graduate?

Do you think the United States should use only metric measurements?

Should the government provide homes for all of the homeless?

Do you believe in life on other planets?

Should the rich pay more taxes?

Should there be video cameras on streets that record people for the Internet?

Should there be seat belts on school buses?

Should the government allow advertisements to be placed on school buses?

Should gambling be allowed in every state?

Should E-Commerce have to pay taxes?

Do we still need a National Guard?

Are planes really safe?

Should there be a time limit for people on welfare?

Should there be a "cut-off" age for people running for president?

Should there be more censorship on television?

PRACTICE ESSAY

(Answers will vary.)

You could have written the practice essay as expository or narrative. If you wrote it as expository you should have followed these guidelines: You should have five paragraphs in your essay. The first is the introduction with the second, third, and fourth being the body. The fifth paragraph would be your summary of the essay. You could have written this essay in two different ways: One, you could have thought of three specific accomplishments that you have had in your life and written about them including main ideas and details. The second way would be for you to have thought of one main accomplishment in your life and given three specific reasons why this was such a great accomplishment for you. You would have used the three specific reasons as your main ideas for the body of the essay.

If you wrote the essay as narrative you should have written the essay in this way: First there should be a three or four paragraph set up. Narrative paragraphs are written in the first person with a sequence of events taking place. You should have listed in your first paragraph your main idea, stating what your greatest accomplishment was. The second and third paragraphs would be a logical sequence of events, explanations, and support telling about your greatest accomplishment. Your last paragraph would be the summarization of the essay.

RUBRIC

This segment will give you some insight on how your essay will be scored.

When you write your essay and submit it to be scored, it will be read by two trained readers. These two readers will base the score they give you on an "overall effectiveness" of the essay. Essays will be assigned a score of 1 to 4, with one being the lowest and four the highest. They will be looking at areas such as:

- **Focus:** The clarity of your ideas to the topic of the essay.
- **Elaboration:** How well you explain and support your ideas or opinions.
- **Organization:** The logical flow and structure of the essay.
- **Conventions:** The standard use of written English.
- **Integration:** The overall effectiveness of the essay.

The readers will not count each mistake that is made and make a deduction of points, but will instead look at the overall effectiveness of the essay for scoring. You may make several small mistakes with grammar or punctuation and still end up with a 4 on the score as long as the essay is well focused, supported, and organized.

Following is the official GED Essay Scoring Guide. This will give you a good idea of how your essay will be graded.

GED Essay Scoring Guide

The GED Testing Service has defined the four levels of GED Essays:

4 – Effective

3 – Adequate

2 – Marginal

1 – Ineffective (It is important to note that a score of 1 will require you to retake the entire Language Arts, Writing, Part I.)

Papers will show *some or all* of the following characteristics.

Upper-half papers make clear a definite purpose, pursued with varying degrees of effectiveness. They also have a structure that shows evidence of some deliberate planning.

Level 4 writing is *competent.*

Papers scored as a 4 are clearly organized with effective support for each of the writer's major points. The writing offers substantive ideas. The surface features are consistently under control, despite an occasional lapse in usage.

Level 3 writing is *sufficient.*

Papers scored as a 3 usually show some evidence of planning or development. Support, though sufficient, tends to be less extensive or convincing than that found in a paper scored as a 4. The writer generally observes the conventions of accepted English usage. Some errors are present, but they are not severe enough to interfere significantly with the writer's main purpose.

Level 2 writing is *acceptable*.

Papers scored as a 2 are characterized by a marked lack of development or inadequate support for ideas. The level of thought apparent in the writing is frequently unsophisticated or superficial, often marked by a listing of unsupported generalizations. Instead of suggesting a clear purpose, these papers often present conflicting purposes. Errors in accepted English usage may seriously interfere with the overall effectiveness of these papers.

Level 1 writing is *insufficient*.

Papers scored as a 1 leave the impression that the writer has not only *not* accomplished a purpose, but has not made any purpose apparent. The dominant feature of these papers is the lack of control. The writer stumbles both in conveying a clear plan for the paper and in expressing ideas according to the conventions of accepted English usage.

Level 0 writing is *not able to be scored*.

The zero score is reserved for papers which are blank, illegible, or written on a topic other than the one assigned.

Now, keeping this scoring guide in mind, study the following treatments of the unfavorable effects on health of smoking.

PAPER 1

The major effects of smoking include a shortened life span. Each year nearly half a million Americans die prematurely as a result of smoking. Smoking is responsible for 30 percent of all cancer deaths in the United States, including those from lung cancer.

Smoking weakens the heart's ability to function, leading to heart attacks and strokes. In addition, tens of thousands die from chronic lung disease linked to smoking.

Women who smoke during pregnancy are ten times more likely to have miscarriages. Also, the babies of smoking mothers tend to have lower birth weights.

Finally, there is the risk of death or severe illness for those who are exposed to second-hand smoke: lung cancer, emphysema, bronchitis, pneumonia, or heart disease.

PAPER 2

Smoking has many unfavorable effects. It affects the health of the smoker in many ways. It results in shortness of breath. It causes tobacco stains.

Smoking becomes a habit that is hard to break smokers become addicted to cigarettes because of the nicotine.

Smoking is also very expensive three packs a day cost about $50 a week which could buy alot of food and necesities.

If you have a family, they are affected by second-hand smoke. Children learn to smoke by imitating there parents.

That's why you shouldn't smoke.

PAPER 3

Smoking has bad affects. Millions of americans smoke they spend a great deal of money on cigarettes.

Smoking is bad for you. It destroys your health and causes Cancer. You may think its grown up to smoke but it really isnt.

Smoking also hurts the ones around you. Who inhale your smoke. Women who are pregnant might hurt they're babies.

Smokers pollute the air. And make it hard for others around them to breath.

This is why you should think twice before you light up.

Paper 1 has excellent organization of materials relating to the subject. Paragraphing is logical. Specific facts are presented, and everything relates directly to the topic. There are no errors in sentence structure, punctuation, or capitalization.

Paper 2 has elements of organization. Each of the first four paragraphs makes a single argument.

This paper has two main weaknesses. First, the arguments are not backed up by any relevant facts. One of the effects mentioned (tobacco stains) is unimportant, while important effects on health are omitted. In addition, there are a number of errors. Paragraph two has a run-on sentence, as has paragraph three. *A lot* is misspelled as *alot*, and *necessities* as *necesities*; also, there should be a comma after *week*. In paragraph four, an incorrect pronoun and verb refer to family—*they are* instead of *it is*, and *there* should be replaced by *their*. Although this paper has good organization, the errors would reduce the rating to a 3.

Paper 3 is poorly organized. Irrelevant material is included (money spent, grown-up feeling). Statements are repeated and not documented (causes cancer). Also, there are many errors in accepted English usage. There are sentence errors—a run-on sentence in the first paragraph, and sentence fragments in the third and fourth paragraphs. There are several spelling errors; *affects* should be *effects*; *its* should be *it's*; *isnt* should be *isn't*; *they're* should be *their*; *breath* should be *breathe*. *Americans*, not *americans*, and *cancer*, not *Cancer*, are correct. Sentences are very short, even childish.

There is no doubt that Paper 1 will receive a 4, but Paper 3 will receive a 1.

SOCIAL STUDIES

CHAPTER 10

Reading and Interpreting Social Studies Materials

GOVERNMENT, HISTORY, ECONOMICS, AND GEOGRAPHY

Reading in the social studies requires a number of skills that are common to all reading materials. When you read in any subject, you want to identify the *main ideas* of the writer. So, too, in social studies you need to get at the key thoughts being expressed.

LOCATING THE MAIN IDEA

If you read too slowly, you may miss the main point because you have gotten too involved in details. It is important, therefore, that you first read the selection through to the end rather quickly *before* you turn to the questions.

Where do you look for the main idea? Most often you will find it in the topic sentence, usually the first sentence in the passage. Sometimes, however, the writer will withhold the main idea until the last sentence, building up to it throughout the entire selection. At other times, the writer will include both a main idea and an important secondary (or subordinate) idea.

FINDING DETAILS

After you have determined the main idea, the next step is to *locate the facts supporting the main idea or details* that flow from the main idea. If, for example, the main idea of a passage is that democracy is the best form of government, the author will undoubtedly provide facts or reasons to support this statement or include facts that show the superiority of democracy to other forms of government. If the main idea is a general conclusion that many persons with physical disabilities have overcome them and become famous, details would probably include such examples as Helen Keller and Franklin D. Roosevelt.

How do you locate a detail? You go back to the selection a second or third time to dig it out of the passage. It most frequently will come in the middle

---

TIP

To train yourself in **locating the main idea**, ask yourself the same questions that will be asked of you on the examination.

1. What is the main idea of the passage?
2. What is the best title for the passage?
3. If I were choosing a suitable headline for the article in a newspaper, what headline would I choose?
4. What is the *topic sentence* of this paragraph or paragraphs; *that is, the sentence that includes the ideas contained in all the other sentences?*

TIP

To train yourself in **locating details**, ask yourself these questions:

1. What examples are given to illustrate the main point?
2. What reasons are offered to support the author's position?
3. What arguments for or against a proposal does the author present?
4. When, where, how did something happen?
5. What did someone do?
6. Why did he or she do it?

or toward the end of the selection. Sometimes clues in the passage steer you to the detail or fact in question. Clues for locating details may read:

> An example is...
>
> One reason is...
>
> An argument in support of (or against)...is...
>
> A reason for...is...

To find the proper detail, it will be necessary for you to *learn how to skim*, that is, to read rapidly to locate the piece of information you are seeking. You can do this only if you know specifically what you need to find in a given selection and limit your reading to finding only that fact.

DETERMINING ORGANIZATION

Note the manner in which the writer organizes his or her material. This will help you to follow the author's thoughts effectively. The writer may organize his or her material chronologically, that is, in the order in which a series of events happened. Alternatively, the writer may organize the material logically by presenting the arguments *for* a position in one paragraph and the arguments *against* in another. Or the writer may present his or her ideas in the order of their importance, with the most important ideas first. This, in fact, is the way a newspaper article is written—"from the top down"—in case the reader doesn't have time to finish it all.

If you can determine the organization of a passage, you can zero in on the relationship between the main parts of a passage.

**CLUES TO FINDING THE RELATIONSHIP
BETWEEN THE MAIN PARTS OF A PASSAGE**

Sequence of ideas is indicated by such words as:

first	next	finally
second	further	

Additional ideas are indicated by such words as:

and	furthermore	likewise
besides	also	in addition

Opposing or contrasting ideas are indicated by such words as:

on the other hand	but	yet
however	still	although

DRAWING CONCLUSIONS

Another step involves *drawing conclusions from the material presented*. Conclusions are often indicated by such words as:

thus	accordingly	consequently
therefore	so	as a result

Sometimes, however, the author does not draw the conclusion, but leaves it to you, the reader, to do so. You infer the conclusion from the materials presented; you draw the inference as a result of details you have noted and the relationships you have determined (time sequence, logical order, cause-and-effect, among others). Thus, if an author indicates that a given president vetoed many bills, you might infer that the president and the Congress differed in their thinking about legislation, perhaps because the Congress was controlled by a political party different from that of the president.

READING CRITICALLY

In addition to drawing conclusions and making inferences, it is essential in social sciences that you react to what you have read. Often you must judge the material you are reading, not merely understand it. Historians, political scientists, economists, sociologists, and anthropologists often present one side of the story, their side, but there is almost always another side. In other words, they may "slant" the material to suit their bias by including only facts and arguments favorable to their own view and omitting everything else. It is essential for you to *read critically*. Do *not* accept everything that is written just because it appears in print.

You must develop the habit of challenging the author by raising questions, judging the completeness and truth of the information presented, and distinguishing fact from opinion.

A *statement of fact* is one that can be proved true by consulting a reliable source of information such as an encyclopedia, an almanac, or an official government document. Here is an example.

EXAMPLE

The federal government spends billions of dollars each year helping states with aid to needy persons: needy through unemployment, disability, or family problems.

This statement can be verified by consulting the official federal budget.

A *statement of opinion or belief* is one that expresses the feelings, thoughts, or beliefs of a person or persons, and that cannot be proved to be true by reference to any reliable source at the present time.

EXAMPLE

It is believed that by the year 2024, population will have outstripped food production and starvation will be widespread.

This is a prediction in the form of a statement or belief attributed to an unidentified source ("It is believed...") that cannot be proved until the year 2024. It is possible that others may have their own beliefs. In any case, the statement is definitely not a fact.

Note that certain words are clues to statements of opinion.

> **TIP**
>
> To train yourself to **make inferences** properly in order to draw a conclusion, ask yourself these questions:
>
> 1. What do I think will happen next? (inference or prediction as to the outcome)
> 2. Putting these arguments together, what conclusion can I reach?
> 3. If one result was caused by something, will a similar effect take place in another situation where the same cause is operating?
> 4. What is the writer suggesting, rather than saying outright?

WORDS THAT ARE CLUES TO STATEMENTS OF OPINION

claim	probably	consider	should (have)
believe	possibly	will be	could (have)
think	might	likely	ought

WORDS THAT PROBABLY REFLECT OPINION RATHER THAN FACT

better	undesirable	desirable
worse	necessary	unnecessary

REMEMBER: Always apply the test, "Can this statement be proved by reference to a reliable source?"

TIP

You can **read critically** if you ask yourself the following questions:

1. Why is the author writing this selection?
2. What is the author trying to get me, the reader, to believe?
3. Is the author presenting a balanced or one-sided view of the situation?
4. Is the author omitting essential information?
5. Is the author appealing to my mind or to my emotions and prejudices?
6. Does the author have some hidden reason for writing what he or she writes?
7. Is the author accurate? Or does he or she deal in half-truths?
8. Does the author use words with specific agreed-upon meanings, or does he or she use words that are "loaded" because they have special meanings?

It is important to distinguish fact from opinion in the printed word when writers unconsciously allow their opinions or biases to enter into their writing. It is even more important to do so when a writer slants his or her material deliberately.

DETECTING PROPAGANDA AND PROPAGANDA TECHNIQUES

When writers deliberately spread ideas or opinions to benefit themselves or institutions to which they belong or to damage opponents or opposing institutions, they are engaging in propaganda. A propagandist tries to influence your thinking or behavior and to turn your opinions and actions in a certain direction. He or she uses words that appeal to your emotions—your fears, your loves, your hates—rather than to your reason, to your ability to think clearly, in order, ultimately, to make you do things in a way you never ordinarily would do.

Six common techniques in propaganda are:

1. *Name-calling.* The writer tries to influence you by attaching a bad name to an individual, group, nation, race, policy, practice, or belief.

   EXAMPLE

   It would be wise to pay no attention to that loony liberal (or retarded reactionary, depending upon the writer's point of view).

   Certain names are loaded with emotional overtones: Fascist, Red, Nazi, Commie. You must note carefully in what way and for what purpose these terms are used. Name-calling is a common propaganda technique.

2. *Glittering generalities.* The writer attaches "good" names to people and policies, in the hope that you will accept them without really looking into the facts.

   EXAMPLE

   The writer appeals to our emotions by using such "good" terms as *forward-looking*, *peace-loving*, *straight-shooting*, and *idealistic*.

   We all love progress, peace, honesty, and idealism so we tend to accept rather than challenge. Always ask the questions "why" and "how" when "good" terms are applied to people and policies.

3. *Transfer.* The writer tries to use the approval and prestige of something or some institution we respect to get us to accept something else in which he or she is interested.

   EXAMPLE

   Most Americans are law-abiding and respect their police officers. One who writes on behalf of an athletic league supported by the local police will try to get you to transfer your approval of the police to the athletic league he or she is sponsoring.

   Always examine the person or institution receiving the transfer on its own merits rather than on the merits of the original institution you love and respect.

4. ***Testimonial.*** Advertisements on television and radio make wide use of testimonials. A top athlete endorses a breakfast cereal. A beautiful actress recommends a cosmetic cream. An ex-senator testifies to the value of a credit card. A testimonial is a recommendation made by someone on behalf of a person, a product, or an institution.

But is the athlete an expert on nutrition? Is the actress an expert on skin care? Is the politician an expert on personal money management? REMEMBER: these people are being paid to make these testimonials. You must ask yourself whether the person making the testimonial is expert enough to do so before you believe what you read or hear.

More subtle is newspaper reporting that is based on *indirect* testimonials.

EXAMPLES

Official circles report...; It was learned from a senior government official...; A reliable source stated...

Always ask *which* circles, *which* official, *which* source. Be careful of any information that comes from a high *unidentified* source.

5. ***Card-stacking.*** The writer attempts to get you to see only one side of a particular issue. To do so, he or she will use half-truths and omit the other side of the argument. Examples occur frequently in "authorized" biographies that present a person's life in glowing terms, including all the good qualities while omitting or toning down the poor ones. When reading about an issue, always note whether both sides have been discussed or whether the cards have been stacked by the writer on one side of the issue only.

6. ***Bandwagon.*** The writer tries to make you go along with the crowd. Since most people like to follow the trend, they will respond favorably to such statements as "Nine out of ten Americans prefer..." or "...sells more... than all other companies put together." In politics, the bandwagon technique is often seen in action in national political conventions. "Join the swing to...."

The bandwagon-approach writer does not want you to think clearly for yourself. You should always ask *why* you should join the others, and not do so because your emotions have gotten the better of you.

> **REMEMBER**
>
> A critical reader
>
> - does not believe everything he or she reads simply because it is in print;
> - accepts as true only statements that can be proved or that are made by reliable authorities;
> - separates fact from opinion, recognizes emotional language and bias, and is aware of slanting by omission.

DETERMINING CAUSE AND EFFECT

A reading skill frequently used in social studies involves determining the relationship between events. Events rarely occur in isolation. They are generally the result of other events that happened earlier.

EXAMPLE

The Japanese bombed Pearl Harbor on December 7, 1941. The United States then declared war on Japan.

The bombing of Pearl Harbor was the cause; the declaration of war was the result or effect of the bombing. Always try, when reading of an event, to determine its cause or causes. *Here is a question involving cause and effect:*

1. President Franklin D. Roosevelt's New Deal policy led to numerous government agencies, created in an effort to combat the effects of the Great Depression. One major result of this policy was to

   (1) weaken the power of the chief executive
   (2) strengthen the policy of laissez-faire
   (3) increase the power of the federal government
   (4) expand the importance of states' rights
   (5) lessen the need for judicial review

ANSWER AND ANALYSIS

The question asks for a result of President Franklin D. Roosevelt's New Deal policy. The opposite results occurred from those listed as Choices 1, 4, and 5; that is, the New Deal strengthened the power of the chief executive; weakened the importance of states' rights, and increased the need for judicial review. Choice 2, the policy of laissez-faire, provides for little or no interference by government in the affairs of business, clearly an incorrect response. Only Choice 3 is correct because the New Deal program called for executive action to advance economic recovery and social welfare.

COMPARING AND CONTRASTING IDEAS AND ORGANIZATIONS

Another frequently needed skill in social studies reading involves the ability to compare and contrast institutions and events. You may be asked to compare American democracy with French democracy, contrast democracy with communism, compare the platforms of the Republicans and Democrats, or contrast the role of women in the eighteenth century with their role in the twentieth.

QUESTION

1. The careers of Theodore Roosevelt and Franklin D. Roosevelt were similar because each man

   (1) was an outstanding military leader before becoming president
   (2) led the cause for international peace, but involved the United States in a war
   (3) succeeded to the presidency upon the death of the preceding president
   (4) believed in a strong presidency and acted accordingly
   (5) represented the same political party

ANSWER AND ANALYSIS

You are asked to compare the careers of two American presidents. Franklin D. Roosevelt was not an outstanding military leader before becoming president. Theodore Roosevelt did not involve the United States in a war. Franklin D. Roosevelt did not succeed to the presidency upon the death of the preceding president. Theodore Roosevelt was a Republican; Franklin D. Roosevelt, a Democrat. Thus Choices 1, 2, 3, and 5 are incorrect. Choice 4 is correct because both Roosevelts were strong presidents: Theodore Roosevelt was a trust buster, had a Square Deal policy, and pursued an expansionist foreign policy; Franklin D. Roosevelt carried out New Deal policies and a Good Neighbor policy with Latin America, and he led the nation for most of World War II.

LEARNING SOCIAL STUDIES VOCABULARY AND DERIVING MEANING FROM CONTEXT

In social studies as in science, vocabulary is of critical importance. Words found in social studies may

- represent complicated ideas, such as *nationalism, referendum, mercantilism;*

- imply a whole set of ideas, such as *feudalism, militarism, bimetallism;*

- have meanings specific to the social studies although they have other meanings as well, such as *Axis, act, shop;*

- come from foreign languages, such as *apartheid, junta, laissez-faire;*

- have meanings that go beyond the usual ones, such as *dove, plank, scab.*

Try to derive the correct meaning from the *context*—the words with which the term appears in a sentence.

You can **check your understanding of the meaning of the vocabulary** in a given selection by asking yourself:

1. What is the key word in the sentence (paragraph, selection)?

2. What is the meaning of the word in *this* sentence (context)?

3. What is the exact meaning (denotation) of the word in this selection?

4. What is the extended meaning (connotation) of the word in this selection? (What does it *suggest* as well as say?)

5. What is the effect of a given word on me?

6. What is the special meaning of this word in social studies?

PRACTICE WITH SOCIAL STUDIES READINGS

A representative selection in each of the social studies follows, together with questions based on it. Read each of the selections and try to answer the questions *without* referring to the answer analyses that follow. Then check your answers by carefully reading the analyses. Each of the sets of questions following the selections contains a question that

- is aimed at testing whether you can *locate the main idea* ("The best title for the selection is...");

- is designed to test your ability to *locate details* ("One difference between _____ and _____ is...");

- requires you to show your *knowledge of social studies vocabulary* ("All of the following words used in economics are correctly paired with their meanings EXCEPT...");

- forces you to *make a conclusion or predict an outcome* ("We can conclude that..." "It is most likely that...").

In addition, there are questions designed to test your ability to

- *find reasons* that the author uses to support an argument;

- *follow the organization* of a selection;

- *identify the position taken by the author* (or any bias he or she may have).

CIVICS AND GOVERNMENT, WITH ANSWERS AND ANSWER ANALYSIS

There are the following four key committees at a political convention:

➤ The *Credentials Committee*. This group decides who is an official delegate entitled to vote.

➤ The permanent *Organization Committee*, which picks the convention's officers, including the chairperson. This official decides who can speak at the convention and who cannot.

➤ The *Rules Committee*, which makes the rules by which the convention and the party organization are run.

➤ The *Resolutions and Platform Committee*, which writes the party platform. Usually, a convention lasts about four days. Typically, a temporary convention chairperson opens the convention with a *keynote address*, which is meant to set the tone of the convention—and quite frequently does. The real business of the day, however, goes on behind the podium, where the Credentials Committee settles disputes over *delegate credentials.*

On the second day the *party platform* is read, debated, and usually voted upon. A *permanent chairperson* is installed, and the convention is asked to approve the reports of its major committees.

On the third day actual *nominations* for presidential candidates are taken. States are called alphabetically at the Republican Convention, by lottery at the Democratic. Each state may nominate one candidate, second a nomination already made, yield (surrender the floor to another state), or pass. After each nomination there is usually a loud demonstration for the nominee.

Balloting begins only after nominations have been closed. A *simple majority*—one more than half the votes—is all that is needed to win. Every Republican presidential candidate since 1948 and every Democratic one since 1952 has won on the first ballot. If no one wins a simple majority on the first ballot, the vote is taken again until a candidate is picked.

By the fourth day a *presidential nominee* has usually emerged. He, in turn, addresses party leaders and tells them whom he prefers for *vice president.* Usually he gets his way.

Finally, the two candidates make their *acceptance speeches*, go through a few ceremonial events, and the *convention ends.*

An explanation of the following words can be found in the "Glossary of Social Studies Terms": *ballot, convention, majority, nominate, party, platform,* and *plurality.*

1. The main idea of the selection on page 276 is

   (1) choosing a president and vice president
   (2) four key committees
   (3) how Republican and Democratic conventions differ
   (4) conventions: American political dramas
   (5) how conventions are organized and run

2. The vice-presidential candidate is chosen by the

   (1) party leaders
   (2) roll-call vote
   (3) Rules Committee
   (4) permanent convention chairman
   (5) presidential nominee

3. In the next convention, it is most likely that the party candidates will be nominated by

   (1) simple majority on the second ballot
   (2) plurality on the second ballot
   (3) two-thirds vote on the first ballot
   (4) simple majority on the first ballot
   (5) plurality on the first ballot

4. The INCORRECTLY paired group below is

   (1) Organization Committee—convention chairperson
   (2) permanent chairperson—keynote address
   (3) nominees—acceptance speeches
   (4) states—nominations
   (5) simple majority—choice of nominee

5. One difference between Republican and Democratic conventions is the way in which

   (1) committees are organized
   (2) convention chairpersons are chosen
   (3) nominations for presidential candidates are made
   (4) balloting takes place
   (5) party platforms are decided

6. The writer of this selection has organized the passage

   (1) logically
   (2) psychologically
   (3) chronologically
   (4) argumentatively
   (5) critically

Answer Key

1. **5**   2. **5**   3. **4**   4. **2**   5. **3**   6. **3**

Answer Analysis

1. **5** Question 1 calls for the main idea of the selection. The possible answers generally fall into several categories. *One of the choices* will be incorrect or irrelevant; that is, it will have nothing to do with the question. *Other choices* will focus on details and not on the main idea. *Still another choice* will be too general, too vague. *The correct answer* will be broad in scope yet specific enough to indicate the main idea or purpose of the article. Choice 5 is correct because it indicates the main idea of the article, which is to explain how conventions are organized by committees and how they are run to accomplish their purposes, namely, nominating a presidential and a vice-presidential candidate and adopting a party platform. Choice 1, choosing a president and vice president, is incorrect since the convention merely nominates. It chooses the presidential and vice-presidential candidates who may become president and vice president if elected. Choices 2 and 3 deal with details; the committee structure and the one point of difference between the Republican and the Democratic conventions. Choice 4 is too broad; conventions may be American political dramas but that is *not* the main idea or purpose of this selection.

2. **5** This question requires you to locate a detail, albeit an important detail, in the passage. Skimming (reading rapidly) through the passage, you will note the term *vice president* for the first time in the next to last paragraph. It is there you will find the correct answer—Choice 5. The presidential nominee tells the party leaders whom he prefers for vice president.

3. **4** Question 3 requires you to predict an outcome because it uses the words "In the next convention, it is most likely...." Since the presidential candidate has won on the first ballot for over twenty years in both parties' political conventions, and since a simple majority is all that is required to win, it is safe to predict that this will be true of future conventions. Therefore, Choice 4 is correct.

4. **2** Question 4 is somewhat tricky. All of the choices contain correct associations but one. Thus, the Organization Committee chooses the convention chairperson; the nominees make acceptance speeches; the states make nominations; a simple majority results in a nomination. Only Choice 2 is in error; the *temporary* chairperson makes the keynote address.

5. **3** Question 5 pinpoints the one difference between the Republican and the Democratic conventions. Skimming to a point halfway through the selection, looking for the words *Republican* and *Democratic*, you find that the actual nominations are made differently—by alphabet in one and by lottery in the other. The correct choice, therefore, is 3.

6. **3** Question 6 calls your attention to the organization of the article. To find the answer, you note how the various paragraphs in the passage follow one another. In this instance, the second paragraph indicates the length of the convention—four days—and tells how it opens. The third paragraph deals with the second day; the fourth paragraph, with the third day. The next to the last paragraph indicates what has happened by the fourth day. Since the passage follows the time sequence of the convention, it is organized chronologically. Choice 3 is the correct answer.

HISTORY, WITH ANSWERS AND ANSWER ANALYSIS

The United States is often considered a young nation, but in fact it is next to the oldest continuous government in the world. The reason is that its people have always been willing to accommodate themselves to change. We have been dedicated to equality, but have been willing to realize it by flexible means. In the European sense of the term, America's political parties are not parties at all, because they do not divide over basic beliefs. Neither wishes to overturn or replace the existing political and economic order; they merely desire to alter it at slower or faster rates of speed.

One of our proudest achievements has been the creation of a system of controlled capitalism, that yields the highest living standards on earth, and has made possible a society as nearly classless as man has ever known. The profit system as it has developed in America shares its benefits with all parts of society: capital, labor, and the consuming masses. Yet even this was the result of trial and error. Unprincipled businessmen had first to be restrained by government, and by the growing power of organized labor, before they came to learn that they must serve the general good in pursuing their own economic interests. Now labor is feeling the restraint.

Even our creed of democracy is not fixed and unchangeable. Thus the statesmen of the early republic, though they strongly believed in private enterprise, chose to make the post office a government monopoly and to give the schools to public ownership. Since then, government has broadened its activities in many ways. Americans hold with Lincoln that "the legitimate object of government is to do for a community of people whatever they need to have done but cannot do at all, or cannot do so well for themselves, in their separate and individual capacities."

An explanation of the following words can be found in "Glossary of Social Studies Terms:" *capitalism, democracy, party, profit, monopoly, republic,* and *standard of living.*

1. The main quality of the United States stressed in this passage is its

   (1) youth
   (2) equality
   (3) high living standards
   (4) profit system
   (5) flexibility

2. The widely held belief about the United States with which the passage mentions disagreement concerns American

   (1) political parties
   (2) capitalism
   (3) private enterprise
   (4) labor
   (5) public ownership

3. All of the following are characteristic of the United States, according to the passage, EXCEPT a

   (1) dedication to equality
   (2) classless society
   (3) belief in democracy
   (4) profit system
   (5) controlled capitalism

4. An agency that performs a function of which Lincoln, according to his quoted words, would most approve is the

   (1) U.S. Office of Education
   (2) U.S. Chamber of Commerce
   (3) National Guard
   (4) Public Service Commission
   (5) Federal Aviation Administration

5. The creation of the U.S. government post office monopoly is cited as an example of a

   (1) replacement of the existing economic order
   (2) restraint of unprincipled businesspersons
   (3) control of organized labor
   (4) flexible view of private enterprise
   (5) system of shared profits

6. According to the passage, which of the following statements is true?

   (1) Our political parties agree on goals but not on methods.
   (2) Business has a larger share of profits than labor.
   (3) Government has tended to restrict its role in American life.
   (4) Americans are conservative where change is required.
   (5) Americans have kept their democratic beliefs intact.

7. The author's view of change in America is

   (1) critical
   (2) cautious
   (3) favorable
   (4) qualified
   (5) unclear

Answer Key

1. **5**   2. **1**   3. **2**   4. **5**   5. **4**   6. **1**
7. **3**

Answer Analysis

1. **5** This question requires you to determine the author's main purpose in writing this passage. Each of Choices 1 through 4 refers to a quality of the United States, but none of them is central to the selection. Flexibility is mentioned in many ways: "willing to accommodate themselves to change"; "flexible means"; "trial and error"; "not fixed and unchangeable."

2. **1** The question calls for selecting a common belief about the United States that is called into question in the passage. While two exceptions to private enterprise are cited, the belief in private enterprise is not challenged. Three other beliefs are mentioned, but none of them except political parties is called into question. The passage states that Europeans would not consider America's political parties parties at all. So Choice 1 is the correct answer.

3. **2** Here location of a detail in the passage is required. Of the five characteristics mentioned, four are true characteristics of the United States. The fifth, a classless society, is not, although a society "as nearly classless as man has ever known" is a quality of American life.

4. **5** This difficult question involves applying the principle stated by Lincoln to contemporary American institutions. What is the principle? That government fills a need for a community that the community itself cannot fill or fill well. Choice 1 is incorrect since education is a function the states have traditionally performed. Choice 2 is incorrect since the U.S. Chamber of Commerce is a private organization, not a federal agency. Choice 3 is incorrect since the National Guard is under state jurisdiction in peacetime. Choice 4 is incorrect because Public Service Commissions are generally state agencies. By the process of elimination, Choice 5 is correct. The Federal Aviation Administration regulates air commerce, including a national system of airports and air traffic control, an interstate function that a state ("community") cannot efficiently perform.

5. **4** This question calls for recall of a detail mentioned in the passage. Although the founders of our republic "strongly believed in private enterprise," they "chose to make the post office a government monopoly." This is an example of how flexible they were. The correct answer is 4. The other choices are irrelevant.

6. **1** Involved here are four statements that are false according to the passage and one that is true. Each statement has to be considered in light of what is said in the passage, and four must be discarded. Choices 3, 4, and 5 contradict what is said: government has actually broadened its role; Americans have always been willing to accommodate to change; our creed of democracy is not fixed. Choice 2 is not answerable solely on the evidence given in the passage, since we are not told the size of the shares of profit that capital and labor receive. Only Choice 1 is true: our political parties wish to retain "the existing political and economic order." They differ, however, on the rate of speed at which to change it.

7. **3** This question requires an inference on your part. "From what I have read," you must ask yourself, "what is the author's view of the issue he discusses?" The issue is change and the author obviously applauds it. Choice 3—favorable—is the correct answer. Why? The reason is found in the first two sentences. All the rest of the passage merely gives examples of change. The author cites the fact that the United States is "next to the oldest continuous government in the world." He is proud of that and he attributes that fact, in the next sentence, to our willingness to accommodate ourselves to change. Therefore, change must be good if it enables our government to survive.

Thus far, we have thoroughly analyzed the answers to two passages in political science and history. We have *located the main ideas* of each selection. We have dealt with the problem of *identifying* various kinds of *details*. In each selection, your *knowledge of social studies vocabulary* was tested. Finally, you were required to *draw inferences and predict outcomes*. The remaining four selections will give you further practice in these reading skills. We will analyze only those questions that introduce new reading techniques or that present special problems. Be certain to check your answers against the correct answers that follow the questions. If you made an error, do not hesitate to go back to the selection and read it through once more.

ECONOMICS, WITH ANSWERS AND ANSWER ANALYSIS

Could the United States fall into the depths of another Great Depression?

Economists can't say for sure. Most feel, however, that past depressions have taught us how to avoid economic disaster.

We've learned, for example, of the need for:

• *Government regulation of the stock market.* The Securities Act of 1933 made stock dealings less of a shell game by bringing them out into the open. The Securities Exchange Act of 1934 set up the Securities and Exchange Commission (S.E.C.), which acts as a sort of official consumer watchdog group. One of its jobs is to warn the investing public against the sort of crazy speculating that preceded the 1929 crash.

- *A permanent Council of Economic Advisers to take the economy's pulse for the government.* The Employment Act of 1946 created the Council of Economic Advisers. Its recommendations in 1949, 1958, 1969, and 1985 observers feel, helped keep the recessions of these years from becoming depressions.

- *A Federal Deposit Insurance Corporation (F.D.I.C.) to promise government backing of bank deposits.* The F.D.I.C. insures certain bank deposits. Such insurance has so far prevented the type of bank runs—panic withdrawals—that forced thousands of banks to close their doors in the early 1930s.

- *A federal relief system for jobless people.* State and local governments struggled to provide relief for the poor in the early years of the Great Depression. For the most part, they failed. They, too, ran out of money.

The New Deal introduced Social Security, a government pension plan. Government insurance followed for workers who are laid off or can't work because of injuries. Veterans' benefits and public assistance (welfare) are two other forms of government help in which Washington became involved during the 1930s.

These *transfer funds*, as they are called, don't merely help the recipients. In the long run, they help the whole economy by giving people buying power. This buying power helps keep up the demand for bonds. Thus, it helps keep factories open and factory workers employed.

For these and other reasons, many economists believe that we are now in better control of the U.S. economy, which is one of the strongest in the world.

> The words *crash, depression, inflation, panic, speculation, welfare,* and *unemployment* are all in the Economics section of the "Glossary of Social Studies Terms."

1. The selection emphasizes

   (1) the effects of the Great Depression
   (2) the contributions of the New Deal
   (3) the strength of the U.S. economy
   (4) ways to avoid economic disaster
   (5) the role of people's buying power

2. All of the following are associated with the New Deal EXCEPT

   (1) Social Security
   (2) Council of Economic Advisers
   (3) veterans' benefits
   (4) welfare
   (5) unemployment insurance

3. All of the following were characteristics of the Great Depression that economists sought to correct EXCEPT

   (1) stock market speculation
   (2) bank failures
   (3) unemployment
   (4) soaring inflation
   (5) poverty

4. The federal government stepped in where state and local governments failed in

   (1) regulating the stock market
   (2) backing bank deposits
   (3) providing relief for the jobless
   (4) providing veterans' benefits
   (5) introducing Social Security

5. Which of the following statements is NOT true?

   (1) The United States avoided depressions in each decade following the Great Depression.
   (2) Bank panics have been avoided since the Great Depression.
   (3) The Securities and Exchange Commission alerts investors to the kind of stock market activity that preceded the Great Depression.
   (4) Transfer funds help the unemployed.
   (5) We have learned how to prevent another Great Depression.

6. We can conclude from the author's presentation that he sees another Great Depression as

(1) inevitable
(2) likely
(3) unlikely
(4) impossible
(5) predictable

Answer Key

1. **4**   2. **2**   3. **4**   4. **3**   5. **5**   6. **3**

Answer Analysis

Let us look at questions 5 and 6.

5. **5** Question 5 gives you five statements, one of which is false. You have to check each statement against the passage. Choice 1 is true since the passage states that the recommendations of the Council of Economic Advisers helped avoid depressions in 1949, 1958, 1969, and 1985. Choice 2 is true since the passage states the Federal Deposit Insurance Corporation "has so far prevented" bank runs. Choice 3 is also true since the Securities and Exchange Commission has, as one of its responsibilities, warned the public against speculation. Choice 4 is true because unemployment insurance is included in transfer funds. Choice 5 is *not* true since economists are not certain we can avoid another Great Depression, although most of them may feel that way.

6. **3** Question 6 asks you to make an inference, one of the most difficult reading skills. The author concludes the article on an optimistic note—"economists believe that we are now in better control" of our economy, which is "one of the strongest in the world." Therefore, we are safe in inferring or drawing the conclusion that the author sees another Great Depression as unlikely, Choice 3.

GEOGRAPHY, WITH ANSWERS AND ANSWER ANALYSIS

Geography may be subdivided into several areas of study.

Physical Geography   In the study of physical (natural) geography, stress is laid upon the natural elements of man's environment. These include topography, soils, earth materials, earth-sun relationships, surface and underground water, weather and climate, and native plant and animal life. Physical geography must also include the impact of man on his physical environment as well as those influences omnipresent in nature.

Cultural Geography   In cultural geography emphasis is placed upon the study of observable features resulting from man's occupation of the earth. These features include population distribution and settlement, cities, buildings, roads, airfields, factories, railroads, farm and field patterns, communication facilities, and many other examples of man's work. Cultural geography is one of the very significant fields of geographic inquiry.

Economic Geography   In economic geography, the relationship between man's efforts to gain a living and the earth's surface on which they are conducted are correlated. In order to study how man makes a living, the distribution of materials, production, institutions, and human traits and customs are analyzed.

Regional Geography   In regional geography the basic concern is with the salient characteristics of areas. Emphasis is placed upon patterns and elements of the natural environment and their relationships to human activities. By using the regional technique in studying geographic phenomena, what otherwise might be a bewildering array of facts is brought into focus as an organized, cohesive pattern.

Systematic Geography   It is also feasible to study the geography of a small area or the entire surface of the earth in systematic fashion. Settlement, climates, soils, landforms, minerals, water, or crops, among others, may be observed, described, analyzed, and explained. Research in systematic geography has proved to be very valuable.

1. This passage describes geography's

   (1) growth
   (2) scope
   (3) importance
   (4) role in the social sciences
   (5) principles

2. The difference among the five areas of geography described is one of

   (1) method
   (2) importance
   (3) emphasis
   (4) recency
   (5) objectivity

3. A student interested in the influence of a geographical feature of a region on available jobs would study

   (1) physical geography
   (2) cultural geography
   (3) economic geography
   (4) regional geography
   (5) systematic geography

4. A meteorologist would likely be most interested in

   (1) physical geography
   (2) cultural geography
   (3) economic geography
   (4) regional geography
   (5) systematic geography

5. An urban sociologist would probably study

   (1) physical geography
   (2) cultural geography
   (3) economic geography
   (4) regional geography
   (5) systematic geography

6. A person studying the problems of the Middle East will use the approach found in

   (1) physical geography
   (2) cultural geography
   (3) economic geography
   (4) regional geography
   (5) systematic geography

7. A conservationist studying the effects of such human activities as strip mining and land erosion would turn to

   (1) physical geography
   (2) cultural geography
   (3) economic geography
   (4) regional geography
   (5) systematic geography

8. That aspect of geography that seeks to study in a planned and orderly way the geography of a small area is

   (1) physical geography
   (2) cultural geography
   (3) economic geography
   (4) regional geography
   (5) systematic geography

Answer Key

1. **2**   2. **3**   3. **3**   4. **1**   5. **2**   6. **4**

7. **1**   8. **5**

Answer Analysis

Four of the questions—3, 6, 7, and 8—deal with definitions. Two call for knowledge of terms in addition to those defined in the passage.

2. **3** Question 2 is a little tricky, but, if you read closely, you will notice that the author uses the words *stress* and *emphasis* in his definitions of the various areas of geography.

   Questions 4 and 5 are, in effect, two-step questions. First, you must define the term in the question. Then, you must recall the definition of the area of geography to which it relates.

4. **1** In question 4, you must know that a meteorologist is concerned with weather. Only then can you identify physical geography as his or her primary interest.

5. **2** In this question, you must know that an urban sociologist studies cities, an area of interest to the cultural geographer.

PRACTICE WITH INTERPRETING TABLES, GRAPHS, MAPS

Since study of the social sciences involves the gathering and interpretation of facts, you will frequently encounter various methods for presenting the facts you need. Most often, these facts will be presented in the form of tables or charts, graphs, or maps. Let us deal with each of these methods in turn.

TABLES

The ability to read tables is an important skill because tables are the most common means of presenting data in the social studies.

What is a table? It is an arrangement of figures, usually in one or more columns, which is intended to show some relationship between the figures. In political science, a table may show the growth of the number of eligible voters in national elections. In economics, a table may show the annual incomes of various groups within the population of a country. A table may also show the relationship between two factors, for example, between the amounts of education of various groups as related to their annual incomes.

First note the title of the table: Sizes, Populations, and Densities of the World's Largest Nations and Regions.

Now, look at the headings of the columns in the table. Six headings are given: Country, Size, Population 1950, Population 2005, People per Square Mile 1950, People per Square Mile 2005.

Next, locate the columns to which each heading is related. In the first column, the different countries are listed. The next column gives their sizes in square miles. The next two columns list population figures for 1950 and 2005, and the last two give the numbers of people per square mile for the same two dates.

Just how do you read a table? First you read the title of the table to determine just what figures are being presented. The title is usually at the top of the column or columns of figures. Let us use the following table as a typical illustration.

Having identified the title, the column headings, and the columns to which they relate, you are now in a position to *locate facts*.

SIZES, POPULATIONS, AND DENSITIES OF THE WORLD'S LARGEST NATIONS AND REGIONS					
1	**2**	**3** Population	**4** (U.N. Estimate)	**5** People per	**6** Square Mile
Country	**Size (sq. mi.)**	**1950**	**2005**	**1950**	**2005**
Russian Federation	6,592,000	103,000,000	143,000,000	15.6	21.7
China	3,700,000	555,000,000	1,316,000,000	150.0	355.6
United States	3,600,000	158,000,000	298,000,000	43.8	82.8
Brazil	3,300,000	54,000,000	186,000,000	16.4	56.4
India	1,200,000	358,000,000	1,103,000,000	298.3	919.2
Japan	143,000	84,000,000	128,000,000	587.4	895.1

QUESTIONS

1. What is the size of the United States?

2. What was the population of India in 1950? What is the U.N. estimate of the population of India in 2005?

3. What was the number of people per square mile in Japan in 1950?

4. Which two countries' populations grew to over 1 billion between 1950 and 2005?

ANSWERS

1. 3,600,000 square miles

2. 358,000,000   1,103,000,000

3. 587.4

4. China and India

ANSWER ANALYSIS

1. The second column from the left lists sizes. Put your finger at the top of that column, and move it down until you locate the figure on a line with United States—3,600,000.

2. Locate the column for population in 1950. Put your finger at the top of the column, and move it down to the figure on a line with India—358,000,000. Do the same for 2005.

3. Locate the column for people per square mile in 1950. Find the number on a line with Japan—587.4.

4. To answer this question, you have to locate two populations, one in 1950 and one in 2005. You also must locate a figure that is over 1 billion. Scan both columns of population figures. Two are over 1 billion, that of China in 2005, and that of India in 2005.

Now you are ready to *find relationships between facts.* This type of question requires you to locate one figure and then relate it to at least one other figure.

QUESTIONS

1. What is the basic trend of the world's population?

2. What is the basic trend in the number of people per square mile?

3. From 1950 to 2005, what country had the smallest increase in population?

4. In what country did the number of people per square mile increase the most?

REMEMBER

Summary of how to read a table

1. Note the title.
2. Look at the column headings.
3. Locate the column to which the other columns are related.
4. Locate facts.
5. Find relationships between facts.
6. Infer conclusions from the facts presented.

ANSWERS AND ANALYSIS

1. Compare column 4 (pop. 2005) with column 3 (pop. 1950). In every instance, the population in 2005 is greater. The conclusion can be reached that population is increasing all over the world.

2. Compare column 6 (people per square mile—2005) with column 5 (people per square mile—1950). The conclusion can be reached that the number of people per square mile is increasing all over the world.

3. Subtracting the figures in column 3 (pop. 1950) from those in column 4 (pop. 2005), it is apparent that the Russian Federation had the smallest increase, 40,0000,000, in population.

4. Comparing the figures in columns 5 and 6 for people per square mile in 1950 and 2005, it is clear that in India the number of people per square mile more than tripled, from 298 to 919.

Now you can proceed to the most difficult skill of all—*inferring conclusions from the facts presented.* Sometimes you can draw a conclusion from the table alone. Other times, you must add facts from your general knowledge.

QUESTIONS

1. What conclusion can you draw from Japan's population figures?

2. What conclusion can you draw about the population in the Russian Federation?

3. What common problems may India and Japan experience?

ANSWERS AND ANALYSIS

1. Japan has the most crowded population in the world, with attendant problems of housing, health, and transportation among others.

2. The population of the Russian Federation is spread over 6,592,000 square miles. This fact will result in problems of distribution of goods and services to the countries of the area.

3. The high population density in each country suggests potential difficulty in providing food, shelter, and other essential services to the inhabitants.

GRAPHS

The Circle (Pie) Graph

Tables, as you have just seen, are composed of columns of figures selected to show the relationship between facts that the social studies writer considers important. Very often, the author will present these same facts in another way so that you can visualize them more readily and draw conclusions more easily. The writer does this by means of a graph.

Let us look at the following set of facts arranged in a table. They concern the principal religions of the world in the year 2000.

PRINCIPAL RELIGIONS OF THE WORLD, 2000	
Buddhist	6%
Christian	33%
Hindu	13%
Islam	18%
No religion	21%
Other	1%
Para-religions	8%

Looking at these facts in table form, you find it hard to draw any ready conclusions. But when you see them in the form of a circle (pie) graph, you are able to immediately visualize the relationships that exist between them.

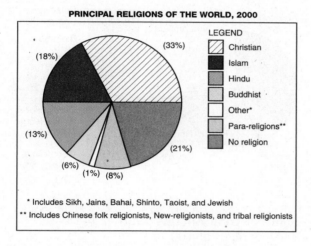

Now use this graph to answer the following questions.

QUESTIONS

1. Which religion has the most followers?

2. Which of the individually named religions has the fewest followers?

3. Which two religions account for more than half of the world's population?

4. Which proportion of the world's people do not practice a religion?

ANSWERS

1. Christian

2. Buddhist

3. Islam and Christianity

4. 21%

ANSWER ANALYSIS

The answers almost leap up at you from the circle graph. The Christian religion has by far the largest slice of the circle; all of the religions combined under "Other" are hardly visible. By visually combining the various slices of the pie, you can see that the Christian and Islamic religions account for just over half of the total pie. By referring to the legend and then back to the pie, you can see that a large slice of the pie represents people who practice no religion. Just by inspection, you can estimate the number at around one-fifth or 20% of the total. The actual figure (21%) is provided.

The circle graph can also help you to compare visually two sets of facts. Here are a circle graph and a graph of another type (the bar graph).

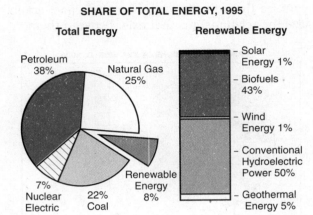

SHARE OF TOTAL ENERGY, 1995

Note the title—Share of Total Energy, 1995
Note the unit used—percent of 100
Note the date—1995
Note the major categories—petroleum, natural gas, renewable energy, coal, nuclear electric
Study both graphs carefully and answer the following questions.

QUESTIONS

1. What are the most important sources of energy?

2. To reduce our dependence on oil imports, the use of which sources would have to be increased?

3. What percent of total energy does conventional hydroelectric power contribute?

ANSWERS AND ANALYSIS

1. Three sources—petroleum, natural gas, and coal—amount to 70% of total energy.

2. The percents of the other sources—natural gas, coal, renewable energy, and nuclear electric—would have to be increased from their current total of 62%.

3. The circle graph tells you that renewable energy contributes 8% of the total energy consumed. Now look at the bar graph. Conventional hydroelectric power contributes half of renewal energy, or 4% of total energy.

The Line Graph

This common type of graph shows relationships between facts by plotting points on a coordinate plane (two lines are involved) and connecting them with straight lines.

As an example, let us construct a line graph based on the following data about world population growth between 1650 and 2000.

Year	World Population in Millions
1650	550
1750	725
1850	1175
1900	1600
1950	2490
2000	6500

To construct the graph, draw a horizontal line and, perpendicular to it, a vertical line. Let:

• the horizontal line (technically known as the *abscissa*) represent the period of years from 1650 to 2000;

• the vertical line (technically known as the *ordinate*) represent world population.

To plot the line graph, start with the first line of data—year 1650, world population 550 million. Go up the ordinate 550, and place a dot there. Then find the next date, 1750, on the abscissa and go up the ordinate and place a dot opposite 725. Next find the date 1850 on the horizontal line and go up to a point opposite 1175. Place a dot there. Continue to do the same thing for each year on the table. Then draw a straight line from dot to dot to complete the graph.

What can you tell or visualize from this line graph?

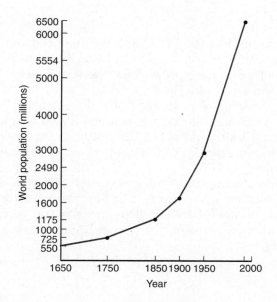

1. What is the trend of the world population?

2. What was the world population in 1900?

3. In what 50-year period was the increase the greatest?

4. In the period covered by the graph, approximately how many times did the population grow?

1. The trend is sharply upward.

2. 1600 million.

3. 1950–2000.

4. About 12 times, from 550 million to 6500 million.

1. The plotted line always trends upward, with the slant becoming steeper in recent decades to indicate accelerating population growth.

2. First find the year 1900 on the abscissa. Then move your finger straight up to the point in line with the ordinate indicating the population. The number is 1600 million.

3. The growth is greatest where the line is steepest—between 1950 and 2000.

4. The population grew from 550 million to 6500 million, or about 12 times.

The Bar Graph

A bar graph is very much like the line graph we just studied. There is the same visual presentation of one set of facts in relation to another set. There is the same horizontal line (*abscissa*) representing one set of facts. The same vertical line (*ordinate*) represents the other set.

For a bar graph, however, you do not put a dot at the point that represents one fact in relation to another, nor do you connect those points by lines. Instead, you make bars of equal width and of heights that indicate the relationship. Thus you could change the line graph you just studied to a bar graph by making a bar for each point identified.

The bar graph below is entitled "Aging Societies." It gives the percentages of population 65 and over for five countries at four different times, two past and two projected. It also indicates by small pie graphs the percentages of health spending in 1993, in each country, for people 65 and over as a share of total health care spending.

AGING SOCIETIES

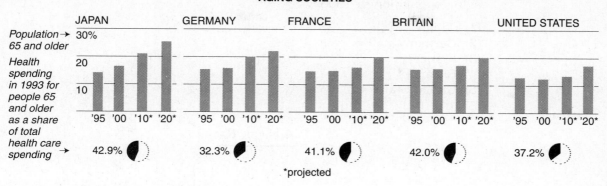

*projected

Source: Organization of Economic Cooperation and Development

Use these graphs to answer the following practice questions.

QUESTIONS

1. In what country will the government have to spend the most in the year 2020 for health care for the aging?

    (1) Japan
    (2) Germany
    (3) France
    (4) Britain
    (5) United States

2. Which country will have the greatest population under 65 in 2020?

    (1) Japan
    (2) Germany
    (3) France
    (4) Britain
    (5) United States

3. Which countries have the most similar aging characteristics?

    (1) Japan and Germany
    (2) Germany and France
    (3) France and Britain
    (4) Britain and the United States
    (5) Japan and the United States

4. Which country will have the least stable growth of population over 65 for the rest of this century?

    (1) Japan
    (2) Germany
    (3) France
    (4) Britain
    (5) United States

5. What country was the least responsive to the health care needs of its aging population in 1993?

(1) Japan
(2) Germany
(3) France
(4) Britain
(5) United States

ANSWER KEY

1. **1**   2. **5**   3. **3**   4. **1**   5. **2**

ANSWER ANALYSIS

1. **1** In 2020, 25% of the population of Japan will be 65 or older, at least 4% more than any other country in the graph.

2. **5** In 2020, the United States will be the only country with an over-65 population below 20%.

3. **3** For France and Britain, percents are nearly identical for 1995, 2000, and 2010. The two countries will have the identical percent of population 65 or older in 2020, and in 1995 differed by less than 1% in percent of health care spending for the elderly as a share of total health care spending.

4. **1** Japan will have an increase in population over 65. The other countries will remain at the same level.

5. **2** The pie graphs show that Germany spent least, approximately 9 to 10% less than France and Britain, for similar numbers of elderly.

Maps

A map is a visual representation of all or part of the surface of the earth. A map may or may not include a number of aids to help you visualize the surface it is depicting. It will always include a *title*. If the map uses symbols, it will always include a *legend* (or key) to give the meaning of those symbols. It may also include:

• latitude and longitude to indicate direction and help you to find a specific location;

• a scale of miles to indicate what distance on the map equals a specific distance in miles on land;

• a grid, or square, usually identified by a set of letters on one axis (vertical or horizontal) and a set of numbers on the other, so that a place can be found in, for example, a grid identified as F 3 or H 7;

Important aids that you must learn to use in order to read a map are its *title* and its *legend* (or key). Since ancient times, maps have played a unique role in presenting information about the world, and maps are extremely useful in locating places and distances in any part of the world.

**PER CAPITA INCOME AND UNEMPLOYMENT
IN THE UNITED STATES**

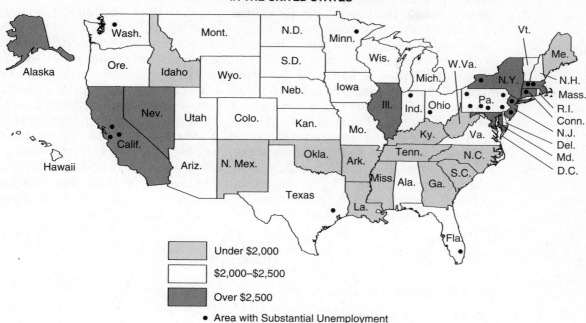

Under $2,000

$2,000–$2,500

Over $2,500

• Area with Substantial Unemployment

In the 1500s Gerardus Mercator, a Dutch mapmaker, coined the word *atlas* to describe a collection of maps. The atlas is unique because only it, with its maps, actually shows *where* things are located in the world. Only on a map can the countries, cities, roads, rivers, and lakes covering a vast area be seen all at once in their relative locations. Routes between places can be traced, trips planned, boundaries of neighboring countries examined, distances between places measured, and the paths of rivers and the sizes of lakes visualized.

Places can be found by looking up the place name in the index at the back of the atlas. There is usually a letter-number key next to the name of the place, **A3**, for example. This will help you find the place on a grid or square on the map. The letters are usually located to the left or right of the map, the numbers to the top or bottom of the map.

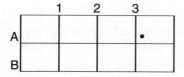

Sometimes, if the place is big enough, you can find it on the map visually.

Distances between places can be figured by using the scale of miles, usually on the bottom of the page.

Place a ruler over the scale to find how many miles a given ruling is, then place the ruler between two places on the map to find the length. For example, if a distance on the scale is 20 miles to one inch and the distance on the map is 1½ inches, the distance is 1½ times 20, or 30 miles between the two points on the map. Determining directions can be done by using a series of lines drawn across the map—the lines of latitude and longitude. Lines of latitude are drawn east and west, from left to right. Lines of longitude are drawn north and south, from top to bottom. The lines of latitude appear as curved lines; the lines of longitude are straight lines that come together toward the top of the map.

Lines of latitude and longitude not only help you find direction, they help you locate places. Parallels of latitude are numbered in degrees north and south of the equator. Lines of longitude are numbered in degrees east and west of an imaginary line running through Greenwich, England, near London. Any place on earth can be located by the latitude and longitude lines running through it. For example, Chicago, Illinois, is located at 41° 53' N (north of the equator), and 87° 40' W (west of the Greenwich prime meridian—the line of 0° 0' longitude).

Maps usually use symbols, points, dots, or stars (for cities, capital cities, or points of interest), or lines (roads, rivers, railroads). Help in understanding the symbols is provided by a legend or key found in an atlas near the map. The map on the previous page is in many respects typical of the maps you will encounter. The following questions will sharpen your skills in map reading.

QUESTIONS

1. What is the *title* of the map?

2. What three indications make up the *legend*?

3. What does ● mean?

4. What is the average per capita income of the population of the state of New York?

5. What is the average per capita income of the population of the state of New Mexico?

6. What is the average per capita income of the population of the state of Iowa?

7. Which state has a larger per capita income, Alaska or Hawaii?

ANSWERS AND ANALYSIS

1. The title of the map is "Per Capita Income and Unemployment in the United States." See the heading above the map.

2. The dark blue areas indicate per capita income over $2,500; the white areas indicate per capita income between $2,000 and $2,500; the light blue areas indicate per capita income under $2,000.

3. The ● indicates an area with substantial unemployment.

4. Since New York is a dark blue area, its per capita income is over $2,500.

5. Since New Mexico is a light blue area, its per capita income is under $2,000.

6. Since Iowa is a white area, its per capita income is between $2,000 and $2,500.

7. Since Alaska is a dark blue area (per capita income over $2,500) and Hawaii is a white area (per capita income between $2,000 and $2,500), Alaska has a larger per capita income than Hawaii.

This map introduces a complication, the idea of substantial unemployment, a feature that is not typical of most maps. That idea is the topic of questions 3–7 that follow.

ADDITIONAL QUESTIONS

1. Per capita income in Maine is most nearly equal to per capita income in

    (1) Washington
    (2) Idaho
    (3) Utah
    (4) Nevada
    (5) Missouri

2. Which generalization is best supported by the map?

    (1) All New England states have per capita incomes of over $2,000.
    (2) All states along the Atlantic seaboard have a high per capita income.
    (3) All southern states have incomes below $2,000.
    (4) All states along the Pacific coast have per capita incomes of $2,000 or over.
    (5) Most states have per capita incomes over $2,500.

3. According to the map, in which state is unemployment a major problem?

    (1) Pennsylvania
    (2) Florida
    (3) Alabama
    (4) Texas
    (5) Washington

4. Which state has both a per capita income of between $2,000 and $2,500, and an area with substantial unemployment?

    (1) Kansas
    (2) Ohio
    (3) Kentucky
    (4) Mississippi
    (5) California

5. Which state has a high per capita income and substantial unemployment?

    (1) Florida
    (2) Louisiana
    (3) Minnesota
    (4) California
    (5) Nevada

6. Unemployment is less of a problem in Indiana than in

    (1) Massachusetts
    (2) Tennessee
    (3) Mississippi
    (4) Louisiana
    (5) Arizona

7. Which conclusion concerning the state of Tennessee is supported by the map?

(1) It is larger than Montana and richer than Mississippi.
(2) It has more unemployment than Georgia and was richer than Kentucky.
(3) It is as rich as Arkansas and poorer than Nevada.
(4) It had less unemployment than Oklahoma and more unemployment than Georgia.
(5) It is smaller than Minnesota and richer than Illinois.

ANSWER KEY

1. **2**	3. **1**	5. **4**	7. **3**
2. **4**	4. **2**	6. **1**	

ANSWER ANALYSIS

1. **2** The answer is Choice 2 since both states are light blue areas, with per capita incomes under $2,000.

2. **4** Choice 4 is correct. California had a per capita income of over $2,500; Washington and Oregon had incomes between $2,000 and $2,500; all have incomes of $2,000 or over per capita. Choice 1 is incorrect since Maine has an income of less than $2,000. Choice 2 is wrong since three states—North Carolina, South Carolina, and Georgia—have incomes lower than $2,000. Choice 3 is incorrect since Texas, Florida, and Virginia have incomes above $2,000. Choice 5 is incorrect; only 10 states have per capita incomes over $2,500.

3. **1** On the map, Pennsylvania has six dotted areas with substantial unemployment; Florida, Washington, and Texas have one each and Alabama has none. Choice 1 is correct.

4. **2** You have to find a white area with a dot. Only Ohio, Choice 2, fits these criteria.

5. **4** You have to find a dark blue area with several dots. Only California, Choice 4, fits this description.

6. **1** You need to locate a state with more than one dot since Indiana has one such dot. The correct answer is Choice 1, Massachusetts, which has two dots.

7. **3** The map compares Tennessee with other states with regard to per capita income *and* unemployment. Choice 1 is wrong since Montana is larger. Choice 2 is wrong since Tennessee is not richer than Kentucky but the same. Choice 4 is wrong since Tennessee has more unemployment than both Oklahoma and Georgia. Choice 5 is incorrect since Tennessee is poorer than Illinois. Choice 3 is correct; both Tennessee and Arkansas have per capita incomes of less than $2,000, while Nevada has a per capita income of over $2,500.

Now it is time for further practice. The following practice exercises will give you ample preparation in reading tables, graphs, and maps for the GED Examination.

ADDITIONAL PRACTICE WITH TABLES, GRAPHS, AND MAPS

Read each of the following questions carefully. Select the best answer.

Questions 1–4 are based on the following map.

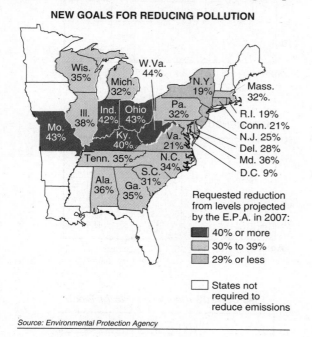

NEW GOALS FOR REDUCING POLLUTION

Requested reduction from levels projected by the E.P.A. in 2007:

- ■ 40% or more
- ▨ 30% to 39%
- ▧ 29% or less
- □ States not required to reduce emissions

Source: Environmental Protection Agency

1. According to the map, the state that probably will have the most pollution is
   (1) Missouri
   (2) Indiana
   (3) Ohio
   (4) Kentucky
   (5) West Virginia

2. The states that have exactly similar goals in the reduction of pollution are
   (1) Michigan, Pennsylvania, Massachusetts
   (2) Missouri, Indiana, Ohio
   (3) Alabama, Georgia, South Carolina
   (4) Virginia, Connecticut, Maryland
   (5) New York, Rhode Island, New Jersey

3. The area with the lowest requested reduction in pollution is
   (1) Virginia
   (2) District of Columbia
   (3) Rhode Island
   (4) New York
   (5) Connecticut

4. Pollution appears to be lowest in the region of
   (1) the Midwest
   (2) the Great Lakes
   (3) the Southeast
   (4) the Middle Atlantic States
   (5) the Deep South

Questions 5–11 are based on the following graphs.

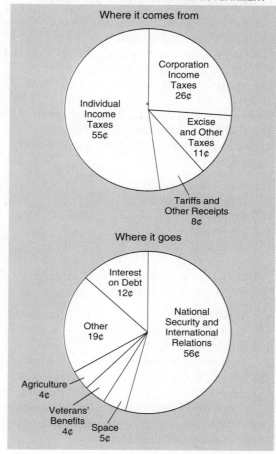

THE BUDGET DOLLAR OF FEDERAL GOVERNMENT

Where it comes from

- Individual Income Taxes 55¢
- Corporation Income Taxes 26¢
- Excise and Other Taxes 11¢
- Tariffs and Other Receipts 8¢

Where it goes

- Interest on Debt 12¢
- Other 19¢
- National Security and International Relations 56¢
- Agriculture 4¢
- Veterans' Benefits 4¢
- Space 5¢

5. Forty-five percent of the national income is derived from
   (1) individual income taxes, excise taxes, and tariffs
   (2) corporation income taxes, excise taxes, and tariffs
   (3) individual income taxes, corporation income taxes, and excise taxes
   (4) individual income taxes, corporation income taxes, and tariffs
   (5) individual income taxes and excise taxes

6. The largest amount of the national income is expended on

    (1) health and welfare
    (2) national security and international relations
    (3) space
    (4) interest on debt
    (5) veterans' benefits

7. The two areas on which equal amounts of the national income are expended are

    (1) agriculture and veterans' benefits
    (2) space and agriculture
    (3) health and welfare and interest on debt
    (4) veterans' benefits and space
    (5) space and all others

8. The amount of income received from the collection of excise and other taxes approximately equals the amount expended for

    (1) interest on debt
    (2) health and welfare
    (3) space
    (4) agriculture
    (5) veterans' benefits

9. What is the biggest source of income for the federal government?

    (1) tariffs
    (2) excise taxes
    (3) corporation taxes
    (4) individual income taxes
    (5) other receipts

10. The combined expenditure for agriculture and veterans' benefits equals that for the income category entitled

    (1) excise and other taxes
    (2) health and welfare
    (3) interest on debt
    (4) tariffs and other receipts
    (5) national security

11. The income from individual income taxes most nearly equals the expenditure for

    (1) national security and international relations
    (2) health and welfare
    (3) space
    (4) veterans' benefits
    (5) all others

Questions 12–15 are based on the following graphs.

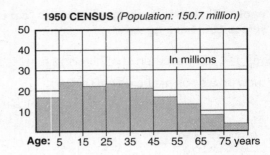

1950 CENSUS (*Population: 150.7 million*)

In millions

Age: 5 15 25 35 45 55 65 75 years

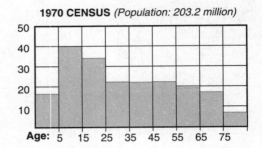

1970 CENSUS (*Population: 203.2 million*)

Age: 5 15 25 35 45 55 65 75

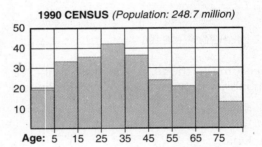

1990 CENSUS (*Population: 248.7 million*)

Age: 5 15 25 35 45 55 65 75

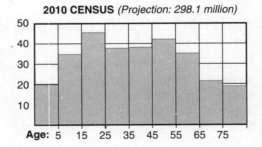

2010 CENSUS (*Projection: 298.1 million*)

Age: 5 15 25 35 45 55 65 75

12. According to the graphs, the population census takes place

    (1) every 10 years
    (2) every 20 years
    (3) every 30 years
    (4) every 50 years
    (5) irregularly

13. The 1990 census reveals that the largest age group is that between

    (1) 5 and 15
    (2) 15 and 25
    (3) 25 and 35
    (4) 35 and 45
    (5) 45 and 55

14. The birth to 5-year group is larger in each census than the

    (1) 5 to 15
    (2) 35 to 45
    (3) 45 to 55
    (4) 65 to 75
    (5) over 75

15. The group that will have grown the most in percentage between 1950 and 2010 is the

    (1) 5 to 15
    (2) 15 to 25
    (3) 25 to 35
    (4) 35 to 45
    (5) over 75

COASTAL LANDS AT RISK

If sea levels rose by 20 inches by the year 2100, as scientists expect, coastal areas would be at risk. Here are some examples of shoreline losses, in square miles.

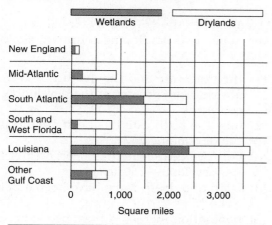

The New York Times

16. According to the graph, if sea levels rose 20 inches by the year 2100, the coastal lands that would be most affected are in

    (1) the South Atlantic
    (2) the Mid-Atlantic
    (3) Louisiana
    (4) Other Gulf Coast
    (5) Florida

17. The coastal drylands that would be most affected are in the

    (1) Mid-Atlantic
    (2) South Atlantic
    (3) South and West Florida
    (4) Other Gulf Coast
    (5) New England

18. Which statement is true, according to the graph?

    (1) The northeast United States would be more affected than the Gulf Coast.
    (2) The East Coast would be more affected than the Gulf Coast.
    (3) The Gulf Coast would be the hardest hit.
    (4) Generally the wetlands would be affected more than the drylands.
    (5) The shoreline is greater on the Atlantic than on the Gulf.

WHERE THE POPULATION GROWS FASTEST
Total world population in billions

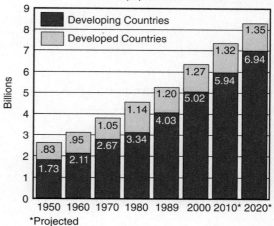

Source: The Washington Post, July 1990 (adapted)

19. Which statement is best supported by the data in the graph?

    (1) The rate of world population growth has begun to decrease.
    (2) The world's population tripled between 1970 and 1989.
    (3) Most of the world's population lives in economically developing countries.
    (4) The population of economically developed countries consumes most of the world's resources.
    (5) The world is nearing zero population growth.

20. Which factor best accounts for the difference in the growth rate between developing and developed countries as shown in the graph?

    (1) increased family planning in developed countries
    (2) increasing pollution in developed countries
    (3) the breakdown of extended families in developing countries
    (4) the rise of single-parent families throughout the world
    (5) the greater likelihood of wars in developing countries

21. The greatest difference in population growth between developing and developed countries took place (or will take place) in the year

    (1) 1980
    (2) 1989
    (3) 2000
    (4) 2010
    (5) 2020

Questions 22–24 are based on the following graphs.

DEVELOPED COUNTRIES

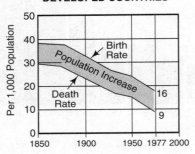

DEVELOPING COUNTRIES

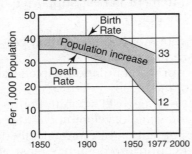

RATE OF POPULATION INCREASE = BIRTH RATE – DEATH RATE
Source: United Nations Population Division

22. Which statement is best supported by the information in the graphs?

    (1) In the years shown, population in both developed and developing countries increased at the same rate.
    (2) By the year 2000, the developing countries will reach the point of zero population growth.
    (3) Population growth in the years shown was due largely to a drop in the death rate.
    (4) Population growth in the years shown was due largely to an increase in the birth rate.
    (5) Population in 2000 will be greater in the developed countries than in the developing countries.

23. According to the graphs, in the developed countries

    (1) the birth rate surpassed the death rate for the years shown
    (2) the death rate surpassed the birth rate for the years shown
    (3) the population is growing at an increased rate
    (4) the birth rate is increasing
    (5) the death rate is increasing

24. According to the graphs, a comparison of developed and developing countries shows that

    (1) the birth rate and the death rate have always been greater in the developing countries
    (2) only the birth rate has been greater in the developing countries
    (3) only the death rate has been greater in the developing countries
    (4) birth and death rates have been similar in both
    (5) population increases have been similar in both

Questions 25–30 are based on the following illustration.

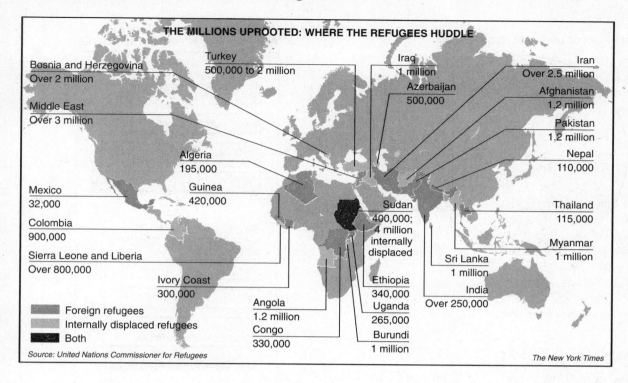

THE MILLIONS UPROOTED: WHERE THE REFUGEES HUDDLE

Bosnia and Herzegovina
Over 2 million

Middle East
Over 3 million

Turkey
500,000 to 2 million

Iraq
1 million

Azerbaijan
500,000

Iran
Over 2.5 million

Afghanistan
1.2 million

Pakistan
1.2 million

Algeria
195,000

Nepal
110,000

Mexico
32,000

Guinea
420,000

Sudan
400,000;
4 million
internally
displaced

Thailand
115,000

Colombia
900,000

Myanmar
1 million

Sierra Leone and Liberia
Over 800,000

Sri Lanka
1 million

Ivory Coast
300,000

Ethiopia
340,000

India
Over 250,000

Angola
1.2 million

Uganda
265,000

Congo
330,000

Burundi
1 million

Foreign refugees
Internally displaced refugees
Both

Source: United Nations Commissioner for Refugees

The New York Times

---

25. According to the map, the country with the largest number of foreign refugees is

   (1) Algeria
   (2) Congo
   (3) Azerbaijan
   (4) Uganda
   (5) Iran

26. The country with the largest number of internally displaced refugees is

   (1) Sudan
   (2) Angola
   (3) Afghanistan
   (4) Pakistan
   (5) Myanmar

27. The European country with the largest number of refugees is

   (1) Turkey
   (2) France
   (3) Italy
   (4) Bosnia
   (5) Greece

28. The number of countries that have over 1 million refugees is

   (1) 3
   (2) 5
   (3) 6
   (4) 8
   (5) 10

29. The continent with the fewest number of refugees is

   (1) North America
   (2) South America
   (3) Europe
   (4) Africa
   (5) Asia

30. The country for which the number of refugees is least precise is

   (1) Colombia
   (2) Algeria
   (3) Turkey
   (4) Nepal
   (5) Thailand

Questions 31–33 are based on the following graph.

SOURCES OF UNITED STATES ENERGY

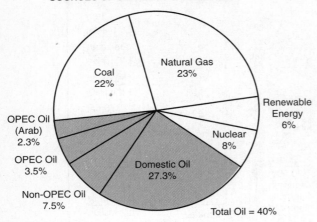

Figures represent estimated percentage of sources for U.S. energy consumption in 2004.

Source: U.S. Department of Energy

Questions 34–35 are based on the following graph.

HEALTH CARE IN THE UNITED STATES

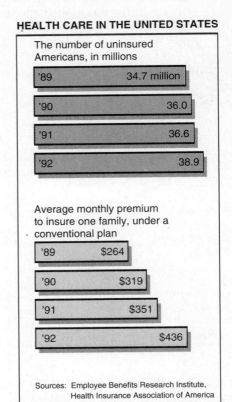

Sources: Employee Benefits Research Institute, Health Insurance Association of America

31. According to the graph,

   (1) oil contributes more to U.S. energy than coal and natural gas
   (2) OPEC (Arab) oil is the smallest contributor to U.S. energy
   (3) OPEC oil exceeds non-OPEC oil as a source of U.S. energy
   (4) natural gas is the largest single source of U.S. energy
   (6) hydro energy and nuclear energy exceed foreign oil as sources of U.S. energy

32. According to the graph, the largest single source of U.S. energy is

   (1) coal
   (2) natural gas
   (3) domestic oil
   (4) nuclear and hydro
   (5) OPEC and non-OPEC foreign oil

33. It can be inferred from the graph that foreign sources account for what percentage of U.S. energy?

   (1) 27.3%
   (2) 26.4%
   (3) 22.3%
   (4) 13.3%
   (5) 10.2%

34. According to the graph, the most valid conclusion that can be drawn is that

   (1) health care is not available for most Americans
   (2) the number of Americans not insured for health has reached a peak
   (3) the premiums for conventional plans for health care cannot be afforded by most Americans
   (4) health care is becoming less available and more costly to American families
   (5) the rate of increases in health care costs is declining

35. The average monthly premium to insure one family

    (1) had its greatest increase from 1989 to 1990
    (2) had its greatest increase from 1990 to 1991
    (3) had its greatest increase from 1991 to 1992
    (4) saw a decrease in the rate of increases
    (5) increased at a rate of 50% in the four-year period 1989–1992

Questions 36–37 are based on the following graph.

PERCENTAGES OF WORKERS WITH YEAR-ROUND FULL-TIME JOBS

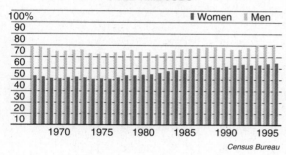

Census Bureau

36. According to the graph, during the period shown:

    (1) the number of men working full time increased dramatically.
    (2) the number of women working full time increased dramatically.
    (3) the number of men working full time fell slightly.
    (4) the total number of men and women working full time leveled off.
    (5) the total number of men and women working full time decreased.

37. From the figures given in the graph, there probably was a recession in the years

    (1) 1967–1973
    (2) 1974–1978
    (3) 1979–1985
    (4) 1985–1990
    (5) 1991–1996

Questions 38–40 are based on the following chart.

ECONOMIC AND SOCIAL PROFILES OF SELECTED COUNTRIES—EAST ASIA

	Populations (Millions est.)		Per Capita Income	GNP (billions of dollars)	Literacy Rate (%)		Doubling Population Time (Years)
	1976	1990	1989	1989	1976	1992	
Japan	113	124	23,730	2,920	99	100	exceeds 100
Korea (South)	36	43.2	4,400	186.5	88.5	96	70
Korea (North)	16	21.8	1,240	28	NA	95	38
China (People's Republic)	852	1,150	360	393	40	73	48
Taiwan (Republic of China)	16.3	20.5	7,480	150	86	94	61

Source: *Encyclopedia Britannica Book of the Year 1992*

38. Which of the following is true according to the chart?

    (1) Taiwan leads China in both per capita income and literacy rate.
    (2) Taiwan is the least populated country.
    (3) North Korea is wealthier than South Korea.
    (4) South Korea leads China in GNP.
    (5) The population of North Korea showed the least growth between 1976 and 1990.

39. The country with the greatest increase in population and literacy rate is

    (1) Japan
    (2) North Korea
    (3) South Korea
    (4) China
    (5) Taiwan

40. Individuals are benefiting most from the GNP in

    (1) Japan
    (2) North Korea
    (3) South Korea
    (4) China
    (5) Taiwan

Answer Key

1. **5**	9. **4**	17. **2**	25. **5**	33. **4**
2. **1**	10. **4**	18. **3**	26. **1**	34. **4**
3. **2**	11. **1**	19. **3**	27. **4**	35. **3**
4. **4**	12. **2**	20. **1**	28. **5**	36. **2**
5. **2**	13. **3**	21. **5**	29. **1**	37. **2**
6. **2**	14. **5**	22. **3**	30. **3**	38. **1**
7. **1**	15. **2**	23. **1**	31. **2**	39. **4**
8. **1**	16. **3**	24. **1**	32. **3**	40. **1**

WHAT'S YOUR SCORE?

_____right,   _____wrong

Excellent	36–40
Good	32–35
Fair	28–31

If you scored lower, you may need more review. Reread the section, "Practice with Interpreting Tables, Graphs, Maps" (page 284), and try again.

Answer Analysis

1. **5** West Virginia has a proposed level of 44%, the highest percentage indicated.

2. **1** All three states have levels of 32%.

3. **2** The District of Columbia, at 9%, has by far the lowest projected level of pollution.

4. **4** The Middle Atlantic states, with the exception of Maryland have projected levels of pollution of less than 30%.

5. **2** These three sources provide 26%, 11%, and 8%, respectively, for a total of 45%.

6. **2** National security and international relations represent 56% of the national expenditure.

7. **1** Four percent is expended on each.

8. **1** Excise and other taxes bring in 11%, 12% is spent on interest on debt.

9. **4** Fifty-five percent of federal income comes from individual income taxes.

10. **4** These add up to 8%, the amount received from tariffs and other receipts.

11. **1** Income from individual income taxes is 55%; expenditure for national security and international relations is 56%.

12. **2** The titles of the bar graphs are the 1950 census, 1970 census, 1990 census, and 2010 census; here is a 20-year gap between them.

13. **3** Over 40 million persons are between 25 and 35.

14. **5** In each census, there are more in the birth to 5-year group than the over-75 group.

15. **2** The 15 to 25 age group will grow from 21% to 46%, more than any other age group.

16. **3** Louisiana would lose about 3600 square miles, at least 1000 square miles more than anywhere else.

17. **2** The loss to South Atlantic drylands would constitute about 900 square miles, hundreds of square miles more than the Mid-Atlantic and South and West Florida.

18. **3** The Gulf Coast and Louisiana would lose about 4300 square miles, the total of all the other areas combined.

19. **3** The graph shows that most of the world's population lives in economically developing nations. In 1989, 4.03 billion, of a total world population of 5.23 billion, or 80% of the total, lived in developing nations.

20. **1** Inspection of the figures shows that the growth rate is higher in developing than in developed nations; people in developing nations have less access to family-planning assistance.

21. **5** In 2020, the gap as shown in the graph is 6.94 minus 1.35 or 5.59 billions, greater than for any other year.

22. **3** While the graph for developed countries shows a steady balance between declining birth and death rates, the graph for developing countries shows a relative population increase that grows from about 1875 to the present because the death rate drops more and more compared with the birth rate.

23. **1** The birth rate line is consistently above the death rate line.

24. **1** The birth rate and the death rate lines for the developing countries have always been higher than those for the developed countries.

25. **5** Iran has over 2.5 million foreign refugees. The other choices all have fewer than half a million.

26. **1** Sudan has 4 million internally displaced persons.

27. **4** Bosnia has over 2 million internally displaced refugees.

28. **5** The following countries have over 1 million refugees—Angola, Iraq, Burundi, Sudan, Sri Lanka, Iran, Afghanistan, Pakistan, Myanmar, and Bosnia.

29. **1** Only Mexico in North America has refugees, and they total 32,000.

30. **3** Turkey's refugee population is indicated as having a range between 500,000 to 2 million.

31. **2** OPEC (Arab) oil, contrary to popular belief, is the smallest contributor to United States energy, 2.3%.

32. **3** Domestic oil counts for 27.3% of United States energy.

33. **4** 13.3% is the total of OPEC and non-OPEC contributions.

34. **4** Health care is becoming less available because fewer and fewer people have insurance and each year it gets more costly for a family.

35. **3** The increase was $85 a month per family—$351 to $436.

36. **2** The percentage of women working full time in 1976 was 40%. In 1996, it was 55%, an increase of 15% in 20 years. The percentage of men in the same period of time grew half as much, from 62% to 70%.

37. **2** The percentage of both men and women working dropped visibly in the years 1974–1978, to 62% and 40%, respectively, from consistently higher levels prior to that period, probably because fewer jobs were available.

38. **1** Inspection of the chart shows that per capita income in Taiwan is 7480, many times that in China, 360. Taiwan had literacy rates of 86 in 1976 and 94 in 1992, much higher than those of China for the same dates.

39. **4** The population of China grew from 852 to 1150 and the literacy rate grew from 40% to 73%; these increases were greater than than those of any other country listed.

40. **1** Japan has a per capita income far greater than that of any other country in the chart. The same is true for its gross national product.

BASICS IN INTERPRETING POLITICAL CARTOONS

Political cartoons, as a distinct art form, first became important in the second half of the nineteenth century. Two cartoonists, in particular, achieved great fame during that period.

Thomas Nast, of *Harper's Weekly*, attacked Tammany Hall in 1869, when Boss Tweed and his Ring were in control of New York City. His most famous cartoon, "The Tammany Tiger Loose—'What are you going to do about it?'" led to the voting out of Ring officials and Tweed's conviction and jailing for grand larceny. This cartoon is below.

Joseph Keppler, who founded *Puck*, the first humorous weekly in the United States, used color to powerful effect in his cartoons. A famous cartoon, "Bosses of the Senate," attacked the financial interests represented in the U.S. Senate. This cartoon is below.

1. Most cartoons deal with a single important issue, usually an election campaign issue, questions of peace or war, or corruption in government.

2. The cartoonist frequently uses an exaggerated likeness, or caricature, of some well-known person or institution, for example, Uncle Sam, as the main focus of attention. Or he or she may use or create a familiar symbol to represent an important idea; a dove for peace, a tiger for Tammany Hall.

3. Reading is kept to a minimum so that the appeal is largely visual. A few words at most are used to drive home an idea, so the visual appeal of the political cartoon is universal. Boss Tweed pointed out that, even if his followers could not read, they could "look at the d____n pictures." Thus the cartoonist presents an issue in simplified form, stripped of all relatively unimportant details, in a way that his readers can understand.

4. The cartoonist graphically presents his or her own point of view or that of a newspaper or magazine. The cartoonist is usually openly anticorruption or antiwar, and portrays the object of his or her criticism in the ugliest manner possible.

Because of the visually appealing use of a caricature and/or a symbol focusing critically on a single important issue, the political cartoon is a powerful means of shaping public opinion. Its appeal to the emotions is difficult to equal, and its influence continues to the present day.

How, then, do you interpret a political cartoon when you encounter it on the High School Equivalency Examination?

Here are a few suggestions, using the Nast and Keppler cartoons.

Step 1. *Identify the caricatures or symbols used in the cartoon.* For historical cartoons, you may need some social studies background. In contemporary cartoons, the caricatures and symbols are easier to identify.

In the Nast cartoon, Boss Tweed, sitting in the gallery under the standard reading TAMMANY SPOILS, is a symbol of political power. The tiger represents Tammany Hall, the corrupt political club, and the woman in the tiger's claws is the dead Republic surrounded by the breakdown of law and the destroyed democratic freedom of the ballot.

Step 2. *Identify the issue being exposed or criticized by the cartoonist.* In the case of Nast, it is the undermining of the democratic process by a corrupt political boss and his cronies. In the Keppler cartoon, it is the taking over of the U.S. Senate by monopolies and trusts.

Step 3. *Determine the point of view being expressed by the cartoonist.* In the Nast cartoon, the snarl on the face of the tiger and the exaggerated size of Boss Tweed show how vicious the cartoonist considers the political boss, his organization (the Tweed Ring), and Tammany Hall to be. In the Keppler cartoon, the bloated stomachs of the trusts and their ugly facial expressions convey the cartoonist's disgust.

Now turn to a third cartoon, study it, and try to answer the questions based on it.

QUESTIONS

1. What issue is the subject of this cartoon?

2. What do the elephant and the donkey represent?

3. What is each trying to do?

4. What point of view is the cartoonist expressing?

ANSWERS AND ANALYSIS

1. The issue is campaign-funding abuse, as indicated on the cookie jar.

2. The elephant is the traditional symbol of the Republican Party; the donkey, of the Democratic Party.

3. Each has a hand in the cookie jar and is trying to extract money for the campaign.

4. The cartoonist finds both parties at fault even though he portrays the equally guilty Republicans expressing disapproval of the Democrats.

PRACTICE WITH INTERPRETING POLITICAL CARTOONS

1. The main purpose of Mike Thompson's cartoon is to

   (1) portray the conflict between Republicans and Democrats
   (2) show the superiority of the Republicans over the Democrats
   (3) show the superiority of the Democrats over the Republicans
   (4) show that Republicans and Democrats are both at fault in campaign fund-raising
   (5) show that Democrats do not feel guilty about their campaign fund-raising

2. The cartoonist achieves his purpose by

   (1) exaggerating the conduct of both parties
   (2) arousing our sympathy for both parties
   (3) portraying the humor of the conduct of both parties
   (4) favoring Republicans over Democrats
   (5) showing the irony of the Republicans' conduct

3. What is the main idea of the cartoon?

   (1) Families that watch television are the most informed about politics.
   (2) The speeches of candidates often fail to attract the voters' attention.
   (3) More voters should watch cable television.
   (4) Television networks are not acting in politically responsible ways.
   (5) Families approve of television coverage of political campaigns.

4. What is the main idea of the cartoon?

   (1) Labor camps remain China's primary method of punishing political prisoners.
   (2) The Chinese consider the United States an ungrateful trading partner.
   (3) Economic development in China has been achieved by ignoring human rights issues.
   (4) The Chinese believe that human rights are unimportant to the United States.
   (5) The United States should benefit from the cheap prices of Chinese products.

5. What is the main idea of the cartoon?

    (1) The electoral college has more value now than it did in the past.
    (2) Only Congress should have the power to elect a president.
    (3) The electoral college decreases the value of a citizen's vote.
    (4) Free elections in the United States have almost disappeared.
    (5) The electorate chooses the electoral college.

6. The point of view expressed in this cartoon is that the 1997 increase in the minimum wage would

    (1) significantly reduce the gap between the rich and the poor
    (2) encourage the poor to appreciate the concern of politicians
    (3) help workers climb the ladder of success
    (4) be unlikely to provide any major benefit to the poor
    (5) lower taxes for workers

ANSWER KEY

1. **4**	3. **2**	5. **3**
2. **5**	4. **3**	6. **4**

ANSWER ANALYSIS

1. **4** Choice 4 is correct because the cartoonist indicates that both parties have their hands in the cookie jar and are guilty of campaign fund-raising abuses. Neither party is superior to the other, nor does either feel guilty.

2. **5** The irony arises from the fact that each party has a hand in the jar, yet the Republican elephant is faulting the Democratic donkey for an abuse of which both are equally guilty.

3. **2** Although the viewers approve of free air time for presidential candidates, they ignore the candidates and view other programs.

4. **3** Labor camps in China violate the human rights of the Chinese who are not free to leave, work long hours under extremely poor conditions, and receive little wages.

5. **3** Since the popular vote is sometimes not reflected in the electoral college vote, the value of the vote of the American citizenry is diminished.

6. **4** Though there is some benefit in the increase of the minimum wage, the gap between the wage and the cost of living is still very large so the benefit is merely a token benefit.

PRACTICE WITH INTERPRETING HISTORICAL DOCUMENTS

Interpreting historical documents means reading them carefully and deciding what is the main purpose behind the document. Sometimes you are simply asked from what the document text was taken. Pay close attention to any vocabulary words that may be mentioned in the text; these may be included in the questions to follow. Many questions ask "which of the following EXCEPT." In cases like these, eliminate the choices that ARE examples of the statement. Then choose the one best answer that is NOT an example.

DOCUMENT 1

THE DECLARATION OF INDEPENDENCE

When in the Course of human events it becomes necessary for one people to dissolve the political bonds which have connected them with another, and to assume among the powers of the earth, the separate and equal station to which the Laws of Nature and of Nature's God entitle them, a decent respect to the opinions of mankind requires that they should declare the causes which impel them to the separation.

We hold these truths to be self-evident, that all men are created equal, that they are endowed by their Creator with certain unalienable

Rights, that among these are Life, Liberty and the pursuit of Happiness. That to secure these rights, Governments are instituted among Men, deriving their just powers from the consent of the governed. That whenever any Form of Government becomes destructive of these ends, it is the Right of the People to alter or to abolish it, and to institute new Government, laying its foundation on such principles and organizing its powers in such form, as to them shall seem most likely to effect their Safety and Happiness.

QUESTIONS

1. The main purpose of the Declaration of Independence is to

    (1) justify separation from another government
    (2) obey laws of nature
    (3) earn a decent respect for others' opinions
    (4) influence the course of human events
    (5) join the powers of the earth

2. All of the following rights are included EXCEPT

    (1) life
    (2) liberty
    (3) pursuit of happiness
    (4) equal opportunity
    (5) safety

3. The Declaration states that governments derive their powers from

    (1) the powers of the earth
    (2) the Laws of Nature
    (3) the Laws of Nature's God
    (4) the opinions of mankind
    (5) the governed

ANSWER KEY

1. **1**   2. **4**   3. **5**

ANSWER ANALYSIS

1. **1** The Declaration states that "a decent respect to the opinions of mankind requires that (a people) should declare the causes which impel them to the separation."

2. **4** All the rights are mentioned except equal opportunity, although that might be interpreted as being included in the pursuit of happiness.

3. **5** It is stated that governments derive "their just powers from the consent of the governed."

DOCUMENT 2

UNITED STATES CONSTITUTION
Amendment VI

In all criminal prosecutions, the accused shall enjoy the right to a speedy and public trial, by an impartial jury of the State and district wherein the crime shall have been committed, which district shall have been previously ascertained by law, and to be informed of the nature and cause of the accusation; to be confronted with the witnesses against him; to have compulsory process for obtaining witnesses in his favor, and to have the Assistance of Counsel for his defense.

QUESTIONS

1. The above passage is

    (1) part of the Declaration of Independence
    (2) part of the Bill of Rights of the Constitution
    (3) part of the Articles of Confederation
    (4) part of the Preamble to the Constitution
    (5) a requirement of the Supreme Court

2. The amendment requires that an accused should have all of the following EXCEPT

    (1) counsel for the defense
    (2) a jury from the state where the crime took place
    (3) witnesses in his favor
    (4) reasons for the trial
    (5) a confidential trial

3. The amendment enumerates the

    (1) civil rights of accused criminals
    (2) responsibilities of the federal government
    (3) duties of the witnesses
    (4) duties of the defense counsel
    (5) duties of the courts

ANSWER KEY

1. **2**   2. **5**   3. **1**

ANSWER ANALYSIS

1. **2** The passage is Amendment VI of the United States Constitution and part of the Bill of Rights.

2. **5** The first four choices are rights of the accused criminal. The last, Choice 5, is prohibited. A speedy and public trial must take place.

3. **1** The amendment gives the civil rights of the accused criminal: a speedy and public trial; an impartial jury, a knowledge of the reasons for his accusation, the right to confront witnesses against him, the right to have witnesses for him, the right to a defense counsel.

DOCUMENT 3

"In the discussions to which this interest has given rise, and in the arrangements by which they may terminate, the occasion has been deemed proper for asserting as a principle in which rights and interests of the United States are involved, that the American continents, by the free and independent condition which they have assumed and maintain, are henceforth not to be considered as subjects for future colonization by any European power. . . . We owe it, therefore, to candor and to the amicable relations existing between the United States and those powers to declare that we should consider any attempt on their part to extend their system to any portion of this hemisphere as dangerous to our peace and safety. With the existing colonies or dependencies of any European power we have not interfered and shall not interfere. But with the governments who have declared their independence and maintain it, and whose independence we have, on great consideration and on just principles, acknowledged, we could not view any interposition for the purpose of oppressing them or controlling in any other manner their destiny by any European power in any other light than as the manifestation of an unfriendly disposition toward the United States."

QUESTIONS

1. The statement that "the American continents . . . are henceforth not to be considered as subjects for future colonization by any European power" is known as

   (1) the Declaration of Independence
   (2) Washington's Message to Congress
   (3) the Articles of Confederation
   (4) the Monroe Doctrine
   (5) the Truman Doctrine

2. The United States would

   (1) retaliate if colonized
   (2) interfere with existing European colonies
   (3) ignore the actions of European powers
   (4) view colonization as an unfriendly act
   (5) break off relations with the interfering European power

3. The passage states that this statement of policy is based on

   (1) the freedom and independence the United States has maintained
   (2) the friendly relations between it and European powers
   (3) its success as a colony
   (4) its right to interfere with European powers
   (5) its control of its destiny

ANSWER KEY

1. **4**   2. **4**   3. **1**

ANSWER ANALYSIS

1. **4** The statement is known as the Monroe Doctrine announced to Congress by President James Monroe on December 2, 1823.

2. **4** The message mentions "an unfriendly disposition" as a consequence.

3. **1** The justification for the doctrine is maintaining the "free and independent condition of the United States."

DOCUMENT 4

UNIVERSAL DECLARATION OF HUMAN RIGHTS
Preamble

Whereas recognition of the inherent dignity and of the equal and inalienable rights of all members of the human family is the foundation of freedom, justice and peace in the world,

Whereas disregard and contempt for human rights have resulted in barbarous acts which have outraged the conscience of mankind, and the advent of a world in which human beings shall enjoy freedom of speech and belief and freedom from fear and want has been proclaimed as the highest aspiration of the common people,

Whereas it is essential, if man is not to be compelled to have recourse, as a last resort, to rebellion against tyranny and oppression, that human rights should be protected by the rule of law,

Whereas the people of the United Nations have in the Charter reaffirmed their faith in fundamental human rights, in the dignity and worth of the human person and in the equal rights of men and women and have determined to promote social progress and better standards of life in larger freedom,

Now, Therefore, The General Assembly proclaims...
This Universal Declaration of Human Rights...

QUESTIONS

1. The Preamble states that the rule of law can

    (1) prevent barbarous acts
    (2) prevent contempt for human rights
    (3) outrage the world's conscience
    (4) disregard human rights
    (5) prevent rebellion against tyranny

2. The purposes of the Universal Declaration are to do all of the following EXCEPT

    (1) protect human rights
    (2) promote freedom of speech
    (3) achieve freedom from fear
    (4) prevent war
    (5) promote social progress

3. The Declaration has as its justification all of the following EXCEPT

    (1) equal rights of men and women
    (2) observance of fundamental freedoms
    (3) justice in the world
    (4) rebellion against tyranny
    (5) dignity and worth of all peoples

ANSWER KEY

1. **5**   2. **4**   3. **4**

ANSWER ANALYSIS

1. **5** It states that the protection of the rule of law will make unnecessary recourse to rebellion against tyranny.

2. **4** War is not mentioned in the Preamble.

3. **4** Rebellion against tyranny is mentioned only as a last resort.

PRACTICE WITH INTERPRETING PHOTOGRAPHS

Interpreting historical photographs means studying them carefully and deciding what is the main purpose behind the photograph. Sometimes you are simply asked from what location the photograph was taken. Pay close attention to every person and item in the photograph. Other questions ask you to identify the photo. Most important, you may be asked the purpose behind the photograph (why it was taken or why it is famous). Take time to analyze the photograph. Identify key political figures, if any, location, and important subjects in the photograph. All of these are important clues to the meaning behind the photograph.

PHOTOGRAPH 1

1. This photograph was taken

   (1) in a courtroom
   (2) at an open air debate
   (3) at a political campaign rally
   (4) at a sports event
   (5) at a celebration

ANSWER ANALYSIS

1. **3** The photograph was taken of President Theodore Roosevelt at a political rally.

PHOTOGRAPH 2

2. This is a photograph of

   (1) a business meeting
   (2) a presidential meeting
   (3) a questioning of a witness
   (4) a public trial
   (5) a political confrontation

ANSWER ANALYSIS

2. **2** President Harry Truman, who succeeded Franklin D. Roosevelt, meets with government officials.

PHOTOGRAPH 3

3. The purpose of this photograph is to depict

   (1) the illegal use of child labor
   (2) factory conditions
   (3) a strict foreman
   (4) ill-clothed children
   (5) oyster shucking

ANSWER ANALYSIS

3. **1** Young children were illegally used in a sweatshop to make clothing.

PHOTOGRAPH 4

4. The purpose of this photograph is to show

   (1) obedient children
   (2) the pledge of allegiance
   (3) objection to saluting the flag
   (4) an American classroom
   (5) equality of the sexes

ANSWER ANALYSIS

4. **2** All of the children are pledging allegiance to the country.

PHOTOGRAPH 5

5. The purpose of this photograph is to picture

    (1) a mathematics class
    (2) a disobedient student
    (3) an inadequate classroom
    (4) a segregated classroom
    (5) neglected children

ANSWER ANALYSIS

5. **4** The photograph depicts a classroom in which Black children are segregated. All the people in the picture are Black—pupils and teacher.

PRACTICE WITH INTERPRETING PRACTICAL DOCUMENTS

Interpreting practical documents means reading a business or government document. Read the entire document carefully, noting lists or words that are bolded. Key points are usually listed and numbered or bulleted. Many of the questions accompanying these documents are to test whether or not you can read and interpret the document. Sometimes the purpose of the document is questioned; the answer to this can often be found in the headline or bolded words.

INTERNAL REVENUE SERVICE PUBLICATION 529

Job Search Expenses

You can deduct certain expenses in looking for a new job in your present occupation, even if you do not get a new job. You cannot deduct these expenses if:

(1) You are looking for a job in a new occupation, or

(2) There was a substantial break between the ending of your last job and your looking for a new one.

You cannot deduct your expenses if you are seeking employment for the first time.

Employment and outplacement agency fees. You can deduct employment and outplacement agency fees you pay in looking for a new job in your present occupation.

Résumé. You can deduct amounts you spend for typing, printing, and mailing copies of a résumé to prospective employers if you are looking for a new job in your present occupation.

Travel and transportation expenses. If you travel to an area and, while there, you look for a new job in your present occupation, you may be able to deduct travel expenses to and from the area. You can deduct the travel expenses if the trip is primarily to look for a new job.

QUESTIONS

1. You can deduct expenses if you are a mechanic

   (1) looking for a new job as a computer programmer
   (2) returning to work after many years
   (3) looking for your first job
   (4) looking for a job in another garage
   (5) going back to school

2. Expenses that can be deducted include all of the following EXCEPT

   (1) cost of distributing your résumé
   (2) travel time primarily for personal activity
   (3) travel looking for a new job in a new area as a mechanic
   (4) travel looking for a new job as a mechanic in your present area
   (5) certain travel and transportation expenses

3. The main purpose of this regulation is to

   (1) get more tax money from job seekers
   (2) ease the burden of job seekers
   (3) catch violators of Internal Revenue Service regulations
   (4) list allowable deductions
   (5) list expenses that are not deductible

ANSWER KEY

1. **4**   2. **2**   3. **2**

ANSWER ANALYSIS

1. **4** It is specifically stated that you can deduct expenses if you are looking for a job in your present occupation. The mechanic, in this case, will still be a mechanic in another garage.

2. **2** The expenses for a trip on personal business cannot be deducted.

3. **2** The instructions of the Internal Revenue Service help job seekers by allowing them to deduct legitimate expenses.

VOTE ON A COUNTY PROPOSITION TO APPROVE AN AMENDMENT TO A LAW

Shall "Local Law" adopted by the County amending the laws of the County Commissioner of Public Works with respect to the local Community College be approved?

BACKGROUND: This local law is subject to a vote because it would change the powers of the Commissioner of Public Works as laid out in the County Charter. All construction projects at the College are now undertaken by the County through its Department of Public Works (DPW). Currently, all College projects are supervised by DPW, which sometimes also performs the work with County workers but often contracts it out. If the law is approved, DPW would no longer have control over public works on the Community College campus; instead, the College would supervise improvement projects directly with its own personnel. The College would no longer pay DPW to supervise improvement projects.

QUESTIONS

1. At present, construction projects at the College are directly performed by

    (1) the County
    (2) the Commissioner of Public Works
    (3) the Department of Public Works
    (4) the Community College
    (5) the contracted personnel

2. The local law, which must be approved by the voters, would give control of improvement projects to

    (1) the Commissioner of Public Works
    (2) the Department of Public Works
    (3) the Community College
    (4) the County Charter
    (5) the County workers

3. The proposed change would affect all of the following EXCEPT

    (1) the Commissioner of Public Works
    (2) the Department of Public Works
    (3) the role of the Community College
    (4) the supervision of the Community College
    (5) local law

ANSWER KEY

1. **3**   2. **3**   3. **4**

ANSWER ANALYSIS

1. **3** Construction projects are now undertaken by the County through its Department of Public Works.

2. **3** The College would supervise improvement projects directly.

3. **4** Supervision *of* the Community College is not mentioned in the passage. Supervision *by* the College is.

ANNUAL REPORT—CORPORATION X

The Company designs, manufactures and markets personal computers and related personal computing and communicating solutions for sale primarily to education, creative, consumer, and business customers. Substantially all of the Company's net sales to date have been derived from the sale of personal computers. The Company manages its business primarily on a geographic basis. The Company's geographic operating segments include the Americas, Europe, Japan, and Asia Pacific. Each geographic segment provides similar hardware and software products and similar services. During 1998, the Company continued and essentially completed a restructuring plan commenced in 1996 aimed at reducing its cost structure, improving its competitiveness, and restoring sustainable profitability. The Company's restructuring actions included the termination of employees, closure of facilities, and cancellation of contracts.

The Company's personal computers are characterized by their ease of use, innovative industrial designs and applications base, and built-in networking, graphics and multimedia capabilities. The Company offers a wide range of personal computing products, including personal computers, related peripherals, software, and networking and connectivity products.

QUESTIONS

1. The annual report of the corporation includes all of the following EXCEPT its

    (1) products
    (2) geographic operating segments
    (3) restructuring actions
    (4) marketing
    (5) cost of products

2. The company's main source of income comes from

    (1) personal computers
    (2) peripherals
    (3) software applications
    (4) networking products
    (5) connectivity products

3. The company's income has come from all of the following EXCEPT

    (1) schools
    (2) corporations
    (3) individual consumers
    (4) investments
    (5) creative customers

ANSWER KEY

1. **5**   2. **1**   3. **4**

ANSWER ANALYSIS

1. **5** The first four choices are mentioned in the report. Cost of products is mentioned nowhere.

2. **1** The report mentions that substantially all the net sales have been from the sales of personal computers.

3. **4** Investments are not mentioned as a source of income. Schools, businesses, and customers—individual and creative—are.

SAFETY BULLETIN OF CORPORATION X
SUBJECT: BACKING OF VEHICLES

It has been estimated that the average driver has his vehicle in reverse less than 1% of the time, but backing produces a substantially greater percentage of vehicle accidents. This is understandable because a driver often has restricted vision while backing.

Backing can be avoided by using a few simple rules:

—Plan your route and make immediate decisions on parking which will keep backing to a minimum.

—Always back into a parking space. This allows full visibility when pulling out.

If backing cannot be avoided:

—Walk behind your vehicle before you enter it.

—Align the mirrors for maximum view.

—Check clearances and know your vehicle.

—Turn your head while backing. Don't rely on mirrors alone.

—Back slowly and be ready to stop at any moment.

—Sound the horn if there is a possibility that someone might walk behind your vehicle.

—Avoid blind-side backing. Backing to the right is dangerous because you are backing blind.

QUESTIONS

1. Proper backing is important because

    (1) it cannot be avoided
    (2) the driver has to do it constantly
    (3) the driver has full visibility
    (4) it is the cause of many avoidable accidents
    (5) the driver makes immediate decisions

2. Backing accidents occur because the driver

    (1) has limited visibility
    (2) backs into a parking space
    (3) backs in slowly
    (4) sounds his horn
    (5) is ready to stop

3. All of the following are possible causes of backing accidents EXCEPT

    (1) inadequate clearance
    (2) reliance solely on mirrors
    (3) blind-side backing
    (4) aligned mirrors
    (5) inadequate visibility

4. The purpose of the bulletin is to remind drivers to

    (1) plan
    (2) always avoid backing
    (3) rely on mirrors
    (4) prevent backing accidents
    (5) walk behind the vehicle

ANSWER KEY

1. **4**   2. **1**   3. **4**   4. **4**

ANSWER ANALYSIS

1. **4** Backing produces a greater percentage of accidents for the time needed for it—1%.

2. **1** The bulletin states that the driver has restricted view while backing.

3. **4** Drivers are reminded to align mirrors to prevent backing accidents. All the other choices are causes.

4. **4** The bulletin is intended to prevent backing accidents by cautioning drivers to avoid backing where possible and to observe safe backing procedures.

United States
Census
2000

U.S. Department of Commerce • Bureau of the Census

This is the official form for all the people at this address. It is quick and easy, and your answers are protected by law. Complete the Census and help your community get what it needs — today and in the future!

Start Here

Please use a black or blue pen.

1. How many people were living or staying in this house, apartment, or mobile home on April 1, 2000?

Number of people

INCLUDE in this number:

- foster children, roomers, or housemates
- people staying here on April 1, 2000 who have no other permanent place to stay
- people living here most of the time while working, even if they have another place to live

DO NOT INCLUDE in this number:

- college students living away while attending college
- people in a correctional facility, nursing home, or mental hospital on April 1, 2000
- Armed Forces personnel living somewhere else
- people who live or stay at another place most of the time

2. Is this house, apartment, or mobile home —
Mark ☒ *ONE box.*

- ☐ Owned by you or someone in this household with a mortgage or loan?
- ☐ Owned by you or someone in this household free and clear (without a mortgage or loan)?
- ☐ Rented for cash rent?
- ☐ Occupied without payment of cash rent?

3. Please answer the following questions for each person living in this house, apartment, or mobile home. Start with the name of one of the people living here who owns, is buying, or rents this house, apartment, or mobile home. If there is no such person, start with any adult living or staying here. We will refer to this person as Person 1.

What is this person's name? *Print name below.*

Last Name

First Name   MI

4. What is Person 1's telephone number? *We may call this person if we don't understand an answer.*

Area Code + Number

5. What is Person 1's sex? *Mark* ☒ *ONE box.*
- ☐ Male   ☐ Female

6. What is Person 1's age and what is Person 1's date of birth?
Age on April 1, 2000

Print numbers in boxes.
Month   Day   Year of birth

→ **NOTE: Please answer BOTH Questions 7 and 8.**

7. Is Person 1 Spanish/Hispanic/Latino? *Mark* ☒ *the* ***"No"*** *box if* ***not*** *Spanish/Hispanic/Latino.*
- ☐ **No,** not Spanish/Hispanic/Latino
- ☐ Yes, Mexican, Mexican Am., Chicano
- ☐ Yes, other Spanish/Hispanic/Latino — *Print group.* ↘
- ☐ Yes, Puerto Rican
- ☐ Yes, Cuban

8. What is Person 1's race? *Mark* ☒ *one or more races* to indicate what this person considers himself/herself to be.
- ☐ White
- ☐ Black, African Am., or Negro
- ☐ American Indian or Alaska Native — *Print name of enrolled or principal tribe.* ↘

- ☐ Asian Indian
- ☐ Chinese
- ☐ Filipino
- ☐ Other Asian — *Print race.* ↘
- ☐ Japanese
- ☐ Korean
- ☐ Vietnamese
- ☐ Native Hawaiian
- ☐ Guamanian or Chamorro
- ☐ Samoan
- ☐ Other Pacific Islander — *Print race.* ↘

- ☐ Some other race — *Print race.* ↘

OMB No. 0607-0856: Approval Expires 12/31/2000

Form **D-1**

→ **If more people live here, continue with Person 2.**

Person 2

Your answers are important! Every person in the Census counts.

1. What is Person 2's name? *Print name below.*
Last Name

First Name   MI

2. How is this person related to Person 1? *Mark* **X** *ONE box.*

- ☐ Husband/wife
- ☐ Natural-born son/daughter
- ☐ Adopted son/daughter
- ☐ Stepson/stepdaughter
- ☐ Brother/sister
- ☐ Father/mother
- ☐ Grandchild
- ☐ Parent-in-law
- ☐ Son-in-law/daughter-in-law
- ☐ Other relative — *Print exact relationship.* ➦

If NOT RELATED to Person 1:

- ☐ Roomer, boarder
- ☐ Housemate, roommate
- ☐ Unmarried partner
- ☐ Foster child
- ☐ Other nonrelative

3. What is this person's sex? *Mark* **X** *ONE box.*

- ☐ Male
- ☐ Female

4. What is this person's age and what is this person's date of birth? *Print numbers in boxes.*

Age on April 1, 2000   Month   Day   Year of birth

➡ **NOTE: Please answer BOTH Questions 5 and 6.**

5. Is this person Spanish/Hispanic/Latino? *Mark* **X** *the "No" box if* ***not*** *Spanish/Hispanic/Latino.*

- ☐ **No,** not Spanish/Hispanic/Latino
- ☐ Yes, Mexican, Mexican Am., Chicano
- ☐ Yes, other Spanish/Hispanic/Latino — *Print group.* ➦
- ☐ Yes, Puerto Rican
- ☐ Yes, Cuban

6. What is this person's race? *Mark* **X** *one or more races* to indicate what this person considers himself/herself to be.

- ☐ White
- ☐ Black, African Am., or Negro
- ☐ American Indian or Alaska Native — *Print name of enrolled or principal tribe.* ➦

- ☐ Asian Indian
- ☐ Chinese
- ☐ Filipino
- ☐ Other Asian — *Print race.* ➦
- ☐ Japanese
- ☐ Korean
- ☐ Vietnamese
- ☐ Native Hawaiian
- ☐ Guamanian or Chamorro
- ☐ Samoan
- ☐ Other Pacific Islander — *Print race.* ➦

- ☐ Some other race — *Print race.* ➦

➡ **If more people live here, continue with Person 3.**

Person 3

Census information helps your community get financial assistance for roads, hospitals, schools, and more.

1. What is Person 3's name? *Print name below.*
Last Name

First Name   MI

2. How is this person related to Person 1? *Mark* **X** *ONE box.*

- ☐ Husband/wife
- ☐ Natural-born son/daughter
- ☐ Adopted son/daughter
- ☐ Stepson/stepdaughter
- ☐ Brother/sister
- ☐ Father/mother
- ☐ Grandchild
- ☐ Parent-in-law
- ☐ Son-in-law/daughter-in-law
- ☐ Other relative — *Print exact relationship.* ➦

If NOT RELATED to Person 1:

- ☐ Roomer, boarder
- ☐ Housemate, roommate
- ☐ Unmarried partner
- ☐ Foster child
- ☐ Other nonrelative

3. What is this person's sex? *Mark* **X** *ONE box.*

- ☐ Male
- ☐ Female

4. What is this person's age and what is this person's date of birth? *Print numbers in boxes.*

Age on April 1, 2000   Month   Day   Year of birth

➡ **NOTE: Please answer BOTH Questions 5 and 6.**

5. Is this person Spanish/Hispanic/Latino? *Mark* **X** *the "No" box if* ***not*** *Spanish/Hispanic/Latino.*

- ☐ **No,** not Spanish/Hispanic/Latino
- ☐ Yes, Mexican, Mexican Am., Chicano
- ☐ Yes, other Spanish/Hispanic/Latino — *Print group.* ➦
- ☐ Yes, Puerto Rican
- ☐ Yes, Cuban

6. What is this person's race? *Mark* **X** *one or more races* to indicate what this person considers himself/herself to be.

- ☐ White
- ☐ Black, African Am., or Negro
- ☐ American Indian or Alaska Native — *Print name of enrolled or principal tribe.* ➦

- ☐ Asian Indian
- ☐ Chinese
- ☐ Filipino
- ☐ Other Asian — *Print race.* ➦
- ☐ Japanese
- ☐ Korean
- ☐ Vietnamese
- ☐ Native Hawaiian
- ☐ Guamanian or Chamorro
- ☐ Samoan
- ☐ Other Pacific Islander — *Print race.* ➦

- ☐ Some other race — *Print race.* ➦

➡ **If more people live here, continue with Person 4.**

QUESTIONS

1. Which of these would be included in answering the census form?

    (1) an inmate in a federal prison
    (2) a person living in Evanston, Illinois, and attending Northwestern University
    (3) a pilot at an Air Force base in Alaska
    (4) a person living in the apartment
    (5) a traveling salesman away most of the year

2. All of the following are asked about EXCEPT

    (1) age
    (2) employment
    (3) telephone number
    (4) race
    (5) date of birth

3. All of the following are mentioned as Spanish/Hispanic/Latino EXCEPT

    (1) Dominican
    (2) Puerto Rican
    (3) Mexican
    (4) Chicano
    (5) Cuban

ANSWER KEY

1. **4**   2. **2**   3. **1**

ANSWER ANALYSIS

1. **4** The form asks for the people living or staying in the apartment. All the others are not to be included.

2. **2** No mention is made of employment. All the other choices are specifically mentioned.

3. **1** Dominicans are not mentioned although they might be included in other Spanish/Hispanic/Latino groupings.

Handling Social Studies Skills Questions

The Social Studies test no longer tests your ability to recall information such as dates, isolated facts, or events. It now emphasizes higher level skills. It does so by testing your ability to understand the written word or graphics, to analyze and apply the given information and ideas, and to evaluate the accuracy of the information and the conclusions based on it.

COMPREHENSION ITEMS

Twenty percent of the test, or about 10 items, require you to understand the meaning and purpose of written material, passages or quotations, and information contained in maps, graphs, tables, and political cartoons. These items test your ability to restate information, summarize ideas, and identify incorrectly stated ideas. The question will usually include a quotation and be followed by the words "This most nearly means" or "The best explanation of this statement is" or "The author believes or suggests."

> **TIP**
>
> Comprehension items require you to understand meaning and purpose.

EXAMPLE

A CODE

Never DO, BE, or SUFFER anything in soul or body, less or more, but what tends to the glory of God.

Resolved, never to lose one moment of time; but improve it the most profitable way I possibly can.

Resolved, to think much, on all occasions, of my own dying, and of the common circumstances which attend death.

Resolved, to maintain the strictest temperance in eating and drinking.

QUESTION

1. The author of the code believes that people should be mainly concerned with

   (1) monetary issues
   (2) luxuries
   (3) patriotism
   (4) spiritual matters
   (5) politics

ANSWER AND ANALYSIS

The passage reflects the ideas of Puritanism, a code that stresses spiritual concerns.

You can answer this question correctly if you read the passage carefully and decide what is being emphasized. Then, look for the answer that identifies that emphasis. In this question, the emphasis is on living for the glory of God, concern for one's manner of dying, and discipline in such material concerns as eating and drinking. The spiritual is stressed. Indeed, you can answer the question even if you do not know it is the Puritan Code that is being quoted. The correct choice is 4.

APPLICATION ITEMS

TIP

Application items require you to understand content and apply it to a particular situation.

Thirty percent of the test, or about 15 items, require you to use information and ideas in a situation other than that indicated to you in the question. Applying information and ideas is a high-level skill because you must not only understand the general content, but also be able to transfer it to the context of a particular situation. In other words, you must go from the general information you are given to a specific case.

EXAMPLE

The principle of judicial review provides for the judiciary to determine the constitutionality of both state and federal laws.

QUESTION

1. Which action best illustrates the principle of judicial review?

   (1) Congress enacts civil rights legislation.
   (2) The Senate approves appointment of federal judges.
   (3) An act of Congress is struck down by the Supreme Court.
   (4) The states refuse to cooperate with the federal authorities in crime control.
   (5) Congress overrides a presidential veto.

ANSWER AND ANALYSIS

The principle of judicial review means the power of the U.S. Supreme Court to rule on the constitutionality of acts of Congress, state legislatures, executive officers, and lower courts. The only choice that involves a court action is Choice 3, a specific application of this principle to an act of Congress. You must apply the principle of judicial or court reexamination to an act of Congress.

The purpose of another form of question or item on the High School Equivalency Examination Social Studies test is to test your ability to apply given information that defines ideas in historical documents, divisions of subject matter in the social studies, systems of government, economics, psychology, and groups of basic concepts in the five areas of the social studies. You will have to

1. understand information that is presented in defined categories, usually five in number;
2. relate a situation, action, or event to those categories;
3. arrive at an application of the information in the categories to the given situation, action, or event.

An illustration will make this clear. In this example, the information presented in defined categories is the central idea of each of five articles of the Bill of Rights, the first ten amendments to the Constitution.

EXAMPLE

The first ten amendments to the Constitution make up the Bill of Rights ratified by Congress in 1791. Parts of five of the amendments read as follows:

(A) Article 1—Congress shall make no law...abridging the freedom of speech or of the press.
(B) Article 2—The right of the people to keep and bear arms shall not be infringed.
(C) Article 5—No person...shall be compelled in any criminal case to be a witness against himself, nor be deprived of life, liberty, or property, without due process of law.
(D) Article 7—The right to trial by jury shall be preserved.
(E) Article 8—Excessive bail shall not be required...nor cruel and unusual punishments inflicted.

The questions that follow deal with three ways in which the given information can be used by three individuals in three different situations.

QUESTIONS

Indicate the amendment (article) most likely to be cited in support of his or her position by

1. an opponent of capital punishment

    (1) Article 1
    (2) Article 2
    (3) Article 5
    (4) Article 7
    (5) Article 8

2. a member of the National Rifle Association

    (1) Article 1
    (2) Article 2
    (3) Article 5
    (4) Article 7
    (5) Article 8

3. a person accused of a criminal act who is testifying at his or her trial

    (1) Article 1
    (2) Article 2
    (3) Article 5
    (4) Article 7
    (5) Article 8

ANSWERS AND ANALYSIS

You must apply the categorized information to each situation.

The correct answer to question 1 is Choice 5. An opponent of capital punishment will cite Article 8's prohibition against cruel and unusual punishment.

The correct answer to question 2 is Choice 2. A member of the National Rifle Association will cite Article 2, "The right of the people to keep and bear arms shall not be infringed."

The correct answer to question 3 is Choice 3. The person on trial might "take the Fifth," citing the provision of Article 5 that "no person...shall be compelled in any criminal case to be a witness against himself."

Try another item set in this format.

EXAMPLE

Psychology is the science of behavior and of human thought processes.
There are a number of closely interrelated branches of human psychology.

(A) Social psychology investigates the effect of the group on the behavior of the individual.
(B) Applied psychology puts to practical use the discoveries and theories of psychology as in industrial psychology.
(C) Clinical psychology diagnoses and treats mental disorders and mental illnesses.
(D) Comparative psychology deals with different behavioral organizations of animals including human beings.
(E) Physiological psychology attempts to understand the effects of body functions on human behavior.

QUESTIONS

Each of the following describes a proposed study. Indicate which branch of psychology is most clearly involved.

1. A company wants to study the effects of music piped into a factory where workers are on an assembly line.

    (1) Social psychology
    (2) Applied psychology
    (3) Clinical psychology
    (4) Comparative psychology
    (5) Physiological psychology

2. A drug rehabilitation center wants to study the role of peer pressure on a teenager in a drug prevention program.

    (1) Social psychology
    (2) Applied psychology
    (3) Clinical psychology
    (4) Comparative psychology
    (5) Physiological psychology

3. A grant is available for a study of schizophrenia, a disorder characterized by hallucinations and delusions.

   (1) Social psychology
   (2) Applied psychology
   (3) Clinical psychology
   (4) Comparative psychology
   (5) Physiological psychology

ANSWERS AND ANALYSIS

The correct answer to question 1 is Choice 2. Applied psychology puts the findings of industrial psychologists to practical use, in this case for people who work on an assembly line.

The correct answer to question 2 is Choice 1. Social psychologists are concerned with the effects of groups, in this case teenagers, who put pressure on their peers to use drugs.

The correct answer to question 3 is Choice 3. Clinical psychologists would apply for the grant because of their interest in schizophrenia, a mental disorder.

ANALYSIS ITEMS

Thirty percent of the test, or about 15 items, require you to break down information into its parts to determine their interrelationships. These items involve the ability to identify cause-and-effect relationships, separate fact from opinion, separate conclusions from supporting statements, and show that you can recognize assumptions on which conclusions are based.

QUESTION

Democracy may be defined as government by the people directly or through representatives chosen in free elections. Which quotation from the Declaration of Independence best describes the fundamental principle of democracy in the United States?

(1) "imposing taxes on us without our consent"
(2) "governments long established should not be changed for light and transient causes"
(3) "depriving us, in many cases, of the benefits of trial by jury"
(4) "deriving their just powers from the consent of the governed"
(5) "quartering large bodies of armed troops among us"

ANSWERS AND ANALYSIS

Not only must you understand the meaning of each possible answer, but you must analyze it to determine which is a *fundamental* principle of government in the United States. First you must understand; then you must analyze.

You have to go through all of the following steps:

Choice 1: imposing taxes without consent—meaning taxation without representation

Choice 2: governments long established should not be changed for light causes—meaning change in government must be for good reason

> **TIP**
>
> Analysis items require you to determine relationships and interrelationships.

Choice 3: benefits of trial by jury—meaning the right to trial by jury

Choice 4: deriving powers from consent of the governed—meaning the government gets its power from those it governs, the people

Choice 5: quartering armed troops—meaning compulsion to keep soldiers in homes

Now the test of a *fundamental* principle of government in the United States must be applied to each.

Choice 1 is not fundamental; it is a grievance.

Choice 2 refers not to the government of the United States, but to changing governments in general.

Choice 3, trial by jury, is an important right, but it is not as fundamental as Choice 4, which states that the U.S. government is a democracy in which the people rule through their elected representatives. This is an absolutely fundamental principle.

Choice 4 is the only correct interpretation that can be made.

Choice 5 refers to unauthorized quartering of soldiers—important, but not fundamental.

EVALUATION ITEMS

Twenty percent of the test, or about 10 items, are the most difficult. You must make judgments about the soundness or accuracy of information. These questions test your ability to determine whether facts are adequately documented or proved, whether they are appropriately used to support conclusions, and whether they are used correctly or incorrectly in the presentation of opinions or arguments.

QUESTION

Which statement is an opinion rather than a fact?

(1) France was involved in the Vietnam conflict before the United States entered it.
(2) There are tensions between mainland China and Taiwan.
(3) Peace will be achieved by regional agreements throughout the world.
(4) Great Britain has become a full member of the European Common Market.
(5) The United States is a member of the North Atlantic Treaty Organization.

ANSWER AND ANALYSIS

Five statements are presented. Four are facts that can be proved or verified by evidence—that France was involved in Vietnam; that mainland China and Taiwan have tensions; that Great Britain is a member of the European Common Market; that the United States is a member of the North Atlantic Treaty Organization. Choice 3, peace will be achieved by regional agreements throughout the world, is an opinion or a hypothesis—not a fact—and it remains to be proved.

TIP

Evaluation items require you to evaluate information presented.

PRACTICE WITH SOCIAL STUDIES SKILLS QUESTIONS

COMPREHENSION

1. During the last 150 years, immigrants were attracted to the United States because manpower needs increased. This occurred when the United States was experiencing periods of

   (1) economic expansion
   (2) economic depression
   (3) war
   (4) political change
   (5) stability

2. "The privilege to be involved and to conduct a business in any manner that one pleases is not guaranteed by the Constitution. The right to engage in certain businesses may be subject to various conditions. Laws regulating businesses have been found to be valid. We find no justification to reject the state law under question."

   Which is best illustrated by the passage?

   (1) residual powers
   (2) legislative consent
   (3) judicial review
   (4) executive order
   (5) executive privilege

3. Which is a basic assumption of the graduated income tax?

   (1) The ability to pay increases as wealth increases.
   (2) Each wage earner should contribute to the government the same percentage of his or her income.
   (3) The middle class should bear the burden of financing the government.
   (4) Citizens should pay the costs of government services in proportion to their use of such services.
   (5) Taxes on the wealthy should not be too great.

4. "In a sense the people of the Third World were forced to help pay for the Industrial Revolution in the West."

   Which statement most clearly supports this viewpoint?

   (1) The colonizing powers encouraged industries in their colonies.
   (2) Western nations depended upon raw materials from their colonies.
   (3) Financial centers of the world blocked investments in these new nations.
   (4) The Third World is now experiencing an Industrial Revolution.
   (5) The Third World supplied most of the manpower needed by the West.

5. "Public opinion is of major significance in social control."

   The author of this statement most probably means that

   (1) the influence of public opinion on government leaders is very limited
   (2) problem solving is simplified when public opinion is not known
   (3) public opinion may be predicted accurately, especially in the time of national crisis
   (4) government officials must pay attention to public opinion in the formulation of policies
   (5) polls provide little help to lawmakers

ANALYSIS

THE BUSINESS CYCLE

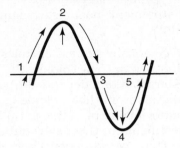

6. If economic indicators place the economy at a point on the cycle between 1 and 2, then the Council of Economic Advisers would most likely suggest which action to the president?

(1) planned deficit spending
(2) increasing income tax rates
(3) lowering interest rates
(4) increasing government expenditures
(5) encouraging higher wages

7. "The showpieces are, with rare exceptions, the industries dominated by a handful of large firms. The foreign visitor, brought to the United States...visits the same firms as do the attorneys of the Department of Justice in their search for monopolies."

The best explanation of this seemingly contradictory behavior is that

(1) only the largest corporations will allow foreign visitors to inspect their factories
(2) both State and Justice Department officials oppose the development of monopolies
(3) the developing countries of the world are interested only in large corporations
(4) the largest corporations often pioneer in research and production methods
(5) small firms do not welcome foreign investment

8. "Why, by interweaving our destiny with that of any part of Europe, entangle our peace and prosperity in the toils of European ambition, rivalship, interest, humor, or caprice?"

Which action by the United States best reflects the philosophy expressed in this quotation?

(1) passage of legislation restricting immigration
(2) rejection of the Treaty of Versailles
(3) enactment of the Lend-Lease Act
(4) approval of the United Nations Charter
(5) membership in the North Atlantic Treaty Organization

9. "If a nation expects to be ignorant and free, in a state of civilization, it expects what never was and never will be."

Which idea is most strongly supported by this statement?

(1) the government's right to tax
(2) universal suffrage
(3) a strong central government
(4) compulsory education
(5) abolition of slavery

10. "Ours is a country where people...can attain to the most elevated positions or acquire a large amount of wealth...according to their talents, prudence, and personal exertions."

This quotation most clearly supports the idea that

(1) upward social mobility and the work ethic are closely related
(2) economic collectivism is part of American life
(3) regulated capitalism reflects private initiative
(4) the United States has a centrally controlled economic system
(5) the U.S. economic system favors the wealthy

APPLICATION

11. Which is the most valid statement concerning the problem of balancing human wants with limited resources?

    (1) It exists only in societies with a free enterprise economy.
    (2) It has been solved in nations with strong governmental controls over economic activity.
    (3) It has become less of a problem with the advancements in technology.
    (4) It exists in all societies, no matter what the economic system.
    (5) It will be solved by the year 2000.

12. A "strict constructionist," one who would permit the federal government to exercise only those powers specifically granted by the U.S. Constitution, would favor which of the following actions?

    (1) the institution of programs for social reform
    (2) annexation of territory by the United States
    (3) bypassing constitutional restraints
    (4) limiting the power of the federal government
    (5) increasing the power of the states

A basic principle of the U.S. Constitution is the division of governmental power in the executive, the legislative, and the judicial branches. Legislative powers are vested in Congress; judicial powers, in the Supreme Court and federal court system; executive powers, in the president and his governmental machinery. Thus, a system of checks and balances exists among the three branches of government.

Each of the following is an example of the system of checks and balances in operation. Identify the one branch that is checking the other by choosing the appropriate response.

13. Congress overrides a presidential veto.

    (1) the executive checks the legislative
    (2) the executive balances the judicial
    (3) the judicial balances the legislative
    (4) the legislative checks the executive
    (5) the legislative checks the judicial

14. The Senate refuses to confirm a presidential nominee for an ambassadorship.

    (1) the executive checks the legislative
    (2) the executive balances the judicial
    (3) the judicial balances the legislative
    (4) the legislative checks the executive
    (5) the legislative checks the judicial

15. The president nominates a Supreme Court justice.

    (1) the executive checks the legislative
    (2) the executive balances the judicial
    (3) the judicial balances the legislative
    (4) the legislative checks the executive
    (5) the legislative checks the judicial

EVALUATION

16. Which statement would be most *difficult* to prove?

    (1) Japan's emperors have reigned but have seldom ruled.
    (2) The workers of the United States are better workers than those of Japan.
    (3) In the post-World War II period, the United States was the source of much cultural borrowing by the Japanese.
    (4) Japanese technology in the 1970s was more advanced than it was in the 1940s.
    (5) The cost of living in Japan has been rising ever since World War II.

17. Which statement would be most *difficult* to prove?

    (1) Popular ideas of third parties in the United States tend to be adopted by the major political parties.
    (2) The Articles of Confederation rendered more authority to the state government than to the federal government.
    (3) The Sherman Antitrust Act was used to reduce the effectiveness of labor unions.
    (4) World War II was necessary in order to end the Great Depression.
    (5) The right to vote has been extended in the twentieth century.

18. Which information about country *X* would be most useful to the head of a government establishing a foreign policy toward country *X*?

    (1) an analysis of the national resources and goals of country *X*
    (2) a file containing the major public statements made by the leaders of country *X* concerning their nation's foreign policies
    (3) an analysis by religious leaders of the major religious groups and beliefs of the people of country *X*
    (4) a newspaper report summarizing the treaties and international agreements of country *X*
    (5) knowledge of the party to which leaders of country *X* belong

19. Which statement expresses an opinion rather than a fact?

    (1) The United States did not join the League of Nations.
    (2) At one time, the United States was on the gold standard.
    (3) President Franklin D. Roosevelt made unnecessary concessions to the Russians at Yalta.
    (4) The Oregon Dispute was settled by extending the 49th parallel to the Pacific Ocean.
    (5) The United States is a member of NATO.

20. "The privilege to be involved and to conduct a business in any manner that one pleases is not guaranteed by the Constitution. The right to engage in certain businesses may be subject to various conditions. Laws regulating businesses have been found to be valid. We find no justification to reject the state law under question."

    Which concept would most likely be REJECTED by the author of this passage?

    (1) laissez-faire
    (2) welfare
    (3) competition
    (4) profit motive
    (5) antitrust legislation

Answer Key

1. **1**	5. **4**	9. **4**	12. **4**	15. **2**	18. **1**
2. **3**	6. **2**	10. **1**	13. **4**	16. **2**	19. **3**
3. **1**	7. **4**	11. **4**	14. **4**	17. **4**	20. **1**
4. **2**	8. **2**				

WHAT'S YOUR SCORE?

	right,	wrong
Excellent		19–20
Good		15–18
Fair		13–14

If your score was low, the explanation of the correct answers below will help. Analyze your errors. Reread the appropriate sections in this chapter. There are more skills questions in the two full-length practice examinations at the end of this book.

Answer Analysis

1. **1** Immigrants have been attracted when there were opportunities for farming on cheap, fertile land; and for jobs in factories and mines and in building transportation lines. Immigration has fallen off during wars, when it was dangerous and difficult to travel, and during depressions, when jobs were not available.

2. **3** Judicial review is the power of the Supreme Court to determine the constitutionality of laws of Congress and the states, and the acts of government executives. The hypothetical decision in the passage is the result of the Supreme Court's being willing to hear a case on appeal from a lower court because a constitutional issue was involved.

3. **1** The graduated income tax raises the *rate* of taxation as one's income increases. For example, a family of four earning $55,000 pays a federal income tax at a higher rate than a similar family having a taxable income of $25,000.

4. **2** From about 1870 on, the growth of European industrialization led to increased demand for African copper, precious woods, diamonds, gold and (later) uranium; and the development of rubber and cocoa plantations by U.S. firms and Western European nations. In Asia, areas such as Malaya and Indonesia furnished rubber, tin, and petroleum to the West.

5. **4** Social controls are composed of two parts. There are, first, the laws against what society defines as criminal actions, such as malicious destruction of property or the sale of narcotics. Those laws are enforced by police and courts to the extent of their ability and efficiency. Then there are the informal controls, based upon the human desire for the good opinion of others, that society exerts upon its members. Teenage fads illustrate the control exerted by group conformity. Public opinion in general is a powerful factor in social control. Political leaders know that they cannot stray too far from public opinion without risking loss of control, for example, with respect to imposing a state sales tax where none exists.

6. **2** A major economic aim of government is to smooth out the extremes of the business cycle in order to avoid "boom and bust." During the period of economic expansion and prosperity indicated in the question, a rise in income tax rates would reduce disposable income, slowing the rate of inflation that can shorten the period of expansion. Another reason for higher tax rates under these conditions is to create a budget surplus to repay part of the national debt.

7. **4** Foreign businesspersons and engineers are interested in both the techniques of large-scale production and the research and development programs that can be afforded only by such large and wealthy firms as Xerox, IBM, Intel, and DuPont. This research is responsible for patents that create monopolies over techniques and products—e.g., xerography, nylon fibers—that may attract the attention of the antitrust division of the Department of Justice.

8. **2** The Treaty of Versailles provided for a League of Nations, but the view expressed in the quotation prevailed. The United States never joined the League of Nations.

9. **4** This statement of Thomas Jefferson strongly supports compulsory education. To implement it, Jefferson designed a system of public education from elementary school through secondary school and then the university.

10. **1** Upward social mobility or movement refers to the potential ability of anyone in America to move up in socioeconomic status. If one has talent, plans carefully ("prudence"), works hard ("personal exertions"), one can advance in American society.

11. **4** The central problem of *all* economic systems is how best to use limited resources to meet unlimited human needs and desires.

12. **4** A *strict construction* would permit the federal government to exercise only the powers specifically delegated in the Constitution, restricting the use of the elastic clause. A *broad construction* would favor more flexibility in the interpretation of the elastic clause, thus leading to more power for the federal government.

13. **4** Legislative powers are vested in Congress, but the president must sign bills enacted by Congress before they become law. The presidential veto is a check of the executive on the legislature. However, Congress may override a president's veto by a two-thirds vote in each house, in which case, as in this item, the legislative branch checks the executive branch.

14. **4** The Constitution provides that a majority vote of the Senate is needed to confirm appointment of ambassadors. In this instance, the legislative branch is exercising a check on the executive.

15. **2** The Constitution grants the president (executive) the power to appoint "judges of the Supreme Court" with the advice and consent of the Senate. The executive branch is given this power over the judicial branch; the Supreme Court cannot choose its own judges.

16. **2** The term *better* involves many factors, and it would be difficult to reach an agreement about *what* was to be measured, let alone *how* to measure the many factors.

17. **4** Each of the other choices can be substantiated by objective, factual evidence, such as examples of minor-party ideas that major parties have adopted, a restrictive list of the powers the Constitution gives to the national government, and examples of the use of the Sherman Act against labor unions. In the twentieth century women and 18-year-olds have been given the vote. The above facts are generally accepted and agreed upon. That is not true for the controversial statement linking the Great Depression and World War II.

18. **1** One nation should understand the purposes and resources of another in order to carry on intelligent dealings with it. An analysis of those items is particularly valuable.

19. **3** We may define a fact as a statement that can be proved or verified and about which most people agree. An opinion is a personal conclusion that may be based on factual information, one's own biases and background, and even wishful thinking. An opinion is not verifiable, and people tend to disagree about opinions; for example, which team will win next year's World Series or Super Bowl game, who is the world's greatest musician, whether a particular presidential action was wise or foolish.

20. **1** The paragraph approves of state laws that regulate business in the public interest. Laissez-faire is an economic policy that provides for little or no interference by government in the affairs of business, so the author of this passage would most likely reject it.

OUTLINE OF STUDY FOR THE SOCIAL STUDIES TEST

Although the Social Studies test does not ask you to recall specific facts, reading passages are based on the topics that are covered in the high school curriculum. The more you know about these topics, therefore, the easier it will be for you to understand the reading passages.

Use the following outline of topics that may appear on the Social Studies test to guide you in your review.

ECONOMICS

I. The meaning of economics

II. How businesses behave

    A. How business is organized

    B. Economic markets

    C. Capitalism

    D. Supply and demand

    E. How prices are determined

    F. Competition and monopoly

III. Production

    A. Role of production

    B. Deciding what and how to produce and distribute

    C. Production of goods and services

    D. Uses and rewards of factors of production

IV. The individual as a consumer

    A. Consumer problems and responsibilities

        1. The American standard of living: wages, working conditions, food, shelter, clothing, health care, educational and recreational activities

        2. Factors influencing price and quality of goods: supply and demand (Note: Simple illustrations; e.g., snowstorm in citrus fruit belt, drought, strikes)

        3. Business organizations as they affect the consumer, independent stores, chain stores, cooperatives

        4. Consumer information services: private and government aids

        5. Consumer protection

            a. Credit associations: origin, functions

            b. Protective legislation: Bureau of Standards, price controls, Food and Drug Administration, grading and labeling

        6. Installment buying: advantages and disadvantages

        7. Advertising: values, government curbs

        8. Inflation; deflation; effects on the consumer

B. Responsibilities of consumers

    1. Saving; budgeting

    2. Economical buying and use of materials and possessions

V. The individual as a worker

  A. Choice of a vocation

    1. Occupational trends

    2. Qualifications and preparation

    3. Employment opportunities

    4. City, state, national, and private employment services

  B. Rights and responsibilities as a worker

    1. Bargaining individually and collectively

    2. Producing efficiently; conserving wisely; consuming intelligently

  C. Problems of capital and labor

    1. Labor's struggle for economic freedom

      a. Against evils of industrialism; against monopoly

      b. Development of trade unionism

    2. Rights and responsibilities of labor and management

    3. Recent trends toward labor-management cooperation

    4. Problems of increasing centralization: large corporations, large labor unions, government controls, and services

  D. Labor and the economy

    1. Labor market—union and nonunion labor

    2. Distribution of income—profit and wages

    3. Collective bargaining, strikes, picketing

    4. Productivity

  E. Government employees

    1. Types of service

    2. Means of securing positions: merit system, history of Civil Service

    3. Economic status and problems

VI. Economics and financial institutions

  A. Money and monetary policy

  B. Banking and interest

  C. Financial institutions other than banks

VII. Government's role in the economy

  A. Taxes and other sources of revenue

  B. Government expenditures

VIII. How the overall economy behaves

   A. Measuring the economy

   B. How the economy grows

   C. Problems of growth

   D. Economic fluctuations—business cycles

   E. Inflation and deflation

   F. Policies for stabilization of the economy

   G. Formulating modern economic policy

IX. United States and the world economy

   A. International trade

   B. Foreign exchange and the balance of payments

X. Other economic systems

   A. Comparative economics

   B. Communism and socialism

   C. Economics of underdeveloped nations

XI. Contemporary problems of the American economy

   A. Social economic problems—poverty in plenty

   B. Economic security

   C. Economy problems of agriculture

   D. Problems of urbanization

XII. Molders of economic thought

   (Adam Smith, John Maynard Keynes, John Stuart Mill, Karl Marx, Thomas Malthus, et al.)

AMERICAN HISTORY

I. Beginnings of America

   A. Old World backgrounds

   B. The new lands

      1. The explorers: their motives, achievements, utilization of natural gateways to America

      2. Geographic factors and their effects on life in new lands

      3. Leaders: Spanish, Portuguese, Dutch, French, English

   C. Colonization and growth of settlements

      1. Reasons for leaving Europe

      2. Diversity of cultural origin; effects on patterns of life in New World

      3. Effects of economic and geographic influences: on agricultural development, growth of commerce and industry, transportation and communication, social and cultural life

    4. Growth of ideals of religious freedom: the Puritans, Roger Williams, the Quakers and William Penn, the Baltimores and Maryland

    5. Characteristic examples of self-government: Virginia, Massachusetts, New York, Pennsylvania, Rhode Island

    6. Conflicting ideals and systems: political, industrial, economic, social

  D. French and Indian War, 1754–1763: causes, effects, significance

  E. Democracy in colonial times

    1. European influences

    2. Contributions of immigrants toward shaping American ideal

    3. Influence of geographic factors

    4. Leaders of early democratic ideals: Patrick Henry, James Otis, Samuel Adams, John Adams, Benjamin Franklin

    5. Zenger case: freedom of the press

  F. Establishing the new nation: growth of democracy

    1. The American Revolution: causes, leaders, events, results

    2. The Declaration of Independence: Thomas Jefferson

    3. The Articles of Confederation, 1781–1789; weaknesses

    4. The Constitution

      a. The Constitutional Convention: main compromises, struggle for adoption

      b. Contributions: James Madison, George Washington, Alexander Hamilton

      c. Adoption; provision for amendment

      d. Study of the Constitution: federal nature of our government; division of powers between federal government and states; separation of powers: executive, legislative, judicial

      e. Bill of Rights: origin, adoption, significance

II. The expansion of the United States

  A. Original extent of thirteen states and territories

  B. Northwest Ordinance, 1787: foundation of our expansion and colonial policy; its effects on later history

  C. Growth of continental United States of America (Louisiana Purchase, Florida Purchase, annexation of Texas, acquisition of Oregon Territory, Mexican Cession)

  D. The frontier

    1. Meaning: description of frontier life, geographic influences

    2. Influence of frontier on American life

    3. Leaders: Daniel Boone, Brigham Young, Kit Carson

  E. Acquisition of territory beyond continental United States (Alaska, Pacific Islands, Hawaii, Guam, Philippines, Caribbean area, Puerto Rico, Panama Canal Zone, Virgin Islands): how acquired, present status

III. Development of democratic way of life

   A. Roots of American democracy in colonial and early American periods

      1. European sources; colonial experience; influence on making of Constitution; Bill of Rights

      2. Problems confronting new nation: organization of federal government, interpretation of Constitution

      3. Federalists vs. Anti-Federalists; beginning of political parties

      4. Leaders: Washington, Hamilton, John Adams, Jefferson, Madison

   B. Jeffersonian Democracy
(Jefferson's ideas on democracy; agrarian versus commercial influences; War of 1812; effects on American life; Era of Good Feeling, 1816–1823)

   C. Jacksonian Democracy

(meaning; evidences in economic, social, and political life; extension of suffrage; humanitarian reforms—care of sick, criminals, needy; early cooperative movement)

IV. National unity versus sectionalism

   A. Factors that promoted nationalism (Monroe Doctrine; Supreme Court decisions; development of an American culture)

   B. Factors that promoted sectionalism (differences in ways of earning a living; industrialism of the North; plantation-holding system of the South; acquisition and settlement of new territory)

   C. Major issues of sectionalism (Tariff; the Bank; internal improvement; admission of new states; slavery)

   D. Slavery (origin; influence of geographic factors on slavery as an institution; effect of inventions [Eli Whitney's cotton gin]; Missouri Compromise; Abolitionists—Garrison, Stowe; growing tension between North and South)

   E. Civil War (election of Abraham Lincoln, 1860; highlights of the war; leaders and events; Emancipation Proclamation; results of war)

   F. Reconstruction Period

      1. Problems: the plight of freed slaves; readmission of the seceded states; the rebuilding of the South; contribution of reconstructed states to South; high taxes and corruption; "carpetbaggers," "scalawags," the Ku Klux Klan

      2. Significance of constitutional amendments: XIII, XIV, XV

      3. Effects of Reconstruction

V. The industrial era

   A. Geographic background

      1. The physiographic regions of the United States: Atlantic Coastal Plain, Appalachian Highlands, Great Central Plain, Cordilleran Highlands

      2. Geographic study of each region: differences in location, climate, topography, natural resources; man's utilization and control of natural environment; effects on life of people, types of industries, products; interdependence of peoples of different regions

3. Geographic reasons for location and growth of big cities: New York, Philadelphia, Boston, Chicago, Denver, Seattle, New Orleans, San Francisco, Detroit, Pittsburgh

B. The Industrial Revolution

1. Meaning

2. Causes: inventions, wealth of raw materials, abundant labor supply, ready markets, capital

3. Inventions

   a. European: textile machinery, steam engine

   b. American: cotton gin, steamboat, sewing machine, telegraph, farming machines, newer processes for steel manufacture, later inventions

4. Effects on social, industrial, and political life

5. Significance in our lives today

C. Development of our business economy

1. America's riches: abundant natural resources; energetic, inventive people

2. Domestic and international trade

   a. Bases of trade: needs of people, climatic variations, unequal distribution of natural resources

   b. Exports; imports; tariffs

3. Development of industries (geographic basis)

   a. Agriculture: chief agricultural regions of the United States, life and problems of the farmer, chief products

   b. Transportation and communication: significance in our industrial development

   c. Commerce

   d. Mining: coal, iron, oil, copper

   e. Manufacturing industries: steel, oil, textiles, automobiles, machinery, motion pictures, radio and television

   f. The factory system: effects on worker, methods of work, and population movements

   g. Growth of cities

D. Recent trends

1. Regional developments: Tennessee Valley Authority, Boulder Dam, Grand Coulee, Bonneville, Missouri Valley

2. Conservation: need for; work of Theodore Roosevelt, Franklin Roosevelt, Gifford Pinchot, Rachel Carson, and others

3. Social legislation: Social Security Act; care of aged, dependent, unemployed

4. Increase of government controls

5. Contemporary contacts of the family with the federal and the state government: taxes, draft, education

VI. Our American heritage

   A. Our democratic institutions and ideals

      1. Division of power between the central government and the states

      2. Bill of Rights and Civil Liberties; Four Freedoms

      3. Development of Women's Rights movement; leaders

      4. Extension of democracy to social and economic life; free tax-supported educational system; legislative restrictions against discrimination in employment

   B. Development of an American culture

      1. Influence of American literature

      2. Influence of science

      3. Growth of art, architecture, and music

   C. Education for democracy

      1. Organs of information and opinion: schools and colleges, newspapers, periodicals, radio, movies, pressure groups

      2. Propaganda: its meaning and recognition

   D. Our people

      1. Story of immigration; "Americanizing" the immigrant

      2. Contribution of various peoples to our culture

      3. Problems of groups of diverse racial, religious, and national origins

      4. Intercultural understandings and appreciations

   E. Democracy vs. totalitarianism

VII. Growth of America as a world power

   A. Our foreign policy

      1. Washington's Farewell Address—isolation and neutrality

      2. Jefferson's "no entangling alliance"

      3. The Monroe Doctrine: origin, provisions, importance

      4. Westward Expansion: Louisiana and Florida purchases; Mexican War; Oregon Treaty

      5. Overseas Expansion: Spanish-American War

      6. America's relations with the Far East and Japan: opening of Japan; Open-Door Policy, 1899

      7. Relations of United States with Latin America; life and culture of people; leaders of several Latin American countries; Pan-Americanism; Good Neighbor Policy; present relations

      8. The Panama Canal: acquisition; construction; importance

   B. The United States and World War I

      1. Origin and causes of World War I

      2. Entry of the United States into the war

    3. Peace problems

    4. League of Nations; Woodrow Wilson

  C. The United States and World War II

    1. Origin and causes of World War II

    2. Reason for U.S. participation

    3. Outcomes of World War II

  D. Post World War II

    1. Emergence of new nations

    2. The Cold War

    3. The Truman Doctrine

    4. The Marshall Plan

    5. Regional organizations: OAS, NATO, CENTO, OAU; Benelux, EU, Colombo Plan, GATT

    6. The Korean War

    7. The Civil Rights and Feminist movements

    8. The spread of nuclear weapons and efforts to contain them

    9. Space exploration

    10. The Vietnam War

    11. The Third World

    12. The War on Terror

VIII. The United States as a member of the United Nations

  A. Historical background of peace movements

  B. Events leading to formation of the United Nations

  C. Organization

  D. Main current problems

  E. Role of United States in world affairs

GEOGRAPHY

I. The individual in his or her relationships to the earth

  A. The earth as the home of man

    1. The earth as a globe: principal features, size, shape, relation to other heavenly bodies, revolution and rotation, inclination of the axis, great circles, the equator and the measurement of latitude, the prime meridian and the measurement of longitude, relative sizes and positions of land masses and water areas, the atmosphere, effects on human living

    2. Representations of the earth

      a. Maps; globes

      b. Types and uses of map projections; relation of map to globe

3. Climate

    a. Climatic controls: latitude, altitude, topography, distance from the sea, prevailing winds, ocean currents (study of major climatic regions of world: tropical rain forest, tropical savanna, tropical desert, maritime, humid continental, continental steppe, continental desert, Mediterranean subtropical, humid subtropical, taiga, tundra, polar ice cap)

    b. Effects on human living: on energy and temperament, on natural resources, on occupations and industries, on population movements

4. Topography

    a. Chief topographical features of earth: plains; plateaus; mountains; valleys; continents; bodies of water—oceans, lakes, seas, rivers

    b. Relation to human living: transportation and communication; population movements

5. Natural resources: their utilization, conservation, effect on human living

6. People: cause and effect of population distribution and movements, present trends

7. The air age: relation of shape of earth to development effects of air age on human living

II. The individual in his or her relationships to the life and culture of peoples of different lands

  A. Latin America, our southern neighbor

    1. Reasons for our interest

    2. Geographic influences: relative location, comparative area, range in latitude, climatic range, topography (mountains—Andes; volcanoes; plateaus—Brazilian highlands, Altiplano; plains—pampas; rivers—Amazon, Orinoco)

    3. Natural regions and countries

    4. People

      a. Composition and distribution of the population, sharp regional differences, effects of racial diversity, economic and social groups; education and culture; role of the church—population trends (fast growth) and movements; contributions to world culture—foods, vocabulary

      b. Utilization of resources for development of industry; mode of life in agricultural, grazing, mining, and limited industrial areas; one-crop countries; big landowners, inadequate food supply; urban centers

    5. Transportation and communication problems (poor topography, lack of roads, and railroads)

    6. Trade relations: characteristic products, imports, exports (only raw materials), world markets, port cities

    7. Significance of region in the world community

B. Canada—our northern neighbor

1. Reasons for our interest; common bonds

2. Natural regions and provinces

3. Geographic influences: relative location (latitudinal factor), comparative area, climatic range, topography, natural resources, effects on life of people

4. People; size and distribution of population; causes and effects of two national cultures; utilization of resources of land and adjacent waters for development of industries; mode of life in different regions; interdependence of regions; newer trends in industrialization; population movements; urban centers

5. Transportation and communication handicaps; effects of air age

6. Trade: characteristic products; imports, exports (agriculture, wheat, automobiles, forest products, fish, furs, minerals); trade relations with United States, Great Britain, other countries; ports

7. Place in British Commonwealth; in world community

C. Northern and western Europe

1. Reasons for our interest

2. Regions and countries included (23 nations in northwest Europe, southern Europe, middle (central) Europe, Scandinavia)

3. Geographic influences; strategic location; comparative area; climatic factors; bodies of water; nature of coastline; variety and location of resources; effects on life of people

4. People: 300 million, composition, distribution (urbanization); low population growth; diversity of skills; multilingual—60 languages, ethnic minority problems; similarities and contrasts in education and culture; life and work in various regions; maximum use of resources of environment (land and sea) for development of industry and agriculture; locations of agricultural areas and industrial centers; contributions of various national groups to world culture; cultural centers

5. Trade: characteristic products, farming, food surpluses; major industrial products, imports, exports, trade centers; role of European Union (EU), role of European Free Trade Association (EFTA), world markets, port cities

6. Transportation and communication facilities; effects of air age

7. Current problems: colonial policies, regional problems, American relations with European countries, trade barriers, postwar problems

8. Significance of region in world community

D. Mediterranean region and Near East, including southwest Asia

1. Reasons for our interest

2. Natural regions and countries

3. Strategic points: Suez Canal, Dardanelles, Bosporus, Gibraltar

4. Mediterranean climate (desert areas of little rainfall); topography—great mountain systems (Alps), major rivers, northern European plains; natural resources—two-thirds of world's oil reserves, effects on life of people

5. People: 400 million, distribution of population (small density); diverse cultural backgrounds; methods of utilizing resources for limited agricultural and limited industrial development; mode of life in different regions; population trends and movements; urban centers

6. Transportation and communication

7. Trade: characteristic products; imports, exports (oil), importance of trade route through Suez Canal; trade centers and ports; world markets

E. Eastern Europe

1. Reasons for our interest

2. Natural regions and countries in the area: Belarus, Bulgaria, Czech Republic, Hungary, Moldova, Poland, Romania, Russia, Slovakia, and Ukraine

3. Geographic influences; comparative area and extent; climatic range; topography—mountains (Carpathians, Urals), rivers (Volga); natural resources—coal, effects on life of people

4. People: size and distribution of population; diversity of nationalities and cultures; utilization of resources: mode of life in agricultural (Ukraine), forest, and mining areas; industry (in Czech Republic) and in the growing manufacturing centers; effects of government land policies; program of expansion

5. Trade: limited foreign trade; emphasis on internal trade; effects of lack of good ports; characteristic products—coal, oil, agriculture; imports and exports

6. Significance of region in world community

F. The Far East

1. Reasons for our interest

2. Natural and climatic regions; countries—China, Japan, India, southeast Asia, south Asia, the two Koreas, Taiwan, the Philippines, Indonesia

3. Geographic influences: relative location; comparative area and extent (one-third of the earth's surface); types of climate: tundra, taiga, grasslands of steppes, monsoons (southeast Asia), tropical rainforests (Indonesia), humid subtropical (south China), humid continental (north China), desert (Gobi); topography—mountains (Himalayas), plateaus (Mongolia), desert (Gobi), active volcanoes, rivers—Yangtze, Yellow, Indus, Ganges, Mekong, deltas; natural resources—coal, oil, iron ore, tungsten; effects on lives of people

4. People: 60% of total world population; unequal distribution (one-third in urban centers); social classes (India), racial and cultural diversity: Mongoloid, Caucasoid, Negroid; high birth rate

5. Mode of life: adverse climatic conditions; utilization of natural resources; types and methods of agriculture—need for intensive soil cultivation, prevalence of subsistence crops; home industries; factors limiting industrial expansion; trends toward industrialization

6. Transportation and communication problems in greater part of region; topographic handicaps

7. Trade: characteristic products—two-thirds agricultural (wheat, rice, spices), imports, exports (tea, silk), world markets reached mostly by air

G. Australia and New Zealand

1. Reasons for our interest

2. Natural regions: western plateau, Red Heart, Great Barrier Reef

3. Geographic influences: remoteness; comparative area—3 million square miles; mild climate; low population destiny; natural resources (iron ore, gold)

4. People: 17 million, including 200,000 aborigines; population concentrated in coastal cities; effects of remoteness on life and culture; mode of life in different regions (cities, outback); high level of industrialization; agricultural regions; urban centers; effects of progressive government

5. Transportation and communication: importance of internal travel by air because of vast distances

6. Trade: 25% of world's wool (sheep-raising in New Zealand), meat (beef, lamb), wheat as principal exports; imports; trade centers, ports, trade relations with United Kingdom and United States

7. Problems of immigration and multiculturalism

8. Place in British Commonwealth; in world community

H. Africa

1. Natural regions and countries

2. Geographic influences: 10% of world area, 5000 miles from north to south, 4600 miles from east to west; second largest continent; climatic range—tropical rain forest, grasslands, desert (Sahara), the Rift Valley, rivers (Nile, Zambezi), effects on life of people

3. People: size, distribution (70% Black); native and European cultures; effects of exploitation by European powers; mode of life in mining, grazing, agricultural regions; handicaps limiting development of resources; special case of South Africa

4. Transportation and communication problems; no railroads; lack of capital

5. Trade: exports—tropical crops, minerals; imports—machinery, manufactured goods; problem of smooth coastline and few natural harbors; lack of skilled labor

6. Potential for future development

III. World Trade

    A. Bases of world trade
(Needs of people; climatic variations; unequal distribution of natural resources)

    B. Importance of trade in our economic, political, and cultural life

    C. Man's role in world trade

        1. Making of goods: raw materials; capital; labor; transportation; inventions and improved processes that make possible better utilization of natural and human resources

        2. Marketing of goods: transportation; land, water, and sky routes; influence of government policies on the flow of goods; effect of trade on group living

        3. Utilization of goods and services; production, consumption, law of supply and demand; surpluses and shortages; effects of prosperity or depression in one region on other regions

        4. Importance of communication and its effect on trade; major agencies of communication; effects of airplane and of computers and other new inventions

    D. Relation of world trade to world peace

IV. Toward a better world

    A. The development of better understanding among peoples; reasons why understanding is essential; factors that tend to foster understanding; factors that tend to foster disunity and conflict; suggested methods of dealing with such problems

    B. Implications of atomic age: peacetime development; atomic energy and war; need for international control of atomic energy

    C. International organization: past efforts to bind people of the world together; creation of the United Nations; functioning of the United Nations; future hopes for world unity

CIVICS AND GOVERNMENT

I. Nature of political systems

    A. Government and society—importance and basic role of government

    B. Types of modern governments

    C. Meaning of democracy

II. American political system

    A. Foundations of American government; modern political and economic systems; heritage

    B. Declaration of Independence and U.S. Constitution

    C. American federalism

III. American political process

    A. Political party system

    B. Right to vote and voter behavior

    C. Nominations and elections

    D. Public opinion and pressure groups (lobbyists)

IV. National executive branch

    A. Office and powers of the president

    B. Functions

    C. Vice president

    D. President's cabinet

V. National legislative branch

    A. Nature, structure, and powers of Congress

    B. Functions

    C. Roles of Congress

VI. National judiciary branch

    A. American system of justice—importance of law and the legal system

    B. Federal court system and role of Supreme Court

    C. Judicial process and administration of law

    D. Civil liberties and civil rights

    E. Goal of equal justice for all

VII. State governments

    A. Nature and functions of state governments

    B. State executive, legislative, and judiciary branches

    C. Financing state and local governments

VIII. Local governments

    A. Importance

    B. Governing the communities—cities, towns, counties

    C. Financing

IX. Government and the general welfare

    A. Federal revenues and expenditures

    B. Money and banking policies

    C. Our government and business—capitalism

    D. Labor and Social Security

    E. Agriculture and conservation

X. The United States in today's world

    A. American foreign policy

    B. U.S. and international organizations

    C. Population explosion; technological revolution; meeting social responsibilities—health, education, welfare, crime, and other social issues

WORLD HISTORY

I. The Dawn of Civilization (c. 3000–1500 B.C.)

   A. Mesopotamia

      1. Sumeria

      2. Babylonia

      3. Assyria

      4. Chaldea

   B. Egypt

      1. Role of Pharaohs

      2. Religion

      3. Sciences

II. The Spread of Civilization (c. 1500–500 B.C.)

   A. Hittites

      1. Iron

   B. Phoenicians

      1. Trade

   C. Hebrews

      1. Jewish monotheism

      2. The Old Testament

      3. The Ten Commandments

   D. Lydians

      1. Coins

   E. Ancient Persians

      1. Zoroasterianism

III. Aegean Civilization (c. 1200 B.C.)

   A. Crete

   B. Troy

IV. Ancient Greece (Hellenic)

   A. Homeric Age (1000 B.C.)

   B. Greek Gods

   C. City States (900 B.C.)

      1. Spartan military

      2. Athenian democracy

         a. Pericles (461 B.C.) "Golden Age"

         b. Architecture

         c. Philosophy

   D. Persian Wars

   E. Peloponnesian Wars

  F. Hellenistic Period

    1. Macedonian conquests

    2. Alexander the Great (334 B.C.)

 V. Ancient Rome

  A. Etruscan

  B. Roman republic (509 B.C.)

    1. Rome conquers Italy

    2. Rome conquers world

    3. The Caesars (49 B.C.)

  C. Roman contributions

    1. Latin language

    2. Religion

    3. Engineering (roads)

  D. Decline and Fall (300–476 A.D.)

    1. Barbarian invasions

 VI. Asia

  A. India (563 B.C.)

    1. Buddha

  B. Chinese Empire (770–256 B.C.)

    1. Confucius

    2. Taoism

 VII. Rise of Christianity (c. 30–529 A.D.)

  A. Christ as Messiah

  B. The New Testament

  C. Spread by Peter and Paul

  D. Papacy created

  E. Monasticism

 VIII. Byzantine Civilization

  A. Constantine (312 A.D.)

  B. Justinian (527 A.D.)

  C. Byzantine Empire (610–1453 A.D.)

 IX. Islam

  A. Mohammed (570 A.D.)

    1. Allah

    2. Mecca

  B. Moslem conquests

  C. Contributions

    1. Mathematics and science

    2. Medicine

X. Medieval Society

    A. Feudalism (800–1250)

        1. The Manor

            a. Lord

            b. Knighthood

        2. Chivalry

    B. Church

        1. The Popes

        2. The Hierarchy

        3. Clergy (Monks)

        4. Crushing of heresy

    C. The Crusades (1096)

        1. Commerce—Guilds

    D. Medieval governments

        1. France—Charlemagne

        2. England—Alfred the Great, William the Conqueror

        3. The Magna Carta (1215)

    E. Culture

        1. Romance languages

        2. Gothic architecture

XI. China

    A. Genghis Khan (1162)

    B. Kublai Khan (1218)

XII. Africa

    A. Kingdom of Songhay

XIII. Renaissance (1350–1600)

    A. Printing (1450)

    B. Art

        1. Painting

            a. DaVinci, Michelangelo, Rembrandt

    C. Literature

        1. Dante—*Divine Comedy*

        2. Cervantes—*Don Quixote*

        3. Chaucer—*Canterbury Tales*

        4. Shakespeare—Plays

    D. Ruling families

        1. Medici

        2. Borgia

       E. Cities

         1. Venice

         2. Florence

XIV. Reformation

       A. Martin Luther (1519)

       B. Protestantism

         1. John Calvin

       C. Anglicanism

         1. Henry VIII (1509)

         2. Elizabeth I (1558)

       D. Catholic Counter-Reformation

         1. The Inquisition

         2. The Jesuits

       E. Religious Wars

XV. Scientific Revolution (1500–1700)

       A. Astronomy—Copernicus

       B. Physics—Galileo

       C. Mathematics—Newton

XVI. European Expansion

       A. Exploration

         1. Portuguese—Prince Henry, Vasco da Gama

         2. Spanish—Columbus, Magellan

       B. The Americas

         1. Mayans (900–1200)

         2. Aztecs (1360)

         3. Incas (1493)

         4. Conquistadors—Cortez, deSoto, La Salle, Pizarro

XVII. Absolute Monarchy

       A. Spain—Ferdinand and Isabella (1479)

       B. France—Louis XIV (1661)

       C. Prussia—Frederick the Great (1740)

       D. Russia—Peter the Great (1682); Catherine the Great (1762); Romanov (1613–1917)

XVIII. Western Civilization

       A. French Revolution (1789–1799)

       B. Napoleon (1799–1815)

       C. The Industrial Revolution

         1. Railroads (1820)

         2. Steel (1856)

    D. The Rise of Nationalism

        1. France—Bourbons

        2. Prussians

        3. Hapsburgs

        4. Kingdom of Italy (1861)

        5. German Empire—Bismarck (1871)

        6. Austria-Hungary (1867)

XIX. Europe (1914–1945)

    A. World War I (1914–1918)

        1. Defeat of Germany

    B. Rise of Communism

        1. Lenin, Stalin

    C. Rise of Nazism

        1. Hitler

        2. The Holocaust

    D. Rise of Fascism

        1. Mussolini

    E. World War II (1939–1945)

        1. Defeat of Germany and Japan

        2. Use of atomic bomb

XX. 1945–Present

    A. Cold War

        1. Marshall Plan, Berlin Wall

    B. NATO vs. Warsaw Pact

    C. Downfall of Soviet Union

    D. People's Republic of China (1949) Mao

    E. Korean War (1950–1953)

    F. Vietnam War (1964–1973)

    G. Cuban Revolution

        1. Castro

    H. Middle East

        1. Emergence of Israel (1948)

        2. Persian Gulf War (1990–1991)

        3. The War on Terror (2001–present)

    I. Achievements in Space

    J. European Community

GLOSSARY OF SOCIAL STUDIES TERMS

In social studies, as in science, vocabulary is of critical importance. The following selected subject-area vocabulary lists consist of words from the five social sciences—history (see below), civics and government (page 365), economics (page 369), and geography (page 372). The definitions have been simplified, and in the simplification some aspects of the definition have been omitted. If a definition is not clear, be certain to consult a dictionary. In any event, be sure to review the section "Learning Social Studies Vocabulary and Deriving Meaning from Context" in Chapter 10 (page 275).

Don't forget: The glossary defines a number of terms that are likely to be used on the test. Be sure to consult the glossary when you encounter unfamiliar terms in the questions in the next chapter.

HISTORY

ABOLITIONIST   one who favored abolishing slavery in the United States prior to the Civil War

AGGRESSION   attack by one country on another without any provocation

ANNEXATION   addition of territory to an already existing country or state

APARTHEID   policy of racial segregation and discrimination against blacks and other non-Europeans practiced by the Republic of South Africa until 1990

APPEASEMENT   policy of giving into the demands of an enemy power in an effort to maintain peace

ARMISTICE   temporary stopping of war by agreement of both sides before a peace treaty is signed

ARYAN   term wrongly used by the Nazis to refer to a person of German or northern European descent

AXIS   in World War II, the countries—Nazi Germany, Fascist Italy, and Japan—that fought against the United States and its allies

BLACKLIST   list of people or organizations to be avoided in trade or denied employment because of government policy or suspected disloyalty

BLOCKADE   action taken to cut off trade and communication with an enemy

BOONDOGGLE   spending of public money to create unnecessary jobs

BOURGEOISIE   the middle class

BOYCOTT   refusal to deal with a country or an organization for political or economic reasons

CHARTER   in colonial times, a grant from the English ruler to a person or corporation giving certain rights and privileges of settlement

CIVIL WAR   American war between the northern and southern states (1861–1865)

COLD WAR   diplomatic and economic conflict between nations short of actual warfare

COLONY   settlement in a distant land that remains under control of the country from which its settlers came

COMPROMISE   agreement in which each side gives up some things it wanted

CONSERVATION   policies and practices that aim at preservation of natural resources such as forests and wildlife

COUP D'ETAT   sudden overthrow of a government by force

DECREE   order of a government or a church

DESEGREGATION   removal of separation of races in public places such as schools

DISARMAMENT   reduction in arms and armed forces as a result of agreement between nations

DISCRIMINATION   prejudice in the treatment of one group, as compared with another, in such matters as jobs, housing, and admission to schools

DOCTRINE   principle or belief or a set of principles or beliefs

DOVE   one who espouses the cause of peace and/or pursues a conciliatory policy in foreign affairs

EDICT   official proclamation or decree

EMANCIPATION   setting free of a slave or anyone else in bondage

EMBARGO   official order preventing ships from entering or leaving the ports of a country for the purpose of commerce

EMIGRATION   movement of a person or persons from one country to settle in another

EMPIRE   group of states, colonies, or territories joined together under the rule of a dominant power

EVOLUTION   theory that plants and animals develop from earlier life forms by the passing down, from one generation to the next, of variations that help them to survive

FAIR DEAL   continuation and development of the principles of the New Deal by the Truman administration

FEMINISM   movement to win for women, rights equal to those of men in political, social, and economic areas

FEUDALISM   medieval (9th to 15th centuries) social and economic organization of society in Europe

GENOCIDE   systematic killing off of an entire national, racial, or cultural group

HAWK   one who advocates an aggressive and warlike approach to foreign policy

HERESY   a religious belief opposed to doctrine established by the church

IMMIGRATION   movement of a person into a new country to settle there

IMPERIALISM   policy of a nation to extend its power by establishing colonies and controlling territories, raw materials, and world markets

INDUSTRIAL REVOLUTION   social and economic changes brought about by the development of large-scale industrial production

INTEGRATION   incorporation of different racial or ethnic groups into free and equal association in a society or an organization

ISOLATIONISM   policy of a country that is based on unwillingness to take part in international affairs

MANDATE   authority given by the League of Nations to one nation to administer a territory or geographic region

MANIFESTO   public declaration by a government of intention to act or of action taken

MEDIEVAL   referring to the period in Europe between the 9th and 15th centuries

MILITARISM   belief that the military should dominate the government and that military efficiency is the ideal of the state

MONARCHY   government in which supreme power rests with a king, queen, or emperor and where such power may be absolute or limited

MONOTHEISM   doctrine that there is only one God

NATIONALISM   doctrine that the interests and security of one's own country are more important than those of other nations or international groups

NAZISM   system in Germany (1933–1945) that controlled all activities of the people, fostered belief in the supremacy of a Fuhrer (Leader), and promoted the German people as a master race and the establishment of Germany as the dominant world power

NEW DEAL   principles and policies of liberal democrats as advocated under the leadership of President Franklin Roosevelt

NONAGGRESSION   referring to an agreement between two nations not to attack one another

OPINIONS, ATTITUDES, AND BELIEFS   a person's preferences or positions on public matters based on thought or emotion: opinions are short-term, attitudes are more lasting, beliefs deal with the more basic values of life

PACIFISM   belief that conflicts between nations should be settled by peaceful means rather than by war

PACT   agreement or treaty between nations

PAN-AMERICANISM belief in political, economic, social, and cultural cooperation and understanding between the nations of North, Central, and South America

PARLIAMENT the legislative body of Great Britain, consisting of the House of Lords and the House of Commons

PARTITION division of a geographic area into two or more countries or into areas annexed to already existing countries

PLEBISCITE direct vote of all eligible voters on an important political issue

PREJUDICE hostile attitude without foundation in fact or knowledge toward an ethnic group or any member of it

PROHIBITION in the United States, the period between 1920 and 1933 when the manufacture and sale of alcoholic drinks was forbidden by federal law

PROPAGANDA systematic spread of ideas or doctrines with a view to convincing others of their truth, using repetition and, in some cases, distortion

PROTECTORATE weaker state protected and in some instances controlled by a stronger state

PROVISIONAL referring to a government that functions temporarily until a permanent government is established

PURITAN Protestant in 16th and 17th century England and America who sought greater reform in the Church of England

QUOTA greatest number of persons who may be admitted, as to the United States or to an institution such as a college

RACE one of three primary divisions of humans—Caucasian, Negro, and Mongoloid—differing in physical characteristics

RATIFICATION granting of formal approval, as to a constitution or a treaty

REACTIONARY extreme conservative, one who opposes progress or liberalism

RECIPROCAL applying by mutual agreement to both parties or countries concerned, as in trade

RECONSTRUCTION period after the Civil War (1865–1877) during which the Confederate states were controlled by the federal government and recognized prior to readmission to the Union

RENAISSANCE period (14th through 16th centuries) of revival in learning and the arts in Europe

REPARATION payment by a defeated nation for damages done to persons and property of the victorious country in a war

SANCTIONS measures taken by a group of nations to force another to stop a violation of international law that it is considered to have made

SATELLITE a small state that is dependent on a larger, more powerful state and must, as a result, maintain similar policies

SECTIONALISM placing of the interests of a section of a country ahead of those of the nation

SEDITION acts that tend to foment rebellion against the existing government

SEGREGATION policy or practice of compelling racial and ethnic groups to live apart from each other

SELF-DETERMINATION right of a people to determine its own form of government independently

SHARECROPPER farmer who does not own land but works it for a share of the crop

SOVEREIGNTY supreme and independent political authority of a state

STATUS QUO the existing political, social, and economic order

STEREOTYPE fixed belief regarding a person, group, or idea that is held by a number of people and allows no individuality or critical judgment

SUFFRAGETTE woman who works actively for the right of women to vote

TOLERATION freedom to hold religious beliefs different from those in authority

TRUSTEESHIP authority from the United Nations to a country to administer a territory or region

VALUES   social principles, goals, or standards held or accepted by an individual, class or society

WHIG   member of a political party that supported limitation of presidential power and opposed the Democrats in the United States (1836–1856); also a person who supported the American Revolution

ZIONIST   supporter of the movement to establish a Jewish national state in Palestine; now, a supporter of the State of Israel

CIVICS AND GOVERNMENT

ACT   document made into law by a legislative body

ADMINISTRATION   term of office of the executive branch of government

AGENCY   bureau that administers a governmental function

ALIEN   one who owes allegiance to a government or country other than the country in which he resides

ALLEGIANCE   duty of a citizen to his or her government

ALLIANCE   formal agreement between nations to achieve a common purpose

AMENDMENT   change or revision made in a constitution or a law

AMNESTY   general pardon to a group of persons, freeing them from punishment for offenses against a government or society

ANARCHY   complete absence of government and law with resulting disorder

APPELLATE   court that can receive appeals and reverse the decisions of lower courts

APPORTIONMENT   allotment of representatives to a group in proportion to their members

APPROPRIATION   money made available by formal act of a legislative body for a specific public purpose

AT-LARGE   official chosen by all the voters of a particular election district

AUTONOMY   self-government

BALLOT   (1) the paper on which a vote is recorded (2) the right to vote

BICAMERAL   legislature made up of two houses, such as a Senate and an Assembly or a Senate and a House of Representatives

BILL   preliminary form of a law proposed to a legislative body

BIPARTISAN   representing or composed of members of two parties

BLOC   combination of legislators or nations that acts as a unit with a common interest or purpose

BOSS   politician who controls a political machine and has influence over legislation and appointments to office

BUREAUCRACY   government that functions through departments that follow given rules and have varying degrees of authority in the organization

CABINET   group of advisers to the head of a country who usually administer governmental departments

CAMPAIGN   program of activities designed to elect a candidate to political office

CAUCUS   closed meeting of party members to decide policy or to select candidates for office

CENSURE   reprimand voted by a governmental body of one of its members or of the government or its cabinet

CENTER   in politics, a party or group that follows policies between the left (which advocates change) and the right (which opposes it)

CHECKS AND BALANCES   system of government that provides for each branch (executive, legislative, and judicial) to have some control over the others

CIVIL LIBERTIES   rights to think, speak, and act without interference that are guaranteed to the individual by law and custom

CIVIL RIGHTS   rights that are guaranteed to the individual by the Constitution and by acts of Congress; e.g., right to vote

CIVIL SERVICE   those in the employ of government who got their positions through open competitive examination on the basis of merit

COALITION   temporary alliance of countries or parties for action to achieve some purpose

COMMISSION government agency with administrative, judicial, or legislative powers

COMMITTEE group chosen by a legislative body to consider a particular law or topic

CONFERENCE meeting of committees from two branches of a legislature to settle differences in a bill they have enacted

CONFIRMATION approval by a legislative body of an act or appointment by an executive

CONGRESS the legislature of the United States, consisting of the Senate and the House of Representatives

CONSERVATIVE person or party that tends to oppose change in government and its institutions

CONSTITUTION system of fundamental laws and principles, written or unwritten, by which a people is governed

CONVENTION gathering of members or delegates of a political group for a specific purpose, such as choosing a candidate for office

DELEGATE (1) representative to a convention (2) person empowered to act on behalf of those who choose him or her

DEMOCRACY government by the people directly or through representatives chosen in free elections

DICTATORSHIP state ruled by one who has absolute power and authority

ELECTION choosing by vote among candidates for public office

EXECUTIVE the branch of government charged with administering the laws of a nation

FASCISM a system of government characterized by power in the hands of a dictator, suppression of opposition parties, and aggressive nationalism (Italy, 1922–1945)

FEDERAL referring to a system of government in which a constitution divides powers between the central government and such political subdivisions as states

FILIBUSTER tactics, such as nonstop oratory, used by a minority in a legislative body to delay action on a bill

FOREIGN POLICY course of action adopted by a country in its dealings with other nations

FREEDOM civil or political liberty

GOVERNMENT established system of political administration by which a country or its subdivisions is ruled

HEARING session of a legislative committee in which evidence bearing on possible legislation is obtained from witnesses

IMPEACH to bring charges against a public official for wrongdoing prior to possible trial and removal from office if a conviction is obtained; **IMPEACHMENT** the act of bringing such charges

INAUGURATION formal induction into office of a public official

INDICTMENT formal accusation of someone with the commission of a crime, usually after investigation by a grand jury of charges made by a prosecutor

INITIATIVE right of a citizen to bring up a matter for legislation, usually by means of a petition signed by a designated number of voters

INJUNCTION court order preventing a person or group from taking an action that might be in violation of the law

JUDICIAL referring to the courts and their functions or to the judges who administer these functions

JURISDICTION authority of a government or court to interpret and apply the law

LAW bill that has been approved by a legislative body and signed by the chief executive

LEFT members of a legislative body who take more radical and liberal political positions than the other members

LEGISLATION laws made by a legislative body, such as a Senate

LEGISLATURE group of persons having the responsibility and authority to make laws for a nation or a political subdivision of it

LIBERAL individual or political party whose beliefs stress protection of political and civil liberties, progressive reform, and the right of an individual to govern him- or herself

LOBBY to attempt to influence legislators to support bills that favor some special group or interest

MACHINE political organization under the leadership of a boss and his lieutenants that controls party policy and job patronage

MAJORITY (1) number of votes for a candidate that is greater than the votes for all the other candidates put together (2) party in a legislative body that commands the largest number of votes

MINORITY political group that is smaller than the controlling group in a government or legislature and does not have the necessary votes to gain control

MUNICIPAL referring to local government such as that of a city, town, or village

MUNICIPALITY city or town that has the power to govern itself

NATURALIZE to give the rights of citizenship to a noncitizen or alien

NEUTRALITY policy of a government that avoids taking sides directly or indirectly in disputes between other nations

NOMINATE to name a candidate for election to public office

ORDINANCE law enacted by local governmental authority

OVERRIDE action taken by a legislative body to enact a law that has been disapproved (vetoed) by the chief executive of a political unit such as a nation or state

PARDON official release from (continued) legal punishment for an offense

PARTISAN position or vote that follows party policy ("the party line")

PARTY organization of persons who work to elect their candidates to political office to further the governmental philosophy and causes in which they believe

PATRONAGE power of a political organization or its representative to give jobs

PETITION request for specific legal or judicial action that is initiated and signed by an interested individual or group of individuals

PLANK one of the items in a party program or platform

PLATFORM statement of the policies and principles of a political party or its candidate for office

PLURALITY number of votes by which the winning candidate in an election defeats his or her nearest opponent

POLL (1) vote as recorded by a voter (2) count of votes cast (3) questioning of a group of people chosen at random on their views on political and other matters

PRECINCT subdivision of a town or city that serves as an election unit

PRESSURE GROUP group of people who seek to change government law or policy through the use of lobbies, propaganda, and media

PRIMARY vote by members of a political party to choose candidates for political office or for some other political purpose

PROGRESSIVE person or party that stands for moderate political and social change or reform

PUBLIC OPINION views of a people, generally as they influence social and political action

QUORUM minimum number of a legislative body that must be present before the body can legally conduct business

RADICAL person or party that stands for extreme political and social change

RATIFY give formal approval to a document such as a treaty or constitution

RECALL right of or action taken by vote of the people or by petition to remove a public official from office

REFERENDUM practice of submitting to direct popular vote a proposed law or an act that has been passed by a legislative body

REFORM political movement designed to correct abuses in government by changes in the law

REGIME form or manner of government or rule

REGISTRATION signing up of a person in his or her election district to enable that person to vote

REGULATE to control or bring under the control of government or a government agency

REPRESENTATIVE member of a legislative body chosen to act on behalf of those who elected him or her to represent them

REPUBLIC government in which power remains with all the citizens, who are entitled to vote and who elect representatives who act for them and are responsible to them

RESOLUTION formal statement of opinion or intention voted by a legislative or other group

REVIEW reexamination by higher judicial authority of the proceedings or decision of a lower court

REVOLUTION complete overthrow, usually by force, of an established government or political system

RIGHT (1) members of a legislative body who hold more conservative views than the other members (2) that which belongs to an individual by law or tradition, such as the right to free speech

SELF-GOVERNMENT government of a people by its own members or their representatives instead of by some outside power

SENIORITY consideration given to length of service in a legislative body in making assignments to important positions or to membership in committees of that body

SOCIAL SECURITY federal system of old age, unemployment, and disability insurance for employed and dependent persons

SOVEREIGNTY supreme and independent power or authority in government

SPEAKER public official who presides over a law-making body such as the House of Representatives or an assembly

STATE any of the political units that constitute the federal government

STATUTE law passed by a legislative body

SUBPOENA written order to a person to appear in court or before a legislative body to give evidence

SUBVERSIVE referring to an act or a person that would tend to overthrow the existing government

SUFFRAGE right to vote in political elections or on political matters

SUMMONS written order to appear in court, addressed to a person who may be involved in or have knowledge of a crime

SUPREME COURT highest federal court whose decisions are final and take precedence over those of all other courts

TENURE (1) length of time a person holds office (2) an individual's right to hold office until retirement or death

TESTIFY to present evidence in a court under oath

TICKET list of candidates nominated for election by a political party

TOTALITARIAN kind of government in which one political party is in power to the exclusion of all others

TREASON betrayal of one's country by actively helping its enemies in their attempt to overthrow it or defeat it in war

TREATY formal agreement, entered into by two or more nations, dealing with commerce or policies

URBAN having to do with a town or city

VETO act or power of a chief executive to turn down a bill passed by a legislative body by actually rejecting it or refusing to sign it

VOTE to cast a ballot or take any other necessary action to express one's choice in an election of a candidate for office or of any proposal for legislative change

ECONOMICS

ARBITRATION attempt to settle, or settlement of, a dispute by submitting it to a third party designated to decide it after hearing evidence presented by both sides

ASSET property and resources of all kinds of a person or a corporation.

AUTOMATION production and distribution of goods automatically by mechanical and electronic, rather than human, means

BALANCE OF PAYMENTS relationship between a nation's outflow of money (imports, foreign aid) and inflow of money (exports, gifts)

BALANCE SHEET financial statement balancing the assets, liabilities and net worth of an individual or a business

BANKING practice of receiving, keeping, lending, or issuing money and making easier the exchange of funds

BANKRUPTCY financial condition in which a person or business is found legally unable to pay creditors

BARTER system of trading in which one good is exchanged for another without the use of money

BUDGET statement of an individual, business, or government in which expected incomes are allocated as expenses in designated necessary areas

BUSINESS buying and selling of commodities and services for a profit

CAPITALISM economic system based on private ownership of the means of production with freedom of private enterprise to earn a profit under free market (competitive) conditions

CARTEL combination of businesses to establish a national or international monopoly by limiting competition

CASTE social class or group formed on the basis of birth or wealth, existing under strict rules within a social system, with little or no movement into or out

CENSUS official count of the population of a country (required every ten years in the United States by the Constitution)

CERTIFICATE document that shows that a person owns stock and is entitled to the benefits and liabilities of a stockholder

COLLECTIVE BARGAINING negotiation between management and labor regarding wages, hours, working conditions, and other benefits

COMMERCE large-scale buying and selling of goods involving transportation of the goods between cities or countries

COMMODITY any good that is bought or sold in a commercial transaction

COMMUNISM economic system based on ownership of all property by the state and, in Marx's view, on equal distribution of economic goods through revolutionary means

COMPENSATION payment given as recompense for an injury or loss, as to a worker who has been hurt on the job

COMPETITION in a free enterprise system, the attempts by rival businesses to get customers for the goods they manufacture or distribute

CONSUMER one who uses goods or services out of need

CONSUMER PRICE INDEX single number that compares consumer prices in one year with prices paid by consumers in previous years

CONTRACT agreement between two or more people or companies to do something, set forth in writing or orally, and enforceable by law

CORPORATION group of individuals who possess shares and have the privileges and obligations of a single person, with limited liability

COST amount of money, labor, and other expenses involved in producing or obtaining goods or services

CRAFT (members of) trade requiring special skills, such as printing

CRASH sudden decline in market values of shares in a business

CREDIT money, based on a person's economic standing, that he or she is allowed to borrow and repay at a later date

CREDITOR person or institution to whom money is owed

CURRENCY money, such as coin or bank notes, that is in circulation in a country

CUSTOMS duty or tax levied by a government on imported and exported goods

CYCLE in business, a sequence of events that occurs and recurs in a given order and involves boom, downturn, depression or recession, and recovery

DEBT obligation of an individual or corporation to pay something to a creditor

DEFICIT amount by which a corporation's or a government's debts are greater than its credits or assets

DEFLATION fall in prices brought about by a decrease in spending

DEMAND desire and ability to pay for goods and services usually within a given price range at a given time

DEPLETION using up of natural resources such as oil and timber

DEPOSIT money put into a bank or given in partial payment for something purchased

DEPRECIATION decrease in value of business property or equipment through "wear and tear"

DEPRESSION period of low business activity, wide unemployment, and falling prices

DEVALUATION lowering of the exchange value of one currency with respect to another by decreasing the amount of gold backing it

DISCOUNT amount deducted from the original price of something sold

DISCRIMINATION unfavorable treatment of persons based on negative prejudgments made without regard to fact

DISTRIBUTION process of making goods and services available to consumers, as well as the promotion of the buying and selling of these goods and services

ECONOMICS science that deals with the production, distribution, and consumption of goods and services

ECONOMIC SYSTEM manner in which a nation's resources are used, and goods and services are produced and distributed

ECONOMY structure and functioning of a nation's economic system

ENTREPRENEUR person who enters into business and risks his or her skills, time, and money in the hope of earning a profit

EQUILIBRIUM market price at which supply equals demand

EXCISE tax on the production, sale or use of certain commodities within a country

EXPORT goods sold by one country to another

EXTENDED FAMILY family that includes other relatives (grandparents, uncles and aunts, cousins, in-laws) beyond the immediate nuclear family (parents and children)

FISCAL having to do with taxes, public revenues, or public debt

FOREIGN EXCHANGE currency that can be used to pay international debts

FRINGE benefit given by an employer that, although not paid directly as wages, involves a cost to the employer

GOODS merchandise

GROSS NATIONAL PRODUCT (GNP) total value of a nation's annual output of goods and services

IMPORT goods brought into by one country from another

INCOME money received by a person or business organization for work or services performed or from investment or property

INDUSTRY businesses as a group that are engaged in manufacturing

INFLATION rise in prices caused by an increase in the amount of money in circulation or by an increase in the amount of spending resulting from greater demand than supply

INPUT amount of money and/or manpower invested in a project or process

INSTALLMENT system of credit in which goods purchased are paid for over a period of time by partial payments

INTEREST (1) charge for money borrowed, usually expressed as a percentage of the money lent (2) money paid to a depositor for money left in a bank for a stated period

INVESTMENT money put into a business or property in the hope of receiving income or earning a profit

LABOR economic group of wage-earning workers

LEVY tax imposed or collected by a government or other authority

LIABILITY debt owed by a business, a corporation, or an individual

LOCKOUT prevention by an employer of his or her workers from working during a dispute

LOSS amount by which the cost of an article sold is greater than the selling price

MANAGEMENT those who direct the affairs of a business or industry

MARGIN difference between the cost and the selling price of a product

MARKET buying and selling of goods or property

MEDIATION entry of a third party into a dispute between management and labor, with the intention of settling it fairly

MERGER combination of two or more businesses or corporations in which one of them eventually controls the other(s)

MONETARY having to do with the money of a country

MONEY coin or paper stamped by government authority, used as a medium of exchange and measure of value

MONOPOLY exclusive control of a product or service in a market so that prices for the product or service can be fixed and competition eliminated

NOTE written promise to pay a debt, such as a promissory note

OBSOLESCENCE process by which the plant and equipment of a business become outdated and can no longer be used efficiently to produce the goods needed

OUTPUT work done or amount produced by a person, machine, or assembly line in a given period

OVERHEAD costs involved in running a business, such as those for rent and electricity

PANIC period in which fear of economic collapse results in frenzied attempts to convert property, goods, and securities into cash

PARTNERSHIP form of business organization in which two or more people put money or property into a business and share the profits or losses

POVERTY extreme lack of the things necessary to sustain life, such as food, shelter, and clothing

PRICE amount of money or its equivalent for which anything is bought, sold, or offered for sale

PRODUCTION creation of economic value by making goods and services available to meet the needs of consumers

PRODUCTIVITY degree of ability to produce goods and services of economic value

PROFIT amount by which the selling price of an article sold is greater than the cost

PROPERTY possessions that may be personal (movable), land or real estate, or securities (stocks and bonds)

PROSPERITY condition in which the economy of a country or a business enjoys a state of well-being

RECESSION period of temporarily reduced business activity

RENT income received by a land or property owner for the use of his or her land or property

RESOURCES natural and human assets that can be used to produce economic goods or provide services

REVENUE income from taxes and other sources that is available for use on behalf of the public

SAVINGS total money saved by an individual or a nation

SCAB employee of a business who continues to work during a strike against that business

SCARCITY gap between the supply of goods produced and human needs

SECURITIES documents, usually bonds or stock certificates, that are evidence of either indebtedness (bonds) or ownership (stocks)

SERVICES duties performed or work done for others that has economic value

SHOP if *open*, a business establishment where workers are employed regardless of union membership; if *union*, one in which labor and management agree that all employees must be union members

SLUM highly crowded area in which housing is rundown, sanitary conditions are poor, and poverty is widespread

SOCIALISM ownership and operation of the means of production and distribution by society rather than by private persons, with all members sharing in the work and the products

SOCIOECONOMIC STATUS position in society based on social and economic factors such as wealth

SPECULATION use of capital to buy and sell stocks, property, commodities, and businesses in situations where above-average risk is taken

STANDARD OF LIVING level of subsistence of a country or an individual that takes into account possession of the necessities and comforts of life

STOCK shares held by an individual in a corporation

STRIKE work stoppage carried out by workers to force the employer to improve working conditions and benefits and/or to increase wages

SUBSIDY sum of money given by a government to a private individual or business in the public interest

SUBSISTENCE lowest level of food, clothing, and shelter needed to sustain life

SUPPLY amount of goods and services available for sale, usually within a given price range at a given time

SURPLUS amount of goods over and above what is needed

SURTAX tax that is added to an already existing tax

TARIFF tax imposed by a country on imported goods

TAX sum that an individual or corporation is required by the government to pay on income or property or an object purchased

TECHNOLOGY use of scientific knowledge in industry and commerce

TRADE buying and selling of economic goods

TRUST combination of corporations in an industry to control prices and eliminate competition

UNDERDEVELOPED NATION country inadequately developed economically and industrially with a relatively low standard of living

UNEMPLOYMENT condition of being out of work

UNION organization of workers that seeks to protect and advance the interests of its members with respect to working conditions and wages, usually through collective bargaining

WAGES money paid to an employee for work done

WEALTH everything having economic value measurable in price

WELFARE referring to a state or nation in which government rather than private organizations assumes the primary responsibility for the well-being of its citizens

WILDCAT referring to a strike that takes place without the permission of the union representing the striking workers

GEOGRAPHY

ALTITUDE elevation of an object above sea level

ANTARCTIC relating to the region near the South Pole

ARCHIPELAGO group of many islands

ARCTIC relating to the region around the North Pole to approximately 65° N

BASIN body of water partly or fully enclosed

BAY inlet of the sea or other body of water, usually smaller than a gulf

BAYOU lake occupying the abandoned part of a stream channel

BLUFF steep rise of ground between bottom land and higher land on the shore of a river, sea, or lake

BUTTE steep-sided, round-topped hill or mountain

CANYON deep, narrow valley with steep sides cut by a river

CLIMATE average weather conditions at a given place over a period of years as evidenced by temperature, precipitation, and winds

CONSERVATION planned management of natural resources to prevent exploitation, destruction, or neglect

CONTINENT one of the great land areas of the earth

CYCLONE violent storm or system of winds rotating about a calm center of low atmospheric pressure, traveling at a speed of 20 to 30 miles per hour and accompanied by rain

DELTA triangular or fan-shaped area of low-lying land formed by deposits at the mouth of a river

DESERT dry, barren expanse of land unable to support normal plant and animal life

DROUGHT prolonged period of lack of rainfall

EARTHQUAKE shaking or trembling of the earth that is volcanic in origin or involves the earth's crust

ECOLOGY science concerned with the interrelationship of organisms and their environments

ELEVATION height above the level of the sea

ENVIRONMENT climatic, soil, and living factors that influence an organism or an ecological community

EQUATOR great circle of the earth that is equidistant from the North and South poles and divides the earth's surface into the Northern and Southern hemispheres

EQUINOX one of two times each year when day and night are everywhere of equal length

EROSION wearing away by the action of water, wind, or glacial ice of the surface features of the earth—mountains, plateaus, valleys, coasts

FAR EAST countries of east Asia, including China, Japan, and Korea, and southeast Asia and the Malay Archipelago

FAULT break in the earth's crust accompanied by a displacement of one side of the break with respect to the other

FAUNA animals or animal life of a region

FJORD narrow inlet of the sea between steep cliffs and extending far into the land

FLORA plants or plant life of a region or special environment

FRONT boundary between differing air masses that differ in temperature

GEYSER hot spring that, from time to time, violently ejects boiling water and steam

GLACIER large mass of ice and snow moving slowly down a mountain or valley

GLOBE spherical model of the earth

GRASSLAND area of grass or grasslike vegetation, such as a prairie

GULF large area of a sea or ocean partially enclosed by land

HABITAT region where a particular plant or animal naturally lives

HIGH center of high atmospheric pressure

HUMIDITY moisture or water vapor in the atmosphere

HURRICANE severe tropical cyclone having winds of over 75 miles per hour and usually involving heavy rains

ISLAND land mass, smaller than a continent, entirely surrounded by water

ISTHMUS narrow strip of land having water at each side and connecting two larger bodies of land

JUNGLE land densely overgrown with tropical vegetation and trees

LAKE relatively large inland body of water, usually fresh

LANDLOCKED surrounded by land, as a bay

LATIN AMERICA part of the Western Hemisphere south of the United States: Mexico, Central America, the West Indies, and South America

LATITUDE distance north or south of the equator, measured in degrees

LEGEND title or key accompanying an illustration or map

LONGITUDE distance in degrees east or west of the prime meridian

LOW region of depressed barometric pressure

MAP representation on a flat surface of all or part of the earth

MARITIME on, near, or living near the sea

MEDITERRANEAN CLIMATE climate characterized by warm, dry summers and rainy winters

MERIDIAN any of the lines of longitude

MESA high, broad, and flat plateau bounded by a steep cliff

METROPOLIS any large, important city

MIDDLE EAST lands from the eastern shores of the Mediterranean and Aegean seas to India

MIGRATION movement of people from one region or country to another, with the intention to settle there

MONSOON seasonal wind that blows over the Indian Ocean from Australia to India

NATURAL RESOURCES forms of wealth supplied by nature, such as coal, oil, and water power

OASIS place in a desert that is fertile because of the presence of water

OCEAN any of the five main divisions of the body of salt water that covers over 70 percent of the earth's surface: Atlantic, Pacific, Indian, Arctic, or Antarctic

PARALLEL imaginary line parallel to the equator and representing degrees of latitude on the earth's surface

PENINSULA land area almost entirely surrounded by water and connected to the mainland by a narrow strip of land

PLAIN extent of level country

PLATEAU elevated tract of fairly level land

POLAR ICE CAP mass of glacial ice that spreads slowly out in all directions from the poles

POPULATION DENSITY number of people in a given area

POPULATION EXPLOSION very great and continuing increase in human population in modern times

PRAIRIE large area of level or slightly rolling grassland that occupies the region between the Ohio and the Mississippi-Missouri rivers

PRECIPITATION rain, snow, sleet deposited on the earth

PRIME MERIDIAN great circle on the earth's surface from which longitude is measured both east and west: 0° longitude

RAINFALL amount of water falling in the form of rain, snow, etc., over a given area in a given period of time

RAIN FOREST dense, evergreen forest occupying a tropical region that has abundant rainfall throughout the year

RANGE a series of connected mountains forming a single system

RAW MATERIAL material still in its natural or original state, before processing or manufacture

REGION large, indefinite part of the earth's surface

RELATIVE HUMIDITY amount of moisture in the air, expressed as a percentage, as compared with the maximum amount that the air could contain at the same temperature

REVOLUTION movement of a heavenly body, as a star or planet, in an orbit or circle

ROTATION turning of a body, such as the earth, around a center point or axis

SCALE   proportion that the size of a feature on a map bears to the actual size of the feature it represents

SEA   large body of salt water wholly or partly enclosed by land

SEASON   any of four divisions of the year, characterized chiefly by differences in temperature, precipitation, amount of daylight, and plant growth

SOLSTICE   either of two points on the sun's path at which it is farthest north or farthest south of the equator

SOUND   wide channel or strait linking two large bodies of water or separating an island from the mainland

STEPPE   in Europe and Asia, vast, usually level plain having few trees

STRAIT   narrow waterway connecting two large bodies of water

SUBCONTINENT   large subdivision of a continent

SUBTROPICAL   referring to regions bordering on the tropical zone

TAIGA   forests of cone-bearing trees in the far north of Europe, Asia, and North America

TEMPERATE ZONE   one of two zones between the tropics and the polar circles

TERRACE   any of a series of flat platforms of earth with sloping sides, rising one above the other, as on a hillside

TERRAIN   natural or surface features of a tract of land

THUNDERSTORM   storm accompanied by thunder and lightning

TIDAL WAVE   unusually large wave sent inshore by an earthquake or a very strong wind

TIDES   alternating rise and fall of the surfaces of oceans and of waters connected with them, caused by the attraction of the moon and sun and occurring twice in approximately 24 hours

TOPOGRAPHY   surface features of a region, including hills, valleys, rivers, lakes, and man-made features: canals, bridges, roads, etc.

TORNADO   violently whirling column of air, extending down from a mass of storm clouds, that usually destroys everything in its rapid advance along a narrow path

TORRID ZONE   area of the earth's surface lying between the Tropic of Cancer and the Tropic of Capricorn and divided by the equator

TRIBUTARY   stream or river flowing into a larger stream or river

TROPICS   area between the Tropic of Cancer and the Tropic of Capricorn, 23½° north and south of the equator

TUNDRA   any of the vast, nearly level, treeless, and marshy plains of the arctic and extreme northern regions

TYPHOON   violent tropical cyclone originating in the west Pacific, especially in the South China Sea, principally from July to October

VALLEY   stretch of low land lying between hills or mountains and usually having a river or stream flowing through it

VOLCANO   cone-shaped mountain built up around a vent to form a crater with lava, cinders, ashes, and gases escaping through the vent from the earth's interior when the volcano is active

WEATHER   general condition of the atmosphere at a particular time and place with regard to temperature, moisture, cloudiness, etc.

WESTERLIES   winds blowing primarily from the west

WIND   air naturally in horizontal motion at the earth's surface, coming from any direction, with any degree of velocity

Social Studies Practice

CHAPTER 12

CIVICS AND GOVERNMENT

Read each of the following selections carefully. After each selection, there are questions to be answered or statements to be completed. Select the best answer.

Questions 1–3 are based on the following passage.

The American Revolution is the only one in modern history that, rather than devouring the intellectuals who prepared it, carried them to power. Most of the signatories of the Declaration of Independence were intellectuals. This tradition is ingrained in America, whose greatest statesmen have been intellectuals: Jefferson and Lincoln, for example. These statesmen performed their political function, but at the same time they felt a more universal responsibility, and they actively defined this responsibility. Thanks to them there is in America a living school of political science. In fact, it is at the moment the only one perfectly adapted to the emergencies of the contemporary world, and one which can be victoriously opposed to communism. A European who follows American politics will be struck by the constant reference in the press and from the platform to this political philosophy, to the historical events through which it was best expressed, to the great statesmen who were its best representatives.

1. This passage deals chiefly with

   (1) the causes of the American Revolution
   (2) Jefferson and Lincoln as ideal statesmen
   (3) the basis of political philosophy in the United States
   (4) democracy versus communism
   (5) a living school of political science

2. According to this passage, intellectuals who pave the way for revolutions are usually

   (1) honored
   (2) misunderstood
   (3) destroyed
   (4) forgotten
   (5) elected to office

3. Which statement is true according to the passage?

   (1) America is a land of intellectuals.
   (2) The signers of the Declaration of Independence were all well educated.
   (3) Jefferson and Lincoln were revolutionaries.
   (4) Adaptability is a characteristic of American political science.
   (5) Europeans are confused by American politics.

Question 4 is based on the following cartoon.

NEUTRALITY

4. The cartoon indicates the foreign policy position of the United States in response to the

(1) start of the League of Nations
(2) collapse of the global economy
(3) beginning of World War II
(4) spread of communism to Eastern Europe
(5) rise of Hitler

Question 5 is based on the following cartoon.

5. The main idea expressed by the cartoon is that

(1) discipline has broken down in the U.S. military
(2) a majority of the people must support the conflict before the United States enters a war
(3) the president's use of military power depends on congressional cooperation
(4) Congress often opposes presidential proposals for increased military spending
(5) only the president can declare war

Question 6 is based on the following cartoon.

"Miss Jones, weren't there any founding MOTHERS?"

6. Which statement best expresses the main idea of the cartoon?

(1) Women have increasingly difficult choices in a modern society.
(2) Women are the dominant force in American education today.
(3) Women made few significant contributions to society until the twentieth century.
(4) Free public education in the United States was established primarily by women.
(5) More emphasis should be placed on the role of women in U.S. history.

Questions 7–9 are based on the following passage.

The average citizen today is knowledgeable about "landmark" court decisions concerning such questions as racial segregation, legislative apportionment, prayers in the public schools, or the right of a defendant to counsel in a criminal prosecution. Too often, however, he thinks that these decisions settle matters once and for all. Actually, of course, these well-publicized court decisions are merely guideposts pointing toward a virtually endless series of vexing legal questions.

For example, this nation could hardly fail to agree that state-compelled racial segregation in the public schools is a denial of the equal protection of the laws guaranteed by the 14th amendment. The real difficulty lies in determining how desegregation shall be accomplished and how to solve the problem of de facto school segregation, perpetuated by the practical if unfortunate realities of residential patterns.

7. According to the author, the effect of many decisions in the courts has been to

   (1) make citizens study the law
   (2) lead to more legal complications
   (3) contradict the Constitution
   (4) deny states' rights
   (5) provide final solutions to many problems

8. The author implies that, so far as important court decisions are concerned, the public today is generally

   (1) disinterested
   (2) mystified
   (3) critical
   (4) well informed
   (5) disapproving

9. As used in the first line of the passage, the word *landmark* most nearly means

   (1) exciting
   (2) just
   (3) significant
   (4) publicized
   (5) legal

Questions 10–12 are based on the following passage.

Among the many effects of democracy's spread through much of the developing world in the last few decades is the birth of a new American industry, democracy promotion. Beginning in the early 1990's, Washington began a wide variety of programs worldwide to help third-world countries democratize, including training election observers, improving parliamentary libraries, persuading political parties to form coalitions, teaching citizens' groups how to lobby, and helping independent newspapers.

But one expert feels that no American democracy consultant can affect the underlying conditions of a country that really determine its democratic progress—concentrations of power and wealth, political traditions, the expectations of its citizens.

The right programs over the long term can do much in countries where a government genuinely wants democracy but lacks expertise—nations such as South Africa, Slovakia, or Chile. In dictatorships, aid to the opposition can keep hope alive. But in nations that enjoyed some democratic progress but fell into strongman rule—such as Peru, Haiti, Cambodia, Kazakhstan, or Zambia—democracy promotion efforts to reform government institutions have been thwarted by leaders who have little interest in sharing power.

10. Increased democracy in the developing world has been a result of

    (1) American democracy promotion
    (2) independent newspapers
    (3) American democracy consultants
    (4) concentrations of power and wealth
    (5) political traditions

11. American democracy promotion is *least* successful

    (1) where interested governments lack expertise
    (2) in dictatorships
    (3) in countries where some democracy exists
    (4) where there is strongman rule
    (5) where government institutions have been reformed

12. American help has included improving all of the following EXCEPT

    (1) elections
    (2) lobbying
    (3) the party system
    (4) government libraries
    (5) expectations of citizens

ECONOMICS

Read each of the following selections carefully. After each selection, there are questions to be answered or statements to be completed. Select the best answer.

Questions 13–15 are based on the following passage.

There are hundreds and thousands of homeless children in this nation—a fivefold increase in the years since 1981. Because they are scattered in a thousand different cities, they are easily unseen. Many of them will never live to tell their stories.

None of these children has committed any crime. They have done nothing wrong. Their only crime is being born poor in a rich nation.

Last year I met a homeless family in Los Angeles. The mother had come there from Ohio to search for rent that she could afford. The father—there was a father, none of these families fit the stereotypes; few people do—the father worked full time, for minimum wage, in a sweatshop making blue jeans, earning $500 a month. The parents couldn't pay their rent and feed their child in Los Angeles on $500. The child was with them in the street—38 days old. I shook my head and asked myself, "Is this the best the United States can do?"

Dr. Martin Luther King, Jr., told us, "I have been to the mountain." But almost every voice that we have heard for 20 years has counseled us to shut that mountain out of mind, and to direct our eyes instead to the attractive flatlands where careers are made, résumés typed, and profits maximized. Our culture heroes have been sleek and agile people; cynical and cold, streamlined for efficient malice, and unweighted by the excess burden of compassion.

"We owe a definite homage to the reality around us," Thomas Merton wrote, "and we are obliged at certain times to say what things are and to give them their right names." The right name for the willingness of a rich nation to leave half a million homeless children in its streets is sheer betrayal of ourselves and our best values.

It has been a long winter. But as with the seasons, so too with a nation: life renews itself.

I like to think another season of compassion is before us. We look to you who graduate this morning to renew this weary earth, to water the soil of the 1990s with the simple but forgotten values of the heart, to heal the ill, house the homeless, feed the hungry, and bring mercy to the frightened mother and her child.

It is not by standing tall, but by bending low—to reach a hand to those who are too frail to stand at all—that good societies are defined.

13. The author focuses on the plight of

    (1) cultural heroes
    (2) sleek people
    (3) homeless children
    (4) cynical and cold leaders
    (5) graduates of a university

14. The many homeless children are unseen because they

    (1) were born poor
    (2) are scattered
    (3) are decreasing in number
    (4) are sleek and agile
    (5) are cynical and cold

15. The author feels that the plight of the homeless is a result of

    (1) betrayal of our values
    (2) national poverty
    (3) obsession with résumés and careers
    (4) propaganda against the poor
    (5) maximized profits

Questions 16–18 are based on the following passage.

Child labor still exists in the United States. Experts say that it is a stubborn problem in every country and will take many years to solve. There are about 200 million children working all over the world. When people talk about child labor, they are talking about children who are being exploited, being forced to work long hours, often under dangerous conditions.

Child labor has been a problem for centuries. During the late 1800s and early 1900s, child labor was common in the United States and Europe. In 1900, more than two million children age 15 and under worked full time, many in dangerous jobs such as coal mining or factory work.

By the 1930s, the United States and other wealthy countries had made two important reforms that greatly reduced child labor. First, they passed and enforced tough laws against it. Second, they made schooling compulsory for all children. History shows that children who go to school have a better chance of becoming healthy adults.

Despite these measures, child labor remains a problem today, especially among poor people and illegal immigrants. Many illegal immigrants work in sweatshops, factories where people labor long hours under terrible conditions.

Even more common than sweatshop workers are migrant farm workers, who move from place to place. Hundreds of thousands of children do "stoop labor." This means they have to bend over all day picking vegetables and fruit.

16. Child labor includes all the children who work EXCEPT

    (1) as migrants
    (2) in sweatshops
    (3) in coal mines
    (4) as servants
    (5) in factories

17. Child labor refers to children who are exploited

    (1) only in the United States
    (2) only in Europe
    (3) in the United States and Europe
    (4) in wealthy countries
    (5) all over the world

18. Efforts to combat child labor have centered on

    (1) better working conditions
    (2) improved pay
    (3) shorter hours
    (4) legal prohibition
    (5) government inspectors

Questions 19–21 are based on the following passage.

Sparked by the debates of President John F. Kennedy's Commission on the Status of Women and by the birth of a new women's movement, a spate of legislation supports women's efforts to overcome job discrimination. In 1963, Congress passed a long-sought Equal Pay Act. The 1964 Civil Rights Act forbade discrimination on the grounds of sex and created an Equal Employment Opportunity Commission that

workers could use to bring suit against employers who did not comply with the law. As a result, a small number of women managed to inch their way into better jobs. By the seventies, medical and law schools, corporate and financial institutions, and political bureaucracies had increased equal access for women.

Poor women, however, did not seem to benefit as much. Those who headed the expanding number of single-parent families searched for ways to combine family life with work. Many women found themselves confined to retail sales, clerical, and service jobs where low wages and part-time work carried no benefits. New immigrants could find jobs only in sweatshops. At the same time, the rising cost of living locked many two-parent families into dual wage earning, with the problem of how to integrate work and family life. As attention shifted from workplace conditions, legislators increasingly advocated such reforms as subsidized child care, paid pregnancy and parental leaves, flextime, and more generous healthcare coverage. Most experts agreed that resolving these family-related issues would be the key to achieving equality in the workplace of the 21st century.

19. According to the passage, for many families equality for women in the workplace depends most on

    (1) the generosity of corporate and financial institutions
    (2) the Commission on the Status of Women
    (3) the rising cost of living
    (4) the ability to integrate work and family life
    (5) the improvement of workplace conditions

20. It can be inferred from the passage that efforts on behalf of women

    (1) had widely differing effects
    (2) improved the lot of most women
    (3) penalized employers
    (4) had little general effect
    (5) overcame conflict in the workplace

21. The major interest of legislators now is in

    (1) workplace conditions
    (2) family-related issues
    (3) better jobs for women
    (4) equal pay for women
    (5) job discrimination

Questions 22–25 are based on the following passage.

Most Americans look at the developing areas of the world without having the slightest idea of the difficulties with which they are faced. We must try to understand what life is like for the almost 4 billion human beings who live in developing nations.

Let us imagine how an American family, living in a housing development on a very low yearly income, could be changed into a family of the underdeveloped world.

Our first step is to strip our American home of its furniture. Everything from the living quarters goes—beds, chairs, tables, television set, lamps. Leave a few old blankets, a kitchen table, a wooden chair. For clothing, each member of the family may keep his oldest suit or dress, plus a shirt or blouse. Permit a pair of shoes for the head of the family, but none for the wife. In the kitchen the appliances have already been taken out, the water and the electric power shut off. The box of matches may stay, as well as a small bag of flour and some sugar and salt. We will leave a handful of onions and a dish of dried beans. All the rest must go—the meat, fresh vegetables, canned goods, crackers.

The house itself must go. The family can move into a small shack. It may be crowded, but they are fortunate to have any shelter at all.

Communication must go next—no more newspapers, magazines, books. They will not be missed, since we are not able to read. In our community, there will be only one radio.

Government services must go also. No more mail delivery or fire protection. There is a school, but it is three miles away and consists of two classrooms. It is not overcrowded, since only half the children in the neighborhood go to school. There are no hospitals or doctors nearby. The nearest clinic is ten miles away.

The human body requires a daily input of at least 2300 calories to make up for the energy used by the body. If we do no better than the Latin American peasant, we will average not more than 2000 to 2100 calories per day and our bodies will run down.

So we have brought our American family down to the very bottom of the human scale. When we are told that more than half the world's population enjoys a standard of living of less than 100 dollars a year, this is what that figure means.

22. The purpose of the author is to describe

    (1) American family life
    (2) the comforts of civilization
    (3) life in developing nations
    (4) the American home
    (5) changes in the family

23. Over half the world's population has

    (1) a daily input of 2300 calories
    (2) crowded classrooms
    (3) kitchen appliances
    (4) a poor living standard
    (5) high-tech machinery

24. The passage implies that Americans

    (1) are well informed
    (2) lack understanding of life in developing nations
    (3) contribute to the problems of developing nations
    (4) distort the realities of life
    (5) provide help to those less fortunate

25. With which of the following necessities is a family in an underdeveloped nation left?

    (1) a house
    (2) a local hospital
    (3) electric power
    (4) government services
    (5) food

HISTORY

Read each of the following selections carefully. After each selection, there are questions to be answered or statements to be completed. Select the best answer.

Questions 26–28 are based on the following passage.

The early Europeans imagined that the Indians of the East were rovers, who lived and hunted at random wherever they pleased. They were mistaken: the tribes had their separate tracts that were marked off by definite boundaries.... But the fundamental difference between the European conception of property and that of the American Indians was that Indian property was held in common. The Indian had no idea of legal title, of the individual ownership of land,

and the white man was incapable of thinking in any other terms. In 1879, a General Allotment Act was introduced in Congress. The object, or ostensible object, was to encourage the Indians to engage in farming by breaking up the reservations. The fragments were to be allotted, a hundred and sixty acres to heads of families and eighty to single persons. The remainder could be bought by the government, and the individual owners, after twenty-five years, were authorized to sell their land....

...But the act was passed in 1887, and had the effect...of depriving the Indians of ninety million of their hundred and forty million acres. Few of them had taken to farming. Even if they had been eager to farm, they had no money to invest in equipment or livestock, and since their allotments were held in trust, they were unable to get commercial credit. If they did not dispose of their property, and it was divided among their descendants, there was soon very little for anybody left.

—Edmund Wilson

26. According to the passage, early Europeans believed natives of the New World to be

    (1) agrarian
    (2) uncivilized
    (3) nomadic
    (4) disorganized
    (5) unprogressive

27. According to the passage, the essential difference between the Native American and European concepts of property is that Europeans believed in

    (1) individual ownership of the land
    (2) governmental control of the land
    (3) breaking up large tracts of land
    (4) farming the land instead of hunting on it
    (5) handing it down to descendants

28. The official purpose of the General Allotment Act of 1879 was to

    (1) introduce new methods of hunting
    (2) encourage Native Americans to pursue a different way of life
    (3) allow the Native Americans to move about more freely
    (4) sell large tracts of land
    (5) consolidate ownership of land

Questions 29–31 are based on the following passage.

Foreign propagandists have a strange misconception of our national character. They believe that we Americans must be hybrid, mongrel, undynamic; and we are called so by the enemies of democracy because, they say, so many races have been fused together in our national life.

They believe we are disunited and defenseless because we argue with each other, because we engage in political campaigns, because we recognize the sacred right of the minority to disagree with the majority and to express that disagreement even loudly. It is the very mingling of races, dedicated to common ideals, which creates and recreates our vitality. In every representative American meeting there will be people with names like Jackson and Lincoln and Isaacs and Schultz and Kovacs and Sartori and Jones and Smith. These Americans with varied backgrounds are all immigrants or the descendants of immigrants. All of them are inheritors of the same stalwart tradition of unusual enterprise, of adventurousness, of courage—courage to "pull up stakes and git moving." That has been the great compelling force in our history.

29. According to the paragraph, our national character thrives because we have

    (1) few disagreements
    (2) majority groups
    (3) shared our wealth
    (4) common ideals
    (5) minority rights

30. Foreign propagandists believe that Americans

    (1) are enemies of democracy
    (2) lack a common heritage
    (3) have a unified national character
    (4) refuse to argue with each other
    (5) are ashamed of foreign descent

31. Foreign propagandists and the author agree that Americans

    (1) are disunited
    (2) have no common tradition
    (3) come from varied backgrounds
    (4) have the courage of their convictions
    (5) are deeply religious

Questions 32–34 are based on the following passage.

Underlying historical events which influenced two great American peoples, citizens of Canada and of the United States, to work out their many problems through the years with such harmony and mutual benefit constitute a story which is both colorful and fascinating. It is a story of border disputes, questions and their solutions, for certainly the controversies and wars of the early years of Canada and the northern colonies of what now is the United States, and after 1783 their continuation through the War of 1812, scarcely constituted a sound foundation for international friendship.

Yet it is a fact that solutions were found for every matter of disagreement that arose, and the two nations have been able to work out peaceful results from the many difficulties naturally arising in connection with a long and disputed boundary line, in many cases not delineated by great natural barriers.

32. The title that best expresses the ideas of this passage is

(1) "A Proud Record"
(2) "Our Northern Neighbor"
(3) "Cooperation with Canada"
(4) "Our Northern Boundary Line"
(5) "The Role of the Loyalists in Canada"

33. Disagreements between Canada and the United States

(1) did not occur after 1800
(2) have been solved in every case
(3) constituted a basis for friendship
(4) were solved principally to America's advantage
(5) resulted from the presence of natural barriers

34. The writer considers the period before 1812

(1) an insurmountable barrier
(2) a time of geographical disputes
(3) the definer of our differences
(4) a cementer of our Canadian friendship
(5) the period that settled our northern boundary

Questions 35–37 are based on the following passage.

The gradual loss of Indian tribal authority was suddenly reversed in 1934 with the passage of the Indian Reorganization Act, which addressed the strengthening of tribal life and government with federal assistance. The act, the product of the thinking of John Collier, commissioner of Indian affairs, put Indian communities then nearing political and cultural dissolution on the road to recovery and growth. Collier, struck by the strength and viability of Indian communal societies in the Southwest (e.g., the Hopis) and appalled by the destructive effects on tribal societies of the allotment system, sought to restore tribal structures by making the tribes instrumentalities of the federal government. In this way, he asserted, tribes would be surrounded by the protective guardianship of the federal government and clothed with the authority.

Indian tribal governments, as Collier foresaw, now exist on a government-to-government basis with the states and the federal government. Although they are financially and legally dependent upon the federal government, they have been able to extend their political and judicial authority in areas nineteenth-century politicians would have found unimaginable.

American Indians, now a rapidly growing minority group, possess a unique legal status (based on treaties and constitutional decisions) and are better educated, in better health, and more prosperous than ever before (despite the persistence of high levels of unemployment, poverty, and disease).

35. The Indian Representative Act was the result of

(1) Indian tribal authority pressure
(2) the allotment system
(3) action by the states
(4) legislation by nineteenth-century politicians
(5) action by a federal employee

36. The Indian Reorganization Act sought to

(1) strengthen tribal government
(2) dissolve Indian communities
(3) widen the allotment system
(4) make tribes independent
(5) give states a more important role

37. Indian tribal governments are now

    (1) stronger politically and judicially
    (2) stronger financially and legally
    (3) weaker communally and culturally
    (4) weaker in tribal structure
    (5) weaker in government relations

Questions 38–40 are based on the following photograph.

Photo © Alfred Eisenstaedt/LIFE

38. This photograph was taken in

    (1) London
    (2) Boston
    (3) New York City
    (4) St. Louis
    (5) Los Angeles

39. What is the subject of the photograph?

    (1) a newlywed couple celebrating their marriage
    (2) a sailor's desire for romance at the end of the war
    (3) a couple celebrating the new year
    (4) accepted public displays of affection in the 1940s
    (5) a famous movie scene

40. What is the purpose of the photograph?

    (1) to show the jubilation at the end of World War II
    (2) to show the jubilation at the end of World War I
    (3) to show the excitement of the soldiers at the end of the Vietnam War
    (4) to show that it was acceptable for people to be affectionate in public
    (5) to show the relationship between soldiers and nurses

GEOGRAPHY

Read each of the following selections carefully. After each selection, there are questions to be answered or statements to be completed. Select the best answer.

Questions 41–43 are based on the table below.

41. From the table, it can be inferred that population growth is

    (1) greatest in Europe
    (2) greatest in developed countries
    (3) led by the United States and Japan
    (4) greatest in the Middle East
    (5) greatest in India

42. The country that had the largest increase in population density by the year 2000 was

    (1) India
    (2) China
    (3) Japan
    (4) Brazil
    (5) the United States

43. It can be inferred from the table that

    (1) Africa is more densely populated than the United States
    (2) Canada has primarily a favorable environment
    (3) Japan is highly industrialized
    (4) India has an unhealthy climate
    (5) the population of North America is growing at a greater rate than that of Latin America

SIZES, POPULATIONS, AND DENSITIES OF THE WORLD'S LARGEST NATIONS AND REGIONS

Country	Size (sq. mi.)	Population (millions) 1992	2000	People per Square Mile 1992	2000
Canada	3,850,000	27.36	30.42	7.1	7.9
China	3,700,000	1,187.99	1,309.74	321.1	353.98
USA	3,600,000	255.16	257.32	70.88	76.48
Brazil	3,300,000	154.11	172.77	46.7	52.36
India	1,200,000	879.55	1,018.67	732.96	848.89
Japan	143,000	124.49	128.06	870.57	895.57
Southeast Asia	1,692,000	461.5	531.01	272.75	313.83
Western Asia	1,830,817	139.27	171.43	76.07	93.64
Africa	11,700,000	681.69	836.15	58.26	71.47

*(Note the increase of population in the eight years that separate the two sets of figures. Scientists estimate that the earth's population will double in less than 50 years.)

Current annual population growth rates for world regions

Africa	2.9%	Latin America	2.0%	Oceania	1.6%
Asia	1.9%	Europe	0.4%	World	1.7%
North America	1.0%	Former Soviet Union	0.8%		

Questions 44–46 are based on the following passage.

Green Seal, a nonprofit organization based in the nation's capital, helps shoppers single out honest environmental claims. The organization develops stringent environmental standards for products ranging from toilet tissue to re-refined motor oil, and then invites companies to let Green Seal test their products. Goods that equal or exceed the standards can print Green Seal's logo—a blue globe overlaid with a green check-mark—on product packaging. Dean says green labeling rewards companies that make environmentally sound products by giving them a presumed competitive edge and encourages more companies to jump on the green wagon.

Launched in 1990, Green Seal is modeled after eco-labeling programs in Germany, Canada, Japan, and nearly 15 other nations. However, most of these programs are government run, while money from foundations and individual donors bankrolls Green Seal. Dean, formerly director of the National Wildlife Federation's Environmental Quality Division, says that private financing frees Green Seal from the political problems that would arise with federal funding: "The 80 percent of the companies that aren't getting certified would be placing pressure on their members of Congress to squeeze the organization to become more lenient."

Green Seal develops technical standards for various categories of products. The staff considers how raw materials used to manufacture a product are obtained and monitors the product's role in the environment throughout its use and disposal. "We ask, where are the key impacts, and what can be done in these areas to make the product less damaging?" explains Dean.

For products such as bathroom and facial tissue, impacts include logging to get the wood used in paper pulp, discharge of chlorine and other toxic chemicals from paper mills into rivers, dumping of waste paper in landfills and air pollution from paper incineration.

Green Seal has set standards for roughly 40 categories of consumer products and has put its label on 23 products from eight companies.

44. Green Seal's logo would be most likely influential with shoppers who are

   (1) seeking bargains
   (2) honest
   (3) interested in politics
   (4) concerned about the environment
   (5) influenced by packaging

45. According to the passage,

   (1) companies seek out Green Seal
   (2) Green Seal is generous in its testing
   (3) Green Seal sets standards for products
   (4) environmental claims are honest
   (5) Green Seal profits from its services

46. Green Seal's staff is most concerned with a product's

   (1) environmental impact
   (2) profitability
   (3) utility
   (4) performance
   (5) cost

Questions 47–49 are based on the following map and passage.

THE MIDDLE EAST AND NORTH AFRICA

It is important to know about the Middle East for many reasons.

1. The Middle East is very rich in oil. It is believed that two-thirds of the world's total oil reserves lie in the Middle East. Oil is vital to industry throughout the world.

2. The Middle East has always been of great importance because it is located at the crossroads of three continents. Trade between Asia, Africa, and Europe has had to pass through the Middle East, and its waterways have been used as trade routes since the beginning of civilization....

3. Some of the earliest civilizations developed in the Middle East....

4. Three of the world's great religions— Judaism, Christianity, and Islam— began in this part of the world. Many places in Israel, Jordan, and Saudi Arabia are thought of as holy by Christians, Moslems, and Jews.

5. Finally, the Jewish state of Israel stands in the middle of the Arab countries of the area. Israel is a democracy in a part of the world where most people have very little voice in their own government....

47. The map reveals that among the following the country with the smallest area is

(1) Egypt
(2) Saudi Arabia
(3) Iran
(4) Jordan
(5) Israel

48. Of the reasons given for knowing about the Middle East, the most important are

(1) political
(2) economic
(3) historical
(4) religious
(5) cultural

49. According to the map and the text, the bodies of water accessible for trade from the Mediterranean Sea include all of the following EXCEPT the

(1) Black Sea
(2) Caspian Sea
(3) Persian Gulf
(4) Arabian Sea
(5) Red Sea

Questions 50–52 are based on the following passage.

The initial impetus for the environmental movement was the growing interest in outdoor recreation in a more natural environment. This led to the creation of the National Preservation System (1964), the National Trails System (1968), and the National Wild and Scenic Rivers System (1968) and to a public purchase program in the Land and Water Conservation Act (1964). By 1989 the wilderness system, the most dramatic result of these measures, had reached 90 million acres.

These programs set a direction in resource management different from the conservation focus on efficient development of material resources. In wilderness areas, no timber was to be cut and no roads built. Wild and scenic rivers were to remain free-flowing with no dams built in them. The programs meant that resources were now prized for their aesthetic rather than their material value.

The environmental movement gave rise to a new appreciative use of wildlife as an object of observation rather than of hunting. This led to a federal endangered species program, nongame wildlife programs fostered by the states, a heightened interest in habitat for wild plants and animals, and a focus on biological diversity of wild resources.

In the environmental era, a new interest arose in curbing pollution—first air and water pollution in the 1950s and 1960s and then pollution from toxic wastes in the 1970s and thereafter.

50. The environmental movement arose from a desire for

    (1) conservation of natural resources
    (2) civilizing the wilderness
    (3) more hunting and fishing
    (4) resource management
    (5) outdoor recreation

51. The most recent efforts in the environmental field have focused on

    (1) curbing toxic chemical wastes
    (2) obtaining profit from natural resources
    (3) land and water conservation
    (4) reducing air and water pollution
    (5) controlling wildlife

52. New appreciation of wildlife has led to

    (1) increased hunting
    (2) increased profits from the sale of furs
    (3) conservation in resource management
    (4) efficient development of material resources
    (5) a federal endangered species program

Questions 53–55 are based on the following passage.

Puerto Rican migration to the city has constituted the largest influx since the great waves of European immigration in the 19th century.

The islander soon found out what early immigrants had learned. Wages were better but prices were higher; houses were dilapidated; crime was rampant; the weather was cold and damp; and the society at large was strange and different.

How to keep one's family together and preserve one's identity were problems faced by every immigrant group, and they are problems faced by New York Puerto Ricans today. Life in the city was not easy, but there was little to return to.

Unlike many other non-English-speaking newcomers to the city, Puerto Ricans are American citizens. As Americans, they have the right to come and go as they please. Also, unlike previous immigrants, Puerto Ricans did not have to sever their ties to the homeland once they arrived in the city. Thus they could maintain, and even constantly renew, contact with their culture.

53. Puerto Rican immigrants differ from other non-English-speaking newcomers to New York City in that they

    (1) have no language problems
    (2) are needed in the factories
    (3) came with high hopes
    (4) are already American citizens
    (5) were unprepared for migration

54. Puerto Ricans faced all the following problems previous immigrant groups faced EXCEPT

    (1) prices outdistancing wages
    (2) inadequate housing
    (3) poor climate
    (4) crime being prevalent
    (5) broken cultural ties

55. The passage implies that, once they immigrated to New York City, Puerto Ricans

    (1) were just like other immigrant groups
    (2) remained outside the normal course of daily life
    (3) had little alternative but to remain
    (4) returned to Puerto Rico in large numbers
    (5) eventually solved the problem of identity

WHAT'S YOUR SCORE?

_____right,	_____wrong
Excellent	50–55
Good	44–49
Fair	38–43

If your score is low for the "Social Studies Practice," you may need more social studies review. The explanations of the correct answers that follow will help you determine where your weaknesses lie. Analyze your errors. Then reread the chapter "Reading and Interpreting Social Studies Materials" at the beginning of this unit and review the areas in which you had the most trouble.

Answer Key

Civics and Government

1. **3**	3. **4**	5. **3**	7. **2**	9. **3**	11. **4**
2. **3**	4. **3**	6. **5**	8. **4**	10. **1**	12. **5**

Economics

13. **3**	16. **4**	18. **4**	20. **1**	22. **3**	24. **2**
14. **2**	17. **5**	19. **4**	21. **2**	23. **4**	25. **5**
15. **1**					

History

26. **3**	29. **4**	32. **3**	35. **5**	37. **2**	39. **2**
27. **1**	30. **2**	33. **2**	36. **1**	38. **3**	40. **1**
28. **2**	31. **3**	34. **2**			

Geography

41. **5**	44. **4**	47. **5**	50. **5**	52. **5**	54. **5**
42. **1**	45. **3**	48. **2**	51. **1**	53. **4**	55. **3**
43. **3**	46. **1**	49. **2**			

Answer Analysis

Civics and Government

1. **3** The theme of the passage is expressed in the fourth sentence. The American statesmen are described as not only performing their political function, but also expressing a more universal responsibility. This is the basis of American political philosophy.

2. **3** The opening words of the passage indicate that intellectuals who lead the way for a revolution are usually devoured, or destroyed, by the forces that are unleashed.

3. **4** The middle part of the passage states that American political science is the only one perfectly adapted to the emergencies of the contemporary world.

4. **3** The cartoon shows that the United States adopted a foreign policy of neutrality in 1939 (see the license plate of the car), the start of World War II.

5. **3** Although a president as commander in chief can use military power, he is limited by law in his power to send troops into combat in foreign lands.

6. **5** The point of the pupil's question is the role of women in the founding of the United States, indicating that more attention should be given the role of women in U.S. history.

7. **2** The passage states that court decisions often lead to "virtually endless series of vexing legal questions."

8. **4** The opening sentence indicates that the average citizen is knowledgeable about important court decisions.

9. **3** *Landmark* refers to a distinguishing feature that guides someone on his or her way. It is, therefore, "significant."

10. **1** The passage calls democracy promotion a new American industry.

11. **4** Democratic progress has been most difficult in nations that fell into strongman rule.

12. **5** It is stated that no democratic consultant can affect the expectations of people.

Economics

13. **3** The author centers his remarks on the "hundreds and thousands of homeless children in this nation."

14. **2** The children are unseen because they are "scattered in a thousand different cities."

15. **1** He calls our leaving a half-million homeless children on our streets a sheer betrayal of ourselves and our best values.

16. **4** Migrants, sweatshops, coal mines, and factories are mentioned. Servants are not.

17. **5** The passage mentions that "there are about 200 million children working all over the world."

18. **4** Tough laws against child labor are mentioned as an important reform.

19. **4** The passage refers to the problem, for dual wage-earning parents, of finding ways to integrate work and family life.

20. **1** Poor women did not benefit as much as a small number of more fortunate women who managed to get better jobs.

21. **2** Legislators are now interested in family-related issues such as paid pregnancy, child care, and health care.

22. **3** The author wants the reader to understand what life is like in developing nations. For this purpose he imagines that a poor American family is transformed into "a family of the underdeveloped world."

23. **4** The article states that over half of the world's population has a standard of living of less than $100 a year.

24. **2** The author implies that most Americans do not understand the life of almost 4 billion persons living in underdeveloped nations. To help them do so, he creates an imaginary family.

25. **5** Families in underdeveloped nations lack houses, nearby hospitals, electric power, and government services. They have a daily food input of 2000 to 2100 calories, but that is not enough to sustain health.

History

26. **3** "The early Europeans imagined that the natives of the New World were rovers...."

27. **1** The author states that the Native Americans had "no idea of...the individual ownership of land, and the Europeans were incapable of thinking in any other terms."

28. **2** According to the author, the object of the General Allotment Act was to "encourage the Native Americans to engage in farming by breaking up the reservations."

29. **4** The passage refers to "the mingling of races, dedicated to common ideals..."

30. **2** The words *hybrid* and *mongrel* indicate the lack of a common heritage.

31. **3** The author concedes that the "mingling of races," which foreign propagandists believe to be true of America, is a fact.

32. **3** The passage emphasizes the fact that Canada and the United States have cooperated to solve many problems.

33. **2** The passage states that solutions have been found for every matter of disagreement.

34. **2** The passage mentions border disputes that occurred through the War of 1812.

35. **5** The passage states that the Indian Reorganization Act was the work of John Collier, the commissioner of Indian affairs.

36. **1** The act sought to restore tribal authority; it "addressed the strengthening of tribal life and government."

37. **2** The passage refers both to the American Indian's unique legal status and his or her being more prosperous than ever before.

38. **3** The photograph was taken in Times Square, in New York City. Notice the landmark buildings behind the couple.

39. **2** The obvious subject of the photograph is a sailor's desire for romance at the end of the war; the photograph shows his excitement to be home.

40. **1** The purpose of this famous photograph was to show that the soldiers were jubilant about the end of the war.

Geography

41. **5** From 1992 to 2000, population growth in India will be over 139 million. China is second with over 121 million.

42. **1** In 2000, India's density per square mile will have had the largest increase: from 732.96 to 848.89.

43. **3** Since Japan has the largest number of people per square mile and high population densities frequently occur in areas of heavy industrialization, it can be inferred that Japan is highly industrialized.

44. **4** Since Green Seal "helps single out honest environmental claims," it would influence shoppers who are concerned about the environment.

45. **3** The article indicates that "the organization develops stringent environmental standards for products."

46. **1** The staff "monitors the product's role in the environment."

47. **5** Israel, about the size of the state of New Jersey, is by far the smallest with an area of 7,992 square miles, less than one quarter the size of Jordan, one fiftieth the size of Egypt, one eightieth the size of Iran, and one hundredth the size of Saudi Arabia.

48. **2** Oil and trade are mentioned first.

49. **2** The Caspian Sea is an inland sea.

50. **5** The initial impetus was a "growing interest in outdoor recreation in a more natural environment."

51. **1** In the 1970s and thereafter, a new interest arose in curbing pollution from toxic chemical wastes.

52. **5** Wildlife was seen as existing, not for being hunted, but for observation so a federal endangered species program was created.

53. **4** Unlike other newcomers to New York City, Puerto Ricans are already American citizens when they arrive.

54. **5** The first four responses are problems all newcomers faced. The exception is Choice 5; Puerto Ricans could maintain and renew contact with their culture.

55. **3** The passage states that, while life in the city was difficult, there was little in Puerto Rico for the immigrants to return to.

SCIENCE

CHAPTER 13

Reading and Interpreting Science Questions

Science questions on the GED Examination may be based on reading passages, graphs, diagrams, or tables. Test-taking tactics are presented through the use of 31 explained examples and step-by-step explanations. These examples represent the types of questions that you are likely to see on the actual GED exam. There is a heavy emphasis on analyzing and interpreting data and applying information. In this and subsequent chapters, you'll find many questions based on graphs, tables, and diagrams, just like you'll see on the actual exam.

There are several types of questions on the Science Test, and each calls for a specific plan of attack.

SINGLE-ITEM QUESTIONS

In this type, a short paragraph is followed by a single question. Your first task in dealing with this kind of question is to identify the main idea or ideas presented. The best way to do this is to start by reading the paragraph and the question quickly, without stopping to be sure you understand every point. This will give you some sense of the content of the question and of the kind of information you will need to answer it. Fix in your mind the main idea of the paragraph.

Next, reread the question carefully. You may be able to select the correct answer at once. If you have any doubt, go back to the paragraph and reread it carefully, searching for the answer to the question.

Practice this technique on the following questions:

1. Growing plants will not develop their green color, caused by the chlorophyll in their leaves, unless they have both sunlight and the necessary genetic system.

   If a seedling growing in dim light turns out to be colorless, what could be done to find out why?

   (1) Give it a new set of genes.
   (2) Add chlorophyll to the soil.
   (3) Graft it onto a green plant.
   (4) Move it into the sunlight.
   (5) Add fertilizer to the soil.

2. Carbon dioxide (CO_2) gas is dissolved in soda water. The molecules of gas dissolve and are invisible while the bottle is sealed. When the cap is removed, however, the liquid foams up with the release of bubbles of CO_2 gas. If the soda water is warm, the bubbling is even more vigorous.

What general rule would explain these observations?

(1) Warm water tends to lower the pressure of the dissolved gas.
(2) CO_2 gas is more soluble at low temperature and high pressure.
(3) CO_2 gas does not dissolve in water when the pressure is too high.
(4) CO_2 gas is not as soluble when the pressure and temperature are too high.
(5) High pressure tends to keep the temperature low.

ANSWERS AND ANALYSIS

1. A quick reading tells you that the main idea deals with the factors involved in the development of a plant's green color. Now go back to the paragraph and read it again. After rereading, you know that the crucial factors are sunlight and genes. This narrows the answer possibilities to Choices 1 and 4. Since there is no way to give the plant a new set of genes, the answer is Choice 4.

2. A quick reading tells you that the main idea concerns the solubility of gases and its dependence on pressure and temperature. Now you have to reread carefully to find out just what this dependence is.

    This question introduces a type of difficulty that you may meet often—the *unstated assumption*. To get the answer to this question, you will have to realize that the pressure in a sealed soda bottle is high. This should be obvious: when you remove the cap from the bottle of soda, gas rushes out. You will often be expected to supply, for yourself, bits of information that are commonly and widely known.

    Adding this piece of information, you can now go back to the passage to find out how temperature and pressure affect the solubility of the gas in the soda. When you take the cap off, you reduce the pressure and the gas comes out of solution, so it is clear that the gas is more soluble when the pressure is high. Since there is more foaming when the soda is warm, the gas is more soluble at lower temperatures. Thus the answer is Choice 2.

MULTIPLE-ITEM QUESTIONS BASED ON READINGS

Some questions require you to read a passage consisting of several paragraphs and then to answer a number of questions about the material. In this case, you need to study the passage carefully *before* you look at the questions. As you read, note two or three main ideas.

To find the main ideas in the passage, look for key words. These are words such as *aorta* and *nucleus* and *ecosystem* that are normally used in a scientific context. Once you have found these words, they should lead you to one or more of the main ideas in the passage.

Passage 1

The annual migration of birds is a complex process that is only partly understood. Some birds that hatch in the Arctic fly thousands of miles to South America each winter, and then return to the place where they were born. The adults make these trips separately from their offspring. The young birds, however, find their way to the correct wintering grounds even though no adult bird shows them the way. No one knows how they are able to do this.

Biologists do understand, however, that in temperate zones the urge to migrate is prompted by a change in the length of daylight. As days grow shorter in the fall, certain physical changes occur in the birds, such as degeneration of the ovaries or testes. These changes are accompanied by restlessness and the urge to fly south.

There is some evidence that birds navigate using many clues, including the earth's magnetic field, the position of the sun in the sky, visible land forms, and even the pattern of the stars at night. How they know the route, however, is a complete mystery. It can be called instinct, but that is simply a word that explains little.

As you read this passage through for the first time, you should identify several key words, such as *migration, degeneration, ovaries, testes, navigate, magnetic field*. Now use these words to locate the main ideas in the passage. They will probably lead you to three main ideas: (1) the changing length of daylight is the signal that prompts migration; (2) birds use a number of clues to navigate; and (3) how they know the route is completely unknown.

Once you have these main ideas firmly fixed in your mind, you are ready to read the questions. Refer to the passage as needed to find the answers.

QUESTIONS

1. What is the most probable factor that prompts birds to migrate north in the spring?

   (1) depletion of the food supply during the winter
   (2) the disappearance of snow from the ground
   (3) the coming of warmer weather
   (4) the increase in the amount of daylight
   (5) the instinct to fly north

2. In an experiment, the testes are removed from birds in the Arctic in the summertime. It is found that the birds then show the typical restlessness that precedes migration. What hypothesis does this suggest?

   (1) Early migration causes the testes to degenerate.
   (2) The length of the day has nothing to do with migration.
   (3) The immediate physiological factor that initiates migration is degeneration of the testes.
   (4) Increasing length of daylight causes the testes to degenerate.
   (5) Restlessness is not a sign that migration is about to begin.

3. What has the study of migration revealed about how birds know what route to follow?

   (1) Young birds learn by following their parents.
   (2) Birds are born with an instinct that tells them the route.
   (3) Birds use several different means of navigation.
   (4) The changing length of daylight gives birds the necessary clues.
   (5) So far, investigation has not given any answers to the question.

4. In the tropics, some birds migrate short distances between wet and dry seasons. How do we know that they do not use the same seasonal clues as temperate-zone birds?

(1) There is no marked temperature variation between winter and summer in the tropics.
(2) Food is available all year round in the tropics.
(3) The testes and ovaries of tropical birds do not change cyclically during the year.
(4) In the tropics, the length of daylight is much the same all year.
(5) Since it is always warm in the tropics, the birds have no definite nesting season.

ANSWERS AND ANALYSIS

1. One of the main ideas tells you that, in the fall, migration is prompted by the decreasing length of daylight. It is surely reasonable to suppose that the reverse is true in the spring, so the answer is Choice 4.

2. This question requires you to analyze a cause-and-effect relationship. Since it deals with the factors that initiate migration, your attention is drawn to the second paragraph, where you find that degeneration of the testes (or ovaries) always precedes migration. The experiment tests whether loss of the testes is an actual cause of the urge to migrate. When it is found that removal of the testes produces premigratory restlessness, the cause-and-effect relationship is established; the answer is Choice 3. Choice 1 is wrong because a cause cannot come after an effect. Choice 2 is wrong because it introduces a factor not tested for in the experiment. Choice 4 is wrong because the length of daylight decreases, not increases, as the summer advances toward fall. Choice 5 is wrong because it violates one of the assumptions on which the experiment was based.

3. One of the main ideas, already extracted from the passage, is Choice 5—the answer. The passage says that Choice 1 is not true, and Choice 2 offers a word, *instinct*, but not an explanation. Choices 3 and 4 are true, but irrelevant to this particular question. Choice 4 deals with the timing of migration, not the route.

4. The seasonal clue used by migrating birds in temperate zones is the change in the amount of daylight. Since there are no seasons to change in the tropics, the correct answer is choice 4. Choices 1, 2, and 5 may be correct statements, but the question concerns seasonal changes, not temperature or the availability of food. Choice 3 may also be true, but it is not a valid answer because the statement cannot be verified with information presented in the passage.

Passage 2

Sickle cell anemia is a hereditary disease of the erythrocytes (red blood cells) that is found chiefly in the people of tropical Africa and their descendants in America. It is characterized by abnormal hemoglobin, the protein that transports oxygen.

People afflicted with this condition are subject to repeated attacks, brought on by conditions in which the erythrocytes receive insufficient oxygen in their passage through the lungs. This may happen during periods of intense physical exertion, or at high altitudes where the oxygen pressure is low. Under these conditions, the abnormal hemoglobin crystallizes, distorting the erythrocytes into a rigid sickle shape. They are then unable to pass through the capillaries. Blockage of the circulation produces a variety of severe symptoms and may result in death.

The gene that produces the abnormal hemoglobin confers a certain benefit on its carriers. Children of a mating between a person with sickle cell anemia and one with normal hemoglobin have some damaged erythrocytes, but not enough to make them ill except under very severe conditions. They benefit by being immune to malaria, which is a devastating and often fatal disease common in Africa and Asia.

This is a complex passage containing many key words: *sickle cell anemia, Africa, erythrocyte, hemoglobin, hereditary, oxygen, capillary, malaria.* Some of these words may be unfamiliar, but you should note that three of them are defined for you. You are told that erythrocytes are red blood cells, hemoglobin is the oxygen carried in these cells, and malaria is a devastating disease. Sickle cell anemia is described in detail through the passage. You are expected to know the meaning of *Africa, hereditary, oxygen,* and *capillary.*

Using these words, you should find the following key ideas: (1) sickle cell anemia is hereditary; (2) it occurs in Africa, where malaria is common; (3) it involves abnormal hemoglobin; (4) attacks occur in conditions of low oxygen supply; (5) sickle cell anemia provides protection against malaria.

Now you are ready to look at the questions.

QUESTIONS

1. Which of the following might be an appropriate treatment for a person suffering an acute attack of sickle cell anemia?

   (1) Administer antimalarial medication.
   (2) Move the person to a high altitude.
   (3) Administer oxygen.
   (4) Make the person exercise strenuously to open the capillaries.
   (5) Remove the sickled erythrocytes.

2. Why does sickle cell anemia produce some benefit in Africa, but not in the United States?

   (1) There is no malaria in the United States.
   (2) The United States has a temperate climate.
   (3) There is more oxygen in the air in the United States.
   (4) The gene for sickle cell anemia is not found in the United States.
   (5) The United States has a lower altitude than Africa.

3. Of the following, in which group is sickle cell anemia likely to appear most frequently?

(1) Americans living in Africa
(2) Americans of African descent
(3) people who have been exposed to malaria
(4) all people living in the tropics
(5) people who have been in close contact with individuals who have sickle cell anemia

4. A test is available to determine whether an individual is a carrier of sickle cell anemia. Someone might take such a test to help him or her decide whether to

(1) move to a tropical climate
(2) take an office job
(3) work at manual labor at a high altitude
(4) go to a hospital for treatment
(5) travel to Africa

5. Natural selection tends to eliminate genes that produce serious illness and no benefit. Which of the following would result in long-range reduction of the amount of sickle cell anemia in the world?

(1) improved sanitation in tropical countries
(2) a new vaccine against the disease
(3) restriction of immigration from Africa
(4) quarantine of affected individuals
(5) complete elimination of malaria in the world

ANSWERS AND ANALYSIS

1. One of the key ideas tells you that attacks are provoked by shortage of oxygen in the blood, so the answer is Choice 3. It should not be necessary to refer to the passage to get this answer.

2. The last paragraph of the passage details the only benefit of sickle cell anemia: protection against malaria in the carriers of the gene. Where there is no malaria, this benefit disappears, and the answer is Choice 1. Choices 3, 4, and 5 are not true, and Choice 2 is irrelevant.

3. One of the key points is that sickle cell anemia is hereditary; another is that it is common in Africa. It follows that people of African descent are most liable to get it. The answer is Choice 2.

4. This is a difficult question, which cannot be answered except by careful reading of the passage. The last paragraph tells you that under severe conditions a carrier may become ill. In the second paragraph you learned that severe conditions mean a limited supply of oxygen, brought on by hard physical exertion or high altitude. The answer is Choice 3, a combination of both these factors.

5. Since the disease is hereditary rather than infectious, Choices 1, 2, and 4 would have no effect. Choice 3 would have no effect in Africa. The only choice left is 5. The question states that natural selection eliminates genes that cause serious illnesses and no benefit. Since the only benefit of sickle cell anemia is immunity to malaria, elimination of malaria should cause the elimination of sickle cell anemia as well.

QUESTIONS BASED ON GRAPHS, DIAGRAMS, AND DATA TABLES

LINE GRAPHS

A line graph is a common way of showing how something changes or to show the relationship between two or more things. This kind of graph uses two scales, one going up the left side of the graph, called the vertical, or y, axis, and another along the bottom of the graph, called the horizontal, or x, axis.

If you are given a line graph on the GED test, read it carefully. Note the title, the labels on the vertical and horizontal axes, and the legend or key if there is one. Take your time, and pay attention to all of the printed material as well as the lines and the scales. Only then will you be ready to answer questions based on the line graph.

Here is a sample for you to work on:

Example

The graph below represents the temperatures of a white sidewalk and a black asphalt driveway on a sunny day. The surfaces are side by side, and the measurements were made during a 24-hour period.

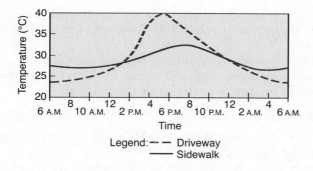

TIP
When looking at a graph, always identify • the x axis • the y axis • the spacing on each axis

What are the features of this graph? The vertical (y) axis represents temperatures between 20 and 40 degrees Celsius. It does not matter whether you are familiar with the Celsius scale of temperature or not. All you need to be able to do is recognize the changes and the intervals from one temperature to another.

The horizontal (x) axis represents the time of day. It is divided into 4-hour intervals for a 24-hour period.

According to the legend, the solid line on the graph represents the temperature of the sidewalk and the dash lines represents the temperature of the driveway. Both temperatures increase during daylight hours and start to decrease in the late afternoon or early evening. It is not necessary that either axis of a graph begin at zero.

Now you are ready for the questions.

QUESTIONS

1. At noon, what was the temperature of the driveway?

   (1) 22°C
   (2) 26°C
   (3) 30°C
   (4) 34°C
   (5) 36°C

2. What is the difference in the times when the two surfaces reach their maximum temperatures?

   (1) The driveway reaches its maximum about 4 hours before the sidewalk.
   (2) The sidewalk reaches its maximum about 4 hours before the driveway.
   (3) The driveway reaches its maximum about 2 hours before the sidewalk.
   (4) The sidewalk reaches its maximum about 2 hours before the driveway.
   (5) Both surfaces reach their maximums at the same time.

3. Where and when does the temperature increase most rapidly?

   (1) the driveway at 4:30 P.M.
   (2) the sidewalk at 5 P.M.
   (3) the sidewalk at 7:30 P.M.
   (4) the driveway at noon
   (5) the driveway at 3 P.M.

4. How do the temperature patterns of the two surfaces compare?

   (1) The driveway is always warmer than the sidewalk.
   (2) The sidewalk is warmer than the driveway at night and cooler in the afternoon.
   (3) The two surfaces are never at the same temperature.
   (4) The sidewalk changes temperature faster than the driveway.
   (5) The driveway is always cooler than the sidewalk.

5. What hypothesis might be advanced on the basis of this graph?

   (1) Radiant heat flows in either direction more easily through a black surface than through a white one.
   (2) Black objects tend to retain heat, while white ones lose it more easily.
   (3) White objects tend to absorb heat more rapidly than black objects do.
   (4) Black objects are always cooler at night than in the daytime.
   (5) White objects are usually cooler than black ones.

ANSWERS AND ANALYSIS

1. Noon is halfway between 10 A.M. and 2 P.M., so start by placing the point of your pencil halfway between these two points on the horizontal scale. Move it straight up until it meets the dashed line, which represents the driveway. Now move the pencil point to the left; it meets the temperature scale at 26°. The answer is Choice 2.

2. The dashed line (driveway) peaks at about 4 P.M. halfway between 2 P.M. and 6 P.M. The solid line (sidewalk) peaks a little before 8 P.M. The difference is fairly close to 4 hours, so the answer is Choice 1.

3. The most rapid change is shown as the steepest slope of the graph. This occurs on the dashed line at about 3 P.M., so the answer is Choice 5.

4. Choices 1 and 5 are wrong by inspection of the graph. Choice 2 is right, because the graph for the driveway rises above the one for the sidewalk at about 1:30 P.M. and falls below it at midnight. Choice 3 is wrong because

the two lines coincide at two times. Choice 4 is wrong because the line for the driveway is always steeper than that for the sidewalk.

5. Since the black surface both warms up and cools down faster than the white one, the answer is Choice 1. Choice 2 is wrong because the black surface cools down faster than the white one. Choice 3 is wrong because the white surface warms up more slowly than the black one. Choices 4 and 5 are wrong because they do not take into account the conditions on which the graph was based, namely, that the two surfaces were in sunlight during the day.

BAR GRAPHS

Whereas a line graph is used to show how something changes, a bar graph is used to compare several quantities. Like a line graph, a bar graph has a vertical axis marked off as a kind of scale. The horizontal axis is used to indicate the different quantities that are being compared.

Look at a bar graph the same way you would a line graph. Read the title and the legend (if any). Then note the information given on the horizontal axis and on the vertical axis.

> **TIP**
>
> Spacing is important on problems illustrated with graphs. Study them carefully.

Example 1

The following bar graphs show the percentages by volume of the sediment sizes found in four different sediment deposits, *A*, *B*, *C*, and *D*.

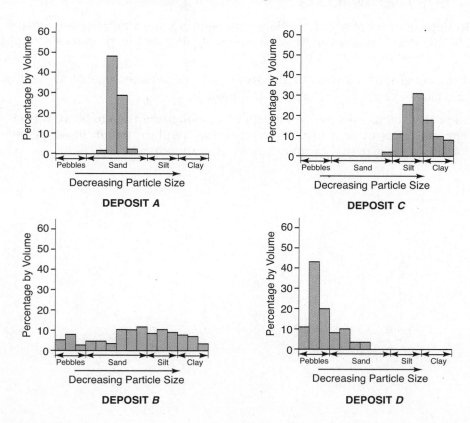

QUESTIONS

1. What is the total percentage of silt in deposit B?

   (1) 7%
   (2) 17%
   (3) 27%
   (4) 37%
   (5) 47%

2. Glaciers carry a wide range of particles. When glacier ice melts, this mixture of material is deposited. In which bar graph(s) is the material most likely deposited by a glacier reflected?

   (1) deposit A
   (2) deposit B
   (3) deposit C
   (4) deposit D
   (5) deposits A and D

3. Smaller particles tend to remain in suspension. In which deposit(s) is there the highest percentage of sediments that would stay in suspension for the longest time before settling?

   (1) deposit A
   (2) deposit B
   (3) deposit C
   (4) deposit D
   (5) deposits A and D

ANSWERS AND ANALYSIS

1. In deposit B there are three bars representing silt. Each deposit is 10% or slightly less. Adding the three deposits of silt together produces a total of a little less than 30%, Choice 3.

2. The only graph that reflects the entire range of particles—pebbles, sand, silt, and clay—carried by a glacier is B, Choice 2.

3. Deposit C contains mostly silt and clay, which are the smallest particles. The materials in deposit C would therefore tend to remain in suspension for the longest period of time. Choice 3 is the answer.

Example 2

The following graph represents the counts of three kinds of leukocytes (white blood cells) in an animal that was administered a standard dose of a drug starting on day 4.

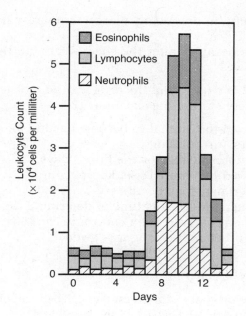

Note that the numbers of the three different kinds of leukocytes are indicated by using different patterns in the bars. Note also that the effect is short lived.

QUESTIONS

1. How long did the medication take to produce its maximum effect?

   (1) 4 days
   (2) 6 days
   (3) 8 days
   (4) 10 days
   (5) 12 days

2. In regard to amount of increase, how did the three different kinds of leukocytes react to the medication?

   (1) All three increased in roughly the same proportion.
   (2) The neutrophils increased proportionally more than the others.
   (3) The eosinophils increased proportionally more than the others.
   (4) There was proportionally less increase in the eosinophils.
   (5) There was proportionally less increase in the lymphocytes.

3. What do the data suggest as to the potential usefulness of this drug?

   (1) It might be used to produce an increase in the leukocyte count in someone suffering from a long-time shortage of leukocytes.
   (2) It is completely useless because the improvement is temporary.
   (3) It is too dangerous because the increase in the leukocyte count is so great.
   (4) It might be useful in producing a large, temporary increase in the availability of leukocytes.
   (5) It is dangerous because, after the effect wears off, the leukocyte count is extremely low.

4. What is the probable reason that the drug was administered from day 4 instead of at the very start of the experiment?

   (1) The delay allowed the animal to become used to its cage and the other conditions of its surroundings.
   (2) The drug was not available for the first 3 days.
   (3) The delay allowed the animal's leukocyte count to rise to normal levels before the experiment was begun.
   (4) The experimenter needed this time to determine the correct dosage.
   (5) The first three days served as a control to establish the pattern of leukocyte count before the drug was given.

ANSWERS AND ANALYSIS

1. Remember that the drug was started on day 4. The peak of leukocyte production was reached on day 10. Day 10 – Day 4 equals 6 days from the time the drug was administered to peak effect, Choice 2.

2. At the peak, the ratios were about 1/4 neutrophils and 1/5 eosinophils, which were not much different from the starting ratios. The answer is Choice 1.

3. In some condition, perhaps a systemic infection, in which the body has a sudden demand for an exceptionally large, temporary supply of leukocytes, this drug might be useful. The answer is Choice 4.

4. Before beginning the experiment, the scientist had to make sure that any changes in the leukocyte count were the result of the medication, and not some other factor. The answer is Choice 5.

PIE CHARTS

A pie chart is a circular graph in which the circle is divided into sections. Pie charts are useful when a particular item of information is a part, that is, a fraction or percentage, of a whole.

The first thing to notice on a pie chart is the labels, which tell you what the various segments represent. Each label is usually accompanied by a number that indicates what part of the whole this segment represents. Next you should note the sizes of the segments to get some idea of which are largest and which are smallest.

Example

The pie chart below indicates the average numbers of macroscopic (large) organisms in one area.

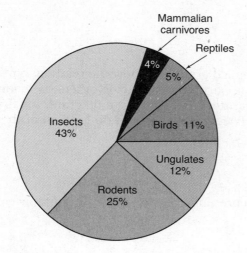

Note that insects, although physically the smallest of the animals represented, are the largest group—43%. Hoofed animals (ungulates) make up 12%.

QUESTIONS

1. Which statement is supported by the chart?

   (1) Birds eat either insects or seeds.
   (2) Most reptiles are carnivores.
   (3) Eighty percent of the ecosystem consists of herbivores.
   (4) The ecosystem in this study was a savannah.
   (5) Insects are important because they are plant pollinators.

2. If the population of carnivores increased by 10%, what would be the result?

   (1) Rodents would increase.
   (2) Ungulates and rodents would decrease, then carnivores would decrease.
   (3) Birds and reptiles would increase, then decrease.
   (4) Ungulates would decrease.
   (5) Ungulates and rodents would increase, then decrease.

ANSWERS AND ANALYSIS

1. Although Choices 1 and 2 are true statements, nothing on the chart indicates what birds or reptiles eat. Choice 4 is an excellent assumption, but noting on the chart proves this statement conclusively. Choice 5 is partly true, but again is not supported by the chart. The best answer is Choice 3. If you know that a great many insects, ungulates (hoofed animals), and rodents eat plants, and if you add up the number represented by their portions of the chart, the total is 80%.

2. There is no reason to suspect that any other population would increase because carnivores did so; therefore Choices 1, 3, and 5 cannot be correct. Choice 4 is a possible answer; however, Choice 2 is more specific and likely as a result of the increase in the population of carnivores. Carnivores feed on ungulates and rodents, and occasionally on some insects. If their population increased, carnivores would need more food, so

the number of prey animals would decrease. When the food level dropped to a point where it could not support such a large population of consumers, however, the number of carnivores would also begin to decline.

DIAGRAMS

Diagrams, sometimes called graphics, show the relationships among the various parts of an object. Some parts may be inside others, be connected to others, or even be completely separate. When you see a diagram, the first things to look for are the connections between parts. Be sure to read all of the labels.

Example

The following diagram represents the human ear. Empty spaces are shown in black.

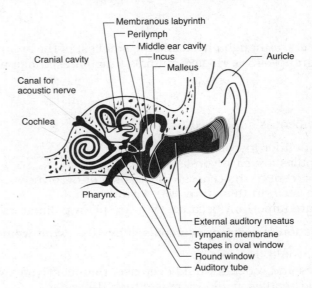

You should see at once that the external auditory meatus is an empty space separated from the middle ear cavity by the tympanic membrane. The middle ear cavity contains three bones.

QUESTIONS

1. The incus is inside the

   (1) malleus
   (2) middle ear cavity
   (3) tympanic membrane
   (4) round window
   (5) auditory tube

2. For a sound wave to get from the external auditory meatus into the pharynx, it would have to go through

   (1) the malleus, incus, and stapes only
   (2) the tympanic membrane, malleus, and middle ear cavity only
   (3) the tympanic membrane, middle ear cavity, and auditory tube only
   (4) the middle ear cavity, round window, and cochlea only
   (5) the tympanic membrane and auditory tube only

3. Ear wax is deposited in the

(1) auditory tube
(2) auricle
(3) middle ear cavity
(4) pharynx
(5) external auditory meatus

ANSWERS AND ANALYSIS

1. The label "Incus" points to something white, a bone. The label "Middle ear cavity" indicates a black area, a cavity. The answer is Choice 2.

2. The path to the pharynx leads through the auditory tube, so that part must be included. Since there is no way to reach the auditory tube without passing through the tympanic membrane and middle ear cavity, the answer is Choice 3.

3. The canal from the outside through the auricle leads into the external auditory meatus, where ear wax is found. The answer is Choice 5.

DATA TABLES

When a series of objects or situations, each having a certain value, is under consideration, a data table is used to make comparison easy. The table is in columns, each column headed by a label that tells what the column contains. If there are numerical data, the column head will also indicate the unit of measure, usually in parentheses. There are no special precautions in reading a data table; just be sure you know what the headings mean.

Example

The following table gives the symbols, atomic numbers, and average atomic weights of the most common elements in the Earth's crust. The atomic number is the number of protons in the atom.

Element	Symbol	Atomic Number	Average Atomic Mass (amu)
Aluminum	Al	13	27.0
Calcium	Ca	20	40.1
Carbon	C	6	12.0
Iron	Fe	26	55.8
Magnesium	Mg	12	24.3
Oxygen	O	8	16.0
Potassium	K	13	39.1
Silicon	Si	14	28.1
Sodium	Na	11	23.0

QUESTIONS

1. How many protons are there in a formula unit of magnesium oxide (MgO)?

   (1) 4
   (2) 8
   (3) 12
   (4) 16
   (5) 20

2. Which of the following groups is arranged in order of increasing atomic mass?

   (1) calcium, iron, potassium
   (2) carbon, oxygen, silicon
   (3) aluminum, carbon, magnesium
   (4) iron, silicon, sodium
   (5) oxygen, calcium, silicon

ANSWERS AND ANALYSIS

1. Just add the 12 in magnesium to the 8 in oxygen; the answer is Choice 5.

2. Choice 2 gives carbon, at 12.0 amu; oxygen, at 16.0 amu; and silicon at 28.1 amu, and is the answer.

OTHERS

There is no limit to the inventiveness of a scientist who sets out to present data. You must expect to meet on the GED Examination an unfamiliar form of graph, table, or diagram. Study it carefully, and make sure you understand the information presented before you tackle the questions based on it.

TIP

In questions, pay close attention to words such as:
• more or less
• increasing or decreasing

Handling Science Skills Questions

The makers of the GED Examination try to test a wide range of skills. You can be asked to do something as simple as restating an idea from the passage, or something as complex as evaluating the scientific validity of an experiment. The questions are generally grouped into four levels of skill: comprehension, application, analysis, and evaluation.

THE FOUR SKILLS

It is not worth your while to try to determine to which of the four levels any one question belongs, or to develop special strategies for each of the four levels. In taking the test, this sort of approach would consume valuable time and require you to use a part of your thinking ability that is best reserved for answering questions. Nevertheless, it is a good idea to become familiar with the four levels of skill that are investigated in the test.

COMPREHENSION

Comprehension is the simplest level. What it comes down to is this: Do you understand the passage, graph, or diagram? Can you rephrase some of the information in it? Can you summarize it? Can you identify a simple implication of the information given?

Here are some examples of the simple comprehension type of question:

QUESTIONS

1. Elements can be either mixed mechanically to form a mixture, or combined chemically to form a compound. In a mixture, the properties of each of the elements present are recognizable. A mixture is rather like a stew in which the carrots, potatoes, and tomatoes are all identifiable. In a compound, however, the original elements are no longer recognizable as themselves, and another form of matter with its own characteristics has been produced.

   Which of the following is NOT a mixture?

   (1) iron filings in sawdust
   (2) sugar water
   (3) vegetable soup
   (4) rust (iron oxide)
   (5) soda water

2. The scientific name of an animal is printed in italic type and has two parts. The first word (capitalized) is the name of the genus to which the animal belongs. The second word (lower case) is the name of its species within the genus. Here are the English and scientific names of five birds:

   A. American robin, *Turdus migratorius*
   B. European robin, *Erithacus rubecula*
   C. European blackbird, *Turdus merula*
   D. Military macaw, *Ara militaris*
   E. Red-breasted blackbird, *Sturnella militaris*

   Of the following pairs, which belong to the same genus?

   (1) A and B only
   (2) D and E only
   (3) B and C only
   (4) A and C only
   (5) C and E only

> **TIP**
>
> In questions, look for opposites in the answer choices. Remember, both can't be true.

3. When you place a solution in a test tube and then spin the test tube very rapidly in a machine called a centrifuge, the materials in the solution will separate, with the densest ones on the bottom and the least dense ones on top.

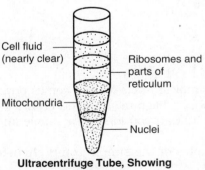

Ultracentrifuge Tube, Showing Various Layers

The diagram above represents the result of spinning a suspension of broken cells in a centrifuge. Which is the correct conclusion?

(1) Ribosomes are more dense than mitochondria.
(2) Nuclei are more dense than mitochondria.
(3) Mitochondria and ribosomes are equal in density.
(4) The cell consists of only solid components.
(5) Nuclei are less dense than mitochondria.

4. The soft body feathers of a bird are useful as insulation, while the stiff feathers of the wings and tail form airfoil surfaces, like those of an airplane wing. If a new species of bird is found that has no stiff feathers, it is safe to assume that it

   (1) cannot fly
   (2) lives in a tropical country
   (3) migrates south in winter
   (4) lives mainly in the water
   (5) is able to run rapidly

5. The table below gives the densities of four kinds of materials found in the Earth:

Substance	Density (g/cm³)
Water	1.00
Petroleum	0.86
Wood chips	0.75
Sand	2.10

If a mixture of all four materials is placed in a cylinder, shaken, and allowed to stand, the materials will settle out with the most dense on the bottom. What will the cylinder look like?

(1) The sand and wood chips will be mixed together on the bottom, and the water will be on top of the petroleum.
(2) The sand will be on the bottom; above will be the water with the wood chips in the layer between the petroleum and the water.
(3) The wood chips will form a layer above the sand on the bottom, and the water will form a layer over the petroleum.
(4) The sand will be on the bottom; the petroleum will form a layer over the water, with the wood chips floating on top.
(5) The water will be on the bottom, with the wood chips floating on it; the petroleum and sand will be mixed above the water.

ANSWERS AND ANALYSIS

1. If you understood the passage, you know that the components of a mixture remain separate and identifiable, while the components of a compound are changed into a new form of matter. The only answer in which the elements have been completely altered is Choice 4, rust, the chemical combination of iron and oxygen. All of the other substances can be separated into their original parts.

2. Since the passage deals only with scientific names, you can ignore the English names. The first word of the scientific name is the same for two birds in the same genus, so the answer is Choice 4.

3. The correct choice is 2 because the most dense particles settle at the bottom after spinning.

4. This question calls for you to make a simple deduction. If the stiff feathers are used in flight, a bird without them cannot fly, so the answer is Choice 1.

5. The materials, top to bottom must be in the sequence of increasing density—wood chips, petroleum, water, sand—so the answer is Choice 4.

APPLICATION

If you have thoroughly understood the information provided in the passage, graph, diagram, or table, you should be able to apply what you have learned. The application questions ask you to use the general principle contained in the information, but to apply that principle to a different situation.

Here are some examples:

QUESTIONS

1. Study the graph below, which shows the percentage distributions of the Earth's surface elevation above, and depth below sea level.

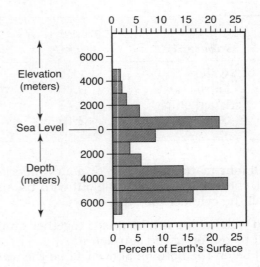

   Approximately what total percentage of the Earth's surface is below sea level?

   (1) 30%
   (2) 50%
   (3) 70%
   (4) 80%
   (5) 90%

2. High-energy sound waves are known to produce long-term damage to the ears, resulting in loss of ability to hear high frequencies. Which of the following individuals is most likely to have good high-frequency hearing after many years of work?

   (1) a rock musician
   (2) an aircraft mechanic
   (3) a riveter
   (4) an accountant
   (5) a sawmill operator

3. A 20-watt fluorescent lamp produces as much light as a 100-watt incandescent bulb. The lighting in a factory is redesigned to provide the same amount of light when half of the incandescent lamps are replaced with fluorescents. What fraction of the cost of lighting is saved?

   (1) 10%
   (2) 20%
   (3) 30%
   (4) 40%
   (5) 80%

4. When an animal eats another that contains PCB pollutants, the PCB concentrates in the predator's liver. The following food relationships exist in a certain ecosystem:

Big fish eat little fish.
Little fish eat plankton.
Wolves eat otters.
Otters eat big fish.

If the water of a pond contains PCB, which of the following will have the greatest concentration of PCB?

(1) otters
(2) wolves
(3) big fish
(4) plankton
(5) little fish

5. Many foods, such as bread, potatoes, and spaghetti, contain high levels of starch. An enzyme in saliva, known as amylose, converts starch to sugar. Which of the following statements is most probably true?

(1) A piece of bread held in the mouth for a long time becomes sweet.
(2) Spaghetti in the mouth causes an increase in the flow of saliva.
(3) If you eat a potato, the enzyme is in your saliva.
(4) If you eat sugar, it can turn to starch in the mouth.
(5) A cookie tastes sweet because it contains starch.

ANSWERS AND ANALYSIS

1. There are more shaded bars below than above sea level on the graph. Adding up the lengths of all the shaded bars below sea level yields a total of about 70%. This represents the total percentage of the Earth's surface below sea level. The correct answer is Choice 3.

2. Again, you cannot get the answer just by looking back at the information. You have to look at the list of choices to figure out who is least likely to have been exposed to loud noise. The answer is Choice 4. All the other occupations involve continuous, loud noises.

3. A complete change to fluorescents would save 80 of every 100 watts. Since only half of the lamps are changed, the saving is half this, 40%; the answer is Choice 4.

4. The concentration of PCB must increase in the sequence plankton, little fish, big fish, otters, wolves, so the answer is Choice 2.

5. If the saliva in the mouth changes the starch in the bread to sugar, you might expect that the bread would begin to taste sweet. Choice 1 is correct. None of the other choices is suggested by the information given.

ANALYSIS

These questions are more complicated. To answer them, you will have to find the relationships among several different items of information. Some of these items will not be given; you will be expected to know things that are general knowledge. It is possible to identify five somewhat different kinds of skills that belong to the general category of analysis:

- Recognizing unstated assumptions
- Using several related pieces of information
- Distinguishing fact from opinion
- Distinguishing cause from effect
- Drawing conclusions from data

Here are some examples of questions requiring analysis:

QUESTIONS

1. A doctor discovers that a patient has blood pressure of 170/110. He tells the patient that medication, accompanied by a reducing diet and limited exercise, will bring the blood pressure down. What has the doctor assumed without actually stating it?

    (1) Blood pressure of 170/110 is dangerous to the health of the patient.
    (2) Medication can bring down blood pressure.
    (3) Medication will reduce the patient's weight.
    (4) The patient has not been exercising at all.
    (5) Blood pressure varies greatly in the population at large.

2. Corals are tiny animals that obtain their energy from their close association with green algae. Fish that eat corals do not live in deep water because

    (1) the pressure is too great in deep water
    (2) the fish that live in deep water eat them
    (3) sunlight does not penetrate into deep water
    (4) there are no currents in deep water to carry nutrients to them
    (5) it is too cold in deep water

3. Someone sees a high waterfall on the side of a cliff and comments about it. Which of the following comments is probably based on opinion rather than fact?

    (1) The waterfall is about 30 meters high.
    (2) The valley into which it falls was carved by a glacier.
    (3) The rock in the mountain is a form of granite.
    (4) The speed of the water at the bottom of the fall is about 25 meters per second.
    (5) A photograph of the fall would be really beautiful.

4. It is found that when a stream becomes more muddy, the population of cat-fish increases. Three possible explanations are offered:

   A. More catfish tend to make the water muddy.
   B. Catfish thrive on invertebrates that live in mud.
   C. Other fish cannot live in muddy water, so catfish have less competition.

   Which of these explanations is (are) feasible?

   (1) A only
   (2) B only
   (3) C only
   (4) A and B only
   (5) B and C only

5. A chemical factory manufacturing a detergent discovers that its product contains a material that is considered a biohazard. Of the following, which can be considered a conclusion based on data?

   (1) The amount of reactant A is twice as great as that of reactant B.
   (2) The temperature of the reaction is 140°C.
   (3) The pH of the reaction mixture is 5.4.
   (4) The problem can be solved by adding an alkali.
   (5) There is a contaminant in reactant A.

ANSWERS AND ANALYSIS

1. Surely the doctor would not bother with the problem if he did not assume that the patient's blood pressure is too high for continued good health, so the answer is Choice 1. Choice 2 is true, but it is not unstated; the doctor told the patient that medication would work. Since there is no reason to believe that the medication is used for weight reduction, Choice 3 is wrong. Choice 4 is wrong because the prescription for limited exercise might just as easily mean that the patient has been exercising too much. Choice 5 is true, but irrelevant.

    If you are asked to find an unstated assumption, do *not* select one that is (a) stated in the information given; (b) untrue; (c) ambiguous; or (d) irrelevant.

2. This is one of the questions in which you are expected to know a few facts and to put some ideas together. You should know that green algae need sunlight to grow, and that corals use energy for growth. The answer is Choice 3. Some of the other answers may be true, but they are irrelevant.

3. "Based on fact" is not the same as "factual." A statement is probably based on fact if it can be derived from one or more facts. Choices 1 and 4 could be determined by measurement or calculation—facts. Choices 2 and 3 could be determined from facts by any competent geologist. Since beauty is in the eye of the beholder, Choice 5 is an opinion.

4. "This question requires you to tell the difference between cause and effect. Is it possible that explanation A is true? No; the water became muddy before the catfish population increased, and a cause can never come after its effect. In both explanation B and explanation C, the water is already muddy, and both are reasonable hypotheses, so the answer is Choice 5.

   This type of question can be tricky. If one event follows another, the one that occurs first may or may not be the cause of the second, even if the second invariably follows the first. The crowing of the rooster does not make the sun rise. In the example given, the sequence of the two events stated in the question establishes only that B and C are possible explanations, not that they must necessarily be true.

5. Fact or conclusion? All the statements except Choice 4 are data, testable and presumably confirmed by measurement. Putting all the known facts together, the engineer might use his knowledge of the process to obtain an overall picture of what is happening. He can then draw the conclusion in Choice 4.

   A conclusion is a general statement that is not obtained from direct observation. It comes from intelligent application of known principles to measurement data.

EVALUATION

We all have our own beliefs and ideas, and most of our beliefs and general thought processes are not scientific. But then, this is how it should be. Science cannot tell you what career to choose or whom to marry, or whether to go to church on Sunday, or who to vote for, or what kind of music to listen to. What science can do, however, is provide highly reliable and accurate answers to specific questions.

On the GED Examination, evaluation questions test your ability to apply the rules of scientific analysis to questions. Before you can do this, though, you need to understand a little about some of the many different kinds of statements that you will encounter.

Fact or Datum

A fact (datum) is something that can be observed and proved to be true.

EXAMPLE

If you measure a piece of wood and it is precisely 8 feet long, you have established a fact. If, however, someone estimates and tells you that the piece is 8 feet long even though it has not been measured, then you have an estimation, not a fact. Another kind of statement is an opinion, as when someone remarks that the piece of wood is an attractive color. Again, you do not have a fact.

You may be asked to determine whether a statement is a valid fact. Sloppy techniques can produce a statement that looks like a fact, but which cannot be supported by evidence or by the experimental process. You will need to be able to identify such statements.

Hypothesis

A hypothesis is an educated guess, the possible answer to a question. It is a purely tentative statement that may be modified or even disproved when more information becomes available.

EXAMPLE

If you find that a type-A shrub in the sunlight grows better than another type-A shrub in the shade, you might propose the hypothesis that type-A shrubs need sunlight for optimum growth. This hypothesis can be tested by a controlled experiment. The most common mistake that people make is to accept a hypothesis as a fact without realizing the need for an experiment to provide proof.

You may have to distinguish between a fact and a hypothesis.

Conclusion

A conclusion may be the result of a controlled experiment. A hypothesis becomes a conclusion when you have tested and verified the initial statement.

EXAMPLE

If the type-A shrub really does grow better in the sunlight during a carefully designed experiment, then it is a reasonable conclusion that this particular plant should be grown in the sun.

You may be asked whether it is reasonable to draw a certain conclusion from a given set of data. You will have to be able to distinguish between a hypothesis and a conclusion.

Generalization

A generalization is a conclusion that can apply to a wide variety of situations.

EXAMPLE

Many experiments with green plants have indicated that all of them, whether a tiny alga cell or an enormous redwood tree, need some sunlight in order to live.

If you are asked whether a certain generalization is reasonable, look to see if it applies to many situations.

Value Judgment

A value judgment is an opinion based on cultural or emotional factors rather than on scientific evidence. Opinions have an important place in our lives, but they cannot be allowed to affect the process of arriving at a scientific conclusion.

EXAMPLE

A certain landowner decided that he should kill every snake on his property because he didn't like snakes. He also killed squirrels and chipmunks for the same reason—he didn't like them.

You will be asked to distinguish value judgments from scientifically valid statements.

Logical Fallacy

A fallacy is a wrong conclusion that results when you use information incorrectly. The most common logical fallacy goes by the imposing name *post hoc ergo propter hoc*, which means "followed by, therefore caused by."

EXAMPLE

I drink a glass of milk for breakfast every morning, and I always get sleepy. Does the milk make me sleepy? Maybe. Or maybe I would become sleepy even if I didn't drink the milk. The way to avoid this kind of fallacy is to perform a controlled experiment and test the possible relationship.

The examples below will give you some idea of the sorts of questions that will test your ability to evaluate scientific statements.

QUESTIONS

1. A proposal to build a dam on a river is opposed by a group of citizens, offering various reasons. Which of the following reasons is based on a value judgment rather than scientific information?

    (1) The river should be preserved because it is a habitat for much beautiful wildlife.
    (2) The cost of the dam will be too high for the amount of electricity it produces.
    (3) It is not possible to dam the river at the site selected because of the surface features of the land.
    (4) The proposed site is on a fault, and the dam could be destroyed by an earthquake.
    (5) The river carries so much silt that the lake formed by it would soon fill up and render the dam useless.

2. The following graph shows the average growths of two groups of rats. The solid line represents a group raised under standard conditions by a supplier of laboratory animals; the dashed line, a group raised in a laboratory and treated with pituitary extract.

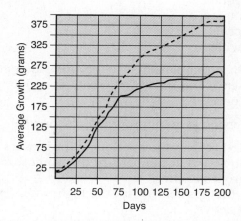

Average growth of 38 untreated rats (control)
- - - - Average growth of 38 rats injected with anterior pituitary extract (experimental)

What is a proper conclusion from the experiment?

(1) It is known that pituitary extract stimulates growth, and the experiment confirms it.

(2) The difference between the control group and the experimental group is so clear that it can be concluded that pituitary extract stimulates growth.

(3) The growths of the two groups are too similar to show that there is any difference in average growth.

(4) The experiment is useless because there is no reason to believe that the same result would be obtained with human beings.

(5) The experiment is inconclusive because there was no attempt to control the heredity of the animals or the conditions under which the experiment was conducted, such as food, water, and physical activity.

3. Over the last hundred years, people have been burning more and more fossil fuel, which releases carbon dioxide into the atmosphere. This excess CO_2 is a cause of global warming, which, according to ecologists, is one of the most serious problems facing us today. Carbon dioxide in the upper atmosphere traps the Sun's heat, in much the same way that the panes of glass hold heat in a greenhouse.

Which graph best represents what most likely happens to the temperature of the Earth's atmosphere as the amount of carbon dioxide in the atmosphere increases over a period of many years?

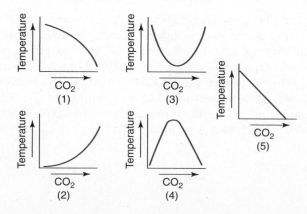

4 Which of the following advertising claims for a toothpaste cannot be confirmed or contradicted by laboratory or clinical tests?

(1) It contains 2% stannous fluoride.
(2) It removes plaque.
(3) It has a fresh taste.
(4) It is not abrasive.
(5) It prevents cavities.

5. A field biologist finds that for three successive winters the beavers in a pond were unusually active and the water level in the pond was exceptionally high in the following spring.

Which of the following is an appropriate response?

(1) She concludes that the winter activity of the beavers raises the water level.
(2) She decides to see what happens to the water level in years in which the beavers are less active.
(3) She suggests the possibility that the high water level makes the beavers more active.
(4) She proposes limiting the winter activity of the beavers so as to avoid flooding.
(5) She suggests that there is no connection between the water level and the activity of the beavers.

ANSWERS AND ANALYSIS

1. The word *beautiful* in Choice 1 is a giveaway, specifying a value judgment. Whoever makes that argument sees an esthetic value in the preservation of wildlife. All the other objections are based on arguments that can be subjected to rigid testing, using established scientific principles.

2. Whether an experiment should have some obvious use is a value judgment that is not at issue here, so Choice 4 is wrong. Choice 1 is wrong because it suggests that the outcome of the experiment was prejudiced in advance. At first this looks like a nice, neat experiment; the difference in growth is marked, and so Choice 3 is wrong. However, Choice 2 is wrong because the controls are inadequate. The rats were not necessarily of the same breed, nor were they raised in the same place. They could differ also in their hereditary endowments, their feeding, and any number of other factors. The results of this experiment could lead to a hypothesis, but not a conclusion, so the answer is Choice 5.

3. Graph (2) shows that, as the amount of carbon dioxide increases, the average temperature of the atmosphere also increases.

4. Taste is a highly subjective value judgment, and what is a fresh taste for one person may be revolting to another, so the answer is Choice 3.

5. Choice 1 is wrong because the evidence is insufficient for a conclusion; the fact that the rising water level followed the activity does not prove a cause-and-effect relationship. Choice 3 is wrong because an effect can never come before a cause. Choice 4 is wrong because there has been no suggestion that flooding is a problem, or that limiting the activity of the beavers will prevent it. Choice 5 is wrong because the evidence is sufficient to suggest the hypothesis that winter activity of beavers raises the water level. More investigation is called for, and Choice 2 is a good idea.

GLOSSARY OF SCIENTIFIC TERMS

In your preparation for the Science test you may on occasion find a term, an expression, or a reference that is not familiar to you. This handy glossary may save you trips to another source of reference. On some occasions your idea of a term may be hazy; you may have known the meaning of it well in the past but have now forgotten. Make it a habit to turn to this glossary to locate clear, succinct definitions. Some students have also used the glossary as a tool for checking up on science information. Your science background will greatly improve if you can find time to develop this habit.

ABIOGENESIS belief that living things may develop from lifeless matter

ACID a compound that dissociates in water to produce hydrogen ions; usually tastes sour; pH less than 7

ACID RAIN rain with an excessively acidic composition that has a harmful effect on fish and other animal and plant life (usually pH < 4.5)

ALLOY homogenous mixture composed of two or more metals (e.g., bronze, steel, brass)

AMOEBA a type of protozoan that has no permanent shape

AMORPHOUS without definite shape

AMPLITUDE the maximum value of a wave or vibration

ANAEROBIC RESPIRATION fermentation, or respiration in the absence of oxygen

ANEMIA condition in which the blood has insufficient red blood cells

ANODE positive electrode of an electrolytic cell; negative terminal of a battery; negative plate of a vacuum tube; site where oxidation occurs

ANTIBIOTIC substance made by a microorganism that kill bacteria.

ANTIBODY a protein, usually in the blood of an organism, that serves to counteract the effects of disease-producing bacteria or viruses

ANTIDOTE a substance used to counteract the effects of poison

ANTISEPTIC a substance that prevents the growth or activity of bacteria

ANTITOXIN substance in the body that neutralizes toxins

APPENDIX wormlike, narrow part of the alimentary canal, in the lower right-hand part of the human abdomen

ARMATURE a piece of metal or a coil of wire that moves back and forth, or rotates, in a magnetic field

ARTERY a muscular vessel carrying oxygenated blood away from the heart to the periphery of the body

ARTHROPODS the phylum consisting of animals with nonliving external skeletons and jointed appendages; insects, spiders, crustaceans

ASCORBIC ACID vitamin C; found in citrus fruits, tomatoes, and green vegetables

ASEPTIC free of live bacteria

ASEXUAL REPRODUCTION producing offspring without union of individuals or germ cells

ASSIMILATION process by which digested food is utilized by the body to build up or repair cells

ASTEROID one of a group of "minor planets" between Mars and Jupiter, of which about 1,500 are known

ATMOSPHERE the whole mass of gases surrounding a planet

ATOM smallest unit of an element, consisting of a nucleus surrounded by electrons

ATOMIC FISSION the breaking down of an atomic nucleus, into two or more parts, with a great release of energy

ATOMIC FUSION the joining of atomic nuclei to form heavier nuclei, such as deuterium (heavy hydrogen) and tritium (another isotype of hydrogen) to make helium, resulting in the release of enormous quantities of energy

AURICLE an upper chamber of the heart that receives blood from the veins—also called the atrium

AUTONOMIC NERVOUS SYSTEM part of the human nervous system that regulates the involuntary activities of the body

AUTOTROPH organism (e.g., a green plant) that nourishes itself by making organic materials out of inorganic

AUXIN a plant hormone

BACILLUS a rod-shaped bacterium

BACTERIA the smallest one-celled organisms, having neither nucleus nor other organelles

BALANCE IN NATURE the interdependence of all plants and animals with their environment

BAROMETER an instrument that measures air pressure

BASAL METABOLISM the rate at which the body's activities are carried on when the body is at rest

BASE chemical compound that produces a salt when it reacts with an acid; an alkali; pH more than 7. Bases turn litmus blue

BEDROCK the solid surface of the Earth's crust, often overlaid by soil or sediments

BENIGN TUMOR a growth that, although abnormal, does not spread and does no particular harm unless it presses a vital organ

BILE a fluid that is secreted by the liver and passes into the small intestine, where it aids in the digestion of fats

BINOMIAL NOMENCLATURE double name used to identify a living organism by genus and species

BIOME a community of plants and animals

BIOPSY the removal of a small part of living tissue for microscopic examination

BRAIN main center of the human nervous system, consisting of cerebrum, cerebellum, and medulla

BRONCHIAL TUBE one of the two branches of the windpipe

CALORIE a unit of measure of heat or other forms of energy (not metric)

CANCER an abnormal growth that, if not detected early and removed or destroyed, will usually, in time, spread widely throughout the body and ultimately cause death

CAPACITOR device that stores electric charge

CAPILLARY a thin-walled tube; one of the tiny blood vessels in the network connecting the arteries and the veins

CARBOHYDRATE a compound consisting of carbon, hydrogen, and oxygen (e.g., starch, sugar)

CARBON DIOXIDE colorless, odorless gas present in the air in small amounts; breathed out from the lungs

CARBON MONOXIDE poisonous gas that prevents oxygen from entering the red blood cells; produced when gasoline is not completely burned

CARCINOMA cancerous growth

CARNIVORE a flesh-eating mammal with long eyeteeth and sharp claws (e.g, cat, lion, dog)

CARTILAGE an elastic, yet hard, tissue composing most of the skeleton of the very young of all vertebrates and the breastbone of adults

CATALYST a substance that speeds up the rate of a chemical reaction without any change in itself

CATHODE negative electrode of an electrolytic cell; positive terminal of a battery; site where reduction occurs

CELL basic unit of plant and animal life, consisting of a small mass of protoplasm, including a nucleus, surrounded by a semipermeable membrane

CELL MEMBRANE the thin outer layer of lipid and protein acting as a cell boundary

CELLULOSE a complex carbohydrate found in the wall of plant cells

CELL WALL the nonliving, rigid wall surrounding the cells of plants, algae, fungi, and bacteria

CELSIUS temperature scale on which 0° is the freezing point of water and 100° is the boiling point; this term has replaced "centigrade"

CHEMOTHERAPY treatment of illness by the use of chemicals (drugs)

CHITIN material forming the exoskeleton of anthropods

CHLOROPHYLL a green pigment that enables green plants to make glucose by the process of photosynthesis

CHLOROPLAST a small green body that contains chlorophyll

CHOLESTEROL fatty substance found in animal fats

CHROMOSOME one of several small, more or less rod-shaped bodies in the nucleus of a cell; contains the hereditary factors (genes)

CLAY finely ground quartz, feldspar, and mica resulting from the erosion of rocks

CLIMATE a composite of weather conditions over a long period of time

COMET heavenly body having a head and tail and traveling in a long, oval orbit around the Sun

COMPOUND substance composed of two or more chemically united elements

CONDENSATION process by which a liquid or solid is formed from a vapor or gas

CONDUCTOR a material (e.g., copper wire) that carries a flow of electrons (electricity)

CONGLOMERATE sedimentary rock made up of a mixture of rounded fragments cemented together by natural substances such as clay

CONSERVATION wise and careful use of natural resources

CONSTELLATION any of the groups of stars and the area of the sky in the group's vicinity to which a definite name has been given (e.g., Ursa Major, the Great Bear)

CORNEA transparent tissue in front of the iris and the pupil of the eye

CORONARY pertaining to the blood vessels of the heart muscle

CORPUSCLE red or white cell in the blood

CORROSION the weakening of a metal by chemical action, such as oxidation

CYCLONE storm or system of winds blowing counterclockwise about a nearly circular region of low air pressure in the Northern Hemisphere and extending over an area covering thousands of square miles

CYCLOTRON instrument used to study the properties of atoms by increasing the speed of atomic particles

CYTOPLASM that part of the cell that lies outside the nucleus; carries on all life activities except reproduction

DECIBEL unit for measuring the relative loudness of a sound

DECIDUOUS vegetation that regularly loses its leaves with the change in seasons

DEHYDRATION loss of water

DEOXYRIBONUCLEIC ACID (DNA) nucleic acid that controls the metabolism of the cell and stores the hereditary information of the cell

DESALINATION removal of salt from a solution, as in the purification of seawater

DIABETES a disease in which the body cannot utilize sugar because of lack of insulin or an inability to properly use insulin

DIAPHRAGM a sheet of muscle that separates the chest cavity from the abdomen and by its movement helps in breathing; also, the vibrating disk of metal in a telephone

DIFFUSION movement from high to low concentration

DIGESTION a process of chemical change that prepares food for absorption by breaking down complex molecules into simpler ones

DISINFECTANT a chemical that kills microbes

DISTILLATION the process of heating a substance until it turns into a gas and then condensing this gas by cooling, usually used to separate substances from a mixture; distillation is a physical change

EBB TIDE outgoing tide

ECHO a reflected sound wave

ECLIPSE cutting off of light from one celestial body by another

ECOLOGY study of the relationships of living things with each other and with their environment

ELECTRIC CURRENT flow of electric charge (e.g., electrons in a wire, ions in a solution)

ELECTROLYSIS chemical breakdown of a compound due to the passage of an electric current through it

ELEMENT a chemical substance made up of one kind of atom; cannot be decomposed by ordinary chemical or physical means (e.g., hydrogen, sodium)

EMBRYO organism in an early stage of development

EMULSIFIER a substance (e.g., soap) that can break large fat droplets into many smaller droplets suspended in water

ENZYME protein that speeds up the rate of a chemical reaction without change to itself

EROSION wearing away of the Earth's surface by water, ice, and winds

ESOPHAGUS (gullet) tube that connects the mouth with the stomach

ESTROGEN female hormone secreted by the ovaries

EVAPORATION escape of molecules from the surface of liquids

EVOLUTION the process by which living things change into other kinds over time

EXCRETION elimination of the wastes of metabolism

FALLOUT radioactive particles that fall to Earth as the result of a nuclear explosion

FARSIGHTEDNESS defect of the eye in which sharper images of objects at a distance are formed than of things nearby

FATTY ACID organic substance whose molecule is a long hydrocarbon chain with a carboxyl group at the end; component of molecules of fats and oils

FAUNA animal life typical of a particular region

FERMENTATION chemical change brought about by enzymes produced by microbes; in the making of beer or wine, yeasts ferment sugars into alcohol and carbon dioxide

FERTILIZATION process that occurs in sexual reproduction when the gametes, a sperm and an egg, unite

FILAMENT fine wire inside an electric light bulb that gives off light and heat when electricity is passed through it

FISSION splitting of the nucleus of an atom with the release of tremendous amounts of energy

FJORD a narrow inlet of the sea between cliffs or steep slopes

FOG a cloud of condensed water vapor formed on or near the ground

FOOD CHAIN pathway of energy through an ecosystem from producers to consumers

FOOD WEB complex feeding relationships within a biological community

FOSSIL remains or impression, in rock or amber, of a plant or animal that lived long ago

FOSSIL FUEL remains of organisms that lived hundreds of millions of years ago; used to release energy on burning (e.g., coal, oil, natural gas)

FRATERNAL TWIN one of two individuals that result from the fertilization of two ova simultaneously by two different sperm

FUNGUS kingdom of plantlike organisms that lack chlorophyll and therefore cannot make their own food

FUSION atomic reaction in which the nuclei of atoms combine and energy is released

GALAXY a large group of billions of stars

GALLBLADDER sac attached to the liver that stores bile

GAMETE one of the two cells that unite in sexual reproduction (e.g., egg or sperm)

GAS phase of matter in which the substance spreads out to fill all the space in its container. Gases have indefinite shapes and volumes.

GASOHOL a motor fuel that consists of nine parts gasoline and one part ethanol

GASTRIC JUICE acid digestive fluid produced by the glands in the walls of the stomach

GENE a part of a DNA molecule that controls the manufacture of a specific protein. Since it is copied and passed on in every cell division, it forms the unit of heredity

GEOTHERMAL ENERGY heat produced in the Earth's interior

GESTATION the period of time necessary for embryo development; pregnancy

GLUCOSE a simple sugar oxidized in the body to give energy

GROUND WATER water that saturates the soil, filling all the space between particles

HALF-LIFE time required for half of any sample of a radioactive material to undergo transformation into other nuclei

HARD WATER water containing a large quantity of dissolved mineral salts (usually calcium and magnesium salts)

HEMOGLOBIN an iron-rich chemical, found in the red blood cells, which carries oxygen to cells

HEMOPHILIA   physical condition in which blood fails to clot properly

HEREDITARY   the tendency of offspring to resemble parents due to the passage of genes in the reproduction process

HETEROTROPH   organism that cannot synthesize food from inorganic material

HIBERNATION   torpid or resting state of an organism throughout some or all of the winter season

HOMEOSTASIS   maintenance of a stable internal environment in an organism

HOMOGENIZE   to distribute the solute in a solution to form a permanent emulsion

HOMO SAPIENS   scientific name for a human being (genus = homo; species = sapiens)

HORMONE   chemical messenger, produced by an endocrine gland, that helps to control and coordinate the activities of the body (e.g., insulin)

HORSEPOWER   a unit for measuring the rate of work, equal to 550 foot-pounds per second

HUMIDITY   amount of water vapor in the air

HUMUS   dead and decaying organic matter found in the soil

HURRICANE   a cyclone with winds of at least 74 miles per hour

HYBRID   a cross between species; an organism with dissimilar genes for a trait

HYDROCARBON   compound containing only hydrogen and carbon atoms

HYDROELECTRIC   referring to the generation of electric energy from falling water

HYDROGEN BOMB   a bomb consisting of deuterium and tritium (isotopes of hydrogen), which are fused into helium, releasing a great deal of energy

HYDROPONICS   soilless growth of plants

HYPOTHESIS   assumption made as a basis for further investigation or research

IDENTICAL TWIN   one of two individuals that result from the division of a single fertilized egg

IMMUNITY   ability of the body to resist or overcome infection

INERTIA   property by which a body at rest remains at rest or a body in motion remains in motion, unless acted upon by a force

INFECTIOUS DISEASE   illness caused by microorganisms

INGESTION   taking in of food

INHALATION   phase of breathing in which air is drawn into the lungs

INSTINCT   complex inborn pattern of involuntary responses

INSULATION   material used to reduce the transfer of heat or to shield a conductor of electricity

INSULIN   hormone secreted by the pancreas that enables cells to use glucose

INTERNAL-COMBUSTION ENGINE   an engine in which the fuel is burned inside the cylinders

INTESTINE   a section of the digestive system below the stomach in which digestion and absorption of nutrients take place

INVERTEBRATE   animal without a backbone

IONOSPHERE   the part of the atmosphere 40–300 miles above the Earth

IRIS   muscular, colored part of the eye, surrounding the pupil

IRRIGATION   supplying of land with water by means of canals and ditches

JET STREAM   swift, high-altitude wind at a height of about 35,000 feet

KIDNEY   one of a pair of bean-shaped organs in the back part of the abdomen that collect the wastes of metabolism from the blood

KILOMETER   unit of distance, equal to about 5/8 mile (1,000 meters)

KINETIC ENERGY   energy possessed by an object because of its motion, depending on its mass and velocity

LACTATION   secretion of milk by the mammary glands

LAGOON   shallow body of water near or communicating with a larger body of water

LARVA   young, usually wormlike stage of an invertebrate

LARYNX   the voice box, located in the upper part of the windpipe, in which the vocal cords are found

LASER   device in which atoms, when stimulated by focused lightwaves, amplify and condense these waves and then emit them in a narrow, intense beam

LATEX   a milky substance from which rubber is made

LATITUDE   the distance due north or south from the Equator, measured in degrees and marked by an imaginary line parallel to the equator

LAVA   liquid rock material that flows out on the surface of the earth from underground sources

LEGUME   a member of the pea family: peas, beans, clover, alfalfa; roots contain nodules with nitrogen-fixing bacteria

LEUKEMIA   a disease of the blood-forming organs: bone, lymph glands, spleen, etc.; characterized by uncontrolled multiplication of white blood cells

LEVER   a rigid rod turning around a fulcrum to increase the force or distance moved of the work input

LICHEN   a complex organism composed of a fungus and an alga in intimate connection, able to live in highly unfavorable conditions

LIGAMENT   tissue joining two or more bones

LIGHT-YEAR   distance that light, traveling at about 186,000 miles each second, travels in one year

LIMESTONE   a type of sedimentary rock, rich in calcium carbonate, that yields lime when heated

LIPID   a fat, oil, or wax

LIVER   largest gland in the body; makes bile, stores extra sugar as glycogen

LOAM   ordinary garden soil; a loose soil made up mainly of clay and sand and a small amount of humus

LODESTONE   natural rock magnet occurring in the Earth

LONGITUDE   distance on the Earth's surface measured in degrees east or west of the Greenwich meridian

LUNAR ECLIPSE   an eclipse that occurs when the full Moon crosses the plane of the Earth's umbra

LYMPH   a nearly colorless liquid containing proteins, found in the lymphatic vessels of the body

LYMPHOCYTE   type of white blood cell involved in immunity

MAGGOT   larva of a fly

MAGMA   molten material from which igneous rocks are derived

MALARIA   a disease of the blood caused by a protozoan and transmitted by the female *Anopheles* mosquito

MALIGNANT TUMOR   a cancerous growth

MAMMAL   a vertebrate that suckles its young

MARINE   referring to saltwater environments

MARSUPIAL   mammal whose young continue development in a pouch after birth

MATTER   substance that occupies space and has mass

MEMBRANE   a thin sheet of tissue; also the outer edge of the cytoplasm of a living cell

METABOLISM   sum total of all chemical activity in an organism

METAMORPHOSIS   the change from larval to adult form, as in insect and amphibian development

METEOR   streak of light in the sky caused by the burning of a meteoroid as it enters the Earth's atmosphere

METEOROID   a small stony or metallic body in outer space

METEORITE   a meteroid that strikes the Earth's surface

METER   a unit of length in the metric system, equal to 39.37 inches (1 m = 100 cm)

MINERAL   chemical element or compound occurring free or found in rocks

MIXTURE   two or more substances mixed together in no definite proportions and not chemically united

MOLD   a filamentous fungus

MOLECULE   smallest unit, composed of one or more atoms, of any pure chemical substance

MOLLUSK a soft-bodied invertebrate; usually has a shell outside the body (e.g., snail, octopus, clam)

MOLTING the process by which an animal sheds its shell, skin, feathers, or other outer covering and grows a new one

NATURAL IMMUNITY resistance to disease produced without medical intervention, as by exposure to the causative organism or by passage of antibodies from mother to offspring

NATURAL SELECTION survival of organisms that are best adjusted to the conditions in which they live

NEARSIGHTEDNESS a defect of the eye in which sharper images of things nearby are formed than of things at a distance

NERVE bundle of nerve fibers held together by connective tissue

NIGHT BLINDNESS a condition in which a person does not see well in dim light, sometimes due to a deficiency of vitamin A

NOVA a star that suddenly becomes brighter than normal and then fades again

NUCLEAR FISSION breakup of a larger nucleus of an atom into two or more smaller nuclei

NUCLEAR FUSION joining of two or more atomic nuclei to form a larger one, with the release of energy

NUCLEAR REACTOR device for splitting an atom in order to produce useful energy or valuable radioactive materials

NUCLEUS (BIOLOGY) specialized chromosome-containing portion of the protoplasm of cells; coordinates cell activities

NUCLEUS (PHYSICAL SCIENCE) positively charged, dense part of an atom containing protons and neutrons

NUTRIENT one of a group of substances in food used to nourish and repair body tissue

OPTIC NERVE nerve that carries impulses from the eye to the brain

ORE rock from which one or more minerals can be extracted

ORGAN group of tissues performing a special function in a plant or an animal

ORGANIC COMPOUND compound containing carbon and hydrogen

ORGANISM any individual living animal or plant

OXIDATION reaction involving the loss of electrons from an atom

OXYGEN colorless, odorless gas that makes up 21% of the air; needed by cells to burn food for energy

OZONE a form of oxygen (O_3), usually formed by an electrical charge

PALEONTOLOGY the study of fossils

PANCREAS a dual gland, near the beginning of the small intestine, that makes the pancreatic juice; also produces the hormone insulin in the cells of the islets of Langerhans

PARASITE animal or plant that obtains its food by living inside or on another living thing (e.g., tapeworm, hookworm, louse, ringworm, many harmful bacteria)

PASTEURIZATION process of heating to kill pathogenic microorganisms

PATHOGEN organism that causes an infectious or parasitic disease

PAYLOAD the contents of an earth satellite or rocket

PENICILLIN antibiotic obtained from a type of mold; used effectively in the treatment of many bacterial diseases

PETRIFIED referring to plant or animal remains that have become like stone

PHARYNX (THROAT) common passageway for air and food

PHOSPHORESCENCE capacity of a substance to emit visible light when stimulated by electrons

PHOTON particle of light

PHOTOSYNTHESIS process by which, in the presence of light, a green plant makes sugar from water and carbon dioxide

PLACENTA structure by which the young are nourished in the body of a mammal

PLANET one of the bodies orbiting the Sun (e.g., Earth, Mars)

PLANETOID one of the many small bodies between the orbits of the planets Mars and Jupiter

PLANKTON minute floating organisms that live at the surface of the ocean and serve as food for large animals

PLASMA the liquid part of the blood; contains antibodies, hormones, and digested foods

PLASTIC synthetic polymer capable of being molded (e.g., cellophane)

POLIO a viral disease that injures the nerve cells in the brain or spinal cord; may result in paralysis of the diaphragm or other muscles

POLLINATION transfer of pollen from the stamen of a flower to a pistil

POLLUTANT substance that contaminates air, water, or soil

POLLUTION accumulation of harmful substances in air, soil, or water

POLYMER giant molecule formed when smaller molecules join together

PRECIPITATION all forms of moisture falling from the sky: hail, snow, rain, and sleet

PREVAILING WIND wind that almost always blows from one direction

PRIMARY LIGHT COLOR one of a group of colors, red, green, and blue, that can be combined to produce all the colors visible to the human eye

PRIMATES order of mammals that includes lemurs, monkeys, apes, and humans

PROGESTRONE hormone produced by the ovaries that regulates the menstrual cycle and the uterus during pregnancy

PROTEIN one of a group of nitrogen-containing organic compounds of large molecular size; important constituent of protoplasm

PROTON positively charged particle found in the nuclei of all atoms

PROTOPLASM all the living substance of a cell

PSYCHIATRIST medical doctor who specializes in mental health

PSYCHOLOGY the study of behavior and learning

PTOMAINE poisonous substance formed by the action of certain bacteria

PULLEY a wheel with a grooved rim, used with a rope or chain to change direction of a pulling force; simple machine

PULSE beat of an artery, produced by the surging of blood out of the heart

PUS yellowish white matter consisting of dead tissue, white blood cells, and bacteria, present in an abscess or boil

QUARANTINE isolation of an individual carrying a contagious disease

QUININE drug once used to prevent and treat malaria

RABIES (HYDROPHOBIA) a dangerous disease of the nervous system caused by a virus; transmitted in the saliva when an infected dog, fox, or similar animal bites a victim

RADAR acronym for radio detection and ranging; device used for the detection of objects by radio waves

RADIANT ENERGY energy in the form of light or other kinds of radiation

RADIANT HEATING a heating system in which hot water or steam pipes set in floors or walls send out heat into rooms

RADIATION process by which energy is transferred in a vacuum

RADIOACTIVITY property of large atomic nuclei that are unstable and break down spontaneously, emitting particles and/or energy

RECYCLE to save and return material so that it can be used again

REFLEX an inborn, immediate response to a stimulus, made without thinking

REFRIGERANT a liquid (e.g., freon) that evaporates easily and therefore is useful in the cooling coils of a refrigerator

REGENERATION regrowth of lost body parts

RELATIVE HUMIDITY ratio of the amount of water vapor actually present in the air to the greatest amount that would be possible at a given temperature

Rh FACTOR a blood protein present in most people; incompatible Rh factors from the parents cause damage to the blood of newborns

ROTATING CROPS farming method in which different plants are sown in the same soil in succeeding years

ROUGHAGE coarse, fibrous food (e.g., bran) that adds bulk to the diet and prevents constipation

RUNOFF surface water that runs to the sea without entering the underground water supply

RUST a fungus related to the smuts; different forms cause plant diseases, such as wheat rust. Also, the oxidized product of iron.

SALINITY   degree of saltiness

SALIVA   a secretion produced by three pairs of glands near the tongue; contains an enzyme that changes starch into sugar

SALT   a compound composed of a positive (metallic) ion and a negative ion other than OH⁻

SATELLITE   natural or artificial body circling the Earth or another planet

SCURVY   a disease characterized by weakness of the capillaries, caused by vitamin C deficiency

SEED   a developed ovule consisting of a protective coat, stored food, and an embryo plant

SHORT CIRCUIT   an accidental direct connection between the two sides of an electric circuit, producing a destructive surge of current

SILT   soil particles intermediate in size between clay particles and sand grains

SMOG   layer of fog that contains smoke and irritating gases

SOFT WATER   water that is relatively free of dissolved mineral salts

SOLAR CELL   a device that produces electricity from the energy of sunlight

SOLAR SYSTEM   the Sun with the group of bodies in space that, held by gravitational attraction, revolve around it

SOLID   phase of matter in which the substance has a definite shape and volume

SOLSTICE   time when the sun seems to reverse its apparent movement north or south of the equator

SOLUBLE   capable of being dissolved

SOLUTION   a homogeneous mixture in which molecules or ions of a substance are evenly or uniformly dispersed in a liquid

SOLVENT   liquid part of a solution in which a substance is dissolved

SOUND BARRIER   the speed at which an airplane overtakes its own sound waves, resulting in violent vibration

SPAWNING   the shedding of eggs and milt into the water during the reproductive process of fish

SPECIES   a group of similar organisms, consisting of populations that can interbreed freely

SPECTRUM   the array of colors or wavelengths into which light is divided, usually by the action of a prism or diffraction grating

SPONTANEOUS COMBUSTION   bursting into flame of a substance because of the accumulated heat of slow oxidation

STATIC ELECTRICITY   electric charge accumulated on an object

STERILITY   complete absence of microscopic life; also, inability to have offspring

STIMULUS   any form of energy to which protoplasm is sensitive

STREPTOMYCIN   antibiotic used to combat infections, such as tuberculosis

SUBATOMIC PARTICLE   particles that make up the atom

SUBLIMATION   change from solid to gas or gas to solid without going through the liquid phase

SULFA DRUG   synthetic drug used to combat certain bacterial infections

SUSPENSION   a cloudy mixture composed of a finely divided solid in a liquid

SWEAT GLAND   gland in the skin that excretes onto the skin surface a fluid consisting of water, salts, and urea

SYMBIOSIS   beneficial relationship between organisms living closely together

SYNTHESIS   building up of compounds from simpler compounds or elements

SYSTEM   group of organs in an organism that deal with the same function

THEORY   scientific principle, more or less acceptable, that is offered in explanation of observed facts

THERMODYNAMICS   study of laws governing heat and energy, and their movement

THERMOMETER   instrument for measuring temperature

THERMONUCLEAR   referring to a nuclear reaction that requires heat in order to occur

THERMOSTAT   device on a heating system that automatically controls temperature

THUNDER   sound following a flash of lightning and caused by the sudden expansion of air in the path of the discharge

THYROID large ductless or endocrine gland in front of and on either side of the trachea in the lower part of the neck

TIDES regular movement of the oceans caused by the gravitational pull of the Moon and Sun

TISSUE group of similar cells and intercellular material that perform similar work

TOPSOIL upper fertile layer of soil, containing humus, that is necessary to plant life

TORNADO one of the most violent of windstorms, noted for its funnel-shaped clouds, high-speed winds, and great destructiveness over a short path and a small area

TOTAL ECLIPSE complete hiding of one heavenly body by another or by the umbra of the shadow cast by another

TOXIN poisonous substance of microbial origin

TRAIT distinguishing quality of a person or thing

TRANSFORMER device for transforming high voltage to low voltage, or low voltage to high voltage

TUBER underground storage stem that produces new plants (e.g., the white potato)

TUMOR an abnormal swelling or enlargement, either benign or malignant

TUNDRA far-northern type of ecological community; water soaked, with permanently frozen ground, bogs, and low plants

TURBINE rotary engine powered by steam, water, or gas

ULTRASONIC SOUND high-pitched sound above the range of human hearing

ULTRAVIOLET RAY high-energy electromagnetic radiation with wavelengths too short to be seen

UMBILICAL CORD structure that connects a mammalian embryo with the placenta

URANIUM heavy, radioactive element present in an ore called pitchblende

VACCINATE to inoculate with dead or weakened germs of a disease, such as smallpox, thereby causing a light attack of the disease but conferring future immunity

VACCINE a substance consisting of dead or weakened bacteria or viruses; used to produce immunity

VEIN a blood vessel that drains the other organs of the body and carries blood toward the heart

VELOCITY the time rate to traverse a distance in a particular direction

VENEREAL DISEASE disease transmitted through sexual intercourse (e.g., syphilis)

VENTRICLE one of the two muscular chambers of the heart that pump blood to parts of the body

VERTEBRATE animal having a backbone (e.g., bird, reptile, fish, dog)

VIRUS submicroscopic disease-causing organism, consisting of a DNA or RNA molecule surrounded by a protein coat

VITAMIN chemical found in foods and needed in small quantities for special body functioning

VOLCANO an opening in the Earth's crust from which molten rock and steam are ejected

VOLT unit of electric potential, equal to 1 joule of energy per coulomb of charge

WARM FRONT boundary between a mass of advancing warm air and a retreating mass of relatively cooler air

WATERSHED area from which a river or lake draws its water

WATER TABLE level below which the soil is saturated with water

WATT unit of power, equal to a joule per second

WAVELENGTH the distance between two points in the same phase on a wave, such as from one crest to the next

WEIGHT measure of the effect of gravity on the mass of an object

WHITE BLOOD CELL leukocyte; blood cell that helps destroy bacteria and other foreign particles that enter the body

YEAST a single-celled fungus, responsible for many kinds of fermentation and certain infections

Science Practice

CHAPTER 15

LIFE SCIENCES

Questions 1–3 refer to the following figure.

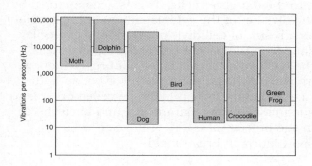

The figure above shows the range of hearing of various animals. Sounds that have a higher pitch or frequency than can be heard are called ultrasonic, whereas those that have a lower pitch or frequency than can be heard are called subsonic. The y axis (horizontal axis) shows the range of frequencies that an animal can hear. Note that the scale is by steps of 10 to accommodate the wide variation in hearing ranges.

1. What is the range of human hearing?

   (1) 10–10,000 Hz
   (2) 20–20,000 Hz
   (3) 10–20,000 Hz
   (4) 20–10,000 Hz
   (5) 10–100,000 Hz

2. Which of the following frequencies would be within the hearing range of both a dolphin and a dog?

   (1) 20 Hz
   (2) 200 Hz
   (3) 2,000 Hz
   (4) 20,000 Hz
   (5) 200,000 Hz

3. Which animal's range of hearing covers the widest variation in frequencies?

   (1) moth
   (2) dog
   (3) human
   (4) frog
   (5) crocodile

Questions 4–7 refer to the following graph.

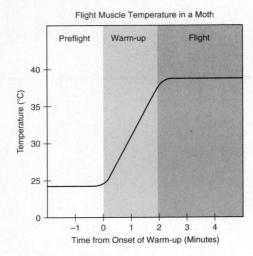

Flight Muscle Temperature in a Moth

The graph above shows the temperature of flight muscles of a sphinx moth before flight, during a warm-up period, and during flight.

4. About how many minutes does it take the sphinx moth to warm up in order to fly?

    (1) 1 minute
    (2) 2 minutes
    (3) 3 minutes
    (4) 4 minutes
    (5) 5 minutes

5. What temperature must the flight muscles be in order for the sphinx moth to be able to fly?

    (1) 24°C
    (2) 30°C
    (3) 35°C
    (4) 38°C
    (5) 42°C

6. Why does the sphinx moth need a warm-up period to get ready for flight?

    (1) It is a cold-blooded animal, and its muscles are not warm enough to generate enough energy when cold.
    (2) It has large wings.
    (3) The muscles need more blood supply to allow them to carry more oxygen to the muscle cells.
    (4) The muscles generally move too slowly to allow the moth to fly.
    (5) Muscle contraction requires a great deal of energy.

7. What is the purpose of the "preflight" section of the graph?

    (1) to show the outside air temperature
    (2) to show the moth's normal body temperature
    (3) to show the muscle temperature when the moth is not preparing to fly
    (4) to show how long it takes the moth to decide to fly
    (5) to show what temperature the moth's muscles will return to

Questions 8–10 refer to the following information.

When a new individual is produced from a single parent cell or from two parent cells, the process of reproduction occurs. This life function differs from all other life processes in that it preserves the species rather than ensuring the survival of the individual. To understand how a cell divides, one must consider the behavior of the nuclear material and the cytoplasm. Mitosis is the process by which the hereditary material of the nucleus is doubled and then distributed into the daughter cells. This is accompanied by the division of the cytoplasmic material so that, as a result of cell division, normally two cells similar to the parent cell are produced. This is the basis of all forms of asexual reproduction, in which a single parent is involved, as is the case in binary fission in single-celled organisms such as amoebas, paramecia, and bacteria, or in the process of budding in yeast cells or sporulation in bread mold.

8. Which life function is more important to the species than the individual?

    (1) growth
    (2) movement
    (3) food manufacture
    (4) reproduction
    (5) protection

9. Which of the following terms does NOT belong with the others?

    (1) fertilization
    (2) budding
    (3) sporulation
    (4) asexual reproduction
    (5) binary fission

10. Which of the following processes is a part of all the others?

    (1) binary fission
    (2) asexual reproduction
    (3) sporulation
    (4) budding
    (5) mitosis

Questions 11–13 refer to the following figures.

Prokaryotic cell

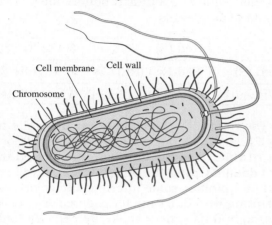

The figures above show a prokaryotic cell and a eukaryotic cell. The questions below ask you to describe some similarities and differences they have.

Eukaryotic cell

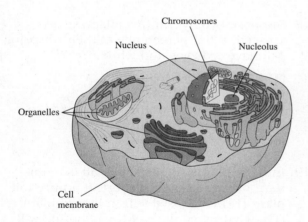

11. Which type of cell has a defined nucleus containing genetic information?

    (1) the eukaryotic cell
    (2) the prokaryotic cell
    (3) neither one
    (4) both the prokaryotic cell and the eukaryotic cell
    (5) it varies with the species from which the cell came

12. Which type of cell has chromosomes?

    (1) the prokaryotic cell
    (2) the eukaryotic cell
    (3) both the prokaryotic cell and the eukaryotic cell
    (4) neither one
    (5) it varies with the species from which the cell came

13. Prokaryotic cells were discovered much later than eukaryotic cells, even though they have been on earth for a much longer time. Which of the following would best explain why this is true?

    (1) Prokaryotic cells have no nucleus.
    (2) Eukaryotic cells have organelles, which are easy to see.
    (3) You can see only the nucleus
    (4) Prokaryotic cells are smaller and require better microscopes to see.
    (5) Eukaryotic cells have a cell membrane to help outline the cell.

Questions 14 and 15 refer to the following passage.

Surprisingly, a fish's caudal (tail) fin, is not used for propulsion. Fins are used primarily for stability and steering. In order to swim, a fish needs to be able to flex its body back and forth very rapidly. To create this motion, a fish's muscles are arranged in a series of waves or segments called myomeres.

Fish have two kinds of muscle fibers, white and red. White myomeres are used for short bursts of swimming. Groupers and other slow-moving fish have almost all white myomeres. Open-sea fish, such as the tuna and mackerel, are capable of cruising at high speed for long periods of time. The blood in their red muscle fibers is rich in a pigment called myoglobin, which can carry large amounts of oxygen. The oxygen nourishes muscle cells, enabling them to work harder for longer periods of time.

14. Cellular respiration requires the oxidation of fuel that is in the form of organic molecules. In the fish, which of the following is (are) responsible for carrying large amounts of oxygen?

    (1) caudal fins
    (2) myomeres
    (3) hemoglobin
    (4) myoglobin
    (5) red muscles

15. On dissecting a fish, a biologist saw that it had large quantities of red muscle fibers. From this observation he can assume that this fish

    (1) lived in a coral reef
    (2) would be good to eat
    (3) came from shallow waters
    (4) was usually slow moving
    (5) came from the open sea

Questions 16 and 17 refer to the following information.

It is well known that plants tend to grow toward the light, a process known as phototropism. Research with plant hormones, known as auxins, has disclosed the mechanisms at work. One such mechanism results in the bending of a stem toward the light. In the grass family, the tip of the growing stem produces an auxin. When light strikes one side of the tip, the auxin moves to the other side. It then diffuses down the stem, where it promotes the elongation of the cells below the tip. As the cells on the dark side elongate, the stem bends toward the light.

16. What causes a stem to turn toward the light?

    (1) phototropism
    (2) the need for light for photosynthesis
    (3) an auxin that controls cell elongation
    (4) the effect of light in stimulating growth
    (5) a plant hormone produced in the dark

17. Which of the following best describes auxins?

    (1) leaf structures
    (2) stem tips
    (3) tropisms
    (4) plant hormones
    (5) light filters

Questions 18–20 refer to the following passage.

If two fruit flies mate and larvae hatch, the physical traits of the offspring will be determined by the genetic makeup of the parents. In the case of fruit flies, the eyes might be either red or white. If only red and white eyes are possible, one color will be the dominant one and will be represented with a capital letter. The other color is called recessive and is shown with a small letter. A chart that shows this is called a Punnett square. A Punnett square for this cross would look like this:

	Red (R)	White (r)
Red (R)	Red Red (RR)	Red White (Rr)
White (r)	Red White (Rr)	White White (r)

The red trait is dominant over the white trait, so if a larva has one gene for R (Red) and one for r (white) from the two parents, the red trait will dominate and the offspring's eyes will be red (not pink or some intermediate color). An offspring with one gene for each color is called a hybrid and its genetic make-up can't be told from the color of its eyes, as either RR or Rr will look red.

18. Suppose two hybrid (Rr) offspring are crossed. What percentage of their offspring will have red eyes and white eyes?

    (1) 25% red, 75% white
    (2) 50% red, 50% white
    (3) 75% red, 25% white
    (4) 100% red, 0% white
    (5) 50% red, 50% pink

19. In bean plants the gene for tall is dominant over the gene for short. If a pure tall plant (TT) is crossed with a hybrid plant (Tt), what percentage of the offspring will be tall?

    (1) 0%
    (2) 25%
    (3) 50%
    (4) 75%
    (5) 100%

20. Brown eye color is dominant over blue eye color. Which combination of parents could have children with blue eyes?

  I. Two brown-eyed parents, both BB
 II. Two brown-eyed parents, both Bb
III. Two blue-eyed parents, both bb

(1) I only
(2) II only
(3) III only
(4) I and III only
(5) II and III only

Questions 21–25 refer to the following article.

The timber wolf occupies an important position in the food chain. Like any other large carnivore, it plays a major role in keeping populations of smaller animals in balance. Its diet includes many rodents. Even as a deer killer, it is more helpfully selective than its rival predator, the human.

The human hunter kills for sport and pride, most often shooting the finest member of the deer herd, but the wolf kills for food alone, picking off the weakest, the oldest, and the sickliest. Thus, humans lower the quality of the herd, but the wolf preserves its health and keeps its numbers geared to the sustaining support of the land. The result is good for the deer, good for the wolf, and good for the browsing area.

Recently a project was launched in Minnesota to extend the range of the wolf. The plan is to trap a small pack of wolves there and then transplant them to a new wild environment in northern Michigan. At one time wolves inhabited this area but are now almost extinct there. The purpose of the project is to have the wolves breed and preserve the species. In this way, Northern Michigan University and several wildlife organizations that are sponsoring the experiment will be doing a service to preserve a creature that is useful in the natural environment. They hope also to explode the myth of the wolf's wickedness.

21. Which deer are killed by the wolf?

(1) the weakest
(2) the strongest
(3) the best specimens
(4) those that eat rodents
(5) the fastest

22. In connection with deer population why is the human race more destructive than the wolf?

(1) The wolf destroys only browsing areas.
(2) The hunter preserves the health of the herd.
(3) The hunter shoots deer for food alone.
(4) The hunter shoots the weakest, the oldest, and the sickliest deer.
(5) The hunter shoots the finest members of the herd.

23. What is the purpose of the Northern Michigan University Project?

(1) trap the wolves in Michigan and export them to Minnesota
(2) increase the range of the wolf in Michigan
(3) increase the number of deer in Michigan
(4) keep wolves out of Michigan
(5) prove the wolf's wickedness

24. Which of the following best describes the wolf's position in the food chain?

(1) important because it keeps the population of its prey in balance
(2) unimportant because it preys mostly on rodents
(3) unimportant because it is a large carnivore
(4) unimportant because it leaves healthy deer alone
(5) important because it lives in the midst of tall timber

25. Two examples of predators mentioned in the selection are

(1) wolf and man
(2) wolf and deer
(3) man and deer
(4) wolf and rodent
(5) rodent and deer

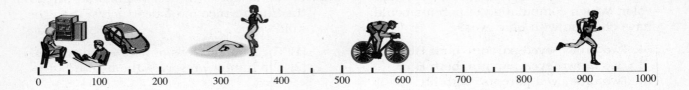

Questions 26–28 refer to the figure above.

The figure above shows the approximate amount of energy used (kilocalories burned) by doing the illustrated activities for one hour. As a rough rule of thumb, burning 3,500 kilocalories is the equivalent of 1 pound of body weight.

26. To lose 1 pound of body weight, a person would have to run for how many hours?

    (1) 1 hour
    (2) 2 hours
    (3) 3 hours
    (4) 4 hours
    (5) 5 hours

27. A person swims and burns 600 calories. How much time bicycling would she have to do in order to burn the same number of calories?

    (1) ½ hour
    (2) 1 hour
    (3) 1½ hours
    (4) 2 hours
    (5) 3 hours

28. Arrange the following from activities that burn the most calories per hour to those that burn the fewest per hour

    (1) swimming, running, writing
    (2) writing, running, swimming
    (3) writing, swimming, running
    (4) running, swimming, writing
    (5) running, writing, swimming

Questions 29–33 refer to the following information.

The higher forms of plants and animals, such as seed plants and vertebrates, are similar or alike in many respects but decidedly different in others. For example, both of these groups of organisms carry on digestion, respiration, reproduction, transport, and growth and exhibit sensitivity to various stimuli. On the other hand, a number of basic differences are evident. Plants have no excretory systems comparable to those of animals. Plants have no heart or similar pumping organ. Plants are very limited in their movements. Plants have nothing similar to the animal nervous system. In addition, animals cannot synthesize carbohydrates from inorganic substances. Animals do not have special regions of growth, comparable to terminal and lateral meristems in plants, which persist throughout the life span of the organism. And finally the animal cell has no wall, only a membrane, but plant cell walls are more rigid, usually thicker, and may be composed of such substances as cellulose, lignin, pectin, cutin, and suberin. These characteristics are important to an understanding of living organisms and their functions and should, consequently, be carefully considered in plant and animal studies.

29. Which of the following do animals lack?

    (1) ability to react to stimuli
    (2) ability to conduct substances from one place to another
    (3) reproduction by gametes
    (4) a cell membrane
    (5) a terminal growth region

30. Plants have rigid cell walls, but animals do not. This is probably related to the difference between animals and plants in the function of

    (1) respiration
    (2) photosynthesis
    (3) excretion
    (4) responsiveness
    (5) locomotion

31. Which of these do only plants possess?

    (1) specialized organs for circulation
    (2) excretory organs
    (3) organs of locomotion
    (4) the ability to manufacture carbohydrates from inorganic materials
    (5) specialized nerve tissue

32. Which of the following do plants lack?

    (1) rigid cell walls
    (2) pumping structures
    (3) special regions of growth
    (4) structures for reproduction
    (5) a digestive process

33. Which of these processes are carried on by plants and animals?

    (1) the synthesis of carbohydrates
    (2) transport
    (3) the manufacture of cellulose
    (4) the production of cutin
    (5) excretion through excretory organs

Questions 34–36 refer to the following figure.

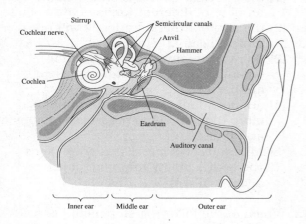

The figure above shows a diagram of the human ear.

34. Which of the following structures are in the middle ear?

    (1) the anvil
    (2) the hammer
    (3) the cochlea
    (4) the anvil and the hammer
    (5) the anvil, the hammer, and the cochlea

35. Which of the following structures would carry information directly to the brain?

    (1) the eardrum
    (2) the cochlea
    (3) the cochlear nerve
    (4) the semicircular canals
    (5) the stirrup

36. A sound wave's signal would be transmitted through structures in which order?

    (1) auditory canal, eardrum, cochlea, hammer
    (2) cochlea, eardrum, hammer, stirrup
    (3) hammer, anvil, cochlea, stirrup
    (4) cochlear nerve, cochlea, eardrum, hammer
    (5) auditory canal, eardrum, stirrup, cochlea

Questions 37–39 refer to the following article.

Plant cells contain specialized chlorophyll containing structures known as chloroplasts. These chloroplasts contain the pigment chlorophyll, which allows the cell to carry out photosynthesis, which is the process by which plants capture and use the sun's energy to sustain themselves. Some plants cells, such as those in *Spirogyra*, contain a single chloroplast. When these cells divide, the chloroplast must divide also, so that each new cell still has one chloroplast. Other plant cells, such as grasses or grains, may have as many as 40 or 50 chloroplasts.

Cells that do not have their chlorophyll stored in well-defined organelles such as chloroplasts are more accurately defined as algae. Many blue-green algae have chlorophyll scattered on specialized membranes throughout the cell, rather than stored in one specialized structure. These specialized membranes are known as chromatophores.

Algae and photosynthetic bacteria that are not exposed to light will rapidly lose their chromatophores and with them the ability to carry out photosynthesis.

37. The main function of chloroplasts in plant cells is to allow the cells to carry out

    (1) cell division
    (2) algal growth
    (3) *Spirogyra*
    (4) photosynthesis
    (5) chromatophores

38. Which of the following statements is correct?

    (1) All chlorophyll in cells is stored in chloroplasts.
    (2) Algae can carry out photosynthesis under all conditions.
    (3) Chromatophores are sites where photosynthesis is carried out.
    (4) Chloroplasts must divide when cells divide.
    (5) Plant cells generally have the same number of chloroplasts.

39. According to the passage, which of the following do not have chloroplasts?

    (1) wheat
    (2) *Spirogyra*
    (3) grass
    (4) blue-green algae
    (5) brown algae

Questions 40–46 refer to the following article.

Whenever microorganisms have successfully invaded the body and are growing at the expense of the tissues, the process is called an infection. The term *infection* should always imply the existence of an abnormal state or unnatural condition resulting from the harmful action of microorganisms. In other words, the simple presence of an organism is not sufficient to cause disease.

Infection may arise from the admission of microorganisms to the tissues through the gastrointestinal tract, through the upper air passages, through wounds made by the contaminated teeth or claws of animals or by contaminated weapons, and by the bite of suctorial insects. Another type of infection sometimes occurs when for some reason the body has become vulnerable to the pathogenic action of bacteria whose normal habitat is the body.

The reaction of the body to the attack of an invading organism results in the formation of substances of a specific nature. The reacting substances that circulate mainly in the blood serum are known as antibodies and are classified according to their activities. Some, known as antitoxins, neutralize poisonous substances produced by the infecting organism. Others, called bacteriolysins, destroy bacteria by dissolving their cell walls. Opsonins or bacteriotropins prepare the bacteria for destruction by phagocytes; precipitins and agglutinins have the property of grouping the invading agents into small clumps of precipitates. The formation of defensive substances is specific for each organism.

40. Which of the following conditions illustrates an infection?

    (1) A guinea pig is exposed to diphtheria toxin.
    (2) A nurse taking care of a tubercular patient inhales some tuberculosis bacilli.
    (3) A man cuts his finger with a dirty knife. He uses no antiseptic.
    (4) A student examines his saliva with a microscope. Under high power he observes some streptococci.
    (5) Malaria parasites in the blood cause chills and fever.

41. Since each antibody is specific for the invading organism, it follows that

    (1) the body can produce only a small number of different kinds of antibodies
    (2) the antidiphtheria antibody will not protect against tetanus
    (3) there are many kinds of invading organisms that cannot be attacked by antibodies
    (4) an individual cannot be immune to more than one kind of disease organism at a time
    (5) immunity to some diseases weakens the body's ability to protect itself against others

42. Which of the following statements is true of phagocytes?

    (1) Opsonins are also called phagocytes.
    (2) Opsonins prepare bacteria for destruction by phagocytes.
    (3) Phagocytes destroy opsonins.
    (4) Bacteriotropins destroy phagocytes.
    (5) Phagocytes prepare bacteria for destruction by opsonins.

43. Which of the following is a correct statement?

    (1) The white blood corpuscles help ward off infection by distributing antibodies to all parts of the body.
    (2) A disease organism that lives in the body of a person always has a bad effect on the person.
    (3) Antibodies are classified according to the type of organism they attack.
    (4) Infection is accompanied by an abnormal state of the body.
    (5) Antitoxins are formed against every organism that enters the body.

44. All of the following are antibodies EXCEPT

    (1) phagocytes
    (2) antitoxins
    (3) bacteriolysins
    (4) opsonins
    (5) precipitins

45. All of the following might result in infection EXCEPT

    (1) inhalation of dust particles
    (2) a drink of contaminated water
    (3) a bite from a mosquito
    (4) a cut with a knife
    (5) a fly landing on the skin

46. By what process do agglutinins destroy invading organisms?

    (1) dissolving
    (2) neutralizing
    (3) clumping
    (4) engulfing
    (5) digesting

Questions 47–49 are based on the following information.

Relationships between organisms are classified according to the way they affect each other. Below are five types of relationships.

    (1) parasitism—a relationship in which one organism lives on another organism and harms it
    (2) commensalism—a relationship in which one organism is benefited and the other is neither harmed nor benefited
    (3) saprophytism—a relationship in which an organism feeds on the dead remains or products of other organisms
    (4) mutualism—a relationship between two organisms in which both organisms benefit from the association
    (5) cannibalism—a relationship in which an organism feeds on the flesh of its own kind

Each of the following statements describes a relationship that refers to one of the categories just defined. For each item, choose the one category that best describes the relationship.

47. The relationship between athlete's-foot fungus and humans is best classified as

    (1) parasitism
    (2) commensalism
    (3) saprophytism
    (4) mutualism
    (5) cannibalism

48. Nitrogen-fixing bacteria enrich the soil by producing nitrates, which are beneficial to green plants. The bacteria live in nodules located on the roots of legumes. These nodules provide a favorable environment for the bacteria to grow and reproduce. The relationship between these bacteria and the leguminous plant is an example of

    (1) parasitism
    (2) commensalism
    (3) saprophytism
    (4) mutualism
    (5) cannibalism

49. Many bacteria or fungi decompose dead plants and animals, releasing ammonia into the environment. This relationship would best be described as

    (1) parasitism
    (2) commensalism
    (3) saprophytism
    (4) mutualism
    (5) cannibalism

Questions 50–55 refer to the following article.

At the beginning of the nineteenth century, it was generally believed that any features of an individual would be passed on to offspring. Thus, if a man lifted weights and had huge muscles, it was believed his children would have huge muscles as well. Jean Lamarck developed a theory of evolution, called the theory of use and disuse, in which this inheritance of acquired characteristics was considered to be the reason for the change in any organism through the generations.

Although Charles Darwin accepted the concept of inheritance of acquired characteristics, he believed that it played only a minor role. The main driving force of evolution, he said, is natural selection. This means that the only individuals that can survive long enough to reproduce are the ones that are optimally adapted to their environment. These adaptations improve generation after generation because only the best adapted individuals pass on the favorable traits to their offspring.

Later, August Weismann's theory suggests that acquired characteristics cannot be inherited because genes are somehow isolated from the rest of the body. Modern genetics has substantiated this theory; the information in the genes is already coded when the organism is born, and nothing that happens to it thereafter can change this coding. Today the theory of inheritance of acquired characteristics is dead, and Darwin's idea of natural selection remains a cornerstone of all theories of evolution.

50. Why was Darwin able to accept the theory of inheritance of acquired characteristics?

    (1) He did not know of Lamarck's work.
    (2) He had not gathered enough information.
    (3) There was good experimental evidence for it.
    (4) There was then no knowledge of the gene.
    (5) Weismann had developed a theory to explain it.

51. How would someone using Lamarck's theory of evolution probably explain the development in South American monkeys of a strong prehensile tail?

    (1) There was a mutation that made the tails strong.
    (2) The gene for a strong tail was dominant.
    (3) The monkeys interbred with other kinds.
    (4) The tail muscles were strengthened by use.
    (5) Strong-tailed monkeys left more offspring.

52. Which of these theories has been discredited by the development of modern genetics?

    (1) There is variation within a species.
    (2) The best adapted individuals survive.
    (3) Inherited features are passed on to offspring.
    (4) Acquired characteristics are inherited.
    (5) Development is controlled by genes.

53. Why have certain strains of bacteria that were susceptible to penicillin in the past now become resistant?

    (1) The mutation rate must have increased naturally.
    (2) The strains have become resistant because they needed to do so for survival.
    (3) A mutation was retained and passed on to succeeding generations because it had high survival value.
    (4) The principal forces influencing the pattern of survival in a population are isolation and mating.
    (5) Penicillin strains became less effective.

54. Which of the following statements is a modern expression of the theory of the continuity of the germ plasm?

    (1) Acquired characteristics may be inherited.
    (2) Genes are not altered to suit environmental demands.
    (3) Natural selection is an important factor in evolution.
    (4) Evolution produces better adapted forms.
    (5) Heredity changes by gene mutation.

55. In any species, which organisms are most likely to survive and reproduce?

    (1) the largest
    (2) the strongest
    (3) the best adapted
    (4) the most prolific
    (5) the most intelligent

Questions 56–60 refer to the following passage.

Most of us are familiar with the role of fats and cholesterol in health. Cholesterol is a white, fatty substance made by animals but not plants. Cholesterol is made by the liver and is essential for proper cell function. In general, the amount of cholesterol in a person's blood is regulated by two types of proteins that transport the cholesterol in the blood.

High Density Lipoprotein, or HDL, is considered "good" in that it tends to promote the removal of fatty deposits from blood vessels, thus decreasing the risk of heart attacks and strokes. Low Density Lipoprotein, or LDL, tends to promote the build-up of fatty deposits within the walls of blood vessels, thus tending to increase the risk of heart attacks and strokes. Fats and oils from animals not only contain cholesterol, but also raise LDL levels. Animal fats also are often saturated, and this too is associated with increased buildup of fatty deposits in blood vessels. Saturated fats from plants (including palm and coconut), while not containing cholesterol, also raise LDL levels. Among the habits that promote HDL level increases are exercise, eating less animal fat, and eating unsaturated or monounsaturated fats and oils such as olive oil or canola oil.

56. Which of the following would likely lower LDL levels in the blood?

    (1) eating bacon
    (2) eating foods cooked in coconut oil
    (3) eating beef
    (4) eating foods cooked in olive oil
    (5) eating lots of cheese and eggs

57. What is the risk caused by high blood levels of cholesterol?

    (1) failure to exercise
    (2) obesity
    (3) heart attacks and strokes
    (4) lack of sufficient HDL
    (5) improper balance of the amounts of HDL and LDL

58. A person who had a history of heart disease in her family would most likely be instructed to eat less of which of the following?

    (1) olive oil
    (2) canola oil
    (3) carrots
    (4) eggs
    (5) soybeans

59. Which of the following is least likely to be a sound medical reason for eating less saturated fat?

    (1) Eating large amounts of saturated fats increases the risk of strokes.
    (2) Eating large amounts of saturated fats increases the risk of heart attacks.
    (3) Saturated fats are components of deposits that block blood vessels.
    (4) People who eat large amounts of saturated fat often don't exercise enough.
    (5) Saturated fats are associated with high blood cholesterol levels.

60. What role does exercise play in benefiting the walls of blood vessels?

    (1) It lowers cholesterol.
    (2) It helps people lose weight.
    (3) It increases LDL levels.
    (4) It increases HDL levels.
    (5) It makes the walls of the blood vessels stronger and less likely to burst.

61. Homologous structures are those that have the same basic structure, but do not necessarily share the same function. They may, however, be indicators of some common ancestor far back on the evolutionary tree. Which of the following are homologous structures?

    (1) the foreleg of a horse and the arm of a human
    (2) the wings of a bee and the wings of a bird
    (3) the legs of a kangaroo and the legs of a grasshopper
    (4) the fins of a fish and the flipper of a whale
    (5) the wings of a bat and the wings of a butterfly

62. The term *metamorphoses* refers to a series of changes undergone from birth to adult. This is a common process in a number of organisms that change from one shape to another as they grow. Which of the following is NOT considered a metamorphosis?

    (1) The eggs of a frog hatch in the water, where the tadpoles must live and go through a series of physical changes before they can move onto the land.
    (2) A trout hatches from an egg and lives for a time as fry before growing into a mature fish.
    (3) A butterfly emerges from a chrysalis after spending the spring as a caterpillar.
    (4) It is much easier to kill flea larvae, with their soft bodies, before they become armored in chitin as adults.
    (5) During an early stage in its life, the jellyfish is attached to the ocean floor and looks rather like a plant. Only later does it become a free-swimming medusa.

63. Which assumption is the basis for the use of the fossil record as evidence for evolution?

    (1) Fossils have been found to show a complete record of the evolution of all mammals.
    (2) In undisturbed layers of the Earth's crust, the oldest fossils are found in the lowest layers.
    (3) All fossils can be found embedded in rocks.
    (4) All fossils were formed at the same time.
    (5) All fossils are found in sedimentary rock.

64. The graph shows the relationship between the number of cases of children with Down syndrome per 1,000 births and maternal age.

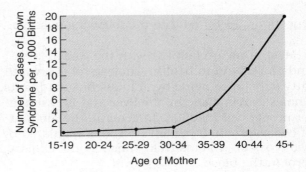

According to the graph, the incidence of Down syndrome

    (1) generally decreases as maternal age increases
    (2) is about nine times less at age 45 than at age 30
    (3) stabilizes at 2 per 1,000 births after age 35
    (4) is greater at age 15 than at age 35
    (5) is about ten times greater at age 45 than at age 30

65. The graph suggests which of the following?

    (1) Older women should be counseled about the risks of having children.
    (2) Older women should not have children.
    (3) Down syndrome will not happen if the mother is young enough
    (4) Older women are more likely to have a child with Down syndrome.
    (5) A 45-year-old mother has a 20% chance of having a child with Down syndrome.

Questions 66 and 67 refer to the food pyramid developed by the USDA, which provides guidelines for healthy diets.

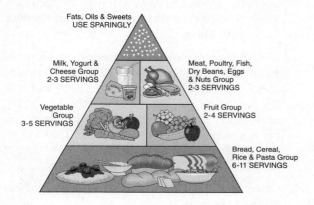

66. According to the pyramid, what types of foods should be eaten most often in a healthy diet?

    (1) grains
    (2) red meats
    (3) fats and oils
    (4) vegetables
    (5) dairy products

67. According to the food pyramid, which of the following combinations would make for a healthy meal?

    (1) a salad and a ham and cheese sandwich
    (2) a glass of milk and a piece of cheese
    (3) an apple and a carrot
    (4) a bowl of rice
    (5) a piece of bread and a bowl of cereal

Questions 68–70 are based on the following graphs.

The graphs show data on some environmental factors acting in a large lake.

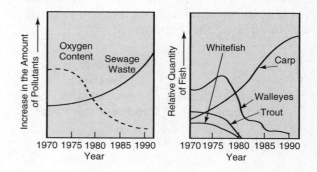

68. Which relationship can be correctly inferred from the data presented?

    (1) As oxygen content decreases, the carp population decreases.
    (2) As oxygen content decreases, the trout population increases.
    (3) Sewage waste and oxygen content are not related.
    (4) As sewage waste increases, oxygen content increases.
    (5) As sewage waste increases, oxygen content decreases.

69. Between what years did the greatest change in the lake's whitefish population occur?

    (1) 1970 and 1975
    (2) 1975 and 1980
    (3) 1980 and 1982
    (4) 1983 and 1985
    (5) 1986 and 1990

70. Which fish species appear(s) able to withstand the greatest degree of oxygen depletion?

    (1) trout
    (2) trout and walleye
    (3) walleye
    (4) whitefish
    (5) carp

Question 71 is based on the following information.

A green plant was placed in a test tube. A light, placed at varying distances from the plant, illuminated the plant. The bubbles of O_2 given off by the plant were counted. The table shows the data collected during this experiment.

Distance of Light from Plant (cm)	Number of Bubbles per Minute Produced by Plant
10	60
20	25
30	10
40	5

71. Which conclusion can be drawn from this investigation?
    (1) As the distance from the light increases, the number of bubbles produced decreases.
    (2) As the distance from the light increases, the number of bubbles produced increases.
    (3) As the distance from the light decreases, the number of bubbles produced decreases.
    (4) As the distance from the light decreases, the number of bubbles produced stays constant.
    (5) There is no relationship between the number of bubbles produced and the distance of the plant from the light.

Questions 72 and 73 are based on the following passage.

A consistent method is used by all scientists to design and conduct an experiment. If the experiment was performed correctly, the system allows any scientist anywhere in the world to duplicate the results. This procedure is called the Scientific Method.

The steps of the Scientific Method are as follows:

1. State the problem or ask a question.

2. Research the subject to see what others have found that might apply to the problem or question.

3. Form a hypothesis; based on the information acquired in step 2, attempt to predict a likely solution to the problem or an answer to the question.

4. Design and perform an experiment. In most situations, two groups of test subjects are used; an experimental group, which will test the factor in question (called the variable), and a control group, which will provide background information about the experimental group if the members of the control group are not exposed to the variable.

5. Observe, measure, and record as the experiment proceeds.

6. Draw conclusions based on the data from the experiment.

7. Repeat the experiment.

72. A botanist was experimenting with two groups of plants. Group 1 was watered with a solution containing a new plant food. Group 2 received plain water with no plant food of any kind. The plant food received by group 1 was the

    (1) control
    (2) variable
    (3) experimental group
    (4) data
    (5) hypothesis

73. A drug company tested a new medication before putting it on the commercial market. Pills without the medication were given to 500 test subjects in group *A*, and pills containing the medication were given to 500 test subjects in group *B*. In this experiment, the individuals in group *A* served as the

    (1) host
    (2) variable
    (3) control
    (4) hypothesis
    (5) generalization

WHAT'S YOUR SCORE?

_____right,	_____wrong
Excellent	65–73
Good	48–64
Fair	37–47

If your score is low, don't get discouraged. Perhaps biology is a difficult subject for you. Try to find out why you failed. The analysis of correct answers that follows will help you to pinpoint your errors. If your mistake was lack of information, turn to the "Glossary of Scientific Terms" (page 423) and look up the meanings of the words you did not understand. If it was a mistake in interpretation, review the analysis of the question.

Answer Analysis

1. **2** The graph shows that the range of human hearing extends from above 10 Hz to above 10,000 Hz. The only choice that covers this range is Choice 2. Note that the scale on the vertical axis is based on orders of 10 (a logarithmic scale), so you have to do a little estimating.

2. **4** The only choice that falls within the hearing range of a dolphin (8,000–100,000 Hz) and a dog (20–60,000 Hz) is 20,000 Hz. Notice that even if your estimation was a bit off, the spacing of the choices would allow you to still get the right answer. Sometimes when you look at a graph it is not necessary to get all of the details. Often the "big picture" is sufficient.

3. **2** Of the choices provided, the widest range of hearing (the longest bar) belongs to the dog.

4. **2** The part of the graph labeled "warm up" extends from 0–2 minutes, and thus lasts 2 minutes.

5. **4** After the warm-up period, and during the flight period, the temperature is above 35°F, but clearly below 40°F. Only Choice 4 fits this range. Notice that if you had thought the correct answer should have been 37°F, you still would have picked Choice 4, because it is the closest.

6. **1** Moths are cold-blooded animals (ectotherms) and their body temperatures mimic their surroundings. By moving its muscles, the moth can generate heat to reach the proper muscle temperature for flight.

7. **3** The preflight part of the graph shows the temperature of the moth's muscles when it is not preparing to fly. This serves as a baseline for reference.

8. **4** Reproduction preserves the species.

9. **1** Fertilization is a sexual process, while all the others are asexual.

10. **5** All reproductive processes must include the division of cells by mitosis.

11. **1** The picture of the eukaryotic cell clearly shows a nucleus, whereas that of the prokaryotic cell does not. This is one of the primary distinctions between the two types of cells.

12. **3** Both types of cells show chromosomes. The prokaryotic cell has chromosomes in the nucleus, whereas the eukaryotic cell does not, but both cell types have genetic material on chromosomes.

13. **4** The figures do not tell you much about what it takes to see the cells. The pictures do indicate that eukaryotic cells are about ten times as large, which should make them easier to see. Smaller cells need better microscopes to be seen. The fact that one type of cell has been on earth longer is irrelevant, even though it is true.

14. **4** According to the passage, a red pigment called myoglobin carries large amounts of oxygen to the muscle cells.

15. **5** Open-sea fish have large quantities of red muscle fibers, which make it possible for these fish to cruise at high speeds for long periods of time.

16. **3** An auxin that controls cell elongation causes the cells on the dark side to elongate, and the stem turns toward the light. Choice 1 is merely the name of the process, not a statement of causation. Choice 2 tells why the bending is useful, but does not explain how it happens.

17. **4** An auxin is a chemical substance that moves through the plant and carries instructions for growth. This is a hormone. Auxim is specifically mentioned as a plant hormone.

18. **3** In this cross, 25% of the offspring will be RR, 50% will be Rr, and 25% will be rr. Since RR and Rr offspring have red eyes (recall that R is dominant over r), 75% will be red-eyed and only those that are rr (double recessive) will be white-eyed.

19. **5** The easiest way to check this is to do a Punnett Square for the cross. It should look like this.

	Tall (T)	Tall (T)
Tall (T)	TT	TT
Short (t)	Tt	Tt

50% of the offspring will be TT (tall) and 50% will be Tt (also tall). Thus all the offspring will be tall. Capital T is dominant over small t.

20. **5** Only a cross in which both parents have a b (blue eye color) gene can produce children with blue eyes. Thus option I can't produce children with blue eyes, but II and III can.

21. **1** The wolf kills only for food and eliminates the weakest, the oldest, and the sickliest deer.

22. **5** Humans kill for sport and pride and try to pick off the finest specimens of the herd.

23. **2** The project is aimed at exporting wolves from Minnesota into northern Michigan to preserve the species and extend the wolf's range there.

24. **1** The wolf occupies an important position in the food chain by keeping populations of smaller animals in balance. In addition, the wolf keeps the number of deer geared to the sustaining support of the land.

25. **1** The end of the first paragraph compares the wolf to its rival predator, the human. It thus identifies both as predators.

26. **4** One pound is the equivalent of 3,500 kilocalories. Because running uses up 900 kilocalories per hour 3,500/900 = 3.9, or just about 4 hours.

27. **2** Someone who swam and burned 600 calories would have been swimming for 2 hours. Bicycling burns calories at the rate of 600 calories per hour, so one hour of bicycling would burn the same number of calories.

28. **4** Choice 4 is the only one that shows the activities in the order from most to least (or top to bottom as shown on this figure).

29. **5** Animals do not have special regions of growth, comparable to terminal and lateral meristems in plants, that persist throughout the life span of the organism.

30. **5** The rigid cell walls severely limit the flexibility of the plant body, so that it is unable to move freely.

31. **4** Green plants have the ability to synthesize carbohydrates from inorganic substances (carbon dioxide and water) in the presence of light.

32. **2** Plants have no heart or similar pumping organ.

33. **2** Food, wastes, and other substances are conducted from one part of a plant or animal to another.

34. **4** The figure clearly shows that the anvil and the hammer are in the middle ear, whereas the cochlea is in the inner ear. It does not matter that not every structure in the middle ear is listed.

35. **3** Nerves are structures that transmit information.

36. **5** Only Choice 5 shows an order from outer ear, through middle ear, and then to inner ear.

37. **4** The first sentence of the passage spells out the role of chloroplasts. Other terms may be mentioned in the passage, but they are not what this particular question asks you for.

38. **3** Choices 1, 2, and 4 refer to situations that may be true, but are not true in all cases. Words like *all* and *must* mean that

there can be no exceptions, and these words can serve as helpful clues in looking for the best answer to a question.

39. **4** Blue-green algae are specifically mentioned as not having chloroplasts. Brown algae (Choice 5) are not mentioned in the passage so that can not be the correct answer.

40. **5** Only in this choice is there evidence that the invading organism has produced a disease process.

41. **2** An antibody is produced in response to a specific invading organism, and will protect only against that one. The body can produce an unlimited variety of antibodies, and the blood usually has many of them.

42. **2** Opsonins prepare bacteria for destruction by phagocytes.

43. **4** Microorganisms that cause an infection produce an abnormal state or unnatural condition. Notice the term is in italics.

44. **1** Phagocytes are white blood cells that destroy bacteria by engulfing them.

45. **5** Unbroken skin is an excellent barrier against the invasion of microorganisms. In some cases, microorganisms may enter through normal body openings; in other cases, through wounds or bites.

46. **3** Agglutinins group or clump invading organisms.

47. **1** The relationship between athlete's-foot fungus and humans is known as parasitism. A parasite is an organism that lives in or on another organism and harms it.

48. **4** The relationship between nitrogen-fixing bacteria and the leguminous plant is an example of mutualism. Mutualism is an association between two organisms that benefits both. In this case, the plant gets nitrogen and the bacteria have a place to live.

49. **3** In a saprophytic relationship, an organism feeds on the dead or decayed remains of other organisms.

50. **4** After Darwin's day, the work of Weismann and others showed that genes (unknown to Darwin) pass unchanged by environmental influences from generation to generation.

51. **4** The theory of use and disuse said that any organ that is used becomes stronger. Although this is true of some organs, the changes are not hereditary and thus have no effect on evolution.

52. **4** With the discovery that heredity is controlled by genes that are sequestered in the germ cells, it became clear that there is no mechanism by which acquired characteristics can be inherited. See that last sentence of the passsage.

53. **3** Bacteria resistant to penicillin developed as a result of mutation. Organisms that did not receive the mutated gene were killed by the antibiotic. Those in which gene mutation occurred survived and passed the mutation on to succeeding generations.

54. **2** Continuity of the germ plasm occurs because no environmental influence affects the genes.

55. **3** Being larger, stronger, more prolific, or more intelligent may or may not promote survival. The general statement in Choice 3 is the only one that applies universally.

56. **4** The other choices all involve animal fats or fats that are saturated. The last sentence of the passage specifically tells you about the benefits of olive oil.

57. **3** The main risk of high levels of cholesterol is heart attacks and strokes. The other things mentioned may be associated (people with high cholesterol often do not get enough exercise) but the cause is the cholesterol levels in the blood.

58. **4** All of the other choices are vegetable products. Only eggs are an animal product and contain cholesterol. A person with a family history of heart disease would want to reduce animal fat intake.

59. **4** All of the statements given are correct, but only Choice 4 is not a direct result. This is an example of a correlation, not a cause and effect. People who eat lots of saturated fat may well not get enough exercise, but the fat intake is not causing them to get too little exercise.

60. **4** The last sentence of the passage states that exercise increases HDL levels.

61. **1** The foreleg of a horse is homologous to the arm of a human. In Choices 2, 3, and 5, a bird or mammal is compared to an

insect, which is structurally quite different. In Choice 4, although both a fish and a whale are aquatic, the whale is a mammal.

62. **2** When a trout hatches from an egg, it looks very much like a little trout. All the other answers describe organisms that go through distinct stages as they mature.

63. **2** *Fossils* are the remains of organisms of the past. When an organism dies, it may be covered by sediment. Sediments are deposited in layers. The layers are compacted into rock. The oldest fossils are found in the lowest layers.

64. **5** According to the graph, the maximum number of Down syndrome cases occurs at age 45: 20 cases per 1,000 births. At age 30, there are 2 cases per 1,000 births. Therefore at age 45, there are ten times as many cases as at age 30.

65. **4** Choices 1 and 2 involve opinions or value statements. Although someone may use the information in the graph to support her view, the graph does not tell people what they should or should not do. Choice 3 is incorrect because even young mothers have a chance of having a child with Down syndrome. Choice 5 is incorrect because the graph shows the number of Down syndrome births per 1,000 births. $(20/1,000) \times 100 = 2\%$, not 20%. Only choice 4 is supported by the information in the graph.

66. **1** The part of the pyramid that shows the greatest number of servings per day is grains (bread, cereal, rice, and pasta).

67. **1** A healthy meal would consist of foods from as many of the groups on the pyramid as possible. The correct answer is choice 1, which includes vegetables, dairy, meat, and grains.

68. **5** According to the graph, oxygen content decreases as sewage waste increases. The organisms that decompose sewage are aerobic organisms, which consume oxygen.

69. **2** There was the greatest change in the whitefish population between 1975 and 1980. The whitefish population disappeared from the lake by 1980.

70. **5** The carp appears to be able to withstand oxygen depletion. The number of carp increased as the oxygen content decreased.

71. **1** According to the table of results, the number of bubbles produced by the plant decreases as the distance from the light increases. The results indicate that there is a relationship between the number of bubbles produced and the distance of the plant from the light.

72. **2** According to the passage, the variable is the part of the experiment that is being tested. In this case, the variable is the plant food.

73. **3** A control is a part of an experiment in which no changes have been made. Group *A* was the control. The individuals in this group received pills that did not contain the medication.

EARTH AND SPACE SCIENCE

Questions 1–3 refer to the following passage.

It is often convenient to classify energy sources as either renewable or nonrenewable. Renewable resources are those that either grow back (such as trees) or that do not get used up, such as wind power, solar power, or hydroelectric power. Nuclear power is also considered renewable, even though the supplies can potentially be depleted. Nonrenewable resources are those that are not replaced by natural processes once they are used up. Fossil fuels, such as coal, petroleum, and natural gas fall into this category. These energy sources were formed over millions or billions of years from the action of great pressure on decayed animal and vegetable matter, such as decayed animals or plants. Our dependence on nonrenewable resources has often meant that we must pay more than we want to for these limited energy sources.

1. Which of the following are nonrenewable resources mentioned in the passage?

   (1) coal, natural gas, and wind
   (2) solar energy and nuclear energy
   (3) coal and petroleum
   (4) petroleum and nuclear energy
   (5) solar power and hydroelectric power

2. Which of the following statements is not directly supported by the passage?

   (1) It takes a great deal of time for coal to be formed.
   (2) Fossil fuels are formed from the decayed remains of plants and animals.
   (3) Trees are considered renewable resources.
   (4) Natural gas is a fossil fuel.
   (5) We may have to go to war to be sure of our oil supplies.

3. Which of the following energy sources will likely become scarcer and more costly in the future?

     I. coal
    II. hydroelectric power
   III. natural gas

   (1) I only
   (2) II only
   (3) I and III only
   (4) II and III only

   (5) I, II and III

4. The Moon is approximately 240,000 miles from Earth. How long would a spacecraft launched from the Moon and traveling at an average velocity of 24,000 miles per hour, take to travel to Earth and back?

   (1) 10 hours
   (2) 20 hours
   (3) 10 days
   (4) 100 days
   (5) 240 days

Questions 5–7 refer to the following information.

The Moon goes through a cycle of four major phases in a period of 4 weeks. As it revolves around the Earth, its orbit takes it first between the Sun and the Earth and then to the other side of the Earth away from the Sun. When the Moon is in the area between the Earth and Sun, the side of the Moon toward us is not lighted directly by the Sun. However, the Moon is slightly visible because of sunlight reflected by the Earth. The light is called earthshine.

APPEARANCE OF THE MOON FROM THE EARTH

New   First Quarter   Full   Third Quarter

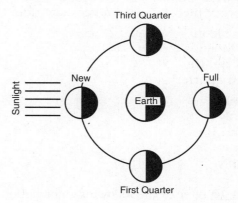

Tides are the result of the gravitational pull of the Moon and the Sun on the freely moving waters of the Earth. Since the Moon is so much closer to the Earth than is the Sun, the Moon has a much greater effect on the tides than does the Sun. The effect is greatest during the periods of the full and new Moon when the Moon and Sun are in direct line with the Earth and exert a pull in the same direction. The result is a *spring tide*, or tide of great range. At the periods of the first and third quarters, the Sun and the Moon pull at right angles and thus oppose each other. Thus the pull of the Moon is lessened, the result being a *neap tide*, or tide of small range.

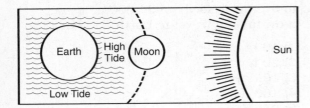

5. Earthshine is illumination seen during which phase of the Moon?

   (1) full
   (2) new
   (3) first quarter
   (4) crescent
   (5) last quarter

6. Why is it possible for an observer on Earth to see the phases of the Moon?

   (1) The Moon revolves around the Sun.
   (2) The Moon rotates on its axis.
   (3) The Earth revolves around the Sun.
   (4) The Earth rotates on its axis.
   (5) The Moon revolves around the Earth.

7. During what phase(s) of the Moon do we have a very high tide and a very low tide?

   A. new Moon
   B. full Moon
   C. first quarter
   D. third quarter

   (1) A only
   (2) B only
   (3) A and B
   (4) C only
   (5) D only

Questions 8–10 refer to the following information.

According to geological evidence, Africa was once a continent of ice, while the Antarctic was a tropical jungle. Paleontologists have also found fossil remains from the same organisms on different continents far apart from each other. For example, the fossil of a medium-sized dinosaur called Kannemyerid has been found in North America, South America, Asia, and India.

Attempts to explain such discoveries have led to the theory of continental drift and plate tectonics. This theory states that the continents of Earth once formed one vast landmass, but later broke away from each other and are still drifting farther apart. Sometimes the geological plates carrying landmasses collide with one another, and we have an earthquake.

Evidence for continental drift lies in a chain of undersea mountains circling the globe. When marine geologists took the temperature in a deep valley running through the middle of this mountain range, they discovered that the valley was much warmer than the surrounding sea. Scientists believe that this is where molten rock is pushed up from within the Earth. As this new rock rises, it spreads out the seafloor, pushing the continents farther apart. More evidence to support this theory was discovered when core samples indicated that the rock nearest the mountains was much younger than rock farther away from the mountains.

8. From the evidence in the article we can infer that a paleontologist

   (1) collects rocks
   (2) studies volcanoes
   (3) maps the ocean floor
   (4) studies fossil remains
   (5) studies plate tectonics

9. The theory that the landmasses of Earth ride on huge geological plates is supported by the occurrence of

   (1) hurricanes
   (2) tidal waves
   (3) continental drifts
   (4) volcanoes
   (5) earthquakes

10. A prehistoric species could range over a number of continents with no problem because at that time

   (1) the continents formed one large landmass
   (2) there were land bridges between the continents
   (3) the oceans were much shallower
   (4) the creatures were excellent swimmers
   (5) large numbers of the animals evolved separately on each continent

Questions 11–13 refer to the following article.

Toward the end of the year 1973, the comet Kohoutek began to make newspaper headlines as it moved toward the Sun at great speed. Predictions were made that it would be more spectacular than Halley's comet, which was last seen in 1910, as well as Ikeya-Seki of 1965 and Bennett's comet of 1970. Kohoutek was first discovered in March 1973 by a Czech astronomer Dr. Lubos Kohoutek, when it was still more than 500 million miles from the Sun. Astronomers reasoned that if it was visible that far away, it would probably prove to be spectacular when it streaked to within 13 million miles of the Sun on December 28. Thus, it was expected to be the third brightest object in the sky, after the Sun and the Moon.

Measurements indicated that Kohoutek's nucleus was 20–25 miles across, its coma about 10,000 miles in diameter, and its tail about 20 million miles in length. The nucleus of a comet is thought to be composed of a clump of "dirty ice"—dust particles, stony matter, and frozen gases, such as water, methane, and ammonia. The coma is a large, hazy cloud formed when the Sun's heat liberates dust and gases from the nucleus as the comet enters the inner part of the solar system. The tail is a long cloud of ions and molecules that may become fluorescent under the influence of the solar wind.

Despite the predictions made for it, the comet Kohoutek turned out to be of such minimum brightness that few people were actually able to see it. The reason for its disappointing appearance may be traced to the fact that it was not the typical "dirty snowball" astronomers had predicted. Whereas the icy head of Halley's comet released streams of dust particles on melting as it approached the Sun, catching the sunlight and reflecting it in orange and yellow bands, Kohoutek turned out to be a relatively clean, blue-white comet.

Astronomers have identified in Kohoutek the molecule methyl cyanide, which is believed essential in star formation; this substance was previously detected only in the vast dust clouds toward the center of the galaxy. Consequently, the conclusion is drawn by some astronomers that comet Kohoutek originated in a dust cloud outside the solar system.

11. What is the composition of the comet Kohoutek?

   (1) a nucleus, a coma, and a tail
   (2) a nucleus, a comet, and a tail
   (3) only a nucleus and a tail
   (4) only a tail
   (5) star dust

12. Why was Kohoutek not as bright as predicted?

   (1) It originated within the solar system.
   (2) It originated outside the solar system.
   (3) It originated in a dust cloud.
   (4) It did not release streams of dust particles on approaching the Sun.
   (5) It contained too much ice.

13. Why was Kohoutek expected to be spectacularly bright?

   (1) Its appearance coincided with the Christmas season.
   (2) It would pass within 13 million miles of the Sun.
   (3) It was first visible when more than 500 million miles from the Sun.
   (4) It was the third brightest object in the sky.
   (5) Its nucleus was very large, about 10,000 miles in diameter.

Questions 14–18 refer to the following article.

One of the contributions of the space age has been a new vantage point for viewing the Earth's surface from distant heights. The Earth can now be viewed by remote sensing, which can be defined as detecting an object from afar without direct contact. All our lives could be influenced by the results of the new era of accomplishment that makes possible such activities as immediate observation of natural and human-made disasters; continuous study of the ocean; monitoring and more efficient management of land, food, and water resources; discovery of additional natural resources; identification of pollution; tracing current flow along coastlines; studying the distribution of fish; and mapmaking.

In July 1972, the Earth Resources Technology Satellite (ERTS-1) was launched to make a systematic surveillance of North America and other areas from space. This unmanned satellite follows a near-polar orbit at an altitude of 920 kilometers and circles the Earth 14 times daily. As it passes overhead, images are transmitted through its various cameras to a number of receiver stations. It also collects and relays information dealing with water quality, snow depth, rainfall, and earthquake activity from about 100 stations located in remote parts of the continent.

In addition to the advantages of viewing the Earth's surface from high altitudes is the value of using infrared photography to study features that would not be visible with ordinary photography. These include plant growth, fungus infections of plants, circulation of sewage in lakes, spread of oil slicks, spawning grounds of sea life, identification of bedrock, surveys of mineral deposits, volcanic activity, and temperature differences in warm water currents, such as the Gulf Stream. It is highly probable that the ultimate benefits to be derived from this program will far exceed the original cost.

14. Which of the following best defines the term *remote sensing*?

    (1) study of fish distribution by the use of sensitive currents
    (2) release of a rowboat to see its path in an ocean current
    (3) study of the Earth's features without direct contact
    (4) measurement of the effect of an atom bomb in causing an earthquake
    (5) measurement of the depth of snow without the use of snowshoes

15. The space age has contributed all of the following values of remote sensing in viewing the Earth's surface EXCEPT

    (1) immediate observation of natural disasters
    (2) continuous surveillance of the oceans
    (3) identification of pollution
    (4) monitoring of food resources
    (5) making accurate observations of the land features of the planet Mars

16. Which of the following describes the orbit of ERTS?

    (1) 14 times daily, at an altitude of 920 kilometers
    (2) 14 times daily, at an altitude of 920 miles
    (3) 41 times daily, at an altitude of 290 miles
    (4) 290 times daily, at an altitude of 41 kilometers
    (5) It is an orbit around the Equator.

17. What can be accomplished by infrared photography?

    (1) Fungus infections of plants can be sterilized.
    (2) Circulation of sewage in lakes can be speeded up.
    (3) The spread of oil slicks can be absorbed.
    (4) The location of mineral deposits can be surveyed.
    (5) The direction of the Gulf Stream can be influenced.

18. Which statement gives correct information about the Earth Resources Technology Satellite?

    (1) The Russians were the first to launch their ERTS in 1954.
    (2) The ERTS was launched in 1972 to make a study of North America.
    (3) In 1972, the Soviet Union applied for permission to survey North America with its ERTS.
    (4) The Apollo project to the Moon was equivalent to the use of the ERTS around the Earth.
    (5) The next use of ERTS is to study the surface of the planet Venus.

Questions 19–23 are based on the following information.

The diagrams show the general effect of the Earth's atmosphere on solar radiation at middle latitudes during the clear-sky and cloudy-sky conditions. The graph shows the percentage of sunlight reflected by the Earth's surface at different latitudes in the Northern Hemisphere in winter on a clear day.

SUNLIGHT IN THE ATMOSPHERE

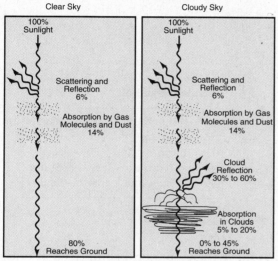

Earth's Surface (45° North Latitude)

**REFLECTION
BY THE EARTH'S SURFACE
(Clear Day)**

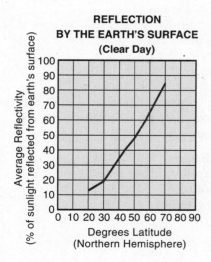

19. Approximately what percentage of the sunlight actually reaches the ground at 45° North latitude on a clear day?

   (1) 100%
   (2) 80%
   (3) 60%
   (4) 40%
   (5) 20%

20. Which factor keeps the greatest percentage of sunlight from reaching the Earth's surface on cloudy days?

   (1) absorption by cloud droplets
   (2) reflection by cloud droplets
   (3) absorption by clear-air gas molecules
   (4) reflection by clear-air gas molecules
   (5) refraction by cloud droplets

21. According to the graph, on a winter day at 70° North latitude, what approximate percentage of the sunlight is reflected by the Earth's surface?

   (1) 55%
   (2) 65%
   (3) 75%
   (4) 85%
   (5) 95%

22. Which statement best explains why, at high latitudes, reflectivity of sunlight is greater in winter than in summer?

   (1) The North Pole is tilted toward the Sun in winter.
   (2) Snow and ice reflect almost all sunlight.
   (3) The colder air holds much more moisture.
   (4) Dust settles quickly in cold air.
   (5) Snow and ice absorb all sunlight.

23. The radiation that passes through the atmosphere and reaches the Earth's surface has the greatest intensity in the form of

   (1) visible-light radiation
   (2) infrared radiation
   (3) ultraviolet radiation
   (4) radio-wave radiation
   (5) invisible light radiation

Questions 24–27 refer to the following data table and information.

Mineral	Color	Luster	Streak	Hardness	Specific Gravity	Chemical Composition
Biotite mica	black	glassy	white	soft	2.8	$K(Mg,Fe)_3(AlSi_3O_{10})(OH_2)$
Diamond	varies	glassy	colorless	hard	3.5	C
Galena	gray	metallic	gray-black	soft	7.5	PbS
Graphite	black	dull	black	soft	2.3	C
Kaolinite	white	earthy	white	soft	2.6	$Al_4(Si_4O_{10})(OH)_8$
Magnetite	black	metallic	black	hard	5.2	Fe_3O_4
Olivine	green	glassy	white	hard	3.4	$(Fe,Mg)_2SiO_4$
Pyrite	brass yellow	metallic	greenish-black	hard	5.0	FeS_2
Quartz	varies	glassy	colorless	hard	2.7	SiO_2

Definitions

Luster: a description of the general appearance of a material's surface

Streak: the color the powdered form of a mineral makes on a piece of white tile

Hardness: a general classification of the ease of a mineral at being scratched by other minerals (soft = easily scratched; hard = not easily scratched)

Chemical Symbols

Al	— Aluminum	Mg	— Magnesium
C	— Carbon	O	— Oxygen
Fe	— Iron	Pb	— Lead
H	— Hydrogen	S	— Sulfur
K	— Potassium	Si	— Silicon

24. Which minerals shown on the chart have a specific gravity greater than 4.0 and are soft?

   I. pyrite
  II. galena
 III. quartz

(1) I only
(2) II only
(3) I and II only
(4) I and III only
(5) I, II, and III

25. Which minerals on the chart contain sulfur?

   I. pyrite
  II. galena
 III. quartz

(1) I only
(2) II only
(3) I and II only
(4) I and III only
(5) I, II, and III

26. A hard glassy mineral comprised of only two different elements could be which of the following?

(1) biotite mica
(2) diamond
(3) olivine
(4) pyrite
(5) quartz

27. Which mineral exists as a different color in powdered form than it does as a solid piece?

(1) galena
(2) graphite
(3) kaolinite
(4) magnetite
(5) pyrite

Questions 28 and 29 refer to the following information.

Since land heats up more rapidly than water, the air pressure over the land is lower. As the heated air rises, it moves out to the ocean and is replaced by the cooler air blowing in from the ocean. The diagram represents a coastal region with daytime wind direction as indicated.

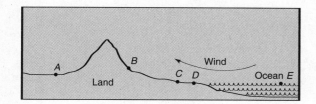

28. Which of the following best explains the direction of the wind?

    (1) the land being cooled during a clear night
    (2) more water vapor in the air over the ocean than in the air over the land
    (3) low pressure over the land and high pressure over the ocean
    (4) warm ocean currents
    (5) high pressure over the land and low pressure over the ocean

29. According to the prevailing wind direction shown in the diagram, which location probably records the highest annual precipitation?

    (1) A
    (2) B
    (3) C
    (4) D
    (5) E

Questions 30–33 are based on the following information.

A cold air mass is more dense than a warm air mass. Since two air masses do not mix, when they meet, the more dense air mass will lift the less dense mass. The boundary between two air masses is called a front.

On Wednesday, the weather service predicted that a cold front was coming and that the warm weather would end by Thursday night. The following graph describes the temperature at 6-hour intervals for 3 days.

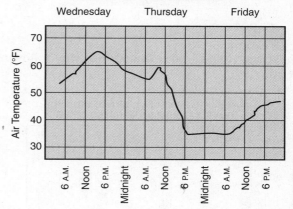

RECORD OF TEMPERATURES

30. What is the lowest temperature reached during this time period?

    (1) 30°F
    (2) 35°F
    (3) 40°F
    (4) 45°F
    (5) 50°F

31. During which interval of time did the temperature vary LEAST?

    (1) 6 P.M. Wednesday to 6 A.M. Thursday
    (2) 6 A.M. to 6 P.M. Thursday
    (3) 6 P.M. Thursday to 6 A.M. Friday
    (4) 6 A.M. to 6 P.M. Friday
    (5) 6 A.M. to noon on Thursday

32. On Thursday, from 9 A.M. to 6 P.M., the approach of which of the following was most probably responsible for the change in temperature?

    (1) warm front
    (2) cold front
    (3) stationary air
    (4) warm air mass
    (5) combination of any of these

33. On Wednesday what was the difference in the temperature from 3 A.M. to noon?

    (1) 4°
    (2) 9°
    (3) 14°
    (4) 19°
    (5) 24°

Questions 34–37 are based on the following graph.

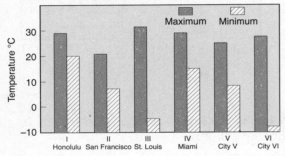

MAXIMUM & MINIMUM AVERAGE MONTHLY TEMPERATURES IN SELECTED CITIES

The graph represents data collected from six cities showing the average maximum and the average minimum temperatures for a 12-month period.

34. Of the following, which location has the highest average maximum monthly temperature?

    (1) I—Honolulu
    (2) II—San Francisco
    (3) III—St. Louis
    (4) IV—Miami
    (5) V—City V

35. Of the following, which location has the greatest difference in average monthly temperatures?

    (1) I—Honolulu
    (2) II—San Francisco
    (3) III—St. Louis
    (4) IV—Miami
    (5) V—City V

36. Between San Francisco and what other city is the variation in temperature extremes greatest?

    (1) Honolulu
    (2) Miami
    (3) St. Louis
    (4) city V
    (5) any of the above

37. To the climate of which city is the climate of city VI most similar?

    (1) I—Honolulu
    (2) II—San Francisco
    (3) III—St. Louis
    (4) IV—Miami
    (5) V—City V

Questions 38 and 39 are based on the following graph.

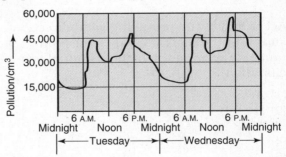

This graph shows the measurements of air pollutants as recorded in a large city for a 2-day period—July 10 and 11.

38. What is a probable cause for the increase in pollutants at 8 A.M. and 5 P.M. on the two days?

    (1) change in amount of sunlight
    (2) occurrence of precipitation
    (3) high wind velocity
    (4) heavy automobile traffic
    (5) cold fronts

39. On the basis of the trends indicated by the graph, at what time on Thursday, July 12, will the greatest amount of pollutants probably be observed?

    (1) 12 noon
    (2) 5 P.M.
    (3) 3 A.M.
    (4) 8 A.M.
    (5) midnight

40. An explosion occurs at the upper surface of an ocean. The sound returns to the original site of the explosion 4 seconds later, after having been reflected from the ocean bottom. If the speed of sound in ocean water is 4,800 feet per second, how deep is the water?

    (1) 4,800 ft.
    (2) 9,600 ft.
    (3) 14,400 ft.
    (4) 19,200 ft.
    (5) 96,000 ft.

WHAT'S YOUR SCORE?

_____right,	_____wrong
Excellent	35–40
Good	25–34
Fair	20–24

If your score is low, don't get discouraged. Perhaps earth science is a difficult subject for you. Try to find out why you failed. The analysis of correct answers that follows will help you to pinpoint your errors. If your mistake was lack of information, turn to the "Glossary of Scientific Terms" (page 423) and look up the meanings of the words you did not understand. If it was a mistake in interpretation, review the analysis of the question.

Answer Analysis

1. **3** Since each choice consists of two or more resources, each resource must be a non-renewable resource in order for that to be the correct choice. Choices with one non-renewable resource and one renewable resource can not possibly be the correct answers. Only Choice 3 meets the criteria for the correct answer.

2. **5** Statement five is an opinion, not a fact, as no mention is made of war or what we may have to do as a result of political changes that affect oil. Make sure that you distinguish facts in an article from opinions, no matter how much they may seem sensible.

3. **3** The question is asking for resources that will get more costly in the future. From reading the passage, you should know that this means nonrenewable resources. Both coal and natural gas are nonrenewable, and Choice 3 includes both of them. Choice 1 includes one of the nonrenewable answers but is not the best choice.

4. **2** This question involves a basic mathematical formula:
   distance ÷ rate = time.
   The question tells us that the average distance from the Moon to Earth is 240,000 miles, and that the average velocity of the spacecraft is 24,000 miles per hour (mph). Substitute these values in the formula:

   $$\frac{240{,}000 \text{ miles}}{24{,}000 \text{ mph}} = 10 \text{ hours} \times 2 \text{ for a}$$

   round trip = 20 hours

5. **2** In discussing the new Moon phase, earth-shine is explained.

6. **5** The diagram illustrates that the phases of the Moon result from the illumination of the Moon's surface by the Sun. Note that about half of the Moon's surface is always facing the Sun. Since the Moon revolves around the Earth, the angle between the Sun, Earth, and Moon changes, resulting in the different phases of the Moon.

7. **3** This question refers to the spring tide, when the gravitational pulls of the Moon and the Sun cause tides of great range.

8. **4** The article states that "paoleontologists have found fossil remains," implying that these scientists study fossils.

9. **5** The second paragraph states that occasionally the plates carrying landmasses collide with each other, causing an earthquake.

10. **1** This answer is given in the second paragraph. There is no mention of land bridges (Choice 2), the depth of the ocean (Choice 3), the creatures' swimming ability (Choice 4), or the animals' evolution on separate continents (Choice 5).

11. **1** A comet consists of three parts—a tightly packed nucleus consisting of frozen gases, dust particles, and stony matter, about 20–25 miles across; a hazy coma around the nucleus, composed of dust transformed into a glowing vapor under the Sun's influence, and 10,000 miles or more in diameter; and the tail, composed of ions and molecules, which stretches out millions of miles in length.

12. **4** A comet with lots of dust is spectacularly visible to the naked eye when it is near the Sun. Light and electrified particles from the Sun blast the dust out of the comet's head, and the dusty tail reflects the yellow sunlight. Apparently Kohoutek did not release much dust.

13. **3** Astronomers reasoned that since comet Kohoutek was already visible at such a great distance from the Sun in March, it would be spectacular by the time it streaked to within 13 million miles of the Sun on December 28.

14. **3** *Remote sensing*, the ability to view the Earth's surface from the vantage point of heights, is a contribution of the space age.

15. **5** No mention is made of studying other planets in this project.

16. **1** The ERTS (Earth Resource Technology Satellite) follows a near-polar orbit at an altitude of 920 kilometers and circles the Earth 14 times daily.

17. **4** The use of infrared photography permits the study of features of the Earth's surface that would not be visible with ordinary photography.

18. **2** ERTS was launched to make a systematic surveillance of North America and other areas from space.

19. **2** The left-hand diagram shows that, when there is a clear sky, 80% of the sunlight reaches the ground.

20. **2** The right-hand diagram indicates that, when the sky is cloudy, cloud reflection returns 30% to 60% of the sunlight. This is greater than the percentage scattered and reflected by the atmosphere (6%), absorbed by gas molecules and dust (14%), or absorbed in clouds (5% to 20%).

21. **4** Find 70° North latitude on the horizontal axis of the graph. Trace upward until you reach the curve. The average reflectivity of sunlight (vertical axis) is 85% for this latitude.

22. **2** Compared to other darker surfaces, snow and ice are both very good reflectors of sunlight. This fact explains why surfaces covered with snow or ice do not heat up as quickly.

23. **1** The atmosphere is a better absorber of infrared, ultraviolet, or radio-wave radiation than of visible light. As a result, the greatest intensity of sunlight passing through the atmosphere and reaching the Earth's surface represents the visible part of the electromagnetic spectrum.

24. **2** Of the minerals listed in the choices, only galena, magnetite, and pyrite have specific gravities greater than 4.0. This lets you eliminate two of the choices. Of the three choices with a specific gravity greater than 4.0, only galena is soft. In a question that asks you to analyze more than one thing, it can be helpful to deal with those items one at a time (in this case, specific gravity then hardness).

25. **3** The chart shows that pyrite is FeS_2 and that galena is PbS, making both of them sulfur-containing minerals. Quartz contains silicon (symbol Si, not S). Make sure to read all material in a table very carefully, as many scientific abbreviations look similar to one another.

26. **5** Here is another case where you are asked to analyze more than one factor. You are looking for a mineral that is hard, glassy, and composed of only two different elements. Of the choices listed, diamond, olivine, and quartz are hard and glassy. The chart tells you that diamond is made of a single type of atom (carbon), while olivine is made of several types of atoms.

Only quartz fits all the criteria for the question.

27. **5** This question is asking you to look for a mineral with a different streak than its original color. You do not need to look at minerals on the table that are not choices for this question. Among the five choices, only pyrite has a different streak than color.

28. **3** As the air above the land heats up, its pressure becomes lower than that of the air above the water. This difference in pressure explains the direction of wind, which moves from high to low pressure.

29. **2** As the air blowing in from the ocean reaches the mountainous area, it tends to rise. As it rises, it cools, causing moisture in the air to condense. This condensation would probably cause location *B* to record the highest annual precipitation.

30. **2** The lowest temperature occurred during the period of time between 6 P.M. Thursday and 6 A.M. Friday. At this time, the temperature remained fairly constant (at about 35°F).

31. **3** The temperature remained almost constant from 6 P.M. Thursday to 6 A.M. Friday, as indicated by the horizontal line on the graph.

32. **2** On Thursday from 9 A.M. to 6 P.M. the temperature dropped steadily. This may have been caused by the approach of a cold front. As the cold front approached, it brought cold air to replace the warm air.

33. **2** On Wednesday at 3 A.M., the temperature was 52°F. By noon, the temperature had risen to 61°F. The temperature, therefore, rose 9°F over a period of 9 hours.

34. **3** The solid bar is tallest for St. Louis, indicating that it has the highest average maximum monthly temperature.

35. **5** In city I, the average maximum temperature is about 29° and the average minimum is about 20°: 29° − 20° = 9°. In city II, the average maximum temperature is about 20° and the average minimum is about 7°: 20° − 7° = 13°. In city IV, the average maximum temperature is about 30° and the average minimum is about 15°: 30° − 15° = 15°. In city V, the average maximum temperature is about 26° and the average minimum is about 9°: 26° − 9° = 17°. City VI has the greatest difference since the average maximum temperature is about 29° and the average minimum is − 8°: 29° − (− 8°) = 37°.

36. **3** Except for city VI (which is not one of the choices), the difference between the length of the two bars is greatest for St. Louis.

37. **3** Cities III and VI have similar maximum and minimum temperatures and would therefore probably have similar climates. However, since climate also depends upon the amount of moisture, it is possible that the two cities have some differences in climates.

38. **4** Automobile emission adds pollutants to the atmosphere. Traffic is heaviest at 8 A.M. and 5 P.M. in most large cities. Changes in the amount of sunlight generally have little or no effect on pollution levels. Precipitation tends to remove some pollutants, such as particulate matter. High winds decrease pollution levels by blowing away polluted air and replacing it with fresh, clean air.

39. **2** Since the pattern indicates that the highest pollution level occurs at 5 P.M., it is reasonable to assume that the highest level will also be reached at that time on the following day.

40. **2** One-half of the 4 seconds is the time that the sound vibrations took to reach the bottom of the ocean:

(2 sec) (4,800 ft/sec) = 9,600 ft.

PHYSICAL SCIENCE (CHEMISTRY)

Questions 1–4 refer to the following information.

A student placed a candle on a tabletop. For the first trial in her experiment, she carefully inverted a 500 ml jar over the candle and measured the time it took for the flame to go out. In trial #2, she repeated the experiment, only this time she filled the jar with exhaled air, rather than room air. For trial #3, she again filled the jar with exhaled air, but only after she had run in place for five minutes. Again, she noted and recorded the time for the flame to go out.

1. The main goal of the experiment was to show which of the following?

   (1) Exhaled air stops the process of combustion.
   (2) Candles go out when covered by jars.
   (3) The composition of exhaled air can vary depending on activity level.
   (4) Exhaled air extinguishes flames effectively.
   (5) Inhaled air has little effect on combustion.

2. Arrange in order from shortest to longest, the length of time the flame would last in each trial.

   (1) 1,3,2
   (2) 1,2,3
   (3) 3,2,1
   (4) 3,1,2
   (5) 2,3,1

3. Which trial served as the control for the experiment?

   (1) one only
   (2) two only
   (3) three only
   (4) one and two only
   (5) two and three only

4. What caused the flame to go out in each trial?

   (1) an increase in carbon dioxide levels
   (2) lack of combustion product levels
   (3) a decrease in carbon dioxide levels
   (4) an increase in oxygen levels
   (5) a decrease in oxygen levels

Questions 5–9 refer to the following figure.

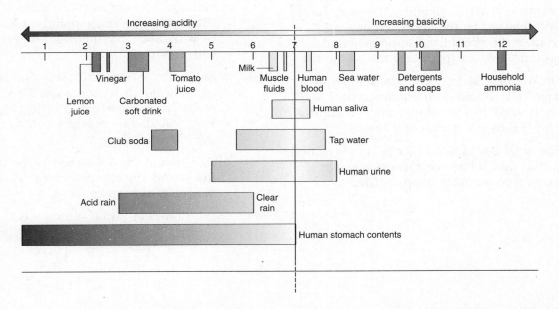

The figure above shows the pH scale and the range of pH values for some common substances. By definition, the lower the pH the more acidic a substance is, and the higher the pH the more basic it is. Neutral substances have a pH of 7. Acids and bases often react to form common ionic compounds known as salts.

5. Which of the following substances is the most basic?

   (1) detergent
   (2) ammonia
   (3) milk
   (4) lemon juice
   (5) club soda

6. According to the chart, which of the following might have a pH that is neutral?

     I. human saliva
    II. sea water
   III. rainwater

   (1) I only
   (2) II only
   (3) III only
   (4) I and II only
   (5) I and III only

7. Which of the following combinations could produce a salt?

   (1) lemon juice and vinegar
   (2) tomato juice and lemon juice
   (3) ammonia and lemon juice
   (4) sea water and ammonia
   (5) detergent and ammonia

8. Which of the following has an acidic pH?

   (1) clear rain
   (2) acid rain
   (3) neither acid rain nor clear rain
   (4) both acid rain and clear rain
   (5) either depending on where the rain falls

9. Which of the following lists shows substances that increase in basicity?

   (1) milk, sea water, tomato juice
   (2) club soda, ammonia, human blood
   (3) acid rain, vinegar, detergent
   (4) milk, human blood, ammonia
   (5) sea water, detergent, lemon juice

10. The three phases of matter are the three states in which matter can exist—as a solid, a liquid, or a gas. Substances change from one to another phase as their temperatures change. Temperature reflects the rate of molecular movement, slow movement indicating colder temperature, and fast movement warmer temperature. For most substances, the freezing temperature and the melting temperature are the same, as are the boiling point and the condensation point.

    Antifreeze is added to the water-filled cooling system of an automobile engine to protect it from the effects of both overheating and freezing. This is possible because antifreeze

    (1) doesn't freeze
    (2) has a much lower freezing temperature than water and a higher boiling point
    (3) consists of alcohols that resist corrosion and can get to all parts of the car's cooling system
    (4) has slower moving molecules than water
    (5) can be used in various amounts to protect against a variety of temperatures

<u>Questions 11–14</u> refer to the following graph.

The graph below shows the solubility of some common salts in 100 grams of water at various temperatures. Solutions with an amount dissolved equal to the graph for that compound are said to be saturated. Those with less are called unsaturated.

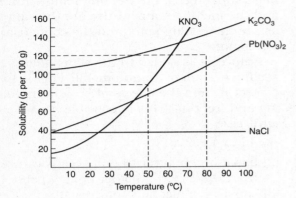

11. How many grams of potassium nitrate (KNO_3) would be able to be dissolved in 100 grams of water at 70°C?

    (1) 30
    (2) 70
    (3) 85
    (4) 100
    (5) 140

12. Which substance on the graph shows no change in solubility with temperature?

    (1) KNO_3
    (2) K_2CO_3
    (3) $Pb(NO_3)_2$
    (4) NaCl
    (5) None of the substances exhibit this property.

13. How many grams of NaCl can dissolve in 200 grams of water at 40°C?

    (1) 19 grams
    (2) 38 grams
    (3) 57 grams
    (4) 76 grams
    (5) 20 grams

14. The symbol for sodium chloride is NaCl, that of potassium carbonate is K_2CO_3, and that of lead chloride is $PbCl_2$. What is the name of the compound $Pb(NO_3)_2$?

    (1) lead carbonate
    (2) lead sodium
    (3) lead nitrate
    (4) potassium nitrate
    (5) lead sodium

<u>Questions 15–20</u> refer to the following article.

Nature has her own ways of purifying water. These methods can be physical, chemical, or biological. As a stream flows, the water becomes cleaner because sediments, for example, are diminished by the addition of more and more water, and they may be deposited along the banks of the stream.

Today, however, in our technologically complex civilization, human activity may cause some dangerous components to remain in stream water. Communities that wish to utilize water from "self-purified" streams have to use precautions, including filtration and chlorination.

Aeration, which may be accomplished in nature by wind action, turbulent flow, and waterfalls, causes an exchange of gases between the atmosphere and the water. In this way hydrogen sulfide, carbon dioxide, and methane are liberated from the water, and oxygen is absorbed from the atmosphere.

Light has an important effect on water. Light stimulates photosynthesis in aquatic plant life, and by this process carbon dioxide is absorbed and oxygen is liberated. Furthermore, the plants remove and use organic material that may be dissolved in the water. Light also has a germicidal effect on the surface of the water, although this effect below the surface is minimal.

A process called sedimentation removes organic bacterial food from water. Sedimentation, which is caused by gravity, occurs when the water is filtered through some fine material such as sand. Sedimentation is most effective in quiet waters.

Some bacteria help clean the water by oxidizing organic material, converting it into basic mineral substances. In the absence of oxygen, other organisms, known as anaerobic bacteria, can split organic compounds and prepare the way for subsequent oxidation. These anaerobic bacteria thrive at the bottom of bodies of water where there is a great deal of concentrated pollution.

Biological cycles also purify water. Protozoa, one-celled animals, thrive on bacteria. As the bacteria are reduced in population, green algae appear. They in turn consume carbon dioxide, nitrates, and ammonia and produce oxygen. Large invertebrate animals, such as worms and mollusks, appear and feed on the deposits at the bottom.

15. Which of the following prevents streams from purifying themselves?

    (1) human activity
    (2) evaporation
    (3) condensation
    (4) filtration
    (5) chlorination

16. What is accomplished by aeration of water?

    (1) loss of oxygen and carbon dioxide
    (2) loss of methane and gain of oxygen
    (3) gain of carbon dioxide and methane
    (4) gain of hydrogen and oxygen
    (5) gain of carbon dioxide and oxygen

17. Which of these causes sedimentation?

    (1) wind action
    (2) bacterial residue
    (3) turbulent water
    (4) gravity
    (5) organic material

18. Which of the following statements is correct in regard to the process of photosynthesis?

    (1) It is carried on by all protozoa.
    (2) Oxygen is necessary for this process to occur.
    (3) Light is necessary for this process to occur.
    (4) Carbon dioxide is given off during this process.
    (5) This process has a germicidal effect on deep stagnant water.

19. Which of these would best remove wastes at the bottom of ponds?

    (1) fish
    (2) aerobic bacteria
    (3) green plants
    (4) anaerobic bacteria
    (5) algae

20. All of the following tend to purify water EXCEPT

    (1) sedimentation
    (2) aeration
    (3) light
    (4) aquatic plants
    (5) bacteria

WHAT'S YOUR SCORE?

_____right,   _____wrong
Excellent   16–20
Good   13–15
Fair   10–12

If your score is low, don't get discouraged. Perhaps chemistry is a difficult subject for you. Try to find out why you failed. The analysis of correct answers that follows will help you to pinpoint your errors. If your mistake was lack of information, turn to the "Glossary of Scientific Terms" (page 423) and look up the meanings of the words you did not understand. If it was a mistake in interpretation, review the analysis of the question.

Answer Analysis

1. **3** The experiment showed that exhaled air can have different effects on a flame, depending on its composition. The composition of the air changed as the student's activity level changed. Since the student varied the air composition by exercising at different levels, studying this must have been the purpose of the experiment.

2. **3** The candle would burn the shortest amount of time in the air after the vigorous exercise, a bit longer when filled with exhaled air, and longer still when filled with inhaled air. Notice that the question asked you to arrange from shortest to longest.

3. **1** A control is a part of the experiment used as a reference point, for comparison. In this case, nonexhaled room air was the starting point for the experiment and was the reference used for comparison.

4. **5** The flame was extinguished by a lack of oxygen. While it is true that there was also an increase in carbon dioxide levels, that alone is not enough to put out a flame. It is the lack of oxygen that caused the flame to go out.

5. **2** 5. The pH scale is set up so that the higher the pH value, the more basic (and less acidic) something is. Ammonia has the highest pH value and thus is the most basic.

6. **1** Only human saliva has a pH that covers the value of 7, which is neutral. Sea water is 8 and rainwater spans a range up to 6.

7. **3** A salt is the product of the reaction of an acid and a base. Thus, you need to find a substance with a pH of less than 7 and with a pH of more than 7. Only Choice 3 meets these criteria.

8. **4** It most likely comes as no surprise that acid rain is acidic, but clear rain is also acidic, although much less so. Clear rain has a pH of about 6, which is just slightly acidic.

9. **4** To find a list that shows increasing basicity, you need to find substances listed from low pH to high pH. Only Choice 4 fits.

10. **2** The answer to this question must be derived by analyzing the information and realizing that, to keep something—in this case, water—from freezing, you have to add a substance that has a much lower freezing point than water. Similarly, to protect the same engine from overheating, you have to add a substance that has a higher boiling point than water. Antifreeze, in combination with water, can accomplish these purposes. Antifreeze and water will freeze at a low enough temperature, so Choice 1 is not valid. Choice 3 is not a good answer because resistance to corrosion is not the subject. If anything, the molecules in antifreeze have to move faster than water molecules, so Choice 4 is incorrect. Choice 5 may or

may not be true, but it is not as logical an answer as Choice 2.

11. **5** The graph shows that at 70°C about 140 grams of potassium nitrate can be dissolved. Notice that you often have to do a little estimating to interpret information on a graph. However, the choices given are designed so that if your estimate is slightly different than that of the test creator, you will still get the correct answer.

12. **4** All of the substances shown on the graph increase in solubility as the temperature increases (they have an upward or positive slope) except NaCl, which remains flat (it shows no change).

13. **4** The graph shows the amount that can be dissolved in 100 grams of water. Since the question deals with twice as much (200 grams of water) you have to double the answer from the graph. The graph shows that about 38 grams can dissolve in 100 grams of water. Doubling this gives 76 grams. Notice that the choices are spaced so that if you estimated slightly differently, only choice 4 would be close to the answer.

14. **3** Lead is Pb and nitrate is NO_3. Combining them gives lead nitrate.

15. **1** Humans are responsible for many forms of water pollution, including those due to industrial processes.

16. **2** During aeration of water, methane and carbon dioxide are liberated, and oxygen is absorbed from the air.

17. **4** Objects heavier than water will drop to the bottom of the water. This is an effect of gravity.

18. **3** Green plants absorb carbon dioxide and liberate oxygen during photosynthesis. The plants need light in order to carry on the process.

19. **4** Anaerobic bacteria thrive in environments, such as the bottom of ponds, where there is little oxygen.

20. **5** While bacteria of decay may at times decompose organic wastes, in this question the other four choices are definite methods of water purification. Another justification for Choice 5 is that bacteria may be pathogenic.

PHYSICAL SCIENCE (PHYSICS)

Questions 1 and 2 refer to the following information.

As you break a beam of light, in one case you may be operating an automatic door opener and in another case you may be setting off a burglar alarm system. Actually your body is breaking a beam of light that is focused on a photoelectric cell.

That beam has been producing a flow of electrons from the photoelectric cell. When your body interrupts the beam, the current stops. The result is to close a relay that starts a motor.

Almost a hundred years ago Heinrich Hertz found that certain substances give off a weak electric current when struck by a beam of light. This is the basis for the electric eye, in which light energy is changed into electricity.

1. Which of the following illustrates a change from mechanical energy to electrical energy?

   (1) electric iron
   (2) steam engine
   (3) fluorescent lamp
   (4) electric eye
   (5) electric generator

2. A photoelectric cell is a device that

   (1) opens doors
   (2) sets off burglar alarms
   (3) breaks a beam of light
   (4) produces electric energy from light
   (5) starts a motor

Questions 3–6 refer to the following chart.

The table below shows the speed of sound in a variety of materials. The temperature is given as well.

Material (Temp)	Speed of sound in meters/second (m/s)
Gases	
Air (0°C)	330
Air (25°C)	346
Air (100°C)	390
Helium (0°C)	972
Hydrogen (0°C)	1,280
Oxygen (0°C)	320
Liquids	
Water (25°C)	1,490
Sea water (25°C)	1,540
Solids	
Copper (25°C)	3,810
Iron (25°C)	5,000

3. What happens to the speed of sound as density increases?

   (1) It is slower as density increases.
   (2) It is faster as density increases.
   (3) It is unaffected by the density of the material.
   (4) It is faster as solids are heated.
   (5) It is slower as solids are heated.

4. What is the likely speed of sound in air at 75°C?

   (1) 316 m/s
   (2) 336 m/s
   (3) 356 m/s
   (4) 376 m/s
   (5) 396 m/s

5. Lead is a solid that is more dense than either copper or iron. Which of the following is a reasonable speed of sound in lead?

(1) 500 m/s
(2) 1,000 m/s
(3) 2,000 m/s
(4) 4,000 m/s
(5) 6,000 m/s

6. The table below shows the molecular masses (in amu) of some common gases at 0°C. What is the likely speed of sound of argon gas at 0°C?

Hydrogen	2
Helium	4
Oxygen	32
Argon	40

(1) 1,200 m/s
(2) 1,000 m/s
(3) 800 m/s
(4) 400 m/s
(5) 200 m/s

Questions 7 and 8 refer to the following information.

Energy can take two forms, potential and kinetic. Potential energy is typically exemplified by an object at rest, its energy ready and waiting to be expressed. Kinetic energy is exemplified by an object in motion. An example of potential energy is a parked car. Kinetic energy is the car in motion.

7. Which of the following is NOT an example of potential energy?

(1) a runner at the starting point
(2) a bag of golf balls
(3) an exercise bicycle
(4) a sleeping child
(5) a falling book

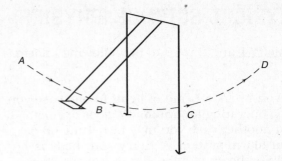

8. As a child on the swing shown in the diagram reaches the highest point (A), the swing seems to hesitate an instant before it begins to fall back. This hesitation is repeated at the other end of the arc (D). How is the energy of this motion expressed in the diagram at the points marked A through D?

(1) potential, kinetic, potential, kinetic
(2) kinetic, potential, kinetic, potential
(3) potential, kinetic, potential, potential
(4) potential, kinetic, kinetic, potential
(5) kinetic, kinetic, potential, potential

Questions 9–11 refer to the following article.

The study of sounds outside the range of normal human hearing is known as ultrasonics. Most people are capable of hearing sounds with a vibrational range of between 20 and 20,000 hertz (vibrations per second). Bats use sounds with a range of greater than 50,000 hertz to help them "see." A bat sends out a sound and it bounces off walls and other objects, returning to the bat's ear. The bat's brain then processes these echoes and determines the location of objects around the bat. In this way, bats can catch food and avoid hidden objects no matter how little light there is.

Sound waves usually reflect back off a hard smooth surface, much like light reflecting off a mirror. Softer materials tend to absorb sounds. Submarines use sonar (sound navigation and ranging) to detect objects in the sea around them. Sound waves are sent out from the submarine and the time it takes the echo to return to the boat can be used to determine the depth of the water, or the distance to an object.

9. Which of the following would be an ultra-sonic sound?

   (1) 20 hertz
   (2) 200 hertz
   (3) 2,000 hertz
   (4) 20,000 hertz
   (5) 200,000 hertz

10. What is a possible way to help reduce echoes in a room?

    (1) Use insulated glass for the windows.
    (2) Have people talk softly.
    (3) Raise the height of the ceiling.
    (4) Hang soft drapes and curtains.
    (5) Use reflective paints.

11. What is the proper name for a reflected sound?

    (1) frequency
    (2) ultrasonic
    (3) echo
    (4) vibration
    (5) Hertz

Questions 12–17 refer to the following information.

Although both a jet engine and a rocket engine operate on the principle of Newton's third law, they differ in that a jet must take in oxygen from the air to burn its fuel, but a rocket must carry its own oxygen. In both engines gases escaping under great pressure in one direction exert a push on the engine in the opposite direction. According to Newton's third law, for each action there is an equal and opposite reaction. You can illustrate the principle by blowing up a rubber balloon and then letting it go as you allow the air to escape. Notice that the balloon moves forward as the air escapes in the opposite direction.

12. Which of the following describes Newton's third law?

    (1) an object at rest
    (2) gravitational force
    (3) objects in uniform motion
    (4) falling bodies
    (5) every force is accompanied by an equal and opposite reaction force

13. What characteristic of rocket engines is NOT characteristic of jet engines?

    (1) method of obtaining oxygen
    (2) method of using oxygen
    (3) reaction to the escaping gases
    (4) application of Newton's third law
    (5) methods involved in the burning process

14. Which of the following would be best explained by Newton's third law?

    (1) A balloon with a lower density than air rises.
    (2) A bat strikes a ball and the bat breaks.
    (3) A sled accelerates while sliding downhill.
    (4) A boat slows down when its engines are turned off.
    (5) A rock, thrown horizontally, falls to the ground.

15. Which of the following is (are) NOT found in an airplane with a jet engine?

    (1) ailerons
    (2) a fuselage
    (3) propellers
    (4) rudders
    (5) flaps

16. What propels jet planes?

    (1) the thrust of hot gases
    (2) propeller blades
    (3) rocket motors
    (4) steam turbines
    (5) any of these

17. Imagine that you are standing on a frictionless ice rink, holding a large, heavy ball. What will happen if you throw the ball forward?

    (1) You will move backwards.
    (2) You will move forward, following the ball.
    (3) You will not move at all.
    (4) How you move depends on how you are standing.
    (5) How you move depends on how heavy the ball is.

Questions 18–20 refer to the following figure.

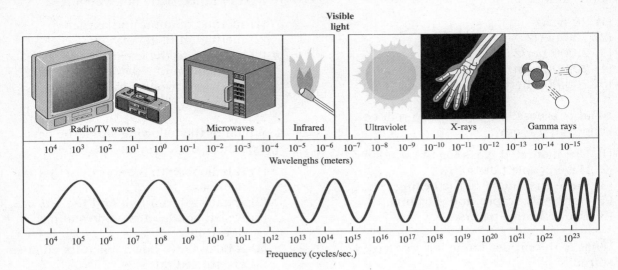

The figure above shows the range of electromagnetic energies known as the electromagnetic spectrum. Each part of the spectrum is characterized by its own wavelength (specified here in meters) and frequency (described here as cycles/sec). A key feature of the spectrum is that the higher the frequency the greater the energy. Notice that each part of the spectrum covers a range.

18. What is the most energetic part of the electromagnetic spectrum?

    (1) microwaves
    (2) gamma rays
    (3) visible light
    (4) radio and TV waves
    (5) x-rays

19. What is the least energetic part of the electromagnetic spectrum?

    (1) blue light
    (2) red light
    (3) radio and TV waves
    (4) gamma rays
    (5) microwaves

TIP

In illustrations, look for patterns. In the one at the top of the page, as wavelength increases, frequency decreases

20. Violet light is more energetic than red light. Which of the following statements about violet light and red light is true?

    (1) Violet light has a longer wavelength than red light.
    (2) Violet light has a lower frequency than red light.
    (3) Violet light has a higher frequency than red light.
    (4) Violet light and red light both have the same frequency, so we see them both equally well.
    (5) Red light is close to infrared light on the spectrum.

WHAT'S YOUR SCORE?

_____right,	_____wrong
Excellent	16–20
Good	13–15
Fair	10–12

If your score is low, don't get discouraged. Perhaps physics is a difficult subject for you. Try to find out why you failed. The analysis of correct answers that follows will help you to pinpoint your errors. If your mistake was lack of information, turn to the "Glossary of Scientific Terms" (page 423) and look up the meanings of the words you did not understand. If it was a mistake in interpretation, review the analysis of the question.

Answer Analysis

1. **5** An electric generator is driven by steam or water power. This rotary mechanical energy is converted into electrical energy. In an electric iron (Choice 1), electrical energy is converted into heat energy when electricity passing through the core heats the element. In a steam engine (Choice 2), steam expands and pushes a piston that is attached to a drive shaft. Thus, heat energy is converted into mechanical energy. In a fluorescent lamp (Choice 3), electrical energy is converted into light energy. The electric current vaporizes some mercury in the lamp, and ultraviolet rays are produced. These rays strike the inner coating of the lamp and cause the chemical phosphorus in it to glow. The electric eye (Choice 4) or photoelectric cell and its operation are described in the selection. Light energy is converted into electric energy.

2. **4** All of the events in the choices do occur, but the photoelectric cell does nothing but produce electricity when light strikes it.

3. **2** Looking at the chart you can see that the speed of sound is least in gases and greatest in solids. Since solids are more dense than liquids, which are more dense than gases, the speed of sound increases as density increases.

4. **4** The speed of sound in air at 75°C must be in between that of air at 25°C and air at 100°C. Since 75°C is closer to 100°C than it is to 25°C, you would expect the speed of sound in air to be closer to 390 m/s than to 346 m/s. Only choice 4 meets this criterion. Notice that choices 1 and 5 are both outside the range of the speeds of sound given and can be eliminated easily.

5. **5** Since lead is more dense than the other two solids, you would expect sound to travel faster in lead than either copper or iron.

6. **5** From a comparison of the chart at the beginning of this block of questions and the molecular masses, you can see that as the molecular mass increases, the speed of sound in that gas decreases. Hydrogen is the lightest gas on the table and is also the one with the greatest speed of sound. Argon is heavier than oxygen so you would expect the speed of sound in argon to be less than in oxygen.

7. **5** The only moving object among the choices is the falling book. All the other objects mentioned are stationary; therefore they are examples of potential energy.

8. **4** The passage mentions that the swing pauses at the highest points, *A* and *D*, where it changes direction. At those times the energy is potential energy. At the other points, *B* and *C*, the energy is kinetic.

9. **5** Ultrasonic sounds are outside the range of human hearing, which is 20 hertz to 20,000 hertz. Choices 1 to 4 are all within that range.

10. **4** Echoes are caused by reflected sound waves and sounds reflect best off hard smooth surfaces. If you wanted to reduce echoes, you would reduce hard smooth surfaces. Drapes and curtains reduce the amount of flat wall space a sound wave could bounce off.

11. **3** The passage gives you the definition of an echo as being a reflected sound wave.

12. **5** For each action there is an equal and opposite reaction.

13. **1** The passage mentions that a rocket must carry its own oxygen supply, but the jet uses the oxygen of the air.

14. **2** When the bat strikes the ball, the ball strikes the bat, causing it to break.

15. **3** In jet engines the force of hot, expanding gases provides the energy that drives the plane forward. In other engines, the blades of the propeller pull against the air as they whirl. Ailerons (Choice 1) are flaps on the rear edge of the wing of the plane that help change the direction of the plane in flight. The fuselage (Choice 2) is the body of the plane. Rudders (Choice 4) are the part used to swing the nose of the plane and prevent it from slipping when making a turn. The flaps (Choice 5) act as brakes in the air and slow down the motion for a smooth landing.

16. **1** According to Newton's third law, the action of the ejected gases produces a reaction that thrusts the plane forward.

17. **1** If you push the ball forward, the ball will push you backward.

18. **2** The figure shows you frequencies and wavelengths for various parts of the electromagnetic spectrum. The information given in addition to the figure tells you that the greater the frequency, the greater the energy. So to find the most energetic part of the electromagnetic spectrum, you would look for the part with the greatest frequency.

19. **3** Use the same approach as in question 18, but in this case you are looking for the least energetic part of the electromagnetic spectrum. This is the section with the smallest frequency or the largest wavelength, which is radio/TV waves.

20. **3** Because violet light is more energetic than red light it must have a higher frequency and a shorter (or smaller) wavelength. Choice 5 is correct but has nothing to do with answering this question.

LANGUAGE ARTS, READING

Reading and Interpreting Literature and the Arts

CHAPTER 16

BASIC READING SKILLS

Reading consists of a complex combination of skills. The writer sets forth his or her ideas using the medium of language consisting of printed words. If the writer has stated the ideas clearly, they have been well organized and well developed. You, the reader, must draw meaning from the ideas expressed on the printed page. In addition, there may be ideas that are implied rather than openly stated. For example, a woman dressed in black is described as *grieving*. The implication is that she has lost a loved one, even if this fact is not stated in so many words.

Reading requires the use of a number of skills so you can decode or derive from the language used the meaning intended by the writer, whether it is explicitly stated or suggested by implication.

These skills are finding the main idea, finding details, and making inferences.

You read to find the main idea of the selection.

You find the main idea in a variety of places. It may be stated directly in the first sentence (easy to find). It may be stated in the final sentence to which the others build up (a bit harder to find). It may have to be discovered within the passage (most difficult); an example (note the underscored words) occurs in the following paragraph:

> Several students were seriously injured in football games last Saturday. The week before, several more were hospitalized. <u>Football has become a dangerous sport.</u> The piling up of players in a scrimmage often
> (5) leads to serious injury. Perhaps some rule changes would lessen the number who are hurt.

TIP

To find the main idea of a passage, ask yourself any or all of these questions:

1. What is the *main idea* of the passage? (Why did the author write it?)
2. What is the *topic sentence* of the paragraph or paragraphs (the sentence that the other sentences build on or flow from)?
3. What *title* would I give this selection?

TIP

To find the main details of a passage, the questions to ask yourself are these:

1. What examples illustrate the main point?
2. What reasons or proof support the main idea?
3. What arguments are presented for or against the main idea?
4. What specific qualities are offered about the idea or subject being defined?
5. Into what classifications is a larger group broken down?
6. What are the similarities and differences between two ideas or subjects being compared or contrasted?

You may also find that the main idea is not directly expressed, but can only be inferred from the selection as a whole.

> The plane landed at 4 P.M. As the door opened, the crowd burst into a long, noisy demonstration. The waiting mob surged against the police guard lines. Women were screaming. Teenagers were yelling for autographs
> (5)   or souvenirs. The visitor smiled and waved at his fans.

The main idea of the paragraph is not expressed, but it is clear that some popular hero, movie or rock star is being welcomed enthusiastically at the airport.

You read to find the details that explain or develop the main idea.

How do you do this? You must determine how the writer develops the main idea. He or she may give examples to illustrate that idea, or may give reasons why the statement that is the main idea is true, or may give arguments for or against a position stated as the main idea. The writer may define a complex term and give a number of aspects of a complicated belief (such as democracy). He or she may also classify a number of objects within a larger category. Finally, the writer may compare two ideas or objects (show how they are similar) or contrast them (show how they are different).

In the paragraph immediately above, you can see that the sentence "You must determine how the writer develops the main idea" *is* the main idea. Six ways in which the writer can develop the main idea follow. These are the details that actually develop the main idea of the paragraph.

You read to make inferences by putting together ideas that are expressed to arrive at other ideas that are not.

In other words, you draw conclusions from the information presented by the author. You do this by locating relevant details and determining their relationships (time sequence, place sequence, cause and effect).

How do you do this? You can put one fact together with a second to arrive at a third that is not stated. You can apply a given fact to a different situation. You can predict an outcome based on the facts given.

READING LITERATURE

There are three periods of literature on the GED examination: pre-1920, 1920–1960, and post-1960. The basic reading skills apply to all types of literature.

Literature after 1960 is easier to read because you are more likely to have shared some of the same experiences as the writer. Also, you are generally more familiar with the language of the writer. Because the selections are drawn from sources that you read quite frequently—newspapers and magazines, for example—they should be no more difficult than the usual materials geared to the high school graduate.

Literature before 1960 differs from the more current literature in a number of ways. The settings are certainly different because they go back at least 40–200 years. Also, the style of writing is more complicated. The vocabulary is less familiar. Some of the subject matter may be dated for today's reader. On the other hand, this type of literature deals with the eternal emotions of love, hate, greed, loyalty, self-sacrifice, joy, fear, among others. And many of the themes are eternal—the relationship of man to his fellow man and woman, of man to God, of man to nature, of man to his family, of man to his country.

Reading literature before 1960 requires patience, but it can be greatly rewarding. Try to imagine the unfamiliar setting. Reread the difficult sentences. Get the meaning of the unfamiliar word from its context. Find the application to life today of the theme of the selection. Continued practice will make these worthwhile tasks easier and the literature more satisfying.

READING PROSE, POETRY, AND DRAMA

In addition to the reading skills required in general reading, to read literary material, additional special skills are necessary, namely the ability to: recognize the mood of the selection and the purpose for which it was written; deal with involved sentences and sentence structure; figure out unusual word meanings from the sentences in which they appear; interpret figures of speech. (See the Glossary of Literary Terms beginning on page 504.)

Read carefully the following treatment of these special skills and then go to the sample reading passages and the questions and analyzed answers based on them to get a feeling for these special, and necessary, skills.

LOCATING THE MAIN IDEA

Depending upon the type of passage—poetry, fiction, essay, drama—the technique of finding the main idea may vary. In the essay, for example, the main idea may very well appear as a straightforward statement, usually expressed in the topic sentence. In this particular case, the trick is to find the topic sentence. In works of fiction, poetry, or drama, the main idea might be found in a line of dialogue or exposition, or within a long, flowing line of verse.

Prose

In reading *prose*, the main unit is the paragraph. Since all the paragraphs you will encounter on the GED examination have been chosen for their "loaded" content—that is, because they contain a number of ideas offering possibilities for questions—it is important that you learn how to locate the main idea. This, in turn, will enable you to understand many of the subordinate (less important) elements of the paragraph—all of which may also be the basis for examination questions.

TIP

To make inferences from a passage, ask yourself the following questions:

1. From the facts presented, what conclusions can I draw?
2. What is being suggested, in addition to what is being stated?
3. What will be the effect of something that is described?
4. What will happen next (after what is being described)?
5. What applications does the principle or idea presented have?

The topic sentence containing the main idea is used in five standard patterns:

1. The topic sentence, expressing the main idea, may introduce the paragraph and be followed by sentences containing details that explain, exemplify, prove, or support the idea, or add interest.

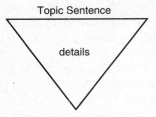

In *Alice in Wonderland*, Lewis Carroll created a world of fantasy out of essentially real creatures, transformed into whimsy by the odd patterns of a dream. Sitting with her sister by a stream, Alice sees a rabbit; as she dozes off, the rabbit becomes larger, dons a waistcoat and a pocket watch, and acquires human speech.

2. The topic sentence may appear at the end of the paragraph, with a series of details leading to the main idea.

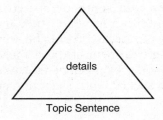

The small, darting rabbit on the riverbank becomes a huge White Rabbit, complete with waistcoat and pocket watch. The cards in a discarded deck become the Queen of Hearts and her court. The real world of Alice Liddell becomes, through the odd patterns of the dream, the fantasy world of *Alice in Wonderland*.

3. The selection may begin with a broad generalization (topic sentence) followed by details that support the main idea and lead to another broad generalization that is called the "summary sentence" (conclusion).

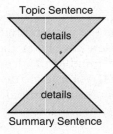

The elements of the real world become, through the strange, shifting patterns of the dream, objects and creatures of curiosity and whimsy. A scurrying rabbit becomes a humanized White Rabbit; a deck of cards becomes the court of the Queen of Hearts; a kitten becomes a chess Queen. In *Alice in Wonderland* reality becomes fantasy and, for a while, fantasy becomes reality.

4. The topic sentence may appear in the body of the paragraph.

When Alice goes through the looking glass, she enters a garden where the flowers speak. In a dark forest, a fawn befriends her. <u>The dream world reverses the events of the real world</u>. The Lion and the Unicorn come off their shield and do battle. The Red Queen, originally a kitten of Alice's pet cat Dinah, gives Alice instructions in etiquette.

5. The selection may contain *no expressed topic sentence* but consist of a series of sentences giving details and implying a central thought.

A deck of cards becomes a royal court. A kitten becomes a chess Queen. A scurrying wild creature becomes a sophisticated courtier, a White Rabbit in vest and pocket watch. A proper Victorian tea party becomes the setting for rude remarks and outrageous behavior.

Poetry

Poetry is a form of literature that is difficult to define. Dictionary definitions are very complicated. One states that a poem is a rhythmical composition, sometimes rhymed, expressing experiences, ideas, or emotions in a style more concentrated, imaginative, and powerful than that of ordinary speech or prose. Another dictionary defines poetry as writing that formulates a concentrated imaginative awareness in language chosen and arranged to create a specific emotional response through meaning, sound, and rhythm. A desk encyclopedia defines poetry as a meaningful arrangement of words into an imaginative emotional discourse, always with a strong rhythmic pattern.

All these definitions stress certain common elements.

1. The content is an experience of the poet, usually emotional, filtered through the poet's imagination.

2. The poet uses a special language that is concentrated, using words that suggest more than their exact meaning.

3. The poet creates rhythmic and sound patterns that contribute to the experience described. He or she frequently, but not necessarily, uses rhyme.

With these elements in mind, let us analyze the sonnet "Ozymandias" by Percy Bysshe Shelley.

WHAT REMAINS OF A ONCE POWERFUL KING

I met a traveler from an antique land
Who said: "Two vast and trunkless legs of stone
Stand in the desert... Near them, on the sand,
Half sunk, a shattered visage lies, whose frown
And wrinkled lip, and sneer of cold command,
Tell that its sculptor well those passions read
Which yet survive, stamped on these lifeless things,
The hand that mocked them, and the heart that fed;
And on the pedestal these words appear:
'My name is Ozymandias, king of kings:
Look on my works, ye Mighty, And despair!'
Nothing beside remains. Round the decay
Of that colossal wreck, boundless and bare
The lone and level sands stretch far away."

The poet meets someone who describes something seen in a desert. It is the colossal wreck of a statue of a powerful king that has decayed over time. The remains consist of several parts—two legs, a shattered face, and the pedestal on which the statue once stood. The poet wants to portray a scene of utter desolation. Only the shattered statue survives amidst the emptiness of the boundless, bare desert sands. The poem gains its power by means of irony—the opposite of what we expect for a powerful king, not a royal palace but a broken statue of a king, is described. The poet creates, in a few words, the character of the king—his frown, his wrinkled lip, his sneer of authority. All of these details lead to the lesson the poet wishes to teach the Mighty: life is brief; human desires are vain; power leads to despair. He does this in 14 lines and 111 words.

Technically the poem has unusual rhyme—*stone* and *frown*, *appear* and *despair*, and the word order in "Nothing beside remains" is unusual. Nevertheless, an emotional response from us results from the picture the poet creates and the message engraved on the pedestal: nothing lasts forever, not even the power of a mighty king.

FINDING DETAILS

Very often questions on reading passages will test your ability to locate relevant details. In a descriptive passage, the author may give a general impression of a scene. Take, as an example, Edgar Allan Poe's famous short story, "The Fall of the House of Usher." The narrator conveys his reaction on seeing the house with these words: "I know not how it was, but, with the first glimpse of the building, a sense of insufferable gloom pervaded my spirit." Two sentences later you learn the details that made him feel that way.

Or, in a passage dealing with the character of the subject of a biography, details will document the point the author is making. Sandburg's biography of Abraham Lincoln contains many passages that follow this pattern. To show the industriousness of Lincoln, Sandburg writes: "Abe knew the sleep that comes after long hours of work outdoors...." You feel almost certain that the "work" that is mentioned will be described in detail, and it is. Among the jobs listed are "clearing timberland," "splitting rails," "harrowing," "planting," "pulling fodder," "helping...house raisings, log-rollings, corn-huskings."

Details are also used to move the plot or story interestingly and smoothly along the way. In Hawthorne's "The Ambitious Guest," there is the sentence, "The simplest words must intimate, but not portray, the unutterable horror of the catastrophe." Immediately there follow the details that tell just how horrible the catastrophe was.

Finally, details are often used to provide reasons for a conclusion that has been reached. Sherlock Holmes, in talking to Dr. Watson about his solution of the case entitled, "The Adventure of the Speckled Band," says, "I had come to these conclusions before ever I had entered his room." Then Holmes proceeds to give the details of why he reached the conclusions.

How do you locate a detail? It may be necessary for you to return to the reading passage many times to dig out the particular detail required to answer a given question. In your search, a number of clues may help you. These involve what are called **transitional words**, words that point out the purpose of the details presented. (See "Chapter 6: Organization" for a complete list of transitions.)

DETERMINING TONE AND MOOD

Tone is the aspect of the author's style that reveals attitude toward the subject. *Mood* is the atmosphere, or emotional effect, created by the manner in which the author presents the material.

To determine the tone or mood of a passage, consider the feelings or attitudes that are expressed. Examine, for example, the following passages:

EXAMPLE

> The room was dark—so dark that even after giving her eyes a while to accustom themselves to the blackness, she could still see nothing. Something soft—she hoped it was only a cobweb—brushed her lip. And the throbbing sound, attuned to her own heavy heartbeat, became stronger and faster.

EXAMPLE

> The room was dark—not dark as it is when your eyes are just not used to blackness, but really *dark* dark. Then some soft creepy thing brushed her lip, and she found herself hoping very hard that it was only a cobweb. And then there was that sound—baBoom, baBoom, baBoom—getting faster and louder all the time like her own heart going thump, thump, thump.

Consider the contrasting moods of the two passages above. The first passage presents a sustained mood of suspense and fear. The woman in the room can see nothing; something strange touches her; she hears a heavy and mysterious sound. We have the feeling that something is going to happen; the indication is that what will happen is dangerous, evil, or deadly.

The second paragraph relates essentially the same event. But we are distracted somewhat from what is happening by several devices. First, we are brought informally into the story—we know what a room is like when it's *really* dark. And the quality of darkness is also expressed informally—it is not pitch dark, or night dark, but "dark dark." "Then something creepy" is felt, and the sounds of the noise and the woman's heart are described—baBoom. The feeling conveyed by these devices is somehow made less frightening by the familiarity of the language, and the general impression is less one of total fear than of "scariness"—an easier emotion to deal with. Thus we have the impression from this second passage that whatever happens will probably not be all that bad or, if it is, it will somehow be easier to overcome.

REMEMBER

Tone is attitude. Mood is atmosphere.

INFERRING CHARACTER

Character is often implied by a person's words or actions, rather than by direct description. This has always been particularly true of drama, where the reader of a play is often called upon to interpret a character's personality without benefit of stage directions or other descriptive material. In the modern novel, too, the trend has been away from utilizing long descriptive passages and more toward allowing the characters' actions, speech, or thoughts (often called "inner dialogue") to reveal their personalities. The reader must rely, therefore, on the hints offered by the playwright or novelist to interpret character—and even then, a wide range of interpretation may be possible.

The following scene from *Life with Father* features Father and his son Clarence.

TIP

Character is inferred from a person's actions or dialogue.

CLARENCE (desperately): I have to have a new suit of clothes—you've got to give me the money for it.

(Father's *account book reaches the table with a sharp bang as he stares at* Clarence *with astonishment.*)

FATHER: Young man, do you realize you're addressing your father?

(Clarence *wilts miserably and sinks into a chair.*)

CLARENCE: I'm sorry, Father—I apologize—but you don't know how important this is to me. (Clarence's *tone of misery gives* Father *pause.*)

FATHER: A suit of clothes is so—? Now, why should a —? (*Something dawns on* Father and *he looks at* Clarence.) Has your need for a suit of clothes anything to do with the young lady?

CLARENCE: Yes, Father.

FATHER: Why, Clarence! (*Suddenly realizes that women have come into* Clarence's *emotional life and there comes a yearning to protect this inexperienced and defenseless member of his own sex.*) This comes as quite a shock to me.

CLARENCE: What does, Father?

FATHER: Your being so grown up! Still, I might have known that if you're going to college this fall—yes, you're at an age when you'll be meeting girls. Clarence, there are things about women I think you ought to know! (*He goes up and closes the doors, then comes down and sits beside* Clarence, *hesitating for a moment before he speaks.*) Yes, I think it's better for you to hear this from me than to have to learn it for yourself. Clarence, women aren't the angels that you think they are! Well, now—first, let me explain this to you. You see, Clarence, we men have to run this world and it's not an easy job. It takes work, and it takes thinking. A man has to be sure of his facts and figures. He has to reason things out. Now, you take a woman—a woman thinks—I'm wrong right there—a woman doesn't think at all! She gets stirred up! And she gets stirred up over the damnedest things! Now I love my wife just as much as any man, but that doesn't mean I should stand for a lot of folderol! By God! I won't stand for it!

CLARENCE: Stand for what, Father?

FATHER (to himself): That's the one thing I will not submit myself to. (*Has ceased explaining women to* Clarence *and is now explaining himself.*) Clarence, if a man thinks a certain thing is wrong to do he shouldn't do it. Now that has nothing to do with whether he loves his wife or not.

What action is taking place? A son is asking his father for money to buy a suit. What is the relationship between father and son? Father scolds his son for doing so; the son is miserable and apologizes. Obviously, the first thing we learn about Father is his lack of understanding of his son's needs. He acts like a dictator and causes his son to "wilt miserably." Next, after realizing his son's newly found interest in girls, he takes it upon himself to teach Clarence about women. Father acts like a know-it-all. "It's better for you to hear this from me than to have to learn it yourself." Then he reveals his prejudices against women: "a woman doesn't think at all!" Finally, his thinking becomes disorganized, he starts telling Clarence about women and ends up trying to convince himself how *he* should deal with them. The conversation, which started out as a request for money from a son to his father, ends in a useless discussion that reveals Father's prejudices.

We are left with a devastating picture of Father's character—a person who is dictatorial, lacking in understanding of his son's needs, filled with prejudices, self-deceptive, and disorganized, who regards himself as all knowing.

We learn all this from a cleverly written page of dialogue between father and son.

INFERRING SETTING

A number of factors are involved in the setting of a selection. These include not only *place* (physical location, type of locale—noisy, crowded, tranquil, etc.), but *time* (of day, of season, of historical period). See what clues to the setting you can find in the following passage.

EXAMPLE

He knew she would be late, but he could not keep himself from hurrying, pushing his way impatiently through the strolling, multilingual crowd. The Germans, their sunburned necks garlanded with camera straps, bargained gutturally with the indifferent women at their stalls, thinking to strike a sharp bargain on the price of a straw handbag or a painted box. The women let them struggle with the unfamiliar numbers, knowing exactly how much they would ultimately settle for. Three American girls, distinguishable by their short hair and madras skirts above sandalled feet and bare legs, dawdled along, giggling at the pleadings of two persistent *pappagalli* who seemed determined to improve international relations at all costs.

The sidestreet leading to the Signoria was hardly less busy, and he found it easier to dodge the small motorbikes bouncing noisily along the cobbled roadway than to struggle against the crowds pouring out of the great museum and onto the narrow sidewalks. He hated these annual floods of holiday-makers and culture-seekers who jammed the streets, the hotels, and the small restaurants so that the year-round residents found it necessary to retreat more than ever to the interiors of their cool, stone houses and their small, closed social circles. The more fortunate natives, of course, headed for Viareggio or the beaches of the South or the Riviera.

He finally found a table at the back of the cafe—a little too close to the bar but partially screened by a box hedge—and ordered a drink. The ancient *piazza* was mostly in shade now, except for the very tops of the towers which had been turned by the sun from the faded buff of the old stone to a rich gold against the blue sky.

> **REMEMBER**
>
> Setting includes place and time.

What can we tell of the setting described? Place: We can immediately pick up a number of clues. Obviously the setting is a city (crowds, sidewalks, a market, a museum). It is also not in the United States, since American girls are particularly distinguishable. By the mention of the Riviera as a nearby vacation spot, we know that we are somewhere in western Europe—but not Germany (the Germans are not familiar with the language). We can narrow the location down even further (although you are not expected to have all this extra information): two foreign words, *pappagalli* and *piazza*, might lead to the educated guess that the country is Italy.

Time: (1) Period—although the city itself is old (cobbled streets, narrow sidewalks, towers in an ancient piazza), the period is more recent. Motorbikes, barelegged girls, camera-carrying tourists all indicate the modern era. (2) Season—we can assume by the dress of the tourists, and by the fact that the natives usually head for the beach during this season, that it is summer. (3) Time of day—The piazza is in shade, except for the tops of the towers. It is unlikely, therefore, to be midday. Since the main character orders a drink in a cafe-bar, and since we have nowhere been given to understand that he has a drinking problem, we can assume it is late afternoon (cocktail time) and he has an appointment with someone for a predinner drink.

You should be made aware that the above passage was prepared solely to give you practice in inferring setting, and that you are not likely to find too many passages on the actual examination that concentrate on such description. However, you should learn to pick up small clues here and there that will give you an idea of the setting in a descriptive passage. Remember that, more often than not, the locale will be inferred rather than actually stated.

READING PROSE

Now let us turn to two representative passages from prose literature. Read these carefully; answer the six questions based on each; compare your answers with those in the answer key; then study the analysis of the answers, particularly for questions those that you answered incorrectly.

Practice in Reading Popular and Classical Prose

WHAT IS ABOUT TO HAPPEN TO BORIS?

The light carriage swished through the layers of fallen leaves upon the terrace. In places, they lay so thick that they half covered the stone balusters and reached the knees of Diana's stag. But the trees were bare; only here and there a single golden leaf trembled high upon the black twigs. Following the curve of the road, Boris's carriage came straight upon the main terrace and the house, majestic as the Sphinx herself in the sunset. The light of the setting sun seemed to have soaked into the dull masses of stone. They reddened and glowed with it until the whole place became a mysterious, a glorified abode, in which the tall windows shone like a row of evening stars.

Boris got out of the britska in front of the mighty stone stairs and walked toward them, feeling for his letter. Nothing stirred in the house. It was like walking into a cathedral. "And," he thought, "by the time that I get into that carriage once more, what will everything be like to me?"

1. The title that expresses the main idea of this passage is

    (1) "The Lure of Autumn"
    (2) "Sphinx in the Sunset"
    (3) "A Mysterious Cathedral"
    (4) "A Terrifying Surprise"
    (5) "An Important Visit"

2. From the description of the house, we may most safely conclude that the house

    (1) is sometimes used as a place of worship
    (2) is owned by a wealthy family
    (3) was designed by Egyptian architects
    (4) is constructed of modern brick
    (5) is a dark, cold-looking structure

3. This story probably takes place in

    (1) the British Isles
    (2) the Far East
    (3) eastern Europe
    (4) southern United States
    (5) the Mediterranean

4. We may most safely conclude that Boris has come to the house in order to

    (1) secure a job
    (2) find out about his future
    (3) join his friends for the holidays
    (4) attend a hunting party
    (5) visit his old family home

5. In this passage, which atmosphere does the author attempt to create?

    (1) pleasant anticipation
    (2) quiet peace
    (3) carefree gaiety
    (4) unrelieved despair
    (5) vague uncertainty

6. From this passage, which inference can most safely be drawn?

    (1) The house was topped by a lofty tower.
    (2) Boris is tired from his journey.
    (3) There is only one terrace before the house is reached.
    (4) The most imposing feature of the house is the door.
    (5) Boris intends to stay at the house for only a short time.

Answer Key

1. **5**   2. **2**   3. **3**   4. **2**   5. **5**   6. **5**

Answer Analysis

1. **5** Boris has come to the house and as he enters, he wonders what changes may take place for him as a result of his visit. To Boris, this will be "an important visit." Choice 1 cannot be correct. Going back to the passage, we find "the trees were bare; only here and there a single golden leaf trembled high upon the black twigs." This and a reference to "layers of fallen leaves" in line 2 are the only indications of season, and "the lure" of the season is not even mentioned. We reject this choice because it states only the setting for the main idea of the selection and background detail at best. It is not the *main* idea. Choices 2 and 3 are incorrect for similar reasons. In each case, a *detail* has been picked out of the selection and offered as the *main* idea. Choice 2 refers to the house, compared in majesty to the Sphinx. Choice 3 also involves a comparison—this time of the house with a cathedral. Choice 4 is completely incorrect. There is no surprise, nor is the selection's mood one of terror. There is anticipation of something about to happen, rather than something surprising that has happened.

2. **2** We can conclude that the house is owned by a wealthy family because there are several terraces, the stone stairs are "mighty," the windows are tall, and there are "masses of stone." Of the possibilities offered, this is the one we may most safely conclude is correct. Choices 1 and 3 are both incorrect, for similar reasons. Each is based on a figure of speech used in the passage, an implied comparison between the house and a cathedral and the stated comparison of the house to the sphinx. These are comparisons in the mind of the writer. Choice 4 is incorrect because it flatly contradicts the passage; the house is built of stone. Choice 5 is incorrect because it, too, contradicts the selection. The stone is not dark; it glows with the light of the setting sun.

3. **3** This question calls on you to draw an inference. The chief character has a Russian name, Boris. He gets out of a britska, and, even if you don't know that this is a kind of open carriage used in eastern Europe, the word suggests a conveyance that immediately eliminates "the British Isles" and "southern United States." It is safe to conclude, because of the name Boris, that the story "probably takes place in eastern Europe."

4. **2** The purpose of the question is to see whether you can determine the purpose of Boris's visit from the *evidence given*. While Choices 1, 3, and 4 may possibly be correct, there is no evidence in the passage to support them. Choice 5 must be considered along with Choice 2. If the selection ended just before the final sentence, the two choices would be equally plausible. But Boris is not merely making a visit. The question he asks himself in the final sentence makes it clear that the visit promises to change his future. Therefore, Choice 2 is the better of the two.

5. **5** Usually this type of question can be quite difficult. It involves not only locating details but also deciding what feeling the author wishes these details to create in you, the reader. Choices 5 and 2 remain possibilities. While "quiet peace" could describe the atmosphere, "vague uncertainty," Choice 5, is clearly superior as the answer. The whole place became "mysterious." Boris feels for his letter, the contents of which we are forced to guess. The uncertainty is climaxed by Boris's question, which asks, in effect, "What will become of me?" Choices 1, 3 and 4 involve some indication of Boris' feelings—of pleasure, of gaiety, of despair, but the passage contains no such indications.

6. **5** This question again calls for an inference, a conclusion that you, the reader, must draw from the facts that are presented. Choice 5 is correct because it represents the inference that "can most safely be drawn." Boris mentions getting back into the carriage. From this *fact* in the passage, we can *infer* that he intends to stay at the house for only a short time. Choices 1, 2, and 4 are not based on any facts in the passage: no tower is mentioned, nor is the door, and Boris's feelings are not described. Choice 3 contradicts the facts in the passage; one terrace is mentioned at the beginning and a main terrace is mentioned later. Clearly there are two terraces.

WHAT IS A CAMP OF WAR-WOUNDED LIKE?

Then the camps of the wounded—O heavens, what scene is this?—is this indeed humanity—these butchers' shambles? There are several of them. There they lie, in the largest, in an open space in the woods, from 200 to 300 poor fellows—the groans and the screams—the odor of blood, mixed with the fresh scent of the night, the grass, the trees—that slaughter-house! O well is it their mothers, their sisters cannot see them—cannot conceive, and never conceiv'd these things. One man is shot by a shell, both in the arm and leg—both are amputated—there lie the rejected members. Some have their legs blown off—some bullets through the breast—some indescribably horrid wounds in the face or head, all mutilated, sickening, torn, gouged out—some in the abdomen—some mere boys—many rebels, badly hurt—they take their regular turns with the rest, just the same as any—the surgeons use them just the same. Such is the camp of the wounded—such a fragment, a reflection afar off of the bloody scene—while all over the clear, large moon comes out at times softly, quietly shining. Amid the woods, that scene of flitting souls—amid the crack and crash and yelling sounds—the impalpable perfume of the woods—and yet the pungent, stifling smoke—the radiance of the moon, looking from heaven at intervals so placid—the sky so heavenly—the clear-obscure up there, those buoyant upper oceans—a few large placid stars beyond, coming silently and languidly out, and then disappearing—the melancholy, draperied night above, around. And there, upon the roads, the fields, and in those woods, that contest, never one more desperate in any age or land—both parties now in force—masses—no fancy battle, no semi-play, but fierce and savage demons fighting there—courage and scorn of death the rule, exceptions almost none.

—Walt Whitman

1. The author's main purpose in writing this selection is to

   (1) express his sympathy for the wounded
   (2) point out the brutal treatment of the rebels
   (3) praise the courage of the fighters
   (4) deplore the horrors of war
   (5) describe the camps of the wounded

2. The author shows his emotions in all of the following ways EXCEPT by

 (1) asking unanswerable questions
 (2) effective use of epithets
 (3) contrasting the battle with its peaceful setting
 (4) including gruesome details
 (5) sympathizing with the surgeons

3. All of the following relate to our sense of smell EXCEPT

 (1) "fresh scent of the night"
 (2) "the odor of blood"
 (3) "the radiance of the moon"
 (4) "the pungent, stifling smoke"
 (5) "the impalpable perfume of the woods"

4. The soldiers are referred to by all of the following EXCEPT

 (1) butchers
 (2) poor fellows
 (3) mere boys
 (4) flitting souls
 (5) savage demons

5. The reader can infer from the final sentence that, for the soldiers, the author has a feeling of

 (1) pity
 (2) contempt
 (3) indifference
 (4) admiration
 (5) resignation

6. That the author is also a poet may be inferred from his

 (1) description of the wounded
 (2) comments on the camps
 (3) conclusions about war
 (4) awareness of the night's beauty
 (5) indignation at what he sees

Answer Key

1. **4**   2. **5**   3. **3**   4. **1**   5. **4**   6. **4**

Answer Analysis

1. **4** The key word in the question is *main*. The question calls for you to identify the "main purpose" of the author. Although it is true that the author expresses his sympathy for the wounded ("poor fellows") and he does describe the camps of the wounded, his main purpose is to use these camps as "a reflection" of the "bloody scene" to express his disgust at the horrors of war. Therefore, Choices (1) and (5) are incorrect. Choice 2

is obviously wrong since the author indicates that the rebel soldiers got the same treatment as the rest. He mentions the courage of the fighters almost incidentally in the last sentence of the selection, so Choice 3 cannot be the main purpose of the author.

2. **5** This question requires you to go back to the selection and to ferret out the details that the possible answers identify. Choice 5 is correct because the one thing the author does *not* do is sympathize with the surgeons, although he does refer to the impartiality with which they treat soldiers on both sides. In the first two lines, the author asks unanswerable questions.

Epithets describe significant qualities of the nouns they modify. We find "horrid" wounds and "desperate" contest, "fierce and savage" demons, as well as such poetic epithets as "melancholy, draperied" night. The bloody battle is indeed contrasted with the "placid," moon and "heavenly" sky. Gruesome detail abounds in the selection.

3. **3** This relatively easy question contains many clues to the answer. *Scent* and *odor* are synonyms of *smell*. While *pungent* may refer to both taste and smell, it is the smell of smoke, rather than its taste, that is obviously referred to here. Perfume, of course, is something that is smelled. The correct choice is 3 because "the radiance of the moon" refers to the sense of sight, not the sense of smell.

4. **1** Careful attention to the details of the passage reveals that the soldiers are referred to as "poor fellows," "some mere boys," "flitting souls," and "fierce and savage demons." The term *butchers' shambles* compares the camp of the wounded with a butchers' slaughterhouse and does not refer at all to the soldiers.

5. **4** The question identifies the specific place where the answer may be found—the final sentence. Study of that sentence gives us two clues to the author's feeling for the soldiers. They are "fierce and savage demons." "Courage and scorn of death" is typical of their fighting. The author does not pity the soldiers in this sentence, nor does he show any indifference to their "desperate" plight. There is no evidence that he is resigned to their having to continue the battle. While he does allude to their ferocity and savagery, he does not show contempt or scorn for the soldiers. Rather, he emphasizes their courage, since it is true that almost all display this quality in the fierce battle. Therefore, his feeling is one of admiration.

6. **4** What details would lead you, the reader, to conclude that any writer has the qualities of a poet? The "Glossary of Literary Terms" beginning on page 508 defines a poem as literature that has "deep emotion; highly imaginative language with figures of speech; distinctive rhythm;... words that mean more than they apparently say" among others. Mere description, comment, and conclusion are not poetic qualities. The writing of a good reporter has all of these features. Anger, while it is a deep emotion, is not as good a clue to the fact that the author is a poet as is his unusual sensitivity to the night's beauty: "the radiance of the moon," "those buoyant upper oceans" (referring to the sky), "the melancholy, draperied night above." The scene is viewed by the light of the moon, the sky is compared to a sea, and the night is compared to a hanging curtain in a way that only a poet could succeed in doing.

SUMMARY OF PROSE INTERPRETATION

When interpreting prose, you should:

1. *Read the selection carefully.*

2. *In **selecting a title** that expresses the main idea, go back to the selection constantly. Arrive at the correct answer by a process of elimination.* Eliminate the one or more possibilities that are clearly incorrect. Eliminate the possibilities that are based on minor details; there will be one or two of these. From the remaining choices, you must select the one that expresses the main rather than the subordinate idea.

3. *In **drawing inferences**, find the clues in the passage from which you can draw the proper conclusion.* The clue may be a name, a place, an adjective, an object, an unusual word. You may have to reread the selection a few times before you locate the clue or the two details that can be linked to make a clue.

4. *In **determining purpose**, ask yourself why the author wrote the passage; what he or she wanted you, the reader, to understand or feel.* After you have read the passage several times, try to define the *total impression* you get from your reading. The purposes of authors at various times may be to inform, to arouse anger, to poke fun at, to evoke pity, to amuse, and to urge to action, among others. Which of these predominates?

5. *In **determining mood**, try to find words that either create an atmosphere or evoke an emotion.* This is related to the author's purpose but may not necessarily be his or her main purpose. *There are two main guides to determining atmosphere: selection of details and use of adjectives and adverbs.*

READING POETRY

SKILL ONE

Use your imagination when reading figurative language. Don't take everything literally in the poem.

Reading poetry requires a special set of skills because the poet uses both a special language and special writing techniques.

In poetry, words are not used in their normal, literal senses. Rather, they are used in such a way that you, the reader, must call on your imagination to fully understand them. Let's consider an example.

"I almost blew my top."

Here the words *blew* and *top* do not have their regular meanings, but are used figuratively to express the idea "I almost went crazy."

In poetry, meaning is frequently compressed into a few words by the use of figures of speech such as metaphors. (See the "Glossary of Literary Terms," page 504.)

"The road was a ribbon of moonlight."

In seven words, the poet Walter de la Mare tells us that the time is night, the moon was shining, and the road is a lighted area surrounded by darker ones.

"The moon was a ghostly galleon."

In six words, the poet tells us that the moon is like a ship, the sky is like an ocean, and the moon creates an eerie, supernatural feeling as it moves across the sky.

In poetry, meaning is closely related to rhythm. For this reason it helps to read poetry aloud.

In poetry, in addition to rhythm, which is always present, you will frequently encounter rhyme. Rhyme, too, often helps to convey meaning. In Edgar Allan Poe's poem "The Raven," the rhyme is repeated in *door, more, Lenore, forevermore,* and *nevermore.*

"'Tis some visitor,' I muttered, 'tapping at my chamber door: Only this and nothing more.'"

The sound itself adds to the atmosphere of mystery.

In poetry, the poet uses sounds in addition to rhyme to help convey meaning. The poet John Masefield describes the effect of the wind with a series of "w" and "wh" sounds. He wants to return

"To the gull's *w*ay and the *wh*ales's *w*ay *wh*ere the *w*ind's like a *wh*etted knife."

This technique is known as alliteration. (See the "Glossary of Literary Terms," page 504.)

Another technique is the use of words whose sounds correspond to their meaning. Here is the way one poet describes the movement of the waters of a river:

"And rushing and flushing and brushing and gushing,

And flapping and rapping and clapping and slapping..."

In poetry, the poem itself has a certain shape or form. The poem can be in a very definite form, such as the sonnet, or in a very loose form. "The New Colossus," by Emma Lazarus, which follows below, is a sonnet with a definite rhythm and a definite rhyme scheme. The form of "The New Colossus" is appropriate because it lends itself to the main ideas expressed in each of the two stanzas of the poem.

Read the following poem carefully and answer the questions based on it. Compare your answers with the answer key: then study the analysis of the answers, particularly for questions that you have answered incorrectly.

SKILL TWO

Picture the images from the poem created by the figures of speech.

SKILL THREE

Read the poem aloud, noting the rhythm which also adds meaning to the poem.

SKILL FOUR

Read the poem aloud, noting the rhyme which also adds meaning to the poem.

SKILL FIVE

Read the poem aloud, noting the sounds of the words.

SKILL SIX

Study the poem's form and structure for meaning.

Practice in Reading Poetry

WHAT DOES THE NEW STATUE REPRESENT?

The New Colossus

Not like the brazen giant of Greek fame,
With conquering limbs astride from land to land;
Here at our sea-washed, sunset gates shall stand
A mighty woman with a torch, whose flame
Is the imprisoned lightning, and her name
Mother of Exiles. From her beacon-hand
Glows world-wide welcome; her mild eyes command
The air-bridged harbor that twin cities frame.
"Keep, ancient lands, your storied pomp!" cries she
with silent lips. "Give me your tired, your poor,
Your huddled masses yearning to breathe free,
The wretched refuse of your teeming shore.
Send these, the homeless, tempest-tost, to me.
I lift my lamp beside the golden door!"

—Emma Lazarus

1. The main idea of the poem is that

   (1) the ancient lands of Europe should serve as a beacon to America
   (2) the Greek statue serves as a model for the American statue
   (3) the mighty are asked to come to these shores
   (4) America welcomes all persecuted freedom-lovers
   (5) the lamp guides those who come to the golden door

2. In the choices below, the incorrectly paired words are

   (1) brazen—of brass
   (2) sunset—east
   (3) beacon—guiding light
   (4) refuse—trash
   (5) pomp—splendor

3. The "mighty woman" and "Mother of Exiles" is the

   (1) United States of America
   (2) city of New York
   (3) Statue of Liberty
   (4) Plymouth Rock
   (5) Golden Gate

4. The title of this poem, "The New Colossus," implies

   (1) similarity to the old
   (2) replacement of the old
   (3) difference from the old
   (4) inferiority to the old
   (5) acceptance of the old

5. The *incorrectly* matched phrase from the poem with the figure of speech or poetic device it demonstrates is

   (1) "Her mild eyes"—epithet
   (2) "Keep, ancient lands, your storied pomp!" cries she—personification
   (3) "shall stand a mighty woman"—inversion
   (4) "world-wide welcome"—alliteration
   (5) "flame is the imprisoned lightning"—simile

6. The form of the poem is that of

   (1) a ballad
   (2) an octet
   (3) an ode
   (4) a sestet
   (5) a sonnet

Answer Key

1. **4**   2. **2**   3. **3**   4. **3**   5. **5**   6. **5**

Answer Analysis

1. **4** Choice 1 is not correct because the reverse is actually true; America's "beacon-hand" as represented in the statue is a beacon to the exiles from the ancient lands of Europe. Nor is Choice 2 correct since the opening line begins "Not like" the Greek statue is the American statue. Choice 3 is incorrect; it is the "tired," "poor," and "homeless" who are welcomed to these shores. While Choice 5 is true as far as it goes, it is not the main idea. Choice A is correct.

2. **2** While this question is seemingly a vocabulary question that requires you to recall the meanings of the words in the five possible answers, the poem does provide hints or context clues to the meanings of several of the words. "From her *beacon*-hand glows world-wide welcome" indicates that light is going forth. The *refuse* is described as *wretched*. Pomp is contrasted with the *poor* and the *refuse*. Therefore, you can conclude that these words are correctly paired. If you deduce from the first verse that an ancient statue is being described, the meaning of *brass* for *brazen* seems logical. But even if you can't, "our"—meaning America's— "sunset gates" must be located in the west, where the sun sets. Choice 2 is the correct answer because sunset is always associated with the west rather than the east.

3. **3** To answer this question, you must draw an inference or conclusion from what is stated indirectly in the poem. What does the poem tell us about the "mighty woman" and "Mother of Exiles"? We learn that she stands "with a torch"; we also learn that "her mild eyes command the...harbor." These facts rule out all possible answers except Choice 3. The United States of America and the city of New York do not, even symbolically, stand "with a torch." Neither Plymouth Rock (a rock) nor the Golden Gate (a bridge) fits the clues contained in the poem.

> **REMEMBER**
>
> *You must read the selection carefully.* **In selecting the main idea,** *you must go back to the selection several times. Arrive at the correct answer by a process of elimination.*

> **REMEMBER**
>
> *Never give up on a question.* **Where the meaning of words is involved,** *carefully study the clues to their meaning given by other nearby words in the passage.*

REMEMBER

In drawing inferences or making deductions from the text, find the clues that can help you. You may have to reread the selection a few times before you find them.

4. **3** This is not a difficult question if you read the poem with care from the very beginning. The new colossus is "not like" the old, according to the very first verse, so Choices 1 and 2 are immediately ruled out. To find the correct answer, you must determine how the poet feels about this new colossus. Since she is "mighty" and since her eyes are "mild," it is obvious that the poet admires the new colossus and finds it superior to the old (which the poet rejects). Therefore, Choices 4 and 5 are also incorrect. It is the "difference" and the fact that the new is "not like" the old that are stressed. Therefore, Choice 3 is correct.

5. **5** It is important for you to refer to the "Glossary of Literary Terms" on page 508 if you haven't mastered the definitions already because all five possible answers are defined in that vocabulary. *Epithet,* an adjective or phrase that identifies a significant quality of the noun it describes, is exemplified by her *mild* eyes, so Choice 1 contains a correctly matched pair. *Personification,* the act of attributing human qualities to a "thing" (in this case the power of speech to a statue), is correctly paired with the quotation from the poem. *Inversion,* reversal of normal word order, applies to "shall stand a mighty woman" because the normal order is "a mighty woman shall stand." "Worldwide welcome" is a perfect example of *alliteration* since the same consonant sound, "w," is repeated at the beginning of two words that follow one another. By elimination, Choice 5 is correct since *simile* is *incorrectly* paired with "flame is the imprisoned lightning." *Like* or *as* is *not* used to make the comparison, so "flame is the imprisoned lightning" is properly called a *metaphor.*

6. **5** Where the form of a poem is required to answer a question, first count the number of lines. Then figure out the rhyme scheme. Here there are 14 lines with a rhyme scheme as follows:

fame	—*a*
land	—*b*
stand	—*b*
flame	—*a*
name	—*a*
hand	—*b*
command	—*b*
frame	—*a*
she	—*c*
poor	—*d*
free	—*c*
shore	—*d*
me	—*c*
door	—*d*

   If you consult the "Glossary of Literary Terms" beginning on page 504, you will find that this form cannot fit the definitions of a ballad (which deals with a simple story) or an ode (which is a lengthy lyric poem). Since the poem has 14 lines, it cannot be an octet (eight lines) or a sestet (six lines). The correct answer must be Choice 5, a sonnet. This poem is actually a fairly good example of an Italian sonnet. The octet or first eight lines present the main idea—the contrast between the new colossus, which represents a welcome to the exiles, and the old colossus, which symbolized conquest—and is in the exact rhyme scheme required. The sestet or second six lines expands the idea by stressing the freedom and opportunity offered to the exiles in contrast to their rejection by the countries from which they came. The rhyme scheme, instead of rigidly following the *c d e c d e* of the Italian sonnet, confines itself to *c d c d c d*, one of the possible combinations.

It should be noted that the sestet of this famous sonnet is inscribed on the base of the Statue of Liberty and is one of the most frequently quoted American poems.

SUMMARY OF INTERPRETATION OF POETRY

The skills needed in reading and interpreting poetry call for you to:

1. To understand the extended meaning of words used figuratively, use your imagination to add to the usual meanings of the words.

2. Since poetry compresses meaning and description into a few words, fill in the suggested meanings and pictures they create by studying the figures of speech used, such as similes and metaphors.

3. Read the poem aloud, since the rhythm will help you determine its meaning.

4. Note the rhymes used, since they will also help you get meaning and feeling from the poem.

5. Note the sounds of the words, since they reinforce meaning.

6. Study the form of the poem, since its subdivisions (stanzas) can help you understand it better.

Note: First, read the poem through quickly to get an overall idea of its meaning and feeling. Then read it more slowly and carefully after you have read the questions based on it.

READING DRAMA

The playwright does not speak directly to the reader in modern drama, as do the novelist and short story writer. Sometimes the playwright sets the scene for those who produce or read the play, and sometimes he or she includes instructions to the actors about mood or action. For the most part, however, the playwright leaves it to the actor and the reader to figure out appearance, character, actions, and feelings. The only real help the playwright should and must give is through the dialogue, the conversation between the characters. From this dialogue alone, you must *imagine the setting*, *visualize the action*, including "hearing" the speech of the actors, and *draw conclusions about their character and motives*. In addition, you must understand the nature of the essence of drama, which is conflict between ideas or characters. This is made clear only through the dialogue. A final point: you may also be asked to predict what is likely to happen on the basis of what you have read.

An analysis of the following scene from a modern American play will illustrate the skills you need to read and understand drama. Reading it aloud will help.

Practice in Reading Drama

HOW DOES WILLY LOMAN'S FAMILY REACT TO HIS DEATH?

REQUIEM

CHARLEY: It's getting dark, Linda.

(Linda doesn't react. She stares at the grave.)

BIFF: How about it, Mom? Better get some rest, heh! They'll be closing the gate soon.

(Linda makes no move. Pause.)

HAPPY (deeply angered): He had no right to do that. There was no necessity for it. We would've helped him.

BIFF: Come along, Mom.

LINDA: Why didn't anybody come?

CHARLEY: It was a very nice funeral.

LINDA: But where are all the people he knew? Maybe they blame him.

CHARLEY: Naa. It's a rough world, Linda. They wouldn't blame him.

LINDA: I can't understand it. At this time especially. First time in thirty-five years we were just about free and clear. He only needed a little salary. He was even finished with the dentist.

CHARLEY: No man only needs a little salary.

LINDA: I can't understand it.

BIFF: There were a lot of nice days. When he'd come home from a trip, or on Sundays, making the stoop, finishing the cellar, when he built the extra bathroom, and put up the garage. You know something, Charley, there's more of him in that front stoop than in all the sales he ever made.

CHARLEY: Yeah, he was a happy man with a batch of cement.

LINDA: He was so wonderful with his hands.

BIFF: He had the wrong dreams. All, all, wrong.

HAPPY: (almost ready to fight Biff): Don't say that.

BIFF: He never knew who he was.

CHARLEY (stopping Happy's movement and reply. To Biff): Nobody dast blame this man. You don't understand. Willy was a salesman. And for a salesman, there is no rock bottom to the life. He don't put a bolt to a nut, he don't tell you the law or give you medicine. He's the man way out there in the blue riding on a smile and a shoeshine. And when they start not smiling back—that's an earthquake. And then you get yourself a couple of spots on your hat, and you're finished. Nobody dast blame this man. A salesman has got to dream, boy. It comes with the territory.

BIFF: Charley, the man didn't know who he was.

HAPPY (infuriated): Don't say that.

BIFF: Why don't you come with me, Happy?

HAPPY: I'm not licked that easily. I'm staying right here in this city, and I'm gonna beat this racket! *(He looks at Biff, his chin set.)* The Loman Brothers!

BIFF: I know who I am, kid.

HAPPY: All right, boy. I'm gonna show you and everybody else that Willy Loman did not die in vain. He had a good dream. It's the only dream you can have—to come out number-one man. He fought it out here, and this is where I'm gonna win it for him.

1. "Requiem" most closely means

    (1) prayer
    (2) regret
    (3) argument
    (4) repetition
    (5) request

2. What has happened prior to this scene?

    (1) The Lomans had an unhappy marriage.
    (2) The brothers did not get along.
    (3) Willy Loman had many friends.
    (4) The Loman family had an easy life.
    (5) Willy Loman was buried.

3. From the dialogue, we can conclude that

    (1) the members of the family differed in their view of Willy Loman.
    (2) the brothers will stick together.
    (3) the family was not tightly knit.
    (4) there was a generation gap in the family.
    (5) everyone blames Willy for his action.

4. Happy defends Willy by saying

    (1) he wanted to be popular.
    (2) he was a family man.
    (3) he wanted to be a top salesman.
    (4) he wanted to build his house.
    (5) he didn't care for himself.

5. The member of the family who differs from the rest is

    (1) Linda
    (2) Biff
    (3) Charley
    (4) Happy
    (5) Willy

6. The irony of the situation is that, at the time of Willy's death, the family is

    (1) splitting up
    (2) united in tragedy
    (3) appreciative of Willy
    (4) in good shape financially
    (5) mutually supportive

Answer Key

1. **1**   2. **5**   3. **1**   4. **3**   5. **2**   6. **4**

Answer Analysis

1. **1** A requiem is a prayer, a Mass for a deceased person, in this case Willy Loman. In this instance, it is a tragic and solemn moment for the family of Willy Loman and, although a prayer is not involved, the Lomans remember and evaluate Willy's life.

2. **5** The clues to the locale of the scene, a cemetery, are: "They'll be closing the gate soon" and "It was a very nice funeral."

3. **1** The brothers differed in their view of their father. Biff criticizes him: "He had the wrong dreams." Happy answers, "Don't say that." Charley adds, "Nobody dast blame this man." The other choices are not true of the family. For example, Charley does not blame Willy at all.

4. **3** Happy defends Willy by saying, "He had a good dream. It's the only dream you can have—to come out number-one man." None of the other choices is supported by the dialogue although Willy was "a happy man with a batch of cement."

5. **2** It is Biff, and Biff alone, who criticizes Willy: "He had the wrong dreams" and "He never knew who he was." It is he who leaves his family and goes off to the city.

6. **4** Linda says, "At this time especially. First time in thirty-five years we were just about free and clear." Dramatic irony is a combination of circumstances or is a result that is the opposite of what might be expected, in this case, death instead of a happier life.

SUMMARY OF INTERPRETATION OF DRAMA READING

The skills needed in reading and interpreting drama call for you to:

1. Imagine the setting. If no stage directions are given, deduce from the speech and dialogue of the characters where the action is taking place.

2. Visualize the action. As the characters speak, figure out *what they are doing* while they are speaking.

3. Determine their motives. Why are the characters speaking as they do? *Why are they doing what they do?*

4. Determine their character and personality. What sort of person talks and acts the way he does? Why?

5. Determine the conflict that is taking place. Since the essence of drama is conflict, who or what is in conflict with whom or what? Is the conflict physical? Is it emotional? Is it a conflict of ideas?

6. Make a prediction on the basis of all of the above what is most likely to happen next.

7. Read the scene aloud, trying to project yourself into the character of each of the roles.

READING COMMENTARY ON THE ARTS

Selections that fall under the term *commentary* are limited to the aspects of contemporary writing that deal with the arts—music, art, theater, movies, television, literature, and dance. They are further limited to selections in which the author comments critically on the arts, discussing the value of the content and the style of these means of expression.

In reading commentaries, try to determine the point of view of the writer and whether his or her evaluation of the artist, the musician, the author, the playwright, the film, the television program, or the dancer is favorable or unfavorable. Also look for the insights of the critic into the meaning and emotion conveyed by the artist or the medium.

The writing style will be that of the author of a piece of popular literature, so sentence structure and vocabulary will be relatively simple. *Here is a helpful hint.* Since critics who comment on the arts are describing their reactions, they resort to many adjectives that express their judgment. Here are a couple of dozen of such adjectives: *adept, authentic, candid, credible, dynamic, eloquent, exquisite, graphic, inane, inept, laudable, lucid, naive, poignant, prosaic, spontaneous, superb, superlative, tedious, timeless, tiresome, trite, vivacious, witty.*

PRACTICE IN READING COMMENTARY ON THE ARTS

WHAT DID THE CREATOR OF THE MUPPETS CONTRIBUTE TO CHILDREN'S TELEVISION?

He built an empire on a discarded green coat and a Ping-Pong ball. Jim Henson, creator of Kermit the Frog and a menagerie of other furry creatures known as the Muppets, revolutionized puppetry and reinvented children's television.

The Muppets charmed audiences of all ages on *Sesame Street*, possibly the most influential children's show ever, and later on *The Muppet Show*, which became the mostly widely watched TV program in the world, attracting 135 million viewers in 100 countries.

Henson succeeded with craftsmanship and showmanship and salesmanship. But above all, he constantly challenged the status quo.

Henson was one of the first producers to use television not merely as a medium but as a tool to enhance his performances.

While earlier puppet programs, such as *Kukla, Fran, and Ollie*, simply pluncked a camera in front of a traditional stage, Henson used a variety of camera lenses to create illusions which made his Muppets more agile and antic.

He also taught his puppeteers to work while using a TV monitor. For the first time, they could see not only their performances as they were unfolding, but also what the viewers could see.

That insight led Henson to create a new, softer-looking style of puppet that was extremely expressive in TV closeups.

Henson's unconventional approach to life came through in his Muppets—a word he coined for the crossbreed of marionettes and puppets he developed in the mid-50s.

While companies like Disney were creating model characters that lived up to the era's model of perfection, such as Bambi, Henson's creatures, such as the proud Miss Piggy, the grumpy Oscar the Grouch, and the uncontrollable Animal, were wildly irreverent.

Henson also applied this irreverent approach to his work. He promoted productivity, not by demanding results, but by encouraging his associates to have fun. He promoted silliness, even chaos, on the set. In fact, he was most satisfied with a scene when it had grown so funny that no one could perform it without busting up, former associates say.

Despite his childlike enthusiasm, Henson was also a pragmatist who tackled situations by approaching them from new angles. He was a problem solver and had a knack for sidestepping complexity and finding a simpler, purer way of doing things.

1. The contributions of Jim Henson, according to the article,

    (1) retained earlier approaches
    (2) added little to current programming
    (3) climbed on the bandwagon of children's television
    (4) imitated Kukla, Fran, and Olllie
    (5) broke new ground in puppetry

2. The reinventing of children's TV was exemplified by the worldwide success of

    (1) *Sesame Street*
    (2) *The Muppet Show*
    (3) *Kukla, Fran, and Ollie*
    (4) Kermit the Frog
    (5) the status quo

3. The most important reason for the success of Jim Henson was

    (1) his craftsmanship
    (2) his showmanship
    (3) his salesmanship
    (4) his unconventional approach
    (5) his charm

4. Henson pioneered in using television

    (1) as a medium
    (2) to improve performance
    (3) as a traditional stage
    (4) to teach tried-and-true methods
    (5) to preserve the familiar puppets

5. Henson's Muppets

    (1) sought perfection
    (2) imitated Disney's creations
    (3) were disrespectful
    (4) were ideal role models
    (5) were static and serious

6. Jim Henson was all of the following EXCEPT

    (1) a man of childlike enthusiasm
    (2) a searcher for simple solutions
    (3) a pragmatist
    (4) an irreverent innovator
    (5) a conformist

Answer Key

1. **5**   2. **2**   3. **4**   4. **2**   5. **3**   6. **5**

Answer Analysis

1. **5** The author stresses Henson's challenging of the status quo and his revolutionizing of puppetry. Since Henson rejected earlier approaches, Choice 1 is wrong. Being dissatisfied with current programming, he searched for something new and came up with Kermit the Frog, adding much to current programs. He didn't climb on the children's TV bandwagon (Choice 3); he reinvented children's TV. Whereas the progam *Kukla, Fran, and Ollie* was static and traditional, Henson injected movement into his characters by new uses of the camera.

2. **2** The audience for Choice 1 is not identified; but for Choice 2, *The Muppet Show*, its worldwide success is mentioned and its domination by the numbers of millions of viewers in a hundred countries. None of the other choices deals directly with the *success* of the Muppets.

3. **4** While Henson's craftsmanship, showmanship, and salesmanship are mentioned, his unconventional approach and unusual characters are stressed. The charm of the Muppets is subordinate to their unusual character.

4. **2** Henson used television not only as a medium but also as a tool to enhance performance. He opposed the tradtional, the tried and true, and the familiar.

5. **3** Henson's Muppets were unlike Disney's characters because they were not perfect, not ideal. They were proud, grumpy, and disrespectful.

6. **5** Henson's childlike enthusiasm, his search for simple solutions, and his irreverence are mentioned, but the major point of the article is Henson's nonconformism, his *not* acting in traditional ways.

READING BUSINESS DOCUMENTS

A new component to the GED examination, reading business documents, requires logical thinking. The types of documents you will find on the examination are business memorandums, company and college handbooks and policies, E-mail messages, letters of recommendation, and so on.

First read the document presented. Then determine the main purpose of the document. Note the topic sentences and the organization of each paragraph. Sometimes you will be asked to determine inferences or meanings that are not directly stated in the text. Because these are everyday types of documents, the language is fairly simple and straightforward. Nonetheless, pay close attention to the details referred to in the questions.

PRACTICE INTERPRETING TECHNICAL OR BUSINESS DOCUMENTS

Read the following excerpt from a voter's registration pamphlet. Then answer the questions that follow.

A Voter's Guide

In order to vote, you must be registered. Simply knowing your specific polling place does not mean you are an officially registered voter. You may find voter registration forms at the following places: library, DMV, post office, city clerk's office, and the county election office. In order to prevent voter fraud, you must register in person, not over the Internet. You must be at least 18 years of age on the date of the election, and you must be a U.S. citizen. Also, bring a picture ID with you.

Deadlines for registration vary from state to state, as do deadlines for requesting and submitting an absentee ballot. It is important that you determine these deadlines several months in advance of the election in which you plan to vote.

1. What is the purpose of the guide?

   (1) to prove that it is difficult to become a registered voter
   (2) to keep underage voters from registering in their states
   (3) to inform a citizen how to register to vote
   (4) to prevent voter fraud
   (5) to name polling locations

2. According to the guide, all of the following are places to register EXCEPT

   (1) county election office
   (2) state clerk's office
   (3) library
   (4) post office
   (5) DMV

3. This guide applies to

   (1) U.S. citizens under 18 years of age
   (2) illegal immigrants
   (3) U.S. residents
   (4) U.S. citizens who are at least 18 years of age
   (5) registered politicians only

Read the following excerpt from a residential lease agreement. Then answer the questions that follow.

Residential Lease Agreement

This lease is dated June 1, 2009, by Landlord John Doe and Tenant Jane Doemont. Both parties agree to the following terms:

1. Term will begin on June 1, 2009 and terminate on May 31, 2010 for 123 Anywhere Street, Sometown, USA.
2. Tenant's lease of $800 is due on the first day of each month, and will be deemed late on the fifth of the month. If lease payment is late, there will be a 10% penalty assessed to the Tenant's lease.
3. Tenant has paid a security deposit of one month's rent upon signing this contract, as well as the first month's rent for a total of $1600. Any damages upon the termination of this lease will be deducted from the security deposit.
4. Pets are not allowed in the property at any time.
5. Tenant is required to report any and all maintenance concerns as soon as possible in order to prevent damage to the property, and the Landlord will make all necessary and reasonable repairs in a timely manner.
6. Tenant is responsible for securing all utilities for the property during the lease term.

I agree to the above terms and conditions as stated.

Signed:

Landlord _____

Tenant _____

4. According to the lease, the Tenant must

(1) report maintenance concerns
(2) pay the lease by the fourth of the month
(3) not keep pets in the apartment
(4) secure his own utilities
(5) all of the above

5. According to the lease, the following reason may terminate the lease:

(1) the Tenant finds another place and gives 2 weeks notice
(2) the Tenant pays the lease on time each month
(3) the ending date of the lease has arrived
(4) the Landlord doesn't like the Tenant's friends
(5) the property is not clean

6. According to the lease, the agreement is binding for

(1) 4 months
(2) 6 months
(3) 8 months
(4) 10 months
(5) 12 months

Answer Key

1. **3**   2. **2**   3. **4**   4. **5**   5. **3**   6. **5**

Answer Analysis

1. **3** The purpose of this guide is to give information on how a citizen may register to vote.

2. **2** The only place not listed in the guide as a place to register is the state clerk's office; the guide stated the "county clerk's office."

3. **4** The guide states that "you must be at least 18 years of age. . . . and a U.S. citizen."

4. **5** The lease agreement states all of the options listed: report maintenance concerns, pay the lease before the fifth of the month, no pets, and secure own utilities; therefore, the correct answer must be "all of the above."

5. **3** The only reason listed that would terminate the lease as stated is that the lease term has expired on the agreed upon date (May 31, 2010).

6. **5** The lease is binding for 12 months, or one year.

Review the basic reading skills presented at the beginning of this chapter for more practice of the skills involved.

GLOSSARY OF LITERARY TERMS

This list includes words used frequently in discussing literature.

ACCENT emphasis given to a syllable or to syllables of a word; used primarily with reference to poetry and also used for the mark (′) that shows this emphasis

ALLITERATION repetition of the same consonant sound at the beginning of two or more words in close proximity ("The fair *breeze blew*, the white *foam flew*...")

ALLUSION offhand reference to a famous figure or event in literature or history ("He opened a Pandora's box.")

AUTOBIOGRAPHY story of a person's life written by him- or herself (Franklin's *Autobiography*)

BALLAD verse form that presents in simple story form a single dramatic or exciting episode and stresses such feelings as love, courage, patriotism, and loyalty ("Sir Patrick Spens")

BIOGRAPHY story of a person's life written by someone else (Boswell's *Life of Johnson*)

CLIMAX high point in the telling of a story, be it in fictional, poetic, or dramatic form (the appearance of Banquo's ghost in *Macbeth*)

COMEDY light form of drama that aims to amuse and/or instruct us and that ends happily (*All's Well That Ends Well*)

DIALOGUE conversation between people in a play

ELEGY lyric poem expressing a poet's ideas concerning death (Gray's "Elegy Written in a Country Churchyard")

EPIC long poem that tells a story about noble people and their adventures centering around one character who is the hero

EPITHET word, such as an adjective, or phrase that effectively identifies a significant quality of the noun it describes (Alexander the *Great*)

ESSAY prose writing that can be recognized by its treatment of any topic, no matter how unimportant, and by its approach—*formal* (containing an analysis with a moral) or *informal* (revealing the personality of the author through his or her humor, bias, and style)

FIGURE OF SPEECH expression used to appeal to the reader's emotions and imagination by presenting words in unusual meaning or context ("My love's like a red, red rose...")

FOOT certain number of syllables making up a unit in a verse of poetry

IMAGE figure of speech, especially a simile or a metaphor

INVERSION reversal of the normal order of words in a sentence ("A king of men am I.")

IRONY figure of speech in which the writer or speaker uses words meaning the exact opposite of what he really thinks (In *Julius Caesar*, Antony attacks Brutus with the words, "Brutus is an honorable man.")

LIMERICK jingle in verse containing five lines, with lines 1, 2, and 5 rhyming and lines 3 and 4 rhyming

LYRIC short poem expressing deep emotion in highly melodic and imaginative verse ("The Daffodils")

METAPHOR figure of speech that compares two things, or a person and a thing, by using a quality of one applied to the other. *Like* or *as* is omitted. ("All the world's a stage.")

METER rhythm patterns in verse

MYTH story of unknown origin, religious in character, that tries to interpret the natural world, usually in terms of supernatural events (the story of Atlas)

NARRATIVE story of events or experiences, true or fictitious. A poem may be narrative, as "The Rime of the Ancient Mariner."

NOVEL lengthy prose story dealing with imaginary characters and settings that creates the illusion of real life (Scott's *Ivanhoe*)

ODE lyric poem of particularly serious purpose written in language that is dignified and inspired (Keats' "Ode on a Grecian Urn")

ONOMATOPOEIA use of words whose sounds resemble and/or suggest their meanings (*buzz, hiss*)

PARADOX statement that seems contradictory, but that may, in fact, be true (In *The Pirates of Penzance*, the hero had only five birthdays although he was 21 years old. He was born on February 29th of a leap year!)

PARODY writing that pokes fun at a serious work by using exaggeration or broad humor in imitation of the serious work

PERSONIFICATION figure of speech where-in an idea or a thing is given human qualities ("Death, be not proud...")

POEM literature that has any or all of the following qualities to a high degree: deep emotion; highly imaginative language with figures of speech; distinctive rhythm; compression of thought; use of the familiar in a symbolic sense; rhyme scheme; words that mean more than they apparently say

REFRAIN word or group of words repeated regularly in a poem, usually at the end of a stanza (*nevermore* in "The Raven")

REPETITION restating of a phrase or line for emphasis

("And miles to go before I sleep

And miles to go before I sleep.")

RHYME in poetry, agreement in the final sounds of two or more words at the ends of lines (*June, moon*)

RHYTHM in poetry and certain kinds of prose, patterns of stress or accent in the units that make up the verse or sentence.

SARCASM figure of speech that is harsh in tone and expresses meaning by use of the opposite ("Excellent" said when a mistake is made.)

SATIRE work that makes fun of a person, an idea, or a social custom or institution by stressing its foolishness or lack of reasonableness (Swift's *Gulliver's Travels*)

SHORT STORY short prose narrative dealing with imaginary characters usually in a single setting, often relating a single incident, and striving for a single effect (Poe's "The Pit and the Pendulum")

SIMILE figure of speech in which two things essentially unlike are compared, with *like* or *as* being used to make the comparison ("...a poem lovely as a tree")

SOLILOQUY speech of a character in a play, uttered when alone on the stage, in which the speaker informs the audience of his or her thoughts or of knowledge the audience needs to follow the action of the play. (Hamlet's "To be or not to be...")

SONNET form of poetry consisting of fourteen verses in which two aspects of an idea are presented

In the *Italian* or *Petrarchan sonnet*, the first aspect of the idea or theme is presented in the first eight lines, which rhyme *a b b a a b b a*; the second aspect of the idea or commentary on the theme is presented in the second six lines, which rhyme (in various combinations) *c d e c d e*. The first eight lines are the *octet*; the second six lines the *sestet*.

In the *Shakespearean sonnet*, the first aspect is presented in the first twelve lines, which rhyme *a b a b c d c d e f e f*; the second aspect is presented in the last two lines, which rhyme *g g*.

STANZA unit in a poem, similar to a paragraph in prose writing, usually consisting of four or more lines

SYMBOL object that represents an idea, either psychological, philosophical, social, or religious (The cross represents Christianity; the Star of David is the symbol of Judaism.)

TRAGEDY form of drama that has any or all of the following qualities: conflict of character that ends unhappily; a person of great and noble character who meets with a sudden fall because of his or her own weakness; a theme that appeals to our emotions of pity and fear (*Othello*)

VERSE single line of poetry

Language Arts and Reading Practice

The Language Arts and Reading Practice test consists of excerpts from pre-1920 literature, 1920–1960 literature, and literature after 1960, as well as poetry, drama, commentary on the arts, and business documents. Each excerpt is followed by multiple-choice questions about the reading material. Read each excerpt first and then answer the questions following it. Refer to the reading material as often as necessary to answer the questions.

Each excerpt is preceded by a "purpose question," which gives a reason for reading the material. Use these purpose questions to help focus your reading. You are not required to answer these purpose questions. They are given only to help you concentrate on the main idea presented in a particular selection.

LITERATURE (PROSE, POETRY, AND DRAMA)

Questions 1–5 refer to the following selection.

WHAT DO WE KNOW ABOUT SWANS?

On Lake Budi some years ago, they were hunting down the swans without mercy. The procedure was to approach them stealthily in little boats and then rapidly—very rapidly—row into their midst. Swans have difficulty in flying; they must skim the surface of the water at a run. In the first phase of their flight they raise their big wings with great effort. It is then that they can be seized; a few blows with a bludgeon finish them off.

Someone made me a present of a swan: more dead than alive. It was of a marvelous species I have never seen anywhere else in the world: a black-throated swan—a snow boat with a neck packed, as it were, into a tight stocking of black silk. Orange-beaked, red-eyed.

They brought it to me half-dead. I bathed its wounds and pressed little pellets of bread and fish into its throat; but nothing stayed down. Nevertheless the wounds slowly healed, and the swan came to regard me as a friend. At the same time, it was apparent to me that the bird was wasting away with nostalgia. So, cradling the heavy burden in my arms through the streets, I carried it to the river. It paddled a few strokes, very close to me. I had hoped it might learn how to fish for itself, and pointed to some pebbles far below, where they flashed in the sand like silvery fish. The swan looked at them remotely, sad-eyed.

For the next 20 days I carried the bird to the river and toiled back with it to my house. One afternoon it seemed more abstracted than usual, swimming very close and ignoring the lure of insects with which I tried vainly to tempt it to fish again. It became very quiet; so I lifted it into my arms to carry it home again. It was breast high, when I suddenly felt a great ribbon unfurl, like a black arm encircling my face: it was the big coil of the neck, dropping down.

It was then that I learned swans do not sing at their death, if they die of grief.

—Pablo Neruda

1. The swan's wounds healed in spite of its lack of

    (1) courage
    (2) nourishment
    (3) intelligence
    (4) shelter
    (5) companionship

2. The narrator implies that the swan's feeling toward him was one of

    (1) apprehension
    (2) trust
    (3) indifference
    (4) compassion
    (5) skepticism

3. The narrator realized that the swan was

    (1) eager to recover its strength
    (2) suspicious of human contact
    (3) angry at its imprisonment
    (4) homesick for its former life
    (5) devoid of feeling

4. What was the swan's reaction to the narrator's attempts to teach it to fish?

    (1) fear
    (2) antagonism
    (3) apathy
    (4) stubbornness
    (5) eagerness

5. According to the narrator, the swan songs of legends do not apply to death caused by

    (1) bludgeoning
    (2) starvation
    (3) heartbreak
    (4) neglect
    (5) exposure

Questions 6–10 refer to the following selection.

WHAT WAS A PARTY GIVEN BY CHINESE WOMEN LIKE?

My idea was to have a gathering of four women, one for each corner of my mah-jongg table. I knew which women I wanted to ask. They were all young like me, with wishful faces. One was an army officer's wife like myself. Another was a girl with very fine manners from a rich family in Shanghai. She had escaped with only a little money. And there was a girl from Nanking who had the blackest hair I had ever seen. She came from a low-class family, but she was pretty and pleasant and had married well, to an old man who died and left her with a better life.

Each week one of us would host a party to raise money and to raise our spirits. The hostess had to serve special *dyansyin* foods to bring good fortune of all kinds—dumplings shaped like silver money ingots, long rice noodles for long life, boiled peanuts for conceiving sons, and of course, many good luck oranges for a plentiful, sweet life.

What fine food we treated ourselves to with our meager allowances! We didn't notice that the dumplings were stuffed mostly with stringy squash and that the oranges were spotted with wormy holes. We ate sparingly, not as if we didn't have enough, but to protest how we could not eat another bite, we had already bloated ourselves from earlier in the day. We knew we had luxuries few people could afford. We were the lucky ones.

6. From the passage, we can conclude that the narrator is

    (1) a young army officer's wife
    (2) a rich girl from Shanghai
    (3) a low-class widow
    (4) a black-haired girl from Nanking
    (5) a girl with fine manners

7. The food incorrectly matched with its happy good fortune is

    (1) noodles—long life
    (2) peanuts—male children
    (3) dumplings—sweet life
    (4) oranges—abundant life
    (5) *dyansyin* foods—good fortune

8. It can be concluded from the passage that the four women

    (1) came from low-class families
    (2) were well off
    (3) were lonely
    (4) were married
    (5) were depressed

9. The approach of the group toward food was that of

    (1) indifference
    (2) resignation
    (3) disinterest
    (4) disgust
    (5) self-deception

10. That these were hard times in China is indicated by all of the following EXCEPT

    (1) they had little money
    (2) they were depressed
    (3) they had meager allowances
    (4) they ate sparingly
    (5) they had fine food

Questions 11–15 refer to the following selection.

WHAT ARE SOME OF THE EFFECTS OF THE HOLOCAUST?

She walked along the river until a policeman stopped her. It was one o'clock, he said. Not the best time to be walking alone by the side of a half-frozen river. He smiled at her, then offered to walk her home. It was the first day of the new year, 1946, eight and a half months after the British tanks had rumbled into Bergen-Belsen.

That February, my mother turned twenty-six. It was difficult for strangers to believe that she had ever been a concentration camp inmate. Her face was smooth and round. She wore lipstick and applied mascara to her large dark eyes. She dressed fashionably. But when she looked into the mirror in the mornings before leaving for work, my mother saw a shell, a mannequin who moved and spoke but who bore only a superficial resemblance to her real self. The people closest to her had vanished. She had no proof that they were truly dead. No eyewitnesses had survived to vouch for her husband's death. There was no one living who had seen her parents die. The lack of confirmation haunted her. At night before she went to sleep and during the day as she stood pinning dresses she wondered if, by some chance, her parents had gotten past the Germans or had crawled out of the mass grave into which they had been shot and were living, old and helpless, somewhere in Poland. What if only one of them had died? What if they had survived and had died of cold or hunger after she had been liberated, while she was in Celle dancing with British officers?

She did not talk to anyone about these things. No one, she thought, wanted to hear them. She woke up in the mornings, went to work, bought groceries, went to the Jewish Community Center and to the housing office like a robot.

11. The policeman stopped the author's mother from walking along the river because

(1) the river was dangerous
(2) it was the wrong time of day
(3) it was still wartime
(4) it was too cold
(5) it was forbidden to do so

12. The author states that her mother thought about her parents when she

(1) walked along the river
(2) thought about death
(3) danced with the officers
(4) was at work
(5) looked into the mirror

13. When the author mentions her mother's dancing with British officers, she implies that her mother

(1) compared her dancing to the suffering of her parents
(2) had clearly put her troubles behind her
(3) felt it was her duty to dance with the officers
(4) felt guilty about dancing
(5) wanted to escape from her past

14. The mother did not discuss her concerns about her loved ones with anyone because she

(1) thought no one was interested
(2) felt it was no one's business
(3) was too shy
(4) did not know anyone
(5) didn't want to hurt anyone

15. The author's purpose in writing this selection is most likely to

(1) inform people about atrocities in the concentration camp
(2) explain the long-range effects of a traumatic emotional experience
(3) enlist active participation in refugee affairs
(4) encourage people to prosecute former concentration camp guards
(5) gain sympathy from her readers

Questions 16–20 refer to the following selection.

HOW HAVE HUMAN BEINGS CORRUPTED THEIR ENVIRONMENT?

I turned on my back and floated, looking up at the sky, nothing around me but cool clear Pacific, nothing in my eyes but long blue space. It was as close as I
(5) ever got to cleanliness and freedom, as far as I ever got from all the people. They had jerrybuilt the beaches from San Diego to the Golden Gate, bulldozed superhighways through the mountains, cut down a
(10) thousand years of redwood growth, and built an urban wilderness in the desert. They couldn't touch the ocean. They poured their sewage into it, but it couldn't be tainted.
(15) There was nothing wrong with Southern California that a rise in the ocean level wouldn't cure. The sky was flat and empty, and the water was chilling me. I swam to the kelpbed and plunged down
(20) through it. It was cold and clammy like the bowels of fear. I came up gasping and sprinted to shore with a barracuda terror nipping at my heels.

I was still chilly a half-hour later,
(25) crossing the pass to Nopal Valley. Even at its summit, the highway was wide and new, rebuilt with somebody's money. I could smell the source of the money when I slid down into the valley on the other
(30) side. It stank like rotten eggs.

The oil wells from which the sulphur gas rose crowded the slopes on both sides of the town. I could see them from the highway as I drove in: the latticed
(35) triangles of the derricks where trees had grown, the oil-pumps nodding and clanking where cattle had grazed. Since 'thirty-nine or 'forty, when I had seen it last, the town had grown enormously, like
(40) a tumor.

16. In the first paragraph, the ocean is a symbol of nature's

   (1) inability to adapt
   (2) resistance to humanity's endeavors
   (3) submission to a mechanized society
   (4) attack on technology
   (5) constant change

17. What are the dominant images in lines 18–21?

   (1) light and dark
   (2) cold and heat
   (3) terror and fear
   (4) death and defeat
   (5) ugliness and hopelessness

18. In this passage, the narrator apparently is trying to

   (1) appeal to legislators for environmental action
   (2) inform readers of what Southern California looks like
   (3) indicate his disapproval of what has been done
   (4) show the potential beauty of the area
   (5) celebrate human progress

19. In the last paragraph, the main idea is developed through the use of

   (1) cause and effect
   (2) contrast
   (3) analogy
   (4) incident
   (5) comparison

20. In the last paragraph, the narrator feels that the growth of the town is

   (1) detrimental
   (2) inevitable
   (3) progressive
   (4) hasty
   (5) necessary

Questions 21–25 refer to the following selection.

HOW DOES THE HAWK'S JOYOUS CRY AFFECT THE WRITER?

I saw him look that last look away
beyond me into the sky so full of light that
I could not follow his gaze. The little
breeze flowed over me again, and nearby
(5) a mountain aspen shook all its tiny
leaves. I suppose I must have had an
idea then of what I was going to do, but
I never let it come up into consciousness.
I just reached over and laid the hawk on
(10) the grass.
He lay there a long minute without
hope, unmoving, his eyes still fixed on
that blue vault above him. It must have
been that he was already so far away in
(15) heart that he never felt the release from
my hand. He never even stood. He just lay
with his breast against the grass.
In the next second after the long minute
he was gone. Like a flicker of light, the
(20) head vanished with my eyes full on him,
but without actually seeing even a
premonitory wing beat. He was gone
straight into that towering emptiness of
light and crystal that my eyes could
(25) scarcely bear to penetrate. For another
long moment there was silence. I could
not see him. The light was too intense.
Then from far up somewhere a cry came
ringing down.
(30) I was young then and had seen little of
the world, but when I heard that cry my
heart turned over. It was not a cry of the
hawk I had captured; for, by shifting my
position against the sun, I was now seeing
(35) further up. Straight out of the sun's eye
where she must have been soaring
restlessly above us for untold hours
hurtled his mate. And from far up, ringing
from peak to peak of the summits over us,
(40) came a cry of such unutterable and
ecstatic joy that it sounds down across
the years and tingles among the cups of
my quiet breakfast table.

21. In line 1, "that last look" suggests that the hawk

(1) has been blinded
(2) expects to be rescued
(3) believes that his death is near
(4) cannot understand what is happening
(5) is looking for sympathy

22. In line 8, the clause "I never let it come up into consciousness" suggests that the freeing of the hawk is

(1) premeditated
(2) impulsive
(3) impossible
(4) accidental
(5) an afterthought

23. In line 11, the minute is "long" to the narrator because he

(1) is thinking of changing his mind
(2) is young and inexperienced
(3) regrets the action he is taking
(4) is not sure what the hawk will do
(5) is impatient

24. In this selection, the natural phenomenon the narrator seems most impressed by is the

(1) deathlike silence
(2) intense light
(3) steady breeze
(4) blue sky
(5) quaking aspen

25. The narrator's most lasting memory is of the

(1) hawk's eyes
(2) bright light
(3) complete stillness
(4) joyous call of the hawk
(5) beauty of the soaring hawk

Questions 26–30 refer to the following selection.

WHAT DANGEROUS MISTAKE WAS NEARLY MADE?

I was vainly trying to go to sleep that evening when I became aware of unfamiliar sounds. Sitting bolt upright, I listened intently.

(5) The sounds were coming from just across the river, and they were a weird medley of whines, whimpers and small howls. My grip on the rifle slowly relaxed. If there is one thing at which scientists are
(10) adept, it is learning from experience; I was not to be fooled twice. The cries were obviously those of a husky, probably a young one, and I deduced that it must be one of Mike's dogs (he owned three half-
(15) grown pups not yet trained to harness, which ran loose after the team) that had got lost, retraced its way to the cabin, and was now begging for someone to come and be nice to it.

(20) I was delighted. If that pup needed a friend, a chum, I was its man! I climbed hastily into my clothes, ran down to the riverbank, launched the canoe, and paddled lustily for the far bank.

(25) The pup had never ceased its mournful plaint, and I was about to call out reassuringly when it occurred to me that an unfamiliar human voice might frighten it. I decided to stalk it instead, and to
(30) betray my presence only when I was close enough for soothing murmurs.

I had assumed the dog was only a few yards away from the far bank, but as I made my way over boulders and gravel
(35) ridges, the sounds seemed to remain at the same volume while I appeared to be getting no closer. I assumed the pup was retreating, perhaps out of shyness. In my anxiety not to startle it away, I kept quiet,
(40) even when the whimpering stopped, leaving me uncertain about the direction to pursue. However, I saw a steep ridge looming ahead of me and I suspected that, once I gained its summit, I would have a
(45) clear enough view to enable me to locate the lost animal. I got down on my stomach (practicing the fieldcraft I had learned in the Boy Scouts) and cautiously inched my way the last few feet.

(50) My head came slowly over the crest — and there was my quarry. He was lying down, evidently resting after his mournful

singsong, and his nose was about six feet from mine. We stared at one another in
(55) silence. I do not know what went on in his massive skull, but my head was full of the most disturbing thoughts. I was peering straight into the amber gaze of a fully grown arctic wolf, who probably weighed
(60) more than I did, and who was certainly a lot better versed in close-combat techniques than I would ever be.

—Farley Mowat

26. What made the sounds so unusual?

(1) They were very loud.
(2) They were a strange mixture.
(3) They were inhuman.
(4) They were coming from across water.
(5) They were persistent.

27. The expression "not to be fooled twice" (line 11) implies that the

(1) narrator was annoyed by a previous mistake
(2) sounds were made by an echo
(3) sounds were a trick
(4) narrator had dealt with canines before
(5) narrator was stubborn

28. The inference in the second paragraph is that Mike is

(1) a forest ranger
(2) a hunter
(3) a dogsled owner
(4) a child
(5) a wildlife biologist

29. What do lines 20 and 21 suggest about the narrator?

(1) He is an animal lover.
(2) He is a clever man.
(3) He is an excellent athlete.
(4) He is a nervous individual.
(5) He is restless.

30. What caused the narrator to lose track of the pup?

(1) the terrain
(2) the darkness
(3) the silence
(4) the distance
(5) the lack of experience

Questions 31–35 refer to the following selection.

HOW CAN YOU IDENTIFY TWO TYPES OF PEOPLE—A AND Z?

There are only two types of people in the world. Type A and Type Z. It isn't hard to tell which type you are.

(5) How long before the plane leaves do you arrive at the airport? Early plane catchers, Type A, pack their bags at least a day in advance, and they pack neatly. If they're booked on a flight that leaves at four in the afternoon, they get up at five-thirty

(10) that morning. If they haven't left the house by noon, they're worried about missing the plane.

Late plane catchers, Type Z, pack hastily at the last minute and arrive at the

(15) airport too late to buy a newspaper.

What do you do with a new book? Type A reads more carefully and finishes every book, even though it isn't any good.

Type Z skims through a lot of books

(20) and is more apt to write in the margins with a pencil.

Type A eats a good breakfast. Type Z grabs a cup of coffee.

Type A's turn off the lights when leaving

(25) a room and lock the doors when leaving a house. They go back and make sure they've locked it, and they worry later about whether they left the iron on or not. They didn't.

(30) Type Z's leave the lights burning and, if they lock the door at all when they leave the house, they're apt to have forgotten the keys.

Type A sees the dentist twice a year,

(35) has an annual physical checkup, and thinks he may have something. Type Z has been meaning to see a doctor.

Type A squeezes a tube of toothpaste from the bottom and rolls it very carefully

(40) as he uses it, and puts the top back on every time.

Type Z squeezes the tube from the middle, and he's lost the cap under the radiator.

(45) Type Z's are more apt to have some Type A characteristics then Type A's are apt to have any Type Z characteristics.

Type A's always marry Type Z's.

Type Z's always marry Type A's.

31. Type A is all of the following EXCEPT

(1) neat
(2) prompt
(3) hasty
(4) early
(5) worried

32. Type Z is all of the following EXCEPT

(1) late
(2) careful
(3) clumsy
(4) prompt
(5) forgetful

33. The author uses all of the following situations to differentiate Type A from Type Z EXCEPT

(1) catching a plane
(2) getting enough sleep
(3) reading a book
(4) getting a physical checkup
(5) leaving a house

34. It can be concluded from the passage that

(1) Type A and Type Z never change their habits
(2) Type A becomes more like Type Z
(3) Type A and Type Z are hardly distinguishable
(4) Type A is superior to Type Z
(5) Type A is more likely to copy Type Z

35. It can be concluded from the passage that

(1) Type A and Type Z are more alike than different
(2) the two types like each other
(3) to two are complete opposites
(4) the two types compete with each other
(5) the two types resemble each other

Questions 36–40 refer to the following selection.

WHAT ARE THE POET'S THOUGHTS ABOUT LIFE?

Alone

This is as philosophical
As keeping the count,
Binoculars trained
For a whale
That will never spout,
This is not the season,
Hamlet knew.

The Pilgrim knew,
As did the Wife of Bath,
This is discovery,
A poem on the Underground
By Sylvia Plath.

This is the season of butchery,
Bullfights without rules,
Lions shot with a precision rifle,
Selective breeding
On Noah's ark.

This is as dark as it gets
In a daylight forest,
As stark
As one isolated note
From an aria,
As lonesome as one straggler goose,
Squawking, 'take me along'.

—Ashok Niyogi

36. The main idea of the poem is

    (1) that it's OK to feel alone
    (2) that being alone is a part of life
    (3) that a soul needs a home
    (4) to compare being alone to different literary figures or current events
    (5) Sylvia Plath writes about being alone, too

37. The poet most likely comes to her conclusion of "aloneness" out of her

    (1) fear of loneliness
    (2) philosophical thoughts
    (3) need for recognition
    (4) envy of others
    (5) political agenda

38. The poet's idea of being alone is compared to

    (1) a season of butchery
    (2) an aria
    (3) a straggler goose
    (4) lions being shot
    (5) Hamlet

39. The poet mentions Sylvia Plath because

    (1) she is comparing Plath's poetry to her idea of being alone
    (2) Plath is the most famous dark poet
    (3) Plath uses the same literary devices as she does
    (4) the poem needs a reference for support
    (5) she is her favorite poet

40. The poem derives its power from effective use of

    (1) metaphor(s)
    (2) irony
    (3) simile(s)
    (4) allusion
    (5) free verse

Questions 41–45 refer to the following selection.

WHAT IS THE POET DETERMINED TO DO?

I've come this far to freedom and I
   won't turn back.
I'm climbing to the highway from my old
dirt track.
     I'm coming and I'm going
     And I'm stretching and I'm growing
And I'll reap what I've been sowing or
   my skin's not black.
I've prayed and slaved and waited and
   I've sung my song.
You've bled me and you've starved me
   but I've still grown strong,
     You've lashed me and you've treed
     me
     You've everything but freed me
But in time you'll know you need me
   and it won't be long.
I've seen the daylight breaking high
   above the bough.
I've found my destination and I've
   made my vow;
     So whether you abhor me
     Or deride me or ignore me
Mighty mountains loom before me and
   I won't stop now.

        —Naomi Long Madgett

41. The poem is a poem of

   (1) praise
   (2) regret
   (3) resignation
   (4) determination
   (5) submission

42. The "destination" is

   (1) freedom
   (2) the highway
   (3) the old dirt track
   (4) the daylight
   (5) mighty mountains

43. The poet has done all of the following EXCEPT

   (1) reaped
   (2) prayed
   (3) slaved
   (4) waited
   (5) sowed

44. The poet will reach her goal because she

   (1) has stretched
   (2) has grown
   (3) will be needed
   (4) is abhorred
   (5) has been beaten

45. The rhyme scheme of the poem in each stanza is

   (1) abbaa
   (2) abbba
   (3) aabba
   (4) ababa
   (5) aaabb

Questions 46–50 refer to the following passage from a work of literature.

HOW FAR CAN A MAN TRAVEL?

Day had broken cold and gray, exceedingly cold and gray, when the man turned aside from the main Yukon trail and climbed the high earth-bank, where a dim and little-travelled trail led eastward through the fat spruce timberland. It was a steep bank, and he paused for breath at the top, excusing the act to himself by looking at his watch. It was nine o'clock. There was no sun nor hint of sun, though there was not a cloud in the sky. It was a clear day, and yet there seemed an intangible pall over the face of things, a subtle gloom that made the day dark, and that was due to the absence of sun. This fact did not worry the man. He was used to the lack of sun. It had been days since he had seen the sun, and he knew that a few more days must pass before that cheerful orb, due south, would just peep above the sky-line and dip immediately from view.

The man flung a look back along the way he had come. The Yukon lay a mile wide and hidden under three feet of ice. On top of this ice were as many feet of snow. It was all pure white, rolling in gentle undulations where the ice-jams of the freeze-up had formed. North and south, as far as his eye could see, it was unbroken white, save for a dark hair-line that curved and twisted from around the spruce-covered island to the south, and that curved and twisted away into the north, where it disappeared behind another spruce-covered island. This dark hair-line was the trail—the main trail—that led south five hundred miles to the Chilcoot Pass, Dyea, and salt water; and that led north seventy miles to Dawson, and still on to the north a thousand miles to Nulato, and finally to St. Michael on Bering Sea, a thousand miles and half a thousand more.

But all this—the mysterious, far-reaching hair-line trail, the absence of sun from the sky, the tremendous cold, and the strangeness and weirdness of it all—made no impression on the man. It was not because he was long used to it. He was a newcomer in the land, a *chechaquo*, and this was his first winter. The trouble with him was that he was without imagination. He was quick and alert in the things of life, but only in the things, and not in the significances. Fifty degrees below zero meant eighty-odd degrees of frost. Such fact impressed him as being cold and uncomfortable, and that was all. It did not lead him to meditate upon his frailty as a creature of temperature, and upon man's frailty in general, able only to live within certain narrow limits of heat and cold; and from there on it did not lead him to the conjectural field of immortality and man's place in the universe. Fifty degrees below zero stood for a bite of frost that hurt and that must be guarded against by the use of mittens, ear-flaps, warm moccasins, and thick socks. Fifty degrees below zero was to him just precisely fifty degrees below zero. That there should be anything more to it than that was a thought that never entered his head.

46. The character demonstrates his lack of imagination by

    (1) his simple gear and clothing
    (2) his understanding of cold weather
    (3) his description of the trail
    (4) his choice of trail to take for his adventure
    (5) his simple attitude toward the cold

47. The trail is described as all of the following EXCEPT

    (1) having an intangible pall
    (2) little traveled in his direction
    (3) mysterious and far-reaching
    (4) steep
    (5) thousands of miles

48. Evidence of the character's hardship is in the amount of

    (1) competitors he must face
    (2) trails he must travel
    (3) warmer temperatures he may experience
    (4) snow and ice he must endure
    (5) uncomfortable clothing he must wear

49. In enduring the weather, the character was

    (1) experiencing this challenge for the first time
    (2) testing his own strength
    (3) acting on a dare
    (4) going on one of many trips
    (5) proving himself to be imaginative

50. The author is describing an adventure that takes place in

    (1) the midwest
    (2) the northeast
    (3) the southwest
    (4) the west
    (5) the northwest

Questions 51–55 refer to the following passage from a play.

ABOUT WHAT WAS
THE AUTHOR EXCITED?

That one, Platero, was in the shape of a watch. You opened the small silver box and it appeared, pressed against the cloth filled with purple ink like a bird in its nest. How exciting when, after pressing it a minute against the fine white and rose of my hand, there appeared the stamp

FRANCISCO RUIZ
MOGUER

How often I dreamed of that stamp belonging to my friend at Don Carlos' school! With a little printing press which I found upstairs in the old office writing desk in my house, I tried to assemble one with my name. But it did not come out well. . .

One day a salesman for office equipment came to my house with Arias, the silver-smith from Seville. What a delightful array of rulers, compasses, colored inks, stamps. They were all shapes and sizes. I broke my money bank and with the five pesetas I found, ordered a stamp with my name and town. What a long week that was! How my heart would beat when the mail coach arrived! What a sweat I was in and how sad, when the mailman moved away in the rain! Finally one night he brought it to me. . . When one pressed on a spring, the stamp appeared, new and resplendent.

Was there anything in the whole house which went unstamped? What was there which did not belong to me that day? . . .
The next day with what happy haste I took everything to school: my books, shirt, hat, boots and hands marked with the words

JUAN RAMON JIMENEZ
MOGUER

51. The name of the author is

(1) Francisco Ruiz
(2) Don Carlos
(3) Arias
(4) Platero
(5) Juan Ramon Jimenez

52. The author got the idea for his rubber stamp from

(1) Francisco Ruiz
(2) Don Carlos
(3) Arias
(4) Platero
(5) Juan Ramon Jimenez

53. The author addresses his story of the rubber stamp to

(1) Francisco Ruiz
(2) Don Carlos
(3) Arias
(4) Platero
(5) Juan Ramon Jimenez

54. The author got the money to pay for the stamp from

(1) Don Carlos' school
(2) Arias, the silversmith
(3) his friend Francisco Ruiz
(4) his old office writing desk
(5) his money bank

55. We know that the author lives in Spain because of

(1) the small silver box
(2) the little printing press
(3) the name of the coins of money
(4) the mail coach
(5) the salesman of office equipment

Questions 56–60 refer to the following selection.

HOW DID RIP VAN WINKLE SEEK COMFORT?

Rip Van Winkle was one of those happy mortals, of foolish, well-oiled dispositions, who take the world easy, eat white bread or brown, which ever can be got with least thought or trouble, and would rather starve on a penny than work for a pound. If left to himself, he would have whistled life away, in perfect contentment; but his wife kept continually dinning in his ears about his idleness, his carelessness, and the ruin he was bringing on his family. Morning, noon, and night, her tongue was incessantly going, and everything he said or did was sure to produce a torrent of household eloquence. Rip had but one way of replying to all lectures of the kind, and that, by frequent use, had grown into a habit. He shrugged his shoulders, shook his head, cast up his eyes, but said nothing. This, however, always provoked a fresh volley from his wife, so that he was fain to draw off his forces, and take to the outside of the house—the only side which, in truth, belongs to a henpecked husband.

Rip's sole domestic adherent was his dog Wolf, who was as much henpecked as his master; for Dame Van Winkle regarded them as companions in idleness, and even looked upon Wolf with an evil eye as the cause of his master's going so often astray....

...For a long while he used to console himself, when driven from home, by frequenting a kind of perpetual club of the sages, philosophers, and other idle personages of the village, which held its sessions on a bench before a small inn, designated by a rubicund portrait of His Majesty George the Third. Here they used to sit in the shade through a long, lazy summer's day, talking listlessly over village gossip, or telling endless, sleepy stories about nothing....How solemnly they would listen to...Derrick Van Brummel, the schoolmaster.

—Washington Irving

56. The story takes place about

(1) 1660
(2) 1770
(3) 1800
(4) 1812
(5) 1848

57. An example of the author's sense of humor may be found in sentences

(1) 2
(2) 3
(3) 4
(4) 5
(5) 6

58. The blame for Rip's conduct was placed by Dame Van Winkle on

(1) Wolf
(2) George the Third
(3) Derrick Van Brummel
(4) the club of sages
(5) other idle villagers

59. Rip may be described by *all* of the following adjectives EXCEPT

(1) henpecked
(2) easygoing
(3) happy
(4) complaining
(5) resigned

60. Rip's only problem was his

(1) poverty
(2) idleness
(3) wife's nagging
(4) wife's evil eye
(5) village companions

Questions 61–65 refer to the following selection.

WHY DID THE AUTHOR GO TO THE WOODS?

I went to the woods because I wished to live deliberately, to front only the essential facts of life, and see if I could not learn what it had to teach, and not, when I came to die, discover that I had not lived. I did not wish to live what was not life, living is so dear; nor did I wish to practise resignation, unless it was quite necessary. I wanted to live deep and suck out all the marrow of life, to live so sturdily and Spartan-like as to put to rout all that was not life, to cut a broad swath and shave close, to drive life into a corner, and reduce it to its lowest terms, and, if it proved to be mean, why then to get the whole and genuine meanness of it, and publish its meanness to the world; or if it were sublime, to know it by experience, and be able to give a true account of it in my next excursion. For most men, it appears to me, are in a strange uncertainty about it, whether it is of the devil or of God, and have *somewhat hastily* concluded that it is the chief end of man here to 'glorify God and enjoy him forever.'

Still we live meanly, like ants; though the fable tells us that we were long ago changed into men; like pygmies we fight with cranes; it is error upon error, and clout upon clout, and our best virtue has for its occasion a superfluous and evitable wretchedness. Our life is frittered away by detail. An honest man has hardly need to count more than his ten fingers, or in extreme cases he may add his ten toes, and lump the rest. Simplicity, simplicity, simplicity! I say, let your affairs be as two or three, and not a hundred or a thousand; instead of a million count half a dozen, and keep your accounts on your thumb-nail.

—Henry D. Thoreau

61. The best statement of why the author went to the woods is that he went to

   (1) discover that he had not lived
   (2) live meanly, like ants
   (3) practice resignation
   (4) reduce life to its simplest terms
   (5) glorify God

62. The author thinks that life should be *all* of the following EXCEPT

   (1) Spartan-like
   (2) complicated
   (3) creative
   (4) noble
   (5) moral

63. All of the following words as used in this selection are correctly defined EXCEPT

   (1) *deliberately*—unhurriedly
   (2) *front*—confront
   (3) *swath*—space
   (4) *mean*—nasty
   (5) *frittered*—wasted

64. The tone of the selection is

   (1) bitter cynicism
   (2) moral indignation
   (3) flippant humor
   (4) quiet resignation
   (5) self-congratulation

65. The author

   (1) wishes to learn from nature
   (2) is afraid of death
   (3) has little regard for life
   (4) seeks reconciliation with God
   (5) celebrates the human life-style

Questions 66–70 refer to the following selection.

WHY DID THE GIRL CLIMB THE TREE?

There was the huge tree asleep yet in the paling moonlight, and small and hopeful Sylvia began with utmost bravery to mount to the top of it, with tingling,
(5) eager blood coursing the channels of her whole frame, with her bare feet and fingers that pinched and held like bird's claws to the monstrous ladder reaching up, up, almost to the sky itself. First she must
(10) mount the white oak tree that grew alongside, where she was almost lost among the dark branches and the green leaves heavy and wet with dew; a bird fluttered off its nest, and a red squirrel ran
(15) to and fro and scolded pettishly at the harmless housebreaker. Sylvia felt her way easily. She had often climbed there and knew that higher still one of the oak's upper branches chafed against the pine
(20) trunk, just where its lower boughs were set close together. There, when she made the dangerous pass from one tree to the other, the great enterprise would really begin.

She crept out along the swaying oak
(25) limb at last and took the daring step across into the old pine tree. The way was harder than she thought; she must reach far and hold fast. The sharp dry twigs caught and held her and scratched her
(30) like angry talons; the pitch made her thin little fingers clumsy and stiff as she went round and round the tree's great stem, higher and higher upward. The sparrows and robins in the woods below were
(35) beginning to wake and twitter to the dawn, yet it seemed much lighter there aloft in the pine tree, and the child knew that she must hurry if her project were to be of any use.
(40) The tree seemed to lengthen itself out as she went up and to reach farther and farther upward. It was like a great mainmast to the voyaging earth; it must truly have been amazed that morning
(45) through all its ponderous frame as it felt this determined spark of human spirit creeping and climbing from higher branch to branch. Who knows how steadily the least twigs held themselves to advantage
(50) this light, weak creature on her way! The old pine must have loved his new dependent. More than all the hawks and bats and moths and even the sweet-voiced thrushes was the brave, beating heart of
(55) the solitary gray-eyed child. And the tree stood still and held away the winds that June morning while the dawn grew bright in the east.

—Sarah Orne Jewett

66. The girl's blood was tingling (line 4) because she was

(1) cold
(2) frightened
(3) excited
(4) ill
(5) clumsy

67. Why did Sylvia climb the oak tree?

(1) to observe the birds
(2) to get closer to the pine tree
(3) to get to the ladder
(4) to chase a squirrel
(5) to observe the sunset

68. Why was the first part of Sylvia's climb easy for her?

(1) The branches were close together.
(2) It was almost daylight.
(3) There was a ladder nearby.
(4) She had climbed the tree before.
(5) She was in good physical shape.

69. In lines 42 and 43, the tree is compared to

(1) a giant's hand
(2) the earth's axis
(3) a part of a ship
(4) a space shuttle
(5) a monument

70. In lines 50 through 55, the pine tree is portrayed as a

(1) kindly protector
(2) solitary sentinel
(3) stern parent
(4) brave soldier
(5) human spirit

Questions 71–75 refer to the following selection.

WHAT ARE FEUDS?

"Don't you know what a feud is?"

"Never heard of it before—tell me about it."

"Well," says Buck, "a feud is this way: A man has a quarrel with another man, and kills him; then that other man's brother kills *him*; then the other brothers, on both sides, goes for one another; then the *cousins* chip in—and by and by everybody's killed off, and there ain't no more feud. But it's kind of slow, and takes a long time."

"Has this one been going on long, Buck?"

"Well, I should *reckon*! It started thirty years ago, or some'ers along there. There was trouble 'bout something, and then a lawsuit to settle it; and the suit went agin one of the men, and so he up and shot the man that won the suit—which he would naturally do, of course. Anybody would."

"What was the trouble about, Buck—land?"

"I reckon maybe—I don't know."

"Well, who done the shooting? Was it a Grangerford or a Shepherdson?"

"Laws, how do *I* know? It was so long ago."

"Don't anybody know?"

"Oh, yes, pa knows, I reckon, and some of the other old people: but they don't know now what the row was about in the first place."...

"Has anybody been killed this year, Buck?"

"Yes; we got one and they got one. 'Bout three months ago my cousin Bud, fourteen year old, was riding through the woods...and sees old Baldy Shepherdson a-linkin' after him with his gun in his hand and his white hair a-flying in the wind;...so at last Bud seen it warn't any use, so he stopped and faced around so as to have the bulletholes in front, you know, and the old man he rode up and shot him down. But he didn't git much chance to enjoy his luck, for inside of a week our folks laid *him* out."

Next Sunday we all went to church, about three mile, everybody a-horseback. The men took their guns along, so did Buck, and kept them between their knees or stood them handy against the wall. The Shepherdsons done the same. It was pretty ornery preaching—all about brotherly love...

—Mark Twain

71. The main purpose of this selection is to

(1) write humorously of Southern mountainfolk
(2) tell the story of the Grangerfords and the Shepherdsons
(3) preach the importance of brotherly love
(4) extol the courage of the narrator
(5) satirize feuds

72. All of the following are true of the Grangerford-Shepherdson quarrel EXCEPT that it

(1) was of long duration
(2) was started by a Grangerford
(3) had an unknown cause
(4) involved courageous people
(5) involved children as well as adults

73. Buck is

(1) the author
(2) a stranger
(3) a Grangerford
(4) a Shepherdson
(5) an impartial observer

74. The church incident is mentioned to

(1) bring out the importance of brotherly love
(2) reaffirm the author's faith
(3) place the blame on neither the Grangerfords nor the Shepherdsons
(4) point up the hypocrisy of those who attended
(5) present the author's view on grace and predestination

75. The attitude of Buck toward feuds is

(1) impartial
(2) critical
(3) unquestioning
(4) regretful
(5) bitter

POETRY

Questions 76–80 refer to the following poem.

WHAT CAN WE LEARN ABOUT OPPORTUNITY?

Opportunity

This I beheld, or dreamed it in a
    dream:—
There spread a cloud of dust along a
    plain;
(5)   And underneath the cloud, or in it,
    raged
A furious battle, and men yelled, and
    swords
Shocked upon swords and shields. A
    prince's banner
(10)
Wavered, then staggered backward,
    hemmed by foes.
A craven hung along the battle's edge,
And thought, "Had I a sword of keener
(15)   steel—
That blue blade that the king's son
    bears—but this
Blunt thing!" he snapped and flung it
    from his hand,
(20) And lowering crept away and left the
    field.
Then came the king's son, wounded,
    sore bestead,
And weaponless, and saw the broken
(25)   sword,
Hilt-buried in the dry and trodden
    sand,
And ran and snatched it, and with
    battle-shout
(30) Lifted afresh he hewed his enemy down,
And saved a great cause that heroic
    day.
              —Edward Roland Sill

76. The main purpose of the poem is to

    (1) tell what happened in a dream
    (2) relate an act of cowardice
    (3) applaud an act of bravery
    (4) teach a lesson in conduct
    (5) tell an interesting story

77. The most logical words to continue the quotation that begins on line 14 are

    (1) "...I could defend myself better."
    (2) "...but I cannot have the blue blade."
    (3) "...I could safely escape."
    (4) "...I could help defeat the enemy."
    (5) "...but what good would it do."

78. The word *craven* as used in this poem means a person who is best described as

    (1) envious
    (2) desirous
    (3) cowardly
    (4) traitorous
    (5) angry

79. Lines 8 and 9 are an example of

    (1) personification
    (2) irony
    (3) metaphor
    (4) simile
    (5) alliteration

80. The poem derives its power by presenting

    (1) a graphic picture of nature
    (2) a stark contrast in behavior
    (3) a description of battle
    (4) an effective use of rhyme
    (5) a human tragedy

Questions 81–85 refer to the following poem.

HOW IS GRIEF AT THE LOSS OF A LOVED ONE EXPRESSED?

Stop All the Clocks

Stop all the clocks, cut off the
telephone,
Prevent the dog from barking with a
juicy bone,
(5)   Silence the pianos and with muffled
drum
Bring out the coffin, let the mourners
come.

(10)   Let aeroplanes circle moaning overhead
Scribbling on the sky the message He Is
Dead,
Put crepe bows round the white necks of
the public doves,
(15)   Let the traffic policemen wear black
cotton gloves.

He was my North, my South, my East
and West,
(20)   My working week, and my Sunday rest,
My noon, my midnight, my talk, my
song:
I thought that love would last for ever: I
was wrong.
(25)

The stars are not wanted now; put out
every one:
Pack up the moon and dismantle the
sun;
(30)   Pour away the ocean and sweep up the
woods;
For nothing now can ever come to any
good.
—W.H. Auden

81. In line 1, the effect of using the one-syllable words *stop* and *cut* is to

(1) conceal the speaker's grief
(2) create an instant picture for the reader
(3) fill the reader with similar suffering
(4) emphasize the shock the speaker has suffered
(5) simplify a complex feeling

82. In line 11, which poetic device is used in the phrase "Scribbling on the sky"?

(1) onomatopoeia
(2) pun
(3) alliteration
(4) simile
(5) metaphor

83. Which statement best summarizes the third stanza?

(1) He was everything to me, but I lost him.
(2) He was with me everywhere I went.
(3) He was always talking or singing.
(4) He was my life, my everything.
(5) He was place and time for me.

84. In which line(s) does the climax of the poem occur?

(1) lines 8 and 9
(2) lines 14 and 15
(3) lines 19 and 20
(4) lines 23 and 24
(5) lines 26 and 27

85. Although the title of the poem is "Stop All the Clocks," the speaker really wants to stop everything that

(1) records time
(2) reflects love
(3) causes grief
(4) continues life
(5) makes sounds

DRAMA

Questions 86–90 refer to this excerpt from a play.

HOW DO MOTHER AND DAUGHTER DIFFER?

DAUGHTER (*gently*): Ma, you worked all your life. Why don't you take it easy?

OLD LADY: I don't want to take it easy. Now that your father's dead and in the grave I don't know what to do with myself.

DAUGHTER: Why don't you go out, sit in the park, get a little sun like the other old women?

OLD LADY: I sit around here sometimes, going crazy. We had a lot of fights in our time, your father and I, but I must admit I miss him badly. You can't live with someone 41 years and not miss him when he's dead. I'm glad that he died, for his own sake—it may sound hard of me to say that—but I am glad. He was in nothing but pain the last few months, and he was a man who could never stand pain. But I do miss him.

DAUGHTER (*gently*): Ma, why don't you come live with George and me?

OLD LADY: No, no, Annie, you're a good daughter.

DAUGHTER: We'll move Tommy into the baby's room, and you can have Tommy's room. It's the nicest room in the apartment. It gets all the sun.

OLD LADY: I have wonderful children. I thank God every night for that. I...

DAUGHTER: Ma, I don't like you living here alone...

OLD LADY: Annie, I been living in this house for eight years, and I know all the neighbors and the store people, and if I lived with you, I'd be a stranger.

DAUGHTER: There's plenty of old people in my neighborhood. You'll make friends.

OLD LADY: Annie, you're a good daughter, but I want to keep my own home. I want to pay my own rent. I don't want to be some old lady living with her children. If I can't take care of myself, I'd just as soon be in the grave with your father. I don't want to be a burden on my children.

86. The daughter's attitude toward the mother is one of

    (1) indifference
    (2) antagonism
    (3) caring
    (4) disrespect
    (5) conciliation

87. The mother's attitude toward the daughter is one of

    (1) antagonism
    (2) disrespect
    (3) indifference
    (4) bitterness
    (5) appreciation

88. The mother wants to

    (1) enjoy her leisure
    (2) forget her past life
    (3) retain her independence
    (4) criticize her children
    (5) forget her husband

89. The mother wants to live alone because

    (1) she wants an easy life
    (2) she doesn't get on well with her children
    (3) she is undecided what to do
    (4) she knows the neighborhood
    (5) she can't take care of herself

90. The daughter offers the mother all of the following EXCEPT

    (1) a sunny room
    (2) a friendly neighborhood
    (3) potential friends of the same age
    (4) independence
    (5) old companions

COMMENTARY ON THE ARTS

<u>Questions 91–95</u> deal with the following selection on the theater.

WHAT IS THE ROLE OF SETTING IN A PLAY'S SUCCESS?

Rain pounds the cobblestone streets—empty except for a handful of urchins hovering around an enormous and imposing mansion. Then come the sounds of laughter and the clinking of champagne glasses. Cut to a shadowy figure in trench coat and snap-brim hat.

The scene is from a recent Broadway hit. It's not so much *An Inspector Calls* competent 50-year-old script or the solid acting that has excited critics and audiences. It's the remarkably inventive and surprising set designed by Ian MacNeil, who, with director Stephen Daldry, has transformed J. B. Priestly's sometimes preachy whodunit into first-rate theater.

MacNeil attributes the triumph of British set design not to artistic superiority but to the art-comes-first atmosphere of England's state-subsidized theaters. "At home, there aren't producers around who second-guess whether audiences want to pay to see it."

The play's most powerful moment is actually a set change: the fall, quite literally, of the house of the family in the play. Not everybody is happy with the fact that the set, not the play, is the thing. From an actor's point of view, says one cast member, "these sets are disturbing and a hindrance. It's not my particular cup of tea."

91. The review indicates that *An Inspector Calls* is good theater because of its

(1) script
(2) acting
(3) direction
(4) sound effects
(5) set

92. *An Inspector Calls* is

(1) a comedy
(2) musical theater
(3) a new play
(4) a mystery
(5) an American play

93. J. B. Priestly is the

(1) author
(2) director
(3) set designer
(4) producer
(5) featured actor

94. The success of the set design for the play is due to

(1) artistic superiority
(2) British producers
(3) union regulations
(4) government assistance
(5) experimentation

95. The reaction of some cast members to the set is

(1) enthusiastic
(2) indifferent
(3) negative
(4) dismissive
(5) predictable

Questions 96–100 refer to the following play.

WHY DO POOR PEOPLE MAKE SUCH EXPENSIVE FUNERALS?

SALESMAN: [*Chewing*] I really don't understand...wherever you look, in all the newspapers, you read the most horrible stories about conditions among the weavers, and you get the impression that all the people here are half-starved. And then you see such a funeral! Just as I came into the village, there were brass bands, school-teachers, children, the pastor, and a whole string of people; my God, you'd think the Emperor of China was being buried. If these people can pay for that...! [*He drinks his beer. Then he puts his glass down and suddenly speaks in a friovolous tone.*] Isn't that so, Miss? Don't you agree with me?

[ANNA *smiles, embarassed, and continues busily with her embroidery.*]

SALESMAN: Those must be slippers for Papa.

WELZEL: Oh, I don't like to wear them things.

SALESMAN: Just listen to that! I'd give half my fortune if those slippers were for me.

MRS. WELZEL: He just don't appreciate such things.

WIEGAND: [*After he has coughed several times and moved his chair about, as if he wanted to speak*] The gentleman has expressed himself mighty well about the funeral. Now tell us, young lady, isn't that just a small funeral?

SALESMAN: Yes, I must say...That must cost a tremendous amount of money. Where do these people get the money for it?

WIEGAND: You'll forgive me for sayin' it, sir, there is no such folly among the poorer classes hereabouts. If you don't mind my sayin' so, they have such exagerated ideas of the dutiful respect and the obligations that's due the deceased and the blessed dead. And when it's a matter of deceased parents, they are so superstitious that the descendants and the next of kin scrape together their last penny. And what the children can't raise, they borrow from the nearest moneylender. And then they're in debts up to their necks; they'll be owing His Reverence the Pastor, the sexton, and everybody else in the neighborhood. And drinks and victuals and all the other necessary things. Oh, yes, I approve of respectful duty on the part of children toward their parents, but not so that the mourners are burdened down the rest of their lives by such obligations.

SALESMAN: I beg your pardon, but I should think the pastor would talk them out of it.

WIEGAND: Beggin' your pardon, sir, but there I would like to interpose that every little congregation has its ecclesiastcal house of worship and must support its reverend pastor. The high clergy get a wonderful revenue and profit from such a big funeral. The more elaborate such a funeral can be arranged, the more profitable is the offeratory that flows from it. Whoever knows the conditions of the workers here-abouts can, with unauthoritative certainty, affirm that the pastors only with reluctance tolerate small and quiet funerals.

96. Which character in the passage seems to see things most clearly?

    (1) The salesman
    (2) Mrs. Welzel
    (3) Welzel
    (4) Wiegand
    (5) Anna

97. What do the italicized portions in the passage signify?

    (1) Directions to the actors
    (2) Asides to the actors
    (3) Directions to the cameraman
    (4) Important parts of the dialogue
    (5) Comments by the playwright

98. Why do the townspeople apparently have such elaborate funerals?

    (1) They have more money than the public has been led to believe.
    (2) They have strong ideas of the respect due to the dead.
    (3) They look upon the funerals as holiday occasions.
    (4) They wish to impress their neighbors.
    (5) They wish to defy the advice of their parents.

99. Wiegand's speech about the church suggests that he views it as an institution that is

    (1) sympathetic to the weavers' needs
    (2) interested only in formal worship
    (3) in favor of small and quiet funerals, rather than large, boisterous ones
    (4) organized to do God's work on Earth
    (5) interested in making money from the people

100. From this passage, the reader can most safely conclude that Anna is

    (1) Wiegand's wife
    (2) Welzel's daughter
    (3) the salesman's friend
    (4) a worker in the weaving mills
    (5) a servant

Questions 101–105 refer to the following passage on film.

WHAT IS HOLLYWOOD REALLY LIKE?

Like other forms of American popular culture, Hollywood is a little world in itself—a subculture of the larger society, but with marked mirror distortions. It has strata of prestige and power, narrowing to a small top group who sit at the peak of the pyramid. They are the studio executives in charge of production. A mass of legendry clings to each of them, and what passes for conversation in Hollywood is likely to be anecdotes, gossip, and malice about them. Their royal position casts a deep shadow on Hollywood, for independent critical judgment is impossible where the employee must also be a courtier. A Hollywood "big shot" is surrounded by yes-men whose function is to give Number One the heady sense of being right. Where one man has the power of life and death there can be none of that responsibility which must mean taking risks in order to make independent choices. No one feels secure in his tenure—not even the top executives, who fear the intrigues of their rivals and the power of the bankers, and these in turn fear the whims and hostility of the movie audience.

The final decisions that affect creativeness are made in the "front office" with an eye on picture budgets that may run into millions of dollars. Everyone connected with a picture, including the director and script writers, knows that two or three million dollars may be at stake: as a result, no one takes risks with ideas, theme, treatment. The phrase "venture capital" has an ironic meaning when applied to Hollywood: since the capital being ventured is big, nothing else can be ventured. This is the nub of Hollywood's timidity. And timidity joins with bureacracy and the money yardstick to form Hollywood's deadly trinity.

The movie colony is always in feverish motion, always coming up with "terrific" ideas for "colossal" successes; yet for all its febrile quality, it is always in danger of becoming stagnant. It isn't a metropolis, yet it feels too important to be content with the life of a small town—nor could it even if it wished, since it is torn away from all the normal activities of a town. Thus Hollywood is one of the loneliest places in the world.

101. The attitude of the author to Hollywood is

    (1) objective
    (2) critical
    (3) admiring
    (4) even-handed
    (5) traditional

102. The structure of Hollywood society

    (1) makes for security
    (2) stifles independent thinking
    (3) encourages risk-taking
    (4) results in group tensions
    (5) reflects the larger society

103. The author implies that the ultimate authority rests with

    (1) the studio executive
    (2) the Hollywood employee
    (3) rivals of the top executives
    (4) the bankers
    (5) the movie audience

104. The word that best describes Hollywood movie-making is

    (1) legendary
    (2) responsible
    (3) venturesome
    (4) independent
    (5) fearful

105. The author points up a contradiction in Hollywood's

    (1) size
    (2) bureaucracy
    (3) success
    (4) creativeness
    (5) conversation

Questions 106–110 refer to the following passage.

WHAT IS THE SECRET OF A MOVIE DIRECTOR'S SUCCESS?

Orson Welles was once asked which director's work he admired. Welles, who had himself made cinematic history on a few occasions, responded: "The old masters, by which I mean John Ford, John Ford, and John Ford."

Welles wasn't alone in his admiration of Ford. His fellow directors awarded Ford Oscars for best director on four different occasions. While a few directors have produced individual films that equal, or perhaps even surpass, Ford's best, no one can match his total body of work.

Over a career spanning five decades, Ford directed 112 feature films, with only a couple of outright failures. Dozens of his films are recognized by critics as classics. The vast majority of the rest remain eminently watchable. *Stagecoach*, *Young Mr. Lincoln*, *The Grapes of Wrath*, *How Green Was My Valley*, *The Searchers*, *The Quiet Man*, *She Wore a Yellow Ribbon*—these are just a few of the classics he made.

Ford, who always protested that he did not aspire to make great art, only entertaining films, shrugged off the praise. He told anyone that would listen that he filled the set with mist and kept the actors in shadows because he didn't have a budget big enough for good sets.

This frugality was a trait that Ford did not abandon even at the height of his success. Another trait that distinguished Ford's filmmaking was his speed. The cavalry film, *She Wore a Yellow Ribbon*, for example, was shot in just 28 days. Most films have a shooting schedule of at least 60 days. His speed and frugality grew out of his character. Ford believed in hard work and was tight with a buck even in his private life. But these traits also seemed to be part of a deliberate strategy on Ford's part.

Because his films were so inexpensive, few of them failed to at least break even. Because he was so prolific, Ford could be certain that, even when one of his films was less-than-successful, he would be back in theaters just a few months later with one that would likely be a hit.

106. Ford's honors came from

    (1) his audiences
    (2) his actors
    (3) his choice of subjects
    (4) his critics
    (5) his fellow directors

107. The reader can infer from his reaction to praise that Ford was

    (1) hungry for recognition
    (2) antisocial
    (3) egocentric
    (4) proud
    (5) modest

108. The reader can infer from Ford's filling the set with mist that he

    (1) didn't have good actors
    (2) didn't have an adequate budget
    (3) had a love for the mysterious
    (4) valued a good set
    (5) was lavish in his direction

109. Ford's speed and frugality were a result of

    (1) necessity
    (2) poor planning
    (3) pressure to succeed
    (4) a purposeful plan
    (5) an unfortunate inefficiency

110. Ford's films were profitable because they were

    (1) made inexpensively
    (2) produced on lavish sets
    (3) made in foreign countries
    (4) notable for artistic quality
    (5) based on classics

Questions 111–115 are based on the following selection.

WHAT IS THE SURPRISING FINDING ABOUT KIDS AND READING?

A new study on how kids use different media could give a parent both apoplexy and cause for joy. The study, titled "Kids and Media at the New Millennium," found
(5) that the technology-savvy generation of 2- to 18-year-olds knows all too well the delights of TV, compact discs, video games and video cassettes—all the latest cyber-gadgetry. But, and here is the silver
(10) lining, reading is still among the youthful set's top three interests despite the glittery allure of fancy electronics.

Watching television is still the most popular pastime. On average, youngsters
(15) spend 2 hours and 46 minutes in front of the tube a day. Second comes listening to music which takes up an average of 1 hour and 27 minutes a day. Reading is 44 minutes a day but it is third, above
(20) watching videos, using a computer for fun, playing video games, and going online.

The phenomenal popularity of the Harry Potter books by J. K. Rowling gave adults one major clue that reading could
(25) entice children and make them forget Nintendo and "The Simpsons" for a while.

The study offers hope that reading is here to stay. The challenge is to figure out how to move it to the top of the charts.
(30) Parents can have a significant influence on TV watching. Just turning off the dial and having a conversation during meal-time could go a long way toward moving television down and reading up on the
(35) popularity scale and families can set aside nightly reading times for everyone in the house.

111. The most encouraging finding of the study is that, for youngsters, a top interest is

(1) video games and cassettes
(2) television
(3) music
(4) reading
(5) family electronics

112. The study found that this generation of youngsters is

(1) knowledgeable about technology
(2) a source of disappointment to parents
(3) wasting time on cyber-gadgetry
(4) reading-illiterate
(5) a cause of concern to parents

113. The study showed that reading is still attractive to youngsters because of

(1) Nintendo
(2) "the Simpsons"
(3) computer games
(4) the delights of television
(5) the Harry Potter books

114. The task for the future according to the study is to

(1) educate them in technology
(2) increase interest in reading
(3) expose them to music
(4) increase family electronics
(5) improve relationships with parents

115. The results of the study are

(1) cause for disappointment
(2) basically negative
(3) inconclusive
(4) hopeful
(5) worrisome

Questions 116–120 refer to the following selection on art.

WHAT WERE LEONARDO DA VINCI'S TALENTS?

Leonardo carried on his studies in mathematics and physics, botany and anatomy, not in addition to his art but as a part of it. To him there was no essential difference between art and science. Both are ways of describing God's one universe. He poured scorn on artists who wish to improve on Nature. Let them improve on themselves; Nature can't be wrong!

But when he came to paint, Leonardo flung over chill, naked fact the glowing cloak of beauty. His knowledge, his technique, his peerless draftsmanship, were concealed like a conjuror's sleight, and he painted like a man in love with life. How he loved it can be seen by turning over his sketchbooks' pages—hundreds of them. Here on one sheet may be seen the dimples and creases in a baby's knee, together with the contorted features of soldiers dying and killing. Here are naked laborers straining, there is a young woman kneeling in prayer. Now he draws the nervous anxiety in the neck tendons of an old pauper, and here he has captured the gaiety of a playing child. It is said that he would follow beautiful or grotesque people around all day to study them. He visited the hospitals to watch old men die, and hastened to see a criminal hanged. Conspicuous for his golden locks topped with a little round black cap, and for his rose-colored cloak streaming like an anemone in the gusty streets, he loitered to watch the innocent greed of a baby at its mother's breast; then secretly, for it was frowned on, he hurried and dissected a human body that his brush might accurately paint "the divine proportion."

Indeed on no science did Leonardo spend so much time as on anatomy. Our muscles he demonstrated to be the levers they are, and he revealed the eye to be a lens. The heart he proved to be a hydraulic pump, and showed that the pulse is synchronized with the heart beat. He was the first discoverer, too, of the moderator bands involved in the contraction of the heart muscles. His many observations in the hospitals led him to the discovery of hardening of the arteries as a cause of death in old age.

116. According to the article, Leonardo da Vinci's life combined interests in

(1) nature and science
(2) technique and inspiration
(3) God and art
(4) science and art
(5) nature and the universe

117. The contradiction in Leonardo implied by the writer found expression in his

(1) scorn of artists
(2) painting
(3) distrust of nature
(4) morbid curiosity
(5) conspicuous clothing

118. The writer admires all of the following about Leonardo EXCEPT his

(1) improvements on nature
(2) technique
(3) knowledge
(4) draftsmanship
(5) painting

119. His sketches of babies, soldiers, and laborers are cited as examples of Leonardo's

(1) concealed technique
(2) love of life
(3) versatility
(4) curiosity
(5) realism

120. Leonardo's scientific studies led to discoveries regarding all of the following EXCEPT the

(1) muscles
(2) eye
(3) heart
(4) pulse
(5) blood

BUSINESS DOCUMENTS

Questions 121–125 refer to the following company memorandum.

Vehicle Expense Reimbursement

TO: Ms. Gratz
FROM: Accounting
RE: Vehicle Expense Reimbursement
DATE: December 2008

Dear Ms. Gratz,

It is essential that any of our personnel who drive company and personal vehicles in connection with company business maintain a detailed record of expenses incurred. It is our desire to be certain that you are reimbursed for any expenditures that you make in this regard, and your good record keeping will make this possible.

Receipts must be submitted for gasoline purchases, parking expenses, and repairs. In addition, we will require your daily record of the number of miles driven, the odometer reading, before and after, and the amount of time spent driving. This information should be included in your weekly report to Mr. Edward Hutson. Please use the attached form for your convenience.

Thank you very much for your cooperation in this matter.

Sincerely,
Gregory Snells

Gregory Snells
Director of Accounting

121. What is the purpose of the letter?

    (1) to reprimand an employee for not following the proper procedure for reporting vehicle expenses
    (2) to reward an employee for correctly submitting a vehicle expense report
    (3) to give reasons for submitting receipts for gasoline
    (4) to request a record of mileage
    (5) to outline the procedure for submitting reimbursed expenditures

122. All of the following are reimbursed expenditures EXCEPT

    (1) parking receipts
    (2) food
    (3) repairs
    (4) gasoline
    (5) auto services

123. Gregory Snells is writing to

    (1) persuade an employee
    (2) inform an employee
    (3) describe or narrate to an employee
    (4) explain to a customer
    (5) persuade a customer

124. Ms. Gratz is probably requesting

    (1) receipts for car repairs
    (2) a raise
    (3) money for expenses she incurred
    (4) a company car
    (5) a leave of absence

125. All employees at this company probably

    (1) enjoy taking a vacation
    (2) have company cars
    (3) don't travel much
    (4) do company business and travel while using their own cars
    (5) request money for extra expenses

Answer Key

Literature/Page 508

1. **2**	14. **1**	27. **4**	40. **4**	53. **4**	66. **3**
2. **2**	15. **2**	28. **3**	41. **4**	54. **5**	67. **2**
3. **4**	16. **2**	29. **1**	42. **1**	55. **3**	68. **4**
4. **3**	17. **3**	30. **3**	43. **1**	56. **2**	69. **3**
5. **3**	18. **3**	31. **3**	44. **3**	57. **5**	70. **1**
6. **1**	19. **2**	32. **1**	45. **3**	58. **1**	71. **5**
7. **3**	20. **1**	33. **2**	46. **5**	59. **4**	72. **2**
8. **5**	21. **3**	34. **1**	47. **2**	60. **3**	73. **3**
9. **5**	22. **2**	35. **2**	48. **4**	61. **4**	74. **4**
10. **5**	23. **4**	36. **4**	49. **1**	62. **2**	75. **3**
11. **2**	24. **2**	37. **2**	50. **5**	63. **4**	
12. **4**	25. **4**	38. **3**	51. **5**	64. **2**	
13. **4**	26. **2**	39. **1**	52. **1**	65. **1**	

Poetry and Drama/Pages 523/525

76. **4**	79. **5**	82. **3**	85. **4**	87. **5**	89. **4**
77. **4**	80. **2**	83. **1**	86. **3**	88. **3**	90. **4**
78. **3**	81. **4**	84. **4**			

Commentary on the Arts/Page 526

91. **5**	96. **4**	101. **2**	106. **5**	111. **4**	116. **4**
92. **4**	97. **1**	102. **2**	107. **5**	112. **1**	117. **2**
93. **1**	98. **2**	103. **5**	108. **2**	113. **5**	118. **1**
94. **4**	99. **5**	104. **5**	109. **4**	114. **2**	119. **2**
95. **3**	100. **2**	105. **1**	110. **1**	115. **4**	120. **5**

Business Documents/Page 532

121. **5** 122. **2** 123. **2** 124. **3** 125. **4**

WHAT'S YOUR SCORE?

_____right, _____wrong

Excellent	108–120
Good	96–107
Fair	84–95

If your score was low, the explanation of the correct answers that follows will help you. Analyze your errors. Then, reread the section on Basic Reading Skills (beginning on page 475), Reading Prose, Poetry, and Drama (page 477), and Reading Business Documents (page 501).

Answer Analysis

Literature/Page 508

1. **2** The passage states that, despite the fact that no food stayed down, "the wounds slowly healed."

2. **2** The swan "came to regard me as a friend."

3. **4** The narrator felt "the bird was wasting away with nostalgia."

4. **3** The swan looked at the pebbles (fish) "remotely."

5. **3** In the last sentence, the narrator says, "Swans do not sing at their death if they die of grief."

6. **1** The author states that one of the women is an officer's wife, *like myself.*

7. **3** The passage does not link dumplings with bringing any specific piece of good fortune. Oranges are associated with sweet life.

8. **5** The author states they had parties "to raise their spirits."

9. **5** They did not notice the poor stuffing of the dumplings and the spotted oranges.

10. **5** The food they ate really wasn't fine. They didn't notice how poor it was.

11. **2** The selection states it was "not the best time to be walking alone by the side of a half-frozen river."

12. **4** The words "during the day as she stood pinning dresses" indicate that this activity took place regularly. Pinning dresses, therefore, must have been her work.

13. **4** The sentence "What if they...had died of cold or hunger...while she was...dancing with British officers?" communicates a sense of guilt.

14. **1** The sentence "No one, she thought, wanted to hear them" indicates that the woman believed others were not interested, not that she did not want to tell them. The fact that she continued to go to the Jewish Community Center proves that answer Choices 3 and 4 are incorrect.

15. **2** The last paragraph describes the long-range effects of the Holocaust. That is what the reader is meant to remember and to understand.

16. **2** The fact that "They poured their sewage into it, but it couldn't be tainted" means that, no matter what else happened around the ocean, nothing could taint it.

17. **3** Terror and fear are indicated by such words and phrases as *chilling*, *clammy*, and *bowels of fear*.

18. **3** The narrator wishes to show how the area has been ruined by the changes he describes.

19. **2** The contrasts are derricks instead of trees and oil-pumps instead of cattle.

20. **1** The clue is found in the last phrase, "like a tumor."

21. **3** "Taking a last look" is an expression that is often used in relation to death or a catastrophic event.

22. **2** To do something "consciously" is to do it "with deliberate thought or awareness." That the speaker did not let the freeing of the hawk "come into consciousness" would mean that it was never planned.

23. **4** The passage states that "He lay there a long minute without hope...his eyes still fixed on that blue vault above him." A minute may seem longer than a minute if it is filled with suspense and uncertainty.

24. **2** We are told the sky is "so full of light that I could not follow his gaze." Later, we are told that the "light was too intense."

25. **4** The passage refers to "a cry of such unutterable and ecstatic joy that it sounds down across the years and tingles...."

26. **2** The sounds were unusual because "...they were a weird medley of whines, whimpers and small howls."

27. **4** The narrator has learned "from experience.... The cries were obviously those of a husky."

28. **3** Mike "owned three half-grown pups not yet trained to harness..."

29. **1** The narrator states, "If that pup needed a friend...I was its man!"

30. **3** In the fifth paragraph, the narrator "kept quiet, even when the whimpering stopped, leaving me uncertain about the direction...."

31. **3** Type A is careful.

32. **1** Type Z is not late. He arrives just on time.

33. **2** Getting enough sleep is not mentioned.

34. **1** Nowhere is any change indicated. The other choices are either untrue or unlikely.

35. **2** That they like each other is evidenced by the observation that they always marry each other.

36. **4** The main idea of the poem is to compare being alone to different literary figures or current events. The poet uses allusions to illustrate what it feels like to be alone.

37. **2** The poet most likely comes to her conclusion of "aloneness" out of her philosophical thoughts. She uses her knowledge of literature and current events to illustrate her concept of being alone in a world full of people who feel the same way.

38. **3** The poet's idea of being alone is compared to a straggler goose who squawks, "take me along." A straggler goose is one who is alone from the rest of the geese.

39. **1** The poet mentions Sylvia Plath because she is comparing Plath's poetry to her idea of being alone.

40. **4** The poem derives its power from effective use of allusion. The poet uses many allusions to literary figures as well as current events.

41. **4** The poet says she "won't stop now."

42. **1** She says "she's come this far to freedom."

43. **1** The poet writes "I'll reap some time in the future."

44. **3** She states, "in time you'll know you need me."

45. **3** The rhyme scheme is a a b b a—in the first stanza back, track, going, growing, black.

46. **5** The character demonstrates his lack of imagination by his simple attitude toward the cold. He thinks of the cold only as a number, but not how he can make himself warm creatively.

47. **2** The trail is described as all of the following EXCEPT little traveled in his direction. He describes the Yukon as the main trail and then briefly mentions a side trail that is little traveled.

48. **4** Evidence of the character's hardship is in the amount of snow and ice he must endure.

49. **1** In enduring the weather, the character was experiencing this challenge for the first time. The author writes, "he was a newcomer in the land . . . and this was his first winter."

50. **5** The author is describing an adventure that takes place in the northwest because the Yukon trail runs through the northwest state of Washington.

51. **5** The stamp bore the author's name and town.

52. **1** The author got the idea from his school friend Francisco Ruiz.

53. **4** The passage starts, "That one, Platero," so the author is addressing Platero.

54. **5** The author broke his money bank to get the five pesetas to pay for the rubber stamp.

55. **3** The peseta is the unit of currency in Spain.

56. **2** See the section "Inferring Setting" (page 489). The reference to the portrait of George III, the reigning monarch at the time just prior to the American Revolution, implies a date of about 1770.

57. **5** The author refers to the outside of the house as "the only side which, in truth, belongs to a henpecked husband."

58. **1** Dame Van Winkle looked upon Wolf with "an evil eye as the cause of his master's going so often astray."

59. **4** The author says that Rip never said anything in response to his wife's nagging.

60. **3** He would be content were it not for his wife's "dinning in his ear."

61. **4** The author states "I went to the woods...to front only the essential facts of life...."

62. **2** The author says, "Our life is frittered away by detail... "Simplicity, simplicity, simplicity!... keep your accounts on your thumb-nail."

63. **4** *Mean* is used here to imply the opposite of *sublime* (used in the next clause), that is, as in the sentence "Still we live meanly, like ants."

64. **2** The author implies that people do not know how to live properly, but they should learn.

65. **1** The author went to the woods to see if he "could not learn what it had had to teach."

66. **3** "Small and hopeful Sylvia" climbed the tree with "tingling, eager blood coursing" through her body.

67. **2** Sylvia "knew that higher still one of the oak's upper branches chafed against the pine trunk...."

68. **4** The first part of Sylvia's climb was easy because "She had often climbed there...."

69. **3** "It was like a great mainmast...." A ship's mast supports its sails.

70. **1** "The old pine must have loved his new dependent."

71. **5** The feud has been going on for years and nobody knows what it is about. The author implies that a trivial event has been blown out of proportion.

72. **2** Buck doesn't know, so we aren't told, who started the feud; only a few old men remember.

73. **3** Buck talks of his cousin Bud's being ambushed by Baldy Shepherdson; we can, therefore, assume that Buck is a Grangerford.

74. **4** To hear a sermon about brotherly love, all the men arrive armed.

75. **3** Buck states, in answer to two questions, "I don't know" and "how do *I* know?"

Poetry and Drama/Pages 523/525

76. **4** The main purpose of the poem is to teach us a lesson in conduct—that, regardless of our station in life, we must make our own opportunities with the resources we have at hand.

77. **4** "I could help defeat the enemy" follows logically from the incomplete thought, "Had I a sword of keener steel."

78. **3** The "craven" hangs along the edge of the battle and creeps away, both actions of a cowardly person.

79. **5** The words "...swords shocked upon swords and shields" provide an example of alliteration, that is, repetition of the same sound.

80. **2** The bravery of the king's son is contrasted with the cowardly behavior of the craven soldier.

81. **4** *Stop* and *cut* are short, sharp words, just as *shock* is, both in sound and meaning.

82. **3** See the "Glossary of Literary Terms" (page 504) for a definition of alliteration. Here the letter *s* is repeated at the beginning of two or more words in close proximity— "scribbling" and "sky."

83. **1** The first three verses establish the importance of the poet's love. The last verse stresses the effects of the loss of that love.

84. **4** All of the emotion that follows from the loss of a loved one is indicated in lines 23 and 24.

85. **4** To the poet, none of the elements mentioned in the final stanza that represent life serve any purpose.

86. **3** The daughter cares; she doesn't like her mother living alone.

87. **5** The mother appreciates her daughter's caring and says, "Annie, you're a good daughter."

88. **3** The mother wants to be independent. She says, "I want to keep my own home."

89. **4** The mother wants to stay where she knows "all the neighbors and the store people."

90. **4** The daughter mentions everything except independence. Her mother doesn't want to be "some old lady living with her children."

Commentary on the Arts/Page 526

91. **5** The review refers to "the remarkably inventive and surprising set."

92. **4** The play is referred to as a whodunit," that is, a mystery.

93. **1** The play's author is J.B. Priestly.

94. **4** The success of the set design is attributed to "the art-comes-first atmosphere of England's state-subsidized theaters."

95. **3** One cast member says the sets are not his "particular cup of tea."

96. **4** Wiegand is the only character who can clarify matters for the salesman. The others hardly talk.

97. **1** These portions call for actions by the actors.

98. **2** Wiegand refers to their "exaggerated ideas of the dutiful respect" for the dead.

99. **5** Wiegand mentions that the clergy get revenue and profit from big funerals.

100. **2** Anna is embroidering slippers for Papa and Welzel says he doesn't like to wear them.

101. **2** The author refers to Hollywood's "marked mirror distortions" of society and its timidity, among other criticisms.

102. **2** It is stated that the position of the studio executives at the top of a pyramid makes independent critical judgment impossible.

103. **5** Executives fear rivals and bankers, who, in turn, fear the movie audience.

104. **5** The author refers to Hollywood's timidity or fearfulness.

105. **1** Hollywood, according to the article, isn't a metropolis nor is it a small town.

106. **5** Ford's fellow directors awarded him Oscars for best director.

107. **5** Ford shrugged off praise (fourth paragraph).

108. **2** Ford filled the set with mist "because he didn't have a budget big enough for good sets."

109. **4** Ford's speed and frugality were "part of a deliberate strategy on [his] part."

110. **1** The author of the article claims that, "Because his films were so inexpensive, few of them failed to at least break even."

111. **4** The passage states that reading is among the youngsters' top three interests.

112. **1** The study found the 2- to 18-year-olds "technology savvy."

113. **5** The popularity of the Harry Potter books indicated that reading could attract children.

114. **2** The challenge for the future is to move reading from third place up to the top, past watching TV and listening to music.

115. **4** It is stated that the study offers hope that reading is here to stay.

116. **4** Leonardo saw no essential difference between art and science.

117. **2** His painting resulted in the contradiction of art disguising reality (nature).

118. **1** Da Vinci hated artists who tried to improve on nature.

119. **2** These sketchbooks' pages show how Leonardo loved life.

120. **5** All are mentioned *except* circulation of the blood, which was discovered later.

Business Documents/Page 532

121. **5** The whole memo outlines the procedure for submitting reimbursed expenditures.

122. **2** The memo does not mention anything about food being reimbursed.

123. **2** Gregory Snells is writing to inform an employee of the procedures for submitting vehicle expense reports.

124. **3** The letter implies that Ms. Gratz has requested money for expenses she incurred while traveling.

125. **4** The employees at this company probably do business and travel while using their own cars, thus prompting the manager to write this memo.

MATHEMATICS

Overview

CHAPTER 18

BASIC FACTS

The Mathematics section of the GED test is divided into two 45-minute examination periods, each containing 25 questions. Before Part I, you will be given a Casio fx-260SOLAR calculator, which you may use only for this section of the examination. Part II is to be completed without a calculator. The kinds of questions you'll be asked are virtually the same in both parts, as is their level of difficulty, which ranges from easy to challenging. Most problems offer multiple-choice answers, but about 10 of the 50 questions require you to calculate answers on your own and then "bubble in" those answers on a grid. You are not required to show your work for either part.

THE "FORMULAS" SHEET

Students are usually relieved when they first hear the testing service provides a 1-page collection of mathematical formulas with every test booklet. That is, until they actually examine the sheet and see how complicated-looking the information appears. The sheet can be a worthwhile aid, but first you must learn how and when to apply the information listed there. Such learning is only accomplished through hard work and dedication. Once it's done, however, you'll be pleasantly surprised to find you won't even need the sheet—much of it will already be committed to memory. You'll be able to move through the test more quickly and confidently.

HOW TO USE THIS SECTION

The section is designed to instruct self-motivated learners of varying abilities. The concepts and exercises within each chapter progress from easy to difficult, and the chapters, as a whole, move from simple (Chapter 19—Numbers and Basic Operations) to challenging (Chapter 24—Geometry).

If you're confident of your knowledge in a particular area, go directly to the Chapter Review exercises at the end of each chapter to test yourself. If you get all questions in the Review right, move on to the next chapter.

If you know that your math skills are pretty rusty, start at the beginning and carefully work your way through all the instruction, examples, and exercises. When you've completed all the review chapters, you're ready for the practice tests and exams at the end of the section.

This section includes a chapter on test-taking strategies specific to the Mathematics part of the GED. However, shortcuts and tips on how to handle operations and problems can be found throughout. Though it's best to save Chapter 25 (Test-taking Strategies) for the end of your study, those students who are especially pressed for time should review it before taking the GED, regardless of how far they've gone in the Mathematics section.

USING THE CASIO FX-260SOLAR CALCULATOR

Before taking Part I, you will be issued a Casio fx-260SOLAR calculator and then given a few minutes to practice using it. You don't have to use the calculator, but it is strongly recommended that you do so. It can really help you to avoid computational errors that lead to incorrect answers and can dramatically reduce the time it takes to solve certain problems, giving you more time to spend on the tougher questions.

If you have had some past experience using a calculator, it will help you in operating the Casio fx-260, which works like virtually all hand-held calculators. If you have never used a calculator, however, it is a good idea to purchase or borrow one to practice on prior to taking the GED. The most effective way to practice is to use the fx-260, which is available in retail stores.

As you do the exercises in the following chapters, use your calculator only occasionally or where indicated by a calculator icon and for Part I sections of Practice Tests. Because you will still be required to do your own calculations for many of the questions, it's important to keep your computational skills strong and avoid overdependence on the calculator.

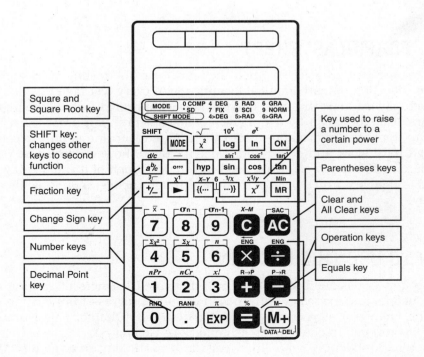

On the previous page is a basic diagram of the Casio fx-SOLAR calculator that will be issued to you. Please note that the calculator has a lot more function keys than you will need to use on the test.

Here are some basic rules to keep in mind when using a calculator:

- Press the keys firmly, checking the display window to make sure you have entered numbers accurately.

- Press AC (or similar key) after completing each problem to completely clear it. Pressing C will erase just the last number entered.

- Numbers and the decimal point will appear on the display window, but operations signs (like + or × or ÷) will not.

Basic Operations

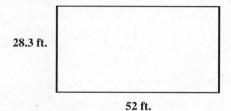

28.3 ft.

52 ft.

How many square feet of carpet are required to cover the entire office floor in the diagram above?

PRESS **28.3,** then ×, then **52,** then =

Answer: 1471.6 sq. ft.

Working with Parentheses

Find: 12(117 ÷ 13) − 68

PRESS **12** × [(⋯ **117** ÷ **13** ⋯)] − **68** =

Answer: 40

Note: The fx-260 has parentheses keys, but some other calculators don't.

Working with Fractions

Broadway	3/4 mile
Alice Avenue	2 1/2 miles
Stockton Street	4 miles

According to the highway exit sign above, how much further past Broadway is Alice Avenue?

PRESS **2** a b/c **1** a b/c **2** − a b/c **3** a b/c **4** =

Answer: 1 3/4 miles

Note: Not all calculators are able to compute fractions.

Working with Signed Numbers

What is the value of the following expression?

$-3(-6 + 8) - (-12)$

PRESS   **3** $\boxed{+/-}$ $\boxed{\times}$ $\boxed{[(\cdots}$ **6** $\boxed{+/-}$ $\boxed{+}$ **8** $\boxed{\cdots)]}$ $\boxed{-}$ **12** $\boxed{+/-}$ $\boxed{=}$

Answer: 6

Note: Some calculators allow you to enter negative numbers using the $\boxed{-}$ key.

Working with Exponents

A container that holds crushed gravel is in the shape of a cube, with each side measuring 17 feet. What is the volume of the container?

PRESS   **17** $\boxed{X^y}$ **3** $\boxed{=}$

Answer: 4,913 cu. ft.

Working with Square Roots

The square root of 138 is between what two whole numbers?

PRESS   **138** $\boxed{\textbf{SHIFT}}$ $\boxed{X^2}$

Answer: between 11 and 12

FILLING IN ANSWER GRIDS

On 10 questions out of the 50 on the test, multiple-choice answers will not be provided. You must come up with an answer yourself and then record it on a grid (see illustration).

Recording Whole Numbers

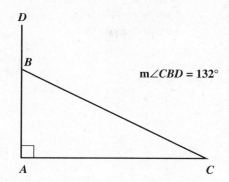

m∠*CBD* = 132°

What is the measure in degrees of ∠*ACB*?
(Using what you will learn about triangles and supplemetary angles in Chapter 24, you calculate the correct answer to be 42°.)

Answer: 42°

You can fill in the answer grid for this response in four different ways; all are correct (see below). Make sure to write the answer in the top horizontal row of boxes and then "bubble in" the corresponding numbers below. Don't worry about including the degrees sign (°); it's unnecessary.

Recording Numbers with Decimals

Sharon and her coworkers want to purchase an MP3 player as a going-away present for their boss. The player costs $86.99. Sharon collects $47.35 from her coworkers and contributes $20 herself. How much more does she need to make the purchase?

Answer: $19.64

1	9	.	6	4

Here, there is only one way to complete the grid. Note that the decimal point *must* be recorded and takes up an entire column. Recording the $ sign is unnecessary.

Recording Fractions

A plumber measures a piece of pipe to be 1 5/8 inches. How much does he need to trim from the pipe to make it fit a connection that is 1 3/8 inches long?

Answer: 2/8 or **1/4**

The grid can be completed in the following ways, all of which are correct.

Recording Points on a Coordinates Plane Grid

Two lines intersect at a point with coordinates of (5, –3). Show the location of the intersecting point on the grid below.

Answer: see grid

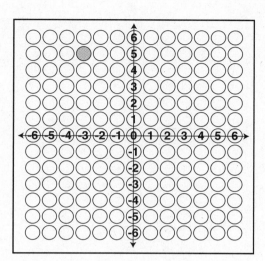

Note: The coordinate plane grid illustrated is just like the rectangular coordinate grid in Chapter 23. However, the x and y axes are not labeled, so it's essential that you memorize which is which. There will most probably be only two questions out of the 50 requiring you to fill in this type of grid.

CHAPTER 19

Numbers and Basic Operations

PLACE VALUES

Say this number out loud to yourself:

$$47,182$$

You should have said, "Forty-seven thousand, one hundred and eighty two." Each **digit** (another word for single numbers between 0 and 9) has its own separate value depending on the place it occupies. Study the chart of place values below until you know it by heart.

PRACTICE—PLACE VALUES

Write each number out in word form—don't worry about spelling.

1. 734
2. 9,008

3. 12,615
4. 7,814,015

ANSWERS

1. seven hundred thirty four

2. nine thousand and eight

3. twelve thousand, six hundred fifteen

4. seven million, eight hundred fourteen thousand, fifteen

Find the value of the digit "7" in each of these numbers and state its value. (For example, in the number 17,412, the "7" has a value of 7,000)

1. 472,812   3. 789,118

2. 31,174   4. 7,018,111

ANSWERS

1. 70,000   3. 700,000

2. 70   4. 7,000,000

ADDITION

Choose the correct setup for adding these three numbers:

87   162   38

```
(a)   87          (b)      38
      162                 162
    +  38              +     87


(c)      162        (d)      162
          38                  38
       +   87               +   87
```

Answer: (d)

When it comes to addition, you must try your best to be neat and accurate in setting up problems. The place values of all the numbers should be lined up precisely so that your answer will be correct. You chose (d) because the digits in the ones column (2,8,7) were lined up directly on top of each other, as were the digits in the tens column (6,3,8). The digit in the hundreds column (1) can stand by itself. The actual computation looks like this:

Step one: Setup
```
              162
               38
           +   87
```

Step two: Add

Ones Column

You always begin an addition problem at the top digit furthest to the right. Here, it's 2. Move down, adding each number in the ones column (2 + 8 + 7 = 17). You can't put the two-digit number 17 directly below the 7 in 87 because there's room for only one digit. Just write down the 7 from the 1<u>7</u> and carry the 1 to the top of the tens column.

Tens Column

Now add the 1 that you carried in with the three numbers from that column (1 + 6 + 3 + 8 = 18). Put the 8 from 1<u>8</u> under the 8 and carry the 1 to the top of the hundreds column.

Hundreds Column

Add that column (1 + 1 = 2). The **sum** is 287. **Sum** means the answer to an addition problem.

```
  1 1
  162
   38
+  87
  287
```

Answer: 287

PRACTICE—ADDITION

Find the sum for the following addition problems.

1.
```
    168
    402
+    43
```

3.
```
  72,416
   4,803
+     92
```

2.
```
  9,104
    586
+   720
```

4.
```
  786
  412
  853
+ 971
```

ANSWERS

1. 613

2. 10,410

3. 77,311

4. 3022

Do You Know Your Basic Addition Facts?

Pay attention to how you're adding and be honest with yourself. Are you using your fingers to count? Are you using "half-steps"?

For example, when you come to a problem like 6 + 7, do you say, "Well, I know 6 + 6 = 12, so add one more on...."? Many GED students begin their study this way, but the successful ones soon realize these methods take too long and cause errors in computation.

The only answer is to memorize these addition facts. Buy some flashcards at a toy store or bookstore, or make your own from index cards, with the help of someone who really knows the facts. Practice until you've got it.

SUBTRACTION

EXAMPLE ONE

Choose the correct setup for the following problem and solve:

168 – 42

a)
```
    168
  –  42
```

b)
```
  168
 –  42
```

c)
```
168
–  42
```

d)
```
   42
 – 168
```

As with addition, accurate place-value arrangement is essential to subtraction. But with subtraction, you must also remember that the larger number goes on top—at least, for now. The correct setup is (b). Here's how to solve it.

Step one: Setup
```
  168
–  42
```

Subtract using the same "column" method you learned in addition.

Step two: Subtract
```
  168
–  42
  126
```

Answer: 126

The answer to a subtraction problem is called **the difference**.

Subtraction Using Borrowing

Subtraction gets a bit more complicated when the process of "borrowing" becomes necessary—that is, when the digit on top is smaller than the digit on the bottom. Consider this example below.

EXAMPLE TWO

724 – 486

Step one: Set-up with larger number on top.

```
  724
– 486
```

Step two: Subtract using borrowing.

Ones Column

The number 4 is smaller than 6, so you need to borrow 1 from the next column over, making 4 in the ones place now worth 14. Subtract the 1 borrowed from the 2 in the tens' place, so it now becomes 1. Since 14 – 6 = 8, put the 8 under the 6 as the first digit in your answer.

Tens Column

You can't subtract 8 from 1 (tens place) so you must borrow from the digit to its left, the 7. Now, 1 becomes 11 and you can subtract 11 – 8 = 3. Enter the 3 as the second digit of your answer. Do the final subtraction in the hundreds column—6 – 4 = 2 and enter the answer.

$$
\begin{array}{r}
{}^{6\,1\,1} \\
724 \\
-\ 486 \\
\hline
238
\end{array}
$$

Answer: 238

Step three: Check. To check subtraction, **add** the answer to the second of the two numbers in the subtraction problem. The sum should equal the top number.

$$
\begin{array}{r}
238 \\
+\ 486 \\
\hline
724
\end{array}
$$

Borrowing and Zeros

Subtraction gets even more complicated when you have to borrow across two or more numbers. Consider the example below.

EXAMPLE

Find the difference between 7003 and 468.

Step one:
$$
\begin{array}{r}
7003 \\
-\ 468 \\
\hline
\end{array}
$$

Step two: Subtract using borrowing.

Notice how you need to move two places over to the 7 to borrow. Then the 1 that was borrowed gets moved to the right *one digit at a time*: first, to the hundreds place, making the 0 a ten and the 7 a 6, then you borrow 1 from that 10 and move it to the 0 in the tens place. Then you borrow 1 from *that* 10, moving it finally to the ones place, making the 3 a 13. Only then can you subtract.

$$
\begin{array}{r}
{}^{6\,9\,9\,1} \\
7003 \\
-\ 468 \\
\hline
6,535
\end{array}
$$

Subtract and find the difference for the following. Check.

1.　475
　　　− 62

4.　10,024
　　　− 8,751

2.　806
　　　− 294

5.　62,400
　　　− 18,519

3.　1413
　　　− 962

ANSWERS

1. 413　　2. 512　　3. 451　　4. 1273　　5. 43,881

MULTIPLICATION

Take a look at how to multiply using this example:

EXAMPLE ONE

306 × 42

```
                    306
                ×    42
2 × 306 = →         612
4 × 306 = →        1224
                 12,852      ← product
```

Answer: 12,852

The answer to a multiplication problem is called a **product**.

Step one: Arrange the problem with the larger number on top.

Step two: Begin multiplying with the bottom number using the digit furthest to the right—in this case, the 2 in 42. Moving from right to left, multiply each of the top digits by 2: 306 × 2 = 612

Step three: Repeat *step two* using the 4 in 42: 306 × 4 = 1,224. Actually, it's 306 × 40, which equals 12,240, but it's common practice to leave off the last zero and shift the entire answer one place to the left. Notice how the 4 in 1,224 is in the tens place.

Step four: Add the two numbers—612 and 1,224—to find the product.

EXAMPLE TWO

406 × 312

$$
\begin{array}{r}
406 \\
\times\ 312 \\
\end{array}
$$

2 × 406 = → 812
1 × 406 = → 406   1-digit shift
3 × 406 = → 1218   2-digit shift
126,672

PRACTICE—MULTIPLICATION

Find the product of the following.

1. 46
   × 13

2. 892
   × 27

3. 404
   × 95

4. 724
   × 106

5. 4302
   × 950

ANSWERS

1. 598
2. 24,084
3. 38,380
4. 76,744
5. 4,086,900

If you understand the steps to multiplication but find you're still getting the wrong answers, you may need to brush up on your multiplication facts. Use flashcards or some other means to help you memorize the multiplication tables up to 12.

TIP

Have problems with your "times" tables? Buy flash cards and practice until you have mastered the times tables up to 12.

DIVISION

Many beginning GED students find division to be the most difficult of the four basic operations. It requires accuracy, neatness, and careful attention to a sometimes complicated step-by-step process.

EXAMPLE ONE

524 ÷ 4

$$
\begin{array}{r}
131 \\
4\,\overline{)524} \\
-4 \\
\hline
12 \\
-12 \\
\hline
04 \\
-4 \\
\hline
0
\end{array}
$$

Answer: 131.

The answer to a division problem is called a **quotient**.

Here's the above process in steps.

Step one: 5 ÷ 4
Step two: 1 × 4
Step three: 5 − 4 = 1
Step four: Bring down the next number, 2

Repeat steps 1–4 until all the numbers are brought down.

Often, there is more than one digit in the **divisor** (the number used to divide). Consider the following example.

EXAMPLE TWO

1,170 ÷ 26

$$
\begin{array}{r}
45 \;\leftarrow \text{quotient}\\
\text{divisor} \rightarrow 26\,\overline{)1170} \;\leftarrow \text{dividend}\\
-104\\
\hline
130\\
-130\\
\hline
0
\end{array}
$$

Of course, 26 doesn't go into 1, so you include the next digit in the dividend. But 26 doesn't go into 11 either. Include the 7, and now you can begin the problem because 26 *does* go into 117. You're not supposed to know, off the top of your head, the answer to 117 ÷ 26. Make an educated guess and do some multiplication on scrap paper to get 4. Notice that the 4 in the quotient goes directly above the 7 in the dividend.

Check: Multiply the quotient by the divisor. The answer should be equal to the dividend. For the last problem, the check would look like this:

$$
\begin{array}{r}
45 \\
\times\ \ 26 \\
\hline
270 \\
90 \\
\hline
1{,}170
\end{array}
$$

Sometimes, numbers don't divide evenly, and there is an amount "left over" called a **remainder**.

EXAMPLE THREE

$75 \div 4$

$$
\begin{array}{r}
18 \\
4\overline{)75} \\
-4 \\
\hline
35 \\
-32 \\
\hline
3 \ \leftarrow \text{remainder}
\end{array}
$$

There are no more numbers in the dividend to bring down. The **remainder**, then, is 3 and the answer would be expressed: 18r3 or 18 remainder 3.

Note: There is a more complete way of dealing with remainders that will be later taught in Chapter 19, Decimals.

Ways of Writing Division

There are a few ways in which division can be expressed. The problem of dividing 96 by 6 can be written:

$$
96 \div 6 \quad \text{or} \quad 6\overline{)96} \quad \text{or} \quad \frac{96}{6}
$$

In the last of these, $\frac{96}{6}$, the fraction bar (—), means "divided by." Read it from top to bottom, and it will soon sound and look like the other two more familiar expressions of division.

Find the quotient and check.

1. $5\overline{)95}$

2. $14\overline{)532}$

3. $\dfrac{1680}{21}$

4. $\dfrac{156}{6}$

5. $32\overline{)933}$

6. $\dfrac{2142}{21}$

7. $92\overline{)21,528}$

ANSWERS

1. 19

2. 38

3. 80

4. 26

5. 29r5

6. 102

7. 234

WORD PROBLEMS USING BASIC OPERATIONS

Almost all of the questions on the GED will be word problems. Read carefully and rely on your common sense to tell you what operations to use. Be aware of certain words and phrases that tell you what to do:

- **Sum, total,** and **all together** usually mean addition.
- **How much more, how much less, find the difference,** and **deduct** indicate subtraction.

EXAMPLE ONE

Carl purchased a computer for $589. In addition, he chose to buy a two-year service contract for $75 and a tech-support option for $35. What is the total cost of Carl's computer purchase?

The words **total** and **in addition** should clue you in to the fact that this is an addition problem:

```
  589     for the computer
   75     for the service contract
+  35     for tech-support option
 $699     for the computer purchase
```

EXAMPLE TWO

The Glenridge Elementary School had an enrollment of 352 first-graders and 413 second-graders. How many more second-graders were there than first-graders?

$$
\begin{array}{rl}
413 & \text{second-graders} \\
-\ 352 & \text{first-graders} \\
\hline
61 & \text{more second-graders}
\end{array}
$$

Multiplication is not often associated with particular words or phrases. Rely on your mathematical sense to determine whether to multiply.

EXAMPLE THREE

Karen can type 65 words per minute. At this rate, find how many words she can type in 15 minutes.

$$
\begin{array}{rl}
65 & \text{words per one minute} \\
\times\ 15 & \text{total minutes} \\
\hline
325 & \\
65\ \ & \\
\hline
975 & \text{words in 15 minutes}
\end{array}
$$

Division is often indicated by words and phrases like **share, split, per, average,** and **grouped into.**

EXAMPLE FOUR

A bagging machine packages 28 oranges per bag. If the machine is loaded with 1,400 oranges, how many full bags will it produce?

$$
\begin{array}{rl}
& \ \ \ \ 50 \quad \text{number of full bags} \\
\text{Oranges \textbf{per} bag} & 28\overline{)1400} \quad \text{total oranges} \\
& -\ 140 \\
& \ \ \ \ \overline{\ \ \ 0}
\end{array}
$$

PRACTICE—SOLVING WORD PROBLEMS

1. Geri cycled a 36-mile loop every day for two weeks. What is the total number of miles she rode during that period?

2. In 1939 there were 4,212 people who lived in the town of Twin Forks. By 2005 there were 32,118 people residing there. What is the difference between Twin Forks' population in 2005 and 1939?

3. Sonia's annual salary is $41,190 and she receives a holiday bonus of $2,670. She also receives $3,219 in stock-option benefits. What are her total earnings for the year?

4. Sean bought 7 CDs, each the same price, for a total of $98. Find the cost for one of the CDs.

5. Shirley was born in 1927. Find her age in 2001.

6. Rob's compact car gets 32 miles per gallon of gas. How far can he travel using 13 gallons of gas?

MULTISTEP WORD PROBLEMS

Multistep problems ask you to use more than one operation to find an answer. You might, for example, need to add a set of numbers, then multiply the sum by another number.

EXAMPLE

The Wilson children were each given a weekly allowance. Tanya, the oldest, received $15, Ed got $10, and Lakisha, the youngest, got $8. Find the total amount the children received after four weeks.

Step one: Find the total allowance for **one** week by adding the amounts of each child.

$$
\begin{array}{r}
15 \\
10 \\
+\ 8 \\
\hline
\$33
\end{array}
\quad \text{for one week}
$$

Step two: Multiply one week's total allowance by 4 (for 4 weeks)

$$
\begin{array}{r}
33 \\
\times\ \ 4 \\
\hline
\$132
\end{array}
\quad \text{combined allowance for 4 weeks}
$$

Gross and **net** are two words you will encounter frequently.

Gross is a total amount **before** deducting taxes, expenses, etc.

Net is the amount remaining **after** deducting taxes, expenses, etc.

EXAMPLE

Tracy's **gross** salary is $450 per week. After her employer deducts $150 for taxes and medical insurance, her **net** salary is $300.

PRACTICE—MULTISTEP WORD PROBLEMS

1. Each month, the Bluesteins pay a home mortgage of $860 and a $318 payment on their car loan. What is the cost of these expenses for one year?

2. Sue is an endurance athlete who likes to run and bike. She can run 6 miles per hour and can bike at 22 miles per hour. In three hours, how much farther can she travel biking than running?

3. Jim's Car Wash grossed $18,230 for one week of operation. However, Jim had the following expenses: $1,205 for workers' salaries, $560 for water and electrical use and $1,582 for supplies and other expenses. What is Jim's *net* profit for the week?

4. The Bevco Bottling Plant produces 192 bottles of soda per minute, which are then packed in cases of 24. How many cases are produced in 10 minutes?

5. Three relatives inherited $86,000. After paying $32,540 in taxes and legal fees necessary to claiming the inheritance, they decided to split the remainder equally among themselves. How much is each of the three relatives' share of the inheritance?

ANSWERS

1. $14,136   2. 48   3. $14,883   4. 80   5. $17,820

SETUPS

Throughout the GED, you will have to respond to setup questions. You won't have to find an answer to the problem, but, instead, will be asked to choose the setup of operations that will allow you to solve it. Setups are usually "friendly" questions; since you don't need to do any calculation to answer them, they take up less time.

EXAMPLE ONE

Bill, Jodi, and Sue decided to share evenly the cost of a computer package that includes the following items: computer and keyboard—$724, monitor—$212, and printer—$159. Which expression below represents what each person had to contribute to the purchase?

(1) ($724 + $212 + $159) + 3

(2) $\dfrac{3}{(\$724 + \$212 + \$159)}$

(3) 3($724 + $212 + $159)

(4) $\dfrac{(\$724 + \$212 + \$159)}{3}$

(5) (3 + $724) + (3 + $212)

The answer is (4) because it's the only one that adds the cost of the computer components together, then divides them among the three people sharing the expense.

PARENTHESES

Parentheses ( ) are a very important part of setups and mathematical computation, in general. They serve to enclose and isolate parts of mathematical sentences. *Do the operations in parentheses first.* Here are some examples of how parentheses work:

$$3(26 + 41)$$

tells you to add 26 + 41, then multiply the sum (67) by 3.

Answer: 201

$$(95 + 26) - (81 + 14)$$

tells you, **first**, to add 95 + 26 = 121 and 81 + 14 = 95 then, **second**, to subtract 121 - 95

Answer: 26

PRACTICE—SETUPS AND PARENTHESES

1. Find the value of 4(46 + 23 - 8)

2. Find the value of $\dfrac{5(19 + 3)}{11}$

3. Serena took her family out to a fast-food restaurant. The bill was $18.24 and the tax was $3.11. Serena gave the cashier $25 to pay the bill. Which of the following expression represents the change Serena received?

   (1) (20 + 5) + (18.24 - 3.11)

   (2) $\dfrac{(18.24 - 3.11)}{25}$

   (3) 25 - (18.24 + 3.11)

   (4) (18.24 - 3.11) - 25

4. A one-way plane ticket from Chicago to Los Angeles is $209 for adults and $159 for children under 10. If the round-trip fare is twice the price of the one-way fare, find the expression that represents a round-trip fare for one adult and one child under 10.

   (1) $\dfrac{(159 + 209)}{2}$

   (2) 2(209 - 159)

   (3) (159 × 1) + (209 × 1)

   (4) 2(159 + 209)

ANSWERS

1. 244   2. 10   3. 3   4. 4

MULTIPLE QUESTIONS ON ONE TOPIC

At some time on the GED, you will be asked two, three, or four questions having to do with one topic or situation.

EXAMPLE

<u>Questions 1–3</u> are based on the following:

Jean is considering whether to join a work-out gym in her neighborhood. The gym offers three different payment options for membership:

Plan A: A monthly fee of $90

Plan B: A one-time fee of $650 at the beginning of membership, which is good for one year.

Plan C: Two payments of $370 each—one at the beginning of the membership and one six months later, also good for one year.

1. How much more would Jean pay annually (for one year) if she chose Plan C over Plan B?

   Simple multistep. Find the difference between the two plans using subtraction.

$$2(370) = \begin{array}{r} 740 \text{ (plan C)} \\ - \ 650 \text{ (plan B)} \end{array}$$

   Answer: $90

2. Which expression represents the difference between Plans A and C if Jean were to use the gym for one year?

   (1) $\dfrac{450}{12} - 12(52)$

   (2) $(90 \times 12) - 2(370)$

   (3) $12(90 + 52)$

   (4) $\dfrac{90}{12} + \dfrac{52}{12}$

   Setup of Plan A has to be 90×12—only answers (2) and (3) have it. "Difference" means subtraction and only (2) has it.

   Answer: 2 $(90 \times 12) - 2(370)$

3. Jean's net monthly income is $1,940. All her living expenses total $1,182. If Jean decides to join the gym using Plan A, what will be the amount remaining from her net income at the end of the month?

Step one: Calculate remaining money *before* joining gym.

$$1940 - 1182 = 758$$

Step two: Subtract monthly gym payment from answer to above step.

$$758 - 90 = \$668$$

Answer: $668

PRACTICE—MULTIPLE QUESTIONS

Questions 1–3 are based on the following:

Walter has an A.M. newspaper route. He drives 88 miles Monday to Friday, 73 miles on Saturday, and 103 miles on Sunday. His van gets 20 miles per gallon of gas.

1. Which of the following represents the number of gallons of gas Walter uses for the weekend?

   (1) $73 + 103 + 88$

   (2) $(73 + 103) + 20$

   (3) $20(73 + 103)$

   (4) $\dfrac{103 + 73}{20}$

   (5) $20 \div (73 + 103 + 88)$

2. Find the total number of miles Walter drives per week.

3. How many more miles does Walter drive during the weekdays compared with the miles he drives on the weekend?

ANSWERS

1. 4   2. 616   3. 264

EXPONENTS

Consider this number: 6^3

The little ^{3} that seems to be floating in the air is called an **exponent**. 6 is called the **base number**. What you're being told to do here is multiply **6 × 6 × 6**. It can also be stated as "6 to the third power."

$$6^3 = 6 \times 6 \times 6$$
$$6 \times 6 = 36 \times 6 = 216$$
$$6^3 = 216$$

Any number to the first power is equal to itself.

EXAMPLE

$$18^1 = 18$$

Sometimes on the GED, you might have to deal with more complex exponent problems like this one:

$$5^4 + 6^2 - 8^1 =$$

Convert each base/exponent pair into a separate number and then perform the operations.

$5^4 = 5 \times 5 \times 5 \times 5 = 625$

$6^2 = 6 \times 6 = 36$

$8^1 = 8$

$625 + 36 - 8 = 653$

PRACTICE—EXPONENTS

Find the value of the following.

1. 7^3

2. 10^4

3. 16^3

4. 28^1

5. 30^2

6. $17^3 + 19^2$

7. $24^2 - 8^3$

8. $20^2 - 5^3 + 2^5$

ANSWERS

1. 343

2. 10,000

3. 4096

4. 28

5. 900

6. 5,274

7. 64

8. 307

SQUARE ROOTS

The square root sign $\sqrt{}$ looks like a cross between a checkmark and a division sign. When you see this: $\sqrt{49}$, you're being asked to find a number that, *multiplied by itself,* will equal 49. Since $7 \times 7 = 49$, 7 is the square root of 49 or $\sqrt{49} = 7$.
Here's how to find square roots of larger numbers.

EXAMPLE ONE

Find $\sqrt{441}$

Step one: Narrow down using multiples of 10.

You know that $10 \times 10 = 100$, but that's too low. Next, try $20 \times 20 = 400$—very close to 441. $30 \times 30 = 900$, which is way over. The square root of 441 must be a number more than 20 and less than 30. So we know $\sqrt{441} = 2\_$

Step two: Find the exact number for the ones digit.

441 ends in a "1." Therefore, the number you choose to accompany your 20, when multiplied by itself, *must end in one.* For example, $1 \times 1 = 1$ (that works, so it could be 21.) $2 \times 2 = 4$ (no) $3 \times 3 = 9$ (no), $4 \times 4 = 1\underline{6}$ (ends in "6"—no) and so on—up to $9 \times 9 = 8\underline{1}$ (ends in "1"—yes). You have two numbers to choose from—21 or 29. Which one is a better guess? 21, of course, because 29 is so close to 30 and you've already seen that 30^2 is 900, which is way over.

Step three: Try it. $21 \times 21 = 441$

Answer: $21 = \sqrt{441}$

EXAMPLE TWO

The value of $\sqrt{34}$ is between what pair of whole numbers?

(a) 16 and 17
(b) 5 and 6
(c) 2 and 3
(d) 9 and 10
(e) 6 and 7

This can be done in your head. Since $5 \times 5 = 25$ is too low and $6 \times 6 = 36$ is just a bit too high, the number has to be between the two. The actual $\sqrt{34}$ is 5.830518... but (b) will answer this question.

Answer: (b)

PRACTICE—SQUARE ROOTS

Solve.

1. $\sqrt{121}$

2. $\sqrt{289}$

3. $\sqrt{529}$

4. $\sqrt{256}$

5. $\sqrt{2704}$

6. $\sqrt{4489}$

7. The value of $\sqrt{28}$ is between what pair of whole numbers?

ANSWERS

1. 11

2. 17

3. 23

4. 16

5. 52

6. 67

7. 5 and 6

FINDING SQUARE ROOTS WITH A CALCULATOR

The calculator makes finding square roots much easier. For Part I square root problems, follow this procedure:

Enter the number whose square root you need to find—for example, 6,084. Then press the "Shift" key in the upper-left corner of the keypad, then press the "x^2" key. The answer will read 78.

ORDER OF OPERATIONS

Do you remember learning *PEMDAS* or "Please Excuse My Dear Aunt Sally?" This is a way of remembering the order of operations for solving complicated mathematical sentences.

PEMDAS or "Please Excuse My Dear Aunt Sally"

1st—**P** stands for **parentheses**

2nd—**E** stands for **exponents**

3rd—**M** stands for **multiplication**

4th—**D** stands for **division**

5th—**A** stands for **addition**

6th—**S** stands for **subtraction**

If you have a problem that asks you to do addition, multiplication, and some work in parentheses, first you would do the work in parentheses, then the multiplication, and finally, the addition. Memorize the order and follow it.

EXAMPLE

Solve: $\dfrac{(5+3)^2}{4} + 27$

Step one: **P** (parentheses) always comes first, so do all work in parentheses.

5 + 3 = 8. Now the problem looks like this:

$$\dfrac{8^2}{4} + 27$$

Step two: **E** (exponents) comes second, so do 8 × 8 = 64

$$\dfrac{64}{4} + 27$$

Step three: **D** (division) is the next operation in the order that has to be performed in this particular problem, so do 64 ÷ 4 = 16

16 + 27

Step four: **A** (addition) is the last step for this problem. So do 16 + 27 = 43

Answer: 43

Evaluate using order of operations.

1. $(43 - 19) + (16 - 14)(4)$

2. $\dfrac{48}{3} - 6$

3. $\dfrac{(6 + 7 + 2)^3}{3}$

Answers

1. 32   2. 10   3. 1125

MEAN AND MEDIAN

Finding the *mean* and *median* of a group of numbers are two operations you must learn for the GED. They both tell you to find the *average* for a group of numbers, but each is a bit different from the other.

EXAMPLE

Tanya is a waitress at the Mercer Street Café. Last week, she worked five days and earned the following tips:

Monday:	$36
Tuesday:	$42
Wednesday:	$28
Thursday:	$60
Friday:	$89

Find the mean (average) amount of her daily tips for the five days she worked.

Step one: Add all of the numbers

$$(36 + 42 + 28 + 60 + 89) = 255$$

Step two: Count how many numbers you just added and divide by the amount of the numbers.

$$5\overline{)255} = 51$$

Answer: Mean amount of tips for the days worked that week is $51. It's true that Tanya never earned $51 on any of the given days she worked that week. The mean indicates that an **average** day's tips for her comes to about **$51**.

> **REMINDER**
>
> **Mean** is interchangeable with the word **average**. Add all of the numbers given, then divide by the amount of numbers.

Median is the middle number in a group of numbers arranged in order. Sometimes this is a very simple operation—just line the numbers up in order and pick the one in the middle. Other times, it's a bit more complicated.

EXAMPLE ONE

For the marking period, Joe's test scores are 86, 66, 75, 81, and 68. What is his median score for the marking period?

Step one: Line the numbers up in order:

66　　68　　75　　81　　86

Step two: Choose the middle number: 75

EXAMPLE TWO

For the next marking period, Joe's test scores are 62, 88, 90, 85, 75, and 83. What is his median score for the marking period?

Step one: Line the numbers up in order:

62　　75　　83　　85　　88　　90

Step two: Choose the middle number—but there's a problem. There *is* no middle number because there are an *even* amount of numbers. In these situations, *choose the* **two** *middle numbers* and average those two:

62　　75　　83　　85　　88　　90

The two middle numbers are 83 and 85.

Sub-step one: 83 + 85 = 168

Sub-step two: 168 ÷ 2 = 84

Answer: Joe's median score for the marking period is 84.

> **TIP**
>
> Median, like the other median on a highway, is the *middle* number in a set of numbers arranged in order.

PRACTICE—MEAN AND MEDIAN

1. Evan is a bike messenger who works three days a week. On Wednesday, he pedaled 32 miles, on Thursday 48 miles, and on Friday 34 miles. What is the mean distance he pedaled during those days?

2. Cara is a real estate broker who does a survey of properties for sale on Beach Street. The prices for four homes are $196,000; $192,900; $201,500; and $191,000. Find the mean sale price for the homes on Beach Street.

3. Competing for the league championship, the Thompson Tigers bowling team members bowl individual games of 189, 207, 217, and 199. What is the mean bowling score for the team?

ANSWERS

1. 38　　　2. $195,350　　　3. 203

NOT ENOUGH INFORMATION IS GIVEN

Sometimes, a question is purposely misleading. It fails to provide enough information for you to calculate the answer.

EXAMPLE

Forestry workers plant trees at the rate of 12 per hour. At that rate, how long will it take two workers to plant 8 acres of cleared land?

(a) 86 hours
(b) 14 hours
(c) 43 hours
(d) 16 hours
(e) not enough information given

The answer is (e). You would need to know how many trees need to be planted in order to calculate an answer. The size of the land is not relevant information.

> **NOTE**
>
> Don't be frequently tempted by the "not enough information is given" response. It is used on only a few occasions during the course of a GED Math section.

PRACTICE—NOT ENOUGH INFORMATION IS GIVEN

One of the following questions does *not* provide enough information; another does.

1. Gerald works at his uncle's restaurant 3 days a week, and gets paid $115 a day plus tips. He works two days a week delivering lumber for $90 a day. What is his average daily pay for a typical week?

   (1) $525
   (2) $105
   (3) $185
   (4) $95
   (5) not enough information is given

2. A plumber buys pipe at $1 a foot. From a 15-foot pipe, he cuts a piece 9 feet long to be used on a job. What is the value of the unused portion?

   (1) $16
   (2) 15 – 11
   (3) $6
   (4) $8
   (5) not enough information is given

ANSWERS

1. 5   2. 3

BASIC GEOMETRY

In this unit, you will deal with the rectangle, square, rectangular container, and cube. The triangle will be mentioned but will be more thoroughly dealt with in Chapter 20. Circles will be dealt with in Chapter 21. Chapter 24 will deal with more advanced geometric concepts.

PERIMETER

The perimeter is the distance around a figure. It's the sum of the lengths of all its sides.

EXAMPLE ONE

Find the perimeter of the triangle below.

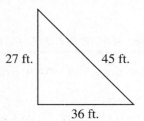

To find perimeter, add the sum of all sides: 27 + 36 + 45 = 108 ft.

Note: Always be aware of the units named in the diagram or asked for in the problem. If it's *feet*, make sure your answer is in *feet*.

EXAMPLE TWO

Find the perimeter of the rectangle below.

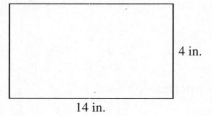

The formula for finding the perimeter of a rectangle is:

$$P = 2(l) + 2(w)$$
$$l = \text{length and } w = \text{width}$$

The *length* of the rectangle is the longer side and the *width* is the shorter side.

You can easily see that a rectangle has two lengths and two widths—two pair of opposite sides—and those opposite sides are equal to each other.

In the rectangle above, the length = 14 in. and the width = 4 in. Now you can use the formula for perimeter:

$$P = 2(l) + 2(w)$$

$$P = 2(14) + 2(4)$$

$$P = 28 + 8$$

$$P = 36 \text{ in.}$$

Answer: Perimeter = 36 in.

EXAMPLE THREE

Find the perimeter of the square below.

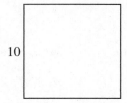

10

The formula for finding the perimeter of a square is:

$$P = 4(s)$$
$$s = \text{side}$$

Unlike a rectangle, all four sides of a square are equal. So, to find a square's perimeter, multiply the one side × 4.

$$P = 4(s) \qquad P = 4(10) \qquad P = 40$$

Note how there is no unit of measure next to the 10. 10 what? You will sometimes see this on the GED. Simply express the answer in terms of a number without a unit of measure.

Answer: $P = 40$

PRACTICE—FINDING PERIMETER

Find the perimeter of the following figures.

1.

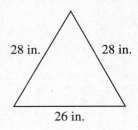

28 in.   28 in.

26 in.

2.

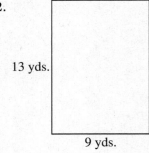

13 yds.

9 yds.

3.

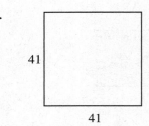

41

41

ANSWERS

1. 82 in.   2. 44 yds.   3. 164

AREA

The area of a figure is the measure of flat surface inside its perimeter.

EXAMPLE ONE

A bedroom is 10 ft. long and 12 ft. wide. How many square feet of carpet will be needed to cover its floor?

　　The bedroom above is rectangular. The formula for the area of a rectangle is:

Step one: Draw a diagram. It's always a good idea to draw a diagram from a word problem about geometry to help visualize what you need to solve.

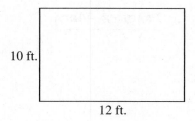

10 ft.

12 ft.

Step two: Using the formula for the area of a rectangle, find the area.

　　$A = lw$

　　$A = 10(12)$

　　$A = 120$ *square* feet.

> **Note:** The word **square (sq.)** must always accompany an answer involving area, regardless of the shape of a figure. There are three ways to express **square**, all of which are correct.
>
> 1. 120 **sq.** ft.
> 2. 120 ft. **sq.**
> 3. 120 ft.^{2}

EXAMPLE TWO

Find the area of the square below.

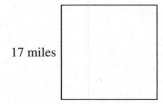

17 miles

> **REMINDER**
>
> $A = l(w)$
> or
> $A = lw$
>
> When letters are pushed right next to each other it means multiply. In this case, **lw** means **length** × **width**

Since all the sides of a square are equal, the formula for the area of a square is:

$$A = s^2$$

$A = s^2$

$A = 17^2$

$A = 17 \times 17$

$A = 289$

Answer: $A = 289$ sq. miles

PRACTICE—AREA

1.

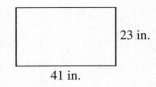

23 in.

41 in.

(a) find perimeter
(b) find area

2.

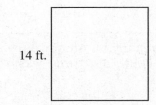

14 ft.

(a) find perimeter
(b) find area

3. How many 1-ft. by 1-ft. square blocks would be required to pave a patio with a length of 20 ft. and a width of 12 ft.?

ANSWERS

1. (a) 128 in.   (b) 943 sq. in.

2. (a) 56 ft.   (b) 196 sq. ft.

3. 240

VOLUME

Volume is the measure of the amount of space inside a three-dimensional fig-ure such as a rectangular container, cube, or sphere. It tells how much these figures can hold.

EXAMPLE ONE

Find the volume for the rectangular container below.

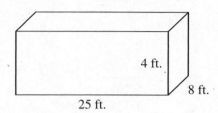

25 ft.   8 ft.   4 ft.

The formula for volume of a rectangular container is:

$$V = lwh$$
$$V = \text{volume}$$
$$l = \text{length}$$
$$h = \text{height}$$
$$w = \text{width}$$
$$(V = l \times w \times h)$$

$V = 25 \times 8 \times 4 = 800$ **cubic** ft. or 800 ft. **cu.** or 800 ft.**³**

EXAMPLE TWO

A cube-shaped container holds sand. How many cubic feet of sand will it hold if one of its sides is 8 feet?

The formula for volume of a cube is:

$$V = s^3 \qquad v = \text{volume} \qquad s = \text{side}$$

Since all sides of a cube are equal, there is no difference between its length, width, and height. Just multiply any side to the third power.

Step one: Draw a diagram.

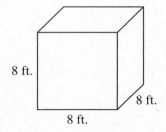

8 ft.   8 ft.   8 ft.

Step two: Do the multiplication.

$8 \times 8 \times 8 = 512$ cu. ft.

MULTIPLYING TIP

A rule in math called the **asso-ciative property** states that it doesn't matter in what order you multiply any three numbers together, the answer will always be the same. So, for finding volume, don't worry about which is the height, length, or width. Just multiply three numbers in any order.

PRACTICE—VOLUME

1. Find the volume of the figure below.

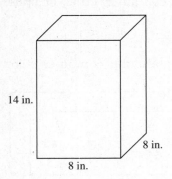

14 in.

8 in.

8 in.

2. What is the difference in volume between a 13-ft. cube and a 10-ft. cube?

ANSWERS

1. 896 cu. in.   2. 1,197 cu. ft.

PRACTICE—REVIEW OF GEOMETRIC FORMULAS

Match the formula used to calculate the following measurements, marking P for perimeter, A for area, and V for volume on the corresponding lines.

1. ____ The amount of wallpaper needed to cover the walls of a room.

2. ____ The amount of water needed to fill a swimming pool.

3. ____ The amount of fencing needed to enclose a yard.

4. ____ The amount of trunk space in a car.

5. ____ The amount of molding need to trim a ceiling.

6. ____ The amount of grass seed needed to plant a new lawn.

ANSWERS

1. A   2. V   3. P   4. V   5. P   6. A

CHAPTER REVIEW

Fill in the answer grids, and use a calculator where indicated.

1. What value does the "6" have in 462,103?

   (1) 600,000
   (2) 60
   (3) 62,000
   (4) 60,000
   (5) 16,000

Questions 2–4 are based on the following:

Jacqueline flies 730 miles on Tuesday, 1,250 miles on Thursday, and 681 miles on Friday.

2. Find the total number of miles she flew for the three days.

3. What is the median number of miles Jacqueline flew?

4. What is the mean number of miles she flew?

5. There are 454 balloons that need to be blown up for the Homecoming Dance. If there are 19 volunteers, how many balloons does each person have to blow up? How many will be left over?

6. For each of its 38 municipal employees, the city of Irvington pays $720 per year to a health insurance provider. What is the total the city pays to purchase its employees' health insurance?

7. A jewelry store sells gold necklaces for $135 each. On Friday, there is a sale on the necklaces, reducing their price by $30. Which expression represents the price of five necklaces and a diamond pendant?

   (1) 5(135)
   (2) 5(135 – 30)
   (3) 5(135 – 30) + 200
   (4) $\dfrac{135 - 30}{5}$
   (5) not enough information given

8. There are three classes of second graders at Rockford Elementary School. One class has 21 students, another has 26, and the last has 25. The principal would like to split the second-grade population into two groups for lunch periods. Which expression represents the separation of the second grade into two groups?

   (1) $2(21 + 26 + 25)$
   (2) $\dfrac{21 + 26 + 25}{2}$
   (3) $(21 + 26) - (25 + 2)$
   (4) $\dfrac{2}{21 + 26 + 25}$
   (5) not enough information is given

9. Traveling at 65 miles per hour, approximately how long will it take Angela to drive 310 miles?

   (1) between 2 and 3 hours
   (2) between 3 and 4 hours
   (3) between 4 and 5 hours
   (4) between 5 and 6 hours
   (5) very close to seven hours

10. Evaluate the following: $5(8^3 - 4^3)$

    (1) 60
    (2) 620
    (3) 2,240
    (4) 1,860
    (5) 185

11. The value of $\sqrt{26}$ is between which of the following pairs of numbers?

    (1) 2 and 13
    (2) 12 and 13
    (3) 4.4 and 4.5
    (4) 5 and 6
    (5) 8 and 9

<u>Questions 12 and 13</u> are based on the following:

The Smithville Auto Parts Store is open Monday–Friday from 9 A.M. to 6 P.M. and Saturday from 9 A.M. to 4 P.M. Tom, the cashier, earns $8 per hour, and Susan, the manager, earns $12 per hour.

12. Which expression represents the total number of hours the store is open during a four-week period?

    (1) $4(9 + 7)$
    (2) $4(9 \times 5) + 4 (7)$
    (3) $(4 + 12) + (5 \times 45)$
    (4) $45 + 7 + 4$
    (5) not enough information is given

13. How much more does Sue make than Tom during a Monday–Saturday workweek?

    (1) $208
    (2) $126
    (3) $52
    (4) $108
    (5) $114

14. Dave operates a snack truck five days a week and uses crushed ice to cool his soft drinks. The following information indicates his ice use by the bucket for each of the days.

    Monday—16
    Tuesday—14
    Wednesday—19
    Thursday—21
    Friday—15

    If the supply house where Dave buys his ice charges him $1.50 per bucket, find the average cost he must pay for ice per day.

    (1) $14.50
    (2) $26.50
    (3) $127.50
    (4) $25.50
    (5) $19.50

15. The diagram below represents a floor plan for an office and storeroom. If both floors are to be covered with 1 sq. ft. vinyl tiles that cost $4 per tile, how much would it cost in dollars to purchase the tiles for both rooms?

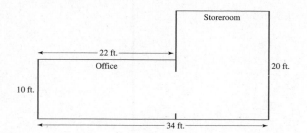

16. The diagram below shows the dimensions of a backyard swimming pool. Which expression represents the maximum volume in cubic ft. of water it can hold?

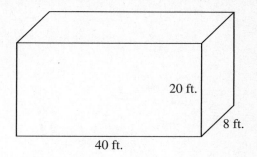

(1) 3(40 + 20 + 8)
(2) 3(8) + 3(40) + 3(20)
(3) (40 × 8) + (40 + 20)
(4) 8 × 20 × 40
(5) not enough information is given

Answers

1. 4	9. 3
2. 2,661	10. 3
3. 730	11. 4
4. 887	12. 2
5. 23r17	13. 1
6. $27,360	14. 4
7. 5	15. $1,840
8. 2	16. 4

Fractions and Measurements

CHAPTER 20

WRITING FRACTIONS

A **fraction** of something means a part of that thing; for example, a pizza pie has eight slices. If you take one slice, that equals $\frac{1}{8}$ (one eighth) of the pie. Two slices equals $\frac{2}{8}$ (two eighths), three slices equals $\frac{3}{8}$ (three eighths), and so on.

In the fraction $\frac{3}{8}$, the top number (3) is called the **numerator**. It tells how many parts you have. The bottom number (8) is called the **denominator** and tells you how many equal parts there are in the whole.

$$\frac{3}{8} \begin{array}{l} \leftarrow \text{numerator} \\ \leftarrow \text{denominator} \end{array}$$

Consider the square below:

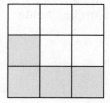

It's one whole divided into nine equal parts. If four of those parts are shaded, as in the diagram above, the shaded area represents $\frac{4}{9}$ of the square.

What fraction of the square is shaded below?

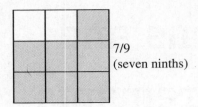

7/9
(seven ninths)

If the entire square is shaded, the fraction represented is $\frac{9}{9}$ or **1**. Any fraction whose numerator and denominator are the same *is equal to one.*

$$\frac{9}{9} = 1 \qquad \frac{12}{12} = 1 \qquad \frac{181}{181} = 1$$

FRACTION TYPES

There are three types of fractions you need to become familiar with: proper fractions, improper fractions, and mixed numbers.

- *Proper fractions* have numerators that are smaller than their denominators and are always less than one. $\frac{1}{3}$, $\frac{5}{6}$ and $\frac{11}{12}$ are proper fractions.

- *Improper fractions* have numerators that are larger than or equal to their denominators. $\frac{7}{3}$, $\frac{9}{6}$ and $\frac{12}{12}$ are improper fractions.

- *Mixed numbers* have a whole number included to the left of the fraction.

  $3\frac{1}{2}$ (three and one-half)

  $5\frac{5}{6}$ (five and five-sixths) are mixed numbers

NOTE

There's nothing wrong or "improper" about improper fractions. That's just a mathematical name given to distinguish them from proper fractions.

PRACTICE—WRITING FRACTIONS

Put an I for improper fraction, P for proper fraction, and M for mixed number on the blank lines next to each number below.

1. ____ $\frac{3}{8}$ 4. ____ $\frac{6}{6}$

2. ____ $\frac{8}{5}$ 5. ____ $\frac{1}{2}$

3. ____ $9\frac{3}{11}$ 6. ____ $12\frac{1}{2}$

ANSWERS

1. **P**   2. **I**   3. **M**   4. **I**   5. **P**   6. **M**

EQUIVALENT FRACTIONS AND
REDUCING TO LOWEST TERMS

Four slices of pizza make up $\frac{4}{8}$ of a pie, which happens also to be $\frac{1}{2}$ the pie.

Therefore, we say $\frac{4}{8}$ is **equivalent** (equal) to $\frac{1}{2}$. Even though the numbers in

both the numerator and denominator are higher, the value of $\frac{4}{8}$ and $\frac{1}{2}$ are the

same. Notice in the fraction $\frac{4}{8}$ that both numerator and denominator can be

divided by 4.

$$\frac{4 \div 4 = 1}{8 \div 4 = 2}$$

This process is called **reducing to lowest terms**. Simply find the largest number that can be used to divide both numerator and denominator, then divide.

EXAMPLE

Reduce the following fractions to lowest terms.

$\frac{5}{25}$ $\quad\quad$ $\frac{6}{9}$

$$5 \div 5 = 1 \quad\quad 6 \div 3 = 2$$
$$25 \div 5 = 5 \quad\quad 9 \div 3 = 3$$

PRACTICE—REDUCING TO LOWEST TERMS

Reduce the following fractions to lowest terms.

1. $\frac{4}{8}$ 4. $\frac{27}{36}$ 7. $\frac{51}{85}$

2. $\frac{12}{16}$ 5. $\frac{16}{48}$

3. $\frac{40}{50}$ 6. $\frac{14}{14}$

ANSWERS

1. $\frac{1}{2}$ 4. $\frac{3}{4}$ 7. $\frac{3}{5}$

2. $\frac{3}{4}$ 5. $\frac{1}{3}$

3. $\frac{4}{5}$ 6. $\frac{1}{1}$

RAISING FRACTIONS TO HIGHER TERMS

When solving problems with fractions, the **answer** must be expressed in lowest terms. However, when working with fractions to solve a problem, you will often have to do the exact opposite—raise them to higher terms while keeping them equivalent. To do this, multiply both the numerator and denominator by the same number.

In virtually all situations where you will raise to higher terms, the denominator will already be determined. You'll just need to figure out the numerator.

EXAMPLES

Convert $\frac{2}{3}$ to sixths

$$\frac{2}{3} = \frac{?}{6} \qquad \frac{2 \times 2}{3 \times 2} = \frac{4}{6}$$

Convert $\frac{5}{8}$ to twenty-fourths

$$\frac{5}{8} = \frac{?}{24} \qquad \frac{5 \times 3}{8 \times 3} = \frac{15}{24}$$

PRACTICE—RAISING TO HIGHER TERMS

Add the appropriate numerator so that the fractions will be equivalent.

1. $\frac{5}{8} = \frac{}{24}$ 4. $\frac{9}{6} = \frac{}{18}$

2. $\frac{3}{8} = \frac{}{16}$ 5. $\frac{7}{8} = \frac{}{56}$

3. $\frac{4}{5} = \frac{}{20}$

ANSWERS

1. **15**   2. **6**   3. **16**   4. **27**   5. **49**

CONVERTING IMPROPER FRACTIONS TO MIXED NUMBERS

Sometimes the solution to a problem will be expressed as an improper fraction, which then must be converted to a mixed number.

EXAMPLE

$$\frac{11}{4} = 2\frac{3}{4}$$

Remember that fractions are division problems, so $\frac{11}{4}$ can be written as $11 \div 4$ or $4\overline{)11}$.

$$4\overline{)11}^{\,2\,r3} \qquad 2\ r3 \text{ is the same as } 2\frac{3}{4}$$

PRACTICE—CONVERTING IMPROPER FRACTIONS TO MIXED NUMBERS

Convert the following improper fractions to mixed or whole numbers. Reduce where necessary.

1. $\frac{15}{2}$ 4. $\frac{56}{7}$ 7. $\frac{33}{9}$

2. $\frac{27}{3}$ 5. $\frac{31}{10}$

3. $\frac{26}{4}$ 6. $\frac{46}{12}$

ANSWERS

1. $7\frac{1}{2}$ 4. **8**   7. $3\frac{2}{3}$

2. **9**   5. $3\frac{1}{10}$

3. $6\frac{1}{2}$ 6. $3\frac{5}{6}$

ADDING AND SUBTRACTING FRACTIONS

Adding and subtracting fractions when the denominators are the same is a simple process. It looks like this:

$$\frac{1}{5} + \frac{3}{5} = \frac{4}{5} \qquad \frac{5}{7} - \frac{3}{7} = \frac{2}{7}$$

Notice the denominators stay the same and the numerators either increase or decrease.

PRACTICE—ADDING AND SUBTRACTING FRACTIONS WITH SAME DENOMINATOR

Solve the following and, where necessary, reduce to lowest terms.

1. $\frac{5}{8} - \frac{3}{8}$

2. $\frac{1}{6} + \frac{3}{6}$

3. $\frac{3}{11} + \frac{5}{11}$

4. $\frac{18}{21} - \frac{4}{21}$

5. $\frac{3}{5} + \frac{4}{5}$

ANSWERS

1. $\frac{1}{4}$

2. $\frac{2}{3}$

3. $\frac{8}{11}$

4. $\frac{2}{3}$

5. $1\frac{2}{5}$

LOWEST COMMON DENOMINATOR

When denominators **differ**, however, fractions can't be added or subtracted until all the denominators are converted to the same number, known as the **lowest common denominator** or **LCD**.

EXAMPLE ONE

Find $\frac{5}{8} + \frac{1}{4}$

The two fractions have different denominators so you can't add them in their present state. Since $\frac{5}{8}$ can't be reduced to quarters, the lowest common denominator that can be used for both fractions is eighths. Both four and eight can divide eight evenly.

Step one: Choose the LCD. Here, it's eighths.

Step two: Convert $\frac{1}{4}$ to $\frac{2}{8}$ by raising to higher terms.

Step three: Add $\frac{5}{8} + \frac{2}{8}$

Answer: $\frac{7}{8}$

EXAMPLE TWO

Find $\frac{1}{2} + \frac{1}{6} + \frac{1}{8}$

Step one: Choose the LCD.
This is a bit more difficult here. None of the denominators in the problem ($\overline{2}$, $\overline{6}$, or $\overline{8}$) can be used as an LCD. You can convert $\frac{1}{2}$ to $\frac{4}{8}$ but you can't convert $\frac{1}{6}$ to eighths ($\overline{8}$) because six doesn't divide evenly into eight; there's a remainder of two. And $\frac{1}{2}$ can be converted to $\frac{3}{6}$, but eighths can't be converted to sixths. You must choose the lowest number all three denominators ($\overline{2}$, $\overline{6}$, and $\overline{8}$) can divide into evenly. This is often a trial-and-error process. You already know 6 and 8 don't work. How about 10? 2 divides 10 evenly, but neither 6 nor 8 does so. How about 12? Both 2 and 6 divide it evenly, but 8 doesn't. How about 16? Both 2 and 8 work, but 6 doesn't. Eventually, you will reach **24**. It is the **lowest** number that all three denominators can divide equally. Therefore, 24 is the **LCD** used for solving the problem. This may seem like a long process, but with some practice, finding the LCD will come more quickly to you.

Step two: Convert $\frac{1}{2}$ to $\frac{12}{24}$, $\frac{1}{6}$ to $\frac{4}{24}$, and $\frac{1}{8}$ to $\frac{3}{24}$

Step three: Add $\frac{12}{24} + \frac{4}{24} + \frac{3}{24}$

Answer: $\frac{19}{24}$

PRACTICE—ADDING AND SUBTRACTING USING LCD

Find the LCD, then add or subtract. Reduce answers to lowest terms where necessary.

1. $\dfrac{2}{7} + \dfrac{3}{21}$

2. $\dfrac{5}{6} - \dfrac{1}{3}$

3. $\dfrac{1}{4} + \dfrac{1}{6}$

4. $\dfrac{5}{7} + \dfrac{3}{4}$

5. $\dfrac{3}{16} + \dfrac{1}{12} + \dfrac{1}{4}$

6. $\dfrac{8}{15} - \dfrac{1}{3}$

7. $\dfrac{7}{10} - \dfrac{1}{3}$

8. $\dfrac{2}{3} + \dfrac{1}{6} - \dfrac{4}{9}$

ANSWERS

1. $\dfrac{3}{7}$

2. $\dfrac{1}{2}$

3. $\dfrac{5}{12}$

4. $1\dfrac{13}{28}$

5. $\dfrac{25}{48}$

6. $\dfrac{1}{5}$

7. $\dfrac{11}{30}$

8. $\dfrac{7}{18}$

COMPARING AND ORDERING FRACTIONS

To compare and order fractions with different denominators: (1) find the LCD, (2) convert fractions by raising to higher terms, where necessary, (3) compare the numerators.

EXAMPLE ONE

Find the larger of the two fractions:

$$\dfrac{2}{5} \qquad \dfrac{1}{3}$$

Step one: Find the LCD: $\dfrac{}{15}$

Step two: Convert: $\dfrac{2}{5} = \dfrac{6}{15} \qquad \dfrac{1}{3} = \dfrac{5}{15}$

Step three: Compare: $\dfrac{6}{15}\left(\dfrac{2}{5}\right)$ is larger than $\dfrac{5}{15}\left(\dfrac{1}{3}\right)$ by $\dfrac{1}{15}$

Answer: $\dfrac{2}{5}$ is larger

EXAMPLE TWO

Arrange the following fractions in order from greatest to least:

$$\frac{7}{8} \quad \frac{5}{6} \quad \frac{7}{12} \quad \frac{3}{4}$$

Step one: Find the LCD: use $\frac{}{24}$

Step two: Convert:

$$\frac{7}{8} = \frac{21}{24} \qquad \frac{5}{6} = \frac{20}{24} \qquad \frac{7}{12} = \frac{14}{24} \qquad \frac{3}{4} = \frac{18}{24}$$

Step three: Compare and arrange in order:

$$\frac{7}{8}\left(\frac{21}{24}\right) \quad \frac{5}{6}\left(\frac{20}{24}\right) \quad \frac{3}{4}\left(\frac{18}{24}\right) \quad \frac{7}{12}\left(\frac{14}{24}\right)$$

PRACTICE—COMPARING AND ORDERING FRACTIONS

Choose the larger fraction in each pair.

1. $\frac{5}{8} \qquad \frac{9}{16}$

2. $\frac{5}{12} \qquad \frac{4}{9}$

3. $\frac{1}{3} \qquad \frac{2}{7}$

4. Arrange the following in order from heaviest to lightest:

$$\frac{1}{4} \text{ lb.} \qquad \frac{3}{8} \text{ lb.} \qquad \frac{3}{5} \text{ lb.} \qquad \frac{3}{10} \text{ lb.}$$

5. Arrange the following in order from shortest to longest:

$$\frac{5}{8} \qquad \frac{7}{32} \qquad \frac{9}{16} \qquad \frac{3}{4}$$

ANSWERS

1. $\frac{5}{8}$

2. $\frac{4}{9}$

3. $\frac{1}{3}$

4. $\frac{3}{5}, \frac{3}{8}, \frac{3}{10}, \frac{1}{4}$

5. $\frac{7}{32}, \frac{9}{16}, \frac{5}{8}, \frac{3}{4}$

WORKING WITH MIXED NUMBERS

ADDITION

EXAMPLE ONE

$$\frac{7}{8} + \frac{5}{8} = \frac{12}{8}$$

This is simple enough. But $\frac{12}{8}$ must be converted to a mixed number.

$$\frac{12}{8} = 1\frac{4}{8} = 1\frac{1}{2}$$
$$\frac{7}{8} + \frac{5}{8} = 1\frac{1}{2}$$

EXAMPLE TWO

$$14\frac{3}{4} + 2\frac{3}{5}$$

Step one: Using LCD, convert the fractions so they can be added.

$$14\frac{3}{4} = 14\frac{15}{20}$$
$$+ 2\frac{3}{5} = 2\frac{12}{20}$$
$$\overline{\phantom{+ 2\frac{3}{5} = } 16\frac{27}{20}}$$

Step two: Convert the fraction to a mixed number

$$\frac{27}{20} = 1\frac{7}{20}$$

and carry the whole number 1 over to the whole-number column, adding it to the 16.

$$16 + 1\frac{7}{20} = 17\frac{7}{20}$$

SUBTRACTION AND "BORROWING"

To subtract mixed numbers, you must be able to "borrow." Here's how to do it.

EXAMPLE

$$5\frac{1}{6} - 2\frac{5}{6}$$

$$5\frac{1}{6}$$
$$-2\frac{5}{6}$$
$$\overline{\phantom{-2\frac{5}{6}}}$$

The problem here is that you can't subtract 5 from 1. You need to borrow from the column to the left, just as you do in working with whole numbers. You borrow 1 from 5, which then becomes 4. Then convert the borrowed one into 6ths.

Remember: $1 = \frac{6}{6}$. Add those borrowed $\frac{6}{6}$ to the $\frac{1}{6}$, which now becomes $\frac{7}{6}$.

$$^4\cancel{5}\frac{1}{6} + \frac{6}{6} = 4\frac{7}{6}$$

$$-2\frac{5}{6}$$

$$2\frac{2}{6} = 2\frac{1}{3}$$

> **REMEMBER**
>
> When borrowing, do NOT simply add a 1 to the numerator as you would with whole numbers. Convert the "borrowed" 1 into a number equal to the fraction's denominator.

Always convert the borrowed 1 into whatever the denominator specifies. If it's 8ths, add $\frac{8}{8}$, or if it's 12ths, add $\frac{12}{12}$ to the existing fraction.

Practice—Adding and Subtracting with Mixed Numbers

Add or subtract. Express answers as mixed numbers where appropriate. Reduce to lowest terms.

1. $\frac{7}{9} + \frac{5}{9}$
2. $12\frac{1}{8} - 5\frac{5}{8}$
3. $\frac{3}{4} + \frac{5}{6}$

4. $41\frac{1}{3} - 18\frac{5}{9}$
5. $16\frac{7}{8} + 12\frac{9}{16}$
6. $36\frac{5}{12} - 19\frac{17}{24}$

7. $9\frac{2}{5} + 8\frac{2}{3} + 7\frac{11}{15}$

Answers

1. $1\frac{1}{3}$
2. $6\frac{1}{2}$
3. $1\frac{7}{12}$

4. $22\frac{7}{9}$
5. $29\frac{7}{16}$
6. $16\frac{17}{24}$

7. $25\frac{4}{5}$

MULTIPLICATION

In one important way, multiplication is a much easier process than adding and subtracting fractions. You don't need to worry about finding a common denominator—simply multiply the numerators of the fractions by each other and then do the same for the denominators. Reduce to lowest terms where necessary.

EXAMPLE ONE

Find $\frac{5}{8} \times \frac{1}{3}$

$$\frac{5 \times 1}{8 \times 3} = \frac{5}{24}$$

When multiplying fractions, all mixed numbers must be converted to improper fractions, and all whole numbers must use $\frac{}{1}$ as a denominator. See the following example.

EXAMPLE TWO

Find $5\frac{3}{4} \times 7$

Step one: Convert to improper fractions

$$5\frac{3}{4} = \frac{23}{4} \qquad 7 = \frac{7}{1}$$

Step two: Multiply

$$\frac{23}{4} \times \frac{7}{1} = \frac{161}{4}$$

Step three: Divide and convert to a mixed number

$$\frac{161}{4} = 40\frac{1}{4}$$

CONVERTING MIXED NUMBERS TO IMPROPER FRACTIONS

How did we get $\frac{23}{4}$ from $5\frac{3}{4}$ in Step one above? Here's how.

Step one: Multiply the denominator of the fraction by the whole number to its left.

$$5\frac{3}{4} \cdot \quad (5 \times 4 = 20)$$

Step two: Take the product of Step one (20) and add it to the numerator.

$$(20 + 3 = 23)$$

Step three: Place the "new" numerator (23) over the same denominator (4).

$$5\frac{3}{4} = \frac{23}{4}$$

PRACTICE—CONVERTING MIXED NUMBERS TO IMPROPER FRACTIONS

Convert the following to improper fractions.

1. $2\frac{3}{8}$

2. $14\frac{1}{2}$

3. $9\frac{6}{7}$

4. $11\frac{3}{4}$

5. $20\frac{13}{16}$

ANSWERS

1. $\frac{19}{8}$

2. $\frac{29}{2}$

3. $\frac{69}{7}$

4. $\frac{47}{4}$

5. $\frac{333}{16}$

USING CROSS-CANCELING IN MULTIPLICATION

This process reduces the size of the numerators and denominators, making multiplication easier. Here's how to do it:

Look at the numerator and its diagonal denominator. See whether there is a number that divides evenly into both. Choose the **highest** number common to both, then divide them by that number. Cross the old numbers out and replace them with the newer (smaller) numbers. Then multiply horizontally (across) to find the answer.

EXAMPLE

Find $\frac{5}{18} \times \frac{9}{20}$

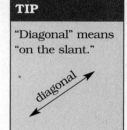

TIP

"Diagonal" means "on the slant."

diagonal

Step one: Look for diagonal relationships. Both 18 and 9 can be divided evenly by 9; both 20 and 5 can be divided evenly by 5.

Step two: Cross out the old numbers and replace them with the new ones.

$$\frac{\overset{1}{\cancel{5}}}{\underset{2}{\cancel{18}}} \times \frac{\overset{1}{\cancel{9}}}{\underset{4}{\cancel{20}}}$$

Step three: Multiply across using the new numbers.

$$\frac{1}{2} \times \frac{1}{4} = \frac{1}{8}$$

Solve, using cross-canceling where possible. Reduce where necessary.

1. $\frac{1}{4} \times \frac{5}{8}$

2. $\frac{5}{6}\left(\frac{8}{15}\right)$

3. $\frac{1}{8}\left(4\frac{2}{3}\right)$

4. $9 \times 5\frac{1}{4}$

5. $\frac{3}{15} \times \frac{5}{18} \times \frac{6}{7}$

6. $11\frac{3}{4} \times \frac{8}{94}$

ANSWERS

1. $\frac{5}{32}$

2. $\frac{4}{9}$

3. $\frac{7}{12}$

4. $47\frac{1}{4}$

5. $\frac{1}{21}$

6. **1**

DIVISION OF FRACTIONS

Division of fractions is not often seen on the GED. The numerator and denominator of the second fraction in the problem (the divisor) is inverted or flip-flopped. Then, you multiply.

EXAMPLE

$\frac{5}{8} \div \frac{1}{4}$

Step one: Invert (flip-flop) the second fraction $\frac{1}{4}$ becomes $\frac{4}{1}$.

Step two: Convert to a multiplication problem $\frac{5}{8} \times \frac{4}{1}$

Step three: Cross-cancel and multiply $\frac{5}{\underset{2}{8}} \times \frac{\overset{1}{4}}{1} = \frac{5}{2}$

Step four: Reduce $\frac{5}{2} = 2\frac{1}{2}$

Answer: $\frac{5}{8} \div \frac{1}{4} = 2\frac{1}{2}$

PRACTICE—DIVISION OF FRACTIONS

Solve.

1. $\dfrac{3}{8} \div \dfrac{3}{4}$ 3. $26 \div \dfrac{2}{5}$

2. $5\dfrac{1}{3} \div \dfrac{4}{15}$ 4. $9 \div 1\dfrac{1}{4}$

ANSWERS

1. $\dfrac{1}{2}$ 3. **65**

2. **20**   4. $\mathbf{7\dfrac{1}{5}}$

REVIEW EXERCISE—BASIC OPERATIONS WITH FRACTIONS

Solve the following.

1. $\dfrac{3}{8} + \dfrac{7}{8}$ 6. $\dfrac{1}{3} \times \dfrac{9}{17}$

2. $\dfrac{8}{11} - \dfrac{5}{11}$ 7. $\dfrac{5}{8}\left(\dfrac{1}{3} + \dfrac{3}{5}\right)$

3. $4\dfrac{1}{4} + 3\dfrac{5}{8}$ 8. $1\dfrac{3}{4}\left(\dfrac{8}{11}\right)$

4. $19\dfrac{1}{3} + 5\dfrac{5}{6} + \dfrac{2}{9}$ 9. $\left(3\dfrac{1}{4} + \dfrac{1}{8}\right) - \left(\dfrac{5}{16} + \dfrac{1}{4}\right)$

5. $8\dfrac{1}{5} - 3\dfrac{3}{5}$ 10. $2\dfrac{5}{8} \div 1\dfrac{1}{4}$

11. Arrange in order from shortest to longest:

$$\dfrac{1}{2} \text{ mile}, \quad \dfrac{5}{12} \text{ mile}, \quad \dfrac{3}{4} \text{ mile}, \quad \dfrac{4}{9} \text{ mile}$$

ANSWERS

1. $\mathbf{1\dfrac{1}{4}}$ 5. $\mathbf{4\dfrac{3}{5}}$ 9. $\mathbf{2\dfrac{13}{16}}$

2. $\mathbf{\dfrac{3}{11}}$ 6. $\mathbf{\dfrac{3}{17}}$ 10. $\mathbf{2\dfrac{1}{10}}$

3. $\mathbf{7\dfrac{7}{8}}$ 7. $\mathbf{\dfrac{7}{12}}$ 11. $\mathbf{\dfrac{5}{12}, \dfrac{4}{9}, \dfrac{1}{2}, \dfrac{3}{4}}$

4. $\mathbf{25\dfrac{7}{18}}$ 8. $\mathbf{1\dfrac{3}{11}}$

USING A CALCULATOR FOR FRACTIONS

A calculator can be a big help with all basic operations involving fractions. There is no need to find the LCD—the calculator does that automatically. It also gives answers in "mixed number" form.

EXAMPLE ONE

$\frac{3}{4} + 1\frac{5}{7}$

Press: $\boxed{3}$ $\boxed{a\,b/c}$ $\boxed{4}$ $\boxed{+}$ $\boxed{1}$ $\boxed{a\,b/c}$ $\boxed{5}$ $\boxed{a\,b/c}$ $\boxed{7}$ $=$

Answer: **2 ⌐ 13 ⌐ 28**   or   **$2\frac{13}{28}$**

A calculator can also convert improper fractions to mixed numbers.

EXAMPLE TWO

Convert $\frac{43}{3}$ to a mixed number.

Press: $\boxed{43}$ $\boxed{a\,b/c}$ $\boxed{3}$ $\boxed{=}$

Answer: $14\frac{1}{3}$

FRACTIONS AND THE ANSWER GRID

It's important to remember that mixed numbers **cannot** be entered on the answer grid.

Let's say the answer to a problem is $4\frac{1}{4}$. You must enter it either as $\frac{17}{4}$ or in its decimal form, 4.25. Converting fractions to decimals will be further discussed in Chapter 21.

Any of these is correct:

TRIANGLES

You already know how to calculate the perimeter of a triangle by adding up its sides. Finding its area is a bit more complicated. First, you must be able to identify two parts of the triangle—the base and the height.

The base is usually the "bottom" of the triangle, the side perpendicular to its height. The corner where the base and height lines meet make a 90-degree angle or square corner.

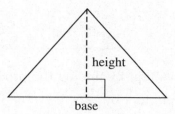

The height is almost always indicated by a vertical (up and down) dotted line. Only when the triangle is a **right triangle** is the height not marked by a dotted line. Study the diagrams below to become acquainted with base and height.

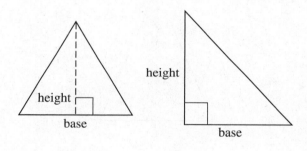

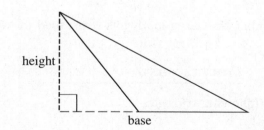

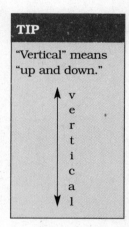

TIP

"Vertical" means "up and down."

AREA OF A TRIANGLE

The formula for area of a triangle is

$$A = \frac{1}{2} bh$$

It's easier to separate this formula into two steps so that is looks like this:

$$\frac{1}{2} (b \times h)$$

Do the work in parentheses first by finding the product of the base times the height, then multiply the product by $\frac{1}{2}$.

EXAMPLE

Find the area of the following triangle.

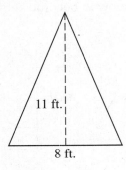

11 ft.

8 ft.

$A = \frac{1}{2} (b \times h)$ $A = \frac{1}{2} (8 \times 11)$ $A = \frac{1}{2} (88)$

$A = 44$ sq. ft. (remember that area is always expressed in **square** units).

PRACTICE—AREA OF A TRIANGLE

Find the area of the following triangles.

1.
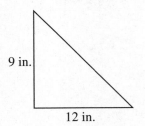

9 in.

12 in.

3.
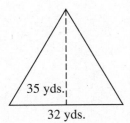

35 yds.

32 yds.

2.
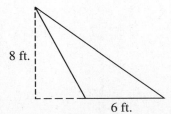

8 ft.

6 ft.

4.

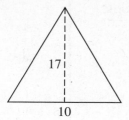

Which expression represents the area of the triangle above?

(a) $17(10 + 2)$

(b) $\dfrac{17}{2} \times \dfrac{1}{10}$

(c) $\dfrac{1}{2}(17 + 10)$

(d) $\dfrac{17 \times 10}{2}$

(e) $\dfrac{1}{2}(17 - 10)$

ANSWERS

1. **54 sq. in.**   3. **560 sq. yds.**

2. **24 sq. ft.**   4. **(d)**

PARALLELOGRAMS

Parallelograms are similar to rectangles. They have four sides, and each pair of opposite sides is parallel and equal. The formula for the area of a parallelogram is:

$$A = bh \text{ (area = base} \times \text{height)}$$

EXAMPLE

Find the area of the parallelogram below.

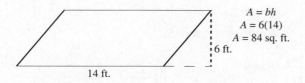

$A = bh$
$A = 6(14)$
$A = 84$ sq. ft.

PRACTICE—PARALLELOGRAMS

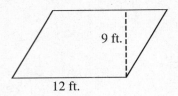

9 ft.

12 ft.

1. Find the area of the above parallelogram.

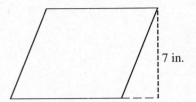

7 in.

2. If the area of the above parallelogram is 56 sq. in., find its base.

ANSWERS

1. **108 sq. ft.**   2. **8 in.**

STANDARD MEASUREMENTS

Many of the GED math questions will test your knowledge of measurement conversions. You should make yourself very familiar with those listed below.

Time
1 year = 12 months = 52 weeks = 365 days

1 week = 7 days

1 day = 24 hours

1 hour = 60 minutes

1 minute = 60 seconds

Liquid Measure
1 pint = 16 ounces (oz.)

1 quart = 32 oz.

1 gallon = 4 quarts

Length
1 ft. = 12 in.   1 yd = 3 ft. = 36 in.

Weight
1 lb. = 16 oz.   1 ton = 2,000 lbs.

Sometimes, you'll need to convert larger units of measure to smaller ones, and vice versa. Some terms can be expressed in two different ways: (1) In two units of measure, and (2) as a fraction or mixed number. Become familiar with both.

EXAMPLE ONE

Convert 40 ounces to quarts.

> **Answer 1:** 40 oz. = 1 qt. 8 oz. (32 oz. is one quart—8 oz. is the "remainder")

> **Answer 2:** 40 oz. = $1\frac{1}{4}$ qts. (32 oz. is one quart—$\frac{8}{32}$ is $\frac{1}{4}$ qt.)

EXAMPLE TWO

Convert $2\frac{1}{2}$ days to hours.

$$2\frac{1}{2}(24) = \frac{5}{2} \times \frac{24}{1} = 60 \text{ hours}$$

PART-TO-WHOLE RELATIONSHIPS

A fraction is representative of a part-to-whole relationship. When converting units of measure this $\frac{\text{part}}{\text{whole}}$ setup is useful.

EXAMPLE

Convert 45 minutes to hours

You know that 45 minutes is less than one hour; therefore, it's going to be a fraction (or part) of the whole hour, which is made up of 60 minutes. To solve, set up a fraction with the part (45) as numerator and the whole (60) as denominator. Then reduce.

$$\frac{45}{60} = \frac{3}{4} \text{ hour}$$

PRACTICE—STANDARD UNITS OF MEASURE

1. Convert 6,500 lbs. to: (a) tons   (b) tons and lbs.

2. Convert 18 months to: (a) years   (b) years and months

3. Convert 260 seconds to: (a) minutes   (b) minutes and seconds

4. Convert 17 ft. to: (a) yards   (b) yards and feet

Using the *part* relationship, convert each of the following measures to a fraction of the whole units indicated.

5. 1 qt. = _____ gallons

6. 28 in. = _____ yd.

7. 18 hrs. = _____ day

8. 9 months = _____ yr.

Using multiplication, convert the following.

9. $6\frac{1}{2}$ tons = _____ lbs.

10. 5 years = _____ months

11. $8\frac{3}{4}$ ft. = _____ inches

12. $19\frac{1}{2}$ qts. = _____ ozs.

ANSWERS

1. (a) **$3\frac{1}{4}$ tons** (b) **3 tons, 500 lbs.**

2. (a) **$1\frac{1}{2}$ years** (b) **1 year, 6 months**

3. (a) **$4\frac{1}{3}$ minutes** (b) **4 min. 20 seconds**

4. (a) **$5\frac{2}{3}$ yds.** (b) **5 yds, 2 ft.**

5. **$\frac{1}{4}$**

6. **$\frac{7}{9}$**

7. **$\frac{3}{4}$**

8. **$\frac{3}{4}$**

9. **13,000**

10. **60**

11. **105**

12. **624**

THE METRIC SYSTEM OF MEASURE

On the GED, you won't be asked to make precise conversions from the standard system to the metric system. But you should familiarize yourself with the following:

Liquid Measure
liter: about 1 qt.

milliliter: $\dfrac{1}{1000}$ of a liter

Weight
gram: $\dfrac{1}{28}$ of an ounce

milligram: $\dfrac{1}{1000}$ of a gram

kilogram: 1000 grams (2.2 lbs)

Length
meter: 39 inches

millimeter: $\dfrac{1}{1000}$ of a meter

kilometer: 1000 meters (.6 of a mile)

WORD PROBLEMS WITH FRACTIONS

PART-TO-WHOLE RELATIONSHIP

The part-to-whole relationship is an important part of setting up solutions to word problems. Here's how to use it.

EXAMPLE ONE

There were 42 people taking the GED exam at Grovesville Center, 28 of whom were men. Find the fractional part of men taking the test.

The **part** you're seeking is the number of men taking the test—28. The **whole** is the total number of people taking the test—42.

$$\frac{\text{part}}{\text{whole}} = \frac{28}{42} = \frac{2}{3}$$

Answer: $\dfrac{2}{3}$ of those taking the test were men.

Sometimes, the **whole** won't be stated; you'll have to figure it out by adding the parts.

EXAMPLE TWO

Jerry packed his suitcase with 10 pairs of black socks, 12 pairs of white socks, and 2 pairs of striped socks. What fractional part of the socks he packed was white?

The **part** is 12, but the **whole** isn't stated. You must add 10, 12 and 2 to get it.

$$\frac{12}{10 + 12 + 2} = \frac{12}{24} = \frac{1}{2}$$

PRACTICE—THE PART-TO-WHOLE RELATIONSHIP

Solve.

1. The Kingsford field hockey team consisted of 27 girls, 18 of whom were seniors. What fractional part of the team was comprised of seniors?

2. Of the 736 registered voters in Youngstown, 552 turned out to vote in the most recent election. What fractional part of the population did *not* vote?

3. A fourth-grade class at Bucksville Elementary School took a poll regarding its favorite ice cream flavors. Fifteen class members chose chocolate as their favorite, 8 chose vanilla, 2 chose pistachio and 5 chose various other flavors. Which expression can be used to find the fractional part of the class favoring chocolate?

   (a) $\dfrac{15}{4} + \dfrac{(8 + 5 + 2)}{4}$

   (b) $\dfrac{30}{15}$

   (c) $\dfrac{15}{15 + 8 + 2 + 5}$

   (d) $\dfrac{(8 + 2 + 15) - 15}{4}$

ANSWERS

1. $\dfrac{2}{3}$ 2. $\dfrac{1}{4}$ 3. **(c)**

"OF" MEANS "MULTIPLY"

This may sound strange, but it's an important thing to remember. The word "of," especially when it appears in a fraction problem, almost always means you need to multiply.

EXAMPLE

At a free concert, $\frac{1}{6}$ of the 636 people who attended were senior citizens. How many senior citizens attended?

$$\frac{1}{6} \textbf{ of } 636 = \frac{1}{6} \times \frac{636}{1} = \frac{636}{6} = 106 \text{ senior citizens}$$

PRACTICE—"OF" MEANS "MULTIPLY"

Solve.

1. The Granville PTA spends $\frac{1}{4}$ of its annual budget on scholarship funds. If the PTA's budget is \$18,240, what fractional part is contributed to scholarship funds?

2. LeeAnn took a history test consisting of 75 questions, $\frac{2}{5}$ of which were multiple choice while the rest were short-answer. How many questions were short-answer?

ANSWERS

1. **4560**   2. **45**

RATIO

Ratio is just another way to express a fractional part of something. It looks a little different (example: the ratio 1:3 is actually $\frac{1}{3}$) and sounds different (you would say 1:3 as "a ratio of one to three") but it acts just like a fraction.

EXAMPLE

There are 54 workers in an office, 18 of whom are men. What is the ratio of men to women in the office?

Step one: The number of women is not stated, so it must be figured out.

54 (total) – 18 men = 36 women

Step two: Set the ratio up in the order it was asked for (men : women) or 18 : 36

Step three: Convert the ratio to a fraction and reduce $\frac{18}{36} = \frac{1}{2}$

Step four: Change back to a ratio when expressing the answer

Answer: 1 : 2 is the ratio of men to women.

1. A computer printer is $238 and its ink cartridge is $34. What is the ratio of the price of the cartridge to the printer?

2. A student takes an exam with 100 questions on it and answers five questions incorrectly. What is the ratio of the number of questions he answered correctly to the number he answered incorrectly?

ANSWERS

1. **7 : 1**   2. **19 : 1**

PROBABILITY

The probability of rolling a 3 using one die (one cube of dice) is said to be 1 in 6 or $\frac{1}{6}$. The numerator represents how many chances there are that a certain event will happen (in this case, rolling a 3) and the denominator represents the total number of possiblities. In this case, there are six different numbers (including the 3) that could come up. It's another use of the part-to-whole relationship.

EXAMPLE

A cooler is packed with 8 cans of ginger ale, 4 cans of root beer, and 12 cans of cola. What is the probability that a person reaching into the cooler will pull out a cola?

Step one: Get a denominator by calculating the total number of possibilities.

$$8 + 4 + 12 = 24$$

use $\frac{}{24}$ as a denominator

Step two: Get a numerator that represents the number of colas there are in the cooler.

$$\frac{12}{24} = \frac{1}{2}$$

Answer: The probability of pulling out a cola is $\frac{1}{2}$.

A root beer?

Step one: Get a denominator $\frac{}{24}$

Step two: Get a numerator $\frac{4}{24} = \frac{1}{6}$

Answer: The probability of pulling out a root beer is $\frac{1}{6}$.

A ginger ale?

$$\frac{8}{24} = \frac{1}{3}$$

Answer: The probability of pulling out a ginger ale is **$\frac{1}{3}$**.

PRACTICE—PROBABILITY

1. There are 6 limes, 5 lemons, and 4 tangerines in a bag. What is the probability of choosing a lemon the first time?

2. There are ten "number" keys on a computer keyboard and 36 "letter" keys. If a person presses a key at random, what is the likelihood that it will be the number 7?

3. You are trying to guess a person's birth date. What is the probability that the person was born in a month beginning with the letter "J?"

ANSWERS

1. **$\frac{1}{3}$**   2. **$\frac{1}{46}$**   3. **$\frac{1}{4}$**

CHAPTER REVIEW

Fill in the answer grids, and use a calculator where indicated.

1. Wuanlee buys Acme stock at $53\frac{1}{4}$ per share. The stock increases $1\frac{3}{8}$. How much is it now worth per share?

    (1) $55\frac{1}{4}$

    (2) $52\frac{7}{8}$

    (3) $54\frac{5}{8}$

    (4) $56\frac{1}{4}$

    (5) $54\frac{1}{4}$

2. According to the pie chart below, what fractional part of Sally's monthly expenses goes to rent?

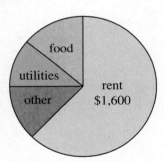

    Total monthly expenses: $2,400

    (1) $\frac{1}{3}$

    (2) $\frac{5}{6}$

    (3) $\frac{1}{2}$

    (4) $\frac{2}{3}$

    (5) $\frac{7}{8}$

3. Ted has the following open-ended wrenches:

    $$\frac{5}{8}, \frac{1}{2}, \frac{15}{32}, \frac{9}{16}$$

    Which represents the correct order, if he wishes to arrange them from smallest to largest?

    (1) $\frac{5}{8}, \frac{15}{32}, \frac{9}{16}, \frac{1}{2}$

    (2) $\frac{1}{2}, \frac{15}{32}, \frac{9}{16}, \frac{5}{8}$

    (3) $\frac{9}{16}, \frac{15}{32}, \frac{1}{2}, \frac{5}{8}$

    (4) $\frac{15}{32}, \frac{1}{2}, \frac{9}{16}, \frac{5}{8}$

4. From a 16-inch length of tubing, Rob cut a piece $4\frac{5}{8}$ inches long. How much is now left from the original piece?

    (1) $12\frac{1}{8}$ inches

    (2) $13\frac{3}{8}$ inches

    (3) $11\frac{3}{8}$ inches

    (4) $11\frac{1}{4}$ inches

    (5) $12\frac{1}{4}$ inches

5. The five members of the Sanford family picked a total of $8\frac{1}{3}$ cartons of blueberries. Which expression would allow the berries to be distributed evenly among each family member?

    (1) $\frac{25}{3} \times \frac{1}{5}$

    (2) $\frac{3}{25} \div \frac{1}{5}$

    (3) $5 \div \frac{25}{3}$

    (4) $5\frac{1}{3} \times \frac{5}{1}$

    (5) $8\frac{1}{3} \times \frac{5}{1}$

6. Find the area of the rectangle below:

$8\frac{2}{3}$ ft.

$14\frac{1}{2}$ ft.

(1) $125\frac{2}{3}$ sq. ft.

(2) $46\frac{1}{3}$ ft.

(3) $138\frac{1}{6}$ sq. ft.

(4) $408\frac{1}{3}$ sq. ft.

(5) $126\frac{1}{4}$ sq. ft.

7. Laura buys 4 yards of fabric at $3.20 a yard. She is making banners that are each 16 inches long. Which expression tells how many banners Laura can cut from the fabric?

(1) $\dfrac{(4 \times 12)3.20}{16}$

(2) $\dfrac{12(4 \times 2)}{4}$

(3) $\dfrac{4(36)}{16}$

(4) $\dfrac{4(3.20)}{2(16)}$

(5) $3.20\,(16)$

8. There are 132 members of the Otis Volunteer Fire Department. At a recent alarm, $\frac{1}{4}$ of the volunteers responded. How many volunteers did *not* respond?

9. Joan's commute to work is $27\frac{1}{4}$ miles each way. Her car averages 26 miles per gallon of gas. Which expression indicates how much gas Joan's car consumes for commutation during a 5-day work week?

(1) $\dfrac{27\frac{1}{4}}{26} \times \dfrac{1}{5}$

(2) $\dfrac{54\frac{1}{4} \times 5}{1}$

(3) $\dfrac{2\left(27\frac{1}{4}\right)}{26} \times \dfrac{5}{1}$

(4) $\dfrac{\left(27\frac{1}{4}\right)5}{13}$

(5) not enough information is given

10. Hector has a summer house where he resides for the months of June, July, and August. Over a three-year period, he followed this schedule, except for one year in which he stayed only in July and August. What fractional part of these three years did Hector reside in his summer house?

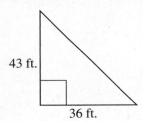

11. Greta planted a triangular garden shown below. She needs to spread fertilizer at the rate of $\frac{3}{4}$ lb. per sq. ft.

Which expression shows how much fertilizer Greta needs to cover the garden?

43 ft.

36 ft.

(1) $\frac{1}{2} \times \frac{36(43)}{1} \times \frac{3}{4}$

(2) $\frac{36 + 43}{1} \times \frac{3}{4}$

(3) $\frac{1}{2} \times \frac{36 + 43}{1} \div \frac{3}{1}$

(4) $36 \times 43 \div \frac{3}{4}$

(5) $\frac{\frac{1}{2}}{x} \times 36(43)$

12. It takes a machine 2 minutes and 15 seconds to assemble one chair. If the machine runs continuously for 6 hours, how many chairs will it produce?

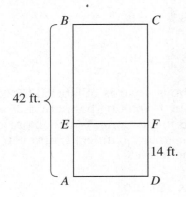

13.

B   C

42 ft.

E   F

14 ft.

A   D

If the length of ▭ ABCD is 42 ft. and the length of ▭ AEFD is 14 ft., what is the ratio of the area of ▭ ABCD to the area of ▭ AEFD?

(1) $\frac{1}{3}$
(2) 5 : 1
(3) 3 : 1
(4) 2 : 1
(5) 3 : 2

14. A traffic light is red for 38 seconds, yellow for 10 seconds, and green for one minute and twelve seconds in a constantly repeating cycle. What is the probability that at the moment a passing pedestrian glances at it, the light will be green?

Answers

1. **3**	6. **1**	11. **1**
2. **4**	7. **3**	12. **160**
3. **4**	8. **99**	13. **3**
4. **3**	9. **3**	14. **3/5 or .6**
5. **1**	10. **2/9 or .22**	

Decimals and Percents

Decimals are just like fractions—they are a way of showing part of a whole number. For example, $\frac{7}{10}$ is written as .7 or 0.7. You can read .7 as "seven tenths," but, more commonly, it is read as "point seven."

Actually, you've been using the decimal system for a long time, perhaps without realizing it. If you have a quarter, two dimes, and three pennies, you know you have $.48 or 48 cents. This .48 represents 48 cents out of one dollar, or $\frac{48}{100}$ or **.48 out of 1.00.**

DECIMAL PLACES

An important part of working effectively with decimals is understanding the **decimal place-value system**. As you move further to the right of the decimal point, the value of the numbers grows smaller. Study the chart below and memorize the values for each place to the right of the decimal point.

Of course, the place-value system could keep moving to the right forever, generating increasingly smaller numbers, but for the purposes of preparing for the GED, we need only worry about working effectively with numbers to the fifth decimal place (100,000ths).

DECIMALS AND FRACTIONAL EQUIVALENTS

Study these fractional equivalents of decimals to better understand the system.

$$.1 = \frac{1}{10} \qquad\qquad .7894 = \frac{7894}{10,000}$$

$$.14 = \frac{14}{100} \qquad\qquad .90023 = \frac{90023}{100,000}$$

$$.235 = \frac{235}{1,000}$$

PRACTICE—WRITING DECIMAL EQUIVALENTS TO FRACTIONS

Write the following fractions as decimals. Refer to the place-value chart above if necessary.

1. $\frac{9}{10}$

2. $\frac{33}{100}$

3. $\frac{507}{1,000}$

4. $\frac{1286}{10,000}$

5. $\frac{17}{100}$

ANSWERS

1. **.9**   2. **.33**   3. **.507**   4. **.1286**   5. **.17**

USING ZEROS WITH DECIMALS

Putting a zero to the **right** of a decimal number does not change its value at all. For example, .7 is equal to .70 or .700 or even .70000000! Which is worth more, seven dimes (.7 or $\frac{7}{10}$) or seventy cents (.70 or $\frac{70}{100}$)? Of course, their value is equal.

However, putting a zero to the left of a number (in between the number and the decimal point) **changes** its value by making it ten times smaller. For example, .07 is ten times smaller than .7. Which is larger, seven dimes (.7) or seven pennies (.07)? Seven dimes (.70) is larger than seven pennies (.07).

Which is larger, .4 or .396? Clearly, .4 is larger. This is often confusing to GED students at first. Try setting these decimals up as fractional equivalents and then compare.

$$.4 = \frac{4}{10} \qquad\qquad .396 = \frac{396}{1,000}$$

If you raise to higher terms for purposes of comparing fractions, you will see that:

$$\frac{4}{10} = \frac{400}{1,000} \text{ is larger than } \frac{396}{1,000} \text{ \textbf{or} .400 is larger than .396}$$

Study these fractional equivalents and decimal comparisons:

$$.06 = \frac{6}{100} \qquad .006 = \frac{6}{1,000} \qquad .6 = .600 \left(\frac{6}{10} = \frac{600}{1,000}\right)$$

$$5.6 = 5\frac{6}{10}$$

.3 is the same as .300

.3 is larger than .299

.3 is much larger than .039

.33 is larger than .3

Practice—Writing and Comparing Decimals with Fractions

Write the decimal equivalent of the following fractions.

1. $\frac{5}{1,000}$

2. $\frac{60}{100}$

3. $\frac{47}{100}$

4. $\frac{71}{100}$

5. $\frac{408}{10,000}$

Write "L" if the first decimal of the pair is larger, "S" if it is smaller, and "E" if the pair is equal.

6. .703   .0788

7. .493   .6

8. 1.08   2.003

9. .52   .5200

10. .01030   .0103

Arrange the following sets of decimals in size order from smallest to largest.

11. 1.8, 1.743, .992, 1.089, 1.81

12. 71.049, 71.2, 70.98, 71.203, 71.0491

Answers

1. **.005**
2. **.6**
3. **.47**
4. **.71**
5. **.0408**
6. **L**
7. **S**
8. **S**
9. **E**
10. **E**
11. **.992, 1.089, 1.743, 1.8, 1.81**
12. **70.98, 71.049, 71.0491, 71.2, 71.203**

ADDING AND SUBTRACTING DECIMALS

These operations are the same as working with whole numbers. Here's what it looks like.

EXAMPLE ONE

5.04 + 12.62 + .88   23.214 – 8.906

```
    12.62              23.214
     5.04           –   8.906
  +   .88              14.308
    18.54
```

Notice: (1) how the place-value columns are perfectly aligned
(2) that the decimal points are moved directly below in the answers.

The only complication with addition and subtraction is this:

EXAMPLE TWO

3.9 + 5 + 4.007

It might be set up: 5
                      4.007
                    + 3.9

It **should** be set up: 5.000
                          4.007
                        + 3.900
                         12.907

Notice how the zeros are added to keep the place–value columns looking aligned to eliminate confusion and to help when there is carrying. This is especially true for subtraction when there is borrowing.

EXAMPLE THREE

5 – 3.03

It **should** be set up: 5.00
                          – 3.03
                           1.97

PRACTICE—ADDING AND SUBTRACTING DECIMALS

Solve the following.

1. 4.09 + 55.369 + 5.6

2. 300 – 186.82

3. 88 + 903.01 + .06 + 12.173

ANSWERS

1. **65.059**   2. **113.18**   3. **1003.243**

> **TIP**
>
> When working with decimals, make sure place columns are aligned. Use decimal points in each number as guides.

MULTIPLYING DECIMALS

You learned in basic operations that it is best to arrange the larger number on top when multiplying, but when working with decimals this is not always the case. Place the number with the *most* digits on top—there's less work to do.

EXAMPLE ONE

Solve   5.4 × 2.13

The number 5.4 is clearly larger than 2.13, but 2.13 has more digits. The problem should be set up this way, then solved using the following steps.

Step one: Don't align the decimals here. Just multiply.

$$
\begin{array}{r}
2.13 \\
\times\ 5.4 \\
\hline
852 \\
1065 \\
\hline
11502
\end{array}
$$

Step two: Count the number of digits to the right of the decimal point in both multiplying numbers. Here, there are three (1 and 3 from 2.13 and 4 from 5.4).

Step three: Put your pen just past the last digit to the right. Here, it's the two. Now move the decimal point to the left the number of digits you counted in Step two (here, it's three). Place the decimal point there.

Answer: 11.502.

PRACTICE—MULTIPLYING DECIMALS

Solve.

1. 4.65(38)
2. .913(4.4)
3. 10.04(.03)

4. (9)1.13
5. 24.28(.01)

ANSWERS

1. **176.7**
2. **4.0172**
3. **.3012**

4. **10.17**
5. **.2428**

TIP

Unlike multiplying whole numbers, multiplying numbers by decimals less than 1 gives a smaller product. See practice problems 2, 3, and 5 as examples.

DIVIDING DECIMALS

When the decimal is in the dividend, all that's needed to be done is to duplicate it (carefully and precisely) directly above to the "shelf" of the dividing sign. Then, divide as you normally would. The decimal is already placed correctly in the answer.

EXAMPLE ONE

91.8 ÷ 54

```
                              1.7   ← quotient
                                    ← shelf
            divisor →    54 ) 91.8  ← dividend
                          -  54
                             378
                          -  378
                               0
```

When the decimal is in the divisor, the process becomes a bit more complicated. You cannot proceed with decimals there. Follow the steps below.

EXAMPLE TWO

30.176 ÷ 7.36

```
                             4.1
               7.36. ) 30.17.6
                    -  2944
                        736
                    -   736
                          0
```

Step one: Move the decimal point in the divisor all the way to the right, making it a whole number. Count the number of places you've moved it. Here, it would be two.

Step two: Now move the decimal in the dividend the same number of spaces as you moved it in Step one.

Step three: Place a decimal on the "shelf" of the dividend just as you did in Example One above. Divide.

Note: Sometimes, you will need to move the decimal point in the dividend, but you will already be at the right end of the number. When this happens, create places to the right by adding zeros. See the following example.

EXAMPLE THREE

62 ÷ 1.25

```
                            49.6
              1.25 ) 62.00.0
                   -  520
                      1200
                   -  1125
                       750
                   -   750
                         0
```

The example above also illustrates another very important concept in division. Previously, you would have ended the division at the second zero in 6200 and expressed the answer as 49 r75. But now that you know how to work with decimals, this rough method of dividing is no longer necessary. Simply add zeros to the right side of the dividend until either:

(1) the dividend divides evenly (as it did in Example Three)

   or

(2) you have carried out the division to the decimal place specified by the question and the answer can then be **rounded off**. See the example below.

EXAMPLE FOUR

Solve and round to the nearest hundredth.

$$\frac{154}{13}$$

$$
\begin{array}{r}
11.846 \\
13\overline{)154.000} \\
-\underline{13} \\
24 \\
-\underline{13} \\
110 \\
-\underline{104} \\
60 \\
-\underline{52} \\
80 \\
-\underline{78} \\
2
\end{array}
$$

To **round off**, always divide one place **past** the place value you were instructed to round. Division was done to the thousandths place, which is one place beyond the hundredths.

Examine the last place to the right. Is the number **5 or higher**? If so, round the next number to the left **up one**. In this example the last number is higher than 5.

Therefore, 11.846 rounded to the nearest hundredth is 11.85. If the number is **lower than 5,** simply leave the last number off and leave the number as it is. See the following examples.

EXAMPLE FIVE

Round the following numbers off to the nearest hundreth.

142.654 becomes 142.65

4.019 becomes 4.02

13.135 becomes 13.14

Solve using division. Round off answers to the nearest hundredth, where necessary.

1. $223.2 \div 12$ 3. $129 \div 5.14$

2. $34.44 \div 32.8$ 4. $\dfrac{67}{14}$

ANSWERS

1. **18.60**   3. **25.10**
2. **1.05**   4. **4.79**

CONVERTING DECIMALS TO FRACTIONS

This is a fairly simple operation. Set the decimal up as a fraction and reduce where necessary.

EXAMPLE

Convert .75 to a fraction

$$.75 = \frac{75}{100} = \mathbf{\frac{3}{4}}$$

CONVERTING FRACTIONS TO DECIMALS

This is a bit more complicated. Remember, once again, that every fraction is a division problem, so that $\frac{1}{4}$ really means $1 \div 4$. Dividing a smaller number by a larger one may look unfamiliar, but it's a very important operation to know. Here's how to do it:

EXAMPLE ONE

Convert $\frac{1}{4}$ to a decimal

Step one: Set $\frac{1}{4}$ up as a division problem and try to divide.

$$4\overline{)1}$$

Step two: You realize you can't divide 4 into 1. You must add a decimal point and a zero to the dividend.

$$4\overline{)1.0}$$

Step three: Transfer the decimal point in the dividend to the "shelf," then divide.

$$\begin{array}{r} .2 \\ 4\overline{)1.0} \\ \underline{-8} \\ 2 \end{array}$$

Step four: Add another zero to the dividend and finish the problem.

$$
\begin{array}{r}
.25 \\
4\,)\overline{1.00} \\
-8 \\
\hline
20 \\
-20 \\
\hline
0
\end{array}
$$

Sometimes, when converting fractions to decimals, you will encounter a never-ending division problem, the answer to which is called a **repeating decimal**. In this situation, carry out division to the nearest thousandth (or whatever the directions indicate) and round off.

EXAMPLE TWO

Convert $\frac{1}{3}$ to a decimal—rounded off to the nearest hundredth.

Step one: $\frac{1}{3} = 3\,)\overline{1}$

Step two: $3\,)\overline{1.0}$ with $.3$ above

Step three:

$$
\begin{array}{r}
.333 \\
3\,)\overline{1.000} \\
-9 \\
\hline
10 \\
-9 \\
\hline
10 \\
-9 \\
\hline
1
\end{array}
$$

Step four: .333 = **.33** rounded to the nearest hundredth

PRACTICE—CONVERTING DECIMALS AND FRACTIONS

Convert the following decimals to fractions and reduce, where necessary.

1. .50

2. .065

3. 2.25

4. .125

5. .367

Convert the following fractions to decimals and round to the nearest hundredth, where necessary.

6. $\frac{4}{5}$

7. $\frac{9}{4}$

8. $\frac{5}{8}$

9. $\frac{3}{32}$

10. $\frac{2}{3}$

ANSWERS

1. $\frac{1}{2}$ 6. **.80**

2. $\frac{13}{200}$ 7. **2.25**

3. $2\frac{1}{4}$ 8. **.63**

4. $\frac{1}{8}$ 9. **.09**

5. $\frac{367}{1,000}$ 10. **.67**

The conversions in the chart below frequently appear on the GED. Memorize as many as you can.

$\frac{1}{3}$ = .333	$\frac{3}{5}$ = .6
$\frac{2}{3}$ = .666 or .67	$\frac{4}{5}$ = .8
$\frac{1}{4}$ = .25	$\frac{1}{8}$ = .125
$\frac{3}{4}$ = .75	$\frac{3}{8}$ = .375
$\frac{1}{5}$ = .2	$\frac{5}{8}$ = .625
$\frac{2}{5}$ = .4	$\frac{7}{8}$ = .875

SCIENTIFIC NOTATION

Scientific notation is a method used by scientists to convert very large or very small numbers to more manageable ones. You will almost certainly be required to do one conversion to scientific notation on the GED. It's an easy operation.

EXAMPLE ONE

A space satellite can transmit from a distance of 46,000,000 miles away. What is the number written in scientific notation?

Step one: Starting at the "imaginary" decimal point to the *right* of the last zero, move the decimal point until only one digit remains to its *left*.

$$46{,}000{,}000 \text{ becomes } 4.6$$

Step two: Count the number of places the decimal was moved left. It's 7 places, which is expressed this way:

$$10^7$$

Step three: Express the full answer in scientific notation this way:

$$46{,}000{,}000 \text{ miles} = \mathbf{4.6 \times 10^7}$$

EXAMPLE TWO

A microorganism is .000056 inch long. What is its length in scientific notation?

Step one: Move the decimal point to the *right* until there is one digit other than zero to the *left* of the decimal.

$$.000056 \text{ becomes } 5.6$$

Step two: Count the number of places moved to the right—it's 5, which is expressed this way, using a *negative sign* with the exponent:

$$10^{-5}$$

Step three: Express the full answer in scientific notation this way:

$$.000056 = \mathbf{5.6 \times 10^{-5}}$$

Consider these other examples to help you get the concept:

$$783{,}000{,}000 = 7.83 \times 10^8$$
$$500{,}000{,}000 = 5 \times 10^8$$
$$.00000923 = 9.23 \times 10^{-6}$$
$$.0005134 = 5.134 \times 10^{-4}$$

Practice—Scientific Notation

Express in scientific notation.

1. 83,000,000
2. .000012

3. 5,160,000,000
4. .0000006

Answers

1. $\mathbf{8.3 \times 10^7}$
2. $\mathbf{1.2 \times 10^{-5}}$

3. $\mathbf{5.16 \times 10^9}$
4. $\mathbf{6 \times 10^{-7}}$

CIRCLES AND CYLINDERS

Now that you know how to multiply decimals, you can work with circles. First, there are important concepts you must understand and vocabulary you must memorize.

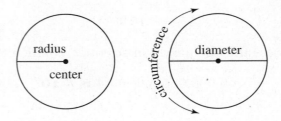

- The **circumference (c)** is the distance around the circle. It's another word for "perimeter."

- The **center** of a circle is its exact middle.

- The **radius (r)** of a circle is a straight line that runs from the exact center of the circle to its circumference.

- The **diameter (d)** is the distance across the circle from a point on the circumference to its opposite side, passing through the center. It is **twice the length of the radius** or **d = 2r**.

CALCULATING RADIUS, DIAMETER, AND CIRCUMFERENCE OF A CIRCLE

Learn the following:

radius = $\dfrac{d}{2}$ (radius = diameter ÷ 2)

diameter = 2r

c = π d (pi × diameter)

π = pi (pronounced "pie"). It is a letter from the Greek alphabet. It represents the number **3.14** and is essential for working with circles. Memorize it.

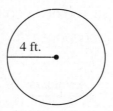

EXAMPLE

Calculate the radius, diameter, and circumference of the above circle.

- radius = 4 ft. (this is stated in the diagram—no calculation is necessary)

- diameter = 2r or 2(4) = 8 ft.

- circumference = πd or 3.14(8) = 25.12 ft.

CALCULATING THE AREA OF A CIRCLE

The formula for calculating the area of a circle is

$$A = \pi(r^2) \text{ or } \pi \times r^2$$

EXAMPLE

Find the area of the following circle.

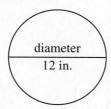

diameter
12 in.

Step one: Find the radius. If $d = 12$ inches then $r = \dfrac{d}{2}$ or 6 inches

Step two: Square the radius (r^2) $6 \times 6 = 36$ inches

Step three: Multiply $\pi \times r^2$

$3.14 \times 36 = 113.04$ **square** inches (even though a circle is round, area is still expressed in terms of **square** units.)

PRACTICE—CALCULATING THE DIMENSIONS OF CIRCLES

Find the radius (r), diameter (d), circumference (c), and area (a) of the following circles. Round to the nearest hundredth, where necessary.

1.

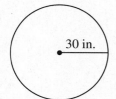

30 in.

2.

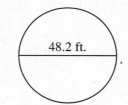

48.2 ft.

ANSWERS

1. **$r = 30$ inches, $d = 60$ inches,**
   $c = 188.4$ inches, $a = 2826$ sq. inches

2. **$r = 24.1$ feet, $d = 48.2$ feet,**
   $c = 151.35$ feet, $a = 1823.74$ sq. feet

CALCULATING THE VOLUME OF CYLINDERS

Like cubes and rectangular containers, cylinders are three-dimensional figures, which are measured by volume. The formula for volume of a cylinder is:

$$V = (\pi\ r^2)\ h \qquad \text{or}$$
$$\text{volume} = (\pi \times \text{radius}^2) \times \text{height}$$

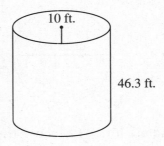

10 ft.

46.3 ft.

EXAMPLE

Find the volume of the above cylinder.

Step one: Find the area on the top (or bottom) circle of the cylinder.

$$A = \pi r^2 = 3.14 \times 10^2 = 314$$

Step two: $A \times h = 314 \times 46.3 = 14{,}538.2$ cubic (cu.) ft. (Always express a volume answer in **cubic** units.)

PRACTICE—VOLUME OF CYLINDERS

Find the volume for the following cylinder.

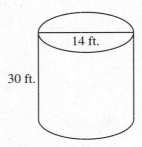

14 ft.

30 ft.

ANSWER

4615.8 cubic feet

PERCENTS

Working with percents is one of the more frequently tested skills on the GED, so it's essential that you become familiar with it.

The percent sign (%) following a number means that the number is a fraction of 100. For example, if you read about the construction of a bridge and the newspaper says, "The project is 60% complete," it means that if the entire bridge-building job were divided into 100 equal parts, 60 of them are complete *or* $\frac{60}{100}$ of the project is complete *or* $\frac{3}{5}$ of the project is complete.

CHANGING PERCENTS TO DECIMALS

This is a simple procedure. Replace the % sign with a decimal point and move it two places **to the left**.

EXAMPLES

1. Change 52% to a decimal (move two places to the left)—52% = .52

2. Change 3% to a decimal (move two places to the left)—3% = .03 (add a zero to occupy the place)

3. Change 90% to a decimal (move two places to the left)—90% = .90 = .9 (drop the zero—it has no value)

4. Change 12.5% to a decimal (move two places to the left)—12.5% = .125

Notice that when there is a decimal point already included in the percent, begin at the decimal point and move it two places to the left.

5. Change 140% to a decimal (move two places to the left)—140% = 1.40

It's generally accepted that 100% means "all full up," but you can use numbers to express **more than 100%.**

Let's say that a boat-building shop constructs four boats in its first year of business, but the next year, the company gets busy, increases its work staff, and builds six boats.

The company has increased its production by 50%. It has built two more boats than the four built the first year—2 is 50% of 4. The next year, it builds eight boats. Now, the company has increased its production by 100% from the first year—4 is 100% or one whole of 4. In the fourth year, the company gets really busy and builds ten boats—that is six more boats than the first year. There is now an increase of 150% from the first year—6 is 150% or $1\frac{1}{2}$ of four. Don't panic if you see percents greater than 100; learn to work with them.

Likewise, it's possible to have less than 1%.

6. Change .5% to a decimal (begin at the decimal point and move two places to the left)—.5% = .005 (it's $\frac{1}{2}$ of 1%)

PRACTICE—CONVERTING PERCENTS TO DECIMALS

Convert the following to decimals.

1. 23%

2. 6%

3. 138%

4. 8.5%

5. 70%

6. 8.25%

7. 238%

8. .6%

ANSWERS

1. **.23**

2. **.06**

3. **1.38**

4. **.085**

5. **.7**

6. **.0825**

7. **2.38**

8. **.006**

CHANGING DECIMALS TO PERCENTS

This is a much simpler process. Move the decimal place two places **to the right** and add a percent sign. See the following examples below:

.14 = 14%

1.23 = 123%

.03 = 3%

.4 = 40%

.825 = 82.5%

.025 = 2.5%

PRACTICE—CHANGING DECIMALS TO PERCENTS

Convert the following decimals to percents.

1. .23

2. 5.03

3. .06

4. .7

5. .567

6. .0015

ANSWERS

1. **23%**

2. **503%**

3. **6%**

4. **70%**

5. **56.7%**

6. **.15%**

CONVERTING FRACTIONS AND PERCENTS

To change **percents to fractions**, simply convert the percent to a decimal and add the appropriate denominator, which would usually be 100, but not always (see last example). Reduce where necessary.

EXAMPLES

$$50\% = \frac{50}{100} = \frac{1}{2} \qquad\qquad 185\% = \frac{185}{100} = 1\frac{17}{20}$$

$$8\% = \frac{8}{100} = \frac{2}{25} \qquad\qquad 12.5\% = \frac{125}{1000} = \frac{1}{8}$$

$$37\% = \frac{37}{100}$$

To change **fractions to percents**, follow the same procedures as you would for converting fractions to decimals. Divide the numerator by the denominator to the 1000ths place. If the numbers don't divide evenly, round to the nearest 100th, then convert the decimal number to a percent.

EXAMPLE ONE

Convert $\frac{4}{9}$ to a percent.

Step one: Divide the numerator by the denominator:

$$9)\overline{4.000}^{\,.444}$$

Step two: Round to the nearest 100th:

$$.444 = .44$$

Step three: Convert decimal to a percent:

$$.44 = \textbf{44\%}$$

EXAMPLE TWO

Convert $\frac{3}{8}$ to a percent.

$$8)\overline{3.000}^{\,.375} \qquad .375 = \textbf{37.5\%}$$

PRACTICE—CONVERTING FRACTIONS AND PERCENTS

Convert problems 1–4 to fractions and reduce where necessary. Convert problems 5–8 to percents.

1. 75%   5. $\frac{7}{10}$

2. 48%   6. $\frac{5}{8}$

3. 225%   7. $\frac{3}{16}$

4. .5%   8. $2\frac{8}{21}$

ANSWERS

1. $\dfrac{3}{4}$ 5. **70%**

2. $\dfrac{12}{25}$ 6. **63%**

3. $2\dfrac{1}{4}$ 7. **19%**

4. $\dfrac{1}{200}$ 8. **238%**

COMPARING AND ORDERING FRACTIONS, DECIMALS, AND PERCENTS

This activity is a summary of all you've learned about conversions. Consider the following examples.

EXAMPLE ONE

Which of the following two numbers have the same value?

$$3\dfrac{3}{8} \qquad 33\% \qquad 37.5\% \qquad 3.33 \qquad \dfrac{3}{8}$$

(1) $3\dfrac{3}{8}$ and 3.33

(2) 33% and 3.33

(3) 37.5% and $3\dfrac{3}{8}$

(4) $\dfrac{3}{8}$ and 33%

(5) 37.5% and $\dfrac{3}{8}$

(1) $3\dfrac{3}{8}$ and 3.33 (no, but close, $3\dfrac{3}{8}$ = 3.375)

(2) 33% and 3.33 (no, 33% = .33)

(3) 37.5% and $3\dfrac{3}{8}$ (no, 37.5% = .375, $3\dfrac{3}{8}$ = 3.375)

(4) $\dfrac{3}{8}$ and 33% (no, 33% = $\dfrac{1}{3}$)

(5) 37.5% and $\dfrac{3}{8}$ (yes, both equal $\dfrac{3}{8}$ or .375 or 37.5%)

EXAMPLE TWO

The following table indicates what part of his or her 12 oz. bottle each infant drank.

Tina—60%

LaShaun—.7

Lina—$\frac{2}{3}$

Which of the following lists the infants according to how much they drank from *least to greatest*?

(1) Tina, Lina, LaShaun

(2) LaShaun, Tina, Lina

(3) LaShaun, Lina, Tina

(4) Lina, LaShaun, Tina

(5) not enough information is given

Convert all numbers to the same scale, choosing the easiest method possible. Here, it would be decimals.

LaShaun—.7 (no conversion necessary)

Tina—60% =.60 or .6

Lina—$\frac{2}{3}$ = .66

Now, the answer is obvious: Tina (.6), Lina (.66), LaShaun (.7) or Choice (**1**).

PRACTICE—COMPARING AND ORDERING DECIMALS, FRACTIONS AND PERCENTS

Choose the correct answer.

1. Which of the following is not the same as 3.25?

(1) $3\frac{25}{100}$

(2) 325%

(3) 3.25%

(4) $3\frac{1}{4}$

(5) 3.250

2. Ed is a sales agent who gets 16% of his salary from commission. Juana gets $\frac{1}{5}$ of her salary from commission and Bill gets $\frac{3}{8}$ of his salary from commission. Which of the following lists the sales agents according to the size of their commissions from smallest to largest?

(1) Ed, Juana, Bill
(2) Bill, Ed, Juana
(3) Juana, Ed, Bill
(4) Bill, Juana, Ed
(5) Juana, Bill, Ed

3. Which expression could be used to compare 35% to $\frac{3}{7}$?

(1) $7 \div 3$
(2) $7 \div 3$ move decimal in the answer two places to the right and add a % sign
(3) $3 \div 7$ move decimal in the answer two places to the right and add a % sign
(4) $7 \times .03$ move decimal in the answer two places to the left and add a % sign

ANSWERS

1. **3**   2. **1**   3. **3**

SOLVING WORD PROBLEMS WITH PERCENTS

All word problems that involve percents, no matter how complicated they may seem, can be reduced to one of these three operations:

> 1. Finding a percent of a number
>
>   30% of 86 = ?
>
> 2. Finding what percent one number is of another
>
>   40 is ?% of 100
>
> 3. Finding a number when a percent of it is given
>
>   30 is 40% of ?

GED students sometimes find it difficult to tell the difference among these three operations and when to apply each to a problem. An aid designed to help you with this difficulty is **the percent triangle**. Once it is understood and memorized, it will guide you through every operation with percents.

The Percent Triangle

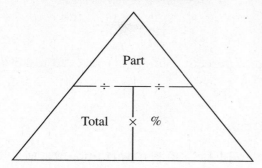

Here's how to use it:

EXAMPLE ONE

What is 30% of 86?

Step one: Decode the problem by labeling its parts. In this problem, you have a **total (86)** and a **% (30%)**. 30% will become .30 (always convert percents to decimals in calculations).

Step two: Using the labeled parts, find the operation on the percent triangle. Notice that **total** and **%** are next to each other at the base of the triangle.

Step three: Perform the operation (either × or ÷) indicated by the separation line between the parts in Step two.

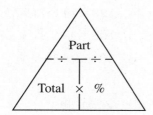

In this case, the × sign separates **total** and %.

$$86 \times .3 = 25.8$$

Answer: 30% of 86 = 25.8

EXAMPLE TWO

32 is what percent of 128?

Step one: Decode and label. 32 is a **part** and 128 is a **total**.

Step two: Find the operation on the triangle. The sign that separates **total** and **part** is a ÷ sign.

Step three: Perform the operation. **Be careful here!** In Example One, the operation was multiplication, so it makes no difference how the numbers are arranged, the answer will always be the same. But when it comes to division, there is a huge difference in the answer if you choose the wrong dividends and divisors. Follow this one simple rule and you shouldn't have problems: When dividing using the triangle, *always place the **part** first*.

TIP
If you know and prefer this method: $$\frac{\text{is}}{\text{of}} = \frac{\%}{100}$$ use it instead of the Percent Triangle.

Therefore, in this example, you would find $32 \div 128$.

$$128\overline{)32.00}^{.25}$$

The problem asks for a percent. Simply convert .25 to 25%.

EXAMPLE THREE

30 is 40% of what number?

Step one: Decode and label. 30 is a **part** and 40% is a %.

Step two: Find the operation on the triangle. A $\div$ sign separates part and %.

Step three: Perform the operation, remembering **part always comes first:** $30 \div .40$

$$.40\overline{)30.00.}^{75}$$

Answer: 30 is 40% of 75

PRACTICE—BASIC WORD PROBLEMS WITH PERCENTS

Label and solve.

1. 40% of 68 is ?
2. 90 is ? % of 135
3. 86 is 12.5% of ?
4. 125% of 80 is ?
5. 108.8 is ? % of 68
6. 30 is 2.5% of ?

ANSWERS

1. **27.2**
2. **67%**
3. **688**
4. **100**
5. **160%**
6. **1200**

WORD PROBLEMS WITH PERCENTS

Don't be intimidated by the length or complexity of percent word problems. Simply repeat the process you just learned. Reduce the sentences down to a short one, label, then perform the operations according to the triangle.

EXAMPLE ONE

Alan earns a salary of $1,420 per month. The rent he pays on his apartment is 44% of his salary. How much is his rent?

Step one: Reduce—all this problem is asking you to find is: 44% of $1,420.

Step two: Label—% × **total**

Step three: Perform the operation—.44 × $1420 = $624.80

Answer: $624.80

EXAMPLE TWO

Lee and Huan went to dinner at the Riverside Restaurant. Not including tax, the bill came to $34.50. The sales tax on the meal was $2.07. What percent of the meal was the sales tax?

Step one: Reduce—$2.07 is ? % of $34.50?

Step two: **Part ÷ total**

Step three: Perform the operation— $34.00)\overline{2.07.00}$ with quotient $.06$

Answer: .06 = 6%

EXAMPLE THREE

Karen has paid her father $2,640, which is 22% of the total she borrowed from him to purchase a car. How much money did Karen originally borrow?

Step one: $2,640 is 22% of ?

Step two: **part ÷ %**

Step three: $2,640 ÷ .22 = $12,000

Answer: $12,000

PRACTICE—BASIC WORD PROBLEMS II

Solve the following.

1. John bought 140 pieces of plywood for a construction job, but 40% of them were warped and had to be returned. How many pieces did John return?

2. Keira invested $43,608 in a mutual fund that paid $432.96 in interest at the end of the year. What was the percent of interest Keira earned from her initial investment?

3. The Baileys drove 280 miles during the first leg of a trip to visit their cousins. The distance represented 32% of the trip. How many miles is the entire trip?

ANSWERS

1. **56**   2. **1%**   3. **875**

MULTISTEP PROBLEMS WITH PERCENTS

Most of the problems involving percents on the GED Math section will be multistep. They require careful attention to wording, but they are usually not much more complicated than the problems in the last exercise.

EXAMPLE ONE

Michelle is a waitress who earns $7 per hour and receives 10% of all tips collected by her and the other waitresses by the end of the day. If she works a six-hour shift and $482.50 is the total collected by the end of the day, what are Michelle's total earnings for the day?

Step one: Calculate her hourly earnings—$7 × 6 = $42

Step two: Calculate her tips—10% of $482.50 = $48.25

Step three: Add $42 + $48.25 = **$90.25**

EXAMPLE TWO

A home-entertainment system, originally priced at $2,500, is on sale for 15% off. One week later, the price of the system is reduced an additional 20% off the discounted price. What is the final sale price of the system?

The "double discount" is a frequently-asked question. Avoid the temptation to add the two discounts together (35%) and then find 65% of $ 2,500. Here's the right way to do it.

Step one: Find the sale price of the first discount—$2,500 × .85 = $2,125

.85 is 100% (full price) – 15% (discount)

Step two: Find the sale price of the second discount—$2,125 × .80 = $1,700

Answer: $1,700

EXAMPLE THREE

There are 3,620 registered voters in Elizabethtown. In the last election, 1,267 did not vote. What percent of the town's registered voters *did* vote?

Step one: Reduce, label and perform the operation.

1,267 is ? % of 3,620, part ÷ whole, 1,267 ÷ 3,620 = .35 or 35%

35% is the percentage that represents those citizens that did not vote.

Step two: Easy. 100% – 35% = 65%

If 35% did *not* vote, then 65% *did* vote.

PRACTICE—MULTISTEP PERCENT PROBLEMS

Solve the following.

1. A businesswoman spends $\frac{1}{5}$ of her travel allotment on airfare and $\frac{3}{10}$ on hotel accommodations. What percent of her allotment is left?

2. Last year's Fourth of July parade was attended by 25,000 people, but this year attendance was only 21,000. What was the percentage of decrease in attendance?

3. A suit was on sale for $142.50, marked down 25% from its original price. What was the original price of the suit?

4. Sarah maintains a savings account of $1,658 that earns 8% annual interest. Dean has a mutual fund with $1,500 that earns 16% interest annually. At the end of one year, whose account earns more interest? How much more?

ANSWERS

1. **50%**

2. **16%**

3. **$190**

4. **Dean—$107.36**

PERCENT OF INCREASE OR DECREASE

In these types of multistep word problems, you need to compare two numbers to find the percent of change.

EXAMPLE ONE

Errol bought stock for $28 per share. In three months, it rose to $49 dollars per share. Find the percent of increase of the stock.

Step one: Find the amount of the increase.

$$49 - 28 = 21$$

The stock increased by $21.

Step two: Find the percent of increase by setting up a proportion;

$$\frac{\text{amount of increase}}{\text{original amount}} = \frac{21}{28}$$

Step three: Convert the proportion to a percent by dividing, as indicated in step 2.

$$21 \div 28 = .75 = 75\%$$

Answer: 75%

EXAMPLE TWO

A college's enrollment drops from 9,152 to 3,520 over the course of ten years. What is the percentage of decrease in enrollment?

Step one: Find the amount of decrease.

$$9,152 - 3,520 = 5,632$$

Step two: $\dfrac{\text{amount of decrease}}{\text{original amount}} = \dfrac{5,632}{9,152}$

Step three: $5,632 \div 9,152 = .615$ or 62%

Answer: 62%

PRACTICE—PERCENT INCREASE OR DECREASE

1. At eight years old, Susanna was 4'2" tall. At fourteen, she is 5'5". Find the percentage of increase in Susanna's height.

2. Harris buys a used car for $8,200. He drives it for six years, then sells it for $1,400. By what percentage has the value of the car decreased?

ANSWERS

1. **30%**   2. **83%**

CHAPTER REVIEW

Fill in the answer grids, and use a calculator where indicated.

1. Tom purchased the following items at the paint store for the prices shown:

   3 gallons of paint—$40.17
   1 wide paintbrush—$6.49
   1 paint roller set—$12.29

   What change did he receive if he gave the clerk $60?

2. A precision laboratory thermometer measures a certain liquid's temperature at 44.014° (degrees) Fahrenheit. If the temperature of that liquid drops by 3.78°, what then would the thermometer read?

   (1) 40.324°
   (2) 47.794°
   (3) 40.234°
   (4) 41.09°
   (5) not enough information is given

3. What is the area in square miles of the property in the diagram below?

   12.4 miles

   9.5 miles

4. John orders $1\frac{3}{4}$ lb. of salami from the deli department. After the clerk places the meat on the digital scale, it reads 1.85 lbs. What must the clerk do to give John the amount he asked for?

   (1) add .62 lb.
   (2) remove .1 lb.
   (3) remove .05 lb.
   (4) add .03 lb.
   (5) add .12 lb.

5. The following library books with their corresponding filing numbers are out of order.

   Book A—913.3
   Book B—913.31
   Book C—913.304
   Book D—913.034

   What is their correct order from lowest to highest?

   (1) A, D, B, C
   (2) C, A, B, D
   (3) D, B, A, C
   (4) D, A, C, B
   (5) A, D, C, B

6.

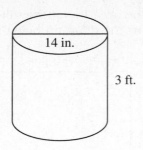

14 in.

3 ft.

Which expression indicates the maximum volume of the waste can in the above diagram?

(1) $36(3.14 \times 7 \text{ in.}^2)$
(2) $3(3.14 \times 14 \text{ in.})$
(3) $(14 \text{ in.} \times 3 \text{ ft.})^2$
(4) $\dfrac{14 \text{ in.}^2 \times 3 \text{ ft.}}{3.14}$
(5) $14 \text{ inches} \times 3.14 \times 3$

7. Janey is training for an upcoming marathon. Her running schedule for the week is as follows:

Monday—6.4 miles

Tuesday—8.3 miles

Wednesday—off

Thursday—7.7 miles

Friday—6 miles

Saturday—10.1 miles

Sunday—off

What is the average distance she runs for the days she *does* train?

(1) between 5 and 6 miles
(2) close to 9 miles
(3) close to 6 miles
(4) close to 8 miles
(5) between 6 and 7 miles

8.

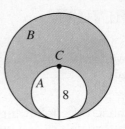

If C represents the center of circle B and the diameter of circle A is 8, which one of the expressions below indicates the area for the shaded portion of the diagram?

(1) $3.14(16 - 8)^2$
(2) $(3.14 \times 8^2) - (3.14 \times 4^2)$
(3) $(8 + 16^2) 3.14$
(4) $(3.14 \times 16) - (3.14 \times 8)$
(5) none of the above

9. Arrange in order from *largest to smallest*:

$\dfrac{9}{16}$ 54% $\dfrac{5}{8}$ .501   1.53

(1) $\dfrac{9}{16}$, 54%, $\dfrac{5}{8}$, .501, 1.53

(2) 1.53, .501, $\dfrac{5}{8}$, $\dfrac{9}{16}$, 54%

(3) 1.53, $\dfrac{5}{8}$, $\dfrac{9}{16}$, 54%, .501

(4) $\dfrac{5}{8}$, $\dfrac{9}{16}$, 54%, 1.53, .501

(5) 1.53, 54%, $\dfrac{5}{8}$, $\dfrac{9}{16}$, .501

10. Which of the following is not equal to 3.6?

(1) $3\dfrac{3}{5}$
(2) 360%
(3) 3.6%
(4) 3.600
(5) $3\dfrac{60}{100}$

11. Tom's gross salary is $760 per week. His salary is taxed at 16%. What is his net salary?

(1) $684
(2) $638.40
(3) $121.60
(4) $690.20
(5) $584

12. On a 56-question examination, Leslie answered 7 questions incorrectly. What percent of the questions did she answer correctly?

13. A delivery of 366 tons of sand to a construction site represents 60% of the sand needed to complete the job. How many more tons of sand need to be delivered?

14. There were 112 consumers who responded to a survey regarding laundry detergent. 38% preferred Brand A, 23% preferred Brand B, 19% preferred Brand C, and the rest were undecided. How many consumers were undecided?

(1) between 18 and 20
(2) between 15 and 18
(3) between 25 and 30
(4) between 24 and 26
(5) between 20 and 23

15. The Ortega family was looking to purchase a computer, originally priced at $1,600, which was discounted 25%. Later that month, it was reduced another 25% off the sale price. Since the Ortegas bought it for cash, they received an additional 5% discount. What was the final price they paid for the computer?

(1) around $1,000
(2) around $850
(3) around $800
(4) around $950
(5) around $900

16. The original price of a coffeemaker is ? dollars. If the price is discounted by 20%, which of the following expressions indicates the discounted price of *three* coffeemakers?

(1) $? \times .80$
(2) $? \times .20$
(3) $3\left(\dfrac{1}{3} \times ?\right)$
(4) $3(.20 \times ?)$
(5) $3(.80 \times ?)$

Answers

1. **1.05**	5. **4**	9. **3**	13. **244**
2. **3**	6. **1**	10. **3**	14. **5**
3. **117.8**	7. **4**	11. **2**	15. **2**
4. **2**	8. **2**	12. **87.5**	16. **5**

Data Analysis

Many questions on the GED—not only in the Math section, but in the Science and Social Studies sections, as well—test your ability to read tables, charts, and graphs.

TABLES

Tables are the simplest forms of graphic representation. Usually, you'll be asked to answer more than one question based on information in the table. Take care to read all the information provided.

EXAMPLE

SCHEDULE FOR TRAIN LEAVING CENTERVILLE AT 4:05 P.M.			
Destination	**Arrival Time**	**Departure Time**	**Fare**
Roxbury	4:20 P.M.	4:22 P.M.	$1.50
Lanesville	4:43 P.M.	4:45 P.M.	$2.10
Hampton	5:10 P.M.	5:12 P.M.	$4.50
Cheshire	5:31 P.M.	5:33 P.M.	$5.25

(double the fare for round-trip price)

The following questions are based on the table.

1. Which is the least expensive destination to travel to from Centerville?

   Look at the "fare" column—it costs only $1.50 to travel to Roxbury.

   Answer: Roxbury

2. How long does it take to travel from Lanesville to Cheshire?

   This is a "clock" question. It's usually best to use an hour marker to help you answer it. The train departs from Lanesville at 4:45, from 4:45 to 5:00 is 15 minutes, and from 5:00 to 5:31 (arrival time in Cheshire) is 31 minutes. Add the two sums together (15 + 31) to get 46 minutes.

   Answer: 46 minutes

3. The fare to Roxbury is what percent of the fare to Hampton?

   This is a basic percent word problem. Just be careful to select the right numbers. When working with tables and charts, it can be helpful to use the straight edge of a piece of paper to read across a row.

   Step one: Reduce—$1.50 is ? % of $4.50?

   Step two: Solve—$1.50 ÷ $4.50 = .33 = 33%

   Answer: 33%

4. James lives in Centerville and commutes to and from a job in Cheshire five days a week. What expression can be used to calculate the cost of his weekly commutation?

   Always read "the fine print." In this case, it tells you that round trips are double the price listed in the "fare" column. Therefore the expression is: **5 (2 × $5.25)**—the "5" represents five days per week.

PRACTICE—TABLES

KINGSFIELD COMMUNITY RECREATION PROGRAM		
Activity	Number of Participants	Enrollment Fee (per person)
Volleyball League	24	$30
Softball League	108	$10
Ballroom Dancing	32	$10
Cooking Class	15	$100
First Aid and CPR	25	$50

Use the chart above to answer the following questions.

1. Which activity attracted the smallest number of participants?

2. What is the difference in total enrollment fees between the cooking class and the softball league?

3. How many of the programs grossed over $1,000 in enrollment fees?

4. Which program netted the greatest profit for the Kingsfield Recreation Program?

5. What was the mean number of participants for the five classes listed?

ANSWERS

1. **Cooking**

2. **$420**

3. **3**

4. **not enough information is given**

5. **40.8 = 41**

BAR GRAPHS

Bar graphs use vertical (up and down) and horizontal (across) "bars" to represent quantities. It's essential that you read all labels and legends ("the fine print"), looking carefully at the base and sides of the graph to see what the bars are measuring and how much they're increasing or decreasing.

EXAMPLE

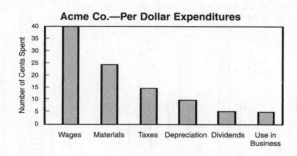

TIP

On the GED test, use a piece of scrap paper as a straightedge to help read graphs accurately.

Before answering any questions, familiarize yourself with the graph and what it means. The Acme Co. may have gross income well over a million dollars, but the graph illustrates how much the company had to pay out *per dollar* in expenses, divided into six different categories. So, as an example, for every dollar the Acme Co. grossed, it had to pay out 15¢ in taxes.

1. How many cents of each dollar did the company use to pay for materials?

   Use the edge of a paper to line up the top of the "materials" bar with the numbers on the left side of the chart. It's very close to 25¢ spent.

   Answer: 25¢

2. How much are the combined expenses of taxes and "uses in business" equal to?

   Taxes = 15¢
   Use in business = 5¢
   15 + 5 = 20¢

   Answer: 20¢ spent per dollar

3. The combined expenses of depreciation, dividends, and use in business represent what percentage of the number of cents spent on wages?

10 + 5 + 5 = 20   (combined expenses)
20 is ? % of 40?   40 (wages)
20 is half of 40 or 50%

Answer: 50%

4. If the Acme Co. reduced its wage payroll by laying off five managers, what would be the new number of cents per dollar spent on wages?

There is no indication of how much these managers are paid nor is there a dollar amount given that reflects total wages. The answer can't be calculated.

Answer: not enough information is given

PRACTICE—BAR GRAPHS

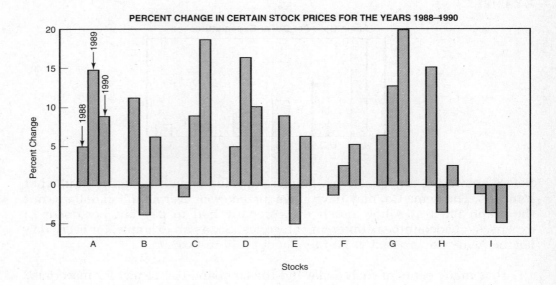

PERCENT CHANGE IN CERTAIN STOCK PRICES FOR THE YEARS 1988–1990

Use the graph above to answer the following questions.

1. Which stocks showed *increases* for every year charted?

2. Which stock had the greatest percentage of change from one year to the next?

3. The percent of change for Stock G in 1990 was how much greater than the percent of change for Stock D in 1988?

4. How much was Stock F worth in 1990?

5. How much greater was Stock G's percent of increase than Stock F's during the three-year period?

   (1) twice as much
   (2) the same
   (3) three times as much
   (4) 1.5 times as much
   (5) not enough information is given

ANSWERS

1. **G**
2. **H**
3. **15%**
4. **not enough information is given**
5. **1**

LINE GRAPHS

Line graphs almost always measure how things increase or decrease over time.
There is often more than one line on a graph, which can cause some confusion. Proceed slowly and carefully.

EXAMPLE

The graph below shows the conversion of farm and forest acreage to housing developments in Granite County.

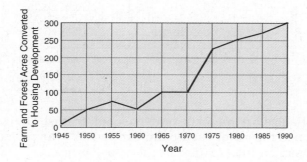

1. How many acres of farm and forest were converted to housing developments in 1955?

   You can't tell **exactly** because the line crosses 1955 about one-third of the way between 50 and 60 acres. But an estimate of 70 acres would be correct.

   Answer: 70 acres

2. During which five-year period was there no increase in conversion?

   That's easy. Look for the place where the line runs horizontally for five years—between 1965 and 1970.

   Answer: 1965–1970

3. During which five-year period were conversions greatest?

   Look for the steepest rise in the line.

   Answer: 1970–1975

4. During which year were the most forest acres converted?

Look carefully at the fine print. There is no special distinction between farm and forest conversion. Therefore, there is **not enough information** given to calculate the answer.

5. What is the difference between the number of acres converted in 1945–1950 and those converted in 1970–1975?

The 1945–1950 conversions are approximately 45 acres, and the 1970–1975 conversions are approximately 125 acres. 125 – 45 = 80

Answer: approximately 80 acres

PRACTICE—LINE GRAPH

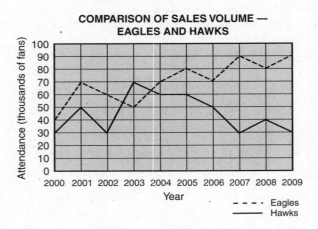

COMPARISON OF SALES VOLUME —
EAGLES AND HAWKS

The Hawks and Eagles are minor-league baseball teams. The graph represents the paid attendance record of each team over a ten-year period. The following questions are based on information in the above graph.

1. During which year did the Hawks' attendance exceed that of the Eagles?

2. In 2007 how many more fans attended Eagles games than Hawks games?

3. By what percent did the Eagles' attendance increase from 2000 to 2004?

4. Between what years was the decrease in attendance the same for both teams?

5. What percent of the ten years covered by the graph did the Eagles' attendance exceed the Hawks'?

ANSWERS

1. **2003**

2. **60,000 more**

3. **75%**

4. **2005–2006**

5. **90%**

PIE CHARTS

Pie charts (sometimes called **circle graphs**) represent the way in which something is divided into parts. As always, try to get the big picture while paying attention to the fine print.

EXAMPLE

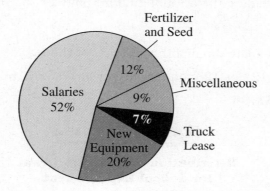

**Annual Expenses for the Golden
Tree Landscaping Corp.**

1. What part of Golden Tree's annual expenses does New Equipment and Fertilizer and Seed represent?

    (1) about $\frac{1}{2}$

    (2) about 20%

    (3) about $\frac{1}{3}$

    (4) about 40%

    First, add the two sections:

    20% + 12% = 32%.

    32% is very close to 33%. You know that 33% of anything is $\frac{1}{3}$.

Answer: (3) about $\frac{1}{3}$

2. Golden Tree establishes a relationship with a new equipment sales company that gives them a 25% discount on all purchases. What would the recalculated percentage of expense be for new equipment using the new supplier?

    New equipment consumes 20% of expenses. If the company now gets a 25% (or $\frac{1}{4}$ off) discount on its purchases, then the percentage will be reduced by $\frac{1}{4}$. $\frac{1}{4}$ of 20% = 5% and 20 – 5 = 15%

Answer: 15%

3. Which section of the chart accounts for equipment repair?

Since none of the sections specify "Equipment Repair," it must be assumed that "Miscellaneous" (which means "other various unnamed items") accounts for it.

Answer: Miscellaneous

4. If Golden Tree's expenses for one year total $62,000, how much does the company pay *per month* for the truck lease?

Step one: Calculate the annual amount paid for the truck lease.

$62,000 × .07 = $4,340

Step two: Calculate the monthly amount of the lease.

$4,340 ÷ 12 (for 12 months of the year) = $361.66

Answer: $361.66

PRACTICE—PIE CHARTS

**Distribution of $62,000 Grant
for School Improvement**

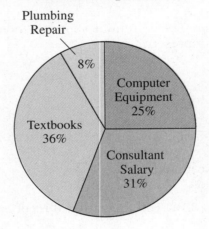

Answer the following questions based on the information provided in the chart above.

1. How many dollars of the grant were spent on plumbing repair?

2. All of the money allotted to computer equipment went to the purchase of five of the same computer systems. How much did each system cost?

3. What expression represents the difference in dollars between money spent on textbooks and that spent on computer equipment?

4. If the grant increased by $21,500 for the following year, how much money would be allotted for consultant salary?

ANSWERS

1. **$4,960**   3. **.11 (62,000)**

2. **$3,100**   4. **$25,885**

CHAPTER REVIEW

Fill in the answer grids, and use a calculator where indicated.

THE EVENING POST—RATES FOR CLASSIFIED ADS

Ads up to 15 words $25
Ads up to 25 words $35
Ads over 25 words $1.50 per word

not including sales tax of 8%

Use the information provided to answer the following questions.

1. How much does it cost to purchase an ad of 12 words, including sales tax?

2. How much more would it cost to purchase an ad of 36 words than two ads of 15 words each, not including tax?

   (1) $4
   (2) $2.75
   (3) $12
   (4) $4.25
   (5) $15

3. *The Evening Post* offers its employees a "one-third off" discount on all classified ads. A worker there wishes to take out a 20-word ad. Including tax, what price will she pay for the ad?

   (1) around $28
   (2) around $20
   (3) around $24
   (4) around $25
   (5) not enough information is given

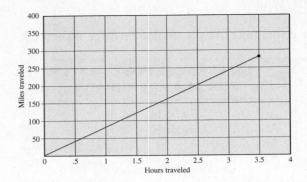

Use the line graph above to answer the following question.

4. In miles per hour, what is the rate of travel represented by the diagonal line?

   (1) between 60 and 70 mph
   (2) between 85 and 90 mph
   (3) between 55 and 60 mph
   (4) between 75 and 80 mph
   (5) not enough information is given

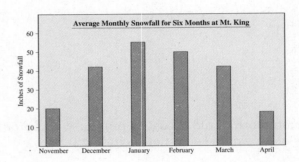

The graph above shows the average monthly snowfall for six consecutive months at a mountain ski resort.

5. How much more snow fell in January than in November?

   (1) 2 ft. 11 in.
   (2) 3 ft. 3 in.
   (3) 2 ft.
   (4) 25 in.
   (5) 2 ft. 3 in.

6. A midwinter thaw melts 30% of the snow that accumulates from November to the end of January. Which expression represents the amount of snow accumulation left immediately *after* the thaw?

   (1) 55 × .30
   (2) .30(20 + 42 +55)
   (3) .70(20 + 42 + 55)
   (4) $\dfrac{20 + 42 + 55}{.30}$
   (5) (.30 × 55) + (20 + 42)

7. By what percent does the snowfall increase from December to January?

How the Residents of Chambersville Heat Their Houses

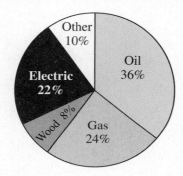

Statistics based on survey of 3,216 households

 8. If 10% of all households in Chambersville that heat with oil shifted to heating with wood, what percent would now heat with wood?

(1) 11.6%
(2) 18%
(3) 2%
(4) 18.3%
(5) 21%

 9. How many households in Chambersville are dependent on gas and oil heat?

(1) 1,930
(2) 1,158
(3) 772
(4) 65%
(5) 1,479

Answers

1. **27**	4. **4**	7. **31**
2. **1**	5. **1**	8. **1**
3. **4**	6. **3**	9. **1**

Algebra

CHAPTER 23

THE NUMBER LINE AND POSITIVE AND NEGATIVE NUMBERS

Consider the number line above. The arrows at each end mean the line extends infinitely in each direction, so that any number imaginable can be found on it. Notice that 0 is at the midpoint of the line.

Up to this point, you have only dealt with positive numbers, but it's now time to introduce negative numbers, which are marked by a "–" sign. The further a number is to the **right** of the number line, the **greater** its value. For example, 3 > 0 (this symbol, >, means "is greater than") because it's further to the right on the number line. Likewise, 0 > –3 (0 is greater than –3) and –2 > –3.

FINDING POINTS ON THE NUMBER LINE

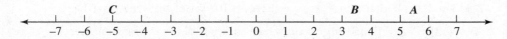

On the GED, you'll be asked to identify points on the number line.

EXAMPLES

1. Which point represents 3.5?

2. Which point represents –5?

3. Which point approximates $\sqrt{28}$?

ANSWERS

1. B—it's halfway between 3 and 4.

2. C—it's right above the –5 marker.

3. $\sqrt{28}$ isn't a whole number. $5 \times 5 = 25$ and $6 \times 6 = 36$ Therefore, $\sqrt{28}$ has to be between 5 and 6. Answer: A is between 5 and 6.

PRACTICE—FINDING POINTS ON THE NUMBER LINE

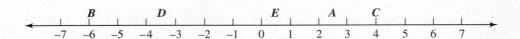

From the above number line, choose the correct letter for the following.

1. .5

2. –3.5

3. $\sqrt{16}$

4. $\sqrt{5}$

5. –6

ANSWERS

1. **E**   2. **D**   3. **C**   4. **A**   5. **B**

ADDING SIGNED NUMBERS

Here are the rules that tell how to add signed numbers. Memorize them.

- If the signs are the same (–,– or +,+) **add** the two numbers and label the answer with that sign.

EXAMPLES

7 + 3 = 10   (Both signs are positive, add, label answer positive.)

–5 + (–3) = –8   (Both signs negative, add, label answer negative.)

- If the signs are different (+,– or –,+), **subtract**. Forgetting for a moment the positive and negative signs, compare the numbers and choose **the larger of the two**. Label the answer with the sign of the "larger" number.

–6 + 5 = –1   (Signs different, subtract, 6 – 5 = 1, compare, 6 is larger than 5, 6 has a negative sign, attach it to answer: –1).

12 + (–7) = 5   (Signs different, subtract, 12 – 7 = 5, 12 is larger and positive so attach sign to answer: +5 or 5).

- When adding **more than two** signed numbers, follow the above rules to get a sum for the first two numbers, then continue to use rules for adding subsequent numbers.

–5 + (–14) + (–6) = –25

Step one: –5 + (–14) = –19

Step two: –19 + (–6) = –25   (Same signs, add, label negative)

5 + (–12) + 7 = 0

Step one: 5 + (–12) = –7

Step two: –7 + 7 = 0   (Different signs, subract 7 – 7 = 0 – 0 never takes a sign)

PRACTICE—ADDING WITH SIGNED NUMBERS

Add the following.

1. 12 + (–8)
2. –14 + (–6)
3. –40 + 13
4. –2 + (–19)

5. 36 + (–1)
6. –26 + 6 + (–15)
7. 8 + (–14) + 30

ANSWERS

1. **4**
2. **–20**
3. **–27**
4. **–21**

5. **35**
6. **–35**
7. **24**

SUBTRACTING SIGNED NUMBERS

Here are the three steps that will help you to subtract signed numbers. Memorize them.

> *Step one:* Change the subtraction problem to an addition problem.
>
> *Step two:* Change the sign of the second number.
>
> *Step three:* Follow the rules of addition you just learned.

EXAMPLE ONE

–16 – 6 = –22

Step one: Change subtraction to addition.

–16 + 6

Step two: Change sign of second number.

–16 + (–6)

Step three: Follow rules of addition. (Same signs, add, 16 + 6 = 22, same sign, attach to answer)

Answer: –22

EXAMPLE TWO

12 – (–7) = 19

Step one: 12 – (–7) becomes 12 + (–7)

Step two: 12 + (–7) becomes 12 + 7

Step three: 12 + 7 = 19

Answer: 19

PRACTICE—SUBTRACTING SIGNED NUMBERS

Solve.

1. –5 – 4
2. 16 – (–18)
3. 12 – 23
4. –20 – 16

5. –4 – (–18)
6. 26 – (–40)
7. 0 – 42
8. 42 – (–5) – 7

ANSWERS

1. **–9**
2. **34**
3. **–11**
4. **–36**

5. **14**
6. **66**
7. **–42**
8. **40**

MULTIPLYING AND DIVIDING SIGNED NUMBERS

Good news. The rules for these operations are much simpler than for addition and subtraction. They are:

> **1.** Signs **alike**—answer is **positive**
>
> **2.** Signs **different**—answer is **negative**

Look carefully at the following examples and see how the rules work.

–3(5) = –15   3(–5) = –15

–3(–5) = 15 $\frac{-15}{-3} = -5$

$\frac{15}{-3} = -5$ (3)(–5)(2) = –30

$\frac{-15}{-3} = 5$ (3)(–5)(–2) = 30

PRACTICE—ADDING AND DIVIDING SIGNED NUMBERS

Solve.

1. $\dfrac{24}{-8}$

2. $\dfrac{1}{4}(-3)$

3. $(-.5)(-6.1)$

4. $\dfrac{-36}{-6}$

5. $(9 - 20)(-18)(-3)$

ANSWERS

1. **-3**

2. $-\dfrac{\mathbf{3}}{\mathbf{4}}$

3. **3.05**

4. **6**

5. **-594**

Use the $\boxed{+/-}$ key on you calculator for negative numbers. It makes working with signed numbers much easier.

WORKING WITH VARIABLES

In a mathematical sentence, a variable is a letter that represents a number. Consider this sentence: $x + 4 = 10$. Here, it's easy to figure out that x represents 6. However, problems with variables on the GED will become much more complex than that, and there are many rules and procedures that need to be learned.

Before you learn to solve equations with variables, you need to perform basic operations with them. Here's some vocabulary that will be helpful.

ADDING AND SUBTRACTING WITH VARIABLES

Consider the following statements:

$x + x = 2x$	but	$x + 1 = x + 1$
$3x + x = 4x$	but	$3x + 1 = 3x + 1$
$4y + 3y = 7y$	but	$4y + 3 = 4y + 3$
$3r - 6r = -3r$	but	$3r - 6 = 3r - 6$
$3rx + 3rx = 6rx$	but	$3r + 3rx = 3r + 3rx$

Remember: x is the same as $1x$

As you can see, only those monomials that have the same variables can be added to or subtracted from each other.

Sometimes, you'll see problems like this:

Evaluate: $a + 3b + 3a$

Answer: $4a + 3b$

> **REMINDER**
>
> $3y$ is called a **monomial**
>
> The 3 in $3y$ is called a **coefficient**
>
> The y is called a **variable**

Evaluate: $5b + 3c - 2b + c$

Answer: 3b + 4c

Do the addition and subtraction with like terms (the ones with exactly matching variables). Anything that stands alone, leave alone.

PRACTICE—ADDING AND SUBTRACTING WITH VARIABLES

Add or subtract the following. If the terms can't be added or subtracted, recopy them.

1. $5x + 12x$
2. $-14a - (-3a)$
3. $25 + 6a$
4. $12st + (-6st)$
5. $3y + 6$
6. $7xy + 8x$

7. $5p + p$
8. $14s - x$
9. $36x - x$
10. $25a + (-6a) - 7$
11. $6a - 3c + a + 2b$
12. $b + 2a + 3b - c$

ANSWERS

1. **17x**
2. **−11a**
3. **25 + 6a**
4. **6st**
5. **3y + 6**
6. **7xy + 8x**

7. **6p**
8. **14s − x**
9. **35x**
10. **19a − 7**
11. **7a − 3c + 2b**
12. **4b + 2a − c**

MULTIPLYING AND DIVIDING WITH VARIABLES

Once again, the rules are different with these operations. You *must* multiply and divide monomials with numbers as well as monomials with different variables. Carefully consider the following examples:

Multiplication

$3(4x) = 12x$ $\qquad$ $3x(4y) = 12xy$

$3x(4yz) = 12xyz$ $\qquad$ $\dfrac{1}{7}(5x) = \dfrac{5x}{7}$

$\dfrac{1}{2}(4a) = \dfrac{4a}{2} = 2a$

As you can see from the examples above, multiply the coefficients and include the variables.

Division

$$\frac{12x}{4} = 3x \qquad \frac{12x}{4x} = 3 \qquad \frac{12xy}{4x} = 3y$$

(The variables cancel each other out.)

PRACTICE—MULTIPLYING AND DIVIDING WITH VARIABLES

Solve.

1. $5(5x) =$

2. $\frac{14s}{7} =$

3. $-5y(6x) =$

4. $\frac{72x}{9x} =$

5. $13x(5y) =$

6. $\frac{48xy}{6y} =$

7. $.36xy(4z) =$

8. $\frac{25abc}{5ac} =$

9. $\frac{1}{5}(15x) =$

10. $\frac{2}{7}(7a) =$

ANSWERS

1. **25x**

2. **2s**

3. **−30xy**

4. **8**

5. **65xy**

6. **8x**

7. **1.44xyz**

8. **5b**

9. **3x**

10. **2a**

VARIABLES AND EXPONENTS

Multiplication

Consider the following:

$x + x = 2x$ but $x(x) = x^2$ and $x^2(x^3) = x^5$

$2(4x) = 8x$ but $2x(4x) = 8x^2$

$2x^2(4x) = 8x^3$

$x(4x^3) = 4x^4$

$5x^3(4x^5) = 20x^8$

$4x^3y^2(5x^2y) = 20x^5y^3$

$3x^5y^3z^4(6x^3yz^2) = 18x^8y^4z^6$

What you *should* see from the above examples is that when multiplying variables with exponents, you *add* the exponents, as long as the bases are the same.

Division

Consider the following:

$$\frac{12x^6y^4}{3x^3y^2} = 4x^3y^2 \qquad \frac{9a^8b^2c^7}{3a^5c} = 3a^3b^2c^6$$

When dividing variables with exponents, **subtract** the exponents.

PRACTICE—VARIABLES AND EXPONENTS

Solve.

1. $x\,(x^3)$

2. $4x(5x)$

3. $\dfrac{16x^4}{4x}$

4. $\dfrac{25s^3}{s}$

5. $3x^3y^2\,(5x^2)$

6. $5ef^2\,(2y^3)$

7. $\dfrac{32a^5bc^3}{8a^4b}$

ANSWERS

1. x^4

2. $20x^2$

3. $4x^3$

4. $25s^2$

5. $15x^5y^2$

6. $10ef^2y^3$

7. $4ac^3$

WORKING WITH PARENTHESES

You already know that $5(6a)$ means $5 \times 6a$, but consider this more complicated statement:

$$5(6a + c)$$

It must be rewritten like this:

$$5(6a) + 5(c) \quad \text{which is} \quad 30a + 5c$$

Each term **inside** the parentheses must be multiplied by the one directly outside. Then the operation specified (in this case, addition) must be carried out.

Consider two more examples:

$3b(6b - 2ac)$ becomes $18b^2 - 6abc$

$\dfrac{1}{3}(6x + 7)$ becomes $\dfrac{6x}{3} + \dfrac{7}{3} = 2x + \dfrac{7}{3}$

Rewrite the following, as in the above examples.

1. $3(5a - 6)$

2. $2(2a + 7)$

3. $5(6r + 7s - t)$

4. $2a^2(5a + 6b)$

5. $3(8x - 5) + \frac{1}{8}(2x + z)$

ANSWERS

1. **$15a - 18$**

2. **$4a + 14$**

3. **$30r + 35s - 5t$**

4. **$10a^3 + 12a^2b$**

5. **$(24x - 15) + \left(\frac{1}{4}x + \frac{z}{8}\right)$**

FINDING VALUES WHEN VARIABLES ARE GIVEN

Consider the following:

EXAMPLE ONE

Find the value of z if $z = 3x + y^2$ where $x = 6$ and $y = -4$

Step one: Replace the variables with numbers

$z = 3(6) + (-4)^2$

Step two: perform the operations in proper order (remember PEMDAS from Chapter 19).

Answer: $z = 18 + 16$ or $z = 34$

EXAMPLE TWO

Find the value of c if $c = 3a^2(b - 5)$ where $a = 3$ and $b = 10$

Step one: $3(3)^2 \times (10 - 5)$

Step two: $(3)(9)(5) = 135$

Answer: $c = 135$

Solve.

1. $c = 4a - 3b$, if $a = 8$ and $b = 5$. Find c.

2. $s = 3q^2 + 2r$, if $q = 6$ and $r = .5$. Find s.

3. $z = 3x^2(y + 8)$, if $x = 10$ and $y = -12$. Find z.

4. $m = \frac{1}{4}n + 3o + 5p^2$, if $n = 16$ and $o = 12$ and $p = 3$. Find m.

5. $c = \dfrac{2a\left(b^2 - 8\right)}{a}$ if $a = 3$ and $b = -5$. Find c.

1. **17**   4. **85**

2. **109**   5. **34**

3. **–1200**

ONE-STEP EQUATIONS

Here's an example of a one-step equation.

$$x + 5 = 29$$

Your goal is to figure out what number can replace x so that both sides of the equation will equal 29. The boundary line of each **side** of the equation is the = sign. So $x + 5$ is on the left side of this equation and 29 is on the right.

To reach your goal in any simple equation, you must reduce one side of the equation to just one variable and the other side to just one number. You accomplish this by performing any of the four basic operations to both sides of the equation.

Here's how it works:

EXAMPLE ONE

$x + 5 = 29$ solve for x

$$x + 5 = 29$$

Step one: $-5 \quad -5$

Step two: $x \quad\quad = 24$

Step three: Check $24 + 5 = 29$

Step one: Since you want to reduce the left side of the equation to just x, you've got to get rid of the "+ 5" in "$x + 5$." The way to get rid of it is to perform its inverse (opposite) by subtracting 5 from that side of the equation. *Remember*, what you do to one side of the equation, you must do to the other side. Therefore, you do 29 – 5.

Step two: Draw a line across the bottom of the entire equation and do the subtraction problems for each side. The result on the left is "$x + 0$." There is no need to write the 0. You have accomplished your goal of reducing one side of the equation to just one variable—x. The result on the right side is 24. Therefore, $x = 24$

Step three: Check. Simply replace the variable with the number, do the math, and make sure both sides of the equation are equal.

The procedure is the same for all other simple equations. Consider the following examples.

EXAMPLE TWO

$a - 19 = 12$ Solve for a.

$$
\begin{array}{rl}
a - 19 = & 12 \\
+\ 19 & +19 \\
\hline
a \quad\ = & 31
\end{array}
$$
    Check: $31 - 19 = 12$

EXAMPLE THREE

$5x = 45$ Solve for x

$$\frac{5x}{5} = \frac{45}{5}$$

$x = 9$ Check: $5(9) = 45$ $45 = 45$

Notice that this equation is a multiplication problem. Again, you do the inverse operation—division—to get rid of the number surrounding x. And, again, what you do to one side you must do to the other.

EXAMPLE FOUR

$$\frac{1x}{3} = 33$$

$$\frac{3}{1} \times \frac{1x}{3} = 33 \times \frac{3}{1}$$

$$x = 99$$

Check: $\frac{1}{3}(99) = 33$ $33 = 33$

In this division problem, once again, you must perform the inverse operation (multiplication) to get rid of the numbers attached to "x." Always multiply by the fraction's **reciprocal** to cancel it out. The reciprocal of $\frac{1}{3}$ is $\frac{3}{1}$—the reciprocal of $\frac{1}{6}$ is $\frac{6}{1}$, $\frac{1}{22}$ is $\frac{22}{1}$, $\frac{3}{8}$ is $\frac{8}{3}$, etc. When you multiply a number by its reciprocal, the product is **1**. Remember, **1x** is the same as **x**.

> **TIP**
>
> Visualize the = sign as a midpoint of all equations, just like the midpoint of a perfectly balanced seesaw.

PRACTICE—ONE-STEP EQUATIONS

Solve for the variable.

1. $51 = x + 20$

2. $x - 43 = 12$

3. $38 = b + 14$

4. $r - 81 = 16$

5. $12t = 96$

6. $\frac{1}{5}p = 14$

7. $118 = 59s$

8. $21 = \frac{1}{3}h$

1. $x = 31$ 5. $t = 8$

2. $x = 55$ 6. $p = 70$

3. $b = 24$ 7. $s = 2$

4. $r = 97$ 8. $h = 63$

MULTISTEP EQUATIONS

These equations are just a bit more complicated because they combine two or three of the procedures just learned into one problem. Consider the following:

EXAMPLE ONE

$5m + 8 = 48$

$$5m + 8 = 48$$
$$\underline{-8 \quad -8}$$
$$\frac{5m}{5} = \frac{40}{5} \qquad m = 8$$

EXAMPLE TWO

$$\frac{3p}{8} + 17 = 38$$

$$\frac{3p}{8} + 17 = 38$$
$$\underline{\phantom{\frac{3p}{8}}-17 = -17}$$
$$\frac{8}{3} \times \frac{3p}{8} = 21 \times \frac{8}{3}$$
$$p = 56$$

EXAMPLE THREE

$$\frac{x}{5} + 12 = 38$$

$$\frac{x}{5} + 12 = 38$$
$$\underline{\phantom{\frac{x}{5}}-12 = -12}$$
$$\frac{x}{5} = 26$$

$$\frac{5}{1} \times \frac{x}{5} = 26 \times \frac{5}{1}$$
$$x = 130$$

EXAMPLE FOUR

$$3p + 7 = 10p$$
$$\underline{-3p \qquad -3p}$$
$$\frac{7}{7} = \frac{7p}{7}$$

$$1 = p$$

What makes this equation different from the previous ones is that it has a variable on both sides. Notice how it's dealt with.

EXAMPLE FIVE

$$6(x - 4) = 36$$

$$
\begin{array}{rcr}
6x - 24 &=& 36 \\
+\ 24 && +24 \\
\hline
\dfrac{6x}{6} &=& \dfrac{60}{6} \\
x &=& 10
\end{array}
$$

Two final notes on solving equations—always do addition or subtraction first, if there is any to be done. *Do not* add or subtract so that one side of the equation equals 0. If it occurs, reexamine the equation and try inverse operation on another number.

PRACTICE—MORE COMPLEX EQUATIONS

Solve for the variable and check.

1. $12a + 6 = 42$
2. $7x - 14 = 14$
3. $\dfrac{r}{9} + 8 = 12$
4. $116 = 15c + 11$
5. $\dfrac{1}{8} m - 27 = 16$

6. $2(x - 9) = 46$
7. $14d = 18 + 8d$
8. $3h + 11 = 38$
9. $4(s + 6) = -28$

ANSWERS

1. $a = 3$
2. $x = 4$
3. $r = 36$
4. $c = 7$
5. $m = 344$

6. $x = 32$
7. $d = 3$
8. $h = 9$
9. $s = -13$

INEQUALITIES

> means **is greater than** $5 > 4$
>
> < means **is less than** $\quad\quad 6 < 8$
>
> ≥ means **is greater than or equal to**
>
> $\quad\quad 5 \geq 5$ and all positive numbers added to it
>
> ≤ means **is less than or equal to**
>
> $\quad\quad 3 \leq 3$ and all positive numbers subtracted from it

Memorize the meanings of the inequality signs.

TIP

The big or open side of the > or < sign is always closest to the bigger number.

PRACTICE—SIMPLE INEQUALITIES

True or False.

1. $\dfrac{1}{4} > \dfrac{1}{8}$

2. $3(5) < 14$

3. $-.5 > 0$

4. $12(3) \geq 36$

5. $\dfrac{12}{7} \leq 1\dfrac{5}{7}, 2, 3$

ANSWERS

1. **True**
2. **False**
3. **False**

4. **True**
5. **True**

EQUATIONS WITH INEQUALITIES

On the GED, you will certainly have to solve equations with inequalities. Proceed exactly as you would with the equations just learned, replacing the = sign with whatever inequality sign is in the equation.

EXAMPLE

$$3s - 4 > 11$$
$$\underline{+ 4 \quad +4}$$
$$\dfrac{3s}{3} \quad > \quad \dfrac{15}{3}$$

Answer: $s > 5$

What this means is that *s* can be checked with any number **greater than** 5. It could be 5.1 or 5,000,000.

Let's use 6.

$3(6) - 4 > 11 = 18 - 4 > 11$

$14 > 11$ is a true statement. It works.

PRACTICE—EQUATIONS WITH INEQUALITIES

Solve and check.

1. $\frac{x}{3} < 12$

2. $5y - 2 > 23$

3. $18 > 3(a - 6)$

4. $12x - 5 \geq 4x + 1$

ANSWERS

1. **$x < 36$**

2. **$y > 5$**

3. **$12 > a$**

4. **$x \geq \frac{3}{4}$**

MULTIPLYING BINOMIALS

$x + 6$ is an example of a binomial. You won't be asked to identify one, nor define the difference between a monomial and a binomial, but you will need to know how to multiply two binomials. It's very much like multiplying regular numbers. Consider this example:

$$(x + 4) \ (x + 3)$$

Step one: Set up like a two-digit multiplication problem

$$
\begin{array}{r}
x + 4 \\
\times \quad x + 3 \\
\hline
+\ 3x + 12 \\
+\ x^2 + 4x \quad\ \\
\hline
x^2 + 7x + 12
\end{array}
$$

Step two: Starting with the lower right term (+3), multiply the two top terms, right (4) then left (*x*). Put the products to each computation in the column where they belong.

$$4 \times 3 = 12 \quad \text{and} \quad x \times 3 = 3x$$

Step three: Now do the same for the lower left term. Just as in numeral multiplication, skip a one-digit space at the far right when entering the second row of products.

$$4 \times x = 4x \quad \text{and} \quad x \times x = x^2$$

Step four: Again, as in numerical multiplication, add the results in columns going downward.

Carefully study the following additional examples of binomial multiplication:

$(x - 7)(x + 2)$

$$
\begin{array}{r}
x - 7 \\
x + 2 \\
\hline
2x - 14
\end{array}
$$

$x^2 - 7x$

$x^2 - 5x - 14$

$(x - 8)(x - 3)$

$$
\begin{array}{r}
x - 8 \\
x - 3 \\
\hline
- 3x + 24
\end{array}
$$

$x^2 - 8x$

$x^2 - 11x + 24$

$(x + 6)(x - 6)$

$$
\begin{array}{r}
x + 6 \\
x - 6 \\
\hline
- 6x - 36
\end{array}
$$

$x^2 + 6x$

$x^2 + 0 - 36$

Since the 0 is unnecessary, $x^2 - 36$.

PRACTICE—MULTIPLYING BINOMIALS

Solve.

1. $(x + 2)(x + 4)$

2. $(x - 6)(x + 3)$

3. $(x - 8)(x - 5)$

4. $(x + 2)(x - 9)$

5. $(x + 9)(x - 9)$

ANSWERS

1. $x^2 + 6x + 8$

2. $x^2 - 3x - 18$

3. $x^2 - 13x + 40$

4. $x^2 - 7x - 18$

5. $x^2 - 81$

FACTORING QUADRATIC EXPRESSIONS

This is the reverse operation of multiplying binomials. You will probably have one problem like this on the test, so it's best to be prepared. A quadratic expression looks like this:

$$x^2 + 10x + 16$$

Here's how to factor it.

EXAMPLE ONE

Factor $x^2 + 10x + 16$

$(x \quad)(x \quad)$ will always be your starting point because $x(x) = x^2$.

You now need to find **one set** of two numbers that, when multiplied, will equal +16 and when added will equal +10.

$16 \times 1 = 16$ but $16 + 1 = 17$—No

$4 \times 4 = 16$ but $4 + 4 = 8$—No

$8 \times 2 = 16$ *and* $8 + 2 = 10$—**Yes**

The factors for the quadratic expression $x^2 + 10x + 16$ are:

$$(x + 8)\ (x + 2)$$

A check will prove it.

EXAMPLE TWO

Factor $x^2 + 2x - 8$

$-8 \times 1 = -8$ but $-8 + -1 = -7$—No

$-4 \times 2 = -8$ but $-4 + (-2) = -2$—No

$4 \times -2 = -8$ *and* $4 + (-2) = +2$—**Yes**

Answer: $(x + 4)\ (x - 2)$

PRACTICE—FACTORING QUADRATIC EXPRESSIONS

Factor the following.

1. $x^2 + 9x + 18$ 4. $x^2 + 9x - 36$

2. $x^2 - 7x + 10$ 5. $x^2 + x - 56$

3. $x^2 - 49$

ANSWERS

1. $(x + 3)\ (x + 6)$ 4. $(x + 12)\ (x - 3)$

2. $(x - 5)\ (x - 2)$ 5. $(x + 8)\ (x - 7)$

3. $(x + 7)\ (x - 7)$

QUADRATIC EQUATIONS

The quadratic equation problems you'll see on the GED all look similar to this:

$x^2 - 12x + 27 = 0$ Solve for x

The key here is that you must come up with **two** different numbers for x that will make the equation work.

EXAMPLE

$x^2 - 12x + 27 = 0$ Solve for x

Step one: Factor the left side of the equation $(x - 9)\ (x - 3)$

Step two: Simply reverse the signs on the two numbers in each binomial factor. -9 becomes 9, -3 becomes 3

Answer: $x = 9,3$

A check of both numbers replacing x is time-consuming. Know the process.

Solve for *x*.

1. $x^2 + 15x + 56 = 0$ 4. $x^2 - 64 = 0$

2. $x^2 - 7x - 30 = 0$ 5. $x^2 - 19x + 60 = 0$

3. $x^2 + 8x - 9 = 0$

ANSWERS

1. **(–7, –8)**   4. **(8, –8)**

2. **(10, –3)**   5. **(15, 4)**

3. **(–9, 1)**

ALGEBRA AND WORD PROBLEMS

PROPORTIONS

This operation is the next logical step after "ratio," which you learned in Chapter 20, Fractions. In its simplest form, the idea is to make two ratios equal, when one of the four parts is unknown.

EXAMPLE ONE

$7 : 2 = x : 6$ solve for *x*

Step one: Set up ratios as fractions

$$\frac{7}{2} = \frac{x}{6}$$

Step two: Cross-multiply and set up the products as two numbers separated by an = sign:

$$7 \times 6 = 42 \quad \text{and} \quad 2 \times x = 2x$$

Set up as $2x = 42$

Step three: Finish the equation by dividing

$$\frac{\cancel{2}x}{\cancel{2}} = \frac{\cancel{42}^{21}}{\cancel{2}^{1}}$$

$$7 : 2 = 21 : 6$$

Answer: *x* = 21

What this means is that 7 has the same numerical relationship to 2 as 21 does to 6.

Let's say you were baking a cake that required you to put in seven cups of milk to two cups of flour. If you wanted to bake a larger cake (in this case, three times larger), you would still follow the same recipe ratio of 7 parts to 2 parts by using 21 cups of milk and 6 cups of flour.

EXAMPLE TWO

The scale on a map is 1 inch to every 150 miles. How far apart in miles are two cities that are 6 inches apart on the map?

Step one: $1 : 150 = 6 : x$

Step two: $\dfrac{1}{150} = \dfrac{6}{x}$

Step three: $900 = x$, making *Step four* unnecessary

Answer: 900 miles

EXAMPLE THREE

In a hotel, the ratio of nonsmoking rooms to rooms where smoking is allowed is 5:2. If there are 350 rooms in the hotel, how many allow smoking?

Step one: Problem! The proportion can't be set up as it has been in the past two examples because the information doesn't match—5:2 gives you two parts (nonsmoking:smoking) but 350 gives you a *total*. You need to compare total (350) to smoking (unknown or x).

The sum of the two parts (5 + 2) will give a total of 7. Now you have equal ratios to compare with.

$$\frac{\text{total}}{\text{smoking}} \qquad \frac{7}{2} = \frac{350}{x}$$

Step two: $7x = 700$

Step three: $\dfrac{7x}{7} = \dfrac{700}{7}$

Step four: $x = 100$

Answer: There are 100 rooms where smoking is allowed

PRACTICE—PROPORTIONS

1. On a construction job, a carpenter uses 26 feet of lumber to build 2 door frames. If he is going to build 5 door frames, how much lumber does he need?

2. The scale on a road map indicates that $\dfrac{1}{4}$ inch equals 20 miles. How far apart in miles are two towns that are $3\dfrac{1}{2}$ inches away on the map?

3. A photograph is 3 inches long by 5 inches wide. If Susan wants to enlarge it so that it is 12 inches long, how wide will the enlargement be?

ANSWERS

1. **65 feet**   2. **280 miles**   3. **20 inches**

SETUPS USING VARIABLES

Problems with variables is, perhaps, the most common type of problem seen on the GED, so understanding it is really important. Much like word problems in Chapter 19, Numbers and Basic Operations, you should rely on your common sense to guide you.

EXAMPLE ONE

Sally can plant x tomato seedlings per row and there are y rows in her garden. Write an algebraic expression that represents the total amount of seedlings that could be planted in the garden.

It should occur to you that this is very much like an "area" question ($l \times w$). What might help you to picture the solution is **to put numbers in place of the variables**. In this case, say Sally can plant 10 seedlings per row and there are 12 rows in the garden. The total number of seedlings would be represented by 10(12) or **xy**.

Answer: xy

EXAMPLE TWO

A class of fourth-graders voted for class president. P students voted for Jake, Q students voted for Ming, and R students voted for Louisa. What fractional part of the class voted for Louisa?

Fractional part is a good clue that this problem should be set up as a fraction and that you're looking for a part-to-whole relationship. Compute the *whole* or total of the class by adding each variable ($P + Q + R$). Remember that the *part* in a part-whole relationship goes on top.

Answer: $\dfrac{R}{P + Q + R}$

EXAMPLE THREE

A carpenter gets paid g dollars per hour and his assistant receives h dollars per hour. On Wednesday, they both worked j hours. Write an expression representing their combined earnings for the day.

If the solution doesn't come to you right away, try replacing variables with number amounts. Let's say the carpenter gets $20 per hour and the assistant gets $12 per hour. They work a total of 7 hours. The phrase "combined earnings" suggests addition and the fact that they *both* worked the same number of hours suggests the use of parentheses. So, 7 hrs. (20 + 12) = combined earnings or:

Answer: $j(g + h)$

PRACTICE—SETUPS WITH VARIABLES

Choose the correct expression for each of the following.

1. A fisherman purchases two fishing rods at b dollars each and a lure for c dollars. He pays with a \$50 bill. What is the amount of change returned?

   (1) $2b - c + 50$
   (2) $50 + (2b - c)$
   (3) $50 + 2(b - c)$
   (4) $50 - (2b + c)$
   (5) $\dfrac{2b + c}{50}$

2. Tom is b years old. How old will he be in 12 years?

   (1) $b - 12$
   (2) $b + 12$
   (3) $12b$
   (4) $b + 12 - x$
   (5) $12 - b$

3. The Wilsons need to drive 350 miles in y hours. How many miles per hour do they need to drive to reach their destination on time?

   (1) $\dfrac{350}{y}$
   (2) $350y$
   (3) $\dfrac{350 + y}{y}$
   (4) $4(350y)$
   (5) not enough information is given

4. A chest has four drawers, three of which contain x sweaters and a fourth that contains y sweaters. What is the total number of sweaters in the chest?

   (1) $3(x + y)$
   (2) $3 + x + y$
   (3) $3xy$
   (4) $x + 3y$
   (5) $3x + y$

5. Lina grosses \$11,000 per month at her yogurt store. Each month she pays out f dollars for rental of the building, g for electric use, and h for other expenses. How much does she net per month?

   (1) $11(f + g + h)$
   (2) $11,000 - (f + g + h)$
   (3) $(f - g - h)11,000$
   (4) $(11,000 - h) - (f + g)$
   (5) not enough information is given

6. There are x girls on a volleyball team. One day, y girls were absent from practice. What fractional part of the team was not absent that day?

   1) $\dfrac{x}{x + y}$

   2) $2x - y$

   3) $\dfrac{x - y}{x}$

   4) $(y + x) - y$

   5) $xy + x$

7. Alicia saves x dollars per month, Dean saves y dollars per month and Sarah saves z dollars per month. What represents their total savings for the year?

   (1) $12(x + y + z)$
   (2) $xyz - 12$
   (3) $30x + 30y + 30z$
   (4) $12 + (x - y - z)$
   (5) not enough information is given

8. Randy invests an equal amount of his salary in two different mutual funds. At the end of the year, Fund A's value increases by 22% but Fund B's value decreases by 6%. What is the total worth of his two funds at the end of the year?

   (1) $(.22 \times A) + (.06 \times B)$
   (2) $(.22 \times A) - (.06 \times B)$
   (3) $.84 (A + B)$
   (4) $.16(A + B) + (A + B)$
   (5) $(.22 \times A) - (.6 \times B)$

ANSWERS

1. **4**	3. **1**	5. **2**	7. **1**
2. **2**	4. **5**	6. **3**	8. **4**

CONVERTING WORDS INTO ALGEBRAIC EQUATIONS

Converting words in algebraic equations is an important skill. To help master it, here is a list of commonly used phrases with numbers and their algebraic translations. Read the left-hand column and cover the right-hand column. Using x as a variable to replace the phrase "a number," predict what the right column will say.

Words	Algebraic Expression
5 plus a number	$5 + x$
12 decreased by a number	$12 - x$
The sum of a number and 6	$x + 6$
16 less than a number	$x - 16$
2.5 more than a number	$2.5 + x$
13 minus a number	$13 - x$
A number increased by 8	$x + 8$
The product of 13 and a number	$13x$
A number divided by 4	$\dfrac{x}{4}$
3 times a number	$3x$
18 divided by a number	$\dfrac{18}{x}$
5 times a number decreased by 7	$5x - 7$
A number times itself	x^2
The square root of a number less 6	$\sqrt{x} - 6$
14 increased by a number, all multiplied by 8	$8(14 + x)$
8 minus a number, all divided by that same number	$\dfrac{8 - n}{n}$

CONVERTING WORDS TO EQUATIONS AND SOLVING

Once you've learned how to solve simple and complex equations, you need to be able to convert sentences into equations and then solve them. Look for the words **is** or **equals**; they mark the place in the equation where the = sign belongs.

EXAMPLE

Three times a number increased by 14 is 23. Convert and solve.

Let $3x$ stand for "3 times a number"

Let + 14 stand for "increased by 14"

Let = 23 stand for "is 23."

Put it all together and solve the equation.

$$3x + 14 = 23$$
$$\underline{- 14 \quad -14}$$
$$\frac{3x}{3} = \frac{9}{3}$$

Answer: $x = 3$

PRACTICE—SOLVING SIMPLE WORD EQUATIONS

Convert and solve for the variable.

1. A number decreased by 16 = 39.

2. 90 divided by a number is 18.

3. 48 equals a number increased by 6, and the sum, all multiplied by 5.

4. A number times itself and added to 23 is equal to 219.

ANSWERS

1. $x = 55$

2. $x = 5$

3. $x = 3\frac{3}{5}$

4. $x = 14$

MULTISTEP ALGEBRAIC WORD PROBLEMS

For some students, word problems requiring several algebraic steps are the most difficult questions on the GED. All these problems need to be converted to multistep equations that then need to be solved.

EXAMPLE ONE

Dolores and her brother Jim have a paper route. Dolores delivers twice as many papers as Jim does. Together, they deliver 117 papers. How many papers does Jim deliver? How many does Dolores deliver?

Step one: Build a box.

$$2x = \text{Dolores}$$
$$x = \text{Jim}$$

We don't know how many papers either person delivered, but we *do* know Dolores delivered twice as many as Jim did. In virtually all of these problems, one of the unknowns, usually the smallest, will be represented by x.

Step two: Write an equation based on the information given.

$$2x + x = 117$$

Step three: Solve the equation.

$2x + x = 117$ becomes $\dfrac{3x}{3} = \dfrac{117}{3}$ $x = 39$

Step four: Return to the box and apply the information to the question asked.

Answer: Jim delivered **39** papers
Dolores delivered 2(39) or **78** papers

EXAMPLE TWO

Three soccer players led the Rhinos in scoring for the season. Henri scored twice as many goals as Fred, and Angelo scored 18 more goals than Fred. If the three combined to score 78 goals, how many did Henri score?

Step one: Build a box.

$$\text{Henri} = 2x$$
$$\text{Fred} = x$$
$$\text{Angelo} = x + 18$$

Step two: $2x + x + (x + 18) = 78$

Step three:
$$
\begin{array}{rcl}
4x + 18 &=& 78 \\
-18 & & -18 \\
\hline
\dfrac{4x}{4} &=& \dfrac{60}{4} \\
x &=& 15
\end{array}
$$

Step four: Henri scored 2(15) or **30** goals.

PRACTICE—MULTISTEP WORD PROBLEMS

Solve.

1. At Oasis College, three times as many freshmen live on campus as those who commute. If there are 988 freshmen, how many commute?

2. A soda vendor sold large sodas for $3 and small sodas for $2. If he sold 182 large sodas and his gross profit for the day was $894, how many small sodas did he sell?

3. Kelly is nine years older than her sister. Kelly's age is one more than twice her sister's age. What is Kelly's age?

4. Two junked cars were sold at auction to a buyer who paid a total of $2,000 for both cars. If the more expensive of the two cars was $240 less than three times the price of the cheaper car, how much was the more expensive car?

ANSWERS

1. **247**   2. **174**   3. **17**   4. **$1,440**

COORDINATE GEOMETRY

FINDING POINTS ON THE RECTANGULAR COORDINATE GRID

Study the diagram below.

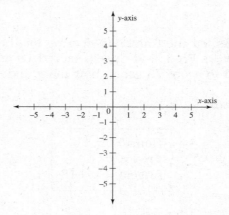

Here, two number lines are set up perpendicular to each other. The horizontal line is the **x-axis** and the vertical line is the **y-axis**. Memorize that.

The diagram below is a more dressed-up version called a rectangular coordinate grid. You must learn to locate points on the grid using two numbers: the **x-coordinate** and the **y-coordinate**.

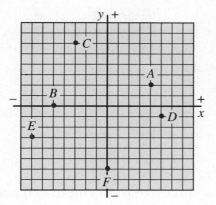

EXAMPLE ONE

Find the coordinates of Point *A*

Step one: Locate the *x*-coordinate (it comes first alphabetically and must be listed first in the answer). Using the darkened *x*-axis zero line as a guide, count the number of ticks (or boxes) on the number line you need to move horizontally (across) from the exact center (0,0) of the graph to the vertical line on which Point *A* is located. It's four horizontal ticks from the center, so the *x*-coordinate is **4**.

Step two: Find the *y*-coordinate. Again, start at dead center but move vertically (up) along the *y*-axis to the horizontal line on which Point *A* is located, counting the ticks as you go. It's two vertical ticks from the center, so the *y*-coordinate is **2**.

Answer: Coordinates for Point A (4,2)

EXAMPLE TWO

Find coordinates for Point *B*

Step One: Find the *x*-coordinate. Counting from dead center, *B* is five ticks away. Notice, though, that it is five steps to the **left** of 0, putting it on the negative side of the number line. The *x*-coordinate is –5.

Step two: Find the *y*-coordinate. Since Point *B* lies directly on the *x*-axis and does not rise above or sink below the 0 line, its *y*-coordinate is 0.

Answer: Coordinates for Point B (–5,0)

Here are coordinates for four more points on the above grid. Try to calculate the coordinates yourself first, and then check your accuracy.

Point *C* (–3,6)   Point *E* (–7, –3)

Point *D* (5, –1)   Point *F* (0, –6)

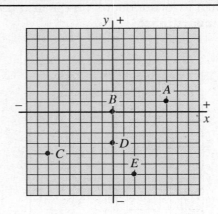

Identify the coordinates of the five points on the grid above.

1. Point A   4. Point D

2. Point B   5. Point E

3. Point C

ANSWERS

1. **(5, 1)**   4. **(0, –3)**

2. **(0, 0)**   5. **(2, –6)**

3. **(–6, –4)**

FINDING THE DISTANCE BETWEEN POINTS

This may look complicated, but it's a very simple operation.

EXAMPLE ONE

Find the distance between Points A and B

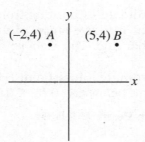

Don't worry because the grid is gone—you don't need it. Since y-coordinates of both points are +4, they both rest on that imaginary horizontal line parallel to the x-axis. To find the distance between the points, you just need to calculate how many ticks there are between the x coordinates. Disregard any + or – sign and **add the sum of the pair of coordinates that aren't the same**. In this case, the pair of y-coordinates are the same (4,4) and the x-coordinates aren't the same (–2,5). Drop the signs and add: 2 + 5 = 7

Answer: The distance between Points *A* and *B* is 7

EXAMPLE TWO

Find the distance between Points *C* and *D*

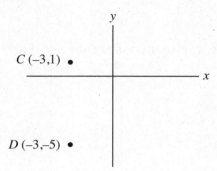

These two points lie on the same imaginary line parallel to the y-axis (–3). The y-coordinates are the pair that's not the same, so drop the – sign and add 5 + 1.

Answer: The distance between *C* and *D* = 6

(In cases where the coordinates are in the same quadrant, simply subtract the smaller coordinate from the larger one.)

PRACTICE—FINDING DISTANCE BETWEEN POINTS

Using the graph below, find the distance between the following sets of points:

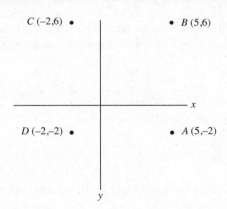

1. *A* and *B*   3. *C* and *B*

2. *D* and *C*   4. *D* and *A*

ANSWERS

1. **8**   2. **8**   3. **7**   4. **7**

FINDING THE SLOPE OF A LINE

This is another operation that looks complicated but isn't. The formula for calculating slope is included on the formula sheet (see page 726) and looks like this:

slope of a line (m) $$m = \frac{y_2 - y_1}{x_2 - x_1}$$

Here's how to apply it.

EXAMPLE

What is the slope of the line that passes through A and B?

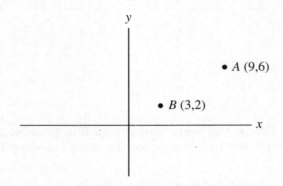

Step one: Write down the formula for slope.

$$m = \frac{y_2 - y_1}{x_2 - x_1}$$

Step two: Replace the letter symbols with the appropriate coordinates. There is no way to tell from the problem which are the $_2$'s and which are the $_1$'s. It's your choice, as long as you remain consistent by assigning one set of coordinates to a number and don't mix them. If, in this case, you decide A will be the $_2$'s and B will be the $_1$'s, then the slope solution will look like this:

$$m = \frac{6 - 2}{9 - 3} = \frac{4}{6} = \frac{2}{3}$$

Step three: Do the math and reduce.

Answer: slope is $\frac{2}{3}$

If you chose the coordinates for Point B as $_1$s and A as $_2$s, the answer would still be the same.

$$m = \frac{2 - 6}{3 - 9} = \frac{-4}{-6} = \frac{2}{3}$$

PRACTICE—FINDING THE SLOPE OF A LINE

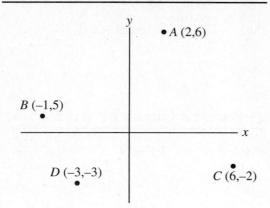

Find the slopes of the lines passing through the following points on the graph.

1. *AC*   3. *AD*

2. *AB*   4. *BD*

ANSWERS

1. **–2**   3. **$1\frac{4}{5}$**

2. **$\frac{1}{3}$**   4. **4**

FINDING A COORDINATE WHEN THE SLOPE IS GIVEN

This is a relatively simple algebra problem that won't be accompanied by a coordinate graph.

EXAMPLE

Find y if the slope of a line passing through points A (5,y) and B (2,3) is equal to 1.

Step one: Set up the formula for slope of a line:

$$m = \frac{y_2 - y_1}{x_2 - x_1}$$

Step two: Insert the slope and the given coordinates. Use y as a variable for the unknown. Again, it's your choice as to whether it's a y_1 or y_2. In this case, we'll make it a $_2$.

$$1 = \frac{y - 3}{5 - 2}$$

Step three: Solve as an equation.

$$1 = \frac{y-3}{5-2} = \frac{(3)}{1} \quad 1 = \frac{y-3}{3}\frac{(3)}{1} = \quad \begin{array}{c} 3 = y - 3 \\ \underline{+3 \quad +3} \\ 6 = y \end{array}$$

Answer: $y = 6$

PRACTICE—FINDING A COORDINATE WHEN SLOPE IS GIVEN

1. Find x if the slope of a line passing through Points A (4,3) and B (x,7) equals 4.

ANSWER

5

CHAPTER REVIEW

Fill in the answer grids, and use a calculator where indicated.

Questions 1 and 2 are based on the following information:

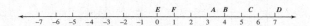

1. The letter on the number line that best represents $\sqrt{32}$ is

   (1) A
   (2) B
   (3) C
   (4) D
   (5) E

2. The variable x in the expression $5x - 7 \geq 13$ is represented on the above number line by

   (1) point B
   (2) all points $< C$
   (3) point A
   (4) point B and all points $>$ point B
   (5) all points $<$ point B

3. Evaluate $(4x + y)(x^2 + 6)$ when $x = -3$ and $y = 5$

   (1) 59
   (2) −63
   (3) 80
   (4) 66
   (5) −105

4.

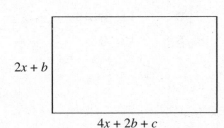

2x + b

4x + 2b + c

   What is the perimeter of the above rectangle?

   (1) $6x + 3b + c$
   (2) $15x_2 + 5b + 2c$
   (3) $2x - b + c$
   (4) $8x + 4b = 2c$
   (5) $12x + 6b + 2c$

5. Given the equation $49 - x = 33$, find $3x$.

6. Given the equation $7a - 28 \geq 56$, find a.

   (1) all numbers < 12
   (2) all numbers > 12
   (3) all numbers ≤ 12
   (4) all numbers ≥ 12
   (5) 14

7. In the equation $x^2 - 8x - 48 = 0$, what are the solutions for x?

   (1) −12, 4
   (2) 6, −8
   (3) 12, −4
   (4) −8, 6
   (5) −6, −4

8. Find x if the slope of a line passing through points A (−2, x) and B (4, 1) equals $\frac{-2}{3}$.

   (1) 3
   (2) $\frac{2}{3}$
   (3) 5
   (4) −6
   (5) −3

9. Tina and Simon visit an amusement park. Both children each pay x dollars for admission. All rides are the same price, represented by y. Tina goes on six rides and Simon goes on four. Which expression represents the total of what both children spent?

   (1) $\frac{6y + 4y}{2}$
   (2) $2(x + 10y)$
   (3) $(6y - 4y) + 2x$
   (4) $2x - 10y$
   (5) $(x + 6y) + (x + 4y)$

10. Nine times a number minus three is equal to five times that same number added to seven. What is the value of the number?

   (1) 2.5
   (2) 7
   (3) 6
   (4) 3
   (5) 13

11. Thomasville and Newtown are 260 miles apart. If the scale on a road map is $\frac{1}{2}$ inch : 40 miles, how far apart in inches will the two towns be on the map?

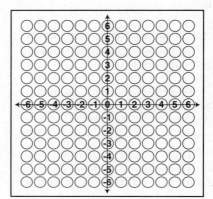

12. John owns three guitars. The most valuable is $25 less than three times the least valuable. The other guitar is worth $16 more than twice the least valuable. All together, the three guitars are worth $1,245. What is the value of the most expensive guitar?

   (1) around $500
   (2) between $650 and $700
   (3) around $600
   (4) around $4,700
   (5) around $550

13. Which point denotes the center of the circle?

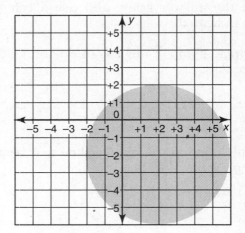

Answers

1. **3**   5. **48**   9. **5**   13. **(2,–2)**

2. **4**   6. **4**   10. **1**

3. **5**   7. **3**   11. **3.25**

4. **5**   8. **3**   12. **3**

Geometry

CHAPTER 24

ANGLES

Learn the following vocabulary.

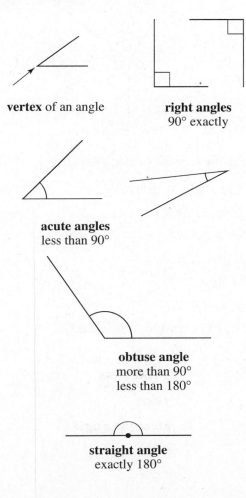

vertex of an angle

right angles
90° exactly

acute angles
less than 90°

obtuse angle
more than 90°
less than 180°

straight angle
exactly 180°

> **NOTE**
>
> ° means degrees in an angle.
>
> m means "measure of" or "number of degrees" in an angle.

On the GED, angles might be referred to in a few different ways.

The angle above might be referred to as ∠*CBA* or ∠*ABC*. Notice how the letter *B*, the one that marks the vertex, is always in the middle of the three letters.

The angle above might be referred to as ∠*x* or m of ∠*x*, with **m** meaning **the measure of** ∠*x*.

PRACTICE—IDENTIFYING ANGLES

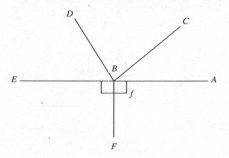

Refer to the above diagram to answer the following.

1. What is m ∠*f* ? (How many degrees?)
2. What kind of angle is ∠*ABC*?
3. What kind of angle is ∠*ABD*?
4. What kind of angle is ∠*EBC*?
5. What is m ∠*EBD* + m ∠*ABD*?
6. What kind of angle is ∠*ABE*?
7. What is m ∠*ABC* if it is equal to $\frac{1}{2}$ m ∠*EBF*?

ANSWERS

1. **90°**
2. **acute**
3. **obtuse**
4. **obtuse**

5. **180°**
6. **straight angle**
7. **45°**

Complementary and Supplementary Angles

Two or more angles are *complementary* if their sum is equal to 90 degrees.

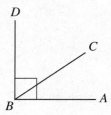

m $\angle ABC$ =   33°
m $\angle CBD$ =   <u>57°</u>
           90°

$\angle ABC$ and $\angle CBD$ are *complementary*

Two or more angles are *supplementary* if their sum is equal to 180°.

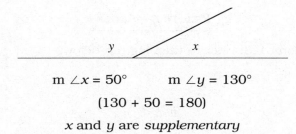

m $\angle x$ = 50°   m $\angle y$ = 130°

(130 + 50 = 180)

x and y are *supplementary*

Bisectors

Any line that *bisects* an angle divides the measure of the angle *in half.*

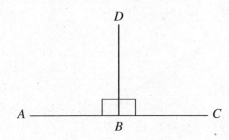

m $\angle ABC$ = 180°

$\overline{BD}$ bisects $\angle ABC$

m $\angle CBD$ = 90°   m $\angle ABD$ = 90°

Vertical Angles

Vertical angles, the ones that appear *opposite* to each other, are equal.

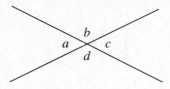

∠*a* is vertical to ∠*c* and ∠*b* is vertical to ∠*d*

∠*a* = ∠*c*

∠*b* = ∠*d*

If, in the above diagram ∠*a* = 60°, then ∠*b* = 120° (supplementary) and ∠*d* = 120° (vertical) and ∠*c* = 60° (vertical).

These concepts will be tested over and over in various ways. Know them.

PRACTICE—ANGLES

To answer questions 1–3, refer to the diagram below.

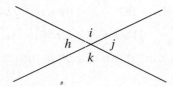

1. What two angles, when separately added to ∠*j*, will equal 180°?

2. What is the sum of all angles in the diagram?

3. What other angle is equal to ∠*i*?

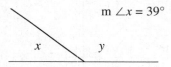

m ∠*x* = 39°

4. In the diagram above, what is m ∠*y*?

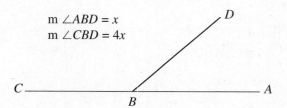

m ∠*ABD* = *x*
m ∠*CBD* = 4*x*

5. In the diagram above, what is m ∠*CBD*? (Hint: 4*x* + *x* = 180)

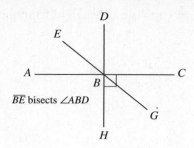

BE bisects ∠ABD

Questions 6 and 7 refer to the diagram above.

6. What is m ∠CBG?

7. Which *two* expressions are true?

   (1) m ∠DBC = 2(∠ABH)

   (2) m ∠DBH = $\dfrac{\angle ABH}{2}$

   (3) m ∠ABC = m of 2(∠CBH)

   (4) 2(∠CBG) = $\dfrac{\angle ABC}{2}$.

ANSWERS

1. **I, K**   5. **144°**

2. **360°**   6. **45°**

3. **K**   7. **3, 4**

4. **141°**

TRANSVERSALS

A **transversal** is a line that cuts across a set of parallel lines. You won't have to know a definition for this type of diagram, but you must thoroughly understand the concepts it illustrates.

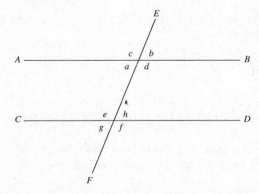

In the above diagram, $\overline{AB} \parallel \overline{CD}$ (∥ means $\overline{AB}$ is parallel to $\overline{CD}$). $\overline{EF}$ is the transversal.

We know that because of the rule of vertical (opposite) angles:

$$\angle c = \angle d \quad \text{and} \quad \angle a = \angle b$$
$$\angle e = \angle f \quad \text{and} \quad \angle g = \angle h$$
Also: $\angle b = \angle g \quad \text{and} \quad \angle c = \angle f$
$$\angle c = \angle e \quad \text{and} \quad \angle b = \angle h$$

PRACTICE—TRANSVERSALS

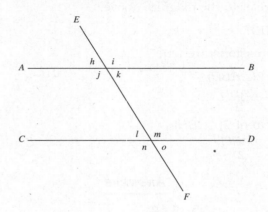

In the above diagram, $\overline{AB}$ is $\parallel$ to $\overline{CD}$.

1. Name all other angles equal to $\angle h$.

2. Name all other angles equal to $\angle n$.

3. If m $\angle o = 36°$, what is m $\angle i$?

4. If m $\angle n = 117°$, what is m $\angle h$?

5. If m $\angle h = 63°$, then what is m $\angle h + \angle n + \angle o$?

6. If m $\angle h$ was expressed as x and m $\angle i$ was expressed as $3x$, which statement would be true?
   (1) $3x - x = 180°$
   (2) $3x + 2x = 180°$
   (3) $4x = 180°$

7. If the answer to question 6 is 3, what is m $\angle i$ in degrees?

8. If m $\angle h = 58°$ and a line is drawn that bisects $\angle n$, what are the measures of the two angles created by the bisection of $\angle n$?

ANSWERS

1. **K, L, O**   5. **243°**

2. **M, I, J**   6. **3**

3. **144°**   7. **135°**

4. **63°**   8. **61°**

TRIANGLES

There are four types of triangles you need to know about.

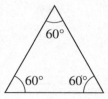

Equilateral triangle—All sides are equal. All angles equal 60°.

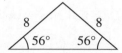

Isoceles triangle (pronounced *I-sosaleez*)—Two sides are equal. Two angles are equal.

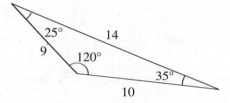

Scalene triangle (pronounced *skayleen*)— No sides are equal. No angles are equal.

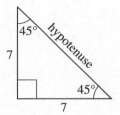

Right triangle—one of the angles is always 90°.
The other two angles can be equal to each other or different, but their sum will always equal 90°.

   The two sides that make up the right angle *can* be equal but don't have to be.

   The third side, the one opposite the right angle, is always longer than the other two and is called the *hypotenuse*.

> The sum of all angles of a triangle always adds up to 180°.

This is a fact that will help you to solve several questions on the GED. Memorize it.

PRACTICE—TRIANGLES

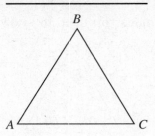

1. In △*ABC* above, ∠*A* = 70° and ∠*B* = 40°. What is the measure of ∠*C*?

2. What kind of triangle is △*ABC*?

3. What kind of triangle is △*DEF* if it has a hypotenuse?

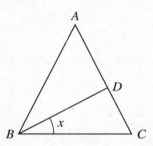

4. △*ABC*, above, is an equilateral triangle. $\overline{BD}$ bisects ∠*ABC*. What is m ∠*x*?

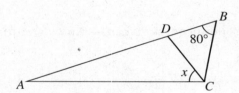

5. △*ABC*, above, is a scalene triangle. ∠*B* = 80°, $\overline{CD}$ bisects ∠*ACB*. What is m ∠*x*?

   (1) 50°
   (2) 25°
   (3) 55°
   (4) 35°
   (5) not enough information is given

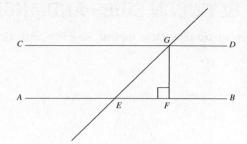

6. In the above diagram, $\overline{AB} \parallel \overline{CD}$, $\overline{GF} \perp \overline{AB}$ and m $\angle EGF = 35°$. What is m $\angle AEG$?

7. In $\triangle ABC$, m $\angle a = 30°$, $\angle B = 60°$, $\angle C = 90°$.

   (a) What kind of triangle is $\triangle ABC$?
   (b) What is the ratio of $\angle A$ to $\angle C$?

      (1) 3:1
      (2) 2:1
      (3) 1:2
      (4) 1:3
      (5) 4:3

8.

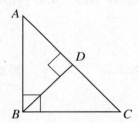

   $AD \perp BD$. If m $\angle DAB = 40°$, what is m of $\angle BCD$? (Clue: Use $\triangle ABC$ to help figure this out. Don't be distracted by DB, which seems to bisect $\angle ABC$).

ANSWERS

1. **70°**

2. **isosceles**

3. **right triangle**

4. **30°**

5. **5**

6. **125°**

7. (a) **right** (b) **4**

8. **50°**

RELATIONSHIPS BETWEEN SIDES AND ANGLES

In a triangle, **the sides opposite two equal angles are also equal.**

EXAMPLE ONE

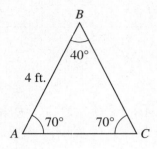

Find $\overline{BC}$

$\overline{BC}$ is **opposite** $\angle A$ $\overline{AB}$ is **opposite** $\angle C$

m $\angle A$ = m $\angle C$ Find $\overline{BC}$

m $\angle A$ = m $\angle C$, so $\overline{AB} = \overline{BC}$; if $\overline{AB}$ = 4 ft., then $\overline{BC}$ = 4 ft.

In a triangle, **the angles opposite two equal sides are equal.**

EXAMPLE TWO

Find x in both figures.

Figure One	**Figure Two**

Where AB is the radius
of the circle

In Figure One, $\overline{AB} = \overline{AC}$. Therefore, $\angle B$ (opposite $\overline{AC}$) = m $\angle C$ (opposite $\overline{AB}$).

Answer: x = 45°

In Figure Two, $\overline{AB}$ and $\overline{BC}$ are both radii (plural of "radius") of the circle. Therefore, $\overline{AB} = \overline{BC}$. So, m $\angle C$ (opposite $\overline{AB}$) = m $\angle A$ (opposite $\overline{BC}$).

Answer: x = 65°

In all triangles except the equilateral, **the longest side is opposite the largest angle and the shortest side is opposite the smallest angle.**

EXAMPLE THREE

In $\triangle ABC$, m $\angle A = x$, m $\angle B = 1.5x$, and m $\angle C = 2.5x$. Which *side* is the longest?

Step one: It might help to draw a diagram. Don't worry about where you place the angles or the scale of the drawing; it'll work out.

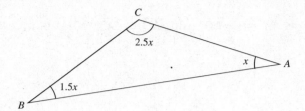

Since the longest side is opposite the largest angle, it has to be $\overline{AB}$.

Answer: $\overline{AB}$

Practice—Relationships Between Sides and Angles

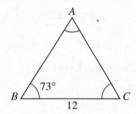

1. In the triangle above, if $\overline{AB} = \dfrac{3}{4}(\overline{AC})$ and m $\angle A = \angle C$, what is the length of $\overline{AB}$?

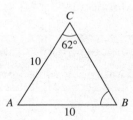

2. In $\triangle ABC$ above, find m $\angle B$.

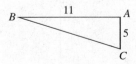

3. The perimeter of $\triangle ABC$ above = 29. Which angle is largest?

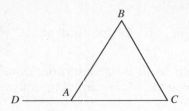

4. In △ABC above m ∠B = 50° and $\overline{AB}$ = $\overline{BC}$. What is m ∠DAB?

5. $\overline{BC}$ and $\overline{AB}$ are the radii of the circle above. If m ∠C = 60°, what kind of triangle is △ABC?

ANSWERS

1. **12**   4. **115°**
2. **62°**   5. **equilateral**
3. **∠A**

SIMILAR TRIANGLES

Similar triangles are *not* equal in size—one could be tiny and one could be huge. What they do have in common is:

> • All their corresponding angles are **equal**
> • All their corresponding sides are **proportional**

EXAMPLE ONE

Is △ABC similar to △DEF?

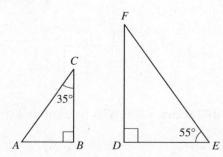

You have the choice of establishing similarity by proving all corresponding angles are equal or all corresponding sides are proportional. In this case, since two angles are already given, go for all angles.

m $\angle B$ = m $\angle D$. That's given in the diagram. Since m $\angle C$ = 35° in $\triangle ABC$, m $\angle A$ must equal 55° (35 + 55 + 90 = 180).

Likewise, since m $\angle E$ in $\triangle DEF$ = 55°, m $\angle F$ must equal 35°.

Now, all corresponding angles are equal: $\angle B$ = $\angle D$, $\angle A$ = $\angle E$, $\angle C$ = $\angle F$.

Answer: $\triangle ABC$ **and** $\triangle DEF$ **are similar.** (This would also mean all sides are proportional.)

EXAMPLE TWO

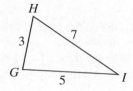

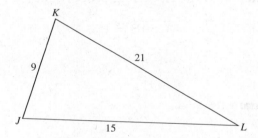

Is $\triangle GHI$ similar to $\triangle JKL$?

It's easy to decide whether to prove similarity through equal angles or proportional sides here. Since you're given all sides, go for sides.

Set up a proportion for one pair of corresponding sides:

$$\overline{GH} : \overline{JK} \ = 3:9 = 1:3$$

A quick look at the lengths of the other pairs of corresponding sides tells you that they are both in the same 1 : 3 proportion to each other.

Answer: $\triangle GHI$ **is similar to** $\triangle JKL$
(This also means their corresponding angles are equal)

EXAMPLE THREE

In the diagram below, $\overline{AB} \parallel \overline{DC}$. Find the length of $\overline{AB}$.

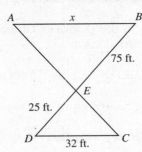

This may seem complicated, but it isn't. A very important fact is that $\overline{AB} \parallel \overline{DC}$, which means $\overline{BD}$ is a transversal.

Step one: Decide whether $\triangle DEC$ and $\triangle AEB$ are similar. Because of the rules governing transversals, you know that $\angle D = \angle B$ and $\angle C = \angle A$. $\angle DEC = \angle AEB$ because they're opposite angles. The two triangles are similar because all three angles are equal. And, their sides are **proportional**.

Step two: Find the length of $\overline{AB}$ using proportion.

$\overline{DE} : \overline{EB}$ = 25:75 = 1:3   so $\overline{DC} : \overline{AB}$ = 1:3

$$\frac{32}{x} = \frac{1}{3} \qquad x = 96$$

Answer: $\overline{AB}$ equals 96 feet.

PRACTICE—SIMILAR TRIANGLES

1. Are the triangles shown below similar?

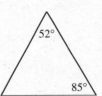

2. If the perimeter of $\triangle DEF$ = 18, are the triangles shown below similar?

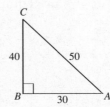

Questions 3 and 4 refer to the figure below.

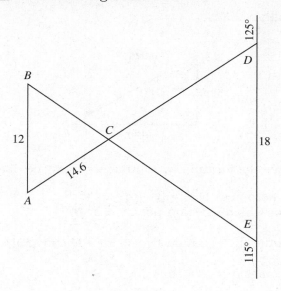

3. $\overline{AB} \parallel \overline{DE}$. What is the length of $\overline{CD}$?

4. What is m $\angle ACB$?

ANSWERS

1. **No**   2. **Yes**   3. **21.9**   4. **60°**

RIGHT TRIANGLES AND THE PYTHAGOREAN THEOREM

Using a formula known as the Pythagorean theorem can help you to figure out the length of unknown sides of right triangles. It's listed on the formula sheet, but you should memorize it anyway.

> Pythagorean theorem: $c^2 = a^2 + b^2$
> where **c** always represents the hypotenuse and **a** and **b** represent the other sides of a right triangle.

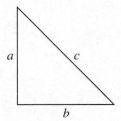

EXAMPLE ONE

What is the length of *EF*?

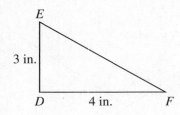

Step one: Replace the formula with numbers from the diagram.

$c^2 = a^2 + b^2$ becomes $c^2 = 3^2 + 4^2$
(it doesn t matter which side you use as **a** or **b**)

Step two: Continue the equation by solving the exponents.

$c^2 = 3^2 + 4^2$ becomes $c^2 = 9 + 16$
$c^2 = 25$

Step three: Find the square root of c^2

$$\sqrt{25} = 5$$

Answer: $\overline{EF}$ **= 5 in.**

EXAMPLE TWO

What is the length of $\overline{AC}$?

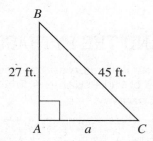

Step one: $c^2 = a^2 + b^2$ becomes $45^2 = 27^2 + b^2$

Step two: 2025 = 729 + b^2
               −729   −729
               1296 = b^2

Step three: Find the square root of b^2

$\sqrt{1296} = 36$

Answer: $\overline{AC}$ **= 36 ft.**

EXAMPLE THREE

A carpenter needs to cut a diagonal support for the frame of a wall pictured below. How long should it be?

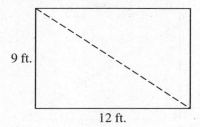

Step one: $c^2 = a^2 + b^2$ becomes $c^2 = 9^2 + 12^2$

Step two: $c^2 = 81 + 144 = c^2 = 225$

Step three: $c = \sqrt{225} = 15$

Answer: 15 feet

EXAMPLE FOUR

Kyla hikes .6 mile due north across a meadow. She then turns and hikes .8 mile due east. How far is she from her starting point?

The "due north" and "due east" phrases are immediate tip-offs that you're working with right triangles and the Pythagorean theorem. Remember that.

Step one: Draw a diagram.

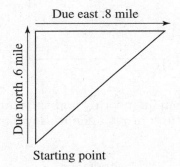

Step two: $c^2 = a^2 + b^2$ becomes $c^2 = .6^2 + .8^2$

$$c^2 = .36 + .64 = c^2 = 1$$

Step three: $c = \sqrt{1} = 1$

Answer: 1 mile

PRACTICE—PYTHAGOREAN THEOREM

1. What is the length of $\overline{BC}$ in the diagram below?

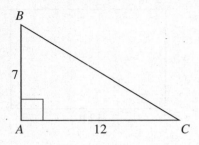

   (1) 15
   (2) 13.6
   (3) $\sqrt{193}$
   (4) 95
   (5) not enough information is given

2. A telephone pole is 40 ft. high and perpendicular to the ground. It needs to be supported by a wire staked into the dirt 30 ft. from the base of the pole and attached to its top. How long is the wire?

3. In the diagram below, what is the length of $\overline{DF}$?

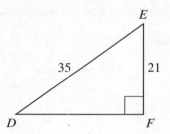

4. A sailboat takes off from its mooring and sails due south for 12 miles, then due east for 16 miles and drops anchor. How far is it from its mooring?

ANSWERS

1. **3**   2. **50 ft.**   3. **28**   4. **20 miles**

GEOMETRY AND PROPORTION

These questions are frequently asked and each is somewhat different from the other. The solutions all rely on your knowledge of geometry and proportion.

EXAMPLE ONE

On line segment $\overline{AC}$, $\overline{BC}$ = 18 inches. $\overline{AB}:\overline{BC}$ = 2:3. What is the length, in inches, of $\overline{AB}$?

Step one: $x : 18 = 2:3$ or $\dfrac{x}{18} = \dfrac{2}{3}$

Step two; Cross-multiply, then solve the proportion.

$$3x = 36 \qquad\qquad \frac{3x}{3} = \frac{36}{3}$$
$$x = 12$$

Answer: $\overline{AB}$ = 12 inches

EXAMPLE TWO

A tree casts a shadow of 72 ft. at the same time that a 6-ft. man's shadow measures 8 ft. How tall is the tree?

Shadow questions are proportion questions. Set up the proportions in the correct order and solve.

Step one: height of tree : shadow of tree
$$x \qquad : \qquad 72$$

height of man : shadow of man
$$6 \qquad : \qquad 8$$

Step two: Convert to fractional proportions, cross-multiply, and solve.

$$\frac{x}{72} = \frac{6}{8} \text{ (reduce) } \frac{x}{72} = \frac{3}{4}$$
$$\frac{216}{4} = \frac{4x}{4}$$
$$x = 54$$

Answer: 54 ft.

EXAMPLE THREE

Based on a survey answered by 900 people, the pie graph above shows where holiday shoppers buy the majority of their gifts. How many people surveyed purchased the majority of their gifts at small shops?

Be careful. The segments of the pie are represented by *degrees*, not percentages. There are 360° in a circle, so:

Step one: Create a proportion.

    Small shop degrees : total degrees
            40°   :   360°

    small shop buyers : total buyers
            x   :   900

Step two: Solve.

$$\frac{40}{360} = \frac{x}{900} \text{ (reduce) } \frac{1}{9} = \frac{x}{900}$$

$$\frac{9x}{9} = \frac{900}{9}$$

$$x = 100$$

Answer: 100 people

EXAMPLE FOUR

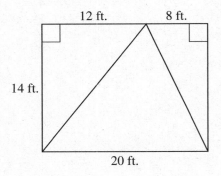

What is the ratio of the area of the triangle to the area of the rectangle?

This may look complicated, but it's quite simple. *Don't* be distracted by the 90° markers or the 12 ft. measurement. *Do* remember your formulas.

Area of a rectangle = *lw*

Area of a triangle = $\frac{1}{2}$ (*bh*)

In the diagram, the length and width of the rectangle are the same as the base and height of the triangle. Since the area of the triangle is *half* the length × width of the rectangle, its area would be half the size of the rectangle's. Therefore, the ratio would be 1:2.

Answer: 1:2

PRACTICE—GEOMETRY AND PROPORTION

1.

If line segment $\overline{AC}$ = 120 ft. and the ratio of $\overline{AB} : \overline{BC}$ = 3:5, what is the length of $\overline{AB}$?

2. A 35-foot telephone pole casts a shadow 21 ft. tall at the same time that a lamppost's shadow measures 12 ft. How tall is the lamppost?

3.

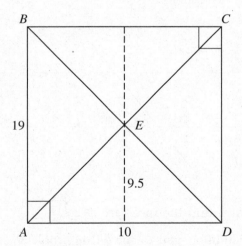

What is the ratio of the combined areas of △*AED* and △*BEC* to the area of ▭ *ABCD*?

4.

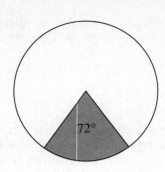

The shaded area of the chart represents the number of Acme employees who bring their children to day-care centers before work. If there are 465 employees at Acme, how many do *not* bring their children to day-care centers before coming to work?

Answers

1. **45 feet**   3. **1 : 2**

2. **20 feet**   4. **372**

GEOMETRY AND ALGEBRA

To answer these challenging problems, you must know facts, formulas and procedures from both disciplines.

EXAMPLE ONE

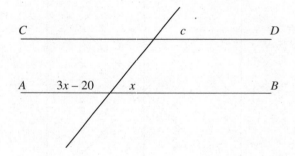

In the diagram above, find the measure of $\angle c$.

The key fact that will allow you to solve this problem is that a straight angle = 180°. You should recognize that $3x - 20$ and x are supplementary.

Step one: Set up an equation and solve for x.

$$3x - 20 + x = 180$$

$$4x - 20 = 180$$
$$+\ 20 \qquad +\ 20$$
$$\frac{4x}{4} = \frac{200}{4}$$
$$x = 50°$$

Step two: Find m ∠*c* based on the measure of ∠*x*

That's easy. The diagram is a transversal—∠*c* = ∠*x*

Answer: m ∠c = 50°

EXAMPLE TWO

In a triangle, the largest angle is 18 more than twice the smallest angle. The other angle is 18 more than the smallest angle. What is the size of the *largest* angle?

The key fact here is that the sum of all angles in a triangle is always 180°.

Step one: Build a box.

Largest ∠ = 2*x* + 18
Middle ∠ = *x* + 18
Smallest ∠ = *x*

Step two: Set up an equation and solve for *x*. Add all the angles together with their sum equaling 180°.

$2x + 18 + x + 18 + x = 180$ becomes

$$4x + 36 = 180$$
$$\underline{- 36 \quad - 36}$$
$$\frac{4x}{4} = \frac{144}{4}$$
$$x = 36$$

Step three: Find the measure of the largest angle. Go back to the box for the "largest angle" sentence: Largest ∠ = 2*x* + 18 and replace *x* with 36.

Answer: largest angle is 90°

PRACTICE—GEOMETRY AND ALGEBRA

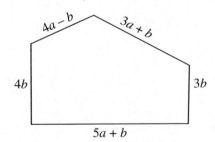

1. What is the perimeter of the figure above?

Questions 2 and 3 are based on the diagram below.

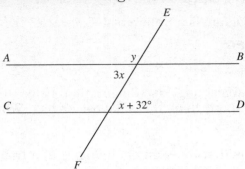

2. Solve for x. (Hint: set up equation using rules of transversals: $3x = x + 32$)

3. What is m $\angle y$?

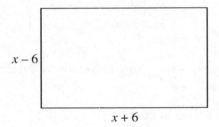

4. If the area of the above rectangle equals 108 sq. ft., find both its length and width.

5. In a scalene triangle, the measure of the largest angle is four more than two times the smallest and the other angle is two more than the smallest. What is the measure of the largest angle?

ANSWERS

1. **$12a + 8b$**

2. **$x = 16°$**

3. **$y = 132°$**

4. **18, 6**

5. **91°**

CHAPTER REVIEW

Fill in the answer grids, and use a calculator where indicated.

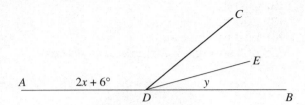

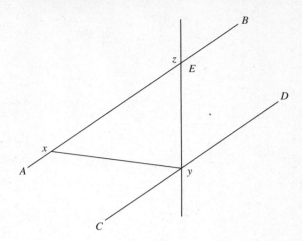

 1. In the diagram above, ∠*ADB* is a straight angle. If m ∠*BDC* = *x* and $\overline{DE}$ bisects ∠*BDC*, what is the measure of ∠*y*?

(1) 29°
(2) 58°
(3) 60°
(4) 26°
(5) not enough information is given

3. In the diagram above, $\overline{AB} \parallel \overline{CD}$ and m ∠*E* = 125°. Which of the following cannot be true?

(1) △*xyz* is a right triangle
(2) △*xyz* is a scalene triangle
(3) △*xyz* is an equilateral triangle
(4) m ∠*z* = m ∠*y*
(5) △*xyz* is an isoceles triangle

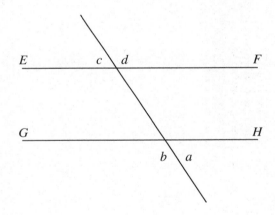

2. In the diagram above, m ∠*a* = 2*x*. Which expression represents m ∠*d*?

(1) $2x + 180°$
(2) $180° - 2x$
(3) $2x - 180°$
(4) $\dfrac{180}{2x}$
(5) $2x(180°)$

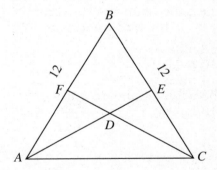

4. In the diagram above, $\overline{AB} = \overline{BC}$, $\overline{AE}$ bisects ∠*BAC*, and $\overline{CF}$ bisects ∠*ACB*. If m ∠*BAC* = 70°, what is the measure in degrees of ∠*D*?

5.

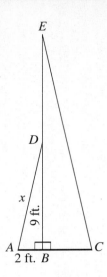

In the above diagram, if $\overline{BE}$ = 18 ft. and $\overline{AC}$ = 6 ft., what is the length of $\overline{EC}$?

(1) $2x - 90°$
(2) $3x$
(3) $x + 18$
(4) $x + 11$
(5) $2x$

6. A bird flies due south from its nest for 5 miles, then due west for 12 miles. How far is the bird from its nest?

(1) 18 miles
(2) 16 miles
(3) 14 miles
(4) between 14 and 15 miles
(5) 13 miles

7. In the line segment $\overline{JL}$ above, the ratio of $\overline{JK} : \overline{KL}$ = 7:2. If $\overline{JK}$ = 35 inches, what is the length of $\overline{KL}$?

(1) $\frac{1}{2}$ ft.

(2) $\frac{3}{4}$ ft.

(3) $\frac{5}{6}$ ft.

(4) 1 ft.
(5) not enough information is given

8. If a building casts a shadow of 120 ft. and, at the same time, a tree's shadow measures 60 ft., how tall is the building?

(1) 100 ft.
(2) 240 ft.
(3) 200 ft.
(4) half the tree's size
(5) not enough information is given

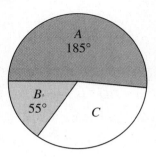

9. In the chart above, what *percent* of the pie is represented by C?

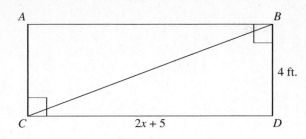

C $2x + 5$ D

4 ft.

Answers

1. **1**
2. **2**
3. **3**
4. **110**
5. **5**
6. **5**
7. **3**
8. **5**
9. **33.3**
10. **29**

10. In the diagram above, $\triangle CDB$ has an area of 58 sq. ft. What is the length in feet of $\overline{CD}$?

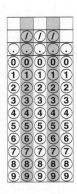

Test-taking Strategies

A sure strategy for success on the Mathematics section of the GED is to learn how to quickly solve every type of problem you might be likely to find there. That means familiarizing yourself with all concepts, formulas, and operations in the seven previous chapters.

Achieving that level of familiarity with the material is not always possible. Furthermore, it's certainly not necessary in order to pass the test. Though requirements vary from state to state, it's safe to say that if you answer at least 30 out of the 50 problems in the section correctly, you'll pass (check with the appropriate agency in your state or region to find out the exact requirements).

Though they are no replacement for knowing the material, here are some test-taking strategies specific to the Math section that should prove helpful.

THE TWO-STEP EVALUATION

"What am I being asked to find?" and "How do I find it?" are the two most important questions you need to answer when approaching any math problem.

Step one: After reading each question, say to yourself,

"I need to find...."

It could be the value of x, the length of side $\overline{AB}$ in $\triangle ABC$, or the percent of questions Susan answered incorrectly on a test. Whatever it is, do *not* proceed with any calculations or attempt to eliminate any of the choices until you feel confident you know what you're being asked to find.

If you're in doubt, carefully reread the problem, paying special attention to the *last sentence*, which tells you specifically what you need to find. If you're still unsure, immediately skip to the next problem.

Step two: Once you are certain of what you need to find, say to yourself,

"I find the answer by doing this: ...."

Avoid reviewing the multiple choices before beginning calculation. There are four wrong answers there that can serve to mislead you. Instead, pause a moment and think carefully. Ask yourself the following:

- Is this a single- or multistep problem?

- What operations and formulas will I use?

- What information given in the problem will be useful?

- Is there a diagram, and, if so, how can it help?

- Do I need to draw my own diagram?

- Is there important information *missing* from the problem that can't be figured out? If so, immediately choose (5) *not enough information is given*, and move to the next problem.

- Is there unnecessary information that must be ignored?

With practice, the answers to these questions will come to you quickly. Begin working, doing your calculations on scrap paper. The scrap paper will *not* be collected, but get in the habit of writing neatly and precisely anyway. Neatness helps in avoiding errors and can aid in making you feel more confident about your work.

Come up with an answer and carefully compare it with the multiple choices. You should find a match among the five offered.

Quick review:

Step one: "I need to find...."

Step two: "I find the answer by doing this: ...."

Try using this way of approaching a problem in the example below.

EXAMPLE

Parking meters in Springfield read: "12 minutes for 25 cents. Maximum deposit—$2.50." What is the maximum time, in hours, that a driver may be legally parked at one of these meters?

(1) 1
(2) 1.2
(3) 120
(4) 2
(5) not enough information is given

Step one: What are you being asked to find?

"I need to find the maximum hours a driver can park."

Not maximum deposit—that's given. Not maximum minutes, even though the information is provided in minutes. You need to find the maximum hours a driver can park, using the information provided.

Step two: How do you find the answer?

"I find the maximum hours a driver can park by doing this:"

Now it's time to think, using the questions listed above. This is a multistep problem. You're given a maximum *deposit*, and from that information you can calculate a maximum *time*. You'll also need to convert maximum minutes to hours. You know 25 cents buys a driver 12 minutes of parking time, so:

(1) 12 min. $\times$ 10 (the number of 25-cent deposits in $2.50) = 120 min.

Now, you need to convert 120 minutes to hours:

(2) $\dfrac{120 \text{ min.}}{60 \text{ min.}}$ = 2 hours

Answer: (4) 2

If you'd reviewed the multiple choices first, you might have been misled. Choice (5) looks tempting because the problem doesn't mention a "maximum *time*" and choice (3) seems appealing because it's the correct number of minutes, not hours. Again, attempt to solve the problem before looking at the answer choices.

Try this two-step evaluation strategy with every problem on the Mathematics section. It should help to keep you focused during a time when anxiety tends to creep in.

SKIPPING AND RETURNING

The questions on the Mathematics section do *not* increase in difficulty; more difficult questions alternate with easier ones in a random pattern throughout the test. It is a far better strategy to direct your time and attention to all the questions you feel confident in answering quickly and correctly than to spend excessive time trying to solve very difficult questions you have a greater chance of getting wrong. Therefore, you should be ready to make a quick judgment about each problem using the Two-step Evaluation.

If you

- are unsure of what you're being asked to find

    or

- you know what you have to find but are unsure how to proceed

    or

- you know what to find and how to proceed, but feel it will take a while to get a correct answer,

skip the problem and go to the next one.

You may find yourself skipping more than half the problems on the test your first time around. That's O.K.

Establish a system for recording your skips. On your answer grid, put a checkmark to the left of each problem you skip and be especially mindful of the problem numbers *at all times* whether skipping or entering answers. You don't want to make the discovery more than halfway through the section that you just entered an answer on the grid space (31) for problem (32)! Careful attention to the question numbers will avoid this problem.

After you finish the last question on your first time through, return to those questions you skipped. Now attempt the ones you know how to solve but initially judged to be too time-consuming. Do not obsess over any one problem. If you divide the 90 minutes allotted for the section by 50 problems, that allows you an average of about 1½ minutes per question. If you feel two minutes have slipped away and you're still not even close to an answer, make your best guess and *move on*. Mark the answer grid with a different symbol—perhaps an X— and return to the question later, if you have time.

PLUGGING IN

There will be a handful of occasions when, after doing a Two-step Evaluation, you decide it's quicker and easier to use the multiple choices to get an answer to the problem instead of calculating an answer on your own. *Plugging in* is a strategy in which you choose what looks like a correct answer from the multiple choices and plug it in to a formula or operation to see if it works.

EXAMPLE

Which of the following is a solution to the inequality:

$3x + 7 > 23$?

    (1) 4
    (2) 6
    (3) 2
    (4) 5
    (5) 4.5

Using the Two-step Evaluation, you'd say to yourself, I need to find the value for "x," which can be gotten by setting up and solving this multistep equation,

    or...

you could go directly to the multiple choices, pick what looks like a correct answer, and plug it in to the inequality. Choice (1) looks good; try plugging it in on paper or in your head.

$$3(4) + 7 > 23 \ldots 12 + 7 > 23 \ldots 19 > 23?$$

Close, but wrong. Try another—choice (4). It's easy to do and you don't have to deal with the decimal that's in choice (5).

$$3(5) + 7 > 23 \ldots 22 > 23$$

Really close, but still not large enough to make the inequality a true statement. However, you now know the answer must be choice (2) because it's the only number larger than choice (5).

Answer: (2) 6

ELIMINATING

Eliminating choices you *know* are wrong so that you can spend more time considering choices that *might* be right is a standard test-taking strategy. Consider this:

EXAMPLE

A hockey team won x games, lost y games, and tied z games. What fractional part of the games played were won?

(1) $\dfrac{x}{x + y + z}$

(2) $\dfrac{x}{xyz}$

(3) $\dfrac{x}{xy}$

(4) $\dfrac{x}{x + y}$

(5) $\dfrac{x}{x - y - z}$

Since x represents the number of games won, it has to be in the numerator. All choices have x as a numerator, so you can't eliminate any yet. But the denominator has to represent a **sum** of all the games, which means **addition** would have to be included. Therefore, choices (2), (3), and (5) can be eliminated. You've narrowed the possibilities down to only two possible choices and, by doing so, have more than doubled your chances of getting the answer correct, even if you have to guess between choices (1) and (4). The correct answer, of course is (1) because it represents the sum of *all* games.

MAKING AN EDUCATED GUESS

It's important to remember that the penalty for a wrong answer is the same as it is for a blank answer. **You have nothing to lose by guessing; it's essential that you fill in every answer on the grid, leaving no blanks.** Sometimes, you might be unsure of how to reach a solution to a problem. In these situations, making an educated guess using common sense and elimination is the only logical strategy you can use.

EXAMPLE

Martin has a piece of lumber 9 ft. 8 in. long. He wishes to cut it into four equal lengths. How far from the edge should he make his first cut?

(1) 2.5 ft.
(2) 2 ft. 5 in.
(3) 2.9 ft.
(4) 29 ft.
(5) 116 in.

The wording in this problem might be confusing to some. "How far from the edge" is an overly complicated way of asking, "How long would the first of the four pieces be?" Also, there are numerous conversions to consider: feet to inches, feet to feet and inches, feet and inches to feet and inches in a decimal setup, etc. Even if you aren't quite sure this problem requires you to divide 9 ft. 8 in. by 4, you can eliminate choices (4) and (5). Common sense tells you that the board is just a bit less than 10 feet. Choice (4)—29 ft.—is almost three times longer than the board's length, and choice (5)—116 inches—is exactly equal to its length. It's impossible to make cuts anywhere on the board using these answers. All the other answers are close. A 60% chance of getting a correct answer (eliminating 2 out of 5 choices, then guessing) is better than a 20% chance (eliminating none and guessing). The correct answer is (**2**).

USING THE FORMULA PAGE

Review the formulas on page 726 now. You will probably notice that most of the information provided there you've already memorized, especially the section on perimeter, area, and volume. If you haven't memorized these formulas but clearly understand when to apply each one, use the page as a study sheet to "lock in" your knowledge. Knowing them is a big time-saver and confidence booster. The same is true for the Pythagorean theorem.

The formulas for distance between points and slope of a line do not need to be committed to memory; use the page.

The formulas for mean and median are poorly written and confusing. If you don't already have these concepts committed to memory, use the explanations in Chapter 19, Numbers and Basic Operations, as your guide. The same can be said for interest, distance, and cost.

USING THE PRACTICE EXAMS

The Practice Test that immediately follows this chapter and the two Practice Exams at the end of the book provide excellent opportunities for you to apply what you have learned. It's important that you create a test-taking environment as similar as possible to the one in which you'll take the GED. Set aside two 45-minute blocks of uninterrupted time, use the answer grids provided and scrap paper, and keep an honest eye on the clock. Pace yourself, take mental note of the strategies mentioned that work for you, and notice successful strategies you come up with on your own.

The practice test and exams all have answers, answer explanations, and references to chapters and subsections in the book where you can find help with a particular problem.

CHAPTER 26

Practice
Mathematics Test

T his test is designed to give you practice in taking the two sections of the Math part of the GED exam. When taking the test, give yourself the benefit of realistic conditions. Select a quiet place, and allow yourself two 45-minute periods for each part. Use a calculator only for the first section. If you finish in less than the allowed time, use the remaining minutes to check your work

After you have completed the test, use the answer key to find your score and then study the solutions and explanations. You may discover new ways to attack problems. Also you will obtain help on the questions that you could not answer, and you will be able to correct any errors that you have made.

Remember that you do not have to get a perfect score to pass the test. If you find that you are weak on a certain topic, review the material in the text on that topic.

FORMULAS

Description	Formula
AREA (A) of a:	
square	$A = s^2$; where s = side
rectangle	$A = lw$; where l = length, w = width
parallelogram	$A = bh$; where b = base, h = height
triangle	$A = \frac{1}{2} bh$; where b = base, h = height
trapezoid	$A = \frac{1}{2}(b_1 + b_2)\, h$; where b = base, h = height
circle	$A = \pi r^2$; where π = 3.14, r = radius
PERIMETER (P) of a:	
square	$P = 4s$; where s = side
rectangle	$P = 2l + 2w$; where l = length, w = width
triangle	$P = a + b + c$; where a, b, and c are the sides
circumference (C) of a circle	$C = \pi d$; where π = 3.14, d = diameter
VOLUME (V) of a:	
cube	$V = s^3$; where s = side
rectangular container	$V = lwh$; where l = length, w = width, h = height
cylinder	$V = \pi r^2 h$; where π = 3.14, r = radius, h = height
square pyramid	$V = \frac{1}{3}(\text{base edge})^2 h$
cone	$V = \frac{1}{3}\pi r^2 h$
Pythagorean theorem	$c^2 = a^2 + b^2$; where c = hypotenuse, a and b are legs, of a right triangle
distance (d) between two points in a plane	$d = \sqrt{(x_2 - x_1)^2 + (y_2 - y_1)^2}$; where (x_1, y_1) and (x_2, y_2) are two points in a plane
slope of a line (m)	$m = \dfrac{y_2 - y_1}{x_2 - x_1}$; where (x_1, y_1) and (x_2, y_2) are two points in a plane
MEASURES OF CENTRAL TENDENCY	mean = $\dfrac{x_1 + x_2 + \ldots + x_n}{n}$; where the x's are the values for which a mean is desired, and n = number of values in the series
	median = the point in an ordered set of numbers at which half of the numbers are above and half of the numbers are below this value
simple interest (i)	$i = prt$; where p = principal, r = rate, t = time
distance (d) as function of rate and time	$d = rt$; where r = rate, t = time
total cost (c)	$c = nr$; where n = number of units, r = cost per unit

PRACTICE TEST, PART I

You have 45 minutes to complete this part. You MAY use a calculator, if needed. Fill in the answer grids where they are provided.

1. In a theater audience of 650 people, 80% were adults. How many children were in the audience?

   (1) 130
   (2) 150
   (3) 450
   (4) 500
   (5) 520

2. On a certain map 1 inch represents 60 miles. If two towns are 255 miles apart, what is the distance, in inches, between the towns on the map?

3. A carpenter has a board 4 feet 3 inches in length. He cuts off a piece 2 feet 8 inches in length. The length of the piece that is left is

   (1) 1 ft. 5 in.
   (2) 2 ft. 7 in.
   (3) 2 ft. 5 in.
   (4) 1 ft. 7 in.
   (5) 2 ft. 3 in.

4. A cardboard crate is 5 feet long, 3 feet wide, and 2 feet tall. What is its holding capacity in cubic feet?

5. 50 kilometers =

   (1) 5,000 miles
   (2) 50,000 centimeters
   (3) 50,000 meters
   (4) 500,000 millimeters
   (5) 1,000 kilograms

6. If O is the center of the circle and m $\angle B$ = 52°, find m $\angle O$.

   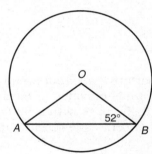

   (1) 52°
   (2) 76°
   (3) 80°
   (4) 94°
   (5) not enough information is given

7. On line segment $\overline{AC}$, $AB : BC = 3 : 5$ and $BC = 20$ inches.

   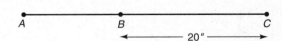

   The length, in inches, of $\overline{AB}$ is

   (1) 3
   (2) 10
   (3) 12
   (4) 15
   (5) 16

8. The diagram below represents a cross section of a pipe. If the diameter of the outer circle is $7\frac{1}{2}$ inches and the diameter of the inner circle is $4\frac{1}{2}$ inches, what is the thickness of the pipe wall, represented by x?

(1) 1 in.
(2) $1\frac{1}{4}$ in.
(3) $1\frac{1}{2}$ in.
(4) 2 in.
(5) 3 in.

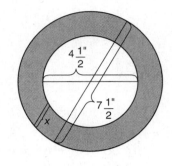

9. Mr. Gray's weekly salary was increased from $400 per week to $500 per week. The percent increase in his salary was

(1) 20%
(2) 25%
(3) 80%
(4) 100%
(5) 125%

10. A shopper buys a loaf of bread at x cents and 2 pounds of coffee at y cents per pound. If she pays with a $20 bill, the number of cents she receives in change is

(1) $2000 - x - y$
(2) $2000 - (x - y)$
(3) $2000 - x + y$
(4) $2000 - (x + 2y)$
(5) $x + y - 2000$

11. The area of a rectangular living room is 240 square feet. If the length of the room is 20 feet, what is the perimeter, in feet, of the room?

(1) 12
(2) 32
(3) 50
(4) 64
(5) not enough information is given

12. A woman buys a Thanksgiving Day turkey weighing 19 pounds 6 ounces. If the turkey sells for $0.88 per pound, how much change does the woman receive from a $20 bill?

(1) $1.95
(2) $2.05
(3) $2.95
(4) $3.95
(5) $4.15

13. A crew of painters can paint an apartment in $4\frac{1}{2}$ hours. What part of the apartment can they paint in $2\frac{1}{2}$ hours? (Round answer to the nearest hundredth.)

Question 14 refers to the chart below.

Planet	Distance from the Sun in Kilometers
Mercury	57,900,000
Venus	108,200,000
Earth	149,600,000
Mars	227,900,000

14. A small planet is discovered halfway between Venus and the sun. What is its distance from the sun in kilometers? Express the distance in scientific notation.

(1) 54.1×10^6
(2) 5.7×10^5
(3) $.541 \times 10^8$
(4) 1.082×10^9
(5) 5.41×10^7

15. The expression $x^2 - 5x + 6$ may be written as

(1) $(x + 3)(x + 2)$
(2) $(x + 3)(x - 2)$
(3) $(x - 3)(x - 2)$
(4) $(x - 3)(x + 2)$
(5) $x(5x + 6)$

16. Joshua earns $72 for typing 20 pages. At the same rate, how much does he earn for typing 15 pages?

   (1) $48
   (2) $54
   (3) $60
   (4) $72
   (5) $84

17. At Adams High School 402 students are taking Spanish and French. If twice as many students take Spanish as take French, how many students take Spanish?

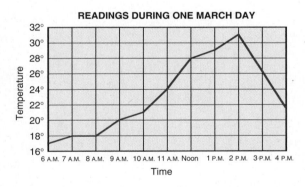

18. According to the graph below, which of the following statements is correct?

READINGS DURING ONE MARCH DAY

Temperature (y-axis: 16° to 32°)
Time (x-axis: 6 A.M. 7 A.M. 8 A.M. 9 A.M. 10 A.M. 11 A.M. Noon 1 P.M. 2 P.M. 3 P.M. 4 P.M.)

   (1) The change in temperature between 7 A.M. and noon was 8°.
   (2) The highest temperature reached during the day was 32°.
   (3) The change in temperature between 8 A.M. and noon was −10°.
   (4) The temperature did not change between 7 A.M. and 8 A.M.
   (5) The temperature at noon was 30°.

19. A shipment of 2,200 pounds of sugar is packed in 40-ounce bags. How many bags will be packed?

   (1) 640
   (2) 750
   (3) 780
   (4) 800
   (5) 880

20. A ship sails 8 miles due east and then 15 miles due north. At this point, how many miles is the ship from its starting point?

21. A book salesman earns 12% commission on sales. Last month he sold a set of 300 textbooks at $20 per book, a group of 20 art books at $50 per book, and a shipment of 400 novels at $25 per book. What was his commission for the month?

   (1) $204
   (2) $1,700
   (3) $2,040
   (4) $17,000
   (5) $20,400

22. Mrs. Alvin bought 120 shares of RST Corporation at $32.75 per share and sold these shares a year later at $36.50 per share. Her profit before paying commission and taxes was

   (1) $400
   (2) $450
   (3) $480
   (4) $520
   (5) $560

23. Mr. and Mrs. Donato went on a vacation motor trip. When the trip started, the odometer reading in their car was 8,947 miles. When the trip was completed the odometer reading was 9,907 miles. How many gallons of gas, to the nearest gallon, were used on the trip?

(1) 36
(2) 38
(3) 40
(4) 41
(5) not enough information is given

24. What is the area of the rectangle below?

$3a^2b^3$

$5a^3b^4$

(1) $16a^{10}b^{14}$
(2) $8a^5b^{12}$
(3) $15a^5b^7$
(4) $15a^6b^{12}$
(5) $16a^6b^{12}$

25. The number of miles per hour needed to cover 120 miles in x hours may be expressed as

(1) $\dfrac{120}{x}$

(2) $\dfrac{x}{120}$

(3) $120x$
(4) $120 + x$
(5) $x - 120$

END OF PART I

PRACTICE TEST, PART II

You have 45 minutes to complete this part. You MAY NOT use a calculator. Fill in the answer grids where they are provided.

26. In 5 years the population of a town decreased from 3,500 to 2,800. The percent of decrease was

    (1) 20%
    (2) 25%
    (3) 30%
    (4) 40%
    (5) 70%

27. Mr. Fox's will provided that his wife receive $\frac{1}{2}$ of his estate, and his three sons divide the rest equally. If each son's share was $8,000, what was the value of the estate?

    (1) $24,000
    (2) $32,000
    (3) $40,000
    (4) $48,000
    (5) $50,000

28. A class has 32 students. On a certain day x students are absent. What fractional part of the class is present on that day?

    (1) $\dfrac{x}{32}$

    (2) $\dfrac{32-x}{x}$

    (3) $\dfrac{x}{32-x}$

    (4) $\dfrac{32-x}{32}$

    (5) $\dfrac{32-x}{32+x}$

29. The Shore Multiplex Theater charges $9 for matinee movies and $12 for evening shows. On one day, 267 matinee tickets and 329 evening tickets were sold. An expression that represents the total receipts, in dollars, for that day is

    (1) 12(267) + 9(329)
    (2) 9(267) + 12(329)
    (3) 21(267 + 329)
    (4) 9(267 + 329) + 12(267 + 329)
    (5) 12(267 + 329)

30. Frank had x dollars. He bought y articles for z dollars each. The number of dollars Frank had left was

    (1) $yz - x$
    (2) $yx - z$
    (3) $x - yz$
    (4) $x + yz$
    (5) $xy + z$

Questions 31 and 32 are based on the following information.

   The fare schedule for Checker Taxi is shown below:

First one-fifth mile	2 dollars
Each one-fifth mile after the first	20 cents

31. How much would a 3-mile trip cost (not including tip)?

    (1) $3.00
    (2) $3.80
    (3) $4.00
    (4) $4.80
    (5) $5.00

32. If a passenger has exactly $10.00, how many miles can she ride and still be able to give the driver a tip of at least $1.00?

    (1) 7 or less
    (2) more than 7 but less than 8
    (3) more than 8 but less than 9
    (4) more than 9 but less than 10
    (5) less than 6

33. In the diagram below, a semicircle surmounts a rectangle whose length is $2a$ and whose width is a. A formula for finding A, the area of the whole figure, is

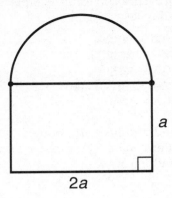

(1) $A = 2a^2 + \dfrac{1}{2}\pi a^2$

(2) $A = 2\pi a^2$

(3) $A = 3\pi a^2$

(4) $A = 2a^2 + \pi a^2$

(5) not enough information is given

34. The graph indicates the way a certain man spends his day. Which one of the following statements is correct?

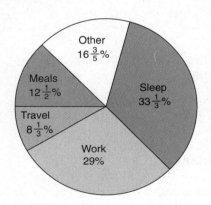

(1) The man works 8 hrs. per day.
(2) The man spends 1 hr. more on meals than he does on travel.
(3) The man sleeps 7 hrs. per day.
(4) The man spends half his time on work and travel.
(5) The man spends 4 hrs. on meals.

35. *ABCD*, shown in the diagram below, is a rectangle. The ratio of the area of $\triangle EDC$ to the area of the rectangle *ABCD* is

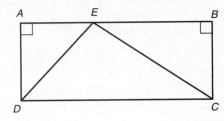

(1) $1:4$
(2) $1:3$
(3) $1:2$
(4) $3:5$
(5) $3:4$

36. If $y = 2x^2(z - 3)$, find the value of y if $x = 5$ and $z = 7$.

(1) 54
(2) 150
(3) 180
(4) 200
(5) 400

37. On a motor trip Mr. Shore covered $\dfrac{2}{7}$ of his total trip distance during the first day by driving 384 miles. The total distance to be covered, in miles, is

(1) 98
(2) 1,244
(3) 1,306
(4) 1,344
(5) 1,500

38. The UNIRING Corp. offers all its cell phone customers a 2% reduction off their monthly bills if they pay online instead of mailing in their payment.

   If Emmy's cell phone bill for March is $106 and a postage stamp is 46 cents, how much does she save by paying online for that month?

39. In a right triangle, the ratio of the two acute angles is 3 : 2. The number of degrees in the larger acute angle is

   (1) 36
   (2) 54
   (3) 72
   (4) 90
   (5) not enough information is given

40. If $3x - 1 < 5$, then x must be

   (1) greater than 2
   (2) less than 2
   (3) greater than 3
   (4) less than 0
   (5) greater than 5

41. If $\overrightarrow{AB} \parallel \overrightarrow{GH}$, m $\angle BDE = 100°$, $\overrightarrow{DJ}$ bisects $\angle BDE$, $\overrightarrow{EJ}$ bisects $\angle DEH$, find m $\angle J$ in degrees.

   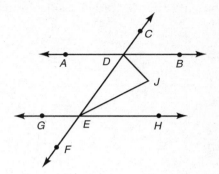

42. A chair was marked for sale at $315. This was a discount of 25% off the original price. What was the original price of the chair?

   (1) $236.50
   (2) $390
   (3) $420
   (4) $450
   (5) $520

43. There are 48 couples at a dance. Each couple consists of 1 male and 1 female. Mr. Fowler selects a female dancing partner for the next dance at random. What is the probability that Mr. Fowler selects his wife?

    (1) $\dfrac{1}{50}$

    (2) $\dfrac{1}{48}$

    (3) $\dfrac{2}{48}$

    (4) $\dfrac{1}{2}$

    (5) $\dfrac{2}{3}$

44. Which inequality is true?

    (1) $\dfrac{4}{5} > \dfrac{2}{3} > \dfrac{5}{7}$

    (2) $\dfrac{5}{7} > \dfrac{2}{3} > \dfrac{4}{5}$

    (3) $\dfrac{4}{5} > \dfrac{5}{7} > \dfrac{2}{3}$

    (4) $\dfrac{2}{3} > \dfrac{4}{5} > \dfrac{5}{7}$

    (5) $\dfrac{5}{7} > \dfrac{4}{5} > \dfrac{2}{3}$

Question 45 refers to the following coordinate graph.

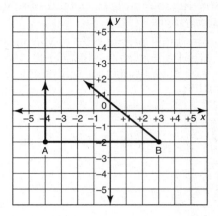

45. At what point on the graph will the line extending from point A intersect with the line extending from point B? Fill in the coordinate grid.

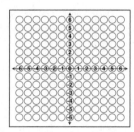

46. A family spent $\dfrac{1}{4}$ of its income for rent and $\dfrac{1}{5}$ of its income for food. What percent of its income remains?

    (1) 40%
    (2) 45%
    (3) 50%
    (4) 52%
    (5) 55%

47. A tree is 24 feet tall and casts a shadow of 10 feet. At the same time a tower casts a shadow of 25 feet. What is the height, in feet, of the tower?

    (1) 45
    (2) 60
    (3) 75
    (4) 80
    (5) 84

48. Mr. Capiello is on a diet. For breakfast and lunch together, he consumes 40% of his allowable number of calories. If he still has 1,200 calories left for the day, his daily calorie allowance is

    (1) 2,000
    (2) 2,200
    (3) 2,400
    (4) 2,500
    (5) 2,800

49. If $3x - y = 11$ and $2y = 8$, then $x =$

    (1) 3
    (2) 4
    (3) $4\frac{1}{2}$
    (4) 5
    (5) 6

50. On the number line below, $\sqrt{7}$ is located at point

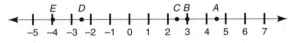

    (1) A
    (2) B
    (3) C
    (4) D
    (5) E

Answer Key

1.	**1**	26.	**1**
2.	**¹⁷⁄₄, or 4.25**	27.	**4**
3.	**4**	28.	**4**
4.	**30**	29.	**2**
5.	**3**	30.	**3**
6.	**2**	31.	**4**
7.	**3**	32.	**2**
8.	**3**	33.	**1**
9.	**2**	34.	**2**
10.	**4**	35.	**3**
11.	**4**	36.	**4**
12.	**3**	37.	**4**
13.	**⁵⁄₉, or .56**	38.	**$2.58**
14.	**5**	39.	**2**
15.	**3**	40.	**2**
16.	**2**	41.	**90**
17.	**268**	42.	**3**
18.	**4**	43.	**2**
19.	**5**	44.	**3**
20.	**17**	45.	**(–4,4)**
21.	**3**	46.	**5**
22.	**2**	47.	**2**
23.	**5**	48.	**1**
24.	**3**	49.	**4**
25.	**1**	50.	**3**

WHAT'S YOUR SCORE?

_____right   _____wrong

Excellent	45–50
Good	39–44
Fair	34–38

If your score was low, the explanation of the correct answers that follows will help you. You may obtain additional help and practice by referring to the review material.

ANSWER ANALYSIS

Following the correct answer are the chapter and section containing the material covered in the question.

1. **1** Chapter 21 (Word Problems)
If 80% of the audience were adults, 100% – 80% = 20% were children. 20% = 0.20, and 0.20(650) = 130

2. **$^{17}/_4$, or 4.25**   Chapter 20 (Ratio)
Let x = number of inches between the towns on the map.
Set up a proportion:

$$\frac{1 \text{ in.}}{60 \text{ mi.}} = \frac{x \text{ in.}}{225 \text{ mi.}}$$

$$60x = 255$$
$$x = \frac{255}{60} = 4\frac{1}{4} = 4.25$$

3. **4** Chapter 20 (Standard Measures)

$$\frac{\begin{array}{r} 4 \text{ ft. } 3 \text{ in.} \\ -2 \text{ ft. } 8 \text{ in.} \end{array}}{} = \frac{\begin{array}{r} 3 \text{ ft. } 15 \text{ in.} \\ -2 \text{ ft. } 8 \text{ in.} \end{array}}{1 \text{ ft. } 7 \text{ in.}}$$

4. **30** Chapter 19 (Basic Geometry and Volume)
v = lwh. The container is 5 ft. long × 3 ft. wide × 2 ft. high. (5 × 3 × 2 = 30 cu. ft.)

5. **3** Chapter 20 (Standard Measures)
Since 1 km = 1,000 m, 50 km = 50,000 m.

6. **2** Chapter 24 (Triangles)

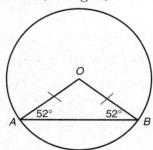

$OA = OB$, since each is a radius.
m∠A = m∠B = 52°
m∠A + m∠B + m∠O = 180°
52 + 52 + m∠O = 180
104 + m∠O = 180
m∠O = 180 – 104 = 76°

7. **3** Chapter 24 (Geometry and Proportion)

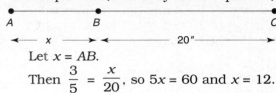

Let $x = AB$.
Then $\frac{3}{5} = \frac{x}{20}$, so $5x = 60$ and $x = 12$.

8. **3** Chapter 21 (Circles)

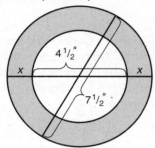

Let x = thickness of the pipe.
Then $x + x + 4\frac{1}{2} = 7\frac{1}{2}$

so $2x = 3$ and $x = 1\frac{1}{2}$ in.

9. **2** Chapter 21 (Percent Increase)

$$\text{Percent increase} = \frac{\text{actual increase}}{\text{original amount}}$$

Actual increase: $500 – $400 = $100

Percent increase: $\frac{100}{400} = \frac{1}{4} = 25\%$

10. **4** Chapter 23 (Setups and Variables)
The shopper gives the storekeeper $20.00, or 2,000 cents. From this amount the storekeeper takes out x cents for the bread and $2y$ cents for the coffee. The result is $2,000 - (x + 2y)$.

11. **4** Chapter 19 (Basic Geometry)
Draw a diagram:

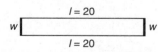

Since $A = lw = 240$, then $20w = 240$, and $w = 12$. Then
$P = 2(l + w) = 2(20 + 12) = 2(32) = 64$.

12. **3** Chapter 20 (Standard Measures)

$$6 \text{ oz.} = \frac{6}{16} = \frac{3}{8} \text{ lb.}$$

19 lb. costs 19($0.88) = $16.72

$\frac{3}{8}$ lb. costs $\frac{3}{\cancel{8}}(\cancel{\$0.88}) = \$0.33$

$19\frac{3}{8}$ lb. costs $16.72 + $.33 = $17.05

Change = $20.00 – $17.05 = $2.95.

13. **⅝, or .56** Chapter 20 (Word Problems)
The part of the apartment painted in $2\frac{1}{2}$ hours =

$$\frac{2\frac{1}{2}}{4\frac{1}{2}} = \frac{5}{2} \div \frac{9}{2} = \frac{5}{2} \times \frac{2}{9} = \frac{5}{9} = .56$$

14. **5** Chapter 21 (Scientific Notation)
To find the halfway mark between Venus and the sun:

$$\frac{108,200,000}{2} = 54,100,000 \text{ km}$$

Then, count the number of places moved to the left until the decimal is at 5.4. That number is 7. Scientific notation for the distance is 5.4×10^7.

15. **3** Chapter 23 (Multiplying Binomials)
The expression $x^2 - 5x + 6$ factors as $(x - 3)(x - 2)$. If you can't factor, check each choice by multiplying out.

16. **2** Chapter 20 (Ratio)
Let x = amount Joshua earns for typing 15 pages.
Set up a proportion:

$$\frac{\text{pages typed}}{\text{dollars earned}} : \frac{20}{72} = \frac{15}{x}$$

$$20x = 15 \times 72 = 1,080, \text{ and}$$
$$x = 1,080 \div 20 = \$54.$$

17. **268** Chapter 23 (Word Problems)
Let x = number of students taking French,
and $2x$ = number of students taking Spanish.
$$x + 2x = 402$$
$$3x = 402$$
$$x = 402 \div 3 = 134$$
$$2x = 2(134) = 268$$

18. **4** Chapter 22 (Line Graphs)
Note on the graph that the temperature neither rose nor fell, that is, it did not change, between 7 A.M. and 8 A.M.

19. **5** Chapter 20 (Standard Measures)
Since there are 16 oz. in 1 lb.
2,200 lb. = 2,200 × 16 = 35,200 oz.
35,200 ÷ 40 = 880

20. **17** Chapter 24 (Pythagorean Theorem)
Use the Pythagorean theorem.
$$x^2 = 8^2 + 15^2$$
$$= 64 + 225$$
$$= 289$$
$$x = \sqrt{289} = 17$$

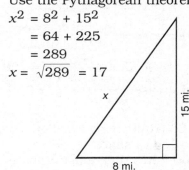

21. **3** Chapter 21 (Word Problems)
Textbook sales: 300 × $20 = $6,000
Art book sales: 20 × $50 = $1,000
Novel sales: 400 × $25 = $10,000
Total sales = $17,000
Commission: 12% of $17,000 = $2,040

22. **2** Chapter 21 (Word Problems)
Profit per share:
$36.50 – $32.75 = $3.75
Total profit: 120 × $3.75 = $450

23. **5** Chapter 19 (Word Problems)
You could subtract to find the number of miles driven, but since the number of miles per gallon is not given, the problem cannot be solved.

24. **3** Chapter 22 (Multiplying Variables)
$A = lw$ Multiply the numbers (5 × 3), but add the like exponents $a^3 + a^2 = a^5$ and $b^4 + b^3 = b^7$
$15a^5b^7$

25. 1 Chapter 23 (Setups with Variables)
Use the relationship
Rate × Time = Distance
or Rate = $\dfrac{\text{distance}}{\text{time}}$
In this case, distance = 120 mi. and time = x
Therefore, the number of miles per
hour is $\dfrac{120}{x}$.

26. 1 Chapter 21 (Percent Decrease)

Percent decrease = $\dfrac{\text{actual decrease}}{\text{original number}}$

Actual decrease: 3,500 – 2,800 = 700

Percent decrease: $\dfrac{700}{3,500} = \dfrac{1}{5} = 20\%$

27. 4 Chapter 20 (Multiplying Fractions)
$8,000 = 1 son's share
$3 × \$8,000 = \$24,000$, amount left to
three sons
$\$24,000 = \dfrac{1}{2}$ of the estate
$2(\$24,000) = \$48,000$, value of the full
estate.

28. 4 Chapter 23 (Setups with Variables)
If there are 32 students in the class
and x students are absent, then
$32 - x$ students are present.
The fractional part of the students
present is $\dfrac{32 - x}{32}$.

29. 2 Chapter 19 (Multistep Word Problems)
To find the total receipts, find the receipts
of the matinee performances and add to
these the receipts of the evening
performances.
$9(267) + 12(329) =$ total receipts

30. 3 Chapter 23 (Setups with Variables)
Frank spent yz dollars.
Subtract yz from x. The result is $x - yz$.

31. 4 Chapter 20 (Word Problems)
Note that, after the first $\dfrac{1}{5}$ mi., the
fare amounts to $1 per mile. Therefore, a
3-mi. trip would cost $2 for the second
and third miles. The first $\dfrac{1}{5}$ mi. would
cost $2, and each of the next $\dfrac{4}{5}$'s would
cost 20 cents each, for a total of $2.80.
The entire 3-mi. trip would cost
$2.00 + \$2.80 = \$4.80$.

32. 2 Chapter 20 (Word Problems)
Taking $1 tip from the $10 available
leaves $9 for the actual travel. The first
$\dfrac{1}{5}$ mi. costs $2, leaving $7. Since
the fare is $1 per mile thereafter,
the trip could be as long as $7\dfrac{1}{5}$ mi.

33. 1 Chapter 24 (Geometry and Algebra)
Area of rectangle = $(2a)(a) = 2a^2$.
Radius of semicircle = $\dfrac{1}{2}(2a) = a$.
The formula for the area of a circle is
$A = \pi r^2$.
Area of semicircle = $\dfrac{1}{2}(\pi a^2)$.
Area of whole figure =
$2a^2 + \dfrac{1}{2}\pi a^2$.

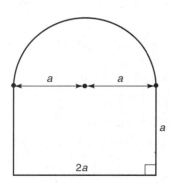

34. 2 Chapter 21 (Percents)
The man spends 12½% (or .125) on meals
in a 24-hour day.
.125 × 24 = 3 hours
.0833 × 24 = 1.99 or 2
The man spends an hour more a day on
meals than on traveling. Some other
choices can be eliminated by common
sense; others must be multiplied as above
before being eliminated.

35. **3** Chapter 24 (Geometry and Proportion)

Area of $\triangle EDC = \frac{1}{2}(DC)h$

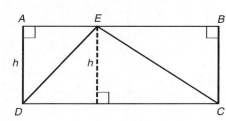

Area of rectangle $ABCD = (DC)h$.
Thus, area of $\triangle EDC$ is equal to one-half area of rectangle $ABCD$. Ratio of area of $\triangle EDC$ to area of rectangle $ABCD = 1 : 2$.

36. **4** Chapter 23 (Finding Values with Given Variables)

$y = 2x^2(z - 3)$
$= 2(5)(5)(7 - 3)$
$= 2(5)(5)(4)$
$= 200$

37. **4** Chapter 20 (Word Problems)

Let x = total distance to be covered.

$\frac{2}{7}x = 384$

$2x = 7(384) = 2,688$

$x = 2,688 \div 2 = 1,344$

38. **$2.58**   Chapter 21 (Percents)

2% of 106 = 106 × .02 = 2.12 + .46
(unused stamp) = $2.58

39. **2** Chapter 24 (Geometry and Proportion)

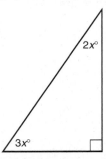

Let $3x$ = measure of the larger angle, and $2x$ = measure of the smaller angle.

$3x + 2x = 90$
$5x = 90$
$x = 90 \div 5 = 18$
$3x = 3(18) = 54°$

40. **2** Chapter 23 (Inequalities)

$3x - 1 < 5$
$3x < 6$
$x < 2$

x must be less than 2.

41. **90**   Chapter 24 (Transversals, Triangles)

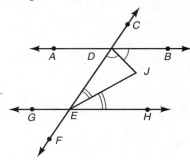

m∠BDE = 100°
Since $\overleftrightarrow{AB} \parallel \overleftrightarrow{GH}$, m∠$BDE$ + m∠DEH = 180°
100 + m∠DEH = 180
m∠DEH = 180 − 100 = 80°

m∠$JDE = \frac{1}{2}$ m∠BDE = 50°

m∠$DEJ = \frac{1}{2}$ m∠DEH = 40°

m∠J + 50 + 40 = 180
m∠J = 180 − 50 − 40 = 90°

42. **3** Chapter 21 (Word Problems)

25% = $\frac{1}{4}$. Selling price of chair

was $\frac{3}{4}$ of original selling price.

Let x = original selling price.

$\frac{3}{4}x = \$315$

$x = \$315 \div \frac{3}{4} = \$315 \times \frac{4}{3} = \$420$

43. **2** Chapter 20 (Probability)

Probability =

$\dfrac{\text{number of successful outcomes}}{\text{number of possible outcomes}}$

In this case, the number of successful outcomes is 1 since, of the 48 women present, only 1 woman is Mr. Fowler's wife. The number of possible outcomes is 48 since there are 48 possible women partners.

Probability = $\frac{1}{48}$

44. 3 Chapter 23 (Inequalities)

$\frac{4}{5} > \frac{5}{7}$ because $4 \times 7 > 5 \times 5$

$\frac{5}{7} > \frac{2}{3}$ because $5 \times 3 > 7 \times 2$

Thus, $\frac{4}{5} > \frac{5}{7} > \frac{2}{3}$ is correct.

Alternative Method:
Convert the three fractions to decimals, to the nearest hundredth.

$\frac{5}{7} = 0.71, \frac{4}{5} = 0.80, -\frac{2}{3} = 0.67$

Therefore, $\frac{4}{5} > \frac{5}{7} > \frac{2}{3}$

45. (–4,4) Chapter 23 (Coordinates)

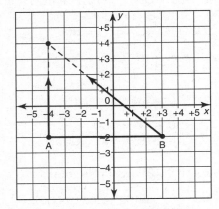

Line starting at point A stays right on the –4 coordinate for x. Use a straight edge (edge of a piece of paper) to trace the diagonal path of line, starting at point B. It intersects A at +4, which is the y coordinate.

46. 5 Chapter 21 (Converting Fractions to Percents)

Fractional part of income spent on

rent and food: $\frac{1}{4} + \frac{1}{5} = \frac{5}{20} + \frac{4}{20} = \frac{9}{20}$

$1 - \frac{9}{20} = \frac{11}{20}$, remaining income,

$\frac{11}{20} = 0.55 = 55\%$.

47. 2 Chapter 24 (Geometry and Proportion)

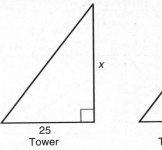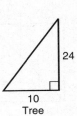

Let x = height of tower.
Set up a proportion.

$\frac{\text{height of object}}{\text{length of shadow}} : \frac{x}{25} = \frac{24}{10}$

$10x = 25(24) = 600$
$x = 600 \div 10 = 60$

48. 1 Chapter 21 (Word Problems)
If Mr. Capiello has consumed 40% of his allowable calories, he has 60% left.
Let x = his daily allowance of calories
$0.60x = 1,200$
$x = 1,200 \div 0.60 = 2,000$

49. 4 Chapter 23 (Working with Variables)
Since $2y = 8$, then $y = 4$.
$3x - y = 11$
$3x - 4 = 11$
$3x = 15$ and $x = 5$

50. 3 Chapter 23 (Points on a Number Line)
Since $2^2 = 4$ and $3^2 = 9$, $\sqrt{7}$ is between 2 and 3. On the number line, only point C lies between 2 and 3.

TWO PRACTICE
EXAMS

ANSWER SHEET FOR THE PRACTICE EXAM

TEST 1: LANGUAGE ARTS, WRITING, PART I

1. ① ② ③ ④ ⑤
2. ① ② ③ ④ ⑤
3. ① ② ③ ④ ⑤
4. ① ② ③ ④ ⑤
5. ① ② ③ ④ ⑤
6. ① ② ③ ④ ⑤
7. ① ② ③ ④ ⑤
8. ① ② ③ ④ ⑤
9. ① ② ③ ④ ⑤
10. ① ② ③ ④ ⑤
11. ① ② ③ ④ ⑤
12. ① ② ③ ④ ⑤
13. ① ② ③ ④ ⑤
14. ① ② ③ ④ ⑤
15. ① ② ③ ④ ⑤
16. ① ② ③ ④ ⑤
17. ① ② ③ ④ ⑤
18. ① ② ③ ④ ⑤
19. ① ② ③ ④ ⑤
20. ① ② ③ ④ ⑤

21. ① ② ③ ④ ⑤
22. ① ② ③ ④ ⑤
23. ① ② ③ ④ ⑤
24. ① ② ③ ④ ⑤
25. ① ② ③ ④ ⑤
26. ① ② ③ ④ ⑤
27. ① ② ③ ④ ⑤
28. ① ② ③ ④ ⑤
29. ① ② ③ ④ ⑤
30. ① ② ③ ④ ⑤
31. ① ② ③ ④ ⑤
32. ① ② ③ ④ ⑤
33. ① ② ③ ④ ⑤
34. ① ② ③ ④ ⑤
35. ① ② ③ ④ ⑤
36. ① ② ③ ④ ⑤
37. ① ② ③ ④ ⑤
38. ① ② ③ ④ ⑤
39. ① ② ③ ④ ⑤
40. ① ② ③ ④ ⑤

41. ① ② ③ ④ ⑤
42. ① ② ③ ④ ⑤
43. ① ② ③ ④ ⑤
44. ① ② ③ ④ ⑤
45. ① ② ③ ④ ⑤
46. ① ② ③ ④ ⑤
47. ① ② ③ ④ ⑤
48. ① ② ③ ④ ⑤
49. ① ② ③ ④ ⑤
50. ① ② ③ ④ ⑤

TEST 2: SOCIAL STUDIES

1. ① ② ③ ④ ⑤
2. ① ② ③ ④ ⑤
3. ① ② ③ ④ ⑤
4. ① ② ③ ④ ⑤
5. ① ② ③ ④ ⑤
6. ① ② ③ ④ ⑤
7. ① ② ③ ④ ⑤
8. ① ② ③ ④ ⑤
9. ① ② ③ ④ ⑤
10. ① ② ③ ④ ⑤
11. ① ② ③ ④ ⑤
12. ① ② ③ ④ ⑤
13. ① ② ③ ④ ⑤
14. ① ② ③ ④ ⑤
15. ① ② ③ ④ ⑤
16. ① ② ③ ④ ⑤
17. ① ② ③ ④ ⑤
18. ① ② ③ ④ ⑤
19. ① ② ③ ④ ⑤
20. ① ② ③ ④ ⑤

21. ① ② ③ ④ ⑤
22. ① ② ③ ④ ⑤
23. ① ② ③ ④ ⑤
24. ① ② ③ ④ ⑤
25. ① ② ③ ④ ⑤
26. ① ② ③ ④ ⑤
27. ① ② ③ ④ ⑤
28. ① ② ③ ④ ⑤
29. ① ② ③ ④ ⑤
30. ① ② ③ ④ ⑤
31. ① ② ③ ④ ⑤
32. ① ② ③ ④ ⑤
33. ① ② ③ ④ ⑤
34. ① ② ③ ④ ⑤
35. ① ② ③ ④ ⑤
36. ① ② ③ ④ ⑤
37. ① ② ③ ④ ⑤
38. ① ② ③ ④ ⑤
39. ① ② ③ ④ ⑤
40. ① ② ③ ④ ⑤

41. ① ② ③ ④ ⑤
42. ① ② ③ ④ ⑤
43. ① ② ③ ④ ⑤
44. ① ② ③ ④ ⑤
45. ① ② ③ ④ ⑤
46. ① ② ③ ④ ⑤
47. ① ② ③ ④ ⑤
48. ① ② ③ ④ ⑤
49. ① ② ③ ④ ⑤
50. ① ② ③ ④ ⑤

TEST 3: SCIENCE

1. ① ② ③ ④ ⑤	21. ① ② ③ ④ ⑤	41. ① ② ③ ④ ⑤
2. ① ② ③ ④ ⑤	22. ① ② ③ ④ ⑤	42. ① ② ③ ④ ⑤
3. ① ② ③ ④ ⑤	23. ① ② ③ ④ ⑤	43. ① ② ③ ④ ⑤
4. ① ② ③ ④ ⑤	24. ① ② ③ ④ ⑤	44. ① ② ③ ④ ⑤
5. ① ② ③ ④ ⑤	25. ① ② ③ ④ ⑤	45. ① ② ③ ④ ⑤
6. ① ② ③ ④ ⑤	26. ① ② ③ ④ ⑤	46. ① ② ③ ④ ⑤
7. ① ② ③ ④ ⑤	27. ① ② ③ ④ ⑤	47. ① ② ③ ④ ⑤
8. ① ② ③ ④ ⑤	28. ① ② ③ ④ ⑤	48. ① ② ③ ④ ⑤
9. ① ② ③ ④ ⑤	29. ① ② ③ ④ ⑤	49. ① ② ③ ④ ⑤
10. ① ② ③ ④ ⑤	30. ① ② ③ ④ ⑤	50. ① ② ③ ④ ⑤
11. ① ② ③ ④ ⑤	31. ① ② ③ ④ ⑤	
12. ① ② ③ ④ ⑤	32. ① ② ③ ④ ⑤	
13. ① ② ③ ④ ⑤	33. ① ② ③ ④ ⑤	
14. ① ② ③ ④ ⑤	34. ① ② ③ ④ ⑤	
15. ① ② ③ ④ ⑤	35. ① ② ③ ④ ⑤	
16. ① ② ③ ④ ⑤	36. ① ② ③ ④ ⑤	
17. ① ② ③ ④ ⑤	37. ① ② ③ ④ ⑤	
18. ① ② ③ ④ ⑤	38. ① ② ③ ④ ⑤	
19. ① ② ③ ④ ⑤	39. ① ② ③ ④ ⑤	
20. ① ② ③ ④ ⑤	40. ① ② ③ ④ ⑤	

TEST 4: LANGUAGE ARTS, READING

1. ① ② ③ ④ ⑤	16. ① ② ③ ④ ⑤	31. ① ② ③ ④ ⑤
2. ① ② ③ ④ ⑤	17. ① ② ③ ④ ⑤	32. ① ② ③ ④ ⑤
3. ① ② ③ ④ ⑤	18. ① ② ③ ④ ⑤	33. ① ② ③ ④ ⑤
4. ① ② ③ ④ ⑤	19. ① ② ③ ④ ⑤	34. ① ② ③ ④ ⑤
5. ① ② ③ ④ ⑤	20. ① ② ③ ④ ⑤	35. ① ② ③ ④ ⑤
6. ① ② ③ ④ ⑤	21. ① ② ③ ④ ⑤	36. ① ② ③ ④ ⑤
7. ① ② ③ ④ ⑤	22. ① ② ③ ④ ⑤	37. ① ② ③ ④ ⑤
8. ① ② ③ ④ ⑤	23. ① ② ③ ④ ⑤	38. ① ② ③ ④ ⑤
9. ① ② ③ ④ ⑤	24. ① ② ③ ④ ⑤	39. ① ② ③ ④ ⑤
10. ① ② ③ ④ ⑤	25. ① ② ③ ④ ⑤	40. ① ② ③ ④ ⑤
11. ① ② ③ ④ ⑤	26. ① ② ③ ④ ⑤	
12. ① ② ③ ④ ⑤	27. ① ② ③ ④ ⑤	
13. ① ② ③ ④ ⑤	28. ① ② ③ ④ ⑤	
14. ① ② ③ ④ ⑤	29. ① ② ③ ④ ⑤	
15. ① ② ③ ④ ⑤	30. ① ② ③ ④ ⑤	

TEST 5: MATHEMATICS, PART I

1. ① ② ③ ④ ⑤

2. ① ② ③ ④ ⑤

3. ① ② ③ ④ ⑤

4. ① ② ③ ④ ⑤

5.

6. ① ② ③ ④ ⑤

7. ① ② ③ ④ ⑤

8. ① ② ③ ④ ⑤

9.

10. ① ② ③ ④ ⑤

11.

12. ① ② ③ ④ ⑤

13.

14. ① ② ③ ④ ⑤

15. ① ② ③ ④ ⑤

16. ① ② ③ ④ ⑤

17. ① ② ③ ④ ⑤

18. ① ② ③ ④ ⑤

19. ① ② ③ ④ ⑤

20. ① ② ③ ④ ⑤

21. ① ② ③ ④ ⑤

22. ① ② ③ ④ ⑤

23.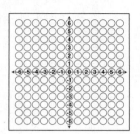

24.

25. ① ② ③ ④ ⑤

TEST 5: MATHEMATICS, PART II

26. ① ② ③ ④ ⑤
27. ① ② ③ ④ ⑤
28. ① ② ③ ④ ⑤
29. ① ② ③ ④ ⑤
30. ① ② ③ ④ ⑤

31.

32. ① ② ③ ④ ⑤
33. ① ② ③ ④ ⑤
34. ① ② ③ ④ ⑤

35.

36. ① ② ③ ④ ⑤
37. ① ② ③ ④ ⑤
38. ① ② ③ ④ ⑤
39. ① ② ③ ④ ⑤
40. ① ② ③ ④ ⑤
41. ① ② ③ ④ ⑤
42. ① ② ③ ④ ⑤

43.

44.

45. ① ② ③ ④ ⑤
46. ① ② ③ ④ ⑤
47. ① ② ③ ④ ⑤
48. ① ② ③ ④ ⑤
49. ① ② ③ ④ ⑤
50. ① ② ③ ④ ⑤

PRACTICE EXAM ONE

TEST 1: LANGUAGE ARTS, WRITING, PART I

DIRECTIONS

The first part of the GED exam measures the test taker's ability to correctly and sufficiently analyze the English language. This section focuses on the written, not spoken, word and consists of both multiple-choice questions and an essay.

The first half of this section consists of multiple-choice questions with paragraphs that have numbered sentences. Some of these sentences contain errors such as usage, sentence structure, and mechanics. Multiple-choice questions follow each of these passages. For questions that refer to sentences that are already correctly written, choose the answer that doesn't change the sentence. Sometimes the best answer is the one that makes a sentence's point of view or verb tense consistent with the rest of the paragraph.

You are given 120 minutes (two hours) for this section of the exam. We recommend that you spend 75 minutes working on the multiple-choice questions, and 45 minutes on the essay. A separate set of directions is given for the essay after the multiple-choice questions.

To mark your answer, darken the corresponding circle on the answer sheet.

FOR EXAMPLE:

Sentence 1: **Participating in a team sport builds trust and self confidence.**

What correction should be made to this sentence?

(1) remove <u>team</u>
(2) insert a hyphen between <u>self</u> and <u>confidence</u>
(3) change <u>builds</u> to <u>build</u>
(4) capitalize <u>team sport</u>
(5) no correction is necessary

In this example, the word *self confidence* requires a hyphen; therefore, answer space 2 would be marked on the answer sheet.

GO ON TO THE NEXT PAGE

TEST 1: LANGUAGE ARTS, WRITING, PART I

<u>Questions 1–9</u> refer to the following paragraphs.

(A)

(1) Safe food must be planned and not left to chance, for the consumer, food safety begins in the marketplace. (2) All cooperative efforts made by states and the U.S. department of agriculture to make available a clean, safe, wholesome food supply will be in vain unless the consumer takes certain precautions to keep it that way. (3) The precautions to be taken by the consumer include care in buying, storing, handling, and cooking food.

(B)

(4) Shop for groceries last after all other errands has been run. (5) Take foods home immediately and don't leave them unattended for a long period of time. (6) Sufficient light in grocery stores is necessary to enable you to adequately view foods four proper selection. (7) Store personnel should make sure that foods are replaced frequently in order to keep it as fresh as possible.

(C)

(8) Under no circumstances buy swollen or leaking cans. (9) The food in a swollen or leaking can may be dangerous to eat or even to taste.

(D)

(10) Ask the checkout clerk to bag cold foods together so that they keep cold longer; interspersed with room-temperature foods, they may warm up quickly.

1. Sentence 1: **Safe food must be planned and not left to <u>chance, for</u> the consumer, food safety begins in the marketplace.**

   Which of the following is the best way to write the underlined portion of this sentence? If you think the original is the best way, choose option (1).

   (1) chance, for
   (2) chance: for
   (3) chance; for
   (4) chance, For
   (5) chance. For

2. Sentence 2: **All cooperative efforts made by states and the U.S. department of agriculture to make available a clean, safe, wholesome food supply will be in vain unless the consumer takes certain precautions to keep it that way.**

   What correction should be made to this sentence?

   (1) insert a hyphen in <u>cooperative</u>
   (2) capitalize <u>department</u> and <u>agriculture</u>
   (3) remove the comma after <u>clean</u>
   (4) change <u>it</u> to <u>them</u>
   (5) no correction is necessary

3. Sentence 3. **The precautions to be taken by the consumer include care in buying, storing, handling, and cooking food.**

   If you rewrote sentence 3 beginning with

   <u>Care in buying, storing, handling and cooking food</u>

   the next words should be

   (1) include
   (2) is
   (3) is among
   (4) would be among
   (5) will be among

4. Sentence 4: **Shop for groceries last after all other errands has been run.**

   What correction should be made to this statement?

   (1) insert a comma after <u>last</u>
   (2) remove the word <u>other</u>
   (3) change <u>run</u> to <u>ran</u>
   (4) change <u>has been</u> to <u>have been</u>
   (5) no correction is necessary

GO ON TO THE NEXT PAGE

TEST 1: LANGUAGE ARTS, WRITING, PART I

5. Sentence 5: **Take foods home immediately <u>and don't</u> leave them unattended for a long period of time.**

   Which of the following is the best way to write the underlined portion of this sentence? If you think the original is the best way, choose option (1).

   (1) and don't
   (2) also don't
   (3) but don't
   (4) however don't
   (5) nevertheless don't

6. Sentence 6: **Sufficient light in grocery stores is necessary to enable you to adequately view foods four proper selection.**

   What correction should be made to this sentence?

   (1) change the spelling of <u>four</u> to <u>for</u>
   (2) insert a comma after <u>stores</u>
   (3) change the spelling of <u>necessary</u> to <u>necessery</u>
   (4) insert a comma after <u>foods</u>
   (5) no correction is necessary

7. Sentence 7: **Store personnel should make sure that foods are replaced frequently in order to keep it as fresh as possible.**

   What correction should be made to this sentence?

   (1) change <u>it</u> to <u>them</u>
   (2) change the spelling of <u>personnel</u> to <u>personal</u>
   (3) change <u>should</u> to <u>might</u>
   (4) change <u>fresh</u> to <u>freshly</u>
   (5) no change is necessary

8. Sentences 8 and 9: **Under no circumstances buy swollen or leaking cans. The food in a swollen or leaking can may be dangerous to eat or even to taste.**

   The most effective combination of sentences 8 and 9 would include which of the following groups of words?

   (1) which contain food that may be
   (2) and the food in a swollen can
   (3) since the food in a swollen can
   (4) being dangerous to eat
   (5) that may be dangerous to eat

9. Which of the following is the thesis statement for the passage?

   (1) sentence 1
   (2) sentence 3
   (3) sentence 4
   (4) sentence 10
   (5) none; thesis statement is implied

<u>Questions 10–18</u> refer to the following paragraphs.

   (1) The traditional family grouping will remain dominant, although the people in the family may change because of divorce, separation, and remarriage. (2) The family with dual careers, both husband and wife working, will increase—particularly among the young. (3) The husband and wife family with no children will also increase.

   (4) Some couples will choose to remain childless, others will spend the major part of their lifetime with no children present because of the possibilities for spacing and limiting family size.

   (5) An increasing number of single-parent families will be formed as a result of divorce, death, abandonment, or the choice of the unwed to rear its children alone. (6) In most cases, the single-parent family will have an employed woman as its head.

GO ON TO THE NEXT PAGE

TEST 1: LANGUAGE ARTS, WRITING, PART I

(7) Because of increased acceptability, more individuals may remain unmarried and establish single households. (8) The single adult living alone will establish close kin or simulated kin networks, relying upon and sharing with others economic and emotional resources to fulfill parentlike roles in an "aunt-uncle" capacity.

(9) These family forms will present different issues and problems for family members.

(10) Families will need information to select wisely the family pattern they want to pursue.

10. Sentence 1: **The traditional family grouping will remain <u>dominant, although</u> the people in the family may change because of divorce, separation, and remarriage.**

    Which of the following is the best way to write the underlined portion of this sentence? If you think the original is the best way, choose option (1).

    (1) dominant, although
    (2) dominant, indeed
    (3) dominant, so
    (4) dominant, therefore
    (5) dominant, nevertheless

11. Sentences 2 and 3: **The family with dual careers, both husband and wife working, will increase—particularly among the young. The husband and wife family with no children will also increase.**

    The most effective combination of sentences 2 and 3 would include which of the following groups of words?

    (1) as well as
    (2) but
    (3) although
    (4) nevertheless
    (5) therefore

12. Sentence 4: **Some couples will choose to remain <u>childless, others</u> will spend the major part of their lifetime with no children present because of the possibilities for spacing and limiting family size.**

    Which of the following is the best way to write the underlined portion of this sentence? If you think the original is the best way, choose option (1).

    (1) childless, others
    (2) childless. others
    (3) childless. Others
    (4) childless; Others
    (5) childless: others

13. Sentence 5: **An increasing number of single-parent families will be formed as a result of divorce, death, abandonment, or the choice of the unwed to rear its children alone.**

    What correction should be made to this sentence?

    (1) change <u>its</u> to <u>their</u>
    (2) change the spelling of <u>families</u> to <u>familys</u>
    (3) remove the comma after <u>abandonment</u>
    (4) change <u>rear</u> to <u>raise</u>
    (5) no correction is necessary

14. Sentence 6: **In most cases, the single-parent family will have an employed woman as its head.**

    What correction should be made to this sentence?

    (1) remove the comma after <u>cases</u>
    (2) remove the hyphen in <u>single-parent</u>
    (3) change <u>will have</u> to <u>has</u>
    (4) change <u>its</u> to <u>it's</u>
    (5) no change is necessary

GO ON TO THE NEXT PAGE

TEST 1: LANGUAGE ARTS, WRITING, PART I

15. Sentence 7: **Because of increased acceptability, more individuals may remain unmarried and establish single households.**

    What correction should be made to this sentence?

    (1) change the spelling of <u>acceptability</u> to <u>acceptibility</u>
    (2) remove the comma after <u>acceptability</u>
    (3) change <u>may remain</u> to <u>will remain</u>
    (4) insert a comma after <u>unmarried</u>
    (5) no correction is necessary

16. Sentence 8: **The single adult living alone will establish close kin or simulated kin networks, relying upon and sharing with others economic and emotional resources to fulfill parentlike roles in an "aunt-uncle" capacity.**

    What correction should be made to this sentence?

    (1) add a comma after <u>close kin</u>
    (2) remove the comma after <u>networks</u>
    (3) change the spelling of <u>resources</u> to <u>resourses</u>
    (4) change <u>to fulfill</u> to <u>fulfilling</u>
    (5) no correction is necessary

17. A new paragraph can

    (1) not be started
    (2) be started after sentence 2
    (3) be started after sentence 5
    (4) be started after sentence 6
    (5) be started before sentence 8

18. Sentence 10: **Families will need information to select wisely the family pattern they want to pursue.**

    What correction should be made to this sentence?

    (1) change <u>will need</u> to <u>will be needing</u>
    (2) change <u>select wisely</u> to <u>wisely select</u>
    (3) change the spelling of <u>pattern</u> to <u>pattren</u>
    (4) change the spelling of <u>pursue</u> to <u>persue</u>
    (5) no correction is necessary

GO ON TO THE NEXT PAGE

TEST 1: LANGUAGE ARTS, WRITING, PART I

<u>Questions 19–27</u> refer to the following paragraphs.

(A)

(1) Drug abuse is like a communicable disease. (2) It spreads—by example, by word of mouth, and by imitation. (3) Drug abuse is certainly increasing, but so is the number of young people who have tried drugs and want out. (4) As we provide treatment services for them, these young people become able to tell other youth that the drug scene is not as great as they thought it was before they got hooked. (5) And, of greater importance, they are believed by they're contemporaries before experimentation becomes habit.

(B)

(6) Parents can help prevent drug usage by setting an example, by knowledge, and by understanding. (7) If they are to talk to their children about drugs they must be informed. (8) usually they know far less about drugs than do their children. (9) Ideally, before their child is tempted to experiment, they will be able to explain to him the undesirability of the drugged life. (10) What is even more convincing to young people, they will have been able to communicate to him the actual damage that a drug abuser does to their body.

19. Sentences 1 and 2: **Drug abuse is like a communicable disease. It spreads—by example, by word of mouth, and by imitation.**

    The most effective combination of sentences 1 and 2 would include which of the following groups of words?

    (1) disease. it spreads
    (2) disease although it spreads
    (3) disease yet it spreads
    (4) disease that spreads
    (5) disease having spread

20. Sentence 3: **Drug abuse is certainly increasing, but so is the number of young people who have tried drugs and want out.**

    What correction should be made to this sentence?

    (1) remove the comma after <u>increasing</u>
    (2) change <u>but</u> to <u>and</u>
    (3) change <u>number</u> to <u>amount</u>
    (4) insert a comma after <u>people</u>
    (5) no correction is necessary

21. Sentence 4: **As we provide treatment services for them, these young people become able to tell other youth that the drug scene is not as great as they thought it was before they got hooked.**

    What correction should be made to this sentence?

    (1) change <u>As</u> to <u>Although</u>
    (2) remove the comma after <u>them</u>
    (3) change <u>become</u> to <u>became</u>
    (4) change <u>thought</u> to <u>think</u>
    (5) no correction is necessary

22. Sentence 5: **And, of greater importance, they are believed by they're contemporaries before experimentation becomes habit.**

    What correction should be made to this sentence?

    (1) remove the commas before <u>of</u> and after <u>importance</u>
    (2) change <u>they're</u> to <u>their</u>
    (3) insert commas before <u>by</u> and after <u>contemporaries</u>
    (4) change <u>becomes</u> to <u>will become</u>
    (5) no correction is necessary

GO ON TO THE NEXT PAGE

TEST 1: LANGUAGE ARTS, WRITING, PART I

23. Sentence 6: **Parents can help prevent drug usage by setting an example, by knowledge, and by understanding.**

    What correction should be made to this sentence?

    (1) change <u>can</u> to <u>could</u>
    (2) change <u>by setting an example</u> to <u>by example</u>
    (3) change the spelling of <u>knowledge</u> to <u>knowlege</u>
    (4) remove the comma before <u>and</u>
    (5) no correction is necessary

24. Sentence 7: **If they are to talk to their children about drugs they must be informed.**

    What correction should be made to this sentence?

    (1) change <u>are to</u> to <u>would</u>
    (2) change <u>their</u> to <u>they're</u>
    (3) insert a comma after <u>drugs</u>
    (4) change <u>informed</u> to <u>informative</u>
    (5) no correction is necessary

25. Sentences 7 and 8: **If they are to talk to their children about drugs they must be <u>informed. usually</u> they know far less about drugs than do their children.**

    Which of the following is the best way to write the underlined portion of this sentence? If you think the original is the best way, choose option (1).

    (1) informed. usually
    (2) informed usually
    (3) informed: usually
    (4) informed—Usually
    (5) informed. Usually

26. Sentence 9: **Ideally, before their child is tempted to experiment, they will be able to explain to him the undesirability of the drugged life.**

    What correction should be made to this sentence?

    (1) change the spelling of <u>ideally</u> to <u>idealy</u>
    (2) remove the comma before <u>before</u>
    (3) change <u>be able</u> to <u>have been able</u>
    (4) change the spelling of <u>undesirability</u> to <u>undesireability</u>
    (5) no correction is necessary

27. Sentence 10: **What is even more convincing to young people, they will have been able to communicate to him the actual damage that a drug abuser does to their body.**

    What correction should be made to this sentence?

    (1) move <u>even</u> to after <u>convincing</u>
    (2) remove the comma after <u>people</u>
    (3) change the spelling of <u>communicate</u> to <u>comunicate</u>
    (4) change <u>their</u> to <u>his</u>
    (5) no change is necessary

GO ON TO THE NEXT PAGE

TEST 1: LANGUAGE ARTS, WRITING, PART I

Questions 28–37 refer to the following paragraphs.

(A)

(1) Statistically, by far the most common type of home accidents are falls. (2) Each year thousands of americans meet death in this way, within the four walls of their home or in yards around their house. (3) Nine out of ten of the victims is over 65, but people of all ages experience serious injuries as a result of home falls. (4) It is impossible to estimate how many injuries result from falls, but it must run into the millions.

(B)

(5) Falls can be a problem for all ages. (6) In the process of growing up, children or teenagers often will fall. (7) Fortunately their bodies are supple, so they may suffer only skinned knees bumps, and bruises. (8) In an older person, however, the same fall may cause a broken arm, leg, or hip, or other injury that requires hospitalization or Medical care. (9) As you get older, you may not fall any more often but the results usually are more serious and may even be fatal.

(C)

(10) Adults fall because they don't look where they're going, are in a hurry, are careless, or thinking about something else. (11) A few inexpensive items such as a suction-type rubber mat or safety strips in the tub, a non-slip mat on the floor, and bathtub handholds can go a long way toward eliminating falls in the bathroom.

28. Sentence 1: **Statistically, by far the most common type of home accidents are falls.**

    What correction should be made to this sentence?

    (1) change the spelling of Statistically to Statisticly
    (2) remove the comma before by
    (3) insert a comma after accidents
    (4) change are to is
    (5) no correction is necessary

29. Sentence 2: **Each year thousands of americans meet death in this way, within the four walls of their home or in yards around their house.**

    What correction should be made to this sentence?

    (1) change americans to Americans
    (2) remove the comma after way
    (3) change within to in
    (4) insert a comma after home
    (5) no correction is necessary

30. Sentence 3: **Nine out of ten of the victims is over 65, but people of all ages experience serious injuries as a result of home falls.**

    What correction should be made to this sentence?

    (1) remove the comma after 65
    (2) change is to are
    (3) change but to and
    (4) change experience to experiance
    (5) no correction is necessary

31. Sentence 4: **It is impossible to estimate how many injuries result from falls, but it must run into the millions.**

    What correction should be made to this sentence?

    (1) change it must run to they must run
    (2) change result to results
    (3) remove the comma after falls
    (4) change but to since
    (5) no correction is necessary

GO ON TO THE NEXT PAGE

TEST 1: LANGUAGE ARTS, WRITING, PART I

32. Sentences 5 and 6: **Falls can be a problem for all <u>ages. In</u> the process of growing up, children or teenagers often will fall.**

    Which of the following is the best way to write the underlined portion of this sentence? If you think the original is the best way, choose option (1).

    (1) ages. In
    (2) ages. in
    (3) ages: In
    (4) ages: in
    (5) ages; In

33. Sentence 7: **Fortunately their bodies are supple, so they may suffer only skinned knees bumps, and bruises.**

    What correction should be made to this sentence?

    (1) change the spelling of <u>Fortunately</u> to <u>Fortunitely</u>
    (2) remove the comma after <u>supple</u>
    (3) change <u>suffer only</u> to <u>only suffer</u>
    (4) insert a comma after <u>knees</u>
    (5) no correction is necessary

34. Sentence 8: **In an older person, however, the same fall may cause a broken arm, leg, or hip, or other injury that requires hospitalization or Medical care.**

    What correction should be made to this sentence?

    (1) remove the commas around <u>however</u>
    (2) change <u>Medical</u> to <u>medical</u>
    (3) insert a colon after <u>cause</u>
    (4) change <u>requires</u> to <u>require</u>
    (5) no correction is necessary

35. Sentence 9: **As you get older, you may not fall any more often but the results usually are more serious and may even be fatal.**

    What correction should be made to this sentence?

    (1) change <u>As</u> to <u>When</u>
    (2) change <u>get</u> to <u>will get</u>
    (3) insert a comma after <u>often</u>
    (4) change <u>more</u> to <u>most</u>
    (5) no correction is necessary

36. Sentence 10: **Adults fall because they don't look where they're going, are in a hurry, are careless, or thinking about something else.**

    What correction should be made to this sentence?

    (1) change <u>don't</u> to <u>doesn't</u>
    (2) change <u>they're</u> to <u>there</u>
    (3) remove the <u>comma</u> after <u>hurry</u>
    (4) insert <u>are</u> before <u>thinking</u>
    (5) no correction is necessary

37. A new paragraph can

    (1) be started after sentence 10
    (2) be started after sentence 8
    (3) be started after sentence 5
    (4) be started after sentence 3
    (5) not be started

GO ON TO THE NEXT PAGE

TEST 1: LANGUAGE ARTS, WRITING, PART I

Questions 38–46 refer to the following paragraphs.

(A)

(1) The only known cure for bikomania, a highly contagious fever sweeping the country from coast to coast, is to ride a bike. (2) Nearly 100 million happy victims, including mom and pop and the kids, now are taking this delightful treatment and pedaling their two-wheelers into an exciting new world of fun and adventure.

(B)

(3) Why buy a bike? Partly because riding a bike benefits both you and you're environment. (4) A bike doesn't foul up the air, makes no noise, keeps you in top physical shape, takes up little room on the road. and is easy to park in a small space. (5) With appropriate accessory's—such as saddle bags, luggage racks, or baskets—a bike can be used on shopping missions, picnic excursions, or bicycle tours.

(C)

(6) What kind of bike should you get? (7) Bewildered by the tantalizing display of racing models with 10-speed gearshifts and lots of fancy gimmicks, your apt to plunge into something you really don't need. (8) Best advice: buy the simplest model that meets your transportation requirements. (9) You need not invest in dropped handlebars, multigear ratios, and special frames that may be too complicated for your purposes.

(D)

(10) Try renting a bike before you buy one. (11) Spend a couple of weekends pedaling various makes over typical terrain in your area; this tryout will answer many of your questions.

38. Sentence 1 should be

(1) left as it is
(2) moved after sentence 8
(3) moved after sentence 5
(4) moved after sentence 3
(5) omitted

39. Sentence 2: **Nearly 100 million happy victims, including mom and pop and the kids, now are taking this delightful treatment and pedaling their two-wheelers into an exciting new world of fun and adventure.**

What correction should be made to this sentence?

(1) remove the comma after <u>victims</u>
(2) capitalize <u>mom, pop</u>
(3) capitalize <u>kids</u>
(4) change the spelling of <u>exciting</u> to <u>exsiting</u>
(5) no correction is necessary

40. Sentence 3: **Why buy a bike? Partly because riding a bike benefits both you and you're environment.**

What correction should be made to this sentence?

(1) change <u>buy</u> to <u>by</u>
(2) insert a comma after <u>and</u>
(3) remove the question mark after <u>bike</u>
(4) change <u>you're</u> to <u>your</u>
(5) no correction is necessary

41. Sentence 4: **A bike doesn't foul up the air, makes no noise, keeps you in top physical shape, takes up little room on the <u>road. and</u> is easy to park in a small space.**

Which of the following is the best way to write the underlined portion of this sentence? If you think the original is the best way, choose option (1).

(1) road. and
(2) road. And
(3) road, and
(4) road, And
(5) road: and

GO ON TO THE NEXT PAGE

TEST 1: LANGUAGE ARTS, WRITING, PART I

42. Sentence 5: **With appropriate accessory's—such as saddle bags, luggage racks, or baskets—a bike can be used on shopping missions, picnic excursions, or bicycle tours.**

    What correction should be made to this sentence?

    (1) change <u>accessory's</u> to <u>accessories</u>
    (2) remove the dashes before <u>such</u> and after <u>baskets</u>
    (3) remove the comma after <u>bags</u>
    (4) change the spelling of <u>excursions</u> to <u>excurshuns</u>
    (5) no change is necessary

43. Sentence 7: **Bewildered by the tantalizing display of racing models with 10-speed gearshifts and lots of fancy gimmicks, your apt to plunge into something you really don't need.**

    What correction should be made to this sentence?

    (1) insert commas before <u>with</u> and after <u>gearshifts</u>
    (2) remove the comma after <u>gimmicks</u>
    (3) change the spelling of <u>your</u> to <u>you're</u>
    (4) change the spelling of <u>really</u> to <u>realy</u>
    (5) no correction is necessary

44. Sentence 8: **<u>Best advice: buy</u> the simplest model that meets your transportation requirements.**

    Which of the following is the best way to write the underlined portion of this sentence? If you think the original is the best way, choose option (1).

    (1) Best advice: buy
    (2) Best advice; Buy
    (3) Best advice; buy
    (4) Best advice, Buy
    (5) Best advice, buy

45. Sentence 9: **You need not invest in dropped handlebars, multigear ratios, and special frames that may be too complicated for your purposes.**

    If you rewrote sentence 9 beginning with

    <u>Nor need you</u>

    the next words should be

    (1) invest in
    (2) dropped handlebars
    (3) multigear ratios
    (4) that may be
    (5) for your purposes

46. A new paragraph can be

    (1) started after sentence 9
    (2) started after sentence 7
    (3) started after sentence 4
    (4) started after sentence 3
    (5) not be started

GO ON TO THE NEXT PAGE

TEST 1: LANGUAGE ARTS, WRITING, PART I

<u>Questions 47–50</u> refer to the following paragraphs.

(A)

(1) At every stage of development, clothes can help establish a person's identity for himself and for those with who he interacts. (2) The childhood game of "dressing up" in parents' clothes provides an opportunity for the child to practice the roles he will be expected to play in adult life.

(B)

(3) The degree to which a person chooses clothes that fit the roles will affect his performance in those roles.

(C)

(4) Clothes are an important factor in developing feelings of self-confidence and self-respect. (5) When you look good, you feel good. (6) For most people, clothes are often a source of positive reaction from others, since in our culture we are more apt to compliment a person on his appearance than on other aspects of the "self."

(D)

(7) Most Americans also recognize that a proper appearance and proper dress are the keys to association with the right crowd, which in turn opens the door to job advancement increased income, and greater prestige.

(E)

(8) Our clothing needs are influenced by a multitude of circumstances. (9) Buying motives are seldom simple.

(F)

(10) The first step in the decision-making process is to make a conscious ordering of the things that are important to us. (11) If a person recognizes and accepts the priorities of his values—for example, that his status and prestige may be more important than his physical comfort—his choice of clothing is not only simplified, but more likely to bring him greater satisfaction.

47. Sentence 1: **At every stage of development, clothes can help establish a person's identity for himself and for those with who he interacts.**

    What correction should be made to this sentence?

    (1) change the spelling of <u>development</u> to <u>developement</u>
    (2) remove the comma after <u>development</u>
    (3) insert a comma after <u>himself</u>
    (4) change <u>who</u> to <u>whom</u>
    (5) no correction is necessary

48. A new paragraph can

    (1) be started after sentence 8
    (2) be started after sentence 5
    (3) be started after sentence 4
    (4) be started after sentence 1
    (5) not be started

49. The thesis statement of the passage is

    (1) sentence 1
    (2) sentence 2
    (3) sentence 7
    (4) sentence 11
    (5) implied

50. Sentences 4 and 5: **Clothes are an important factor in developing feelings of self-confidence and self-respect. When you look good, you feel good.**

    The most effective combination of sentences 4 and 5 would include which of the following groups of words?

    (1) self-respect, moreover, when
    (2) self-respect, although, when
    (3) self-respect, nevertheless, when
    (4) self-respect, therefore, when
    (5) self-respect, since, when

GO ON TO THE NEXT PAGE

TEST 1: LANGUAGE ARTS, WRITING, PART II

This part of the Writing Skills test is intended to determine how well you write. You are asked to write an essay that explains something, presents an opinion on an issue, or concentrates on retelling a personal experience.

Prompt

Throughout one's life there is usually someone who has influenced us in such a way that leaves a lasting postive impression. This may have been a family member, teacher, or special friend who may have helped you through a rough time. Because of this person's influence, you may feel that your life has become richer in ways of personal happiness or success.

Discussion Question

Think of one person in your life who has been an influence to you in such a way that your life is better today. Why has this person been such an influence on you?

DIRECTIONS

Write an essay of about 250 words in which you recount this personal event. Give supporting details in your essay. You have 45 minutes to write on this topic.

Check Yourself

- Read carefully the prompt, discussion question, and directions.
- Decide if the prompt is expository, persuasive, or narrative.
- Plan your essay before you begin.
- Use scratch paper to prepare a simple outline.
- Write your essay on the lined pages of a separate answer sheet.
- Read carefully what you have written and make needed changes.
- Check for focus, elaboration, organization, conventions, and integration.

END OF EXAM

TEST 2: SOCIAL STUDIES

DIRECTIONS

This section is made up of multiple-choice questions, most of which are based on readings that will often include a figure, graph, or chart. Study the information given to answer each question correctly.

Answering the multiple-choice questions should take you no longer than 70 minutes. It's best not to spend too much time on one question. There is no penalty for incorrect answers so be sure to answer every question.

To mark your answer, darken the corresponding circle on the answer sheet.

FOR EXAMPLE:

Early colonists of North America looked for settlement sites that had adequate water supplies and were accessible by ship. For this reason, many early towns were built near

(1) mountains   ① ② ● ④ ⑤
(2) prairies
(3) rivers
(4) glaciers
(5) plateaus

The correct answer is "rivers"; therefore, answer space 3 would be marked on the answer sheet.

GO ON TO THE NEXT PAGE

TEST 2: SOCIAL STUDIES

Questions 1–3 are based on the following passage.

The term *genocide*, a joining of the Greek *genos*, meaning race or tribe, and the Latin suffix *-cide*, or killing, was coined in 1946 by a distinguished international legal scholar, Professor Raphael Lemkin.

The mass murder of six million Jews by the Nazis was the most vivid, violent, and tragic expression of genocide. But this century alone has seen others—Armenians, Gypsies, Chinese, Slavs. Some 20 million people have been slaughtered because of their racial, religious, or ethnic backgrounds.

In the language of the United Nations Convention on the Prevention and Punishment of the Crime of Genocide, *genocide* means certain specifically defined acts *"committed with intent to destroy, in whole or in part, a national, ethnical, racial or religious group, as such."*

1. The word *genocide* literally means

    (1) mass murder
    (2) race killing
    (3) slaughter
    (4) convention
    (5) ratification

2. According to this passage, genocide involves intent to destroy *all* of the following EXCEPT

    (1) nations
    (2) races
    (3) ethnic groups
    (4) political groups
    (5) religious groups

3. All of the following have been subjected to genocide EXCEPT

    (1) Jews
    (2) Nazis
    (3) Slavs
    (4) Gypsies
    (5) Chinese

Questions 4–6 are based on the following passage.

We come then to the question presented: Does segregation of children in public schools solely on the basis of race, even though the physical facilities and other "tangible" factors may be equal, deprive the children of the minority group of equal educational opportunities? We believe that it does.

"Segregation of white and colored children in public schools has a detrimental effect upon the colored children. A sense of inferiority affects the motivation of a child to learn. Segregation with the sanction of law, therefore, has a tendency to [retard] the educational and mental development of Negro children and to deprive them of some of the benefits they would receive in a racial[ly] integrated school system."

Whatever may have been the extent of psychological knowledge at the time of *Plessy v. Ferguson*, this finding of the Kansas court is amply supported by modern authority. Any language in *Plessy v. Ferguson* contrary to this finding is rejected. We conclude that in the field of public education the doctrine of "separate but equal" has no place.

4. "We" (first paragraph) refers to

    (1) the plaintiff
    (2) the defendant
    (3) the Congress
    (4) the Supreme Court
    (5) Plessy and Ferguson

5. Segregation of children in grade or high school is rejected for

    (1) historical reasons
    (2) political reasons
    (3) physical reasons
    (4) psychological reasons
    (5) economic reasons

GO ON TO THE NEXT PAGE

TEST 2: SOCIAL STUDIES

6. The passage implies that *Plessy v. Ferguson*

   (1) called for integration
   (2) stated that separate facilities were unequal
   (3) was based on outmoded psychology
   (4) was constitutional
   (5) applied only to private schools

7. This photograph is known for how it

   (1) sparked additional protest against America's involvement in the Vietnam War
   (2) showed American soldiers murdering innocent civilians in Vietnam
   (3) showed the inhumane treatment of the Koreans by the Americans
   (4) showed the careless judgment of a soldier
   (5) falsely represented Americans who hated the Vietnam War

8. "Without our two great political parties cutting across economic and geographic interests, democracy as we know it could never have been made to function." The author of this statement probably meant to suggest that

   (1) political parties in the United States tend to represent sectional interests
   (2) each political party appeals to a different social class
   (3) there is no significant difference between the Democratic and Republican parties
   (4) an important feature of the U.S. political system is the broadly based appeal of the two political parties
   (5) only a two-party system can function in a democracy

Question 9 is based on the following cartoon.

9. What is the main idea of this 1994 cartoon?

   (1) White South Africans can no longer vote in their own country.
   (2) Free elections are the key to true democracy in South Africa.
   (3) People who fail to vote in South Africa's elections may be arrested.
   (4) Blacks can control elections by casting multiple votes.
   (5) Slavery has been abolished in South Africa.

GO ON TO THE NEXT PAGE

TEST 2: SOCIAL STUDIES

Questions 10–11 are based on the following graph.

Economic Growth

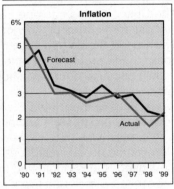

Inflation

Source: *The New York Times*

Questions 12 and 13 are based on the following graph.

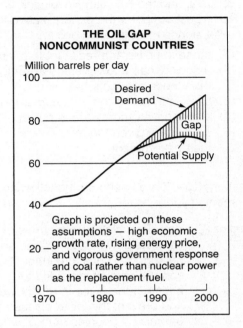

**THE OIL GAP
NONCOMMUNIST COUNTRIES**

Million barrels per day

Desired Demand

Gap

Potential Supply

Graph is projected on these assumptions — high economic growth rate, rising energy price, and vigorous government response and coal rather than nuclear power as the replacement fuel.

10. Forecasts of economic growth have consistently

(1) overestimated economic growth from 1990–1998
(2) underestimated economic growth from 1990–1998
(3) overestimated economic growth from 1996–1999
(4) underestimated economic growth from 1996–1999
(5) forecast correctly economic growth from 1990–1999

11. Forecasts of economists have

(1) overestimated inflation
(2) underestimated inflation
(3) generally been accurate on inflation
(4) been less accurate than forecasts of economic growth
(5) been as accurate as those for economic growth

12. Based on the information in the graph, the demand of noncommunist countries for oil will begin to exceed the supply of oil in about the year

(1) 1980
(2) 1985
(3) 1990
(4) 1995
(5) 2000

13. A valid conclusion that can be drawn from the data in the graph is that the noncommunist countries (western Europe and Japan) would

(1) have serious economic problems if alternative sources of energy are not developed
(2) avoid any gap between oil supply and demand by increasing oil production
(3) have until the year 2000 to make major changes in energy policies
(4) be unable to solve their energy problems
(5) use less oil because of its high price

GO ON TO THE NEXT PAGE

TEST 2: SOCIAL STUDIES

14. A study of the causes of the American Revolution of 1776, the French Revolution of 1789, and the Russian Revolution of 1917 best supports the generalization that revolution is most likely to occur when

    (1) those in power are resistant to change
    (2) a society has a lower standard of living than those around it
    (3) a society has become industrialized
    (4) stable governments are in power
    (5) people are given too much voice in their government

Questions 15–17 are based on the following statements by four historians.

Speaker A: American history is a series of conflicts between the haves and have-nots. Those in control of our society have always tried to maintain their wealth and power and prevent the lower classes and oppressed peoples from getting justice.

Speaker B: The American experience is unique in the story of nations. Due especially to the presence of a large, unused frontier during most of our history, we have been spared many of the problems and conflicts found in the rest of the world.

Speaker C: American history is a series of compromises between groups who have disagreed, but never over basic issues. From the writing of the Constitution to the decision to withdraw from Vietnam, extremists have represented only a minority view; the majority of the American people have usually favored compromise and moderate solutions to problems.

Speaker D: In every crisis of American history a great person, often a president, has risen above party politics and personal interest to lead the nation in the direction of greatness. We owe everything to those famous Americans who have governed us in the past.

15. Which speakers would be most likely to agree that the American Revolution cannot be compared with the French Revolution because the American Revolution did not involve a basic class struggle?

    (1) A and D
    (2) B and C
    (3) B and D
    (4) C and D
    (5) A and C

16. With which statement about the United States would Speaker B most likely agree?

    (1) The United States has one of the highest crime rates in the world.
    (2) The United States has not experienced some of the problems of other nations, mainly because of the availability of space.
    (3) Large cities in the United States tend to have more progressive social policies than small towns.
    (4) Many of the social institutions found in the United States originated in Europe.
    (5) The United States has few social problems.

17. The most valid inference to be drawn from the statements of the four speakers is that

    (1) all the facts should be known before a conclusion is drawn
    (2) historians must be free of personal bias
    (3) a study of history enables people to predict future events
    (4) historians disagree over interpretation of events
    (5) only one of the speakers is correct in his views

GO ON TO THE NEXT PAGE

TEST 2: SOCIAL STUDIES

<u>Question 18</u> is based on the following chart.

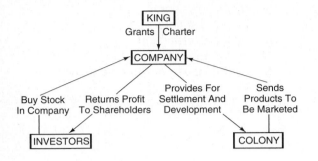

18. Which is a valid conclusion that can be drawn from the information in the chart?

   (1) The main purpose of the system illustrated was to benefit the colonies.
   (2) Nationalism was the motivating factor in English colonization.
   (3) The profit motive was a strong force in colonization.
   (4) The opportunity to own land attracted many settlers to the colonies.
   (5) Inducements were offered to prospective settlers.

<u>Questions 19 and 20</u> are based on the following passage.

   The task of economic policy is to create a prosperous America. The *unfinished task of prosperous Americans is to build a Great Society*.
   Our accomplishments have been many; these tasks remain unfinished:
   —to achieve full employment without inflation;
   —to restore external equilibrium and defend the dollar;
   —to enhance the efficiency and flexibility of our private and public economies;
   —to widen the benefits of prosperity;
   —to improve the quality of American life . . .

   —Lyndon B. Johnson

19. Former President Lyndon B. Johnson felt that the most important first step in the war against poverty is

   (1) full employment
   (2) a sound dollar
   (3) private and public economics
   (4) our natural defense
   (5) efficiency in government

20. The speech implies that America's prosperity

   (1) is threatened
   (2) is at its peak
   (3) must be retained
   (4) must be broadened
   (5) threatened Johnson's war against poverty

<u>Questions 21 and 22</u> are based on the following cartoon.

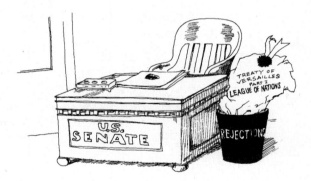

GO ON TO THE NEXT PAGE

TEST 2: SOCIAL STUDIES

21. Which aspect of the United States Government is best illustrated by the cartoon?

    (1) system of checks and balances
    (2) veto power of the president
    (3) congressional committee system
    (4) civilian control of the military
    (5) veto power of the Senate

22. The actions of the Senate are authorized

    (1) by the president
    (2) by popular vote
    (3) by the Constitution
    (4) by the Bill of Rights
    (5) by the House of Representatives

Questions 23–25 are based on the following chart.

Nations	Birthrate (per 1000)	Infant Mortality Rate (per 1000 births)
Uganda	47.35	67.83
Somalia	45.13	116.70
Angola	45.11	187.49
Cambodia	26.90	70.89
Ethiopia	37.98	95.32
Pakistan	29.74	72.44
Canada	10.78	4.75
France	12	4.26
Denmark	11.13	4.56
Italy	8.7	5.94
Germany	8.2	4.16
Japan	9.4	3.26

Source: Information Please Almanac, 2006

23. Which is a valid generalization based on the information in the chart?

    (1) In developing nations, the infant mortality rate decreases as the birthrate increases.
    (2) Industrialized nations have lower birthrates and infant mortality rates than developing nations.
    (3) Decreasing the infant mortality rate will limit population growth in developing nations.
    (4) Industrialized nations have higher population densities than developing nations.
    (5) Developing nations have ten times the infant mortality of industrialized nations.

24. According to the chart, the lowest birthrates are found mostly in

    (1) western Europe
    (2) Southeast Asia
    (3) North America
    (4) Africa
    (5) Latin America

GO ON TO THE NEXT PAGE

TEST 2: SOCIAL STUDIES

25. According to the chart, the highest infant mortality rates are in

    (1) western Europe
    (2) Southeast Asia
    (3) North America
    (4) Africa
    (5) Latin America

---

26. From the point of view of an environmentalist, which is probably the most significant argument against offshore drilling for oil?

    (1) There is little need to take such natural resources from the ocean waters.
    (2) Oil corporations are falsely advertising an oil shortage in order to expand their drilling operations.
    (3) The potential oil to be found is not worth the capital investment needed to extract it.
    (4) The possible harm to the balance of nature is more important than a gain in energy.
    (5) Coal is a preferable resource to oil.

27. Topography deals with surface features of a region, including its landforms and rivers, lakes, etc., and with man-made features such as canals, bridges, and roads. According to this definition, the topography of a region includes its

    (1) climate
    (2) plants
    (3) animals
    (4) mountains
    (5) inhabitants

Questions 28–30 are based on the following passage.

A Continental army and Congress composed of men from all the states, by freely mixing together, were assimilated into one mass. Individuals of both, mingling with the citizens, spread principles of union among them. Local prejudices lessened. By frequent contact, a foundation was laid for the establishment of a nation out of varied materials. Intermarriages between men and women of different states were much more common than before the war, and became an additional cement to the Union. Unreasonable jealousies had existed between the inhabitants of the eastern and of the southern states; but on becoming better acquainted with each other, these in a great measure subsided. A wiser policy prevailed. Men of liberal minds led the way in discouraging local differences, and the great body of the people, as soon as reason got the better of prejudice, found that their best interests would be best promoted by union.

28. The passage deals principally with the

    (1) prejudices in America at the time of the Revolution
    (2) frictions between the sections during the Revolution
    (3) positive social and political results of the Revolution
    (4) triumph of union over local differences
    (5) fear of the Church of England

29. Prior to the Revolution

    (1) a spirit of cooperation existed in the colonies
    (2) reason prevailed over prejudice
    (3) regional rivalry was present
    (4) most Americans knew one another
    (5) religious freedom was the general rule

GO ON TO THE NEXT PAGE

TEST 2: SOCIAL STUDIES

30. The passage implies that

    (1) self-interest has little to do with prejudice
    (2) social contact helps do away with prejudice
    (3) Americans were generally very much alike
    (4) trade discourages social contact
    (5) Congress was a divisive instrument

Questions 31–33 are based on the following passage.

Since the days when the fleet of Columbus sailed into the waters of the New World, America has been another name for opportunity, and the people of the United States have taken their tone from the possibilities of expansion open to them. But never again will such gifts of free land offer themselves. Each frontier did indeed furnish a new field of opportunity, a gate of escape from the bondage of the past. What the Mediterranean Sea was to the Greeks, breaking the bond of custom, offering new experiences, calling out new institutions and activities, that, and more, the ever-retreating frontier has been to the United States. And now, four centuries from the discovery of America, at the end of a hundred years of life under the Constitution, the frontier has gone, and with its going has closed the first period of American history.

31. The term *frontier* as used in this passage means

    (1) the New World
    (2) American energy
    (3) movement
    (4) the expansive nature of American life
    (5) the availability of free land

32. The attitude of the author to the frontier is one of

    (1) admiration
    (2) regret
    (3) indifference
    (4) restraint
    (5) suspicion

33. References in the passage lead to the conclusion that it was written approximately in the year

    (1) 1865
    (2) 1875
    (3) 1890
    (4) 1900
    (5) 1920

GO ON TO THE NEXT PAGE

TEST 2: SOCIAL STUDIES

Questions 34 and 35 are based on the following cartoon.

34. Which political system is referred to in the cartoon?

    (1) feudalism
    (2) monarchy
    (3) democracy
    (4) communism
    (5) fascism

35. The "giant lumbering creature" symbolized by the hammer and sickle is

    (1) NATO
    (2) OPEC
    (3) the USSR
    (4) OAS
    (5) the UN

36. Which statement best illustrates the principle of multiple causation of human behavior?

    (1) To each according to his or her needs.
    (2) Environment and heredity are constantly interacting.
    (3) Geographic differences account for variations in civilizations.
    (4) Wealth and power go together.
    (5) Habit results from repeated acts.

Questions 37 and 38 are based on the following passage.

Since 1750, about the beginning of the Age of Steam, the earth's population has more than tripled. This increase has not been an evolutionary phenomenon with biological causes. Yet there was an evolution—it took place in the world's economic organization. Thus 1,500,000,000 more human beings can now remain alive on the earth's surface, can support themselves by working for others who in turn work for them. This extraordinary tripling of human population in six short generations is explained by the speeded-up economic unification that took place during the same period. Thus most of us are now kept alive by this vast cooperative unified world society.

GO ON TO THE NEXT PAGE

TEST 2: SOCIAL STUDIES

37. The writer considers trade necessary for

    (1) travel
    (2) democracy
    (3) political unity
    (4) self-preservation
    (5) the theory of evolution

38. The basic change that led to the greatly increased population involves

    (1) new explorations
    (2) economic factors
    (3) biological factors
    (4) an increase in travel
    (5) the growth of world government

---

39. The number of Native American men and women in professional life has multiplied remarkably in the past generation. Movement back and forth from the Native American to the white world has become freer. At the same time, the long-standing conviction that sooner or later all Indians would become totally assimilated into the standardized stream of American life has steadily lost ground. Most experts today feel that Native American tribes and communities will retain separate identities for a long, long time into the future—and most experts believe that is good, not bad.

    There is a difference of opinion regarding Native Americans'

    (1) status as wards of the United States
    (2) status as citizens
    (3) assimilation into American life
    (4) property holdings
    (5) tribes and communities

40. "The parties agree that an armed attack against one or more of them in Europe or North America shall be considered an attack against them all. . . ."

    This quotation is most closely associated with which concept?

    (1) collective security
    (2) intervention
    (3) ultimatum
    (4) appeasement
    (5) aggression

41. Social mobility refers to a society in which an individual can and often does change in social status. Which best illustrates social mobility in the United States?

    (1) A midwestern farm family buys a farm in California.
    (2) The son of a president of a large manufacturing plant becomes a company executive.
    (3) The daughter of an unskilled immigrant worker becomes a teacher.
    (4) A woman whose parents are both college professors receives a graduate degree.
    (5) A New Yorker moves to Boston.

42. Cultural diversity, a variety of cultural patterns, is generally the result of

    (1) actions by the government of the area
    (2) the desire of the inhabitants to develop original ideas and styles
    (3) competition among the people for control of food sources
    (4) migrations to the area by various groups
    (5) reciprocal regional agreements

43. Culture shock is the confusion experienced by someone encountering unfamiliar surroundings, a strange community, or a different culture. Which situation is the best example of culture shock?

    (1) the refusal of the Amish to drive motor vehicles
    (2) the hippies' rejection of the "Establishment" in the 1960s
    (3) the difference in lifestyles between European and western American Indian tribal groups
    (4) the initial reaction of a U.S. Peace Corps participant arriving in a developing nation
    (5) the generation gap

GO ON TO THE NEXT PAGE

TEST 2: SOCIAL STUDIES

44. An extended family is a group of relatives by blood, marriage, or adoption living in close proximity or together, especially if three generations are involved.

    Which is usually a characteristic of societies that have the extended family as their basic unit?

    (1) The society tends to be highly industrialized.
    (2) The roles of the family members are economically and socially interdependent.
    (3) The government usually provides incentives to increase family size.
    (4) The functions of the family unit are defined mainly by the government.
    (5) The family becomes widely dispersed geographically.

45. Pluralism is the existence within a society of groups distinctive in ethnic origin, cultural patterns, or religion. Maintaining stability in a pluralistic society is difficult because

    (1) individuals are often forced to deal with the views of others that may challenge their own ideas
    (2) there is usually no well-defined order of governmental authority
    (3) new members in the society are often unwilling to obey established laws of the society
    (4) the wide variety of citizens' abilities hinders the management of labor resources
    (5) there are differing degrees of respect for authority

Questions 46 and 47 are based on the following passage.

Adults who like to think of America's young as a bunch of lazy, cigarette-packing television addicts may be disappointed by a major new study that finds the adolescents in the United States smoke and watch television less than those in many other industrialized nations. The study, conducted by the World Health Organization, finds that American teenagers exercise less than their peers elsewhere. And they eat more junk food. But American young people measure up rather well, certainly better than they are depicted in much of the mass media.

American children fared well, or at least in the middle, in at least two respects. Eleven-year-olds tried cigarettes at about the same rate as children in other countries. But the 15-year-old Americans smoked less than their counterparts, ranking 24th of 28 in the daily rate of smoking (about 12%). The highest rates were in Austria and France. American youths also watched a little less television than most of their counterparts: 15-year-olds ranked 20th and 11-year-olds ranked 6th.

46. American teenagers, according to the study, are much better than teenagers abroad in their

    (1) food habits
    (2) exercise habits
    (3) smoking habits
    (4) image in the mass media
    (5) addiction to drugs

47. Fifteen-year-old Americans did better in the study than the 11-year-olds in

    (1) exercising
    (2) avoiding junk food
    (3) avoiding smoking
    (4) an addiction to TV
    (5) avoiding smoking and watching TV

48. Mountains and coasts have served to restrict settlements; rivers and plains, to extend them. Each of these natural features has placed a characteristic imprint on the society that it dominated, largely fashioning its mode of life, its customs, morals, and temperament.

    The passage implies that

    (1) mountains and coasts are unfriendly to human beings
    (2) mountains and rivers exert equal influences on society
    (3) mountains and plains have similar effects on settlement
    (4) natural features result from the society that evolves within them
    (5) geographic features influence the society that develops

GO ON TO THE NEXT PAGE

TEST 2: SOCIAL STUDIES

<u>Questions 49 and 50</u> are based on the following tables.

TABLE *A*

Question: "Here are two suggestions that people have made to improve stability and order in this country. For each, would you favor or oppose such a step being taken?"

Suggestions	Percent of Public		
	Favor	Oppose	Not Sure
A law should be passed allowing police officers to search a home without a warrant in an emergency, as when they are looking for drugs.	32	65	3
The government should be given authority to use wiretaps and other electronic surveillance to gather evidence against citizens suspected of criminal activity, even if a court does not authorize such activity.	27	68	5

TABLE *B*

Question: "Do you feel the federal government should be allowed to engage in wiretapping and electronic surveillance if, in each case, it had to go to court beforehand to obtain court permission, or don't you feel the federal government should ever be allowed to engage in wiretapping or electronic surveillance?"

Response	Percent of Public
Should be allowed	63
Should not be allowed	28
Not sure	9

---

49. The information in Table *A* indicates that most people questioned

    (1) were undecided on the issues in question
    (2) supported the idea of a search without a warrant only in an emergency
    (3) favored protecting their privacy
    (4) favored permitting the government to investigate their lives
    (5) favored electronic eavesdropping over searches

50. A valid conclusion based on both tables is that the results of opinion surveys

    (1) tend to obscure the issues
    (2) are purposely biased by the pollsters
    (3) can vary according to the way the issue is presented
    (4) show that public attitudes are generally consistent
    (5) tend to be inconclusive

END OF EXAM

TEST 3: SCIENCE

DIRECTIONS

You are given 80 minutes to complete the Science section of the GED. This section is focused on your knowledge of general scientific concepts. All questions are in multiple choice format and require the test taker to study the given information (graph, figure, charts, etc.) to reach a correct answer.

You will not be penalized for incorrect answers, so remember to answer every question.

To mark your answer, darken the corresponding circle on the answer sheet.

FOR EXAMPLE:

Which of the following is the smallest unit?

(1) solution
(2) molecule
(3) atom
(4) compound
(5) mixture

① ② ● ④ ⑤

The correct answer is "atom"; therefore, space 3 would be marked on the answer sheet.

TEST 3: SCIENCE

<u>Questions 1–6</u> are based on the following article.

The study of ecology, the branch of biology that deals with the interrelations between living things and their environment, is most important today. The environment must be considered from the point of view of physical factors, such as temperature, soil, and water, and biotic factors, which are the living organisms.

Ecologists organize groups of living things into populations, communities, ecological systems, and the biosphere. A *population* consists of organisms of the same species living together in a given location, such as all the oak trees in a forest or all the frogs of the same species in a pond. A *community* consists of populations of different species, living together and interacting with each other.

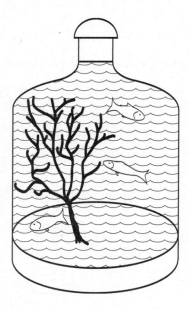

The accompanying diagram illustrates a simple community. It pictures a large bottle with a layer of mud on the bottom. The bottle was filled with pond water, and several fish and some green plants were added. The bottle was then made airtight. The members of this community will thrive as long as the balance is maintained.

1. Which of the following consists of a single species?

   (1) biosphere
   (2) community
   (3) ecosystem
   (4) biome
   (5) population

2. The fact that living things can survive in an airtight bottle illustrates the

   (1) need for green plants in our environment
   (2) need for physical factors in a community
   (3) balance within a population
   (4) need for biotic factors in a community
   (5) interrelations between living things and the environment

3. When species of plants and animals are introduced into a new habitat, they often become pests there, even though they were not pests in their native habitats. The most probable reason for this is that in the new habitat they

   (1) have fewer natural enemies or competition
   (2) have a much lower mutation rate
   (3) develop better resistance to the new climate
   (4) learn to use different foods
   (5) have more predators

4. If the airtight container and its contents were weighed each day for several days, it would be found that the total weight would

   (1) increase gradually
   (2) remain the same
   (3) decrease gradually
   (4) decrease for the first few days and then increase
   (5) increase for the first few days and then decrease

GO ON TO THE NEXT PAGE

TEST 3: SCIENCE

5. All of the following are biotic factors affecting the balance of the airtight container EXCEPT

   (1) the concentration of minerals in solution
   (2) the number of fishes in the water
   (3) the kinds of protozoa in the water
   (4) the kinds of plants in the bottle
   (5) the presence of crustaceans in the mud

6. Many different species of organisms interacting in a particular environment is an example of a

   (1) population
   (2) biosphere
   (3) community
   (4) biome
   (5) species

Questions 7–10 refer to the following graph.

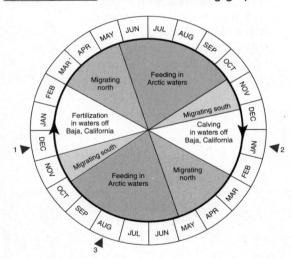

The graph above shows the gray whale's 2-year breeding cycle. Arrow one shows the peak period of fertilization for the whale. Arrow two shows the peak period for births of whale calves, and arrow three shows the period when the whale calves stop drinking milk from their mothers, also known as the weaning period.

7. How many months out of the year are gray whales feeding in Arctic waters?

   (1) 1 month
   (2) 2 months
   (3) 3 months
   (4) 5 months
   (5) 8 months

8. At what age do gray whale calves first migrate south?

   (1) 2 months
   (2) 4 months
   (3) 6 months
   (4) 10 months
   (5) 12 months

9. About how many months after conception are gray whale calves born?

   (1) 1 month
   (2) 5 months
   (3) 7 months
   (4) 13 months
   (5) 16 months

10. In its first year of life, how many months will a gray whale calf spend in the waters of Baja California?

   (1) 1 month
   (2) 2 months
   (3) 5 months
   (4) 8 months
   (5) 9 months

GO ON TO THE NEXT PAGE

TEST 3: SCIENCE

Questions 11–15 refer to the following article.

The human brain is a truly amazing organ. It allows us to process signals coming in from our world, such as smells, tastes, sounds, and sights, and it controls our responses to the world around us. From actions we do not think about at all, such as reflexes, to the most complex thought patterns, such as creating music or solving difficult equations, the brain is in charge. All this is done by a 3-pound organ made of 10 billion specialized cells called neurons. The neurons use a combination of electrical and chemical signals to process information and elicit responses.

The brain is actually composed of two sides, or hemispheres, the left and the right. At first glance the two sides appear to be the same, but each has its own specialized areas of function. The left side of the brain is actually what controls the right side of the body, while the right side of the brain is responsible for the left side of the body. In addition, each side of the brain has specific functions it controls. They are summarized in the table below. The two halves of the brain can "communicate" with each other via the *corpus callosum*, a bundle of nerve fibers that connects the two sides. This allows information to pass from one side of the brain to the other.

11. A person who suffered an injury to the right side of her brain would likely have diminished abilities to do which of the following?

   (1) arrange a series of pictures in order
   (2) solve algebraic equations
   (3) keep track of time
   (4) use the right leg and foot
   (5) musical ability

12. Cells that make up the brain are called

   (1) neurons
   (2) hemispheres
   (3) ganglions
   (4) callosums
   (5) processors

13. The left side of the brain controls which of the following functions?

   (1) musical ability
   (2) mathematical reasoning
   (3) holistic thinking
   (4) intuition
   (5) imagination

LEFT HEMISPHERE	RIGHT HEMISPHERE
Right side of the body	Left side of the body
Spoken language	Imaginative thought and synthesis
Written Language	Insight and awareness
Numerical and mathematical skills	Musical and artistic skills
Scientific and logical reasoning	Three-dimensional thought and analysis
Linear thinking—ordering and organizing	Holistic thought
Logic	Intuition
Sense of time	Nonverbal communication

GO ON TO THE NEXT PAGE

TEST 3: SCIENCE

14. A person who suffers a stroke that damages part of her left hemisphere may be able to regain some use of that part of the brain. Which brain structure would probably be responsible for allowing information to pass from the undamaged hemisphere to the damaged one?

    (1) the neurons
    (2) the corpus callosum
    (3) the tissue cells
    (4) the nerve fibers
    (5) the Broca's region

15. Which of the following is/are involved in the transmission of nerve signals?

    I. chemical signals
    II. electrical signals
    III. hemisphere signals

    (1) I only
    (2) II only
    (3) III only
    (4) I and II only
    (5) II and III only

16. Scientists admit that they still have a great deal to learn about the human brain. What they do know so far is that the nervous system is composed of neurons that carry signals throughout the body. The junction between neurons is called a synapse. A long, thin part of the neuron, called an axon, actually carries the signal. Unlike the wires in an electrical circuit, which sends signals by movement of electrons, the biological circuit of the nervous system dispatches information by means of ions of potassium and sodium, called neurotransmitters.

    In the biological circuit of the nervous system, a signal passes from

    (1) transmitter to neuron to synapse
    (2) neuron to axon to synapse
    (3) axon across synapse to axon
    (4) neuron to neuron across axon
    (5) axon to synapse by way of neuron

Questions 17 and 18 refer to the following graph.

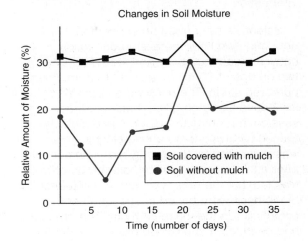

Changes in Soil Moisture

The graph above shows the relative moisture content of soil covered with mulch and soil not covered with mulch.

17. Which statement best summarizes the effects of mulch coverings on soil?

    (1) Mulch lowers the moisture content and increases the range of moisture content.
    (2) Mulch lowers the moisture content and decreases the range of moisture content.
    (3) Mulch raises the moisture content and increases the range of moisture content.
    (4) Mulch raises the moisture content and decreases the range of moisture content.
    (5) Mulch has no effect on moisture content, but it does decrease the range of moisture content.

18. Between which days was it most likely to have rained the most?

    (1) 0 and 5
    (2) 5 and 10
    (3) 10 and 15
    (4) 15 and 20
    (5) 20 and 25

GO ON TO THE NEXT PAGE

TEST 3: SCIENCE

<u>Questions 19–22</u> refer to the following information.

Scientists performed an experiment to determine whether there is a connection between learning ability and food. They took two groups of 20 mice each, all from the same purebred strain. The mice were deprived of food for 3 days and then given a standard learning session in running through a maze. They were trained by giving them a mild electric shock whenever they took a wrong turn. Immediately after each learning session, one group of mice was fed, but the other was not. A week later, all of the mice were tested to see whether they could still run the maze correctly. The group that had been fed had retained this ability, but the other group had not.

19. The probable reason that the scientists used only mice from the same pure-bred strain is so that

    (1) the mice would all be the same size
    (2) the mice would all be the same color
    (3) the experiment could be repeated with the same mice
    (4) genetic differences would not affect the outcome of the test
    (5) the experiment wouldn't cost as much

20. A finding is a proven result obtained as part of an experiment. Which of the following could be considered a valid finding?

    (1) Mice remember better if they are fed immediately after each training session.
    (2) Mice remember better if they are fed and then allowed some time to think about the training.
    (3) Experiments with mice have nothing to do with human learning processes.
    (4) Mice used in experiments have to be from the same purebred strain.
    (5) Mice do not need to be fed in order to learn.

21. The use of an electric shock in the teaching process is

    (1) necessary to keep the mice alert
    (2) cruel and should not be allowed
    (3) a way to show the mice that they have taken a wrong turn in the maze
    (4) designed to elicit a predetermined response
    (5) part of the variable

22. It was noted that the mice could learn to run the maze more readily if it was well illuminated. This information is

    (1) not relevant to their experiment
    (2) vital to the experiment
    (3) an assumption made by someone who observed the experiment
    (4) a result of the experiment
    (5) an important finding

<u>Questions 23–25</u> refer to the following passage.

As scientists plan longer and longer experiments to be carried out in space, the issues of long-term survival in space become much more significant. When trips to space lasted only a few days, it was relatively easy to provide for all the needs of the crew. Now, however, we must develop long-term methods for maintaining proper air pressure in the cabin, providing clean, breathable air, providing protection from gamma and X-ray radiation emitted by the stars (and our own Sun), dealing with the unique problems of weightlessness, as well as providing food and removing waste products.

Air pressure can be maintained by using a series of air locks to connect the passenger cabin to the outside. A similar system is used in submarines, to keep air in and water out of the cabin.

Since humans can live only a matter of minutes without oxygen, the problem of a constant production of safe air is of major importance. One solution has been to use green plants, which take up the carbon dioxide waste products, and produce oxygen as a

TEST 3: SCIENCE

by-product of photosynthesis. It is also possible, that if enough plants were grown, they could help with food as well. Another option is to use chemical oxygen generation systems. These are good in the short term, but eventually run out of materials.

We rarely think of needing protection from radiation. Our ozone layer does an excellent job of protecting us from ultraviolet radiation given off by the sun and from other forms of radiation as well. To date, we do not know if we can effectively shield astronauts from the high radiation doses they will likely receive in space over the long term.

Weightlessness is known to cause a loss of calcium from bones, making them weak and brittle, and to atrophy muscles. There are also documented weaknesses in blood vessels. One possible solution is to develop an artificial gravity.

Lastly, we must find ways to provide for basic food and water needs. Not only does a person use about 1 kilogram (2.2 pounds) of oxygen per day, but he or she also needs about .5 kilograms of food and 2 kilograms of water daily. While it is possible to transport compressed oxygen, water, and food for short trips, any efforts to establish long-term space colonies will require an ability to generate oxygen, food, and water in space as it will be impossible to transport them into space. Recycling will be a priority.

23. A five-minute loss of which of the following functions in a spaceship would have the greatest consequences?

    (1) loss of water production
    (2) loss of food
    (3) loss of oxygen
    (4) loss of artificial gravity
    (5) loss of gamma radiation shielding

24. A space station needs to provide for 10 people for 3 weeks. How much oxygen is needed?

    (1) 10 kilograms
    (2) 21 kilograms
    (3) 30 kilograms
    (4) 210 kilograms
    (5) 442 kilograms

25. Which of the following concerns for an astronaut in space is probably of the least concern to a person on Earth?

    (1) food loss
    (2) air pressure
    (3) weightlessness
    (4) air quality
    (5) exposure to ultraviolet radiation

Questions 26–31 refer to the following passage.

Acid rain, more properly known as acid precipitation, is a man-made environmental problem that is known to be escalating. The source of acid rain is oxides of sulfur and nitrogen that dissolve in water, lowering the pH to such an extreme that damage to living and nonliving things results. Often the source of acid rain is pollutants from factories or automobiles. The gases produced by fuel combustion react with water vapor in the air and produce acids such as sulfurous acid, sulfuric acid, and nitrous acid. Burning of coal, oil, and natural gas is especially likely to cause an increased amount of acid rain. In addition to man-caused sources of acid rain, volcanic eruptions and some bacterial decay also produce these acidic oxides which lower the pH of water.

Scientists measure the acidity of an object using the pH scale. The scale ranges from 0 to 14, with a pH of 7 being considered neutral. A pH less than 7 is acidic and one more than 7 is basic or alkaline. Normal rain has a pH of about 5.6. It is not neutral because rainwater naturally dissolves a small amount of carbon dioxide from the air and becomes slightly acidic.

Acid rain becomes a serious problem when the pH of the precipitation becomes less than 3.5. There have been reported pH's of 1.3 in some areas. These extremely acidic conditions kill fish and plants, and may render lakes and soil totally uninhabitable. Young fish not only are killed by such acidic waters, but any fish that may survive are usually not able to reproduce. Sometimes, nature provides a means of neutralizing these acidic waters via naturally alkaline ammonia compounds or calcium compounds such as limestone.

GO ON TO THE NEXT PAGE

TEST 3: SCIENCE

The table below gives the pH of some common substances:

pH	SUBSTANCE
1.1	Battery acid
2.8	Household vinegar
5.5	Normal rainwater
7.0	Distilled water
8.2	Baking soda
11.6	Household ammonia
13.9	Lye

26. Which of the following mineral formations would be most effective at neutralizing acid rain?

    (1) nitrogen
    (2) oxygen
    (3) calcium carbonate
    (4) magnesium acetate
    (5) baking soda (sodium bicarbonate)

27. Which of the following is not a cause of acid precipitation?

    (1) automobile engines
    (2) gasoline-powered lawnmowers
    (3) burning of coal
    (4) hydroelectric plants
    (5) burning of natural gas

28. According to the passage, which of the following is the most basic?

    (1) ammonia
    (2) lye
    (3) distilled water
    (4) normal rainwater
    (5) battery acid

29. Which pair of substances would likely neutralize each other?

    (1) lye and ammonia
    (2) vinegar and battery acid
    (3) vinegar and ammonia
    (4) ammonia and calcium carbonate
    (5) distilled water and rainwater

30. Which of the following responses to an acid rain-caused fish kill would have the best chance of preventing the problem from reappearing?

    (1) restocking the lake with heartier fish
    (2) allowing the stronger fish to survive and then reproduce
    (3) seeding clouds so that the rain falls elsewhere
    (4) reducing the amount of air pollution created
    (5) adding large amounts of ammonia to the lake to neutralize the acid

31. Which of the following compounds does not dissolve in water and cause acid rain?

    (1) sulfur dioxide
    (2) sulfur trioxde
    (3) carbon dioxide
    (4) nitrogen dioxide
    (5) nitrogen monoxide

32. Which of the following is the most likely reason why spraying pesticides on plants when they are not needed may cause more harm than good?

    (1) Pesticides are costly.
    (2) Certain pests may be selected for and develop an immunity to the pesticide in the future.
    (3) People may not apply pesticides in the proper manner.
    (4) Pesticides may interact with fertilizers.
    (5) Pesticides may not work well.

33. Amniote vertebrates are generally classified into three orders: Reptilia, Aves (birds), and Mammalia. Of the following, which group of three animals contains one member of each order?

    (1) ostrich, American robin, Norway rat
    (2) Beluga whale, black-footed ferret, box turtle
    (3) timber rattlesnake, fence lizard, leopard
    (4) African lion, sea otter, herring gull
    (5) house sparrow, garter snake, African elephant

GO ON TO THE NEXT PAGE

TEST 3: SCIENCE

34. Gases dissolve best at lower temperatures and at higher pressures. Based on this information, which set of conditions would cause a carbonated beverage to go flat (lose its dissolved carbon dioxide gas) the fastest?

    (1) high temperature and low pressure
    (2) high temperature and high pressure
    (3) low temperature and low pressure
    (4) low temperature and high pressure
    (5) high temperature and any pressure

Question 35 is based on the following graph.

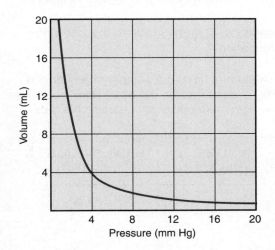

35. This graph represents the relationship of the pressure and volume of a given mass of a gas at constant temperature. When the pressure equals 8 millimeters of mercury (mm Hg), what is the volume, in milliliters (mL)?

    (1) 1
    (2) 2
    (3) 4
    (4) 8
    (5) 16

Ions are electrically charged particles that are formed when certain compounds are dissolved in water. These solutions will conduct electricity. The Swedish scientist Svante Arrhenius coined the term *ion* (which means wanderer) to explain why solutions of electrolytes will conduct an electric current. When an electrolyte forms into a solution, it dissolves or dissociates into ions, a process called ionization. If a substance does not ionize, it will not conduct an electric current.

Electrolytes include most acids, bases, and salts. Some conductors include hydrogen and sodium chloride, copper sulfate, and potassium nitrate. Substances that are not electrolytes include distilled water, sugar water, and most organic compounds.

36. Which of the following is a nonelectrolyte?

    (1) HNO_3 (nitric acid)
    (2) HCl (hydrochloric acid)
    (3) H_2SO_4 (sulfuric acid)
    (4) C_3H_8 (propane gas)
    (5) NaCl (table salt)

37. Which of the following compounds in the liquid phase can be considered an electrolyte?

    (1) H_2O (distilled water)
    (2) CO_2 (carbon dioxide)
    (3) NaCl (sodium chloride)
    (4) CuO (oxidized copper)
    (5) H_2O_2 (hydrogen peroxide)

GO ON TO THE NEXT PAGE

TEST 3: SCIENCE

38. An object accelerates (changes its speed) only if the forces acting on it in one direction are greater than the forces in the opposite direction. All of the following objects will accelerate EXCEPT

    (1) a gas balloon in which the buoyant force is greater than its weight and air resistance
    (2) a man in a parachute when the air resistance is less than his weight
    (3) an airplane in horizontal flight when the thrust of the engine is equal to the drag of the air
    (4) a ball striking a wall, in which the force of the ball on the wall is equal to the force of the wall on the ball
    (5) a rocket fired straight up, when the engine thrust is equal to the air resistance

39. The four giant planets, Jupiter, Saturn, Uranus, and Neptune (in that order), are very far from the Sun; only the dwarf planet Pluto is farther. The *Voyager* space explorer found that Neptune and Uranus are surrounded by rings like those of Saturn. What hypothesis would be suggested by the discovery that Pluto has no rings?

    (1) All large planets have rings, and small ones do not.
    (2) Rings are present around any planet that is far from the Sun.
    (3) Rings are distributed at random, regardless of the size or position of the planet.
    (4) Large planets may have rings, but small ones do not.
    (5) Pluto has lost its rings because it is so far from the Sun.

40. Wind can carry dry sand, blowing it against bedrock and eroding the rock into fantastic shapes. What kind of ecosystem is most likely to have wind-eroded rocks?

    (1) seashore
    (2) desert
    (3) prairie
    (4) tundra
    (5) deciduous forest

41. In a tank with water contaminated with bacteria, a surgical wound in a frog's skin heals much more rapidly than a similar wound on a fish. Any of the following might be a possible explanation EXCEPT

    (1) The bacteria in the tank are not harmful to frogs.
    (2) Some chemical in the frog's skin defends against bacteria.
    (3) The frog's immune system responds efficiently to the bacteria.
    (4) Frog skin has a much better ability to regenerate than the skin of a fish.
    (5) The water contains some chemical substance that promotes healing.

Questions 42 and 43 refer to the following information.

A student heated a sample of a hydrated mineral and removed the water from the sample. The data table below summarizes his data:

TIME (MINUTES)	MASS OF SAMPLE (GRAMS)
0	20.00
1	18.65
2	15.19
3	12.07
4	12.01
5	12.01
6	12.00

42. At the end of the heating process, what mass of water had been removed from the mineral?

    (1) 0.00 grams
    (2) 8.00 grams
    (3) 12.00 grams
    (4) 20.00 grams
    (5) 100.00 grams

GO ON TO THE NEXT PAGE

TEST 3: SCIENCE

43. What percentage of the sample was water at the start of the experiment?

    (1) 0.0%
    (2) 20.0%
    (3) 40.0%
    (4) 60.0%
    (5) 80.0%

44. In a reflex, an impulse starts at a sense organ, passes through sensory neurons to the brain or spinal cord, then goes through motor neurons to a muscle or a gland. What is the sequence of organs in the reflex that causes tears to flow when the cornea of the eye is irritated?

    (1) cornea–tear gland–brain–sensory neuron–motor neuron
    (2) cornea–brain–motor neuron–sensory neuron–tear gland
    (3) cornea–sensory neuron–brain–motor neuron–tear gland
    (4) tear gland–cornea–motor neuron–brain–sensory neuron
    (5) brain–cornea–sensory neuron–motor neuron–tear gland

45. In a certain area, DDT-resistant mosquitoes now exist in greater numbers than 10 years ago. What is the most probable explanation for this increase in numbers?

    (1) DDT causes sterility in mosquitoes.
    (2) Mosquito eggs were most likely to have been fertilized when exposed to DDT.
    (3) DDT acted as a reproductive hormone for previous generations of mosquitoes.
    (4) DDT serves as a new source of nutrition.
    (5) Genetic differences permitted some mosquitoes to survive DDT use.

46. A scientist studying fossils in undisturbed layers of rock identified a species that, he concluded, had changed little over the years. Which observation probably would have led him to this conclusion?

    (1) The simplest fossil organisms appeared only in the oldest rocks.
    (2) The simplest fossil organisms appeared only in the newest rocks.
    (3) The same kind of fossil organisms appeared in old and new rocks.
    (4) No fossil organisms of any kind appeared in the newest rocks.
    (5) Few fossil organisms appeared in the oldest rock.

47. In sexual reproduction, the original chromosome number must be reduced in order that members of the next generation will have the same chromosome number as their parents. For this reason, each reproductive cell—egg or sperm—has only half as many chromosomes as the other cells in the organism. The pollen grain of a wheat plant produces a sperm nucleus with 14 chromosomes. How many chromosomes will there be in the egg nucleus and in a leaf cell?

    (1) 14 in the egg nucleus, 28 in a leaf cell
    (2) 14 in both the egg nucleus and leaf cells
    (3) 28 in both the egg nucleus and leaf cells
    (4) 7 in the egg nucleus, 14 in a leaf cell
    (5) 7 in the egg nucleus, 28 in a leaf cell

48. A salmon will die after laying thousands of eggs, depositing them in the open water. A robin lays about 4 eggs and cares for the young when they hatch. It is reasonable to assume that

    (1) there are far more salmon than robins in the world
    (2) far more salmon than robins die before reaching adulthood
    (3) more food is available for growing salmon than for young robins
    (4) salmon do not reproduce until they are much older than adult robins
    (5) robins are better parents than salmon

GO ON TO THE NEXT PAGE

TEST 3: SCIENCE

49. Corn plants that are grown in the dark will be white and usually much taller than genetically identical corn plants grown in light, which will be green. The most probable explanation for this finding is that the

    (1) corn plants grown in the dark are all mutants for color and height
    (2) expression of a gene may be dependent on the environment
    (3) plants grown in the dark will always be genetically albino
    (4) phenotype of a plant is independent of its genotype
    (5) genotype is independent of its phenotype

50. Potatoes can be reproduced either by cuttings of the tubers or by seed formed sexually. Why would an agriculture specialist decide to go to the trouble of growing potatoes from seed?

    (1) to produce the largest possible crop
    (2) to try out a new fertilizer
    (3) to reduce the difficulty of planting
    (4) to produce new varieties
    (5) to protect the new plants from insects

END OF EXAM

TEST 4: LANGUAGE ARTS, READING

DIRECTIONS

This section of the exam consists of questions based on articles about literature, excerpts from different literary periods (pre-1920, 1920–1960, and post-1960 literature), and business documents. Each of these excerpts will be followed by multiple-choice questions you must answer.

You should read each excerpt carefully before answering the accompanying questions and refer to the passages as often as necessary to help you answer the questions.

Before each excerpt is a "purpose question" designed to show you why you're reading the passage, and what to focus on. These purpose questions do not need to be answered as they are only there to help you in your reading.

You will not be penalized for incorrect answers so be sure to answer every question. This section's questions should take you no more than 65 minutes.

To mark your answer, darken the corresponding circle on the answer sheet.

FOR EXAMPLE:

> The sunshine sparkled
> On the blue green sea
> Like white Christmas lights
> In the downtown square

The poet uses which literary device in line 3?

(1) alliteration
(2) simile
(3) metaphor
(4) personification
(5) rhythm

The correct answer is "simile" because the poet uses "like" when comparing the sea to the lights; therefore, answer space 2 would be marked on the answer sheet.

GO ON TO THE NEXT PAGE

TEST 4: LANGUAGE ARTS, READING

Questions 1–5 refer to the following passage.

HOW DID A CHILD REACT TO AUGUST WEATHER?

I grew up near the Atlantic Ocean among marshes and estuaries, only a few miles back from a low-lying coast. I remember the month of August with a special kind of
(5) pleasure. At this time of year, mainland, marshland, and ocean would blend together into a grey, hot, humid haze. My mother would open all the windows, pull all the blinds, and hope to catch a sea breeze, but
(10) no breeze stirred. The dogs lay under the tables and panted; the cats lurked in the cool tunnels of the earth cellar. August was a time to do nothing and be proud of it.

But I also remember August with a bit of
(15) anxiety. August was the time of hurricanes and polio. Hurricanes and polio were different in many ways but were alike in that both were very bad things that usually happened to other people. During my
(20) childhood, I was lucky enough never to get polio. But we had bad hurricanes three times.

The hurricanes were pretty scary for the adults, but for a child, they were mostly a lot
(25) of fun. First, there was all the getting ready: buying candles and flashlight batteries and food, filling the car with gasoline, helping neighbors board up the only plate-glass window in the neighborhood, and making
(30) sure the buildings were closed up snug and everything loose was stashed away.

Then there was watching for the storm. I remember my father pointing out to me the eerie sky with its banners of cirrus clouds
(35) radiating out of the south, and I remember the strange feel of the air. The first breezes of the hurricane were so mild, so moist, so soft as to be barely distinguishable from the feel of one's own skin.
(40) The storm itself wasn't so bad, except I had to stay indoors. I remember peering through windows watching the water sheet down outside, the ocean tide creep up in

the back marsh, and the trees lash back
(45) and forth. Every time the wind let up I would say, "Is this the eye of the hurricane? Can I go outside and see the eye?"

—Calvin Simonds

1. The mood in lines 1 through 13 is expressed chiefly through the use of

   (1) descriptive details
   (2) sequential order
   (3) figurative language
   (4) simple sentences
   (5) objective observation

2. Why was the narrator "proud" (line 13) to do nothing in August?

   (1) He was lazy.
   (2) It was easier to keep cool.
   (3) He was observing animals' actions.
   (4) It was proper August behavior.
   (5) He was afraid of hurricanes.

3. The narrator characterizes hurricanes and polio as reasons for

   (1) fearing the weather
   (2) being concerned in August
   (3) discussing misfortunes
   (4) helping the neighbors
   (5) staying indoors

4. In the fourth paragraph, the narrator suggests that the early stages of a hurricane are

   (1) unpredictable
   (2) obvious to the eye only
   (3) apparent in the atmosphere
   (4) felt before they are seen
   (5) frightening for children

5. Which words best describe the narrator's memories of August?

   (1) confusing events
   (2) conflict and danger
   (3) contrasting feelings
   (4) freedom and relaxation
   (5) expectancy and fulfillment

GO ON TO THE NEXT PAGE

TEST 4: LANGUAGE ARTS, READING

Questions 6–10 refer to the following passage.

WHO ARE THE MOST RECENT SEEKERS AFTER THE AMERICAN DREAM?

New immigrants are trying all over to integrate themselves into the system. They have the same hunger. On any given day, there are millions throughout the world who are applying to come to the United States and share the American Dream. The same battles.

Sometimes the whole family saves up and gives the bright young man or the bright young woman the family savings. It even goes in hock for a year or two. They pin all their hopes on this one kid, put him on a bus, let him go a thousand miles. He doesn't speak a word of English. He's only seventeen, eighteen years old, but he's gonna save that family. A lot rides on that kid, who's a busboy in some hotel.

He's gonna be the first hook, the first pioneer coming into an alien society, the United States. He might be in Chicago. He works as a busboy all night long. They pay him minimum or less, and work him hard. He'll never complain. If he makes a hundred a week, he will manage to send back twenty-five.

After the kid learns a bit, because he's healthy and young and energetic, he'll probably get another job as a busboy. He'll work at another place as soon as the shift is over. He'll try to work his way up to be a waiter. He'll work incredible hours. He doesn't care about union scale. He doesn't care about conditions, about humiliations. He accepts all this as his fate.

He's burning underneath with this energy and ambition. He outworks the U.S. busboys and eventually becomes the waiter. Where he can maneuver, he tries to become the owner and gives a lot of competition to the locals.

The only thing that helps me is remembering the history of this country. We've always managed, despite our worst, unbelievably nativist actions, to rejuvenate ourselves, to bring in new people. Every new group is scared of being in the welfare line or in the unemployment office. They go to night school. They learn about America. We'd be lost without them.

I see all kinds of new immigrants starting out all over again, trying to work their way into the system. They're going through new battles, yet they're old battles. They want to share in the American Dream. The stream never ends.

6. The attitude of the author toward the new immigrant is

   (1) critical
   (2) skeptical
   (3) cautious
   (4) enthusiastic
   (5) cynical

7. The approach to immigration by the immigrant family is to

   (1) come as a unified family
   (2) send a promising youth
   (3) borrow from relatives
   (4) expect the worst
   (5) bank on a senior member

8. From the passage, it can be inferred that

   (1) other family members will follow the pioneer
   (2) the family will be abandoned
   (3) the family will despair of achieving the American Dream
   (4) the family will give up their efforts
   (5) the family will be frightened by feeling alien

9. The American Dream, as illustrated in this article, allows newcomers to

   (1) make a lot of money
   (2) be exploited
   (3) move upward in society
   (4) be welcomed enthusiastically
   (5) be victims of exclusion

10. The history of America indicates that immigrants

   (1) benefit the United States
   (2) are losing faith
   (3) are easily discouraged
   (4) expect help
   (5) seek welfare

GO ON TO THE NEXT PAGE

TEST 4: LANGUAGE ARTS, READING

Questions 11–15 are based on the following selection.

HOW DOES AN ELDERLY COUPLE CELEBRATE A SABBATH MEAL?

Both of them had eaten sparingly during the day so that they would have an appetite for the Sabbath meal. Shmul-Leibele said the benediction over the raisin wine and
(5) gave Shoshe the cup that she might drink. Afterwards, he rinsed his fingers from a tin dipper, then washed hers, and they both dried their hands with a single towel, each at either end. Shmul-Leibele lifted the
(10) Sabbath loaf and cut it with the bread knife, a slice for himself and one for his wife.

He immediately informed her that the loaf was just right, and she countered: "Go on, you say that every Sabbath."
(15) "But it happens to be the truth," he replied.

Although it was hard to obtain fish during the cold weather, Shoshe had purchased three-quarters of a pound of pike from
(20) the fishmonger. She had chopped it with onions, added an egg, salt and pepper, and cooked it with carrots and parsley. It took Shmul-Leibele's breath away, and after it he had to drink a tumbler of whiskey.
(25) When he began the table chants, Shoshe accompanied him quietly. Then came the chicken soup with noodles and tiny circlets of fat which glowed on the surface like golden ducats. Between the soup and the
(30) main course, Shmul-Leibele again sang Sabbath hymns. Since goose was cheap at this time of year, Shoshe gave Shmul-Leibele an extra leg for good measure. After the dessert, Shmul-Leibele washed
(35) for the last time and made a benediction. When he came to the words: "Let us not be in need either of the gifts of flesh and blood nor of their loans," he rolled his eyes upward and brandished his fists.

11. We know that Smul-Leibele is religious because

   (1) he says a benediction
   (2) he offers Shoshe a drink
   (3) he washes his hands
   (4) he slices the loaf
   (5) he offers Shoshe a slice

12. We can deduce the relationship between husband and wife from

   (1) his compliment to her
   (2) his appetite
   (3) his benedictions
   (4) his hymns
   (5) his drink of whiskey

13. The Sabbath rituals included all of the following EXCEPT

   (1) blessing the wine
   (2) rinsing fingers
   (3) raising the loaf
   (4) drinking whiskey
   (5) singing hymns

14. Shmul-Leibele prayed that he could

   (1) continue to be with Shoshe
   (2) have food and drink
   (3) be free of moneylenders
   (4) need the gifts of flesh and blood
   (5) be blessed with long life

15. The purpose of the selection is to

   (1) describe the relationship between husband and wife
   (2) stress the importance of prayer
   (3) describe a Sabbath meal
   (4) stress the couple's poverty
   (5) stress the couple's loneliness

GO ON TO THE NEXT PAGE

TEST 4: LANGUAGE ARTS, READING

Questions 16–20 are based on the following selection.

WHAT HAPPENS AT THE REUNION OF TWO SISTERS?

"Oh, Lottie, it's good to see you," Bess said, but saying nothing about Lottie's splendid appearance. Upstairs Bess, putting down her shabby suitcase, said "I'll sleep
(5) like a rock tonight," without a word of praise for her lovely room. At the lavish table, top-heavy with turkey, Bess said, "I'll take light and dark both," with no marveling at the size of the bird, or that there was turkey for two
(10) elderly women, one of them too poor to buy her own bread.

With the glow of good food in her stomach, Bess began to spin stories. They were rich with places and people. . . Her face reflected
(15) her telling, above all, the love she lived by that enhanced the poorest place, the humblest person.

Then it was that Lottie knew why Bess had made no mention of her finery, or the shining
(20) room, or the twelve-pound turkey. She had not even seen them. Tomorrow she would see . . . Lottie as she really looked. Tonight she saw only what she had come seeking, a place in her sister's home and heart.

(25) She said, "That's about enough for me. How have the years used you?"

"It was me who didn't use them," said Lottie wistfully. "I saved for them. I forgot the best of them would go without my ever
(30) spending a day or a dollar enjoying them. That's my life story in those few words, a life never lived. Now it's too near the end to try."

Bess said, "To know how much there is to know is the beginning of learning to live.
(35) Don't count the years that are left us. At our time of life it's the days that count. You've got too much catching up to do to waste a minute of a waking hour feeling sorry for yourself."

16. Bess

    (1) took note of her sister's appearance
    (2) envied her sister's finery
    (3) appreciated her welcome
    (4) was oblivious of her surroundings
    (5) was satisfied by what she saw

17. Bess was seeking

    (1) rich people
    (2) rich places
    (3) a place in her sister's home
    (4) a lavish table
    (5) an escape from poverty

18. Lottie looked back on her life

    (1) happily
    (2) regretfully
    (3) with satisfaction
    (4) with nostalgia
    (5) longingly

19. Bess will probably

    (1) take advantage of Lottie
    (2) teach Lottie how to live
    (3) feel sorry for herself
    (4) regret her past life
    (5) count her remaining years

20. Lottie will probably

    (1) change her way of life
    (2) be too old to change
    (3) continue to feel sorry for herself
    (4) count her remaining years
    (5) live in the past

GO ON TO THE NEXT PAGE

TEST 4: LANGUAGE ARTS, READING

Questions 21–25 refer to the following poem.

WHY DOES THE POET OBJECT TO A PHOTOGRAPH?

To a Photographer

I have known love and hate and work and fight;
I have lived largely, I have dreamed and planned,
And Time, the Sculptor, with a master hand
Has graven on my face for all men's sight
Deep lines of joy and sorrow, growth and blight,
Of labor and of service and command
—And now you show me this, this waxen, bland
And placid face, unlined, unwrinkled, white.
This is not I—this fatuous thing you show,
Retouched and smoothed and prettified to please.
Put back the wrinkles and the lines I know;
I have spent blood and tears achieving these,
Out of the pain, the struggle and the wrack
These are my scars of battle—put them back!

—Berton Braley

21. It can be assumed from the poet that

    (1) the poet has taken a photograph
    (2) the poet has been shown a photograph of himself
    (3) a faithful photograph has been taken of him
    (4) the poet is still young
    (5) the poet is a dreamer

22. The poet wishes everyone to know that he has

    (1) led a quiet life
    (2) experienced hardships
    (3) been unsuccessful
    (4) maintains a youthful appearance
    (5) aged gracefully

23. The passage of time has left the poet with a face that is

    (1) lined
    (2) placid
    (3) ashen
    (4) smooth
    (5) bland

24. The poet is

    (1) content with his lot
    (2) resentful of time
    (3) proud of his scars
    (4) desirous of youth
    (5) untrue to himself

25. The poem is written in the form of a

    (1) ballad
    (2) dialogue
    (3) lyric
    (4) limerick
    (5) sonnet

GO ON TO THE NEXT PAGE

TEST 4: LANGUAGE ARTS, READING

Questions 26–30 refer to the following excerpt from a play.

WHY DOES A CANDIDATE DECIDE NOT TO RUN FOR OFFICE?

GRANT: I'm not going to kid anybody along. I never have.

KAY (pleadingly): Grant, everybody here tonight was thinking of the future—which is how to get you elected. It's stupid right now to think in any other terms.

(Grant unbuttons his coat and takes it off. Kay turns to Conover in alarm.)

CONOVER (going to Grant): I've got to talk to these people, and that means you've got to talk to me.

GRANT: I'm talking to a lot of people in my speech Thursday night. You'll be one of them. I promised myself when I went into this that I'd appeal to the best in the American people. The only advice I've ever had from any of you was to appeal to their worst. And that's what both parties are starting to do today. Let's end rationing. Who cares if Europe starves? Let's lift price ceilings—suppose it does bring inflation. Let's lower taxes and all get rich.

CONOVER: I see. You're the only honest man in politics.

GRANT: No, Jim! We have some good men. There are some wonderful men in the Senate and in the House, too—Democrats and Republicans. But, Jim, there aren't enough of them to shape party policies, so, to get votes, both parties are out to buy the American public. I can't do that, Jim. So I'm afraid I can't be of any use to you.

KAY: Well, Grant, I won't accept that decision. Oh, Grant, we've always talked these things out together. All right, we won't discuss it any more tonight. You're upset. I'll be in touch with you tomorrow. Come on, Jim. (She exits.)

CONOVER: I think Kay's right, Grant. You'd better sleep on it. I can stay over another day.

GRANT: No, Jim, I've made up my mind.

CONOVER: Grant, in this country we play politics—and to play politics you have to play ball . . . .(He exits.)

GRANT: Thank God that's settled. I hope they're all listening in Thursday night because I'm going to burn their ears off. Any candidate for any office who threatens world peace for a few votes—there's the international criminal for you. I'll take care of them Thursday night—and from now on.

26. You can deduce from what Kay and Conover are saying that

    (1) they disagree with each other
    (2) they agree with Grant
    (3) they agree with the American people
    (4) they disagree with Grant
    (5) they think well of Grant

27. Grant is implying

    (1) he won't play politics
    (2) he will lift price ceilings
    (3) he will lower taxes
    (4) he will buy the American public
    (5) he'll get rich

28. Grant is critical of

    (1) all Republicans
    (2) all Democrats
    (3) Congress
    (4) the American public
    (5) both political parties

29. Grant feels that the American public

    (1) can be bought
    (2) can be fooled
    (3) can be appealed to
    (4) plays politics
    (5) is cynical about politicians

30. Grant will

    (1) be a candidate for public office
    (2) compromise his principles
    (3) attack dishonest candidates
    (4) go along with Kay and Conover
    (5) drop out of politics

GO ON TO THE NEXT PAGE

TEST 4: LANGUAGE ARTS, READING

Questions 31–35 refer to the following passage.

WHAT IS THE MEANING OF THE FATHER'S ACT?

So it was with a heart full of longing and hope that my father led us to school on that first day. He took long strides in his eagerness, the rest of us running and hopping to keep up.

At last the four of us stood around the teacher's desk; and my father, in his impossible English, gave us over in her charge. . . . I venture to say that Miss Nixon was struck by something uncommon in the group we made. . . . My little sister was pretty as a doll, with her clear pink-and-white face, short golden curls, and eyes like blue violets when you caught them looking up. My brother . . . stood up straight and uncringing before the American teacher, his cap respectfully doffed. Next to him stood a starved-looking girl with eyes ready to pop out, and short dark curls that would not have made much of a wig for a Jewish bride.

All three children carried themselves rather better than the common run of "green" pupils that were brought to Miss Nixon. But the figure that challenged attention to the group was the tall, straight father, with his earnest face and fine forehead, nervous hands eloquent in gesture, and a voice full of feeling. This foreigner, who brought his children to school as if it were an act of consecration, was not like other aliens, who brought their children in dull obedience to the law; was not like the native fathers, who brought their unmanageable boys, glad to be relieved of their care. I think Miss Nixon guessed what my father's best English could not convey. I think she divined that by the simple act of delivering our school certificates to her he took possession of America.

—Mary Antin

31. The best title for this selection is

    (1) "Our First Day at School"
    (2) "America: Land of Opportunity"
    (3) "We Were Different"
    (4) "A Father's Faith in Education"
    (5) "Americanization of the Alien"

32. From their use in the passage, all of the following words are correctly paired EXCEPT

    (1) *charge*—care
    (2) *uncommon*—unusual
    (3) *doffed*—removed
    (4) *consecration*—dedication
    (5) *divined*—heavenly

33. The author's father regarded school in the United States as all of the following EXCEPT

    (1) an act of dedication
    (2) a parental responsibility
    (3) a legal obligation
    (4) a source of hope
    (5) a stake in America

34. The incorrect group of words describing the persons in the passage is

    (1) the author's sister—blonde and beautiful
    (2) the author's brother—erect and respectful
    (3) the author's father—calm and sincere
    (4) the author—observant and plain-looking
    (5) Miss Nixon—sensitive and understanding

35. As used in this passage, *green* means

    (1) inexperienced
    (2) frightened
    (3) disobedient
    (4) sallow-complexioned
    (5) immigrant

GO ON TO THE NEXT PAGE

TEST 4: LANGUAGE ARTS, READING

<u>Questions 36–40</u> refer to the following letter of recommendation.

January 2003

To Whom It May Concern:

(A)
(1) This will confirm that Shawn Black has been employed by Smith Incorporated for approximately 4 years.

(B)
(2) During his tenure of employment, he has displayed a unique ability to identify and solve problems. (3) He has been instrumental in helping to streamline our marketing department. (4) His experience in the marketing and advertising area has been a valuable asset, one that can be of great value to any company using his services. (5) His ideas are fresh and unique, always on the cutting edge in his field.

(C)
(6) He is a loyal employee and always places the welfare of the company above all else. (7) His long hours and his patience with employees under him and with management make him an ideal employee. (8) If available, he can certainly count on reemployment with our firm, should the opportunity arise.

(D)
(9) Any company considering this individual for employment has my most enthusiastic recommendation. (10) If his performance here is any indication, he is destined to achieve new heights in his career and set new records for his future employer. (11) If you have any questions, please do not hesitate to contact me at (310) 555-9902.

Sincerely,

Kristoph Peterson

Kristoph Peterson
Marketing Manager

36. According to the letter, the employee, Shawn Black, is

    (1) unemployed and seeking unemployment insurance
    (2) requesting an application for employment with Smith Incorporated
    (3) writing a letter of recommendation for his employee, Kristoph Peterson
    (4) no longer working for Smith Incorporated, but seeking employment elsewhere
    (5) receiving a letter of reprimand for his behavior at Smith Incorporated

37. According to the letter,

    (1) Kristoph Peterson was not pleased with Shawn Black's performance on the job
    (2) Shawn Black is submitting his letter of resignation to Kristoph Peterson
    (3) Shawn Black is an excellent candidate for any job in the marketing or advertising field
    (4) Shawn Black was highly recommended for any job in the accounting department
    (5) Kristoph Peterson accepted Shawn Black's letter of resignation

38. The letter implies that Shawn Black

    (1) has excellent communication skills
    (2) has excellent accounting skills
    (3) has applied to Smith Incorporated
    (4) has not impressed his employer
    (5) has not worked to the best of his ability

GO ON TO THE NEXT PAGE

TEST 4: LANGUAGE ARTS, READING

39. The author feels that

    (1) he has been let down by Shawn Black because he is seeking employment elsewhere
    (2) Shawn Black is seeking a career in the accounting field
    (3) Shawn Black will not be loyal to his next company
    (4) Shawn Black will make an excellent employee for any company
    (5) he wants to hire Shawn Black next time he applies for the job

40. The letter implies that Kristoph Peterson felt what about Shawn Black's performance?

    (1) frustration
    (2) excitement
    (3) distrust
    (4) displeasure
    (5) pleasure

END OF EXAM

TEST 5: MATHEMATICS

DIRECTIONS

The Mathematics portion of the GED exam consists of both multiple-choice and alternate format questions. The goal of this section is to measure your general math skills and problem-solving abilities. Each question is based on a short reading that could include a diagram, graph, or chart.

The questions in this section should take you no longer than 45 minutes. There's no penalty for incorrect answers so be sure to answer every question. Also, be careful not to spend too much time on each question.

Formulas you need are given on page 796. Only some of the questions will require you to use a formula. Not all the formulas given will be needed.

The questions will give you varying amounts of information—some will provide more information than you need to solve the problem, while some questions will not provide enough to solve the problem. When a question does not provide enough information to solve the problem, then the correct answer will be "Not enough information is given."

You may use a calculator on Part 1.

To mark your answer, darken the corresponding circle on the answer sheet.

FOR EXAMPLE:

If a grocery bill totaling $15.75 is paid with a $20.00 bill, how much change should be returned?

(1) $5.26   ① ② ● ④ ⑤
(2) $4.75
(3) $4.25
(4) $3.75
(5) $3.25

The correct answer is "$4.25"; therefore, answer space 3 would be marked on the answer sheet.

GO ON TO THE NEXT PAGE

TEST 5: MATHEMATICS

FORMULAS

Description	Formula
AREA (A) of a:	
square	$A = s^2$; where s = side
rectangle	$A = lw$; where l = length, w = width
parallelogram	$A = bh$; where b = base, h = height
triangle	$A = \frac{1}{2}bh$; where b = base, h = height
trapezoid	$A = \frac{1}{2}(b_1 + b_2)h$; where b = base, h = height
circle	$A = \pi r^2$; where π = 3.14, r = radius
PERIMETER (P) of a:	
square	$P = 4s$; where s = side
rectangle	$P = 2l + 2w$; where l = length, w = width
triangle	$P = a + b + c$; where a, b, and c are the sides
circumference (C) of a circle	$C = \pi d$; where π = 3.14, d = diameter
VOLUME (V) of a:	
cube	$V = s^3$; where s = side
rectangular container	$V = lwh$; where l = length, w = width, h = height
cylinder	$V = \pi r^2 h$; where π = 3.14, r = radius, h = height
square pyramid	$V = \frac{1}{3}(\text{base edge})^2 h$
cone	$V = \frac{1}{3}\pi r^2 h$
Pythagorean theorem	$c^2 = a^2 + b^2$; where c = hypotenuse, a and b are legs, of a right triangle
distance (d) between two points in a plane	$d = \sqrt{(x_2 - x_1)^2 + (y_2 - y_1)^2}$; where (x_1, y_1) and (x_2, y_2) are two points in a plane
slope of a line (m)	$m = \dfrac{y_2 - y_1}{x_2 - x_1}$; where (x_1, y_1) and (x_2, y_2) are two points in a plane
MEASURES OF CENTRAL TENDENCY	mean = $\dfrac{x_1 + x_2 + \ldots + x_n}{n}$; where the x's are the values for which a mean is desired, and n = number of values in the series
	median = the point in an ordered set of numbers at which half of the numbers are above and half of the numbers are below this value
simple interest (i)	$i = prt$; where p = principal, r = rate, t = time
distance (d) as function of rate and time	$d = rt$; where r = rate, t = time
total cost (c)	$c = nr$; where n = number of units, r = cost per unit

GO ON TO THE NEXT PAGE

TEST 5: MATHEMATICS, PART I

Directions: You will have 45 minutes to complete this section. You may use a calculator.

1. Luisa worked 40 hours and earned $8.10 per hour. Her friend Joan earned $10.80 per hour at her job. How many hours did Joan have to work in order to equal Luisa's earnings for 40 hours?

   (1) 20
   (2) 25
   (3) 30
   (4) 252
   (5) Not enough information is given.

Question 2 is based on the following figure.

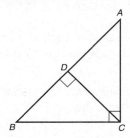

2. △ABC is a right triangle, and $\overline{CD} \perp \overline{AB}$. If the measure of ∠CAD = 40°, what is the measure of ∠DCB?

   (1) 10°
   (2) 20°
   (3) 40°
   (4) 50°
   (5) 90°

3. The number of students in a class is x. One day 5 students were absent. What fractional part of the class was present?

   (1) $\dfrac{x}{5}$

   (2) $\dfrac{5}{x}$

   (3) $\dfrac{5}{x-5}$

   (4) $\dfrac{x+5}{5}$

   (5) $\dfrac{x-5}{x}$

4. The gasoline gauge shows that a gasoline tank is $\dfrac{1}{3}$ full. In order to fill the tank, 16 gallons of gasoline are added. How many gallons of gasoline does the tank hold when full?

   (1) 20
   (2) 24
   (3) 30
   (4) 32
   (5) 48

Question 5 is based on the following figure.

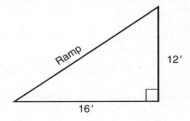

5. What is the length, in feet, of the ramp?

   Mark your answer in the circles on the grid on the answer sheet.

GO ON TO THE NEXT PAGE

TEST 5: MATHEMATICS, PART I

6. At a luncheon, 48 half-pints of fruit juice are served. What is the cost, at $3.50 per gallon, of these servings of fruit juice?

   (1) $6.00
   (2) $7.00
   (3) $10.50
   (4) $12.50
   (5) $15.00

7. If $5x - 1 = 34$, then $2\frac{1}{2} x$ is equal to

   (1) 7
   (2) 14
   (3) $16\frac{2}{3}$
   (4) 17
   (5) $17\frac{1}{2}$

Question 8 is based on the following figure.

8. If $AC = 18$ inches and $BC = 8$ inches, the ratio $AB:BC$ is equal to

   (1) 2:1
   (2) 4:5
   (3) 3:2
   (4) 5:4
   (5) Not enough information is given.

9. A rectangular living room has a floor area of 322 square feet. If the length of the room is 23 feet, what is the perimeter in feet?

   Mark your answer in the circles on the grid on the answer sheet.

10. Fatima saw a digital camera priced at $280 at the Triangle Store. She then saw an advertisement for the same camera at Computer Central, announcing 20% off on all merchandise. What additional information does Fatima need to make a wise buying decision?

    (1) The Triangle Store has a better reputation than Computer Central.
    (2) The sales tax on digital camera purchases is 5%.
    (3) Both stores have a $5 delivery charge.
    (4) The name of the manufacturer of the digital camera is Optomix.
    (5) The price of the digital camera at Computer Central is $280.

11. A crew can load a truck in 3 hours. What part of the truck can they load in 45 minutes?

    Mark your answer in the circles on the grid on the answer sheet.

12. Given the equation $x^2 + x - 6 = 0$, which of the following give(s) a complete solution of the equation?

    (1) 2
    (2) 2 and −3
    (3) −2 and 3
    (4) 2 and 3
    (5) 3 and −3

GO ON TO THE NEXT PAGE

TEST 5: MATHEMATICS, PART I

13. Mrs. Edwards buys 40 feet of woolen material to use for scarfs. How many scarfs each 3 feet 4 inches in length can she cut from this material?

    Mark your answer in the circles on the grid on the answer sheet.

14. Henry has $5 more than Bob, who has the same amount of money as Tom. Together, all three have $65. How much money does Bob have?

    (1) $10
    (2) $12
    (3) $15
    (4) $20
    (5) Not enough information is given.

15. A motel charges $89.00 per day for a double room. In addition, there is a 9.5% tax. How much does a couple pay for several days' stay?

    (1) $198.86
    (2) $208.20
    (3) $246.60
    (4) $288.95
    (5) Not enough information is given.

16. If the square of a number is added to the number increased by 4, the result is 60. If n represents the number, which equation can be used to find n?

    (1) $n^2 + 4 = 60$
    (2) $n^2 + 4n = 60$
    (3) $n^2 + n + 4 = 60$
    (4) $n^2 + 60 = 4n + 4$
    (5) $n^2 + n = 64$

17. Evaluate $(6 \times 10^5) \div (4 \times 10^3)$.

    (1) 20
    (2) 100
    (3) 150
    (4) 1,500
    (5) 2,000

18. The measures of the angles of a triangle are in the ratio $3:2:1$. What is the measure of the largest angle of the triangle?

    (1) 65°
    (2) 70°
    (3) 72°
    (4) 80°
    (5) 90°

GO ON TO THE NEXT PAGE

TEST 5: MATHEMATICS, PART I

Question 19 is based on the following figure.

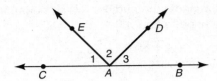

19. If m∠1 = 36° and m∠2 = 2(m∠3), then m∠3 equals

   (1) 36°
   (2) 40°
   (3) 44°
   (4) 48°
   (5) Not enough information is given.

20. Mrs. Adams bought 4 pounds of beef and $3\frac{1}{2}$ pounds of chicken for $21.99. If the beef costs $4.29 per pound, what was the cost of the chicken per pound?

   (1) $1.29
   (2) $1.34
   (3) $1.38
   (4) $1.49
   (5) $1.52

21. A carpenter earns $22 per hour, and his assistant earns half as much. Which of the following expressions represents how many dollars both men earned on a job that took 9 hours?

   (1) $9(22) + 9(\frac{1}{2})$

   (2) $9(22) + 9(10)$
   (3) $22(8) + 9(9)$

   (4) $22(\frac{1}{2}) + 9(\frac{1}{2})$

   (5) $9(22) + 9(11)$

22. The difference in estimated weights between two asteroids is 63,150,000,000 tons. What is this number expressed in scientific notation?

   (1) 631.5×10^8
   (2) 63.15×10^9
   (3) 6315×10^7
   (4) 6.315×10^{10}
   (5) 6.315×10^{-10}

23. A lines passes through a point whose coordinates are (−4,−2). Show the location of the point.
   Mark your answer on the coordinate plane grid on the answer sheet.

24. Mr. Barnes has invested $12,000 in bonds that pay interest at the rate of 9% annually. What is Mr. Barnes's annual income expressed in dollars from this investment?
   Mark your answer in the circles on the grid on the answer sheet.

25. Which of the following numbers is a solution of the inequality $3x + 2 < 14$?

   (1) 3
   (2) 4
   (3) 5
   (4) 6
   (5) 7

END OF EXAM

TEST 5: MATHEMATICS, PART II

Directions: You will have 45 minutes to complete questions 26–50. You may NOT use a calculator; otherwise, directions are the same as in Part I. You MAY refer to the *Formulas* sheet.

Question 26 is based on the following graph.

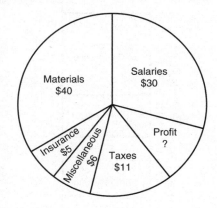

26. The graph shows what happens to each $100 taken in by a small business firm. How many dollars out of each $100 taken in represent profit?

    (1) $5
    (2) $6
    (3) $7
    (4) $7.5
    (5) $8

Question 27 is based on the following figure.

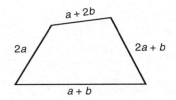

27. What is the perimeter of the figure?

    (1) $6a + b$
    (2) $5a + 5b$
    (3) $6a + 4b$
    (4) $4a + 4b$
    (5) $3a + 5b$

28. Ben scored 7 more points than Jack in a basketball game. Paul scored 2 points less than Jack in the same game. If the three boys scored a total of 38 points, how many points did Jack score?

    (1) 5
    (2) 9
    (3) 11
    (4) 14
    (5) 15

Question 29 refers to the following diagram.

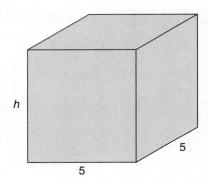

29. A commercial recycling bin (shown above) in the form of a rectangular solid has a square base 5 feet in length and a height of h feet. If the volume of the rectangular solid is 200 cubic feet, which of the following equations may be used to find h?

    (1) $5h = 200$
    (2) $5h^2 = 200$
    (3) $25h = 200$
    (4) $h = 200 \div 5$
    (5) $h = 5(200)$

GO ON TO THE NEXT PAGE

TEST 5: MATHEMATICS, PART II

<u>Question 30</u> is based on the following figure.

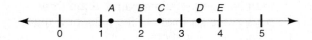

30. Which point on the number line represents the closest approximation to the square root of 12?

    (1) *A*

    (2) *B*

    (3) *C*

    (4) *D*

    (5) *E*

<u>Question 31</u> is based on the following figure.

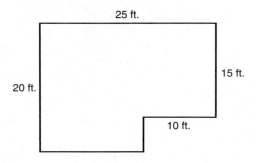

31. The diagram represents a large living room. What is the area, in square feet, of the room?

    Mark your answer in the circles on the grid on the answer sheet.

<u>Questions 32 and 33</u> are based on the following graph.

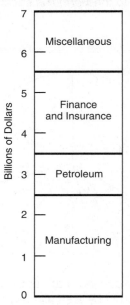

32. What Americans spend per year on video games is equal to 50% of foreign investment in finance and insurance. How much do Americans spend annually on video games?

    (1) $300 million

    (2) $1.5 billion

    (3) $1 billion

    (4) $2 billion

    (5) $.75 billion

GO ON TO THE NEXT PAGE

TEST 5: MATHEMATICS, PART II

33. How much more is invested in manufacturing than in petroleum?

   (1) $$1\frac{1}{2}$ million

   (2) $$3\frac{1}{2}$ million

   (3) $0.5 billion

   (4) $$1\frac{1}{2}$ billion

   (5) $$3\frac{1}{2}$ billion

34. Evaulate $y^2(4x - y)$ if $y = -2$ and $x = 8$

   (1) −18
   (2) 18
   (3) 86
   (4) 96
   (5) 136

35. On a road map, $\frac{1}{4}$ inch represents 8 miles of actual road distance. The towns of Alton and Waverly are represented by points $2\frac{1}{8}$ inches apart on the map. What is the actual distance, in miles, between Alton and Waverly?

   Mark your answer in the circles on the grid on the answer sheet.

36. At a certain time of day, a man 6 feet tall casts a shadow 4 feet in length. At the same time, a church steeple casts a shadow 28 feet in length. How high, in feet, is the church steeple?

   (1) 30
   (2) 32
   (3) 42
   (4) 48
   (5) 56

Question 37 and 38 are based on the following table.

Nutrition Facts for Tastee Chips	
Serving Size 1 oz. (10 chips)	
	% Daily Value
Total 6 g	**9%**
Saturated Fat 0.5 g	**3%**
Cholesterol 0 mg	**0%**
Sodium 110 mg	**5%**
Total Carbohydrates 19 g	**6%**
Dietary Fiber 1 g	**5%**

37. If Kristen eats 15 chips, what percent of the daily value of total carbohydrates has she consumed?

   (1) 9%
   (2) 12%
   (3) 3%
   (4) 33%
   (5) 28.5%

38. The Tastee Company introduces new Tastee Chips *Light,* claiming the product has "half the saturated fat" of the original, described above. How many grams of saturated fat should the *light* chips have for this claim to be true?

   (1) 1 gram
   (2) .05 gram
   (3) 1.5 grams
   (4) .2 gram
   (5) .25 gram

GO ON TO THE NEXT PAGE

TEST 5: MATHEMATICS, PART II

Question 39 is based on the following figure.

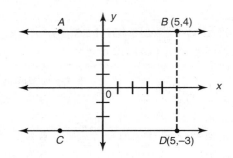

39. In the figure $\overleftrightarrow{AB}$ and $\overleftrightarrow{CD}$ are both parallel to the x-axis. The coordinates of B are (5,4) and the coordinates of D are (5,–3). The perpendicular distance between $\overleftrightarrow{AB}$ and $\overleftrightarrow{CD}$ is

(1) –2

(2) 5

(3) 6

(4) 7

(5) 10

Question 40 is based on the following graph.

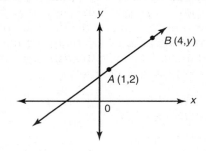

40. If the slope of $\overleftrightarrow{AB}$ is 1, what is the value of y?

(1) 1

(2) 2

(3) 3

(4) 4

(5) 5

Questions 41–43 are based on the following graph.

The graph shows the number of gallons of paint sold by a local hardware store in 1 week.

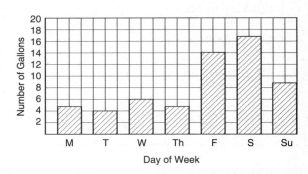

41. How many gallons of paint were sold on Wednesday?

(1) 3

(2) 4

(3) 5

(4) 6

(5) 7

42. By what percent did sales increase on Saturday compared with Tuesday?

(1) about 50%

(2) more than 300%

(3) between 150% and 200%

(4) 100%

(5) 400%

43. What was the total amount, in gallons, of paint sold by the store that week?
Mark your answer in the circles on the grid on the answer sheet.

GO ON TO THE NEXT PAGE

TEST 5: MATHEMATICS, PART II

Question 44 is based on the following figure.

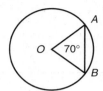

44. *O* is the center of the circle, and the measure of ∠*O* is 70°. What is the measure in degrees of ∠*OAB*?

Mark your answer in the circles on the grid on the answer sheet.

Question 45 is based on the following table.

Time	3:00 P.M.	4:00 P.M.	5:00 P.M.
Distance covered (miles)	80	124	168

45. Sylvia took a trip by car. The table shows the mileage she covered during one afternoon. If she drove at a steady rate, how many miles had she covered at 4:15 P.M.?

(1) 30
(2) 132
(3) 135
(4) 140
(5) Not enough information is given.

46. The following is a list of ingredients used in making cornmeal crisps:

1 cup of yellow cornmeal

$\frac{1}{2}$ cup of sifted flour

$\frac{2}{3}$ teaspoon of salt

$\frac{1}{4}$ teaspoon of baking powder

2 tablespoons of melted shortening

$\frac{1}{3}$ cup of milk

If Joan decides to make a larger batch of cookies by using a full cup of milk, she will have to use

(1) 1 cup of sifted flour
(2) 2 teaspoons of salt
(3) 3 teaspoons of baking powder
(4) 3 tablespoons of melted shortening
(5) $2\frac{1}{2}$ cups of yellow cornmeal

TEST 5: MATHEMATICS, PART II

Question 47 is based on the following graph.

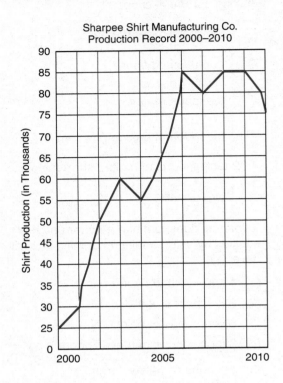

Sharpee Shirt Manufacturing Co.
Production Record 2000–2010

47. In what year did Sharpee experience a $10,000 decrease in sales from the previous year?

(1) 2000
(2) 2004
(3) 2006
(4) 2007
(5) 2010

48. A house and a lot cost $200,000. If the house cost 3 times as much as the lot, how much did the house cost?

(1) $115,000
(2) $120,000
(3) $140,000
(4) $150,000
(5) $175,000

Question 49 is based on the following figure.

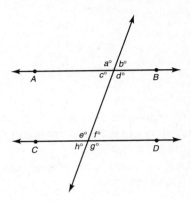

49. If $\overleftrightarrow{AB}$ is parallel to $\overleftrightarrow{CD}$, each of the following is true EXCEPT

(1) $a = d$
(2) $b = f$
(3) $c = b$
(4) $f = c$
(5) $b = g$

Question 50 is based on the following figure.

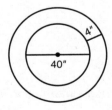

50. A flower bed is circular in shape with a concrete border. If the diameter of the flower section is 40 inches and the width of the concrete border is 4 inches, what is the area, in square inches, of the border? (Leave your answer in terms of π.)

(1) 16π
(2) 176π
(3) 180π
(4) 200π
(5) 240π

END OF EXAM

ANSWER KEYS, SUMMARIES OF RESULTS, AND SELF-APPRAISAL CHARTS

TEST 1: LANGUAGE ARTS, WRITING, PART I/PAGE 747

I. CHECK YOUR ANSWERS, using the following answer key:

1. **5**	10. **1**	19. **4**	28. **4**	37. **1**	46. **5**
2. **2**	11. **1**	20. **5**	29. **1**	38. **1**	47. **4**
3. **3**	12. **3**	21. **5**	30. **2**	39. **2**	48. **5**
4. **4**	13. **1**	22. **2**	31. **1**	40. **4**	49. **1**
5. **1**	14. **5**	23. **2**	32. **1**	41. **3**	50. **5**
6. **1**	15. **5**	24. **3**	33. **4**	42. **1**	
7. **1**	16. **5**	25. **5**	34. **2**	43. **3**	
8. **1**	17. **1**	26. **3**	35. **3**	44. **1**	
9. **1**	18. **5**	27. **4**	36. **4**	45. **1**	

II. SCORE YOURSELF:

Number correct:

Excellent	_____	
	45–50	
Good	_____	
	39–44	
Fair	_____	
	33–38	

III. EVALUATE YOUR SCORE: Did you get at least 35 correct answers? If not, you need more practice for the Language Arts, Writing, Part I test. In any event, you can improve your performance to Excellent or Good by analyzing your errors.

IV. ANALYZE YOUR ERRORS: To determine your areas of weakness, list the number of correct answers you had under each of the following categories (which correspond to the content areas of the Language Arts, Writing, Part I test), and compare your score with the average scores specified in the right-hand column. Review the answer analysis section beginning on page 813 for each of the questions you got wrong, and give yourself more practice in your weak areas before attempting Practice Exam Two.

Content Areas	Items	Your Score	Average Score
Sentence Structure	1, 3, 5, 8, 10–12, 19, 25, 32, 35, 45, 50		8
Usage	4, 7, 13, 23, 26–28 30–31, 36, 43, 47		8
Mechanics			
Possessives/contractions/ homonyms	6, 22, 40, 42		3
Punctuation	24, 33, 41, 44		3
Capitalization	2, 29, 34, 39		3
Organization	9, 17, 37–38, 46, 48, 49		5
No correction	14–15, 16, 18, 20–21		3

Total _____

TEST 2: SOCIAL STUDIES/PAGE 760

I. CHECK YOUR ANSWERS, using the following answer key:

1. **2**	11. **3**	21. **1**	31. **5**	41. **3**
2. **4**	12. **3**	22. **3**	32. **1**	42. **4**
3. **2**	13. **1**	23. **2**	33. **3**	43. **4**
4. **4**	14. **1**	24. **1**	34. **4**	44. **2**
5. **4**	15. **2**	25. **4**	35. **3**	45. **1**
6. **3**	16. **2**	26. **4**	36. **2**	46. **3**
7. **1**	17. **4**	27. **4**	37. **4**	47. **4**
8. **4**	18. **3**	28. **4**	38. **2**	48. **5**
9. **2**	19. **1**	29. **3**	39. **3**	49. **3**
10. **4**	20. **4**	30. **2**	40. **1**	50. **3**

II. SCORE YOURSELF:

Number correct:

Excellent	_____
	45–50
Good	_____
	40-44
Fair	_____
	35–39

III. EVALUATE YOUR SCORE: Did you get at least 35 correct answers? If not, you need more practice for the Social Studies test. In any event, you can improve your performance to Excellent or Good by analyzing your errors.

II. ANALYZE YOUR ERRORS: To determine your specific weaknesses, list the number of correct answers you had under each of the following categories (which correspond to the content areas of the Social Studies test), and compare your score with the average scores specified in the right-hand column. Review the answer analysis section beginning on page 816 for each of the questions you got wrong, and give yourself more practice in your weak areas (including the "Glossary of Social Studies Terms"), before attempting Practice Exam Two.

Content Areas	Items	Your Score	Average Score
Civics and Government	1–6, 8–9, 21–22, 34–36, 39, 41–47, 49–50		11
Economics	10–13, 19–20		4
History	7, 14–18, 28–33, 40		9
Geography	23–27, 37–38, 48		6

Total _____

TEST 3: SCIENCE/PAGE 773

I. CHECK YOUR ANSWERS, using the following answer key:

1. **5**	11. **5**	21. **3**	31. **3**	41. **5**
2. **5**	12. **1**	22. **1**	32. **2**	42. **2**
3. **1**	13. **2**	23. **3**	33. **5**	43. **3**
4. **2**	14. **2**	24. **4**	34. **1**	44. **3**
5. **1**	15. **4**	25. **3**	35. **2**	45. **5**
6. **3**	16. **3**	26. **4**	36. **4**	46. **3**
7. **4**	17. **4**	27. **4**	37. **3**	47. **1**
8. **1**	18. **4**	28. **2**	38. **3**	48. **2**
9. **4**	19. **4**	29. **3**	39. **4**	49. **2**
10. **2**	20. **1**	30. **4**	40. **2**	50. **4**

II. SCORE YOURSELF:

Number correct:

Excellent	_____
	44–50
Good	_____
	38–43
Fair	_____
	32–37

III. EVALUATE YOUR SCORE: Did you get at least 32 correct answers? If not, you need more practice for the Science test. In any event, you can improve your performance to Excellent or Good by analyzing your errors.

IV. ANALYZE YOUR ERRORS: To determine your specific weaknesses, encircle the number of each question you got wrong. This will reveal the specific science area that needs emphasis in planning your study program. After studying the answer analysis section beginning on page 820 for each of the questions you got wrong, list the terms that you feel need further explanation and study them in the "Glossary of Scientific Terms" beginning on page 423. Then give yourself more practice in your weak areas before attempting Practice Exam Two.

Content Areas	Items	Your Score	Average Score
Biology	1–22, 32, 33, 41, 44, 45, 47–50		22
Earth Science	23–25, 37, 39, 40, 46		3
Chemistry	26–31, 34, 36, 37, 42, 43, 51–57		10
Physics	35, 38		7

Total _____

TEST 4: LANGUAGE ARTS, READING/PAGE 785

I. CHECK YOUR ANSWERS, using the following answer key:

1. **1**	9. **3**	17. **3**	25. **5**	33. **3**
2. **4**	10. **1**	18. **2**	26. **4**	34. **3**
3. **2**	11. **1**	19. **2**	27. **1**	35. **5**
4. **3**	12. **1**	20. **1**	28. **5**	36. **4**
5. **3**	13. **4**	21. **2**	29. **3**	37. **3**
6. **4**	14. **3**	22. **2**	30. **3**	38. **1**
7. **2**	15. **3**	23. **1**	31. **4**	39. **4**
8. **1**	16. **4**	24. **3**	32. **5**	40. **5**

II. SCORE YOURSELF:

Number correct:

Excellent ﹐_____
36–40

Good _____
32–35

Fair _____
28–31

III. EVALUATE YOUR SCORE: Did you get at least 28 correct answers? If not, you need more practice for the Language Arts, Reading test. You can improve your performance to Excellent or Good by analyzing your errors.

IV. ANALYZE YOUR ERRORS: To determine your specific weaknesses, first list the number of correct answers you had under each of the following categories and compare your score with the average scores in the right-hand column. After studying the answer analysis section beginning on page 824 for each of the questions you answered incorrectly, study the material in the sections "Basic Reading Skills" and "Reading Prose, Poetry, and Drama" as well as the "Glossary of Literary Terms" (page 504) to strengthen your weak areas before attempting Practice Exam Two.

Reading Skills	Items	Your Score	Average Score
Locating the Main Idea	6, 15, 26, 28, 31		3
Finding Details	2–3, 7, 11, 13–14, 16–17, 25, 27–29, 33–34, 36–37, 40		12
Inferring Meaning	4–5, 12, 18–20, 22–23, 32, 35		6
Making Inferences	8–10, 17, 21, 24, 26–27, 38–39		7
Determining Tone and Mood	1, 13–14		2
Inferring Character	5, 30		1

Total _____

Now, to see how your scores in the content area of Language Arts, Reading test compare with the average scores in the right-hand column, list your score for each of the following:

Literary Forms	Items	Your Score	Average Score
Prose Fiction	11–20		7
Prose Nonfiction	1–10, 31–40		15
Poetry	21–25		3
Drama	26–30		3

Total _____

TEST 5: MATHEMATICS/PAGE 795

I. CHECK YOUR ANSWERS, using the following answer key:

Part I

1. **3**	
2. **3**	
3. **5**	
4. **2**	
5. **20**	
6. **3**	
7. **5**	
8. **4**	
9. **74**	
10. **5**	
11. **1/4 or .25**	
12. **2**	
13. **12**	
14. **4**	
15. **5**	
16. **3**	
17. **3**	
18. **5**	
19. **4**	
20. **3**	

21. **5**
22. **4**
23.

24. **1,080**
25. **1**

Part II

26. **5**
27. **3**
28. **3**
29. **3**
30. **4**

31. **450**
32. **3**
33. **4**
34. **5**
35. **68**
36. **3**
37. **1**
38. **5**
39. **4**
40. **5**
41. **4**
42. **2**
43. **60**
44. **55**
45. **3**
46. **2**
47. **5**
48. **4**
49. **5**
50. **2**

II. SCORE YOURSELF:

Number correct:

Excellent	_____
	40–50
Good	_____
	32–49
Fair	_____
	28–31

III. EVALUATE YOUR SCORE: Did you get at least 38 correct answers? If not, you need more practice for the Mathematics test. In any event, you can improve your performance to Excellent or Good by analyzing your errors.

IV. ANALYZE YOUR ERRORS: To determine your specific weaknesses, list the number of correct answers you had under each of the following categories, and compare your score with the average scores specified in the right-hand column. After studying the answer analysis section beginning on page 826 for each of the questions you got wrong, give yourself more practice in your weak areas before attempting Practice Exam Two.

Content Areas	Items	Your Score	Average Score
Numbers and Basic Operations	1, 4, 9, 11, 13, 16, 17, 22, 34, 48		5
Fractions and Measurements	6, 20, 35, 46		2
Decimals and Percents	10, 15, 24		2
Data Analysis	26, 29, 30, 32, 33, 37 38, 41–43, 45, 47		7
Algebra	3, 7, 8, 12, 14, 21, 25 28, 36		5
Geometry	2, 5, 18, 19, 23, 27, 31 39, 40, 44, 49, 50		7

Total _____

Your Total GED Score

The Language Arts, Writing Test _____

The Social Studies Test _____

The Science Test _____

The Language Arts, Reading Test _____

The Mathematics Test _____

Total _____

ANSWER ANALYSIS

TEST 1: LANGUAGE ARTS, WRITING, PART I/PAGE 747

1. **5** This change is necessary to correct the run-on sentence.

2. **2** *Department of Agriculture* must be capitalized.

3. **3** The singular subject *Care* requires the singular verb *is*. *Among* is necessary because the verb *include* implies other precautions that are not mentioned.

4. **4** The correct verb to agree with the subject *errands* is *have*.

5. **1** The original is correct because two equally important ideas require two independent clauses connected by a coordinate conjunction. Since the clauses express similar, not opposing, ideas, *and*, rather than *but*, is the correct conjunction.

6. **1** The correct homonym is *for; four* is the number.

7. **1** The correct pronoun to agree with the noun *foods* is *they*.

8. **1** The use of the two adjective clauses *which contain food that may be* avoids the repetition of *swollen or leaking can*.

9. **1** The first sentence is the thesis statement because it is a general statement about food safety beginning in the marketplace; all other sentences relate to that one idea.

10. **1** The original is correct. The second idea, "the people in the family may change," is in opposition to the first, so *although* is necessary. The comma after *dominant* must be retained.

11. **1** This combination eliminates repetition of the words *will also increase*.

12. **3** This is necessary to avoid the run-on sentence.

13. **1** The correct pronoun to agree with the noun *families* is *their*, meaning "belonging to them."

14. **5** No correction is necessary.

15. **5** No correction is necessary.

16. **5** No correction is necessary.

17. **1** No new paragraph is needed in this passage.

18. **5** No correction is necessary.

19. **4** The sentences are best combined by an adjective clause, *that spreads*, which modifies *disease*.

20. **5** No correction is necessary.

21. **5** No correction is necessary.

22. **2** The correct homonym is *their*, meaning "belonging to them."

23. **2** To achieve parallelism with *knowledge* and *understanding*, a noun, *example*, must be used.

24. **3** A comma is needed after a lengthy introductory clause.

25. **5** This change is necessary to prevent a run-on sentence.

26. **3** The proper sequence of tenses requires the future perfect tense *will have been* since this action precedes *is tempted*.

27. **4** The pronoun, *his*, must agree in number with its antecedent, *drug abuser*.

28. **4** The verb, *is*, must be singular because its subject, *type*, is singular.

29. **1** *Americans* should be capitalized.

30. **2** The correct verb to agree with the subject *nine* is *are*.

31. **1** The correct pronoun to agree with the noun *injuries* is *they*.

32. **1** The correct pronoun to agree with noun *injuries* is *they*.

33. **4** A comma is used to separate items in a series.

34. **2** *Medical* should not be capitalized in the sentence because it is not a proper pronoun.

35. **3** The sentence is a run-on sentence and requires a comma before the conjunction *but*.

36. **4** The insertion of *are* is necessary to parallel *are in a hurry* and *are careless*.

37. **1** After sentence 10, a new topic begins; therefore, a new paragraph should be started.

38. **1** No correction is necessary.

39. **2** *Mom* and *Pop* should be capitalized since they are proper nouns.

40. **4** The proper homonym is *your*, meaning "belonging to you."

41. **3** A comma, not a period, is necessary before the final verb in the series, which cannot be a separate sentence.

42. **1** The correct spelling is *accessories*.

43. **3** *You're*, which is a contraction of *you are*, is required in this sentence.

44. **1** The original is the best way. The colon is used because it introduces the advice.

45. **1** *Invest in* is required by the sense of the sentence.

46. **5** No new paragraph is needed in this passage. All ideas have been clearly organized.

47. **4** *Whom* is necessary since this word is the object of the preposition *with* and must be in the objective case.

48. **5** No new paragraph is needed in this passage. All ideas have been clearly organized.

49. **1** Sentence 1 is the thesis statement because it generally states "clothes can help establish a person's identity. . . ." All other sentences relate to this one idea.

50. **5** *Since* would be required because the second idea is the result of the first.

TEST 1: LANGUAGE ARTS, WRITING, PART II/PAGE 759

SAMPLE ESSAY

I have known a great many people in my life, but the one person that has had the greatest influence on my life would be my father. He taught me that hard work really pays off, small things really matter, and love lasts more than a lifetime.

My father taught me that hard work really pays off. He worked day and night in a small mining company barely making enough to feed a family of seven. I never heard him complain as he brought home his weekly pay and handed it to my mother to buy food and necessities. I remember how hard and how long he had to work to be able to buy me a new coat for winter. It made me appreciate it all the more.

My father taught me that small things in life really matter. He didn't have a lot of material possessions to offer me, but would often save me back a part of his lunch. He knew that I met him at the end of the driveway every day to carry his lunchbox and I would always look in to see if there was something for me. There usually was.

My father taught me that love lasts more than a lifetime. I found this out when he passed away. I will never forget the love that he had for me and my family and I for him. His lunchbox remains on the shelf as a reminder of the times we shared.

My father was a wonderful person who influenced my life more than he will ever know. It was both a privilege and an honor to be his daughter.

TEST 2: SOCIAL STUDIES/PAGE 760

1. **2** As indicated in the first paragraph, the word *genocide* is the joining of the Greek *genos*, meaning race or tribe, and the Latin suffix *-cide*, meaning killing.

2. **4** The third paragraph gives the scope of the term *genocide* as including the intent to destroy a national, ethnical, racial, or religious group. It does not refer to political groups, as such.

3. **2** Genocide was practiced on a large scale by the Nazis in the destruction of six million Jews. Other groups that have been subjected to genocide, as mentioned in the second paragraph, are Armenians, Gypsies, and Chinese.

4. **4** This obviously is a ruling of a court. Therefore of the choices given, only Choice 4, the Supreme Court, could be correct. Incidentally, this selection is part of the important decision of the Supreme Court on the subject of desegregation of schools.

5. **4** The passage indicates that to separate children in grade and high schools solely because of race is to generate a feeling of inferiority in minority children. This is a psychological reason for rejecting segregation.

6. **3** The first sentence of the final paragraph indicates that modern psychological knowledge does not support the *Plessy* v. *Ferguson* decision and, by implication, indicates that psychological knowledge at the time of *Plessy* v. *Ferguson* no longer applies.

7. **1** The image is a Pulitzer prize-winning photograph by Bill Pierce. His photo captured the South Vietnamese military officer's quick and brutal execution of an undercover Vietcong soldier. His photograph sparked even more protest against America's involvement in the Vietnam War.

8. **4** Both the Democrats and Republicans include supporters from all sections of the nation and from various social and ethnic backgrounds. Each contains leaders and members whose political views range from conservative to moderate to liberal. To gain control of the government, a political party needs the support of a majority of the American voters, and thus must have broad appeal. The Democrats have usually drawn support from labor and minority groups; the Republicans, from businesspeople and wealthier farmers. Party differences have been greater on domestic issues (e.g., tax cuts and spending for social programs) than on foreign policy.

9. **2** The cartoon refers to the first free elections in South Africa, which took place in 1994, when a new constitution provided equal rights to vote for all South Africans. The shackle falling from the arm of the black voter symbolizes the freedom that came with the right to vote.

10. **4** In the graph of economic growth, the line for actual growth is much higher for 1996–1999, about 3.6%, than the forecast of about 2.4%.

11. **3** The lines for actual and forecast inflation nearly coincide, indicating the accuracy of the economists' forecasts.

12. **3** The gap between the fast-rising "desired demand" and the "potential supply," which levels off, is first noticeable on the graph at about 1990.

13. **1** Western European countries and Japan would lack fuel for their industries, and production would drop, with resultant unemployment and depression.

14. **1** Such resistance is often expressed by *denying* the formal methods for peaceful change. Failure to permit evolutionary change may result in revolution.

15. **2** Speaker *B* holds that the frontier made U.S. history unique; he would see only dissimilarities between the French and American revolutions. Speaker *C* stresses historical compromise between conflicting American groups.

16. **2** Speaker *B* would most likely agree that the existence of the American frontier provided a *safety valve* for those who wanted to leave the more crowded East. Such space was unavailable in the European countries from which most Americans or their forebears had come.

17. **4** The different historical perspective of each historian will assign differing causes and results to the same major events.

18. **3** The company's charter gave it a monopoly over colonization and trade in an area, with profits being shared by the shareholders and the King.

19. **1** President Johnson mentioned full employment as the first of America's unfinished tasks and the first goal that must be achieved in the national interest.

20. **4** President Johnson listed the widening of the benefits of prosperity as one of the tasks that remained unfinished.

21. **1** While the president is authorized to negotiate treaties, two-thirds of the Senate must ratify any treaty he negotiates. This is the system of checks and balances.

22. **3** The role of the Senate is authorized in Section 3 of Article 1 of the Constitution.

23. **2** A valid generalization from the chart is that industrialized nations have lower birth rates and infant mortality rates than developing nations. The first six nations of the chart are developing nations, whereas the last six are industrialized nations. The average birth rate of the developing nations is four times greater than that of the industrialized nations. The difference between infant mortality rates is even greater, from Uganda's, which is 12 times greater than Italy's, to Angola's, which is 57 times greater than Japan's.

24. **1** According to the chart, the lowest birthrates are found mostly in western Europe. Four of the six industrialized nations with low birthrates are in western Europe.

25. **4** Uganda, Somalia, Angola, and Ethiopia, four of the six countries with the highest infant mortality, are in Africa.

26. **4** Oil spills have repeatedly ruined the recreational value of beaches and destroyed fish and birdlife, causing both economic and ecological damage.

27. **4** The definition states that topography deals with the surface features of a region.

28. **4** The passage alludes to "principles of union," "cement to the Union," and "their best interests would be best promoted by union."

29. **3** The passage refers to "reasonable jealousies" between the people of the eastern and the southern states.

30. **2** Jealousies "subsided" when inhabitants of different states became better acquainted.

31. **5** The frontier's passing coincides with the end of gifts of free land.

32. **1** The author lists all the contributions of the frontier—escape from the past and opportunity for new experiences, among others.

33. **3** It was written one hundred years after the Constitution (1789) and four hundred years after the discovery of America (1492).

34. **4** The cartoon refers to the collapse of communism in the early 1990s. The hammer and sickle is a symbol of the Soviet Union. A series of symbols is arranged to look like the rib cage of the skeleton of a dinosaur, and the wording in the cartoon implies that communism, like the dinosaur, could not adapt to change.

35. **3** The hammer and sickle is the symbol of the former Union of Socialist Soviet Republics (USSR).

36. **2** Heredity and environment each represents various factors contributing to the behavior of individuals and groups. No *single* factor can be isolated and identified as determining human actions.

37. **4** It is trade that keeps us alive.

38. **2** Increased population was due to speeded-up economic unification.

39. **3** Two views regarding assimilation of Native Americans into American life are mentioned—a belief that total assimilation is inevitable, and a belief that Native Americans will keep separate identities for a long time into the future.

40. **1** Collective security calls for nations to coordinate their military strength to protect one another from aggression.

41. **3** Social mobility is the movement of individuals up or down in social and economic status in society, largely on ability and effort. Choice 3 is an example of social mobility.

42. **4** Cultural diversity, a variety of cultural patterns, exists where different peoples come together frequently and intermingle. Migration is a principal means of bringing this diversity about.

43. **4** Culture shock results from rapid social change—movement to a more developed society or movement to a less developed one. Choice 4 is an example of the latter.

44. **2** An extended family includes grandparents, uncles, aunts, and cousins. Out of economic necessity, they may live together and survive because of their dependence on one another.

45. **1** A pluralistic society encourages coexistence of peoples of various ethnic heritages, usually holding differing views on important issues.

46. **3** The study found that United States adolescents smoke less than those in many industrialized nations.

47. **4** The 15-year-olds ranked 20th, 14 places lower than 11-year-olds. They are less addicted to TV.

48. **5** The passage states that geographic natural features leave their imprint on society.

49. **3** In Table *A*, 65% opposed home searches without a specific warrant; 68% opposed electronic surveillance of citizens without a court order.

50. **3** Table *B* shows that 63% would allow the federal government to eavesdrop with specific court permission. When the same question was asked negatively in Table *A*, 68% opposed electronic eavesdropping without such permission.

TEST 3: SCIENCE/PAGE 773

1. **5** The article defines a population as a group of organisms of the same species living together in a given location. An ecosystem (or ecological system) consists of the living commun-ity of a region and its nonliving environment. The biosphere is that portion of the earth in which ecosystems function. A community consists of populations of different species.

2. **5** The diagram illustrates a simple community consisting of populations of different species living together and interacting with each other.

3. **1** The factor that helps to keep a population in check is natural *predators*. Both predators and prey are adapted to each other and to the environment. If an organism is introduced into a new habitat, it will have few natural enemies or predators. Its population increases.

4. **2** In this simple community the plants carry on photosynthesis, whereby they give off oxygen and make food for themselves and the fish. The fish breathe and supply carbon dioxide to the plants, which they need for the process of photosynthesis. The wastes produced by the fish are acted upon by bacteria in the mud and produce nitrates for the plant. As long as these interrelationships are maintained, the total weight of the container and its contents will remain the same.

5. **1** A biotic factor is one concerned with living things. Minerals are not living.

6. **3** A *community* is a particular environment in which organisms of different species live and interact. A community is a self-maintaining unit in which energy and food materials are recycled.

7. **4** The chart shows a 2-year cycle, but for either year, the whales spend 5 months in Arctic waters.

8. **1** The whales are born in January (arrow 2) and by March they are migrating north. This is a span of 2 months.

9. **4** Gray whales conceive in December (arrow 1), and calves are born in January, 13 months later. Keep in mind that this figure shows a 2-year cycle.

10. **2** In its first year of life, only the first 2 months are spent in the waters off Baja California. The rest of that year is spent living in Arctic waters or migrating to and from those waters.

11. **5** This question is asking you to find a function that is specific to the right side of the brain. Choices 1 to 4 are all found in the list of left-brain functions, while musical ability, Choice 5, is a right-brain function and is the correct answer.

12. **1** Nerve cells, such as those that make up the brain are known as neurons. Notice that the term is defined for you near the end of the first paragraph. As is often the case with a GED question, the information you need is given in the passage.

13. **2** The left side of the brain is responsible for mathematical reasoning, as the table tells you.

14. **2** In order for functions to move from one side of the brain to the other, there must be some communication between the two sides. The passage explains that the *corpus callosum* is responsible for this.

15. **4** Both chemical and electrical signals are mentioned in the passage. Hemisphere signals are not mentioned at all.

16. **3** The passage says that the axon is the part of the neuron that carries the signal from neuron to neuron, and that the synapse is the junction between neurons. Each of the other choices contains an error.

17. **4** The graph shows that soil covered with mulch has a higher moisture content and less range (variation) of moisture content than soil not covered with mulch.

18. **4** Rain would probably increase the moisture content, so look for the part of the graph where moisture content increased the most, which is days 15–20. Note that this is true for both soil covered by mulch and soil not covered by mulch.

19. **4** Neither size nor color was a factor in this experiment, nor was the cost an issue. The same mice could not be reused; the variable in this experiment is learning, and the mice had already been influenced. Choice 4 is the best answer.

20. **1** This choice is a conclusion that can be drawn from the experiment. All the other choices are irrelevant or erroneous.

21. **3** This answer is given in the passage.

22. **1** The issue of illumination was not part of the experiment and is therefore irrelevant.

23. **3** As important as the other functions are, losing oxygen would have the most immediate damage. Humans can live only a matter of minutes without oxygen, but can go much longer without food or water.

24. **4** Each person needs a kilogram of oxygen a day. Multiply 1 kilogram per person per day times 10 people times 21 days to get 210 kilograms.

25. **3** Weightlessness would not be concern for people on Earth.

26. **3** The passage specifically mentions calcium compounds as being natural neutralizers of acid rain.

27. **4** Hydroelectric plants do not burn fossil fuels to generate electricity. All of the other choices are specifically mentioned as contributing to acid rain.

28. **2** The chart chows that the highest pH substance listed is lye, the most basic. The information is almost always provided to you. Your job is to take the information given in the passage and use it to answer the questions.

29. **3** Neutralization requires an acid and a base. The only combination listed among the choices that has an acid and a base is Choice 3. Choice 1 consists of two acids, and Choice 2 of two bases. Choice 4 also contains two bases. Distilled water is neutral and will not be involved in a neutralization.

30. **4** The best approach would be to reduce or stop the problem at its source. The other choices would do nothing to prevent the same problems from reappearing again.

31. **3** The passage specifically mentions that carbon dioxide dissolving in water does not cause acid rain. It also tells you that oxides of nitrogen and sulfur are leading causes of acid rain. Choices 1, 2, 4, and 5 are oxides of nitrogen and sulfur.

32. **2** When pesticides are applied to plants many pests will be killed but some may have a natural resistance to the pesticide and will not be killed. If they reproduce, their offspring will be more likely to be unaffected by the pesticide.

33. **5** Reptilia: garter snake; Aves: house sparrow; Mammalia: African elephant.

34. **1** Soda will lose its carbonation fastest at higher temperatures and lower pressure. This is the result of the carbon dioxide gas "undissolving" under those conditions.

35. **2** Locate the given pressure, 8 mm, along the horizontal axis. Move up the 8 mm line until the graph curve is reached. On the vertical axis at the left, you will find that the volume at this point is approximately 2 mL.

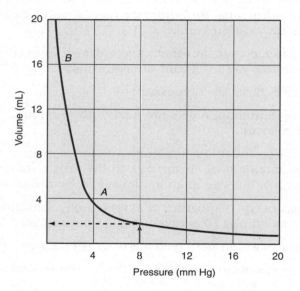

36. **4** Propane (C_3H_8) is an organic compound. HNO_3, H_2SO_4, and HCl are acids. NaCl is a salt.

37. **3** The only solution among the answers that is specifically identified in the passage as an electrolyte is sodium chloride.

38. **3** In horizontal flight, the engine thrust pushes the plane forward and air drag holds it back; if they are equal, there will be no change in speed. In Choices 1 and 2 one of the vertical forces is greater than the other. Choice 4 is wrong because the force acting on the wall has nothing to do with the speed of the ball. Choice 5 is wrong because it takes no account of the pull of gravity.

39. **4** No small planets have rings, but all the large planets except Jupiter have them. Choice 1 is wrong because Jupiter has no rings. Choice 2 is wrong because Pluto has no rings. Choice 3 is wrong because a definite trend is apparent. Choice 5 is wrong because there is no reason to believe that Pluto ever had rings.

40. **2** Only in deserts is dry sand on the surface, where it can be picked up and carried by the wind.

41. **5** If some such substance is present, there is no reason to suppose that it would affect frogs differently from fish.

42. **2** The original sample had 20.00 grams total. At the end of the heating process, 12.00 grams were left; thus, 8.00 grams must have been water that evaporated away.

43. **3** The percentage that was water was 8.00 grams water/20.00 grams total or .4 which is 40%.

44. **3** The impulse starts with irritation of the cornea, goes through a sensory neuron to the brain, and then passes through a motor neuron to the tear gland.

45. **5** That DDT-resistant mosquitoes now exist in greater numbers than 10 years ago means that genetic differences permitted some mosquitoes to survive DDT use. Mosquitoes that did not survive DDT use died off. Those with survival power lived and reproduced others with similar survival power. The result was an increase in the numbers of DDT-resistant mosquitoes in the species.

46. **3** Fossils are found in sedimentary rocks, which are laid down in layers. The oldest layers are closest to the Earth's crust, and the youngest layers are near the surface. To conclude that a species had not changed very much over the years, the unchanged fossils of that species must have been distributed throughout the layers.

47. **1** Gametes—eggs and sperms—have half as many chromosomes as somatic cells, such as leaf cells. The somatic cell number is produced at fertilization.

48. **2** Under normal circumstances, the total number of adult robins or of adult salmon does not change rapidly. Each adult pair, on the average, produces enough eggs to replace itself, so only two eggs survive to adulthood for each adult pair.

49. **2** Corn plants grown in the dark are white. The most probable explanation is that the expression of the gene for color may depend on the environment. That these plants have the genetic information for chlorophyll production can be assumed because they are genetically identical to the plants grown in the light. Light is needed to activate the chlorophyll gene.

50. **4** In sexual reproduction, new properties can be produced by recombination of the genes of the two parents.

TEST 4: LANGUAGE ARTS, READING/PAGE 785

1. **1** In the first paragraph, the writer describes "the hot, humid haze" and other details of August in his surroundings.

2. **4** The writer states that "August was a time to do nothing and be proud of it."

3. **2** The writer remembers August "with a bit of anxiety because it "was the time of hurricanes and polio."

4. **3** ". . . I remember the strange feel of the air. The first breezes of the hurricane were so mild, so moist, so soft as to be barely distinguishable from the feel of one's own skin."

5. **3** August is remembered as a time of both pleasure and anxiety. The hurricanes were scary for adults, but they were "a lot of fun" for the narrator.

6. **4** The author states "we'd be lost without" new groups.

7. **2** The family sends a bright young man or woman.

8. **1** Other family members will come with the money the youth is sending back.

9. **3** The newcomer progresses from busboy to waiter and then tries to become the owner.

10. **1** The United States rejuvenates itself by bringing in new people.

11. **1** As a religious person, Shmul-Leibele blesses the Lord for his food.

12. **1** Shmul-Leibele compliments Shoshe, saying, "the loaf is just right."

13. **4** Whiskey was not part of the ritual. Shmul-Leibele drank it because the fish course took his "breath away."

14. **3** He prayed "not to be in need . . . of their loans."

15. **3** Its purpose is to describe the Sabbath meal of an elderly Jewish couple.

16. **4** Lottie realizes Bess hadn't "seen" her shining room.

17. **3** Bess saw only a place in her sister's home and heart.

18. **2** Lottie felt that she had not really lived.

19. **2** Lottie says to Bess that she's going to let her show her how to live.

20. **1** Lottie is going to try to catch up with life.

21. **2** The poet is reacting to a "fatuous thing" (a photograph of himself) that he has been shown by a photographer.

22. **2** The poet has "spent blood and tears" and experienced "pain, the struggle and the wrack."

23. **1** Time "has graven . . . deep lines of joy and sorrow" on his face.

24. **3** The poet wants his "scars of battle" to be put back into the photograph.

25. **5** The 14-line poem is a sonnet with the rhyme scheme *a b b a a b b a c d c d e e.*

26. **4** Kay says to Grant, "I won't accept that." Conover says, "I think Kay's right."

27. **1** Grant implies that he won't play ball and states that he will go ahead with his speech.

28. **5** Grant says that "to get votes, both parties are out to buy the American people."

29. **3** Grant promises himself that he would appeal to the best in the American people.

30. **3** Grant says he'll take care of any candidate who threatens peace from now on.

31. **4** See the section "Locating the Main Idea." The opening and closing lines refer to the father's devotion to education.

32. **5** *Divined* means "guessed," not "heavenly."

33. **3** The father is described as "not like other aliens, who brought their children in dull obedience to the law . . . ."

34. **3** The author's father is described as "eager," with "nervous hands eloquent in gesture, and a voice full of feeling." He is evidently sincere, but not in the least calm.

35. **5** Here *green* means immigrant, new to the United States.

36. **4** According to the letter, Shawn Black is mentioned as an employee who performed well at Smith Incorporated, but is "destined to achieve new heights in his career and set new records for his future employer"; thus, he is seeking employment with a different company.

37. **3** According to the letter, many of Shawn Black's positive qualities are mentioned, implying that he is an excellent candidate in the marketing field.

38. **1** The letter saying that Shawn Black's "patience with employees under him and with management make him an ideal employee" implies that he has great communication skills.

39. **4** The author of the letter states that "any company considering this individual for employment has my most enthusiastic recommendation."

40. **5** The letter states that the author gives his "most enthusiastic recommendation" for Shawn Black, implying that he is pleased with his job performance at Smith Incorporated.

TEST 5: MATHEMATICS/PAGE 795

Part I

1. **3** Luisa earned a total of 40($8.10) = $324. To find the number of hours Joan would take to earn $324, divide $324 by $10.80: 324.00 ÷ 10.80 = 30

2. **3** Since m∠ACB = 90° and m∠CAD = 40°, then m∠B = 180° – 90° – 40° = 50°. In △BCD, m∠CDB = 90° and m∠B = 50°. Therefore, m∠DCB = 180° – 90° – 50° = 40°.

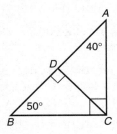

3. **5** If the class has x students and 5 students are absent, then $x - 5$ students are present:

$$\frac{x-5}{x}$$

4. **2** If the tank is $\frac{1}{3}$ full, it is $\frac{2}{3}$ empty.

Let x = capacity of tank.

$\frac{2}{3}x = 16$, so $x = 16 \div \frac{2}{3} = 16 \times \frac{3}{2} = 24$.

5. **20**   Let x = length of ramp.
Use the Pythagorean theorem to obtain the equation:
$x^2 = 12^2 + 16^2 = 144 + 256 = 400$
$x = \sqrt{400} = 20$

6. **3** 48 half-pints = 24 pt.
Since 2 pt. = 1 qt., 24 pt. = 12 qt.
Since 4 qt. = 1 gal., 12 qt. = 3 gal.
3($3.50) = $10.50

7. **5** You do not need the value of x, you need the value of $2\frac{1}{2}x = \frac{5}{2}x = \frac{5x}{2}$.

Since $5x - 1 = 34$, then $5x = 35$, and $\frac{5x}{2} = \frac{35}{2} = 17\frac{1}{2}$.

8. **4** If AC = 18 and BC = 8 then AB = 18 – 8 = 10.
The ratio $AB:BC$ = 10:8, or 5:4.

9. **74**   Let x = width of room.

$23x = 322$

$x = 322 \div 23 = 14$

Perimeter = 23 + 14 + 23 + 14 = 74 ft.

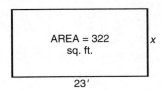

10. **5** To determine the price that Computer Central charges for the digital camera, Fatima must know the price from which the store deducts 20%.

11. **1/4 or .25**   If a crew can load a truck in 3 hrs., it can load $\dfrac{1}{3}$ of the truck in 1 hr. In 45 min., or $\dfrac{3}{4}$ hr., the crew can load $\dfrac{3}{4} \times \dfrac{1}{3} = \dfrac{1}{4} = .25$ of the truck.

12. **2** $x^2 + x - 6 = 0$

$(x + 3)(x - 2) = 0$

$x + 3 = 0 \text{ or } x - 2 = 0$

$x = -3 \text{ or } x = 2$

The correct choice is (2).

13. **12**   40 ft. = 40 × 12 = 480 in.

3 ft. 4 in. = 3(12) + 4 = 36 + 4 = 40 in.

480 ÷ 40 = 12 scarfs

14. **4** Let x = amount of money Bob has. Then x is also the amount that Tom has, and $x + 5$ = amount that Henry has.

Since $65 = x + x + x + 5 = 3x + 5$, then $3x = 60$, and $x = \$20$.

15. **5** You cannot compute the cost unless you are told the number of days that the couple stays at the motel. This information is not given.

16. **3** Let n = number.

Then n^2 = square of number, and $n + 4$ = number increased by 4.

The equation is $n^2 + n + 4 = 60$.

17. **3** $6 \times 10^5 = 600,000$

$4 \times 10^3 = 4,000$

$600,000 \div 4,000 = 600 \div 4 = 150$

18. **5** Let x, $2x$, and $3x$ be the measures of the three angles. Then:

$$3x + 2x + x = 180$$
$$6x = 180$$
$$x = 180 \div 6 = 30$$
$$3x = 3(30) = 90°.$$

19. **4** Let $x = m\angle 3$, and $2x = m\angle 2$.

$$m\angle 1 + m\angle 2 + m\angle 3 = 180°$$
$$36 + 2x + x = 180$$
$$3x + 36 = 180$$
$$3x = 180 - 36 = 144$$
$$x = 144 \div 3 = 48°$$

20. **3** The beef costs $4(\$4.29) = \$17.16$.

The chicken costs $\$21.99 - \$17.16 = \$4.83$.

To find the cost per pound of chicken, divide $\$4.83$ by $3\frac{1}{2}$, or by 3.5.

$$4.83 \div 3.5 = \$1.38$$

The chicken costs $\$1.38$ per pound.

21. **5** The carpenter earns $\$16$ per hour or $9(16)$ dollars for 9 hrs. of work.

The assistant earns $\$8$ per hour or $9(8)$ for 9 hrs. of work.

Together they earned $9(16) + 9(8)$ dollars.

22. **4** To express a number in scientific notation, express it as the product of a number between 1 and 10 and a power of 10. In this case, the number between 1 and 10 is 6.315. In going from 6.315 to 63,150,000,000, you move the decimal point 10 places to the right. Each such move represents a multiplication by 10. Thus, the entire movement of the decimal point represents multiplication by 10^{10}, and, $63,150,000,000 = 6.315 \times 10^{10}$.

23. **(–4,–2)** For the x coordinate (–4), count four places to the right of dead center (where the x and y lines intersect), then, for the y coordinate (–2), count two places down. Bubble in the appropriate grid.

24. **1,080** $\$12,000 \times 0.09 = \$1,080$

25. **1** $3x + 2 < 14$

$$3x < 12$$
$$x < 4$$

The only choice less than 4 is 3.

Part II

26. **5** Add the amounts given: $11 + 6 + 5 + 40 + 30 = \$92$

    $\$100 - \$92$ leaves $\$8$ for profit.

27. **3** To find the perimeter of the figure, find the sum of the lengths of its sides.

    $2a + a + b + 2a + b + a + 2b = 6a + 4b$

28. **3** Let x = number of points scored by Jack,

    $x + 7$ = number of points scored by Ben, and

    $x - 2$ = number of points scored by Paul.

    $$x + x + 7 + x - 2 = 38$$
    $$3x + 5 = 38$$
    $$3x = 38 - 5 = 33$$
    $$x = 33 \div 3 = 11$$

29. **3** Use the formula $V = lwh$.

    In this case, $l = 5$, $w = 5$, and $h = h$.

    Therefore, $V = 5 \times 5 \times h = 25h$ and $25h = 200$.

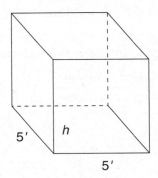

30. **4** Since $3^2 = 9$ and $4^2 = 16$, $\sqrt{12}$ is between 3 and 4. Only point D lies

    between 3 and 4.

31. **450**   Divide the floor space into 2 rectangles by drawing line segment NM.

    Area of a rectangle = lw

    Area of large rectangle = $20 \times 15 = 300$ sq. ft.

    Area of small rectangle = $10 \times 15 = 150$ sq. ft.

    Total area of floor space = $150 + 300 = 450$ sq. ft.

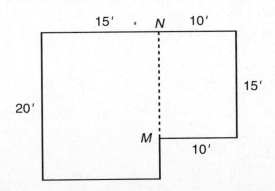

32. **3** Foreign investment on finance and insurance = $2 billion. If Americans spend 50% (or half) of that on video games, then they spend $1 billion.

33. **4** Foreign investment in manufacturing = 2\frac{1}{2}$ billion

Foreign investment in petroleum = $1 billion

Difference = 1\frac{1}{2}$ billion

34. **5** Replace the variables with their given values.

$-2^2(32 - (-2) = 4(34) = 136$

35. **68** Since $\frac{1}{4}$ in. represents 8 mi., 1 in., represents $4 \times 8 = 32$ mi.,

and 2 in. represents $2 \times 32 = 64$ mi. $\frac{1}{8}$ in. $= \frac{1}{2}$ of $\frac{1}{4}$ in., so $\frac{1}{8}$ in.

represents 4 mi.

Then $2\frac{1}{8}$ in. represent $64 + 4 = 68$ mi.

36. **3** Let x = height of steeple. Set up a proportion:

$$\frac{\text{height of object}}{\text{length of shadow}} : \frac{x}{28} = \frac{6}{4}.$$

$4x = 6(28) = 168$

$x = 168 \div 4 = 42$ ft.

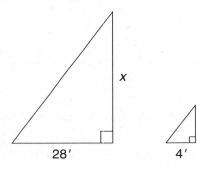

37. **1** Ten chips is equal to 6% of total carbohydrates. Therefore, 5 chips would be half of that—or 3%.

10 + 5 = 15 chips, and 6% + 3% = 9%

38. **5** Half of .5 g is .25 g.

39. **4** To find the distance between two points on the same vertical line, subtract their y-coordinates: $4 - (-3) = 4 + 3 = 7$.

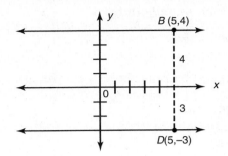

40. **5** Slope $= \dfrac{y_2 - y_1}{x_2 - x_1}$

In this case, $y_2 = y$, $y_1 = 2$, $x_2 = 4$, and $x_1 = 1$.

Therefore, $\dfrac{y - 2}{4 - 1} = 1$

$$(3) \quad \dfrac{y - 2}{3} = 1 \, (3)$$

$$y - 2 = 3$$

$$y = 3 + 2 = 5.$$

41. **4** The top of the bar for Wednesday is at 6 on the vertical scale.

42. **2** Saturday's sales were more than 16 gallons, and Wednesday's sales were 6 gallons. For percent increase, find the actual amount of increase ($16 - 4 = 12$), and divide it by the original amount,

$$\dfrac{12}{4} = 3 = 300\%.$$

Because Saturday's sales were more than 16 gallons, the answer is 2.

43. **60** The tops of the bars for Monday through Sunday are at 5, 4, 6, 5, 14, 17, and 9. These add up to 60.

44. **55** Let $x = \mathrm{m}\angle OAB$

$OA = OB$ since radii of the same circle have equal measures.

Therefore, $\mathrm{m}\angle OAB = \mathrm{m}\angle OBA$.

$$x + x + 70 = 180$$

$$2x + 70 = 180$$

$$2x = 180 - 70 = 110$$

$$x = 110 \div 2 = 55$$

45. **3** Between 3:00 P.M. and 4:00 P.M., Sylvia drove $124 - 80 = 44$ mi.

Since she was driving at a steady rate for the entire trip, in the $\dfrac{1}{4}$ hr.

from 4:00 to 4:15 she drove another $\dfrac{1}{4}(44) = 11$ mi.

Therefore, at 4:15 P.M. she had driven $124 + 11 = 135$ mi.

46. **2** If Joan uses a full cup of milk instead of $\frac{1}{3}$ cup, she must multiply the measure of each ingredient by 3.

$3\left(\frac{2}{3}\right) = 2$ teaspoons of salt.

47. **5** This information can be read directly on the graph.

48. **4** Let x = cost of lot, and

$3x$ = cost of house.

$x + 3x = 200,000$

$4x = 200,000$

$x = 200,000 \div 4 = 50,000$

$3x = 3(50,000) = \$150,000$

49. **5** In the figure below, the four obtuse angles all have the same measure, and the four acute angles also have the same measure:

$$a = d = e = g \quad b = c = f = h$$

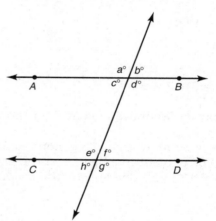

Checking the choices, you see that they are all correct except (5): $b \neq g$

50. **2** Radius of outer circle = $\frac{1}{2}(48) = 24$ in.

Radius of inner circle = 20 in.

Use the formula $A = \pi r^2$.

Area of outer circle = $\pi \times 24 \times 24 = 576\pi$

Area of inner circle = $\pi \times 20 \times 20 = 400\pi$

Area of border = $576\pi - 400\pi = 176\pi$

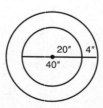

ANSWER SHEET FOR THE PRACTICE EXAM

TEST 1: LANGUAGE ARTS, WRITING, PART I

1. ① ② ③ ④ ⑤
2. ① ② ③ ④ ⑤
3. ① ② ③ ④ ⑤
4. ① ② ③ ④ ⑤
5. ① ② ③ ④ ⑤
6. ① ② ③ ④ ⑤
7. ① ② ③ ④ ⑤
8. ① ② ③ ④ ⑤
9. ① ② ③ ④ ⑤
10. ① ② ③ ④ ⑤
11. ① ② ③ ④ ⑤
12. ① ② ③ ④ ⑤
13. ① ② ③ ④ ⑤
14. ① ② ③ ④ ⑤
15. ① ② ③ ④ ⑤
16. ① ② ③ ④ ⑤
17. ① ② ③ ④ ⑤
18. ① ② ③ ④ ⑤
19. ① ② ③ ④ ⑤
20. ① ② ③ ④ ⑤

21. ① ② ③ ④ ⑤
22. ① ② ③ ④ ⑤
23. ① ② ③ ④ ⑤
24. ① ② ③ ④ ⑤
25. ① ② ③ ④ ⑤
26. ① ② ③ ④ ⑤
27. ① ② ③ ④ ⑤
28. ① ② ③ ④ ⑤
29. ① ② ③ ④ ⑤
30. ① ② ③ ④ ⑤
31. ① ② ③ ④ ⑤
32. ① ② ③ ④ ⑤
33. ① ② ③ ④ ⑤
34. ① ② ③ ④ ⑤
35. ① ② ③ ④ ⑤
36. ① ② ③ ④ ⑤
37. ① ② ③ ④ ⑤
38. ① ② ③ ④ ⑤
39. ① ② ③ ④ ⑤
40. ① ② ③ ④ ⑤

41. ① ② ③ ④ ⑤
42. ① ② ③ ④ ⑤
43. ① ② ③ ④ ⑤
44. ① ② ③ ④ ⑤
45. ① ② ③ ④ ⑤
46. ① ② ③ ④ ⑤
47. ① ② ③ ④ ⑤
48. ① ② ③ ④ ⑤
49. ① ② ③ ④ ⑤
50. ① ② ③ ④ ⑤

TEST 2: SOCIAL STUDIES

1. ① ② ③ ④ ⑤
2. ① ② ③ ④ ⑤
3. ① ② ③ ④ ⑤
4. ① ② ③ ④ ⑤
5. ① ② ③ ④ ⑤
6. ① ② ③ ④ ⑤
7. ① ② ③ ④ ⑤
8. ① ② ③ ④ ⑤
9. ① ② ③ ④ ⑤
10. ① ② ③ ④ ⑤
11. ① ② ③ ④ ⑤
12. ① ② ③ ④ ⑤
13. ① ② ③ ④ ⑤
14. ① ② ③ ④ ⑤
15. ① ② ③ ④ ⑤
16. ① ② ③ ④ ⑤
17. ① ② ③ ④ ⑤
18. ① ② ③ ④ ⑤
19. ① ② ③ ④ ⑤
20. ① ② ③ ④ ⑤

21. ① ② ③ ④ ⑤
22. ① ② ③ ④ ⑤
23. ① ② ③ ④ ⑤
24. ① ② ③ ④ ⑤
25. ① ② ③ ④ ⑤
26. ① ② ③ ④ ⑤
27. ① ② ③ ④ ⑤
28. ① ② ③ ④ ⑤
29. ① ② ③ ④ ⑤
30. ① ② ③ ④ ⑤
31. ① ② ③ ④ ⑤
32. ① ② ③ ④ ⑤
33. ① ② ③ ④ ⑤
34. ① ② ③ ④ ⑤
35. ① ② ③ ④ ⑤
36. ① ② ③ ④ ⑤
37. ① ② ③ ④ ⑤
38. ① ② ③ ④ ⑤
39. ① ② ③ ④ ⑤
40. ① ② ③ ④ ⑤

41. ① ② ③ ④ ⑤
42. ① ② ③ ④ ⑤
43. ① ② ③ ④ ⑤
44. ① ② ③ ④ ⑤
45. ① ② ③ ④ ⑤
46. ① ② ③ ④ ⑤
47. ① ② ③ ④ ⑤
48. ① ② ③ ④ ⑤
49. ① ② ③ ④ ⑤
50. ① ② ③ ④ ⑤

TEST 3: SCIENCE

1. ① ② ③ ④ ⑤
2. ① ② ③ ④ ⑤
3. ① ② ③ ④ ⑤
4. ① ② ③ ④ ⑤
5. ① ② ③ ④ ⑤
6. ① ② ③ ④ ⑤
7. ① ② ③ ④ ⑤
8. ① ② ③ ④ ⑤
9. ① ② ③ ④ ⑤
10. ① ② ③ ④ ⑤
11. ① ② ③ ④ ⑤
12. ① ② ③ ④ ⑤
13. ① ② ③ ④ ⑤
14. ① ② ③ ④ ⑤
15. ① ② ③ ④ ⑤
16. ① ② ③ ④ ⑤
17. ① ② ③ ④ ⑤
18. ① ② ③ ④ ⑤
19. ① ② ③ ④ ⑤
20. ① ② ③ ④ ⑤

21. ① ② ③ ④ ⑤
22. ① ② ③ ④ ⑤
23. ① ② ③ ④ ⑤
24. ① ② ③ ④ ⑤
25. ① ② ③ ④ ⑤
26. ① ② ③ ④ ⑤
27. ① ② ③ ④ ⑤
28. ① ② ③ ④ ⑤
29. ① ② ③ ④ ⑤
30. ① ② ③ ④ ⑤
31. ① ② ③ ④ ⑤
32. ① ② ③ ④ ⑤
33. ① ② ③ ④ ⑤
34. ① ② ③ ④ ⑤
35. ① ② ③ ④ ⑤
36. ① ② ③ ④ ⑤
37. ① ② ③ ④ ⑤
38. ① ② ③ ④ ⑤
39. ① ② ③ ④ ⑤
40. ① ② ③ ④ ⑤

41. ① ② ③ ④ ⑤
42. ① ② ③ ④ ⑤
43. ① ② ③ ④ ⑤
44. ① ② ③ ④ ⑤
45. ① ② ③ ④ ⑤
46. ① ② ③ ④ ⑤
47. ① ② ③ ④ ⑤
48. ① ② ③ ④ ⑤
49. ① ② ③ ④ ⑤
50. ① ② ③ ④ ⑤

TEST 4: LANGUAGE ARTS, READING

1. ① ② ③ ④ ⑤
2. ① ② ③ ④ ⑤
3. ① ② ③ ④ ⑤
4. ① ② ③ ④ ⑤
5. ① ② ③ ④ ⑤
6. ① ② ③ ④ ⑤
7. ① ② ③ ④ ⑤
8. ① ② ③ ④ ⑤
9. ① ② ③ ④ ⑤
10. ① ② ③ ④ ⑤
11. ① ② ③ ④ ⑤
12. ① ② ③ ④ ⑤
13. ① ② ③ ④ ⑤
14. ① ② ③ ④ ⑤
15. ① ② ③ ④ ⑤

16. ① ② ③ ④ ⑤
17. ① ② ③ ④ ⑤
18. ① ② ③ ④ ⑤
19. ① ② ③ ④ ⑤
20. ① ② ③ ④ ⑤
21. ① ② ③ ④ ⑤
22. ① ② ③ ④ ⑤
23. ① ② ③ ④ ⑤
24. ① ② ③ ④ ⑤
25. ① ② ③ ④ ⑤
26. ① ② ③ ④ ⑤
27. ① ② ③ ④ ⑤
28. ① ② ③ ④ ⑤
29. ① ② ③ ④ ⑤
30. ① ② ③ ④ ⑤

31. ① ② ③ ④ ⑤
32. ① ② ③ ④ ⑤
33. ① ② ③ ④ ⑤
34. ① ② ③ ④ ⑤
35. ① ② ③ ④ ⑤
36. ① ② ③ ④ ⑤
37. ① ② ③ ④ ⑤
38. ① ② ③ ④ ⑤
39. ① ② ③ ④ ⑤
40. ① ② ③ ④ ⑤

TEST 5: MATHEMATICS, PART I

1. ① ② ③ ④ ⑤

2. ① ② ③ ④ ⑤

3. ① ② ③ ④ ⑤

4.

5. (grid)

6. ① ② ③ ④ ⑤

7. (grid)

8. ① ② ③ ④ ⑤

9. ① ② ③ ④ ⑤

10. ① ② ③ ④ ⑤

11. ① ② ③ ④ ⑤

12. ① ② ③ ④ ⑤

13. (grid)

14. ① ② ③ ④ ⑤

15. ① ② ③ ④ ⑤

16. (grid)

17. ① ② ③ ④ ⑤

18. ① ② ③ ④ ⑤

19. ① ② ③ ④ ⑤

20. ① ② ③ ④ ⑤

21. ① ② ③ ④ ⑤

22. ① ② ③ ④ ⑤

23. ① ② ③ ④ ⑤

24.

25. (grid)

TEST 5: MATHEMATICS, PART II

26. ① ② ③ ④ ⑤

27. ① ② ③ ④ ⑤

28. ① ② ③ ④ ⑤

29. ① ② ③ ④ ⑤

30. ① ② ③ ④ ⑤

31. ① ② ③ ④ ⑤

32. ① ② ③ ④ ⑤

33. ① ② ③ ④ ⑤

34. ① ② ③ ④ ⑤

35.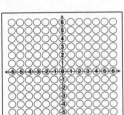

36. ① ② ③ ④ ⑤

37. ① ② ③ ④ ⑤

38. ① ② ③ ④ ⑤

39.

40. ① ② ③ ④ ⑤

41. ① ② ③ ④ ⑤

42.

43. ① ② ③ ④ ⑤

44. ① ② ③ ④ ⑤

45. ① ② ③ ④ ⑤

46. ① ② ③ ④ ⑤

47. ① ② ③ ④ ⑤

48. ① ② ③ ④ ⑤

49. ① ② ③ ④ ⑤

50. ① ② ③ ④ ⑤

PRACTICE EXAM TWO

TEST 1: LANGUAGE ARTS, WRITING, PART I

DIRECTIONS

The first part of the GED exam measures the test taker's ability to correctly and sufficiently analyze the English language. This section focuses on the written, not spoken, word and consists of both multiple-choice questions and an essay.

The first half of this section consists of multiple-choice questions with paragraphs that have numbered sentences. Some of these sentences contain errors such as usage, sentence structure, and mechanics. Multiple-choice questions follow each of these passages. For questions that refer to sentences that are already correctly written, choose the answer that doesn't change the sentence. Sometimes the best answer is the one that makes a sentence's point of view or verb tense consistent with the rest of the paragraph.

You are given 120 minutes (two hours) for this section of the exam. We recommend that you spend 75 minutes working on the multiple-choice questions, and 45 minutes on the essay. A separate set of directions is given for the essay after the multiple-choice questions.

To mark your answer, darken the corresponding circle on the answer sheet.

FOR EXAMPLE:

Sentence 1: **When returning an item to a retail store, you must bring in your original dated store receipt.**

What correction should be made to this sentence?

(1) remove the comma after <u>store</u>
(2) insert a hyphen between <u>retail</u> and <u>store</u>
(3) change <u>receipt</u> to <u>reciept</u>
(4) capitalize <u>retail store</u>
(5) no correction is necessary

In this example, the sentence is correct as is and does not require correction; therefore answer space 5 would be marked on the answer sheet.

TEST 1: LANGUAGE ARTS, WRITING, PART I

<u>Questions 1–10</u> refer to the following paragraphs.

(1) Each year more young men and young women are recognizing the rewards in nursing and enroll in nursing programs, but the demand for nurses continues to outstrip the supply.

(2) If you join the personnel of a hospital you can choose among absorbing fields. (3) You can concentrate on work with children, in obstetrics, in surgery, or on the fascinating new techniques of orthopedics, which calls so heavily for a nurse's skill and imagination.

(4) Since Florence Nightingale went to the crimea over a hundred years ago, nurses have been an enormously mobile group. (5) If one wants to travel, many posts are open to you, both in this country and abroad. (6) You can choose foreign service with the World Health Organization, with our own goverment's foreign operations or with one of our armed services.

(7) Schools need nurses. (8) Many married nurses who want time in the afternoon with her own children find part-time positions ideal and easy to get. (9) Private practice bring its special rewards in choice of hours and cases.

(10) Opportunities in community and public health programs that require a bachelor's degree from an accredited school are growing rapidly. (11) A visiting nurse has a fascinating career, moving through many homes each day and leaving order and comfort behind.

1. Sentence 1: **Each year more young men and young women are recognizing the rewards in nursing and enroll in nursing programs, but the demand for nurses continues to outstrip the supply.**

   What correction should be made to this sentence?

   (1) change the spelling of <u>recognizing</u> to <u>reconizing</u>
   (2) change <u>enroll</u> to <u>are enrolling</u>
   (3) remove the comma before <u>but</u>
   (4) change <u>but</u> to <u>and</u>
   (5) no correction is necessary

2. Sentence 2: **If you join the personnel of a hospital you can choose among absorbing fields.**

   What correction should be made to this sentence?

   (1) change <u>join</u> to <u>will join</u>
   (2) change the spelling of <u>personnel</u> to <u>personel</u>
   (3) insert a comma after <u>hospital</u>
   (4) change the spelling of <u>choose</u> to <u>chose</u>
   (5) no correction is necessary

3. Sentence 3: **You can concentrate on work with children, in obstetrics, in surgery, or on the fascinating new techniques of orthopedics, which calls so heavily for a nurse's skill and imagination.**

   What correction should be made to this sentence?

   (1) change the spelling of <u>concentrate</u> to <u>consentrate</u>
   (2) change the spelling of <u>children</u> to <u>childern</u>
   (3) remove the comma after <u>surgery</u>
   (4) change <u>calls</u> to <u>call</u>
   (5) no correction is necessary

4. Sentence 4: **Since Florence Nightingale went to the crimea over a hundred years ago, nurses have been an enormously mobile group.**

   What correction should be made to this sentence?

   (1) change <u>went</u> to <u>had gone</u>
   (2) capitalize <u>crimea</u>
   (3) remove the comma after <u>ago</u>
   (4) change the spelling of <u>enormously</u> to <u>enormusly</u>
   (5) no correction is necessary

GO ON TO THE NEXT PAGE

TEST 1: LANGUAGE ARTS, WRITING, PART I

5. Sentence 5: **If one wants to travel, many posts are available to you, both in this country and abroad.**

   What correction should be made to this sentence?

   (1) change <u>one wants</u> to <u>you want</u>
   (2) remove the comma after <u>travel</u>
   (3) change the spelling of <u>available</u> to <u>availible</u>
   (4) remove the comma after <u>you</u>
   (5) no correction is necessary

6. Sentence 6: **You can choose foreign service with the World Health Organization, with our own goverment's foreign operations, or with one of our armed services.**

   What correction should be made to this sentence?

   (1) change the spelling of <u>foreign</u> to <u>forign</u>
   (2) remove the capitals from <u>World Health Organization</u>
   (3) remove the comma after <u>Organization</u>
   (4) change the spelling of <u>goverment's</u> to <u>government's</u>
   (5) no correction is necessary

7. Sentence 8: **Many married nurses who want time in the afternoon with her own children find part-time positions ideal and easy to get.**

   What correction should be made to this sentence?

   (1) change <u>who</u> to <u>whom</u>
   (2) insert a comma after <u>nurses</u>
   (3) remove the hyphen from <u>part-time</u>
   (4) change <u>her</u> to <u>their</u>
   (5) no correction is necessary

8. Sentence 9: **Private practice bring its special rewards in choice of hours and cases.**

   What correction should be made to this sentence?

   (1) insert a comma after <u>hours</u>
   (2) change <u>its</u> to <u>it's</u>
   (3) change the spelling of <u>special</u> to <u>speshal</u>
   (4) change <u>bring</u> to <u>brings</u>
   (5) no correction is necessary

9. Sentence 10: **Opportunities in community and public health <u>programs that require</u> a bachelor's degree from an accredited school are growing rapidly.**

   Which of the following is the best way to write the underlined portion of this sentence? If you think the original is the best way, choose option (1).

   (1) programs that require
   (2) programs who require
   (3) programs that do require
   (4) programs that are requiring
   (5) programs that will require

10. Sentence 11: **A visiting nurse has a fascinating career, moving through many homes each day and leaving order and comfort behind.**

    What correction should be made to this sentence?

    (1) change the spelling of <u>fascinating</u> to <u>fasinating</u>
    (2) remove the comma after <u>career</u>
    (3) change the spelling of <u>through</u> to <u>thorough</u>
    (4) insert a comma after <u>order</u>
    (5) no correction is necessary

GO ON TO THE NEXT PAGE

Practice Exam 2

TEST 1: LANGUAGE ARTS, WRITING, PART I

<u>Questions 11–19</u> refer to the following paragraphs.

(1) Nutritional food buying emphasizes the "Basic Four." (2) Backpacking also has its basic four, these being, in order of importance, hiking shoes, the backpack, sleeping gear, and shelter.

(3) Selection of hiking shoes should be your first concern. (4) Even a one-day hike can be misery without comfortable shoes.

(5) Today's hikers prefer a shoe that is six inches high, is made of leather, and thick sturdy composition soles. (6) Break the shoes in thoroughly on short walks before going on any extended hike.

(7) When purchasing a backpack, you will find an almost bewildering array of makes, styles, and materiels to choose from. (8) The backpacking frame must have both shoulder straps and a waist strap. The latter strap being of such design as to permit much of the weight of the pack to rest on the sturdy hip bones rather than on the more fragile shoulder bones.

(9) The sleeping bag and its two accessories (ground cloth and mattress) are next on the list of basics.

(10) The fourth and last of the basic four is the tent or other emergency shelter. (11) An inexpensive shelter is the plastic tube tent.

11. Which sentence is the topic sentence?

    (1) sentence 11
    (2) sentence 7
    (3) sentence 3
    (4) sentence 2
    (5) sentence 1

12. Sentence 2: **Backpacking also has its basic four, these being, in order of importance, hiking shoes, the backpack, sleeping gear, and shelter.**

    What correction should be made to this sentence?

    (1) change <u>its</u> to <u>it's</u>
    (2) change the colon to a semicolon
    (3) change <u>being</u> to <u>are</u>
    (4) remove the comma after <u>gear</u>
    (5) no correction is necessary

13. Sentences 3 and 4: **Selection of hiking shoes should be your first concern. Even a one-day hike can be misery without comfortable shoes.**

    The most effective combination of sentences 3 and 4 would include which of the following groups of words?

    (1) concern, also even
    (2) concern, although even
    (3) concern, because even
    (4) concern, if even
    (5) concern, whereas even

14. Sentence 5: **Today's hikers prefer a shoe that is six inches high, is made of leather, and thick sturdy composition soles.**

    What correction should be made to this sentence?

    (1) remove the apostrophe from <u>today's</u>
    (2) insert a comma after <u>shoe</u>
    (3) remove the comma after <u>high</u>
    (4) insert <u>has</u> before <u>thick</u>
    (5) no correction is necessary

15. Sentence 6: **Break the shoes in thoroughly on short <u>walks before</u> going on any extended hike.**

    Which of the following is the best way to write the underlined portion of this sentence? If you think the original is the best way, choose option (1).

    (1) walks before
    (2) walks, before
    (3) walks: before
    (4) walks. before
    (5) walks. Before

GO ON TO THE NEXT PAGE

TEST 1: LANGUAGE ARTS, WRITING, PART I

16. Sentence 7: **When purchasing a back-pack, you will find an almost bewildering array of makes, styles, and materiels to choose from.**

    What correction should be made to this sentence?

    (1) remove the comma after <u>backpack</u>
    (2) change the spelling of <u>almost</u> to <u>allmost</u>
    (3) remove the comma after <u>makes</u>
    (4) change the spelling of <u>materiels</u> to <u>materials</u>
    (5) no correction is necessary

17. Sentence 8: **The backpacking frame must have both shoulder straps and a waist <u>strap. The</u> latter strap being of such design as to permit much of the weight of the pack to rest on the sturdy hip bones rather than on the more fragile shoulder bones.**

    Which of the following is the best way to write the underlined portion of these sentences? If you think the original is the best way, choose option (1).

    (1) strap. The
    (2) strap. the
    (3) strap, The
    (4) strap, the
    (5) strap: the

18. Sentence 9: **The sleeping bag and its two accessories (ground cloth and mattress) are next on the list of basics.**

    If you rewrote sentence 9 beginning with

    <u>Next on the list of basics</u>

    the next word(s) should be

    (1) the sleeping bag
    (2) its two accessories
    (3) ground cloth and mattress
    (4) are
    (5) is

19. Sentences 10 and 11: **The fourth and last of the basic four is the tent or other emergency shelter. An inexpensive shelter is the plastic tube tent.**

    The most effective combination of sentences 10 and 11 would include which of the following groups of words?

    (1) shelter of which an inexpensive shelter is
    (2) shelter such as the inexpensive plastic tube tent
    (3) shelter whose inexpensive shelter is
    (4) shelter: an inexpensive shelter is
    (5) shelter; an inexpensive shelter is

Questions 20–27 refer to the following paragraphs.

(A)

(1) We were born to be creative in a world rich in creative design rich in natural resources rich with innovative people who consider creativity fun and a responsibility, in a world of rich endowments from nature and man's creative urge. (2) Crafts is one of the rich heritages of our nation. (3) In pioneer days the itinerant craftsman traveled from home to home, selling his wares and earning his bed and board by weaving fabric or a coverlet or hand carving wooden items for the kitchen or barn.

(B)

(4) If people become involved in these early crafts, they may become interested in "trying their hands." (5) They have not only all the rich natural resources and related contemporary subject matter, but they also have man-made materials and efficient, fast equipment to aid them in their creativity. (6) Their products are limited only by their imagination, skill, and knowledge of design.

(C)

(7) If they live in a wooded area and like to collect the unusual from nature's wonders, they may begin to reproduce the pine and nut "kissing balls" and christmas wreaths. (8) If the male member of their family loves to hunt, they may create with feathers. (9) Feather wreaths were made at an early date.

GO ON TO THE NEXT PAGE

TEST 1: LANGUAGE ARTS, WRITING, PART I

20. Sentence 1: **We were born to be creative in a world rich in creative design rich in natural resources rich with innovative people who consider creativity fun and a responsibility, in a world of rich endowments from nature and man's creative urge.**

    What correction should be made to this sentence?

    (1) insert commas after <u>design</u> and <u>resources</u>
    (2) change the spelling of <u>innovative</u> to <u>inovative</u>
    (3) remove the comma after <u>responsibility</u>
    (4) insert a comma after <u>nature</u>
    (5) no correction is necessary

21. Sentences 2 and 3: **Crafts is one of the rich heritages of our nation. In pioneer days the itinerant craftsman traveled from home to home, selling his wares and earning his bed and board by weaving fabric or a coverlet or hand carving wooden items for the kitchen or barn.**

    What correction should be made to this sentence?

    (1) change <u>Crafts is</u> to <u>Crafts are</u>
    (2) insert a hyphen between <u>hand</u> and <u>carving</u>
    (3) insert a comma after <u>fabric</u>
    (4) remove the comma after <u>home</u>
    (5) no correction is necessary

22. Sentence 3 should be

    (1) omitted
    (2) placed first
    (3) placed after sentence 5
    (4) placed last
    (5) left as it is

23. Sentence 4: **If people become involved in these early crafts, they may become interested in "trying their hands."**

    What correction should be made to this sentence?

    (1) change <u>become</u> to <u>became</u>
    (2) change <u>they</u> to <u>one</u>
    (3) change <u>may</u> to <u>might</u>
    (4) change <u>hands."</u> to <u>hands</u>".
    (5) no correction is necessary

24. Sentence 5: **They have not only all the rich natural resources and related contemporary subject matter, but they also have man-made materials and efficient, fast equipment to aid them in their creativity.**

    What correction should be made to this sentence?

    (1) place <u>not only</u> before <u>have</u>
    (2) change the spelling of <u>contemporary</u> to <u>contemperary</u>
    (3) change <u>but</u> to <u>although</u>
    (4) change the spelling of <u>equipment</u> to <u>equiptment</u>
    (5) no correction is necessary

25. Sentences 5 and 6: **They have not only all the rich natural resources and related contemporary subject matter, but they also have man-made materials and efficient, fast equipment to aid them in their <u>creativity Their</u> products are limited only by their imagination, skill, and knowledge of design.**

    Which of the following is the best way to write the underlined portion of this sentence? If you think the original is the best way, choose option (1).

    (1) creativity Their
    (2) creativity, their
    (3) creativity. their
    (4) creativity. Their
    (5) creativity: Their

GO ON TO THE NEXT PAGE

TEST 1: LANGUAGE ARTS, WRITING, PART I

26. Sentence 7: **If they live in a wooded area and like to collect the unusual from nature's wonders, they may begin to reproduce the pine and nut "kissing balls" and christmas wreaths.**

    What correction should be made to this sentence?

    (1) change <u>live</u> to <u>lived</u>
    (2) change <u>like</u> to <u>would like</u>
    (3) remove the comma after <u>wonders</u>
    (4) capitalize <u>christmas</u>
    (5) no correction is necessary

27. Sentences 8 and 9: **If the male member of the family loves to hunt, they may create with feathers. Feather wreaths were made at an early date.**

    The most effective combination of sentences 8 and 9 would include which of the following groups of words?

    (1) feather and feather wreaths
    (2) feathers because feather wreaths
    (3) feathers although feather wreaths
    (4) feathers, which were made into wreaths
    (5) feathers made at an early date

<u>Questions 28–36</u> refer to the following paragraphs.

(A)

(1) Housing is the hub of the family's private world, the nature of housing has a direct effect on the quality of family life. (2) It effects the health, time, and energy required to rear a family and care for its members, self-related attitudes, morale, and satisfaction with one's station in life. (3) It also affects the way in which one family relates to another, to the neighborhood, and to the community.

(B)

(4) Families do not want, expect, or require dwellings that is identical. (5) Families with limited means are more interested in securing clean, safe, and reasonably comfortable housing than to find quarters that are especially psychologically stimulating. (6) At the same time many families having greater incomes can take

basic shelter for granted and proceed to satisfy higher level needs in housing.

(C)

(7) Nevertheless, as a nation we are being more and more concerned with housing that does far more than support physical survival. (8) In other words, essentially all American families are upgrading their housing goals and expectations. (9) And the dominant housing image remains the single-family house.

(D)

(10) Only when families are more articulate in identifying their needs and when builders and public policy become more sensitive to human needs will the nation have a variety of good housing designed, built, and serviced in line with family purposes.

28. Sentence 1: **Housing is the hub of the family's private <u>world, the</u> nature of housing has a direct effect on the quality of family life.**

    Which of the following is the best way to write the underlined portion of this sentence? If you think the original is the best way, choose option (1).

    (1) world, the
    (2) world. the
    (3) world; The
    (4) world: The
    (5) world. The

29. Sentence 2: **It effects the health, time, and energy required to rear a family and care for its members, self-related attitudes, morale, and satisfaction with one's station in life.**

    What correction should be made to this sentence?

    (1) change the spelling of <u>effects</u> to <u>affects</u>
    (2) change the spelling of <u>its</u> to <u>it's</u>
    (3) remove the comma after <u>members</u>
    (4) change the spelling of <u>morale</u> to <u>moral</u>
    (5) no correction is necessary

GO ON TO THE NEXT PAGE

TEST 1: LANGUAGE ARTS, WRITING, PART I

30. Sentence 3: **It also affects the way in which one family relates to another, to the neighborhood, and to the community.**

    What correction should be made to this sentence?

    (1) change <u>also</u> to <u>nevertheless</u>
    (2) insert a comma after <u>way</u>
    (3) remove the comma after <u>another</u>
    (4) change the spelling of <u>neighborhood</u> to <u>nieghborhood</u>
    (5) no correction is necessary

31. Sentence 4: **Families do not want, expect, or require dwellings that is identical.**

    What correction should be made to this sentence?

    (1) change the spelling of <u>families</u> to <u>family's</u>
    (2) remove the comma after <u>want</u>
    (3) change <u>is</u> to <u>are</u>
    (4) change the spelling of <u>identical</u> to <u>identicle</u>
    (5) no correction is necessary

32. Sentence 5: **Families with limited means are more interested in securing clean, safe, and reasonably comfortable housing than to find quarters that are especially psychologically stimulating.**

    What correction should be made to this sentence?

    (1) remove the comma after <u>clean</u>
    (2) change <u>to find</u> to <u>in finding</u>
    (3) change the spelling of <u>especially</u> to <u>especialy</u>
    (4) change the spelling of <u>psychologically</u> to <u>phsycologically</u>
    (5) no correction is necessary

33. Sentence 6: **At the same time many families having greater incomes can take basic shelter for granted and proceed to satisfy higher level needs in housing.**

    What correction should be made to this sentence?

    (1) insert a comma after <u>incomes</u>
    (2) change <u>can</u> to <u>must</u>
    (3) insert a comma after <u>granted</u>
    (4) change the spelling of <u>proceed</u> to <u>procede</u>
    (5) no correction is necessary

34. Sentence 7: **Nevertheless, as a nation we are being more and more concerned with housing that does far more than support physical survival.**

    If you rewrote sentence 7 beginning with

    <u>Housing that does far more than support physical survival</u>

    the next words would be

    (1) as a nation
    (2) we are being
    (3) we, as a nation,
    (4) concerns us, as a nation,
    (5) we are concerned

35. Sentences 8 and 9: **In other words, essentially all American families are upgrading their housing goals and expectations. And the dominant housing image remains the single-family house.**

    The most effective combination of sentences 8 and 9 would include which of the following groups of words?

    (1) expectations but the single-family house remains
    (2) expectations since the single-family house remains
    (3) expectations although the single-family house remains
    (4) expectations with the single-family house remaining
    (5) expectations despite the single-famiy house remaining

GO ON TO THE NEXT PAGE

TEST 1: LANGUAGE ARTS, WRITING, PART I

36. Sentence 10: **Only when families are more articulate in identifying their needs and when builders and pubic policy become more sensitive to human needs will the nation have a variety of good housing designed, built, and serviced in line with family purposes.**

   If you rewrote sentence 10 beginning with

   <u>The nation</u>

   the next words should be

   (1) are more articulate
   (2) identifying their needs
   (3) become more sensitive
   (4) will have
   (5) serviced in line

<u>Questions 37–45</u> refer to the following paragraphs.

(A)
(1) Auto insurance can be bought in the form of a bundle of coverage, or each section in the bundle can be bought seperately.

(B)
(2) Liability, the core of an auto policy, pays for bodily injury and property damage to others when you are legally responsible for the accident. (3) Liability coverage, stated separately for bodily injury and property damage, pay for other people's injuries—not yours.

(C)
(4) Medical payments cover you and your passengers' medical fees regardless of who was to blame for the accident. (5) The uninsured motorist coverage offers protection to you, your spouse, and resident children if you are stricken by an uninsured motorist or a hit and run driver while driving or walking.

(D)
(6) Collision pays for damage to your car when you hit another vehicle or an object like a tree, telephone pole, etc. (7) Collision coverage is usually sold in the form of a deductible. (8) The larger the amount of the deductible, the less the premium.

(E)
(9) Losses caused by fire, wind, theft, vandalism, collision with animals, explosions, flood, and lightning are covered by the comprehensive coverage feature.

(F)
(10) Accidental Death and Dismemberment coverage pays a lump sum for death in a car accident, loss of a limb, blindness, fractures, and dislocations, plus a disability benefit each week.

37. Sentence 1: **Auto insurance can be bought in the form of a bundle of coverage, or each section in the bundle can be bought seperately.**

   What correction should be made to this sentence?

   (1) change the spelling of <u>insurance</u> to <u>insurence</u>
   (2) insert a comma after <u>bought</u>
   (3) change <u>or</u> to <u>and</u>
   (4) change the spelling of <u>seperately</u> to <u>separately</u>
   (5) no correction is necessary

38. Which transitional word(s) could be added to sentence 2?

   (1) First of all,
   (2) However,
   (3) In addition to,
   (4) Nevertheless,
   (5) On the other hand,

39. Sentence 3: **Liability coverage, stated separately for bodily injury and property damage, pay for other people's injuries—not yours.**

   What correction should be made to this sentence?

   (1) remove the comma after <u>coverage</u> and <u>damage</u>
   (2) change <u>pay</u> to <u>pays</u>
   (3) change <u>people's</u> to <u>peoples</u>
   (4) remove the dash after <u>injuries</u>
   (5) no correction is necessary

GO ON TO THE NEXT PAGE

TEST 1: LANGUAGE ARTS, WRITING, PART I

40. Sentence 4 should be

    (1) placed first
    (2) placed last
    (3) left as it is
    (4) placed after sentence 10
    (5) omitted

41. The main idea of this passage is

    (1) stated in sentence 1
    (2) stated in sentence 10
    (3) stated in sentence 3
    (4) stated in sentence 2
    (5) not stated; it's implied

42. A new paragraph can be

    (1) started after sentence 7
    (2) started after sentence 6
    (3) started after sentence 4
    (4) started after sentence 2
    (5) not started

43. Sentences 7 and 8: **Collision coverage is usually sold in the form of a <u>deductible</u>. <u>The</u> larger the amount of the deductible, the less the premium.**

    Which of the following is the best way to write the underlined portion of this sentence? If you think the original is the best way, choose option (1).

    (1) deductible. The
    (2) deductible. the
    (3) deductible; The
    (4) deductible; the
    (5) deductible, The

44. Sentence 9: **Losses caused by fire, wind, theft, vandalism, collision with animals, explosions, flood, and lightning are covered by the comprehensive coverage feature.**

    If you rewrote sentence 9 beginning with

    <u>The comprehensive coverage feature</u>

    the next word(s) would be

    (1) losses caused
    (2) causes losses
    (3) collision
    (4) explosions
    (5) covers

45. Sentence 10: **Accidental Death and Dismemberment coverage pays a lump sum for death in a car accident, loss of a limb, blindness, fractures, and dislocations, plus a disability benefit each week.**

    What correction should be made to this sentence?

    (1) change <u>benefit</u> to <u>benifit</u>
    (2) remove the comma after <u>dislocations</u>
    (3) change <u>pays</u> to <u>pay's</u>
    (4) change <u>Accidental Death and Dismemberment</u> to <u>Accidental death and dismemberment</u>
    (5) no correction is necessary

GO ON TO THE NEXT PAGE

TEST 1: LANGUAGE ARTS, WRITING, PART I

<u>Questions 46–50</u> refer to the following paragraphs.

(A)

(1) How do you find help, when you require it, in your community, assuming that you or your family just cannot meet your own needs or solve your own problems.

(B)

(2) It's not easy, but it can be done. (3) Most Americans, in most communities, can find most of the kinds of help they may need within their local area.

(C)

(4) In just about every city in the Nation, there is a classified phone directory called the Yellow Pages and, if any public, voluntary, or private (for profit) services agencies exist, they will be listed under the heading: "Social Services Organizations."

(D)

(5) In the Washington, D.C., directory, for example, the organizations under this heading number in the hundreds and ranges from Big Brothers through Family Service to Young Adult Rehabilitation Council. (6) In your phone book there may be only four agencies listed where he can call for help, or there may be 400. (7) The longer the list, unfortunately, the more difficult it is to decide from organization names which one can help you with your particular problem.

(E)

(8) Strangely enough, the best place to call or see is your county or local public welfare office (in some areas called social services or public assistence), whether you can or cannot afford to pay for the help you need. (9) Under the Social Security Act, all Federally funded local welfare agencies provide information and referral services without regard for welfare eligibility by reason of poverty, etc.

(F)

(10) Just a word about a very special problem: the problem of where a non-English-speaking person can be sent for help. (11) Because of the increasing awareness of this problem, a number of self-help organizations have recently come into existence in communities where there are significant numbers of ethnic minorities.

46. Sentence 1: **How do you find help, when you require it, in your community, assuming that you or your family just cannot meet your own needs or solve your own problems.**

    What correction should be made to this sentence?

    (1) remove the comma after <u>help</u>
    (2) remove the comma after <u>it</u>
    (3) remove the comma after <u>community</u>
    (4) place a question mark after <u>problems</u>
    (5) no correction is necessary

47. Sentence 2 should be

    (1) placed first
    (2) placed last
    (3) omitted
    (4) moved after sentence 10
    (5) left as it is

48. Sentence 4: **In just about every city in the Nation, there is a classified phone directory called the Yellow Pages and, if any public, voluntary, or private (for profit) services agencies exist, they will be listed under the heading: "Social Services Organizations."**

    What correction should be made to this sentence?

    (1) remove the capital in <u>Nation</u>
    (2) change the spelling of <u>directory</u> to <u>directry</u>
    (3) remove the capitals in <u>Yellow Pages</u>
    (4) change the colon to a semicolon after <u>heading</u>
    (5) no correction is necessary

TEST 1: LANGUAGE ARTS, WRITING, PART I

49. Sentence 5: **In the Washington, D.C., directory, for example, the organizations under this heading number in the hundreds and ranges from Big Brothers through Family Service to Young Adult Rehabilitation Council.**

    What correction should be made to this sentence?

    (1) remove the capital from <u>Brothers</u>
    (2) remove the comma after <u>D.C.</u>
    (3) change <u>ranges</u> to <u>range</u>
    (4) remove the comma after <u>Washington</u>
    (5) no correction is necessary

50. Sentence 6: **In your phone book there may be only four agencies listed where he can call for help, or there may be 400.**

    What correction should be made to this sentence?

    (1) change <u>your</u> to <u>their</u>
    (2) change <u>he</u> to <u>you</u>
    (3) change <u>there</u> to <u>they're</u>
    (4) remove the comma after <u>help</u>
    (5) no correction is necessary

GO ON TO THE NEXT PAGE

TEST 1: LANGUAGE ARTS, WRITING, PART II

This part of the Writing Skills test is intended to determine how well you write. You are asked to write an essay that explains something, presents an opinion on an issue, or concentrates on retelling a personal experience.

Prompt

Each year in the United States thousands of immigrants are allowed into the country and are naturalized to become citizens. These immigrants come to the United States from many different countries. They come here for many reasons such as religious freedom, political reasons, or opportunities.

Discussion Question

What is your opinion on this issue? Do you feel that the United States should put a limit on the number of immigrants that come into the United States or should we continue allowing people to enter and become citizens?

DIRECTIONS

Write an essay of about 250 words in which you recount this personal event. Give supporting details in your essay. You have 45 minutes to write on this topic.

Check Yourself

- Read carefully the prompt, discussion question, and directions.
- Decide if the prompt is expository, persuasive, or narrative.
- Plan your essay before you begin.
- Use scratch paper to prepare a simple outline.
- Write your essay on the lined pages of a separate answer sheet.
- Read carefully what you have written and make needed changes.
- Check for focus, elaboration, organization, conventions, and integration.

END OF EXAM

TEST 2: SOCIAL STUDIES

DIRECTIONS

This section is made up of multiple-choice questions, most of which are based on readings that will often include a figure, graph, or chart. Study the information given to answer each question correctly.

Answering the multiple-choice questions should take you no longer than 70 minutes. It's best not to spend too much time on one question. There is no penalty for incorrect answers so be sure to answer every question.

To mark your answer, darken the corresponding circle on the answer sheet.

FOR EXAMPLE:

Early colonists of North America looked for settlement sites that had adequate water supplies and were accessible by ship. For this reason, many early towns were built near

(1) mountains
(2) prairies
(3) rivers
(4) glaciers
(5) plateaus

The correct answer is "rivers"; therefore, answer space 3 would be marked on the answer sheet.

GO ON TO THE NEXT PAGE

TEST 2: SOCIAL STUDIES

Questions 1–3 are based on the following passage.

The true principle of a republic is that the people should choose whom they please to govern them. . . . This great source of free government, popular election, should be perfectly pure, and the most unbounded liberty allowed. Where this principle is adhered to; where, in the organization of the government, the legislative, executive, and judicial branches are rendered distinct; where, again, the legislature is divided into separate houses, and the operations of each are controlled by various checks and balances, and, above all, by the vigilance and weight of the state governments, —to talk of tyranny, and the subversion of our liberties, is to speak the language of enthusiasm. This balance between the national and state governments . . . is of the utmost importance. . . . I am persuaded that a firm union is as necessary to perpetuate our liberties as it is to make us respectable. . . .

—Alexander Hamilton

1. According to the passage, which one of the following did Mr. Hamilton believe?

   (1) States should determine voting qualifications.
   (2) Suffrage should be granted to all adult males.
   (3) Suffrage should be limited.
   (4) Suffrage should be unrestricted.
   (5) United States senators should be appointed by the state legislatures.

2. Hamilton considered all of the following as safeguards of free government EXCEPT

   (1) popular elections
   (2) separation of the branches of government
   (3) separate legislative houses
   (4) checks and balances
   (5) sovereignty of state governments

3. Hamilton believed that the most important characteristic of a republic is

   (1) popular election
   (2) states' rights
   (3) national militia
   (4) federal taxation
   (5) checks and balances

Questions 4–6 are based on the following passage.

The political party organization is designed to influence voters to support its candidates. Its base of direct operations is, therefore, the voting district, where approximately 700 citizens cast their ballots.

Ordinarily, the enrolled party members choose two committeepersons at the annual fall primary in September, but in presidential election years this action is taken at the spring primary in June. This county committee may by rule, however, set the term at two years; it may demand equal representation of the sexes so that there will be one committeeman and one committeewoman in each district; it can provide for as many as four committee members from a large district as long as the representation is proportional. The important point is that the primary is, for each party, an election for its own officers.

4. All of the following statements about committeepersons are true EXCEPT that

   (1) two are chosen at the September primary
   (2) the elections take place at the June primary during a presidential election year
   (3) the term of office may be set at two years by the county committee
   (4) a large district may have four committee members
   (5) women may not serve on the committee

GO ON TO THE NEXT PAGE

Practice Exam 2

TEST 2: SOCIAL STUDIES

5. The purpose of the primary election is

   (1) to designate the primary candidate
   (2) to ensure proportional representation
   (3) to equalize the vote of the sexes
   (4) for each party to elect its own officers
   (5) for the nomination of four committeepersons per district

6. It can be inferred from the passage that

   (1) the role of committeepersons is relatively unimportant
   (2) each committeeperson represents about 350 voters
   (3) committeepersons serve for two years
   (4) the county committees consist of equal numbers of men and women
   (5) all candidates for committeeperson have equal chances for election

Questions 7 and 8 are based on the following cartoon.

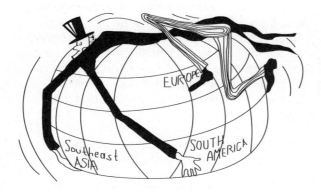

7. The U.S. involvement in Europe indicated in the cartoon most probably refers to the role of the United States in the

   (1) Alliance for Progress
   (2) Common Market
   (3) Nuclear Test-Ban Agreement
   (4) North Atlantic Treaty Organization
   (5) Helsinki Agreement

8. On the basis of the cartoon, it can be concluded that the cartoonist

   (1) questions the U.S. role of "world policeman"
   (2) favors U.S. imperialism
   (3) supports the foreign policy of the United States
   (4) opposes a return to an isolationist policy
   (5) is expressing concern for world survival

Question 9 refers to the following photograph.

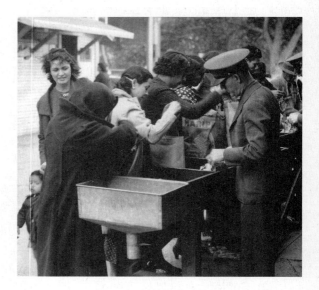

9. Where are these people being searched?

   (1) at a train station
   (2) at a border crossing
   (3) in a Nazi war camp
   (4) in a local market place
   (5) outside their homes

GO ON TO THE NEXT PAGE

TEST 2: SOCIAL STUDIES

Questions 10–12 refer to the following graph.

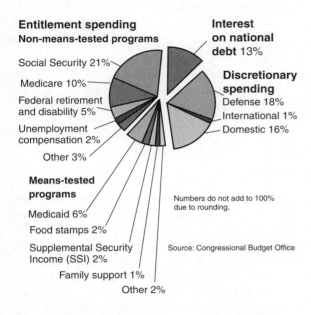

Entitlement spending
Non-means-tested programs

Social Security 21%
Medicare 10%
Federal retirement and disability 5%
Unemployment compensation 2%
Other 3%

Interest on national debt 13%

Discretionary spending
Defense 18%
International 1%
Domestic 16%

Numbers do not add to 100% due to rounding.

Means-tested programs

Medicaid 6%
Food stamps 2%
Supplemental Security Income (SSI) 2%
Family support 1%
Other 2%

Source: Congressional Budget Office

10. Entitlements are government programs providing benefits to members of certain groups. Members of some groups have to be examined (means test) before they can receive benefits. According to the graph, the largest single item of federal spending is

    (1) Social Security
    (2) defense
    (3) interest on the national debt
    (4) Medicare
    (5) Medicaid

11. Of the means-tested programs, the largest is

    (1) Medicaid
    (2) Social Security
    (3) food stamps
    (4) family support
    (5) other

12. The percentage of federal spending going to entitlements is

    (1) 87%
    (2) 54%
    (3) 41%
    (4) 35%
    (5) 13%

Question 13 is based on the following cartoon.

Give me your scientists, your doctors, your teachers, but keep your huddled masses to yourselves.

Adapted from *World Press Review*. November 1980

13. The above cartoon, which appeared in a newspaper published in India, is using the statement attributed to the Statue of Liberty to

    (1) convince the reader of the value of education in the United States
    (2) criticize the United States for not accepting poor immigrants
    (3) deplore the immigration policies in less developed countries
    (4) publicize the need for professionals in the United States
    (5) support the imposition of immigration quotas for professionals

GO ON TO THE NEXT PAGE

TEST 2: SOCIAL STUDIES

Questions 14–16 are based on the following passage.

It is said that growth by merger adds nothing to the economy in the way of new investment, whereas so-called "grass roots" growth does. This, too, is not necessarily so. In many cases, a company has the available capital and several other ingredients of success for a new venture, but can only get some missing ingredient—such as qualified technical manpower—by acquiring another company. In such a case the merging of two companies means a new investment which would not have taken place by the "grass roots" method.

Actually, corporate diversification in the past has served to enhance competition, and it will continue to do so. No company today can confidently look upon its established competitors as being its only future competitors. Tomorrow their ranks may be joined by others now in wholly unrelated industries. If new competitors do enter by acquisition or otherwise, it will be only because they think in the long run they can market a better product, or sell at a lower price, and make a profit by doing so.

14. A reason that is offered for the need to merge is to

    (1) meet new competition
    (2) increase diversification
    (3) increase available capital
    (4) provide for "grass roots" growth
    (5) extend consumer choice

15. The author maintains that growth by merger is sometimes necessary to

    (1) acquire capital
    (2) reduce competition
    (3) make a new investment
    (4) gain technically qualified personnel
    (5) add to the economy

16. Motivations for merger mentioned in this passage include all of the following EXCEPT

    (1) marketing a better product
    (2) selling at a lower price
    (3) making a profit
    (4) getting a missing ingredient
    (5) meeting current competition

Questions 17–19 are based on the following passage.

Americans are the western pilgrims, who are carrying along with them the great mass of arts, sciences, vigor, and industry which began long since in the East. They will finish the great circle. The Americans were once scattered all over Europe. Here they are incorporated into one of the finest systems of population which has ever appeared and which will hereafter become distinct by the power of the different climates they inhabit. The American ought therefore to love this country much better than that in which either he or his forefathers were born. Here the rewards of his industry follow with equal steps the progress of his labor.
His labor is founded on the basis of nature, *self-interest*. Can it want a stronger allurement?

17. The attitude of the author toward the American is one of

    (1) caution
    (2) inquiry
    (3) enthusiastic approval
    (4) self-interest
    (5) prejudice

18. The author predicts that Americans will be unique because of

    (1) a new way of life
    (2) a new government
    (3) a different environment
    (4) their own labors
    (5) self-interest

GO ON TO THE NEXT PAGE

TEST 2: SOCIAL STUDIES

19. The American should be loyal to his new country, according to this passage, because he

    (1) is a new man
    (2) has a new alma mater
    (3) is a western pilgrim
    (4) fled Europe
    (5) benefits from his own labors

20. Which has been an important result of improved means of communication and travel?

    (1) Changes in one part of the world can greatly affect other parts of the world.
    (2) Countries have become more nationalistic.
    (3) Barriers to international trade have been abolished.
    (4) There is less need for international organizations.
    (5) Isolationism has been eradicated.

Question 21 is based on the following cartoon.

21. According to the cartoon, a problem of political elections in the United States is that

    (1) candidates have few serious issues to consider
    (2) candidates offer simplistic solutions in television campaigning to gain votes
    (3) most voters demand quick solutions to national problems
    (4) television reporting of candidates and their campaigns is biased
    (5) these television viewers believe what they are seeing and hearing

Questions 22 and 23 are based on the following graph.

DISTRIBUTION OF WORLD POPULATION BY MAJOR REGIONS 1990 AND 2025 (PROJECTED)

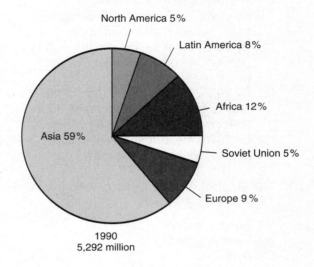

North America 5%
Latin America 8%
Africa 12%
Soviet Union 5%
Europe 9%
Asia 59%

1990
5,292 million

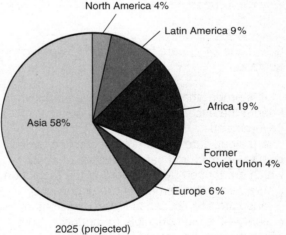

North America 4%
Latin America 9%
Africa 19%
Former Soviet Union 4%
Europe 6%
Asia 58%

2025 (projected)
8,504 million

GO ON TO THE NEXT PAGE

TEST 2: SOCIAL STUDIES

22. According to the graph, which of the following statements is correct?

    (1) The population of the world will double between 1990 and 2025.
    (2) The distribution of the world's population by regions will remain the same between 1990 and 2025.
    (3) By 2025, there will be a major shift in population from the former Soviet Union to Europe.
    (4) By 2025, Africa's percentage of the world's population will increase more than any other region's percentage.
    (5) By 2025, the former Soviet Union's population will lose the most.

23. The greatest decrease in population from 1990 to 2025 will be in

    (1) North America
    (2) Latin America
    (3) Asia
    (4) the former Soviet Union
    (5) Europe

Questions 24–26 are based on the following quotation.

It is proper that you should understand what I deem the essential principles of our government. . . .
    a jealous care of the right of election by the people—a mild and safe corrective of abuses which are lopped by the sword of the revolution where peaceable remedies are unprovided;
    absolute acquiescence in the decisions of the majority—the vital principle of republics, from which there is no appeal but to force, the vital principle and immediate parent of despotism;
    a well-disciplined militia—our best reliance in peace and for the first moments of war, till regulars may relieve them;
    the supremacy of the civil over the military authority;
    economy in the public expense, that labor might be lightly burdened;
    the honest payment of our debts and sacred preservation of the public faith;
. . . freedom of religion;
    freedom of the press;
    freedom of person under the protection of the *habeas corpus*;
    and trial by jury impartially selected. . . .

—Thomas Jefferson, Inaugural Address

24. All of the following principles mentioned by Jefferson are found in the Bill of Rights EXCEPT

    (1) freedom of religion
    (2) freedom of the press
    (3) the right of election by the people
    (4) a well-disciplined militia
    (5) trial by jury

25. An example of the "supremacy of the civil over the military authority" is the

    (1) operation of the National Guard
    (2) Pentagon
    (3) President as Commander-in-Chief
    (4) National Security Agency
    (5) National Security Council

26. The alternative to the "right of election by the people," according to the passage, is

    (1) force
    (2) despotism
    (3) war
    (4) peaceable remedies
    (5) revolution

GO ON TO THE NEXT PAGE

TEST 2: SOCIAL STUDIES

Questions 27 and 28 are based on the following passage.

A map is a presentation on flat surface of all, or a part of, the earth's surface, drawn to scale. A map, in order to accomplish fully the objectives for which it was intended, should generally possess certain essentials. These are a title, a legend, direction, scale, latitude and longitude, and a date. . . .

A legend should define the symbols used on a map to explain the colors or patterns employed.... Since a legend unlocks map details, key is probably an appropriate synonym.

Scale may be defined as the ratio between map distance and earth distance. Scale may be shown as a fraction, for example, $\frac{1}{62,500}$, that is, one unit on the map represents 62,500 units on the earth's surface . . .

A compass rose showing direction is a desirable feature on every map. This directional feature can be eliminated on certain maps where both parallels indicating latitude and meridians indicating longitude are straight lines at right angles to each other.

27. "Drawn to scale" as used in this passage means

    (1) the direction of the parallels and meridians
    (2) the relationship between map distance and earth distance
    (3) linear scales
    (4) verbal scales
    (5) latitude and longitude

28. A compass rose is associated with

    (1) a map title
    (2) a legend
    (3) scale
    (4) direction
    (5) latitude and longitude

29. Which statement best supports the argument for expansion of federal power at the expense of state power in the United States?

    (1) The economic interdependency of all sections of the United States has increased the number and complexity of national problems.
    (2) A uniform penal code is needed in order to insure equal enforcement of the law.
    (3) The federal government with its system of checks and balances is a better guarantee of individual freedom than state governments.
    (4) Increases in population have made it almost impossible for state governments to function efficiently.
    (5) Corruption is more likely to take place at the state governmental level.

30. ". . . the words used are used in such circumstances and are of such a nature as to create a clear and present danger that they will bring about the substantive evils that Congress has a right to prevent . . . . The most stringent protection of free speech would not protect a man in falsely shouting 'fire' in a theatre and causing a panic."

This quotation best reflects the view that freedom of speech is

    (1) guaranteed by the Constitution
    (2) subject to limitations
    (3) clearly dangerous and evil
    (4) likely to cause panic
    (5) impossible to protect

GO ON TO THE NEXT PAGE

TEST 2: SOCIAL STUDIES

31. "... it necessarily became the great object of political economy to diminish as much as possible the importation of foreign goods for home consumption and to increase as much as possible the exportation of the produce of domestic industry."

    Although these words were written in 1776, they apply as well to current U.S. efforts to deal with the problem of the

    (1) decline in the gross national product
    (2) increase in the tariff rates
    (3) surplus in the federal budget
    (4) deficit in the balance of payments
    (5) cost of living

Question 32 is based on the following cartoon.

32. According to the cartoonist, which is a likely result of permitting the Energy Mobilization Board to determine government policy?

    (1) a massive rebuilding program to aid urban areas
    (2) nullification of the benefits of current environmental laws
    (3) an increase in off-shore drilling to lessen our dependence on foreign oil
    (4) land-clearing and home building projects to relieve unemployment among construction workers
    (5) government-sponsored work projects to combat inflation

Questions 33 and 34 are based on the following graph, which shows the relationship of supply and demand for consumer goods and services in five model economies.

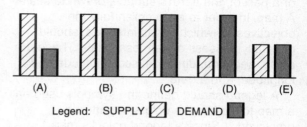

Legend: SUPPLY [hatched] DEMAND [gray]

33. If model B were representative of the economy of the United States, which government action would most likely lead to a balance between supply and demand?

    (1) freeze on wages
    (2) limits on consumer credit
    (3) decrease in income tax rates
    (4) increase in sales taxes
    (5) increase in interest rates

34. Which model economy is most similar to the economic situation in the United States during the years 1929–1939?

    (1) A
    (2) B
    (3) C
    (4) D
    (5) E

GO ON TO THE NEXT PAGE

TEST 2: SOCIAL STUDIES

<u>Questions 35 and 36</u> refer to the following passage.

Latin America has a rich and varied cultural heritage. It was brought into world history by Columbus, was colonized and made a part of Western culture by European powers, and was successful (with a few exceptions) in securing independence during the revolutionary era of George Washington and Simon Bolivar. Latin America differs, however, from the United States in carrying over from pre-Columbian times an Indian population whose cultural influence has intermingled with that of the European. Latin America was colonized primarily by Spanish and Portuguese. They brought to the area a Catholic religious tradition, an agricultural way of life with a land-owning wealthy class, and an influential military class. Independence resulted in twenty separate countries, the Spanish-speaking portion alone being divided into eighteen states, the Portuguese portion being represented by Brazil, and Haiti, which emerged from a long period of French rule.

35. The countries that colonized Latin America brought with them all of the following EXCEPT

    (1) a religious tradition
    (2) an agricultural way of life
    (3) a military class
    (4) a largely Spanish-speaking population
    (5) an Indian population

36. All of the following peoples are represented in the population of Latin America EXCEPT

    (1) Spanish
    (2) Portuguese
    (3) United States
    (4) French
    (5) Indian

<u>Questions 37–39</u> are based on the following graphs.

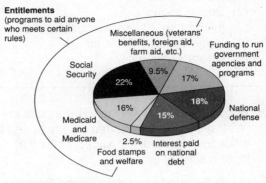

Source: U.S. Office of Management and Budget

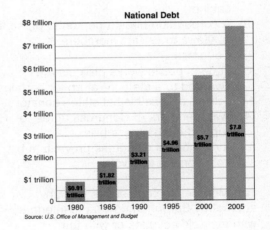

Source: U.S. Office of Management and Budget

37. The largest jump in the national debt occurred between

    (1) 1980–1985
    (2) 1985–1990
    (3) 1990–1995
    (4) 1995–2000
    (5) 2000–2005

38. Of the budgeted money as depicted in the pie graph, entitlements received about

    (1) $\frac{3}{4}$

    (2) $\frac{2}{3}$

    (3) half

    (4) $\frac{1}{3}$

    (5) $\frac{1}{4}$

GO ON TO THE NEXT PAGE

Practice Exam 2

TEST 2: SOCIAL STUDIES

39. The largest part of federal spending is for

    (1) national defense
    (2) Social Security
    (3) interest on the national debt
    (4) Medicare and Medicaid
    (5) veterans' benefits

40. Which situation in the United States is an illustration of lobbying, that is, attempting to influence legislators to support bills that favor a special group?

    (1) A defeated candidate for the Senate is appointed a member of the president's cabinet.
    (2) A corporation hires a person to present its views to certain members of Congress.
    (3) Federal public works projects are awarded to a state in return for certain political actions by that state's senators.
    (4) Two members of Congress agree to support each other's bills.
    (5) A member of Congress prevents a bill from coming to a vote.

41. The Monroe Doctrine states that any attempt by European powers to interfere with their old colonies or with the independence of a republic in the Western Hemisphere would not be tolerated by the United States, nor would any attempt by them "to extend their system to any portion of this hemisphere."

    Which event best illustrates the application of the Monroe Doctrine in United States foreign policy?

    (1) the United States joining the North Atlantic Treaty Organization (NATO)
    (2) President Truman's involving the United States in the Berlin airlift
    (3) President Kennedy's response to the Cuban missile crisis
    (4) Congress' declaration of war against Germany in World War II
    (5) the sale by the United States of AWACs to Saudi Arabia

42. In the United States, changes in occupational titles from busboy to dining room attendant and stewardess to flight attendant illustrate an attempt to deal with the problem of

    (1) racism
    (2) ethnocentrism
    (3) sexism
    (4) age bias
    (5) unionism

Question 43 is based on the following chart.

Income and Management Level of Men and Women Managers*

Income	Men	Women
Income in early career	$ 68,480	$57,210
Income in midcareer	102,540	83,370
Management level		
Top level management	23%	9%
Upper-middle management	33	43
Lower-middle management	21	22
Supervisory management	8	10
Nonmanagement	15	16

Source: "The Impact of Gender as Managerial Careers Unfold," by Joy A. Schneer, Rider University, and Frieda Reitman, Pace University, *Journal of Vocational Behavior.*
*Excludes self-employed.

43. The data in the table show that

    (1) women earn less than men at every managerial level
    (2) men outnumber women on every managerial level
    (3) income in midcareer is comparable for men and women
    (4) fewer women than men become supervisors
    (5) fewer women than men become top-level managers

GO ON TO THE NEXT PAGE

TEST 2: SOCIAL STUDIES

<u>Questions 44–46</u> are based on the following passage.

The numbing row upon row of identical houses, the busy highways leading up to those houses clogged with cars, gas stations, fast-food restaurants, and strip malls are all features of America's suburbs. Traffic jams are all too common since most suburban areas are miles away from good public transportation.

All these things added together have a name: suburban sprawl. Sprawl happens when too many homes, businesses, and shopping centers are built on the fringes of metropolitan areas too quickly.

The costs and consequences of poorly planned development are clear and common. Alarmed by the loss of green space, voters approved nearly 200 state and local ballot initiatives to buy $7 billion of open space. Sprawl is also a major source of traffic congestion and air pollution. It also destroys water quality. The Chesapeake Bay is rapidly being lost to development. Sprawl threatens more than the environment. It also helps destroy older cities and suburbs.

Most Americans want to control sprawl by saving green spaces, redeveloping urban areas, and investing more money in mass transit.

44. Suburban sprawl is caused by all of the following EXCEPT

    (1) housing
    (2) cars
    (3) businesses
    (4) mass transit
    (5) shopping malls

45. Sprawl is chiefly the result of

    (1) increased population
    (2) poor development planning
    (3) public transportation
    (4) inadequate housing
    (5) family travel

46. Efforts to control sprawl include

    (1) more gas stations
    (2) more fast-food restaurants
    (3) more green space
    (4) more highways
    (5) more strip malls

<u>Question 47</u> is based on the following table.

TAX TABLE	
Income	Tax Percentage Rate
$0– 3,000	0
3,001– 8,000	10
8,001–14,000	20
14,001–20,000	25

47. The income tax shown in the table above is best described as

    (1) graduated
    (2) negative
    (3) proportional
    (4) regressive
    (5) universal

48. "We must bring the benefits of Western civilization and Christianity to the less fortunate."

This idea has been used to justify

    (1) imperialism
    (2) nationalism
    (3) socialism
    (4) feudalism
    (5) regionalism

49. "Nations strive to prevent any one country from becoming all-powerful and domineering."

Which concept is referred to by this statement?

    (1) militarism
    (2) imperialism
    (3) national sovereignty
    (4) balance of power
    (5) appeasement

GO ON TO THE NEXT PAGE

TEST 2: SOCIAL STUDIES

Question 50 is based on the following chart.

POPULATIONS OF WORLD REGIONS

Region	1980	1990	2000
Asia	2,583,477,000	3,112,695,000	3,712,542,000
Africa	477,231,000	642,111,000	866,585,000
Europe*	749,973,000	786,966,000	818,378,000
Latin America**	362,685,000	448,076,000	538,439,000
North America	251,909,000	275,866,000	294,712,000
Oceania	22,800,000	26,481,000	30,144,000
World	4,448,048,000	5,292,195,000	6,260,800,000

*Includes the former USSR
**Includes Mexico, Central America, and the Caribbean

50. The chart reveals that

    (1) over half of the world's population between 1990 and 2000 lives in Asia
    (2) most of the world's population lives in the Americas
    (3) the largest population growth is in North America
    (4) the smallest population growth is in Latin America
    (5) the population growth is steadiest in Africa

END OF EXAM

TEST 3: SCIENCE

DIRECTIONS

You are given 80 minutes to complete the Science section of the GED. This section is focused on your knowledge of general scientific concepts. All questions are in multiple-choice format and require the test taker to study the given information (graph, figure, charts, etc.) to reach a correct answer.

You will not be penalized for incorrect answers, so remember to answer every question.

To mark your answer, darken the corresponding circle on the answer sheet.

FOR EXAMPLE:

Which of the following is the smallest unit?

(1) solution
(2) molecule
(3) atom
(4) compound
(5) mixture

① ② ● ④ ⑤

The correct answer is "atom"; therefore, space 3 would be marked on the answer sheet.

GO ON TO THE NEXT PAGE

TEST 3: SCIENCE

Questions 1–3 refer to the following figure.

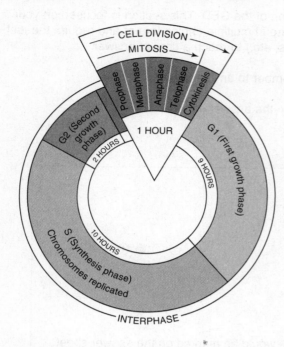

The figure above shows the cell cycle. It shows the typical amount of time spent in each stage of the cell cycle.

1. Mitosis, or cell division, is the time when cells divide to create new cells. About what percentage of the cell cycle is devoted to mitosis?

   (1) 5%
   (2) 20%
   (3) 40%
   (4) 60%
   (5) 75%

2. Which stage of the cell cycle is further subdivided into more stages?

   (1) G1 (first growth phase)
   (2) G2 (second growth phase)
   (3) S (synthesis phase)
   (4) Mitosis
   (5) All of the stages are subdivided

3. Interphase is another name for the time in the cell cycle that is not devoted to mitosis. In a typical cell cycle, how many hours long is the interphase?

   (1) 9 hours
   (2) 10 hours
   (3) 12 hours
   (4) 19 hours
   (5) 21 hours

GO ON TO THE NEXT PAGE

TEST 3: SCIENCE

<u>Questions 4–7</u> refer to the following figure, which describes the major components of blood, their amounts, and their functions.

Plasma 55%	
Constituent	**Major functions**
Water	Solvent for carrying other substances
Ions (blood electrolytes)	
Sodium	Osmotic balance,
Potassium	pH buffering, and
Calcium	regulation of
Magnesium	membrane
Chloride	permeability
Bicarbonate	
Plasma proteins	
Albumin	Osmotic balance, pH buffering
Fibrinogen	Clotting
Immunoglobulins (antibodies)	Defense
Substances transported by blood	
Nutrients (such as glucose, fatty acids, vitamins)	
Waste products of metabolism	
Respiratory gases (O_2 and CO_2)	
Hormones	

Separated blood elements

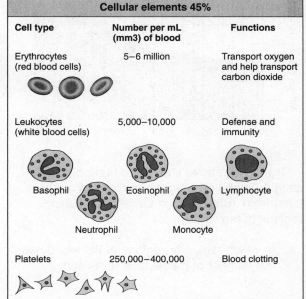

Cellular elements 45%		
Cell type	**Number per mL (mm3) of blood**	**Functions**
Erythrocytes (red blood cells)	5–6 million	Transport oxygen and help transport carbon dioxide
Leukocytes (white blood cells)	5,000–10,000	Defense and immunity
Basophil	Eosinophil	Lymphocyte
Neutrophil	Monocyte	
Platelets	250,000–400,000	Blood clotting

4. Which of the following is not a major function of plasma proteins in the blood?

   (1) membrane permeability
   (2) clotting
   (3) osmotic balance
   (4) pH buffering
   (5) defense

5. 5. Improper functioning or regulation of which of the following might lead to poor regulation of membrane permeability?

   (1) albumin
   (2) fibrinogen
   (3) platelets
   (4) lymphocytes
   (5) chloride ion levels

6. In any given mm^3 of blood, what is the approximate ratio of the number of red blood cells (erythrocytes) to white blood cells (leukocytes)?

   (1) There are about 1,000 red blood cells for each white blood cell.
   (2) There are about 1,000 white blood cells for each red blood cell.
   (3) There are about 10 red blood cells for each white blood cell.
   (4) There are about 10 white blood cells for each red blood cell.
   (5) There are about equal numbers of red and white blood cells.

7. Which of the following are involved in the clotting process?

   I. platelets
   II. neutrophils
   III. fibrinogen

   (1) I only
   (2) II only
   (3) III only
   (4) I and III only
   (5) I, II, and III

Practice Exam 2

GO ON TO THE NEXT PAGE

TEST 3: SCIENCE

<u>Questions 8–11</u> refer to the following graph.

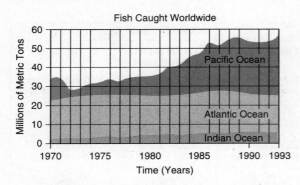

The graph above shows the number of fish caught (based on weight in millions of metric tons) from 1970–1993 in three major fishing regions of the world.

8. In which region or regions of the world has the number of metric tons remained constant?

   (1) The Atlantic Ocean
   (2) The Indian Ocean
   (3) The Pacific Ocean
   (4) The Atlantic Ocean and the Indian Ocean
   (5) The Pacific Ocean and the Indian Ocean

9. Approximately how many millions of metric tons of fish were taken from all three oceans in 1980?

   (1) 5
   (2) 20
   (3) 25
   (4) 35
   (5) 50

10. What percentage of fish was obtained from the Pacific Ocean in 1980?

   (1) 5%
   (2) 10%
   (3) 30%
   (4) 50%
   (5) 70%

11. In what year did the Pacific Ocean first become the major source of fish?

   (1) 1974
   (2) 1978
   (3) 1982
   (4) 1986
   (5) 1990

<u>Questions 12–14</u> refer to the following graph.

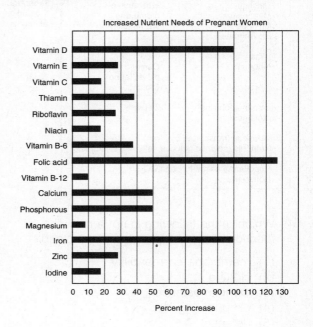

Pregnant women need much higher amounts of many vitamins and minerals to support changes in their bodies and the developing fetus. This graph shows the percentage increase in several vitamins and minerals during pregnancy.

GO ON TO THE NEXT PAGE

TEST 3: SCIENCE

12. What three vitamins and minerals undergo the greatest percentage increase during pregnancy?

    (1) Vitamin D, iron, and folic acid
    (2) Iron, folic acid, and calcium
    (3) Iron, folic acid, and vitamin B6
    (4) Vitamin D, iron, and calcium
    (5) Iodide, iron, and niacin

13. The normal recommended amount of vitamin C is 1,000 milligrams (mg) per day for a nonpregnant woman. During pregnancy, how much vitamin C does a woman need?

    (1) 20 mg
    (2) 200 mg
    (3) 1,200 mg
    (4) 2,000 mg
    (5) 2,400 mg

14. What is the percent increase in dietary calcium needs during pregnancy?

    (1) 10%
    (2) 30%
    (3) 50%
    (4) 70%
    (5) 150%

Questions 15–17 refer to the following information.

Water will change from one phase to another as its temperature changes. In its gaseous form, steam, water has its highest temperature. Water in this form will not change into liquid unless a certain amount of heat is removed. An example is the condensation of water on a bathroom mirror while someone takes a shower. The surface of the mirror is a lot cooler than the warm, steamy air in the bathroom. Water vapor in the air turns into drops of liquid when it touches the cold surface of the mirror. This occurs because the cool mirror cools the air, and cool air cannot hold as much water as warm air.

The diagram represents a sealed plastic container with two Celsius thermometers, one of which is in a glass cup containing ice and water. The purpose of this demonstration is to study the behavior of water vapor and the temperature at which air becomes saturated by water (the dew point).

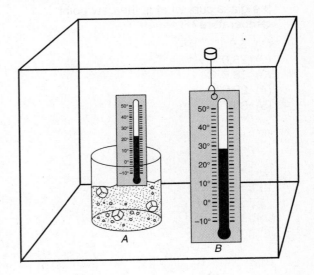

TEST 3: SCIENCE

15. What is the temperature of the air in the box?
    (1) 23.0°C
    (2) 25.0°C
    (3) 26.0°C
    (4) 28.0°C
    (5) 30.0°C

16. Why have droplets of water formed on the outside of the glass cup?
    (1) Glass cups always accumulate water droplets on the outside when they are filled with water.
    (2) The air near the glass cup has become saturated with water.
    (3) Water has seeped through the pore spaces in the glass cup.
    (4) The relative humidity of the air near the glass cup is approaching 0 percent.
    (5) The dew point temperature was not reached.

17. If the water droplets have just appeared on the glass cup, what is the dew point temperature?
    (1) 5.0°C
    (2) 23.0°C
    (3) 28.0°C
    (4) 29.0°C
    (5) 30°C

Questions 18–20 refer to the following article.

Although we often observe the condensation of water vapor on cold surfaces, we seldom think of solid substances going directly to the vapor state. It is possible to change some solids directly to gases by heating them. Instead of melting, these solids go directly into the vapor state because the connections between molecules in these substances are very weak, allowing them to evaporate readily. A good example of such a substance is naphthalene (mothballs). You may have noticed that, over time, mothballs slowly decrease in size. This occurs because of the weak intermolecular forces. The process in which a solid passes directly to the gaseous phase without melting or changing back to the solid state is called sublimation.

18. Condensation is a change from the
    (1) gaseous phase to the solid phase
    (2) gaseous phase to the liquid phase
    (3) liquid phase to the gaseous phase
    (4) liquid phase to the solid phase
    (5) solid phase to the liquid phase

19. Some substances evaporate more easily than others because they
    (1) condense on cold surfaces
    (2) can be heated at atmospheric pressure
    (3) do not change from solid to liquid
    (4) pass from solid state to vapor state
    (5) have weak intermolecular forces

20. Sublimation is a change directly from the
    (1) solid phase to the gaseous phase
    (2) solid phase to the liquid phase
    (3) liquid phase to the gaseous phase
    (4) gaseous phase to the liquid phase
    (5) liquid phase to the solid phase

GO ON TO THE NEXT PAGE

TEST 3: SCIENCE

<u>Questions 21–23</u> refer to the following figure and information.

The figure below shows the relative shape and volume of solids, liquids, and gases. In a solid, the particles are rigidly held in place, giving a solid a fixed volume and a fixed shape. In a liquid, the forces holding particles together are weaker, giving liquids the ability to change shape. The volume of a liquid does not change with the container. In other words, 100 ml of a liquid will have a volume of 100 ml no matter what container it is in. In a gas, the particles are held together very weakly, if at all. Gases take on the shape and volume of the container they are in. Materials that have the ability to flow, such as gases and liquids, are called fluids.

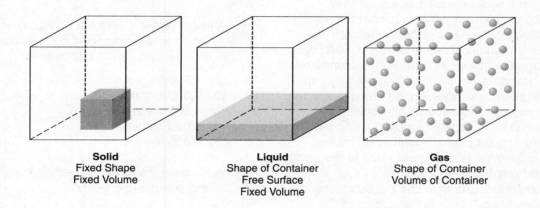

Solid
Fixed Shape
Fixed Volume

Liquid
Shape of Container
Free Surface
Fixed Volume

Gas
Shape of Container
Volume of Container

21. A substance that has a fixed volume but an indefinite shape is

   (1) a solid
   (2) a liquid
   (3) a gas
   (4) a fluid
   (5) either a solid or a liquid

22. Which of the following would be classified as a fluid?

   I. solid
   II. liquid
   III. gas

   (1) I only
   (2) II only
   (3) III only
   (4) I and II only
   (5) II and III only

23. In order for a material to be compressible, there must be space between the particles. Which state(s) of matter would be *incompressible*?

   (1) solid
   (2) liquid
   (3) gas
   (4) solid and liquid
   (5) liquid and gas

Practice Exam 2

GO ON TO THE NEXT PAGE

TEST 3: SCIENCE

<u>Questions 24–26</u> refer to the following article.

Sound waves travel best through denser materials. The speed of sound in air is about 340 meters/second, while the speed of sound in water is about 1,500 meters/second. A rock hitting a solid surface underwater will be very loud, even at a large distance. This is because water, being denser than air, is a better conductor of sound waves. This property of sound waves has been used by navies around the world to identify enemy submarines. Using sensitive listening devices, it is possible to hear the sounds generated by propellers in the submarines at distances of many kilometers. In fact, each class of submarine makes its own unique sound and some detectors are so sensitive that they can tell the differences between the propellers of two nearly identical submarines. This makes the sound of the propeller almost like a fingerprint, allowing that submarine's path to be tracked. Such knowledge was of great value to our ships in World War II.

Sound waves are also used to determine distances to objects or to the bottom of the ocean. A sound wave is sent from the ship to the ocean floor, where it is reflected back. By knowing the speed of sound in water (1,500 meters per second) and the time it took to travel to the ocean floor and then back up, it is possible to calculate the distance to the ocean floor. If a signal took four seconds to travel to the ocean floor and bounce back to the ship, then one would know that it took two seconds to go down and two seconds to come back up. Since sound waves go 1,500 meters per second, the ocean floor would be calculated at 1,500 meters/second times 2 seconds = 3,000 meters (about 1.9 miles deep). A similar strategy is used to find the distance to objects such as schools of fish or ships.

24. The reason submarines can detect other underwater objects is largely due to which of the following?

    (1) Submarines can get very close to these objects.
    (2) Sound travels very well through water.
    (3) It is possible to determine the distance to objects using sound waves.
    (4) Sound waves are affected by propellers.
    (5) Our navy has used sound waves to detect enemy submarines.

25. A sound wave is sent out by a ship and the reflected wave is detected six seconds later. How deep is the ocean floor?

    (1) 1,500 meters
    (2) 3,000 meters
    (3) 4,500 meters
    (4) 6,000 meters
    (5) 9,000 meters

26. In which of the following materials would sound waves travel best?

    (1) air
    (2) helium gas
    (3) water
    (4) oil
    (5) steel

GO ON TO THE NEXT PAGE

TEST 3: SCIENCE

Questions 27 and 28 refer to the following table.

APPROXIMATE SWIMMING SPEEDS OF SOME COMMON FISH

Common Name	Scientific Name	Length (in.)	Speed (mph)
Barracuda	*Sphyraena barracuda*	73	30
Cod	*Gadus callarius*	22	4.2
Eel	*Anguilla vulgaris*	24	2.8
Flounder	*Pleuronectes flesus*	11	2.4
Goldfish	*Carassius aurataus*	5	3.6
Lemon shark	*Negaprion brevirostris*	75	6
Lemon sole	*Pleuronectes microcephalus*	3.5	.26
Mackerel	*Scomber scombrus*	14	5.4
Rainbow trout	*Salmo irideus*	8	3.4
Sea trout	*Salmo trutta*	14	5.4

27. Which of the following statements is supported by information in the table?

   (1) The larger the fish, the faster it swims.
   (2) Some small fish can swim faster than larger fish.
   (3) Sharks are predators and have to swim fast.
   (4) The size of a fish is not related to its speed.
   (5) Saltwater fish are faster than freshwater fish.

28. Other than the two species of trout, which of the following fish are probably related?

   (1) flounder and mackerel
   (2) goldfish and mackerel
   (3) flounder and lemon sole
   (4) lemon shark and lemon sole
   (5) cod and mackerel

GO ON TO THE NEXT PAGE

TEST 3: SCIENCE

29. Commercial fishermen have all the advantages of technology to help them increase their catch. They use locators to find the largest schools and miles of nets to scoop the fish out of the water. Because of overfishing, among other reasons, fish populations all over the world are declining, and the average size of fish that are caught is smaller. This statement is also true of game fish. There are no longer spectacular swordfish of over 1,000 pounds, or giant sea bass weighing 500 pounds. Also, some other fish that were once quite common have become rare.

All of the statements below are opinions EXCEPT

(1) no one should be allowed to fish American waters except Americans
(2) there has to be some other explanation for the decline in game fish; no one could possibly catch enough of them to cause the populations to decline
(3) the oceans are big enough for everybody to take all the fish he or she wants
(4) if fishermen would allow enough larger breeder fish to go free, the populations might increase
(5) the U.S. Department of Fish and Game needs to tell fishermen how many fish they can catch

Questions 30–32 are based on the following graphs.

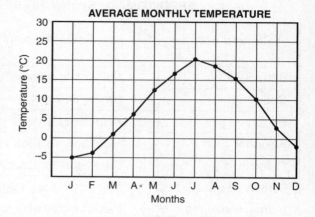

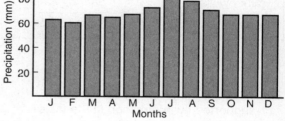

The two graphs represent average monthly temperature and total monthly precipitation from January through December for a city located near the center of a continent.

30. Between which two consecutive months is there the least change in the average temperature?

(1) January and February
(2) February and March
(3) May and June
(4) October and November
(5) December and January

GO ON TO THE NEXT PAGE

TEST 3: SCIENCE

31. The average temperature and the total precipitation during the month of September (S on the horizontal axis of the graphs) were

    (1) 7°C; 60 mm
    (2) 15°C; 50 mm
    (3) 16°C; 68 mm
    (4) 21°C; 68 mm
    (5) 21°C; 80 mm

32. Which best describes the climate pattern of this location?

    (1) hotter and wetter in summer than in winter
    (2) hotter in summer than in winter, with no pronounced wet or dry season
    (3) wetter in summer than in winter, with fairly constant temperature throughout the year
    (4) dry and cold during the winter months
    (5) dry and warm during the summer months

Questions 33 and 34 are based on the following graph.

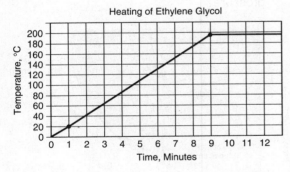

Heating of Ethylene Glycol

The graph above shows the heating of ethylene glycol, the most common component of commercial antifreeze as it is heated for 12 minutes. Ethylene glycol is liquid at room temperature. At 198°C, it starts to boil.

33. In this experiment, how long did the ethylene glycol warm up before it started to boil?

    (1) 3 minutes
    (2) 6 minutes
    (3) 9 minutes
    (4) 12 minutes
    (5) 15 minutes

34. Suppose a similar experiment was done with water. Water boils at 100°C. What would the temperature of boiling water be after boiling for 5 minutes?

    (1) 20°C
    (2) 95°C
    (3) 100°C
    (4) 105°C
    (5) 198°C

35. Pure water has a pH of 7. Acids have pH values lower than 7, and alkalis or bases have values higher than 7. A gardener knows that the plants she grows need soil with a pH of 7.5. If the pH of the soil is 6.5, what action might she take?

    (1) Use only pure water in watering the plants.
    (2) Add a mild acid to the soil.
    (3) Add a mild alkali to the soil.
    (4) Use tap water, which has a pH of 6.5.
    (5) Use an organic fertilizer that becomes acid when it decays.

Practice Exam 2

TEST 3: SCIENCE

Question 36 is based on the following diagram.

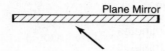

Plane Mirror

36. The arrow in the diagram represents an object in front of a plane mirror. The image formed in a plane mirror must obey the rule that every point on the image is just as far behind the mirror as the corresponding point on the object. Which of the following arrows represents the image?

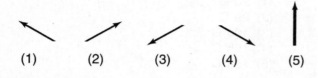

(1)   (2)   (3)   (4)   (5)

Questions 37 and 38 are based on the following chart.

The Sources of Energy
Source: U.S. Dept. of Energy

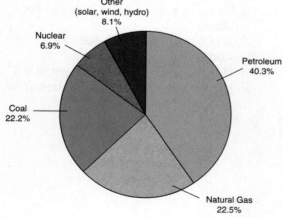

Other (solar, wind, hydro) 8.1%

Nuclear 6.9%

Petroleum 40.3%

Coal 22.2%

Natural Gas 22.5%

The pie chart shown describes the percentage of energy sources in the United States in 1998.

37. Coal, natural gas, and petroleum are collectively known as fossil fuels. About what percentage of energy sources came from fossil fuels?

(1) 22.2%
(2) 22.5%
(3) 40.3%
(4) 62.8%
(5) 85.0%

38. What was the largest energy source in 1998?

(1) Nuclear
(2) Petroleum
(3) Coal
(4) Hydroelectricity
(5) Natural gas

39. The figure below is known as a phase diagram, which shows the state of matter a substance will have at a given temperature and pressure combination. Various other points on a phase diagram may also be labeled. What state of matter would carbon dioxide (CO_2) be in at 25 °C and 0.5 atm of pressure?

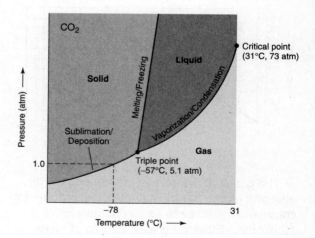

(1) solid
(2) liquid
(3) gas
(4) solid and gas
(5) liquid and gas

GO ON TO THE NEXT PAGE

TEST 3: SCIENCE

Questions 40–49 are based on the following information.

Behavior in living organisms is the pattern of activities in response to stimuli of the environment. Below are five types of behavior.

(1) reflex act—a simple, inborn, automatic response
(2) instinct—a complex behavior pattern performed without learning
(3) conditioned behavior—a changed stimulus produces the original response
(4) habit—a conscious response becomes automatic after constant repetition
(5) learned behavior—a complex process involving reasoning and insight

Each of the following items refers to one of these types of behavior. For each item choose the category that best describes the one type of behavior. A category may be used more than once in answering the following questions.

40. In January, I find myself dating checks with the old calendar year. This type of behavior is best described as

(1) reflex act
(2) instinct
(3) conditioned behavior
(4) habit
(5) learned behavior

41. Students are asked to write their names as many times as they can in 2 minutes. Then they are asked to do the same using the other hand. Comparisons are made regarding quality of performance and number of copies made. This type of behavior is best described as

(1) reflex act
(2) instinct
(3) conditioned behavior
(4) habit
(5) learned behavior

42. The brain of a frog is destroyed in a painless fashion. Some absorbent cotton is dipped in vinegar (five percent acetic acid) and then placed on the frog's thigh. The leg reacts. This type of behavior is best described as

(1) reflex act
(2) instinct
(3) conditioned behavior
(4) habit
(5) learned behavior

43. Joan holds a square of wire mesh closely to her face. Although Martin warns her that he is about to throw a wad of paper at her, when he throws the ball of paper she blinks. This type of behavior is best described as

(1) reflex act
(2) instinct
(3) conditioned behavior
(4) habit
(5) learned behavior

44. Stanley and Lynda finish a difficult crossword puzzle in 60 minutes. Florence and Regina need more time to do the same puzzle. This type of behavior is best described as

(1) reflex act
(2) instinct
(3) conditioned behavior
(4) habit
(5) learned behavior

45. A robin raised in an incubator builds a nest much like those of wild robins. This type of behavior is best described as

(1) reflex act
(2) instinct
(3) conditioned behavior
(4) habit
(5) learned behavior

GO ON TO THE NEXT PAGE

TEST 3: SCIENCE

46. A newborn baby cries when it is uncomfortable, but an older baby will cry just to get attention. This type of behavior is best described as

    (1) reflex act
    (2) instinct
    (3) conditioned behavior
    (4) habit
    (5) learned behavior

47. A dolphin is rewarded with extra food each time it performs a trick. This type of behavior is best described as

    (1) reflex act
    (2) instinct
    (3) conditioned behavior
    (4) habit
    (5) learned behavior

48. After a passage is read to a class very slowly, it is read so that the class could copy what they hear but they are told NOT to cross the t's and NOT to dot the i's. Then the number of errors are reported. What is the kind of behavior that causes the errors?

    (1) reflex act
    (2) instinct
    (3) conditioned behavior
    (4) habit
    (5) learned behavior

49. Persons who have used this book to prepare for the GED have attained satisfactory scores on the test. This type of behavior is best described as

    (1) reflex act
    (2) instinct
    (3) conditioned behavior
    (4) habit
    (5) learned behavior

Questions 50 refers to the following information.

About 100 years ago, two German scientists studying the function of the pancreas as an organ of digestion removed the entire pancreas from several dogs. A short time later some assistants observed that swarms of flies hovered around the cages that housed these dogs. Many regard this as the initial, but accidental, step in diabetes research. However, it was not until 1922 that Banting and Best showed that the pancreas produces the hormone insulin, which is essential for the proper use of sugar by the body. They concluded that if insulin is lacking, diabetes results.

50. The cages around the group of dogs not given the pancreas surgery did not seem to attract as many flies. This statement should be classified as

    (1) the problem statement
    (2) a hypothesis
    (3) an observation
    (4) an assumption
    (5) irrelevant information

END OF EXAM

TEST 4: LANGUAGE ARTS, READING ·

DIRECTIONS

This section of the exam consists of questions based off of articles about literature, excerpts from different literary periods (pre-1920, 1920–1960, and post-1960 literature), and business documents. Each of these excerpts will be followed by multiple-choice questions you must answer.

You should read each excerpt carefully before answering the accompanying questions and refer to the passages as often as necessary to help you answer the questions.

Before each excerpt is a "purpose question" designed to show you why you're reading the passage, and what to focus on. These purpose questions do not need to be answered as they are only there to help you in your reading.

You will not be penalized for incorrect answers so be sure to answer every question. This section's questions should take you no more than 65 minutes.

To mark your answer, darken the corresponding circle on the answer sheet.

FOR EXAMPLE:

Company policy states that extended leave requests must be pre-approved by your supervisor at least three weeks in advance. In emergency situations, call your supervisor as soon as possible with an explanation of your circumstance. Remember, if you do not have enough leave days banked, your pay may be docked.

The policy implies that

(1) you will not be paid on extended leave   ① ② ③ ● ⑤
(2) supervisors cannot grant leave
(3) advance notice is required for all types of leave
(4) extended leave may be granted with pay if leave is available
(5) you will not be paid while on emergency leave

The correct answer is that extended leave may be granted if leave is available; therefore, answer space 4 would be marked on the answer sheet.

GO ON TO THE NEXT PAGE

Practice Exam 2

TEST 4: LANGUAGE ARTS, READING

Questions 1–5 refer to the following passage.

HOW SHOULD ONE HANDLE THE PROBLEM OF CORRECTING OTHERS?

Miss Manners is constantly besieged by people who want to know the tactful manner of pointing out their friends' and relatives' inferiorities. These people, their loved ones report to Miss Manners, chew with their mouths open, mispronounce words, crack their knuckles, spit, belch, and hum tunelessly to themselves. They have bad breath and runs in their stockings. They are too fat, dress badly, and do their hair all wrong.

How can those who love these people dearly, for reasons that are not clear, and who wish to help them, for reasons that unfortunately are clear, politely let them have it?

The answer is that they cannot, certainly not politely. There are times, in certain trusting relationships, when one can accomplish this impolitely. One can sometimes say, "Cracking your knuckles drives me up the wall, and if you do it one more time I'll scream," or "Have a mint— there's something wrong with your breath," or "What's that thing on your left front tooth?" No reasonable person should take offense at these remarks. Because they are so frank, they do not seem to carry a history of repulsion long predating the offense. Also they deal with matters that are more or less easily correctable (although Miss Manners knows some determined knuckle crackers she suspects aren't half trying to stop), and which it is plausible to assume the offenders hadn't noticed.

What is unacceptable is to criticize things a person cannot easily remedy or may not want to. People who you think are too fat either disagree about what too fat is, are trying to do something about it, or are not trying to do something about it. In no case is it helpful for them to know that other people consider them too fat.

It is admittedly difficult to arrest the pleasure of correcting and advising long enough to ask oneself who will feel better after the correction is delivered—the person issuing it, or the one who gets it full in the face? But it is well worth the effort, not only for kindness' sake, but because it is a law of nature that he who corrects others will soon do something perfectly awful himself.

1. The selection deals mainly with

   (1) correcting others
   (2) inferior people
   (3) unacceptable behavior
   (4) trusting relationships
   (5) forcing changes in behavior

2. Unattactive behavior includes all EXCEPT

   (1) bad breath
   (2) loud talk
   (3) cracking knuckles
   (4) inappropriate vocabulary
   (5) spitting

3. According to the passage, people who criticize do so out of

   (1) spite
   (2) revenge
   (3) feelings of superiority
   (4) repulsion
   (5) love

4. Those who correct others should focus on

   (1) matters offenders notice
   (2) matters offenders take offense at
   (3) matters indicating inferiority
   (4) easily correctable matters
   (5) matters carrying a history of repulsion

5. The one who criticizes should consider

   (1) politely letting them have it
   (2) things easily remedied
   (3) both the criticizer and the criticized
   (4) the pleasure of correcting
   (5) only those who agree on the behavior criticized

GO ON TO THE NEXT PAGE

TEST 4: LANGUAGE ARTS, READING

Questions 6–10 are based on this selection from a play.

HOW DIFFICULT IS IT TO CHANGE A PERSON?

PICKERING: You're certainly not going to turn her head with flattery, Higgins.

MRS. PEARCE: [uneasy] Oh, don't say that, sir: there's more ways than one of turning a girl's head; and nobody can do it better than Mr. Higgins, though he may not always mean it. I do hope, sir, you won't encourage him to do anything foolish.

HIGGINS: [becoming excited as the idea grows on him] What is life but a series of inspired follies? The difficulty is to find them to do. Never lose a chance: it doesn't come every day. I shall make a duchess of this draggle-tailed guttersnipe.

LIZA: [strongly deprecating this view of her] Ah-ah-ah-ow-ow-oo!

HIGGINS: [carried away] Yes: in six months—in three if she has a good ear and a quick tongue—I'll take her anywhere and pass her off as anything. We'll start today: now! this moment! Take her away and clean her, Mrs. Pearce. Monkey Brand, if it won't come off any other way. Is there a good fire in the kitchen?

MRS. PEARCE: [protesting]. Yes; but—

HIGGINS: [storming on] Take all her clothes off and burn them. Ring up Whiteley or somebody for new ones. Wrap her up in brown paper til they come.

LIZA: You're no gentleman, you're not, to talk of such things. I'm a good girl, I am; and I know what the like of you are, I do.

HIGGINS: We want none of your Lisson Grove prudery here, young woman. You've got to learn to behave like a duchess. Take her away, Mrs. Pearce. If she gives you any trouble wallop her.

LIZA: [springing up and running between Pickering and Mrs. Pearce for protection] No! I'll call the police, I will.

MRS. PEARCE: But I've no place to put her.

HIGGINS: Put her in the dustbin.

LIZA: Ah-ah-ah-ow-ow-oo!

PICKERING: Oh come, Higgins! be reasonable.

Pygmalion by George Bernard Shaw, 1916

6. Mr. Higgins is trying to

   (1) create a regal wardrobe for Liza
   (2) modernize Liza and teach her to work
   (3) teach Liza how to be social
   (4) understand how Liza speaks
   (5) make Liza like a duchess in speech and appearance

7. In the quote by Mr. Higgins, "inspired follies" probably means what?

   (1) encouraged foolishness
   (2) religious events
   (3) funny plays
   (4) dramatic tragedies
   (5) one-act comedies

8. In regard to Mr. Higgins' help, Liza is probably

   (1) joyous and grateful
   (2) ungrateful but curious
   (3) excited but hesitant
   (4) naïve and suspicious
   (5) nervous and angry

9. When he said, "Take all [Liza's] clothes off and burn them," Higgins was hinting at the symbolic process of

   (1) acting like a queen
   (2) Liza's completely leaving behind her old self
   (3) getting a fresh, new wardrobe
   (4) learning a new language
   (5) decontamination due to an infectious disease

10. The attitude of Mr. Higgins to Liza is one of

    (1) sympathy
    (2) selective help
    (3) intolerance
    (4) impatience
    (5) ignorance

GO ON TO THE NEXT PAGE

Practice Exam 2

TEST 4: LANGUAGE ARTS, READING

<u>Questions 11–15</u> refer to the following passage.

HOW DID ONE VILLAGE BRING DISASTER ON ITSELF?

On a morning in early spring, 1873, the people of Oberfest left their houses and took refuge in the town hall. No one knows why, precisely. A number of rumors had raced through the town during recent weeks, were passed on and converted to news; predictions became certainties. On this particular morning, fear turned into terror, and people rushed through the narrow streets, carrying their most precious possessions, pulling their children and dashing into the great hall. The doors were nailed shut, and men took their turns watching out the window. Two days passed. When no disaster came, the fear grew worse, because the people began to suspect that the danger was already in the hall, locked inside. No one spoke to anybody else; people watched each other, looking for signs. It was the children who rang the great bell in the first bell tower—a small band of bored children found the bell rope and swung on it—set the bell clanging. This was the traditional signal of alarm, and in a moment the elders were dashing in panic to all the other bell towers and ringing the bells. For nearly an hour, the valley reverberated with the wild clangor—and then, a thousand feet above, the snow began to crack, and the avalanche began; a massive cataract of ice and snow thundered down and buried the town, silencing the bells. There is no trace of Oberfest today, not even a spire, because the snow is so deep; and, in the shadow of the mountains, it is very cold.

11. Which element is especially significant in this passage?

    (1) dialogue
    (2) setting
    (3) illustrations
    (4) levels of usage
    (5) rhythm

12. Which is the most valid conclusion regarding the theme of the passage?

    (1) It is a minor feature of the passage.
    (2) It is not related to the plot.
    (3) It is related to the topic sentence.
    (4) It is stated, rather than implied.
    (5) It is implied, but not stated.

13. That the alarm, traditionally sounded to avert danger, became the apparent cause of the avalanche is an example of

    (1) irony
    (2) simile
    (3) satire
    (4) personification
    (5) exaggeration

14. The effect of the last phrase of the passage, "it is very cold," depends mainly on

    (1) rhythm
    (2) rhyme
    (3) comparison
    (4) connotation
    (5) sound

15. Which word best expresses the main idea of the passage?

    (1) faith
    (2) suspicion
    (3) nostalgia
    (4) disaster
    (5) rumors

GO ON TO THE NEXT PAGE

TEST 4: LANGUAGE ARTS, READING

Questions 16–20 refer to the following poem.

HOW DOES THIS POET FEEL ABOUT HIMSELF?

EVERY GOOD BOY DOES FINE

I practiced my cornet in a cold garage
Where I could blast it till the oil in drums
Boomed back; tossed free-throws till I
    couldn't move my thumbs;
(5) Sprinted through tires, tackling a headless
    dummy.
In my first contest, playing a wobbly solo,
I blew up in the coda, alone on stage,
And twisting like my hand-tied necktie, saw
    the judge
(10) Letting my silence dwindle down his scale.

At my first basketball game, gangling away
    from home
A hundred miles by bus to a dressing
    room,
(15) Under the showering voice of the coach, I
    stood in a towel,
Having forgotten shoes, socks, uniform.

In my first football game, the first play
    under the lights
(20) I intercepted a pass. For seventy yards, I
    ran
Through music and squeals, surging, lifting
    my cleats,
(25) Only to be brought down by the safety
    man.
I took my second chances with less care,
    but in dreams
I saw the bald judge slumped in the front
(30)   row,
The coach and team at the doorway, the
    safety man
Galloping loud at my heels. They watch
    me now.

(35) You who have always horned your way
    through passages,
Sat safe on the bench while some came
    naked to court,
Slipped out of arms to win in the long run,
(40) Consider this poem a failure, sprawling flat
    on a page.

16. The "I," or speaking voice of the poem, probably regards himself mainly as

  (1) an athlete
  (2) a musician
  (3) a loser
  (4) a wit
  (5) a critic

17. In relation to the content of the poem, its title is an example of

  (1) personification
  (2) allegory
  (3) sensory language
  (4) irony
  (5) an epithet

18. In the final stanza, the reader is asked to

  (1) make an improper judgment
  (2) feel sorry for the poet
  (3) feel superior to the poet
  (4) agree with the poet
  (5) admire the poet

19. In line 9, "twisting like my hand-tied necktie" is an example of

  (1) a striking contrast
  (2) a vague reference
  (3) an implied meaning
  (4) an overused symbol
  (5) a vivid comparison

20. With which group of words does the poet address the reader directly?

  (1) "I practiced my cornet" (line 1)
  (2) "In my first contest" (line 7)
  (3) "in dreams I saw the bald judge" (lines 28 and 29)
  (4) "some came naked to court" (lines 37 and 38)
  (5) "Consider this poem a failure" (line 40)

GO ON TO THE NEXT PAGE

TEST 4: LANGUAGE ARTS, READING

Questions 21–25 refer to the following poem.

HOW SHOULD WE LIVE OUR LIVES?

BARTER

Life has loveliness to sell—
All beautiful and splendid things,
Blue waves whitened on a cliff,
Climbing fire that sways and sings,
(5) And children's faces looking up
Holding wonder like a cup.

Life has loveliness to sell—
Music like a curve of gold,
Scent of pine trees in the rain,
(10) Eyes that love you, arms that hold,
And for your spirit's still delight,
Holy thoughts that star the night.

Spend all you have for loveliness,
Buy it and never count the cost.
(15) For one white singing hour of peace
Count many a year of strife well lost,
And for a breath of ecstasy
Give all you have been or could be.

—Sara Teasdale

21. The main idea of the poem is to urge us

  (1) to be cautious in life
  (2) to avoid strife
  (3) to despise the ugly part of life
  (4) to enjoy life's treasures
  (5) not to become involved

22. The beauty of nature is indicated in line

  (1) 3
  (2) 6
  (3) 10
  (4) 12
  (5) 16

23. There is a simile in line

  (1) 2
  (2) 4
  (3) 8
  (4) 10
  (5) 16

24. The poet includes the spiritual in life with the words

  (1) "climbing fire"
  (2) "children's faces"
  (3) "arms that hold"
  (4) "holy thoughts"
  (5) "year of strife"

25. The word *barter* means exchange by trade without money. In the poem the exchange is

  (1) personal commitment for life's beauty
  (2) a year of strife for ecstasy
  (3) spirit's delight for peace
  (4) children's faces for wonder
  (5) music for a curve of gold

GO ON TO THE NEXT PAGE

TEST 4: LANGUAGE ARTS, READING

Questions 26–30 are based on the following document.

WHAT IS THE COMMONWEALTH OF VIRGINIA'S POLICY ON ALCOHOL AND OTHER DRUGS?

The Commonwealth of Virginia's Policy 1.05 on Alcohol and Other Drugs states that the following acts by employees are prohibited:

(A)

I. the unlawful or unauthorized manufacture, distribution, dispensation, possession, or use of alcohol and other drugs in the workplace;

II. the impairment on the workplace from the use of alcohol or other drugs (except the use of drugs for legitimate medical purposes);

III. action which results in the criminal conviction for:
- a violation of any criminal drug law, based upon conduct occurring either on or off the workplace, or
- a violation of any alcoholic beverage control law, or law which governs driving while intoxicated, based upon conduct occurring in the workplace;

IV. the failure to report to their supervisors that they have been convicted of any offense, as defined in III above, within five calendar days of the conviction.

(B)

– Included under this policy are all employees in Executive Branch agencies, including the Governor's Office, Office of the Lieutenant Governor, and the Office of the Attorney General.

(C)

– The workplace consists of any state owned or leased property or any site where official duties are being performed by state employees.

(D)

– Any employee who commits any prohibited act under this policy shall be subject to the full range of disciplinary actions, including discharge, and may by required to participate satisfactorily in an appropriate rehabilitation program.

(E)

– A copy of the entire Commonwealth of Virginia's Policy on Alcohol and Other Drugs may be obtained from your agency human resource office.

(F)

CERTIFICATE OF RECEIPT

Your signature below indicates your receipt of this policy summary of Policy 1.05, Alcohol and Other Drugs. Your signature is intended only to acknowledge receipt; it does not imply agreement or disagreement with the policy itself. If you refuse to sign this certificate of receipt, your supervisor will be asked to initial this form indicating that a copy has been given to you.

26. ALL of the following are unacceptable according to the policy EXCEPT

(1) distribution of drugs on work site
(2) manufacturing of drugs on work site
(3) abuse of illegal drugs
(4) abuse of alcohol
(5) use of prescription drugs

27. The purpose of the policy is

(1) to arrest drug dealers
(2) to stop drinking on the job
(3) to discontinue manufacturing illegal drugs
(4) to allow prescription drugs in the workplace
(5) inform employees of the company's policy on alcohol and other drugs

GO ON TO THE NEXT PAGE

TEST 4: LANGUAGE ARTS, READING

28. According to the document, who is included in this policy?

    (1) some employees in Executive Branch agencies
    (2) just the Governor's Office employees
    (3) all of the workers at the Office of the Attorney General
    (4) all employees in Executive Branch agencies, including the Governor's Office, Office of the Lieutenant Governor, and the Office of the Attorney General.
    (5) all employees who receive a copy of this policy

29. Any employee caught committing any prohibited act under this policy may be subject to ALL of the following EXCEPT

    (1) discharge
    (2) disciplinary action
    (3) participation in a rehabilitation program
    (4) immediate release from the company
    (5) a review of the offense by a manager

30. If an employee refuses to sign the "certificate of receipt," then

    (1) he will be fired
    (2) his supervisor will file it without a signature
    (3) he will be arrested
    (4) he will receive a pay cut
    (5) his supervisor will initial the form as receipt for him

Questions 31–35 refer to the following passage.

HOW DOES THE AUTHOR FEEL ABOUT PRIZE FIGHT CROWDS?

The fight crowd is a beast that lurks in the darkness behind the fringe of white light shed over the first six rows by the incandescents atop the ring, and is not to
(5) be trusted with pop bottles or other hardware.

People who go to prize fights are sadistic.

When two prominent pugilists are
(10) scheduled to pummel one another in public on a summer's evening, men and women file into the stadium in the guise of human beings, and thereafter become a part of a gray thing that squats in the dark until, at
(15) the conclusion of the bloodletting, they may be seen leaving the arena in the same guise they wore when they entered....

As a rule, the mob that gathers to see men fight is unjust, vindictive, swept by
(20) intense unreasoning hatreds, proud of its swift recognition of what it believes to be sportsmanship. It is quick to greet the purely phony move of the boxer who extends his gloves to his rival, who has slipped or been
(25) pushed to the floor, and to reward this stimulating but still baloney gesture with a pattering of hands which indicates the following: "You are a good sport. We recognize that you are a good sport, and
(30) we know a sporting gesture when we see one. Therefore we are all good sports, too. Hurrah for us!"

GO ON TO THE NEXT PAGE

TEST 4: LANGUAGE ARTS, READING

The same crowd doesn't see the same boxer stick his thumb in his opponent's eye (35) or try to cut him with the laces of his glove, butt him or dig him a low one when the referee isn't in a position to see. It roots consistently for the smaller man, and never for a moment considers the desperate (40) psychological dilemma of the larger of the two. It howls with glee at a good finisher making his kill. The Roman hordes were more civilized. Their gladiators asked them whether the final blow should be (45) administered or not. The main attraction at the modern prize fight is the spectacle of a man clubbing a helpless and vanquished opponent into complete insensibility. The referee who stops a bout to save a slugged (50) and punch-drunken man from the final ignominy is hissed by the assembled sportsmen.

31. The writer of this passage is

    (1) disgusted
    (2) jovial
    (3) matter-of-fact
    (4) satiric
    (5) optimistic

32. As used in line 26, which action is referred to as a "baloney gesture"?

    (1) pushing the opponent to the floor
    (2) shaking hands with the opponent
    (3) touching gloves with the downed opponent
    (4) smiling at the opponent
    (5) digging the opponent a low blow

33. The "desperate psychological dilemma" of the bigger man (lines 39–40) is caused by the crowd's

    (1) rooting for the smaller man, but cheering a good finisher
    (2) cheering a good finisher, but hissing at the referee
    (3) applauding a friendly gesture, but rooting for the smaller man
    (4) hissing at the referee, but howling at a good finisher
    (5) applauding a friendly gesture, but cheering a helpless opponent

34. Which group of words best indicates the author's opinion?

    (1) *referee, opponent, finisher*
    (2) *gladiators, slugged, sporting gesture*
    (3) *stimulating, hissing, pattering*
    (4) *beast, lurks, gray thing*
    (5) *spectacle, psychological dilemma, sportsmen*

35. The author states that the prize fight audience is

    (1) sportsmanlike
    (2) fair
    (3) civilized
    (4) uninvolved
    (5) vengeful

Practice Exam 2

GO ON TO THE NEXT PAGE

TEST 4: LANGUAGE ARTS, READING

<u>Questions 36–40</u> refer to the following commentary on literature.

WHAT HERITAGE DID WILLA CATHER LEAVE TO US?

Willa Cather (1873–1947) grew up to be a major American writer, but today many people still do not know her face. Critics rank her with our great modern novelists—Faulkner, Hemingway, Fitzgerald—and she was certainly esteemed in her own time. Supreme Court Justice Oliver Wendell Holmes praised *My Antonia* as a book that "makes the reader love his country more."

Miss Cather wrote that novel and 11 others. Her books still have this effect on readers, for she had the power to elevate ordinary people and places. No one has described the American West with more passion and clarity. In every sentence, her feeling for the earth surges beneath a strong, disciplined prose. This is from *My Antonia:*

We were talking about what it is like to spend one's childhood in little towns like these, buried in wheat and corn, under stimulating extremes of climate: burning summers when the world lies green and billowy beneath a brilliant sky, when one is fairly stifled in vegetation, in the colour and smell of strong weeds and heavy harvests; blustery winters with little snow, when the whole country is stripped bare and grey as sheet-iron. We agreed that no one who had not grown up in a little prairie town could know anything about it. It was a kind of freemasonry, we said.

Willa Cather became the voice of an unsung people, the generation of immigrants who settled our western frontier. Today many writers regard that history as tragic, a paradise lost through careless greed. Cather believed that America's promise would endure: *We come and go, but the land is always here. And the people who love it and understand it are the people who own it—for a little while.*

36. The author implies impatience with
    (1) lack of modern recognition of Cather's work
    (2) lack of critical acclaim for Cather's work
    (3) lack of appreciation by her contemporaries
    (4) Cather's stature as a writer
    (5) Cather's patriotism

37. The author admires Cather's
    (1) huge output
    (2) popular success
    (3) unusual subject matter
    (4) objectivity
    (5) earthiness

38. In the excerpt from *My Antonia*, Cather stresses a childhood rooted in a small town's
    (1) repression
    (2) activity
    (3) passion
    (4) natural characteristics
    (5) brutal hardships

39. The author implies praise for all of the following characteristics of Cather's work EXCEPT her
    (1) style
    (2) passion
    (3) clarity
    (4) effect on her readers
    (5) unusual subjects

40. Cather's view of America was
    (1) cynical
    (2) resigned
    (3) tragic
    (4) optimistic
    (5) regional

END OF EXAM

TEST 5: MATHEMATICS

DIRECTIONS

The Mathematics portion of the GED exam consists of both multiple-choice and alternate format questions. The goal of this section is to measure your general math skills and problem-solving abilities. Each question is based on a short reading that could include a diagram, graph, or chart.

The questions in this section should take you no longer than 45 minutes. There's no penalty for incorrect answers so be sure to answer every question. Also, be careful not to spend too much time on each question.

Formulas you need are given on page 888. Only some of the questions will require you to use a formula. Not all the formulas given will be needed.

The questions will give you varying amounts of information—some will provide more information than you need to solve the problem, while some questions will not even provide enough to solve the problem. When a question does not provide enough information to solve the problem, then the correct answer will be "Not enough information is given."

You may use a calculator on Part 1.

To mark your answer, darken the corresponding circle on the answer sheet.

FOR EXAMPLE:

If a grocery bill totaling $15.75 is paid with a $20.00 bill, how much change should be returned?

(1) $5.26   ① ② ● ④ ⑤
(2) $4.75
(3) $4.25
(4) $3.75
(5) $3.25

The correct answer is "$4.25"; therefore, answer space 3 would be marked on the answer sheet.

GO ON TO THE NEXT PAGE

TEST 5: MATHEMATICS

FORMULAS	
Description	**Formula**
AREA (A) of a:	
square	$A = s^2$; where s = side
rectangle	$A = lw$; where l = length, w = width
parallelogram	$A = bh$; where b = base, h = height
triangle	$A = \frac{1}{2}bh$; where b = base, h = height
trapezoid	$A = \frac{1}{2}(b_1 + b_2)h$; where b = base, h = height
circle	$A = \pi r^2$; where π = 3.14, r = radius
PERIMETER (P) of a:	
square	$P = 4s$; where s = side
rectangle	$P = 2l + 2w$; where l = length, w = width
triangle	$P = a + b + c$; where a, b, and c are the sides
circumference (C) of a circle	$C = \pi d$; where π = 3.14, d = diameter
VOLUME (V) of a:	
cube	$V = s^3$; where s = side
rectangular container	$V = lwh$; where l = length, w = width, h = height
cylinder	$V = \pi r^2 h$; where π = 3.14, r = radius, h = height
square pyramid	$V = \frac{1}{3}(\text{base edge})^2 h$
cone	$V = \frac{1}{3}\pi r^2 h$
Pythagorean theorem	$c^2 = a^2 + b^2$; where c = hypotenuse, a and b are legs, of a right triangle
distance (d) between two points in a plane	$d = \sqrt{(x_2 - x_1)^2 + (y_2 - y_1)^2}$; where (x_1,y_1) and (x_2,y_2) are two points in a plane
slope of a line (m)	$m = \dfrac{y_2 - y_1}{x_2 - x_1}$; where (x_1,y_1) and (x_2,y_2) are two points in a plane
MEASURES OF CENTRAL TENDENCY	mean = $\dfrac{x_1 + x_2 + \ldots + x_n}{n}$; where the x's are the values for which a mean is desired, and n = number of values in the series
	median = the point in an ordered set of numbers at which half of the numbers are above and half of the numbers are below this value
simple interest (i)	$i = prt$; where p = principal, r = rate, t = time
distance (d) as function of rate and time	$d = rt$; where r = rate, t = time
total cost (c)	$c = nr$; where n = number of units, r = cost per unit

GO ON TO THE NEXT PAGE

TEST 5: MATHEMATICS, PART I

Directions: You will have 45 minutes to complete this section. You MAY use a calculator.

1. A salesman earns $300 per week plus a 5% commission on all sales. One week, his sales amounted to $15,000. What were his earnings that week?

   (1) $700
   (2) $850
   (3) $900
   (4) $1,050
   (5) $2,150

2. How much does Jane pay for 1 pound 12 ounces of apples at $1.96 per pound?

   (1) $3.43
   (2) $3.60
   (3) $3.64
   (4) $3.72
   (5) $3.96

3. One morning Martin drove 80 miles in 2 hours. After lunch, he covered 100 miles more in 3 hours. What was his average rate of speed, in miles per hour, for the 5 hours of driving?

   (1) 35
   (2) 36
   (3) 37
   (4) 45
   (5) Not enough information is given.

4. A picture 8 inches long and 6 inches wide is to be enlarged so that its length will be 12 inches. What is the width, in inches, of the enlarged picture?

   Mark your answer in the circles on the grid on the answer sheet.

5. A man bought ABC stock at $19.625 per share and sold it at $23.25 per share. What was his profit on 80 shares before deductions for commission and taxes?

   Mark your answer in the circles on the grid on the answer sheet.

6. A solution of the inequality $3x - 1 < 5$ is

   (1) 3
   (2) 2
   (3) 1
   (4) 5
   (5) $2\frac{1}{2}$

7. A theater has 850 seats, 60% of which are in the orchestra. How many seats are NOT in the orchestra?

   Mark your answer in the circles on the grid on the answer sheet.

8. In a right triangle, the ratio of the measures of the two acute angles is $4:1$. What is the measure, in degrees, of the larger acute angle?

   (1) 50
   (2) 54
   (3) 70
   (4) 72
   (5) Not enough information is given.

GO ON TO THE NEXT PAGE

TEST 5: MATHEMATICS, PART I

9. If 18 feet 10 inches is cut from a wire that is 25 feet 8 inches long, what is the length of the wire that is left?

   (1) 6 ft. 1 in.

   (2) 6 ft. 2 in.

   (3) 6 ft. 9 in.

   (4) 6 ft. 10 in.

   (5) 7 ft. 2 in.

10. Bill earns m dollars per month, and Angelo earns n dollars per month. How many dollars do both men earn in 1 year?

    (1) $12mn$

    (2) $12m + n$

    (3) $12(m + n)$

    (4) $12n + m$

    (5) $12n - m$

11. A boat travels due east for a distance of 15 miles. It then travels due north for a distance of 20 miles, at which point it drops anchor. How many miles is the boat from its starting point?

    (1) 23

    (2) 25

    (3) 29

    (4) 30

    (5) 35

12. Joan and Maria earn money by babysitting. If Joan earns twice as much as Maria and the two girls earn a total of $42, how much does Maria earn?

    (1) $8

    (2) $10

    (3) $12

    (4) $14

    (5) Not enough information is given.

Question 13 is based on the following table.

The table gives the instructions that accompany an income tax form.

If your taxable income is:		
At least	**But not more than**	**Your tax is**
0	$3,499	2% of the amount
$3,500	$4,499	$70 plus 3% of any amount above $3,500
$4,500	$7,499	$100 plus 5% of any amount above $4,500
$7,500		$250 plus 7% of any amount above $7,500

13. How much tax in dollars is due on a taxable income of $5,800?

    Mark your answer in the circles on the grid on the answer sheet.

GO ON TO THE NEXT PAGE

TEST 5: MATHEMATICS, PART I

14. Given the formula $x = 2a(b + 7)$, find x if $a = 3$ and $b = 5$.

    (1) 13
    (2) 72
    (3) 108
    (4) 120
    (5) 210

15. A school has 18 classes with 35 students in each class. In order to reduce class size to 30, how many new classes must be formed?

    (1) 2
    (2) 3
    (3) 5
    (4) 6
    (5) 8

16. A committee consists of 7 women and 4 men. If a member of the committee is chosen at random to act as chairperson, what is the probability that the choice is a woman?

    Mark your answer in the circles on the grid on the answer sheet.

17. A bag of potatoes weighing 5 pounds 12 ounces costs $2.07. What is the cost of 1 pound of potatoes?

    (1) $0.36
    (2) $0.38
    (3) $0.40
    (4) $0.45
    (5) $0.48

Question 18 is based on the following figure.

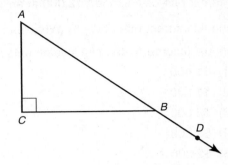

18. If $\overleftrightarrow{AC}$ is perpendicular to $\overleftrightarrow{CB}$ and $m\angle CBD = 125°$ then $m\angle A$ equals

    (1) 15°
    (2) 20°
    (3) 35°
    (4) 45°
    (5) Not enough information is given.

19. In a large class 80 students took a test. When the test papers were rated, it was found that 10% of the students had A papers, 25% had B papers, 30% had C papers, 15% had D papers, and the rest failed. How many students failed the test?

    (1) 10
    (2) 12
    (3) 15
    (4) 16
    (5) Not enough information is given.

Practice Exam 2

GO ON TO THE NEXT PAGE

TEST 5: MATHEMATICS, PART I

20. A man invests $20,000 at an annual interest rate of 7%, and $12,000 at an annual interest rate of $7\frac{1}{2}$%. What was his annual income on the two investments?

   (1) $1,400
   (2) $1,500
   (3) $2,000
   (4) $2,300
   (5) $2,800

21. How many 4-inch by 8-inch bricks are needed to build a walk 6 feet wide and 24 feet long?

   (1) 54
   (2) 600
   (3) 648
   (4) 840
   (5) 1,000

22. Pete Rossini has just graduated from college with honors. He has been offered four jobs with the following pay provisions:
   A. $54,000 for the first year
   B. $1,070 per week for the first year
   C. $4,070 per month for the first year
   D. $4,000 per month for the first 6 months and an increase of 10% for the last 6 months

   Which of the above offers will give Pete Rossini the greatest income for the first year?

   (1) A
   (2) B
   (3) C
   (4) D
   (5) Not enough information is given.

23. A clothing dealer bought two dozen jackets at $48 each. The next month she bought 15 more jackets at $48 each. Which of the following expressions gives the total number of dollars the dealer spent for the jackets?

   (1) 24 × 48 + 15
   (2) (24 × 48) × 15
   (3) 24 + 48 × 15
   (4) 48(24 + 15)
   (5) 24 + (48 + 15)

24. One car travels at an average speed of 48 miles per hour. A slower car travels at an average speed of 36 miles per hour. In 45 minutes how many more miles does the faster car travel than the slower car?
   Mark your answer in the circles on the grid on the answer sheet.

Question 25 is based on the following graph.

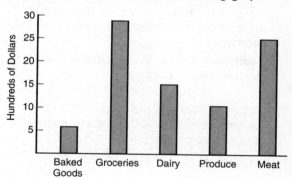

25. By how many dollars do the sales in the meat department exceed the sales in the dairy department?
   Mark your answer in the circles on the grid on the answer sheet.

END OF EXAM

TEST 5: MATHEMATICS, PART II

Directions: You will have 45 minutes to complete questions 26–50. You may NOT use a calculator; otherwise, directions are the same as in Part I. You MAY refer to the *Formulas* sheet.

Question 26 is based on the following figure.

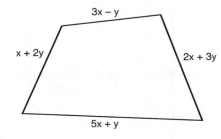

26. What is the perimeter of the figure?

   (1) $11x + 5y$

   (2) $10x + 5y$

   (3) $11x + 4y$

   (4) $9x - y$

   (5) $8x + 3y$

27. On January 1, a 280-gallon oil tank was $\frac{7}{8}$ full; on January 31 it was $\frac{1}{4}$ full. How many gallons of oil were used during the month?

   (1) 70

   (2) 105

   (3) 175

   (4) 210

   (5) Not enough information is given.

28. Express 2,750,389 in scientific notation.

   (1) 27.50389×10^5

   (2) 275.0389×10^3

   (3) 27.50389×10^6

   (4) 0.2750389×10^7

   (5) 2.750389×10^6

29. A basketball team has won 50 games of 75 played. The team still has 45 games to play. How many of the remaining games must the team win in order to win 60% of all games played during the season?

   (1) 20

   (2) 21

   (3) 22

   (4) 25

   (5) 30

Question 30 is based on the following diagram.

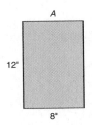 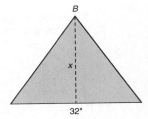

Area of ▭ A = Area of △ B

30. Which of the following expressions will provide the height (x) of △B?

   (1) $\frac{1}{2}(32x) = 12(8)$

   (2) $(12 \times 2) + (8 \times 2) = 3(32) + x$

   (3) $\frac{1}{2}(32x) = 8x(24)$

   (4) $16x^2 = 96$

   (5) $\frac{1}{2}(32) = \frac{20}{2}$

GO ON TO THE NEXT PAGE

TEST 5: MATHEMATICS, PART II

31. The weights of the 11 men on the Panthers football team are 201,197,193, 212, 205, 207, 195, 214, 198, 203, and 184 pounds. What is the median weight, in pounds, of a player on this team?

    (1) 199
    (2) 200
    (3) 201
    (4) 203
    (5) 205

Question 32 is based on the following graph.

Distribution of Expenses for Sales of
$240,000 Triad Technologies Group

32. How many dollars were spent for labor?

    (1) $4,800
    (2) $9,600
    (3) $48,000
    (4) $96,000
    (5) $960,000

Question 33 is based on the following graph.

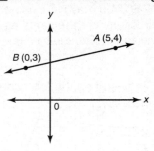

33. What is the slope of the line passing through points A (5,4) and B (0,3)?

    (1) $\dfrac{1}{10}$

    (2) $\dfrac{1}{5}$

    (3) $\dfrac{3}{5}$

    (4) $\dfrac{4}{5}$

    (5) 5

34. A relay team consists of three runners who each run a different distance around a 400-meter track. The first runner runs 4 laps around the track, the second runs 6 laps, and the third runs 2 laps. What is the total distance run by the relay team?

    1) 48,000 meters
    2) 4.8 kilometers
    3) 480 millimeters
    4) 9,600 meters
    5) 48 kilometers

GO ON TO THE NEXT PAGE

TEST 5: MATHEMATICS, PART II

Question 35 is based on the following graph.

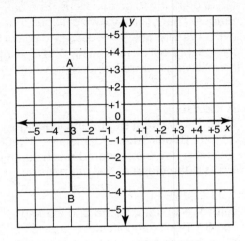

35. Line $\overline{AB}$ is the left side of a rectangle whose length is 7 units. If the rectangle's width is 6 units, at what point will the upper-right corner of the rectangle be located?

Mark your answer on the coordinate grid on your answer sheet.

36. If $3x - 1 = 11$, what is the value of $x^2 + x$?

   (1) 12
   (2) 15
   (3) 16
   (4) 18
   (5) 20

37. A bell rings every 2 hours, a second bell rings every 3 hours, and a third bell rings every 4 hours. If all 3 bells ring at 9:00 A.M., at what time will all 3 bells next ring?

   (1) noon
   (2) 6:00 P.M.
   (3) 9:00 P.M.
   (4) 10:00 P.M.
   (5) Not enough information is given.

38. A family spends 20% of its monthly income on food, 23% on rent, and 42% on other expenses and saves the balance. If the family saves $360 per month, what is its monthly income?

   (1) $2,000
   (2) $2,200
   (3) $2,400
   (4) $2,500
   (5) $28,800

Question 39 is based on the following figure.

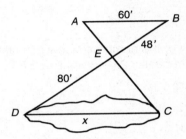

39. To measure the distance (DC) across a pond, a surveyor takes points A and B so that $\overrightarrow{AB}$ is parallel to $\overrightarrow{DC}$. If $AB = 60$ feet, $EB = 48$ feet, and $ED = 80$ feet, and $\triangle ABE$ is similar to $\triangle DEC$, find DC, in feet.

Mark your answer in the circles on the grid on the answer sheet.

Practice Exam 2

TEST 5: MATHEMATICS, PART II

40. A dozen eggs cost x cents. What is the cost, in cents, of 3 eggs at the same rate?

    (1) $\dfrac{x}{3}$

    (2) $\dfrac{x}{4}$

    (3) $\dfrac{3x}{4}$

    (4) $\dfrac{x}{12}$

    (5) $3x$

41. Each of the numbers below is a solution of the inequality $2x + 3 > 7$ EXCEPT

    (1) 10
    (2) 5
    (3) 4
    (4) 3
    (5) 0

Question 42 is based on the following figure.

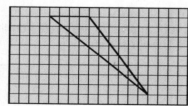

42. What is the area, in square graph units, of the triangle?

    Mark your answer in the circles on the grid on the answer sheet.

43. Shandra Gordon is a bright high school senior planning to go to college. She has narrowed her choice to two colleges that she favors equally. She has decided to select the college that will be less costly and is using the following facts to help her arrive at a decision.

    COLLEGE A
    Tuition — $9,480, Board and lodging — $6,320. Books and incidentals — $1,200. Shandra has been offered a scholarship of $4,200 per year.

    COLLEGE B
    Tuition — $9,200, Board and lodging — $6,150. Books and incidentals — $1,200. Shandra has been offered a scholarship of $3,200 per year.
    Shandra has also been offered a part-time job working in the college library.
    What additional information does Shandra need in order to make a choice?

    (1) how many miles she lives from each college

    (2) which college has the better reputation

    (3) how many scholarships each college grants

    (4) how much she can earn by working in the library at College B

    (5) which college has better athletic facilities

GO ON TO THE NEXT PAGE

TEST 5: MATHEMATICS, PART II

44. A room is 24 ft. long, 18 ft. wide, and 9 ft. high. Which of the following expressions represents the number of square yards of wallpaper needed to paper the four walls of the room?

(1) $\dfrac{(lwh)}{9}$

(2) $\dfrac{(lw)+(hw)}{3}$

(3) $\dfrac{8(lw)+4h}{3}$

(4) $\dfrac{4(lw)+4h}{3}$

(5) $\dfrac{2(lh)+2(wh)}{9}$

45. A man drives x miles the first day, y miles the second day, and z miles the third day. The average mileage covered per day is

(1) $\dfrac{xyz}{3}$

(2) $\dfrac{xy+z}{3}$

(3) $x + y + z$

(4) $\dfrac{x+y+z}{3}$

(5) $3xyz$

46. A plumber must cut a pipe 64 inches long into two parts so that one part is 8 inches longer than the other part. Find the length, in inches, of the larger part.

(1) 28

(2) 30

(3) 36

(4) 40

(5) Not enough information is given.

47. After working 4 hours, Frank has made 21 machine parts. Which expression represents the number of parts he can make in 7 hours?

(1) $\dfrac{7(21)}{4}$

(2) $\dfrac{7(4)}{21}$

(3) $7(21)$

(4) $\dfrac{4(21)}{7}$

(5) $7(4)\,(21)$

48. A storage box in a form of a rectangular solid has a square base. If V represents the volume of the box, x represents the length of a side of the base, and y represents the height of the box, which of the following equations expresses the relationship among V, x, and y?

(1) $V = 2xy$

(2) $V = xy^2$

(3) $V = 2xy^2$

(4) $V = x^2y$

(5) $V = x + xy$

GO ON TO THE NEXT PAGE

Practice Exam 2

TEST 5: MATHEMATICS, PART II

49. In his will, Mr. Adams left $\frac{1}{4}$ of his estate to his wife and the remainder to his son and his daughter. If the son received $36,000 as his share, what was the total value of the estate?

   (1) $45,000
   (2) $72,000
   (3) $80,000
   (4) $90,000
   (5) Not enough information is given.

Question 50 is based on the following information.

A 3-foot-wide walkway is built around a swimming pool that is 20 feet by 30 feet, as shown in the figure below.

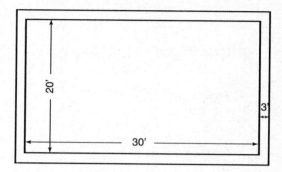

50. In order to determine how much flagstone to buy, the homeowner needs to know the total area, in square feet, of the walkway.

   Which of the following expressions represents this area?

   (1) (23)(33)
   (2) (26)(36)
   (3) (23)(33) − (20)(30)
   (4) (26)(36) − (20)(30)
   (5) (26)(36) − (23)(33)

END OF EXAM

ANSWER KEYS, SUMMARIES OF RESULTS, AND SELF-APPRAISAL CHARTS

TEST 1: LANGUAGE ARTS, WRITING, PART I/PAGE 837

I. CHECK YOUR ANSWERS, using the following answer key:

1. **2**	10. **5**	19. **2**	28. **5**	37. **4**	46. **4**
2. **3**	11. **4**	20. **1**	29. **1**	38. **1**	47. **5**
3. **4**	12. **5**	21. **1**	30. **5**	39. **2**	48. **1**
4. **2**	13. **3**	22. **5**	31. **3**	40. **3**	49. **3**
5. **1**	14. **4**	23. **5**	32. **2**	41. **1**	50. **2**
6. **4**	15. **1**	24. **1**	33. **5**	42. **3**	
7. **4**	16. **4**	25. **4**	34. **4**	43. **4**	
8. **4**	17. **4**	26. **4**	35. **4**	44. **5**	
9. **1**	18. **4**	27. **4**	36. **4**	45. **4**	

II. SCORE YOURSELF:

Number correct:

Excellent _____
45–50

Good _____
40–44

Fair _____
35–39

III. EVALUATE YOUR SCORE: Did you get at least 35 correct answers? If not, you need more practice for the Language Arts, Writing, Part I test. In any event, you can improve your performance to Excellent or Good by analyzing your errors.

IV. ANALYZE YOUR ERRORS: To determine your areas of weakness, list the number of correct answers you had under each of the following categories (which correspond to the content areas of the Language Arts, Writing, Part I test), and compare your score with the average scores specified in the right-hand column. Review the answer analysis section beginning on page 905 for each of the questions you got wrong, and give yourself more practice in your weak areas before attempting the actual GED Exam.

Content Areas	Items	Your Score	Average Score
Sentence Structure	13, 15, 17–19, 25, 27–28, 34–36, 43–44		8
Usage	1, 3, 5, 7, 8, 14, 21, 24 31–32, 39, 49–50		8
Mechanics			
Spelling (homonyms, contractions, possessives)	6, 16, 29, 37		3
Punctuation	2, 20, 33, 46		3
Capitalization	4, 26, 45, 48		3
Organization	11, 22, 38, 40–42, 47		5
No correction	9–10, 12, 23, 30		3

Total _____

TEST 2: SOCIAL STUDIES/PAGE 850

I. CHECK YOUR ANSWERS, using the following answer key:

1. **4**	11. **1**	21. **2**	31. **4**	41. **3**
2. **5**	12. **2**	22. **4**	32. **2**	42. **3**
3. **1**	13. **2**	23. **5**	33. **3**	43. **5**
4. **5**	14. **1**	24. **3**	34. **1**	44. **4**
5. **4**	15. **4**	25. **3**	35. **5**	45. **2**
6. **2**	16. **5**	26. **5**	36. **3**	46. **3**
7. **4**	17. **3**	27. **2**	37. **5**	47. **1**
8. **1**	18. **3**	28. **4**	38. **3**	48. **1**
9. **2**	19. **5**	29. **1**	39. **2**	49. **4**
10. **1**	20. **1**	30. **2**	40. **2**	50. **1**

II. SCORE YOURSELF:

Number correct:

Excellent _____
45–50

Good _____
40–44

Fair _____
35–39

III. EVALUATE YOUR SCORE: Did you get at least 35 correct answers? If not, you need more practice for the Social Studies test. In any event, you can improve your performance to Excellent or Good by analyzing your errors.

II. ANALYZE YOUR ERRORS: To determine your specific weaknesses, list the number of correct answers you had under each of the following categories (which correspond to the content areas of the Social Studies test), and compare your score with the average scores specified in the right-hand column. Review the answer analysis section beginning on page 908 for each of the questions you got wrong, and give yourself more practice in your weak areas (including the "Glossary of Social Studies Terms"), before taking the actual GED Exam.

Content Areas	Items	Your Score	Average Score
Civics and Government	1–6, 9, 24–26, 29–30, 40		9
Economics	10–12, 14–16, 31, 33–34, 43, 47		8
History	7–8, 13, 17–19, 39, 41–42, 44–46, 48–50		11
Geography	20–23, 27–28, 32, 35–38		8

Total _____

TEST 3: SCIENCE/PAGE 863

I. CHECK YOUR ANSWERS, using the following answer key:

1. **1**	11. **4**	21. **2**	31. **3**	41. **4**
2. **4**	12. **1**	22. **5**	32. **2**	42. **1**
3. **5**	13. **3**	23. **4**	33. **3**	43. **1**
4. **1**	14. **3**	24. **2**	34. **3**	44. **5**
5. **5**	15. **4**	25. **3**	35. **3**	45. **2**
6. **1**	16. **2**	26. **5**	36. **3**	46. **3**
7. **4**	17. **2**	27. **2**	37. **5**	47. **3**
8. **4**	18. **2**	28. **3**	38. **2**	48. **4**
9. **4**	19. **5**	29. **4**	39. **3**	49. **5**
10. **3**	20. **1**	30. **1**	40. **4**	50. **3**

II. SCORE YOURSELF:

Number correct:

Excellent _____
44–50

Good _____
38–43

Fair _____
32–37

III. EVALUATE YOUR SCORE: Did you get at least 32 correct answers? If not, you need more practice for the Science test. In any event, you can improve your performance to Excellent or Good by analyzing your errors.

IV. ANALYZE YOUR ERRORS: To determine your specific weaknesses, encircle the number of each question you got wrong. This will reveal the specific science area that needs emphasis in planning your study program. After studying the answer analysis section beginning on page 911 for each of the questions you got wrong, list the terms that you feel need further explanation and study them in the "Glossary of Scientific Terms" beginning on page 423. Then give yourself more practice in your weak areas before taking the actual GED Exam.

Content Areas	Items	Your Score	Average Score
Biology	1–11, 27–29, 33, 34, 40–50		19
Earth Science	12–17, 30–32		8
Chemistry	18–20, 35		2
Physics	21–26, 36–39		8

Total _____

TEST 4: LANGUAGE ARTS, READING/PAGE 877

I. CHECK YOUR ANSWERS, using the following answer key:

1. **1**	9. **2**	17. **4**	25. **1**	33. **1**
2. **4**	10. **2**	18. **1**	26. **5**	34. **4**
3. **5**	11. **2**	19. **5**	27. **5**	35. **5**
4. **4**	12. **5**	20. **5**	28. **4**	36. **1**
5. **3**	13. **1**	21. **4**	29. **4**	37. **5**
6. **5**	14. **4**	22. **1**	30. **5**	38. **4**
7. **1**	15. **4**	23. **3**	31. **1**	39. **5**
8. **5**	16. **3**	24. **4**	32. **3**	40. **4**

II. SCORE YOURSELF:

Number correct:

Excellent _____
36–40

Good _____
32–35

Fair _____
28–31

III. EVALUATE YOUR SCORE:
Did you get at least 28 correct answers? If not, you need more practice for the Language Arts, Reading test. You can improve your performance to Excellent or Good by analyzing your errors.

IV. ANALYZE YOUR ERRORS:
To determine your specific weaknesses, first list the number of correct answers you had under each of the following categories and compare your score with the average scores in the right-hand column. After studying the answer analysis section beginning on page 915 for each of the questions you answered incorrectly, study the material in the sections "Basic Reading Skills" and "Reading Prose, Poetry, and Drama" as well as the "Glossary of Literary Terms" (page 504) to strengthen your weak areas before taking the actual GED Exam.

Reading Skills	Items	Your Score	Average Score
Locating the Main Idea	6, 12, 15, 21, 25, 30		4
Finding Details	1–2, 5, 8–9, 13, 20, 22–24, 28, 32–33, 35, 37–39		11
Inferring Meaning	3, 7, 14, 19, 27–29		4
Making Inferences	4, 8–10, 13, 17–18, 26, 29–30, 34, 36, 40		9
Determining Tone and Mood	31		1
Inferring Character	16		1
Inferring Setting	11		1

Total _____

Now, to see how your scores in the content area of Language Arts, Reading test compare with the average scores in the right-hand column, list your score for each of the following:

Literary Forms	Items	Your Score	Average Score
Prose Fiction	11–20, 26–30		11
Prose Nonfiction	1–10, 31–40		13
Poetry	16–25		7
Drama	6–10		3

Total _____

Note: While Commentary on the Arts is a content area in itself, the commentary, as written, is in the form of prose nonfiction.

TEST 5: MATHEMATICS/PAGE 887

CHECK YOUR ANSWERS, using the following answer key:

Part I

1. **4**
2. **1**
3. **2**
4. **9**
5. **290**
6. **3**
7. **340**
8. **4**
9. **4**
10. **3**
11. **2**
12. **4**
13. **165**
14. **2**
15. **2**
16. **7/11 or .64**
17. **1**
18. **3**
19. **4**
20. **4**

21. **3**
22. **2**
23. **4**
24. **9**
25. **$1,000**

Part II

26. **1**
27. **3**
28. **5**
29. **3**
30. **1**
31. **3**
32. **4**
33. **2**
34. **2**
35.

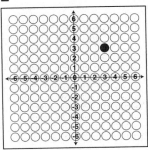

36. **5**
37. **3**
38. **3**
39. **100**
40. **2**
41. **5**
42. **16**
43. **4**
44. **5**
45. **4**
46. **3**
47. **1**
48. **4**
49. **5**
50. **4**

II. SCORE YOURSELF:

Number correct:

Excellent _____
40–50

Good _____
32–49

Fair _____
28–31

III. EVALUATE YOUR SCORE: Did you get at least 38 correct answers? If not, you need more practice for the Mathematics test. In any event, you can improve your performance to Excellent or Good by analyzing your errors.

IV. ANALYZE YOUR ERRORS: To determine your specific weaknesses, list the number of correct answers you had under each of the following categories and compare your score with the average scores specified in the right-hand column. After studying the answer analysis section beginning on page 917 for each of the questions you got wrong, give yourself more practice in your weak areas before attempting Practice Exam Two.

Content Areas	Items	Your Score	Average Score
Numbers and Basic Operations	3, 5, 9, 15, 21–24, 28 31, 37, 47		7
Fractions and Measurements	2, 16, 17, 27, 34, 49		3
Decimals and Percents	1, 7, 19, 20, 29, 38		3
Data Analysis	13, 25, 32, 39, 43, 44, 50		4
Algebra	4, 6, 10, 12, 14, 26, 36, 40, 41, 45, 46		6
Geometry	8, 11, 18, 30, 33, 35, 42 48		5

Total _____

Your Total GED Score

The Language Arts, Writing Test _____

The Social Studies Test _____

The Science Test _____

The Language Arts, Reading Test _____

The Mathematics Test _____

Total _____

ANSWER ANALYSIS

TEST 1: LANGUAGE ARTS, WRITING, PART I/PAGE 837

1. **2** *Are enrolling* is necessary to parallel *are recognizing*.

2. **3** A comma is used after an introductory clause.

3. **4** The plural verb *call* must be used to agree with the plural subject *techniques*.

4. **2** The name of a specific place such as Crimea is capitalized.

5. **1** You cannot shift pronouns that refer to the same person in the same sentence. Use either *you* or *one* throughout the sentence.

6. **4** The correct spelling is *government's*.

7. **4** The pronoun that agrees with the noun *nurses* is *their*.

8. **4** The subject *practice* agrees with the verb *brings*.

9. **1** The original is the best way.

10. **5** No correction is necessary.

11. **4** Sentence 2 states the *four basic elements*. All of the other sentences elaborate on that one idea.

12. **5** No correction is necessary.

13. **3** *Because* is correct since the second sentence states the reason for the first.

14. **4** *Has* must be inserted for parallel structure with *is six inches high, is made of leather*.

15. **1** The original is the best way.

16. **4** The correct spelling is *materials*.

17. **4** The comma is necessary to avoid the sentence fragment beginning with the *waist strap*.

18. **4** A plural verb is needed since the new subject, *the sleeping bag and its two accessories*, is plural.

19. **2** The second sentence names an example of the *tent* mentioned in the first sentence, so *such as* is used.

20. **1** Commas are used to separate items in a series.

21. **1** The plural subject *Crafts* agrees with the verb *are*.

22. **5** Sentence 3 follows a logical order within the passage.

23. **5** No correction is necessary.

24. **1** The correlatives *not only* and *but also* must be followed by parallel elements.

25. **4** The period is necessary to prevent a run-on sentence.

26. **4** Holidays, such as Christmas, are capitalized.

27. **4** The second sentence becomes an adjective clause modifying *feathers*.

28. **5** The period and capital are necessary to avoid a run-on sentence.

29. **1** The correct spelling in this sentence is *affects*.

30. **5** No correction is necessary.

31. **3** The plural verb *are* is needed to agree in number with *dwellings*, the antecedent of *that*.

32. **2** *In finding* is necessary for parallel structure with *in securing*.

33. **5** No correction is necessary.

34. **4** *Concerns* must follow since the new subject, *housing*, requires a verb.

35. **4** A participial phrase is used to describe *are upgrading*.

36. **4** The sense of the sentence requires the verb *will have* after the new subject, *nation*.

37. **4** The correct spelling is *separately*.

38. **1** The only transition word(s) that would fit with this sentence are *First of all* because that sentence is the first point in the passage.

39. **2** The singular subject *coverage* requires the verb *pays*.

40. **3** Sentence 4 should be left as it is, since it follows a logical order of organization.

41. **1** This passage is about different kinds of auto insurance that can make up a bundle. The other sentences describe each kind.

42. **3** A new paragraph can be started after sentence 4 because a new topic is introduced: *uninsured motorist coverage*.

43. **4** The semicolon is needed to prevent a sentence fragment starting with *The larger*.

44. **5** The new subject *feature* requires the verb *covers*.

45. **4** *Accidental death and dismemberment* is not a proper noun and should not be capitalized.

46. **4** A question mark is used after a sentence that asks a question.

47. **5** Sentence 5 should be left as it is because it follows a logical order in the passage.

48. **1** Only the names of specific countries are capitalized; *nation* is a common noun.

49. **3** The subject *organizations* agrees with the verb *range*.

50. **2** The pronoun *you* matches the first pronoun, *your*.

TEST 1: LANGUAGE ARTS, WRITING, PART II/PAGE 849

SAMPLE ESSAY

I feel very strongly that immigrants have a right to become citizens of the United States. There are several reasons why I believe this, but three of the reasons are: the United States is known as a culturally diverse society, we are in a sense all immigrants, and everyone should have the right to make choices.

The United States is known as a culturally diverse society. The reason for this is because of the great diversity of people that have entered into the United States through the immigration process. People have been coming into the United States in waves for centuries.

When we check our own ancestors we find that each of us has forefathers from other countries. Unless a person is one hundred percent native American, then somewhere through time an ancestor has come from another country to the United States.

Everyone in the world should have a right to make choices. Some countries don't allow their citizens to make their own choices, which in turn creates a stalemate in society. People need to be allowed to follow their dreams.

I'm glad no one told my ancestors they weren't allowed to come into the United States to become citizens. If they had, I might not be part of a culturally diverse society or be able to make my own choices.

TEST 2: SOCIAL STUDIES/PAGE 850

1. **4** Hamilton believed in unrestricted suffrage, that is, right of voting, on the part of the people, as stated in his opening sentence.

2. **5** Rather than sovereignty of governments, Hamilton emphasized "balance between the national and state governments."

3. **1** Hamilton mentioned popular election as "this great source of free government" to be kept "perfectly pure."

4. **5** Women are permitted to serve. In fact, as stated in the middle of the second paragraph, the county committee may require equal representation of the sexes in each district.

5. **4** The end of the second paragraph contains the statement giving the purpose of the primary.

6. **2** If about 700 citizens cast their ballots in a voting district for two committeepersons, the inference can be drawn that each committeeperson represents half of the voters, or about 350.

7. **4** Of the choices given, the United States has direct involvement with Europe only in NATO, a military alliance created in 1949 as a shield against further Communist expansion or aggression. Under the North Atlantic Pact, a mutual defense agreement, an attack on any NATO member is considered an attack on all.

8. **1** The exaggerated, uncomfortable, and desperate position of Uncle Sam is meant to be critical. Note the arms stretched to reach Southeast Asia and South America, the left leg raised to touch Europe, and the outer lines beyond the globe and human figure, showing both to be unstable. The implication is that the United States cannot continue in this position.

9. **2** Typically, at border crossings, guards in uniform had travelers place their purchases in wooden bins to be searched.

10. **1** Social Security accounts for 21%, 3% more than defense, which is the second largest program.

11. **1** Of the means-tested programs, the largest is Medicaid, three times more in percentage than either food stamps or Supplemental Security Income.

12. **2** The total of entitlement spending, both means-tested and non-means tested, is 54%, slightly more than the interest on the national debt and discretionary spending combined.

13. **2** The quotation is a perversion of the original poem, which reads "Give me your tired, your poor, your huddled masses," that is inscribed on the Statue of Liberty. By changing it to welcome only the educated, the cartoonist is criticizing the United States for not accepting poor immigrants.

14. **1** The second paragraph points out that corporate diversification (by merger) will continue to be necessary to meet new competitors.

15. **4** The third sentence mentions that a company can sometimes get qualified technical manpower only by acquiring another company.

16. **5** The passage emphasizes future, rather than established, competitors as creating a motivation to merge.

17. **3** The author uses such terms as *finest* to describe the American population.

18. **3** He predicts that Americans will become "distinct" because of the "different climates" they inhabit.

19. **5** In America, the rewards of work are readily available.

20. **1** The world is becoming a "global village" according to Marshall McLuhan, as a result of this aspect of the Industrial Revolution.

21. **2** The cartoon indicates that candidates for office can afford only 30 seconds on TV because of the cost to propose simple solutions to very complicated problems. That is hardly enough.

22. **4** The graphs project that, by 2025, Africa's percentage of the world's population will increase by 7%, from 12% in 1990 to 19% in 2025 which is more than any other region's percentage.

23. **5** North America, the former Soviet Union, and Asia will each decrease by 1%; Latin America will increase 1%; Europe will have the largest decrease—3%.

24. **3** All of the others are mentioned in the Bill of Rights: freedom of religion—Amendment 1; freedom of the press—Amendment 1; a well-disciplined militia—Amendment 2; trial by jury—Amendment 7.

25. **3** "The President shall be Commander-in-Chief of the Army and Navy . . . and of the Militia" according to the United States Constitution.

26. **5** Elections by the people correct abuses that otherwise would have to be "lopped by the sword of revolution."

27. **2** Scale is the ratio between distance as shown on a map and the actual distance on the earth.

28. **4** The passage states that a compass rose shows direction.

29. **1** Problems like those of inflation, recession, and shortages of fuel or fertilizer cannot possibly be handled by individual state governments.

30. **2** This is the famous "clear and present danger" doctrine stated by Justice Oliver Wendell Holmes in the case of *Schenck v. U.S.* (1919). When the right to free speech endangers the common good, the common good prevails and free speech must be limited.

31. **4** The balance of payments involves all the economic transactions that a nation and its people have with the rest of the world, including the trade and investments of businesses, the tourism of citizens, and the economic and military grants and loans of government. A deficit in the balance of payments reflects a net cash flow out of a nation as a result of all the above exchanges. The quotation says that such a deficit might be minimized or reversed by increasing exports and decreasing imports.

32. **2** Those who favor development of new energy sources tend to give a low priority to the need to protect our environment and to conserve our natural resources.

33. **3** Model *B* shows an economy that could lead to depression if supply and demand were not brought into balance. A balance could result from a decrease in income tax rates, which would increase consumer demand.

34. **1** In 1929–1939, the great depression in the United States was characterized by huge supply and little demand because of high unemployment. This situation is depicted in model *A*.

35. **5** The Indian population was carried over from the time before Columbus discovered the Americas.

36. **3** The United States had no role in settling or colonizing Latin America.

37. **5** The national debt jumped $2.1 trillion between 2000 and 2005, the largest jump for any period on the graph.

38. **3** Entitlements, including Social Security, Medicaid, and Medicare received 50% of the budgeted money, half of the pie.

39. **2** The largest single part of federal spending is for Social Security, 22%.

40. **2** Lobbying is the use of politically experienced persons to influence lawmakers by providing financial support, testifying at hearings, supplying information, and drafting legislation on behalf of interested parties.

41. **3** The Monroe Doctrine, a statement that any attempt by European powers to intervene in the Western Hemisphere would be regarded as dangerous to the peace and safety of the United States, was applied by President Kennedy to Russia's attempt in 1962 to establish a missile base in Cuba.

42. **3** Sexism, the exploitation and domination of one sex by the other, more traditionally of women by men, has been countered by the Women's Liberation Movement and by legislation. Women, on the basis of preference and ability, now enter occupations, previously closed to them.

43. **5** Top-level management has 23% men and only 9% women.

44. **4** Investing in mass transit is mentioned as one of the ways to control sprawl.

45. **2** Sprawl is mentioned as the result of poorly planned development.

46. **3** The passage mentions both buying open spaces and saving green space.

47. **1** The tax is graduated because it divides the taxed population into income groups with increasing tax percentage rates by stages for groups with increasing incomes.

48. **1** Imperialism is the policy of acquiring colonies or of establishing political and economic control of foreign areas.

49. **4** The cooperation of nations to prevent any one country from becoming dominant is a definition of the term *balance of power*.

50. **1** In 1990, Asia had approximately 31/53 of the world's population. In 2000, it had 37/63. Both are over 50%.

TEST 3: SCIENCE/PAGE 863

1. **1** The entire cell cycle is 22 hours, and only 1 hour is for mitosis. 1/22 is just under 5%, so this must be the correct answer.

2. **4** The figure shows that mitosis is subdivided into more stages, whereas the other phases of the cell cycle are not.

3. **5** The cell cycle is 22 hours long, as it is shown in the figure: 1 hour is for mitosis, and the rest, 21 hours, is for interphase

4. **1** Plasma proteins are described as carrying out all of the functions except for membrane permeability, choice 1.

5. **5** Membrane permeability is controlled by ion concentrations, as shown on the chart. Of the choices provided, only chloride is an ion.

6. **1** The chart shows that in 1 μl (mm³) of blood there are about 5,000,000 red blood cells and 5,000 white blood cells. This is a ratio of 1,000:1.

7. **4** Clotting involves platelets and fibrinogen, but neutrophils are not mentioned as having any role in the clotting process.

8. **4** The graph shows that the number of metric tons of fish from the Indian Ocean has not changed much over the time period shown. The same can be said about the Atlantic Ocean. There has been a large increase in the fish taken from the Pacific Ocean.

9. **4** The total number of millions of metric tons in 1980 is between 30 and 40 million metric tons, making choice 4 the best choice.

10. **3** In 1980, the total amount of fish from all three oceans was about 35 million metric tons. The catch from the Pacific Ocean was about 12 million metric tons, and 12/35 is about 30%. Notice how even if you had estimated a bit differently, choice 3 would have still been the best choice.

11. **4** It is not until after 1985 (in this case 1986) that the Pacific Ocean became the largest source of fish.

12. **1** The graph clearly shows that vitamin D, folic acid, and iron are the three nutrients that have the greatest increase. Notice how these three really stand out on the graph. Most questions of the GED ask you to find clear distinctions. You should not expect to make a distinction of a 1% difference on a graph such as this.

13. **3** Vitamin C needs to increase by about 20%. This means that if a non-pregnant woman needs 1,000 mg, the increase will be 20% of 1,000 mg, or 200 mg. The total need will be 1,200 mg.

14. **3** The graph shows that the increase in calcium needs is 50%, making choice 3 the best choice.

15. **4** The temperature of the air is indicated on the thermometer marked *B*. The scale is marked in units of 10°, and the mercury has risen to the fourth subdivision between 20° and 30°. Therefore the reading is 28°.

16. **2** The temperature of the ice-water mixture (23°) is lower than the temperature of the air in the box (28°). Therefore, the air near the glass cup will be cooled below the temperature of the surrounding air. At this lower temperature, the amount of moisture the air can hold decreases. The droplets of water represent the excess moisture that has condensed out of the air.

17. **2** The dew point temperature is the temperature at which the air becomes saturated (as shown by the water droplets). Since the temperature of the air near the cup is the same as that of the ice-water mixture, the reading of 23°C on thermometer *A* is the dew point temperature.

18. **2** A change from the gaseous phase to the liquid phase is called condensation. A change from the liquid phase to the gaseous phase is called evaporation. A change from the solid phase to the liquid phase is called melting or fusion.

19. **5** The passage says that naphthalane, for example, vaporizes easily because of weak intermolecular forces.

20. **1** When any solid substance sublimes it changes to the vapor (or gas) phase of that same substance.

21. **2** Liquids have fixed volumes but their shapes can change with the container they are in.

22. **5** The passage states that both liquids and gases are fluids.

23. **4** An incompressible material has little space between particles. This is true for both liquids and solids. Gases are highly compressible.

24. **2** The reason sound detection works so well underwater is that sound travels well in water, since water conducts sound well. Some of the other choices are true statements, but they are not the reason submarines can detect underwater objects.

25. **3** If it took six seconds for the sound wave to travel to the ocean floor and reflect back, then it must have taken half that time, or three seconds for the sound wave to travel in one direction. Multiply 1,500 meters per second times 3 seconds to get 4,500 meters. A very similar example is provided within the passage. Very often you will find worked-out sample problems for any calculations you need to do.

26. **5** Sound travels best in denser materials. Of the materials listed, steel is by far the densest and is the one in which sound would travel best.

27. **1** The largest fish on the chart swim faster than the smaller fish. In fact, the slowest fish, the lemon sole, is also the smallest. While size and speed may not actually be connected in this way, from the figures on the chart one may hypothesize that they are.

28. **3** The scientific names of the flounder and the lemon sole indicate that they belong to the same genus, *Pleuronectes*, and therefore are probably related.

29. **4** Being careful that enough breeders survive to replace the fish taken is a logical solution to the problem of declining populations. The other answer choices are opinions.

30. **1** Observe that there is almost no change in temperature between the months of January and February. The temperature in January is –5°C, and in February it is just above –5°C.

31. **3** In September the average temperature was just above 15°C and can be estimated to be 16°C. The precipitation for September was between 60 mm and 80 mm and can be estimated to be 68 mm.

32. **2** The graph for temperature shows a pronounced rise in the summer months, while the bars for moisture are all about the same size.

33. **3** It is not until 9 minutes have passed that the ethylene glycol reaches 198°C, at which time it will start to boil.

34. **3** The boiling ethylene glycol stays at 198°C. The temperature of a billing liquid does not change. Thus boiling water will stay at 100°C while it is boiling.

35. **3** Since alkalis have a high pH, adding an alkali will raise the pH of the soil. Choices 2 and 5 add acid, thus lowering the pH. Pure water could raise the pH, but never higher than pH 7. The tap water has the same pH as the soil, so it would make no change at all.

36. **3** For a plane mirror, every point of the image is as far behind the mirror as the corresponding point of the object is in front. This is indicated in the following sketch. Note that Choice 3 closely points in the same direction as the image. In addition, the angle of the incoming ray equals that of the outgoing ray.

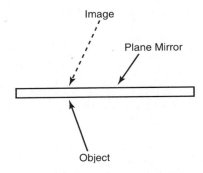

37. **5** To get the total from the three sources that qualify as fossil fuels, petroleum, natural gas, and coal must be added together, giving the total of 85% and making choice 5 the best answer.

38. **2** The pie chart clearly shows petroleum to be the largest energy source in 1998.

39. **3** At a temperature of 25°C and a pressure of .25 atm, the carbon dioxide would be in the lower right section of the graph, indicating it is a gas. As with all GED graphs, if your estimate is slightly different it will not affect the answer significantly.

40. **4** After the calendar year has been written on various documents for 365 days, writing these dates becomes automatic, and so, without thinking, the error is made in the early days of the new year.

41. **4** Habit formation leads to efficiency. This explains why the names were written more neatly and in greater number with the hand normally used.

42. **1** The brain is not involved in reflex acts. A reflex is a simple, quick, automatic act that involves the neurons and the spinal cord.

43. **1** See explanation for question 42.

44. **5** Solving a crossword puzzle involves the higher senses of memory and reasoning.

45. **2** Nest building is a complex activity, involving finding materials and constructing the nest. Through instinct, the incubator robin does things right the first time, even though it has never seen a nest.

46. **3** On previous occasions when the baby cried, adult attention was forthcoming. The infant cried in response to pain, but for the older baby crying was conditioned behavior.

47. **3** All training of animals is the result of conditioning. The dolphin associates the reward (food) with the performance of the trick.

48. **4** Dotting *i*'s and crossing *t*'s has been learned by extensive practice, forming a habit that is hard to disobey.

49. **5** The higher senses are involved in the studying and remembering necessary for satisfactory GED scores.

50. **3** This is an important observation that led to further research.

TEST 4: LANGUAGE ARTS, READING/PAGE 877

1. **1** Ways to correct others' behavior without hurting their feelings is the main subject of the article.

2. **4** All are mentioned except inappropriate vocabulary. This is different from mispronouncing words, which is one of the behaviors mentioned in the passage.

3. **5** The article refers to people who love those they correct dearly and work to help them.

4. **4** If it is unacceptable to criticize things a person cannot correct as the passage states, then it is acceptable to criticize behavior the person can correct.

5. **3** The article mentions the feelings of both the person receiving the criticism and the person giving it.

6. **5** Mr. Higgins is trying to make Liza like a duchess in speech and appearance, as indicated when he specifically says to Liza, "You've got to learn to behave like a duchess."

7. **1** The meaning of inspired follies can be inferred from the quotes surrounding the phrase. Mr. Higgins meant that life is made up of a series of foolish events, encouraged by something or someone.

8. **5** In regard to Mr. Higgins' help, Liza is probably nervous and angry, as indicated by her reaction to every negative comment Higgins makes.

9. **2** Higgins was hinting at the symbolic process of Liza's completely leaving behind her old self. By burning her old clothes, it was a way to leave behind her past ways.

10. **2** The attitude of Mr. Higgins to Liza is one of selective help. He is about to help her, but only for his own purpose of proving to Pickering that he is the better phonetic language teacher.

11. **2** The setting of Oberfest at the foot of the snow-covered mountains is especially significant because of its contribution to the tragic ending.

12. **5** Nowhere is any theme (the essential subject) of the incident stated. The theme—that people, through actions based on rumor and fear, bring about their own destruction—is left to the reader to deduce from the evidence presented by the author.

13. **1** In addition to the meaning given in the "Glossary of Literary Terms" on page 508, irony also refers to a combination of circumstances that results in the opposite of what might be expected to happen. That is true of this selection; the alarm, which should summon help, brings the opposite—destruction.

14. **4** The word *cold* has two meanings in this context: a literal or denotative meaning of very chilly as applied to climate, and an extended or connotative meaning, lifeless.

15. **4** Oberfest was buried beneath the snow without a trace.

16. **3** "I" failed as a cornetist, a basketball player, and a football player.

17. **4** The title, a way of remembering E, G, B, D, F—the notes of the musical staff, describes the opposite of what happened to the poet.

18. **1** The reader is asked to consider the poem a failure, which it definitely is not.

19. **5** The poet compares his physical posture on stage to his "hand-tied necktie."

20. **5** The poet says to the reader, "Consider this poem a failure."

21. **4** Lines 2–6 and 8–12 list life's treasures, which the poet urges us to enjoy.

22. **1** Line 3 refers to "blue waves whitened on a cliff."

23. **3** In line 8, music is compared to a curve of gold. Since the word *like* is used, this comparison is a simile.

24. **4** The poet indicates that "holy thoughts" will delight the spirit.

25. **1** The poet urges the reader to "give all you have been or could be" for life's loveliness.

26. **5** The policy states that the *use of drugs for legitimate medical purposes* is acceptable.

27. **5** The purpose of the policy is simply to inform employees of the company policy on alcohol and other drugs.

28. **4** The company states that *all employees in Executive Branch agencies, including the Governor's Office, Office of the Lieutenant Governor, and the Office of the Attorney General* are subject to its policy.

29. **4** The policy states nothing about immediate release from the company.

30. **5** The policy states that an employee who refuses to sign the "certificate of receipt" will have his supervisor initial the form, indicating that a copy of the form has been given to the employee.

31. **1** The author's negative feelings are indicated by the use of such words as *beast* and *sadistic*, and *vindictive*.

32. **3** The action referred to is "the purely phony move of the boxer who extends his gloves to his rival" on the floor.

33. **1** The passage states that the mob "roots consistently for the smaller man" and "howls with glee at a good finisher making his kill."

34. **4** The author's opinion is evident in the use of such words as *beast*, *lurks*, and *gray thing*.

35. **5** The author describes the mob (audience) as "vindictive."

36. **1** The word *still* indicates the author is surprised that many do not know this major American writer.

37. **5** The author refers to Cather's "feeling for the earth."

38. **4** The excerpt refers to the town's "burning summers" and "blustery winters."

39. **5** Cather "had the power to elevate ordinary people and places."

40. **4** "Cather believed that America's promise would endure," states the passage.

TEST 5: MATHEMATICS/PAGE 887

Part I

1. **4** $0.05 \times \$15{,}000 = \$750$ commission
   $\$300 + \$750 = \$1{,}050$ total salary

2. **1** 12 oz. $= \dfrac{12}{16}$ lb. of apples $= \dfrac{3}{4}$ lb. $= .75$

   Cost of 1.75 lbs. of apples: $1.75\,(\$1.96) = \$3.43$

3. **2** To obtain the average rate of speed, divide the total distance covered by the total driving time.
   Total distance $= 80 + 100 = 180$ mi.
   Total time $= 2 + 3 = 5$ hr.
   $180 \div 5 = 36$ mph.

4. **9** Let $x =$ width of enlarged picture.

   Set up a proportion: $\dfrac{\text{length of picture}}{\text{width of picture}} : \dfrac{8}{6} = \dfrac{12}{x}$

   $8x = 6(12) = 72$
   $x = 72 \div 8 = 9$ in.

5. **290** $23.25 - 19.625$ (use your calculator!) $= 3.625$

   3.625 is profit for 1 share
   $\times\ 80$
   $\$290$

6. **3** $3x - 1 < 5$
   $\quad 3x < 6$
   $\quad\ x < 2$

   Of the choices given, the only choice less than 2 is 1.

7. **340** $850 \times 0.60 = 510$ seats in orchestra
   $850 - 510 = 340$ seats not in orchestra

8. **4** Let $4x =$ measure of larger acute angle, and $x =$ measure of smaller acute angle.
   $4x + x = 90$
   $\quad 5x = 90$
   $\quad\ x = 90 \div 5 = 18$
   $\ 4x = 4(18) = 72°.$

9. **4** 25 ft. 8 in. = 24 ft. + 12 in. + 8 in.
                      = 24 ft. 20 in.

   24 ft. 20 in.
   – 18 ft. 10 in.
   ───────────────
    6 ft. 10 in.

10. **3** Bill earns m dollars per month.

   Angelo earns n dollars per month.

   Together Bill and Angelo earn $(m + n)$ dollars per month.

   In 1 year, Bill and Angelo earn $12(m + n)$ dollars.

11. **2** Use the Pythagorean theorem.
$$x^2 = (15)^2 + (20)^2$$
$$= 225 + 400 = 625$$
$$x = \sqrt{625} = 25 \text{ mi.}$$

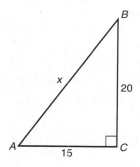

12. **4** Let x = Maria's earnings, and $2x$ = Joan's earnings.
$$x + 2x = 42$$
$$3x = 42$$
$$x = 42 \div 3 = \$14$$

13. **165** $5,800 – $4,500 = $1,300

   Tax is $100 + 5% of $1,300 = 100 + 0.05(1,300) = 100 + 65 = $165

14. **2** $x = 2a(b + 7)$
$$= 2(3)(5 + 7)$$
$$= 2(3)(12)$$
$$= 72$$

15. **2** The number of students in the school is $18 \times 35 = 630$. If there are to be 30 students in a class, the number of classes needed is $630 \div 30 = 21$.

   Therefore, the number of new classes needed is $21 – 18 = 3$.

16. **7/11 or .64**   Since there are 7 women among the 11 committee members, the probability of choosing a woman is $\dfrac{7}{11}$.

17. **1** 12 oz. $= \dfrac{12}{16} = \dfrac{3}{4}$ lb.

5 lb. 12 oz. $= 5\dfrac{3}{4} = \dfrac{23}{4}$ lb.

If $\dfrac{23}{4}$ lb. cost \$2.07, then 1 lb. costs $\$2.07 \div \dfrac{23}{4}$.

$2.07 \div \dfrac{23}{4} = 2.07 \times \dfrac{4}{23} = \$0.36$

18. **3** $m\angle CBD = 125°$

$m\angle ABC = 180° - 125° = 55°$

$m\angle A + m\angle ABC = 90°$

$\qquad m\angle A + 55° = 90°$

$\qquad\quad m\angle A = 90° - 55° = 35°$

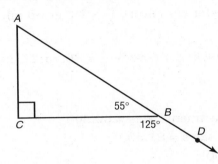

19. **4** 10% + 25% + 30% + 15% = 80%, so 80% passed, and 20% failed.

20% of 80 = 0.20(80) = 16

20. **4** \$20,000 × 0.07 = \$1,400

\$12,000 × 0.075 = \$900

\$1,400 + \$900 = \$2,300

21. **3** Width of walk is 6 ft., or 6 × 12 = 72 in. Width of each brick is 4 in. Number of bricks that can be fitted along the width is 72 ÷ 4 = 18.

Length of walk is 24 ft., or 24 × 12 = 288 in. Length of each brick is 8 in. Number of bricks that can be fitted along the length is 288 ÷ 8 = 36.

18 × 36 = 648

22. **2** Calculate the yearly income for each choice.

    A. $54,000

    B. $1,070 × 52 (weeks in a year) = $55,640

    C. $4,070 × 12 = $48,840

    D. $4,000 × 6 = $24,000 (first half-year)
       +
      $4,000 × 1.10 (raise) = 4,400 × 6 = $26,400 (second half-year)
      $24,000 + $26,400 = $50,400

    B or 2 is correct.

23. **4** First, the dealer bought 2(12) or 24 jackets at $48 each. The following month, she bought 15 jackets at $48. In all, she bought (24 + 15) jackets at $48, spending a total of 48(24 + 15) dollars.

24. **9** 45 min. = $\frac{45}{60}$, or $\frac{3}{4}$ hr.

    At 48 mph, the faster car covers $\frac{3}{4}$ × 48, or 36 mi.

    At 36 mph, the slower car covers $\frac{3}{4}$ × 36, or 27 mi.

    36 – 27 = 9 mi.

25. **$1,000**   Meat department sales = $2,500

    Dairy department sales = $1,500

    Difference = $1,000

Part II

26. 1 Perimeter of figure is $x + 2y + 3x - y + 2x + 3y + 5x + y = 11x + 5y$.

27. 3 $\dfrac{7}{8} - \dfrac{1}{4} = \dfrac{7}{8} - \dfrac{2}{8} = \dfrac{5}{8}$

$\dfrac{5}{8} \times 280 = 175$ gal. used

28. 5 To express a number in scientific notation, express it as the product of a number between 1 and 10 and a power of 10. In this case, the number between 1 and 10 is 2.750389. In going from 2.750389 to 2,750,389, you move the decimal point 6 places to the right. Each move represents a multiplication by 10 and 6 moves represents a multiplication by 10^6. Thus, $2{,}750{,}389 = 2.750389 \times 10^6$.

29. 3 The team has played 75 games and will play 45 more games.

$75 + 45 = 120$

60% of $120 = 0.6 \times 120 = 72$

The team must win 72 games, and it has already won 50 games.

Therefore, the team must win $72 - 50 = 22$ more games.

30. 1 Because the areas of both figures are equal to each other, write an equation for both areas using an "equals" sign.

$\dfrac{1}{2}(b \times h) = lw$

Then fill in the dimensions given in the diagram: $\dfrac{1}{2}(32x) = 12(8)$

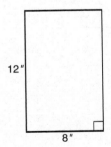
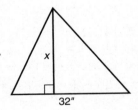

31. 3 To find the median weight, arrange the weights in increasing order and identify the middle weight. In order of increasing size, the weights are as follows: 184, 193, 195, 197, 198, 201, 203, 205, 207, 212, 214 lb.

The median (sixth) weight is 201 lb.

32. 4 40% of the total expenses of $240,000 went for labor.

$0.40(\$240{,}000) = \$96{,}000$

33. **2** Slope = $\dfrac{y_2 - y_1}{x_2 - x_1}$

In this case $y_2 = 4$, $y_1 = 3$, $x_2 = 5$, and $x_1 = 0$.

Slope = $\dfrac{4 - 3}{5 - 0} = \dfrac{1}{5}$

34. **2** First, find the sum of all laps around the track: $4 + 6 + 2 = 12$

12×400 meters (1 lap) = 4,800 meters

1000 meters = 1 kilometer

$\dfrac{4,800}{1,000} = 4.8$ kilometers

35. **(3,3)** Starting from the upper-left corner (point A) of what would be a rectangle, count 6 units (boxes) to the right on the same x plane. You will arrive at point 3,3 on the coordinate grid, as the answer key indicates.

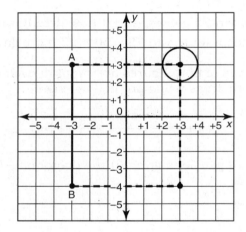

36. **5** $3x - 1 = 11$

$\qquad 3x = 11 + 1 = 12$

$\qquad x = 12 \div 3 = 4$

$x^2 + x = (4)^2 + 4 = 16 + 4 = 20$

37. **3** The first bell rings at 9:00 A.M., 11:00 A.M., 1:00 P.M., 3:00 P.M., 5:00 P.M., 7:00 P.M., 9:00 P.M.

The second bell rings at 9:00 A.M., 12:00 noon, 3:00 P.M., 6:00 P.M., 9:00 P.M.

The third bell rings at 9:00 A.M., 1:00 P.M., 5:00 P.M., 9:00 P.M.

All 3 bells will ring again at 9:00 P.M.

38. **3** Expenditures: $20\% + 23\% + 42\% = 85\%$

Savings: $100\% - 85\% = 15\%$

Let x = family's monthly income. Then $0.15x = \$360$, so $x = \$360 \div 0.15 = \$2,400$

39. **100**   Let $x = DC$.

Since $\triangle ABE$ is similar to $\triangle CED$, the lengths of their corresponding sides are in proportion.

$$\frac{x}{60} = \frac{80}{48}$$

$48x = 80(60) = 4800$

$x = 4800 \div 48 = 100$ ft.

40. **2** Since 12 eggs cost x cents, 3 eggs cost $\frac{3}{12}$, or $\frac{1}{4}$, as much: $\frac{1}{4}x = \frac{x}{4}$.

41. **5** Since $2x + 3 > 7$, then $2x > 4$, and $x > 2$. Of the choices listed, only 0 is *not* greater than 2.

42. **16**   Use the formula for the area of a triangle:

$$A = \frac{1}{2}bh.$$

In this case, $b = 4$ and $h = 8$.

$$\text{Area} = \frac{1}{2}(4)(8) = 16$$

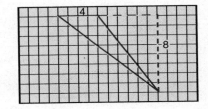

43. **4** To make a sound financial decision, Shandra must know how much she can earn by working in the College *B* library.

44. **5** It always helps to draw a diagram when none is provided in the question. There are two pairs of walls, and each pair has a different area to be calculated then added.

Pair 1 = 2(24 × 9) or   2(*lh*)

                    +

Pair 2 = 2(18 × 9) or   2(*wh*)

The sum of the pairs provides the total square *feet* of wallpaper needed, but it must then be divided by 9 to get total square *yards*.

9 sq. ft. = 1 sq. yd.

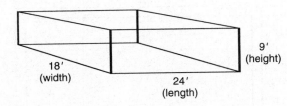

45. **4** To find the average, divide the total mileage by the total time.

Total distance = $x + y + z$

Total time = 3 days

Average = $\dfrac{x + y + z}{3}$

46. **3** Let x = length of shorter part, and $x + 8$ = length of longer part.

$x + x + 8 = 64$

$2x + 8 = 64$

$2x = 64 - 8 = 56$

$x = 56 \div 2 = 28$

$x + 8 = 28 + 8 = 36$

47. **1** Let x = number of machine parts Frank can make in 7 hr.

Set up a proportion: $\dfrac{4}{21} = \dfrac{7}{x}$

$4x = 7(21)$

$x = \dfrac{7(21)}{4}$

48. **4** Use the formula $V = lwh$.

In this case, $l = x$, $w = x$, and $h = y$

$V = x(x)y$ $V = x^2y$

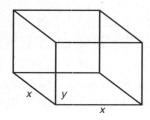

49. **5** To find the value of the estate, you need to know either the daughter's share or the fractional part of the estate received by the son. Neither item of information is given.

50. **4** As you can see from the figure below, to find the area of the white walkway, you need to subtract the area of the inner rectangle, (20)(30) sq. ft., from the area of the outer rectangle, (26)(36) sq. ft.:
(26)(36) − (20)(30) sq. ft.

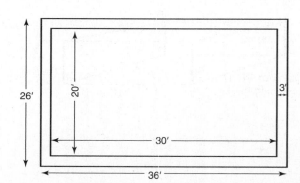

Acknowledgments

The authors gratefully acknowledge the kindness of all organizations concerned with the granting of permission to reprint passages, charts, graphs, and outlines.

We are indebted to Scholastic Magazines, Inc. for their kind permission to reproduce passages from **Senior Scholastic** that formed the basis for original questions interpreting items to be analyzed in social studies. Sources and permissions for charts and graphs appear on the appropriate pages throughout the book courtesy of the following organizations: U.S. Department of Agriculture; U.S. Department of Health, Education, and Welfare—Office of Education; U.S. Bureau of the Budget; Social Security Administration; Census Bureau; and Bureau of Labor Statistics.

The copyright holders and publishers of quoted materials are listed below.

"Elegy for Jane," copyright 1950 by Theodore Roethke, from **Collected Poems of Theodore Roethke** by Theodore Roethke. Used by permission of Doubleday, a division of Random House, Inc.

Passage from **A Raisin in the Sun**, by Lorraine Hansberry. Copyright © 1958 by Robert Nemiroff, as an unpublished work. Copyright © 1959, 1966, 1984 by Robert Nemiroff. Copyright renewed 1986, 1987 by Robert Nemiroff. Used by permission of Random House, Inc.

Passage from **Memoirs of Chief Red Fox**, by Chief Red Fox. Copyright © 1971. Reprinted by permission of W.W. Red Fox.

Passage from **Paths to the Present**, by Arthur M. Schlesinger, Sr. Reprinted by permission of Arthur Schlesinger, Jr.

Passage from Arthur H. Doerr and J. L. Guernsey, **Principles of Geography— Physical and Cultural**, Second Edition Revised. Copyright © 1975 by Barron's Educational Series, Inc.

Table from **Let's Review Global Studies**, Second Edition. Copyright © 1994 by Barron's Educational Series, Inc.

Photographs from Corbis-Bettmann Archive.

Excerpt from a speech by Jonathan Kozol, Boston College, May 1969. Copyright Jonathan Kozol.

Passage from "What It Is Like to Be Underdeveloped," in **Global Studies, Vol. 1,** Second Edition. Copyright © 1993 by Barron's Educational Series, Inc.

Excerpts from "The Iroquois Resurgence" from APOLOGIES TO THE IROQUOIS by Edmund Wilson. Copyright © 1959, 1960 by Edmund Wilson. Reprinted by permission of Farrar, Straus and Giroux, LLC.

Excerpts from **The Reader's Companion to American History**, edited by Eric Foner and John A. Garraty. Copyright © 1991 by Houghton Mifflin Company. Reprinted by permission of Houghton Mifflin Company. All rights reserved.

Passage from "Green Seal of Approval," by Michael Lipske, in **National Wildlife**, June–July 1994, pp. 22–23.

Map and Passage from Erwin Rosenfeld and Harriet Geller, **Afro-Asian Culture Studies**, Second Revised Edition. Copyright © 1976 by Barron's Educational Series, Inc.

Passage from **Life With Father**, by Clarence Day, copyright 1935 by Clarence Day and renewed 1963 by Mrs. Katherine B. Day. Used by permission of Alfred A. Knopf, a division of Random House, Inc.

"Requiem" from **Death of a Salesman**, by Arthur Miller. Copyright © 1949, renewed © 1977 by Arthur Miller. Used by permission of Viking Penguin, a division of Penguin Group (USA) Inc.

Article from **Investor's Business Daily**, December 1, 1997 and April 21, 1994. © 2009 Investor's Business Daily, Inc. Republished with permission.

"The Joy Luck Club," from **The Joy Luck Club** by Amy Tan. Copyright © 1989 by Amy Tan. Used by permission of G.P. Putnam's Sons, a division of Penguin Group (USA) Inc.

Passage from **A Few Minutes with Andy Rooney**. Copyright © 1981 by Atheneum Publishers.

Passage from **Star by Star**, by Naomi Long Madgett. Copyright © 1972 by Harlo Press.

Passage from **Platero and I**, by Juan Ramon Jimenez Moguer. Copyright © by Philip Duschenes.

Passage from "The Mother," in **Television Plays**, by Paddy Chayevsky. Copyright © 1955 by Simon and Schuster, Inc.

Passage from "Destruction Men," by Michael Goldstein. **New York Magazine**, May 28, 1994.

Passage from **America as a Civilization**, by Max Lerner. Copyright © 1957, 1985 by Max Lerner. Reprinted by permission of Simon and Schuster, Inc.

Cartoon from **United Media**, 1994.

Poem "To a Photographer," by Berton Braley. Copyright © 1965 by Berton Braley.

From **State of the Union** by Howard Lindsay and Russell Crouse, copyright 1946 by Howard Lindsay and Russell Crouse. Used by permission of Random House, Inc.

Passage from **Principles of Geography—Physical and Cultural**, Second Revised Edition, by Arthur Doerr and J. L. Guernsey. Copyright © 1975 by Barron's Educational Series, Inc.

Passage from "Willa Cather: Voice of the Frontier," by William Howarth. Copyright © 1982 by National Geographic Society.

Passage from *A Lost Lady*, by Willa Cather. Copyright 1997 by http://cather.classicauthors.net/LOSTLADY/LOSTLADY1.html.

"Digging Limestone" © 1982; first published in *North American Review*; collected in the author's *In Limestone Country* (Beacon Press, 1991); reprinted by permission of the author.

Reprinted with the permission of The Free Press, a Division of Simon & Schuster, Inc., from *The Black Death* by Robert Gottfried. Copyright © 1983 by The Free Press. All rights reserved.

Passage from "Menagerie, A Child's Fable" from *The Sorcerer's Apprentice* by Charles Johnson. Copyright © 1977, 1979, 1981, 1982, 1983, 1984, 1985, 1986 by Charles Johnson. Reprinted by permission of Georges Borchardt, Inc., on behalf of the author.

Excerpt by Leonel T. Castillo from *Literary Cavalcade*. Copyright © by Scholastic Inc. Reprinted by permission of Scholastic Inc.

Excerpt from "Why I Write" from *Such, Such Were The Joys* by George Orwell, copyright 1953 by Sonia Brownell Orwell and renewed 1981 by Mrs. George K. Perutz, Mrs. Miriam Gross, and Dr. Michael Dickson, Executors of the Estate of Sonia Brownell Orwell, reprinted by permission of Houghton Mifflin Harcourt Publishing Company. World rights for "Why I Write" by George Orwell granted by permission of Bill Hamilton as the Literary Executor of the Estate of the late Sonia Brownell Orwell and Secker & Warburg, Ltd.

How to Use the CD-ROM

The software is not installed on your computer; it runs directly from the CD-ROM. Barron's CD-ROM includes an "autorun" feature that automatically launches the application when the CD is inserted into the CD-ROM drive. In the unlikely event that the autorun feature is disabled, follow the manual launching instructions below.

Windows®

Insert the CD-ROM and the program should launch automatically. If the software does not launch automatically, follow the steps below.
1. Click on the Start button and choose "My Computer."
2. Double-click on the CD-ROM drive, which will be named **GED**.
3. Double-click **GED.exe** application to launch the program.

Macintosh®

1. Insert the **GED** CD.
2. Double-click the **GED** CD-ROM icon on your desktop.
3. Double-click on the **GED** file.

SYSTEM REQUIREMENTS

The program will run on a PC with:
Windows® Intel® Pentium II 450 MHz
or faster, 128MB of RAM
1024 X 768 display resolution
Windows 2000, XP, Vista
CD-ROM Player

The program will run on a Macintosh® with:
PowerPC® G3 500 MHz
or faster, 128MB of RAM
1024 X 768 display resolution
Mac OS X v.10.1 through 10.4
CD-ROM Player
Browser with Adobe® Flash® Player installed